THE GARDEN
FLOWER BOOK

bay books

THE GARDEN
FLOWER BOOK

CONTENTS

Growing Perennials

GROWING PERENNIALS

Many of the loveliest and best-loved flowering plants are perennials. Like annuals, perennials provide a colorful display, but they have the advantage that they don't need to be changed at least twice a year. Perennials are easy-care plants which have a major place in low-maintenance gardens.

Perennials remain alive for a number of years, unlike annuals which usually last only one season, and biennials which grow and flower through a second season or year. Perennials form a variable group in terms of their size and foliage, flower shape, style, and color. In fact, there is a perennial to suit almost every climate, aspect, and soil, and some can even be grown in containers. Perennials can also be planted among shrubs, to form a background for bulbs or annuals, or in their own separate areas. Perennial borders make lively, exciting features.

ABOVE: The white form of the purple coneflower showing its attractive, recurved petals.

LEFT: A tender, bright pink argyranthemum, and scabious, in the foreground add perennial interest to this colorful, mixed border featuring soft hues offset by green.

PERENNIALS COMBINE with annuals to form a free-flowing, rich, colorful border, a highlight of mid-summer in this gorgeous cottage garden. A pink shrub rose is flanked by two varieties of aster, while deep blue delphiniums add scale and height at the back.

EVERGREEN OR HERBACEOUS?

Some perennials are evergreen but many are herbaceous. Most herbaceous perennials grow rapidly during spring and summer to flower during the summer and the fall. After flowering they gradually die back to the crown or fleshy roots, and they remain dormant during cold winters. Since most of the hardy herbaceous perennials come from climates with very severe, cold winters, they die down naturally in the fall. In warmer areas, where they do not become completely dormant and some growth continues year round, the plants do not live as long. However, it is simple to renew these perennials as division is easy, and most increase rapidly. In time, a few can even become invasive.

PLANTING PERENNIALS

Soil preparation

Because perennials are long-term plants and because they are close planted, good soil preparation is essential. Although some perennials, such as astilbes and hostas, enjoy damp soil, many prefer well-drained conditions. If you are planting any of the latter group, check your drainage before planting. Dig some holes in the bed, fill them with water and see how long

PERENNIALS FOR SUN AND SHADE

SUNNY BORDERS

• Agapanthus	• Hemerocallis
• Delphinium	• Miscanthus
• Diascia	• Oenothera
• Eryngium	• Papaver
• Gypsophila	• Sedum
• Helenium	• Stachys

SHADY BORDERS

• *Alchemilla mollis*	• *Gunnera manicata*
• Aquilegia	• Helleborus
• Bergenia	• Hosta
• Candclabra primula	• Polygonatum
• Digitalis	• Primula
• Epimedium	• Pulmonaria
	• Rodgersia (dappled)

PURE WHITE shasta daisies light up the summer garden, putting on a strong display from early summer to early fall.

A HIGH STONE WALL marks the boundary of this meadow garden filled with golden fern-leaf yarrow, daisies, and purple loosestrife.

it takes to drain away. If there is still water in the holes 12 hours later, you will need to improve the drainage by installing a system of sub-soil drains.

If the soil is very heavy clay, which remains wet but not waterlogged for a long time, you should dig in some gypsum, about 10.5oz per sq yd. Digging in large quantities of decayed manure or compost a few weeks before planting will also improve clay soils, and it is a must in sandy soils that have poor moisture and nutrient retention.

Thorough weeding of the area is essential, too, as it is difficult to remove weeds in densely planted beds. Remove the weeds you can see, dig or fork over the area again, water, and wait for the next lot of weeds to emerge. You may need to repeat this step if the area has been neglected for any length of time. Hand weeding or spraying with glyphosate should eliminate most weeds, but you will need to be persistent to control oxalis, bindweed and ground elder. This sounds like a lot of work when you are eager to plant out your garden, but it will be worth the wait and the effort in the long run.

Planting perennials from containers

Garden centers and nurseries will stock some perennials, especially when they are in flower. These can be planted in your yard like any other container-grown plant. When the plant is removed from its pot, loosen the rootball a little so that the roots can extend into the surrounding soil. It is essential that the planting hole is about twice the width of the container and approximately the same depth. The soil level around the plant should be exactly the same as it was in the container. Give a thorough soaking after planting. Also apply a deep mulch to the soil around the plant.

Planting bare-rooted perennials

There are also nurseries that specialize in perennials. These nurseries usually advertise in popular gardening magazines, have detailed catalogs with thorough plant descriptions, and sell by mail-order. Plants are delivered during their dormant season, which for the majority is from late fall through the

THESE GOLDEN-YELLOW, green-tipped spikes of a red hot poker cultivar provide a strong focus in this pastel border.

THE TALL, VERTICAL CLUMP of pink dahlias and the midnight blue spires of delphinium provide a colorful mix. They form a bright imaginative backdrop for the rich mix of annuals and perennials edging this beautiful garden bed, clearly illustrating the versatility of perennials.

winter. Plants are mailed, bare-rooted, or in small pots, having been carefully packed and labelled. On arrival, they should be planted at once. However, if the ground is frozen, or you are not ready to plant them, either unpack and water them (if necessary), and store in a bright, cool, frost-free place, or "heel in" as a temporary measure. To do this, dig a trench large enough to contain the plant roots in a sheltered part of your yard. Finally, lay the plants on their sides, cover the roots with soil, and lightly water them.

When planting bare-rooted plants, again make sure the hole is at least twice the width of the rootball, and deep enough to take the roots without kinking them. If some roots are very long, trim them cleanly with pruning shears. Hold the plant in the hole in one hand and fill the hole, poking soil between the roots. Sometimes you can make a slight mound in the center of the hole so that the roots can be spread out over it, keeping the crown high. Make sure the crown of the plant is not buried: if necessary, lift the plant and push more soil in around the roots.

Water thoroughly immediately after planting if the soil is dry, but until the plants have developed plenty of shoot growth they will not require too much watering. The area around the plants should be mulched. If the soil has been well prepared, feeding at this time is not necessary but you may give a very light sprinkling of general fertilizer if you wish.

CARE OF PERENNIALS

Perennial plantings in areas that have been well prepared need little maintenance. You must deadhead through the flowering season to prolong blooming, and cut back or tidy up after flowering. Established perennials will only need watering in prolonged dry spells, and feeding in spring as growth commences. When they become too crowded they are divided between fall and late winter, or early spring. This may be only necessary every three or four years. For details, see plant entries in the A-Z section.

Watering

Never give perennials a light watering because it will encourage surface rooting at the expense of a deep, root system. The plants need big, strong roots to sustain several years of growth, and benefit most from being given a deep, regular watering. On sandy soils choose such perennials as sedum, oenothera, and dianthus that tolerate dry conditions. A deep mulch around the plants will help conserve moisture, as will adding quantities of organic matter to the soil as the mulch breaks down.

Feeding

Perennials should not need a lot of feeding. Apply an all-purpose plant food as growth begins; if the soil has been well prepared this should be enough for the whole growing season. If your soil is very poor though, you may like to use a slow-release granular fertilizer to feed plants through the growing season, or to apply a second helping of plant food as the flower buds start to appear. A mulch of decayed manure or compost around the plants serves two functions. It improves the soil condition, and also supplies small amounts of nutrients to the plants.

Keep the entire area free of weeds until the plants cover the ground. This will ensure that any fertilizer you apply will feed your perennials and not any unwanted weeds. Avoid high nitrogen fertilizers as they tend to promote leaf growth at the expense of flowers. Rose food is ideal.

THE PENSTEMONS AND SALVIAS in the foreground make a gorgeous foil for the stiff, upright growth of Russell lupins.

Cutting flowers and deadheading

A number of perennials make very good cut flowers, and many are grown for the cut flower trade. The various daisies, chrysanthemums, Russell lupins, delphiniums, pinks, and Peruvian lilies are just a few of the perennials that are commercially grown. Regularly picking the flowers will help to ensure a long succession of bloom. If the flowers are not removed they will mature, most setting seed so that the flowering cycle will finish abruptly as the plant decides its reproductive work is over. If you do not want to take cut flowers, remember to deadhead regularly.

Exceptions to this rule are plants such as cardoon and globe thistle that have decorative seedheads. Some gardeners prefer to leave them on the plant. Many remain attractive even when dry, and they can add interest to the garden in late fall and winter, especially when covered in frost or snow.

AFTER FLOWERING

After the flowering season is over, perennials can be cut back almost to the ground. If you live in an area prone to heavy frosts, some of the more tender perennials will then need to have the crown of the plant covered. A thick layer of straw, or fall leaves, held in place by a few sticks in windy sites, will protect them from winter damage.

Alternatively, you could leave some stems sticking out of the ground to create extra, interesting shapes over winter. Grasses are especially invaluable. They are at their best when covered with frost or snow, or when helping to cast a web of shadows from the low winter sun. The birds also benefit from the seedheads.

THE BRIGHT, HOT COLORS of orange and yellow feature in this very effective planting, which shows up so impressively against the cool green of the lawn. The large clump of red hot pokers and a generous drift of deep apricot-orange geum are especially notable.

INCREASING YOUR STOCK OF PERENNIALS

Division

Clumps of perennials are divided either when they become congested, or when you want to plant sections elsewhere in the garden. In general, most perennials need dividing about every three or four years, possibly longer. Division is done after flowering or while the plants are dormant.

If you want some pieces to plant elsewhere you can sever a section with a knife, or put a spade through the clump, and lift away what you want. This might lose some of the peripheral pieces but the process is quick and simple. Otherwise, dig up the whole clump, shake off the excess soil, and pull the clump apart or cut it into sections. Replant the sections immediately, trimming off very long roots. Remember that the outer growths are the youngest to be saved, and that the center of the plant may have died, in which case it can be discarded. You may need to divide very large, heavy clumps by pushing two garden forks, back to back, into the center to prize it apart. A sharp spade may also be used but this needs a lot of force and will, of course, result in the loss of some sections of plant. This may not be of any consequence with vigorous perennials.

If you are unable to replant at once or have pieces to give away, wrap them in damp newspaper or hessian and keep in a shaded, sheltered spot, giving time to decide where to plant them. "Heeling in," as described on the previous page, is another way to store plants temporarily, and they are less likely to dry out. They can, of course, be potted up in a good quality potting mix.

Taking cuttings

Many perennial plants can be grown from cuttings and a number, including geraniums and diascias, are among the easiest plants to strike. Others that will grow readily from cuttings include penstemons and sedums.

Make a mix of two or three parts of coarse sand and one of peat, or peat substitute compost. Put the prepared mix in clean pots, preferably no larger than 4in across. A pot of this size will take a good number of cuttings. They should not be forced to sit in soil that remains wet when watered, which would rot the roots.

Take tip cuttings of unflowered shoots, no more than 2–4in long. Cut, do not tear, pieces from the parent plant. Take the cuttings early in the morning, placing the pieces in a clean plastic bag, and quickly put in a cool, shady place. Trim the cuttings by removing the lower leaves, allowing just a very few to remain on top. Cleanly cut the base of the cutting below a node (leaf junction). Another aid to rooting is to "wound" the cutting by carefully scraping about ³⁄₈in of the outer bark or stem cover at the base of the stem. Hormone rooting powders can also be used but are not usually necessary with most perennials.

Use a clean stick or pencil to make a hole in the compost. Put the cutting in the hole and carefully firm the surrounding mix. Once all your cuttings are in the pot you can water them thoroughly and put the pot in a warm, sheltered place out of direct sun. In warm months geraniums and daisies may be well rooted after three weeks, but many plants can take a considerable time. Check regularly to see if the cuttings need water but do not keep them wet or, as explained they will rot.

DIVIDING A CLUMP

Step 1: Use a garden fork to lift the whole perennial clump from the soil.

Step 2: Separate matted clumps by inserting two garden forks, back to back, firmly into the clump.

Step 3: First press the fork handles together, and then force them apart to split the clump in two. Repeat until the clumps are the size you want.

Step 4: Use pruning shears to cut off dead, rotten or damaged roots. The clumps will now be ready for replanting.

STRIKING A CUTTING

Step 1: Take a cutting just below a leaf node or joint. Use a sharp knife or pruning shears so that the cutting is not bruised. Trim it if necessary.

Step 2: Make a hole in the compost with your finger and insert the cutting into it. Firm the soil gently around it. If you are placing more than one cutting in the pot, plant them around the edge, giving them plenty of space.

Step 3: Water the cuttings in well, but take care not to dislodge them. Make sure the water is draining away well as the cuttings will rot if the soil remains wet.

Step 4: To make a humid atmosphere and keep the soil and cuttings moist, make a frame of sticks or wire tall enough to cover the cuttings. Place a polythene bag over the frame, and stand the pot out of direct sunlight.

A ROMANTIC GARDEN PATH is bordered by old-fashioned favorites, including perennial daisies and scented pinks.

Taking root cuttings

A number of plants, including perennials such as sea lavender, romneya, and perennial phlox, can be grown from root cuttings. As the plant will be disturbed when the cuttings are taken, this task is best done in winter.

• Remove the soil from around the base of the plant until you reach the roots. Trace them back until they are $\frac{1}{8}-\frac{3}{16}$in thick, and cut off some cleanly with a sharp knife or pruning shears. Immediately place them in a plastic bag so they do not dry out.

• Wash the soil from the roots and cut them into 1–2in lengths. If you intend to plant them vertically you will need to know which way is up; cut all the tops straight across and the bottoms at an angle.

• Place the cuttings vertically in a container, or lay them in horizontally and cover with about $\frac{3}{16}$in of John Innes No.1. Water thoroughly and check regularly to see whether further watering is needed.

• Once good shoots have appeared, your new plants can be potted up individually into small pots or planted into the ground. It is important to keep the cuttings moist, but if you saturate the compost the roots will rot.

WHAT CAN GO WRONG?

Perennials can be attacked by a number of insect pests and diseases, and problems that occur on specific plants will be discussed in the individual plant entries. Slugs and snails are among the worst pests for herbaceous perennials since they can destroy newly emerging growth as it appears in spring. If each successive burst of leaves is destroyed, the plant will eventually give up. You must search for and destroy these pests, perhaps picking them off by hand, or using bait or beer traps.

Overwatering or poorly drained heavy soils can also damage or kill perennials, especially if they are too wet during their dormant period when there is no foliage to transpire moisture from the plant. Waterlogged soils also provide ideal conditions for the growth and spread of various soil-borne, root-rotting fungi. A few plants, such as astilbe and hosta, actually enjoy damp or boggy ground, but most enjoy conditions with good drainage.

Yellow leaves

• Plants may have been overwatered or they may be too dry. You are actually more likely to overwater a perennial in a pot than in a border. They may also need feeding if this has not been done for some time. Try a light application of fertilizer; in warm weather there should be an improvement within two to three weeks. Toward the end of the growing season you can expect to see some leaves yellowing as they finish their useful life. Do not worry if a few leaves, especially down towards the ground, become brown or yellow during the active spring period.

Curled or distorted leaves

• Keep a regular check against aphids. They can be a terrible problem. They are small, sap-sucking insects that may be black, brown, green, or clear. They cluster thickly on the new growth of plants, sucking out the sap. This may cause curling or distortion of leaves, and flowers may fail to open if the sap has been sucked from the buds or they, too,

A HEALTHY display of violets.

may be distorted. Close inspection usually reveals these tiny insects; they can be squashed and wiped off the stems, hosed off or sprayed with insecticidal soap or pyrethrum-based sprays. Aphids need to be controlled as they also transmit virus diseases from plant to plant.

Silvery mottling on foliage

• Silver markings or discoloration of foliage may be the first sign of thrip attack. These tiny insects attack plant tissue and suck the sap. Unlike most sap-sucking insects they attack the top, not the under leaf. There are several different types that cause plant damage. They are readily recognizable, usually having black bodies and wings edged with hairs. Apart from the physical damage, some thrips are also responsible for transmitting virus diseases from plant to plant. Since many thrips use weeds as hosts it is important to keep them out of your beds and borders. If thrips are causing damage, make sure that the plants are not stressed through lack of water. When spraying, use an appropriate contact or systemic insecticide.

Curled and browned flowers

• Check plants for thrips because they can attack pale-colored flowers. For their control, see "Silvery mottling on foliage."

TAKING ROOT CUTTINGS

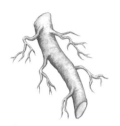

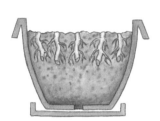

Step 1: To take root cuttings from most perennials, trace the roots back and cut out a section some ⅛–³⁄₁₆in thick.

Step 2: Wash any soil from the roots and cut them into sections 1–2in long. Mark the top of each so you know which way up to plant them.

Step 3: Place the root cuttings vertically in a container, making sure that they are the right way up. Water them in thoroughly.

Alternatively, if plants have thin roots, take cuttings in the same way but lay them horizontally and cover with a thin layer of compost.

Holes in leaves or on leaf edges

• If your plants have chewed edges or large areas of leaf missing, check for snails. They are the most likely culprits. Pick the snails off and destroy them, or use a bait if you do not have a pet.

• If there is no sign of snails, start looking for caterpillars. Chewing insects such as caterpillars can do a great deal of damage in quite a short time because they can be such voracious feeders. They can be well camouflaged, lying along leaf margins or hiding under leaves. Try first to find and destroy them, but if the damage continues, dust the plants with derris.

Mottled leaves

• Leaf mottling may be the result of mite damage. Mites are not true insects, having eight legs like other members of the arachnid family. Mites are sap suckers, and foliage attacked by mites appears mottled and discolored. With the aid of a magnifying glass the tiny creatures and their clear circular eggs can sometimes be seen on the underside of leaves. If severe mite attacks go unnoticed initially, there may be fine webbing on the underside of foliage too. Sometimes with light attacks hosing under the leaves every two to three days is enough to reduce their population to an acceptable, non-

damaging level. Mites are much worse in warm, dry weather or on plants that may be sheltered by the overhanging eaves of a house. Make sure that plants are well watered and well nourished. If mite numbers do reach unacceptable levels, clearly getting out of hand, you may need to spray with an appropriate insecticide. Many general, broad spectrum insecticides are useless against mites.

Gray/white powder on leaves

• This is probably caused by the common fungal disease, powdery mildew. In humid areas this disease is a constant problem. For plants that are very susceptible to powdery mildew, much work is being done to breed plant-resistant varieties. Meanwhile, it may be necessary to spray with a fungicide such as carbendazim or copper oxychloride or, alternatively, you can dust the plants with sulfur. If you have any

A VIBRANT show of argyranthemums.

kind of problem with powdery mildew, avoid watering the plants late in the day so that you do not increase the humidity around them overnight.

Black or dark spots on leaves

• There are many strains of fungal leaf spots that can attack a wide range of plants. If only a few leaves are affected, remove and destroy them. Avoid watering late in the day and, where possible, avoid splashing the foliage which will spread the fungal spores. Many fungal leaf spots respond well to simple fungicides such as copper oxychloride, but there are other effective fungicides available to the home gardener.

Yellow spots on top of leaves

• Yellow spots on the upper side of leaves that have blisters, or pustules on the underside, are likely to be some form of rust. There is an enormous number of rust strains, and they can attack a wide range of plants and perennials, including chrysanthemums. It is a good idea to remove the worst affected leaves immediately, and to avoid overhead watering which quickly splashes the spores around, increasing contamination. Copper oxychloride will control some rusts, though you may find you need to use a more specific fungicide.

PLANNING A PERENNIAL GARDEN

Many perennials have a long flowering period, and well-planned beds of perennials can display a succession of flowers over many months. This does, however, take a good deal of planning and usually some trial and error.

If you are planting a large area, it's best to design it on paper first, so that you can place the tallest plants at the back or in the center of the bed, also giving you time to devise your color scheme. You can experiment by using a variety of plants, all with flowers in one color or shades of one color, or you may opt for a planting of bright contrasts. Whatever scheme you choose, allow for plenty of plants to create a full, rich scene. A well-planted perennial border or garden is close-planted, so that every bit of soil is covered, providing foliage and floral interest throughout the season.

ABOVE: These rich purple spikes belong to the spectacular Salvia "Ostfriesland," *a cultivar of* Salvia nemorosa.

LEFT: True perennials, such as purple Liatris spicata, *and the yellow daisies of* Coreopsis verticillata, *mix well with annual red strawflowers and* Dahlia "Bishop of Llandaff."

THE LUSH GREEN SCENE, composed of hostas, candelabra primulas, and other shade-tolerant perennials, in a fern-filled woodland garden on the mild west coast of Scotland. Such a scene can easily be reduced and modified for the borders in a shaded city yard.

USING PERENNIALS

Perennials are among the most versatile of plants, and the vast majority of gardeners use them in conjunction with permanent plantings of shrubs, annuals, and bulbs. They are plants that require far less work and maintenance than annuals, while still giving a great deal of seasonal color and interest. In fact many low-growing perennials, such as penstemon, lamb's ears, pinks, and bergenia, make excellent border plantings, while taller growers, such as phlox and *Acanthus mollis*, can be planted among shrubs. Long-flowering plants, such as achillea and corydalis, can be used to give color between seasonal annual displays. They also give interest to a garden bed where bulbs have finished flowering and are in the process of dying down.

PERENNIAL BORDERS

Traditionally, perennials have often been close planted in a border. To get an idea of how a well-grown perennial border should look, visit the great public gardens. Gardeners have been refining the art of perennial borders for a very long time, and both first-time and experienced gardeners will find plenty of new, imaginative ideas in these schemes. Specialist nurseries often have special exhibit beds where you can also see how well various perennials combine.

FORMAL GARDENS

It is difficult for a perennial garden to look really formal, but many of the best perennial schemes have been informally planted within a formal framework. Some are enclosed within walls, while many are contained within low, formally trimmed hedges. The garden beds are laid out in strict geometric style, resembling an ornate piece of embroidery when viewed from above, their angular shapes defined by tightly pruned hedges, often of box or lavender. Sometimes the garden beds are also defined by close-mown paths of grass.

Probably the closest one can get to a formal perennial scheme is by creating a mirror-planting effect. Each part of the design mirrors the next, and the sections are divided by paths of grass, brick, gravel, or stone. For a mirror planting to be successful, the whole of the area must be in full sunlight, otherwise there is absolutely no chance of growth rates and flowering times being the same, or as near as one can get to that, given that you are dealing with living plant material.

PLANT ARRANGEMENT

Perennials come in many shapes and sizes, which is a great advantage when planning a garden. If your perennial garden is to be sited against a picket or wall you might decide to place the tallest growers at the back. This both forms a backbone and gives you the space to stand back and fully appreciate them. So, for example, the long tall spears of delphiniums generally stand behind their lower-growing neighbors. If you are designing an island bed, the tall plants are traditionally placed in the center for a formal effect, or slightly off-center so it does not look quite so inflexibly schematic. Smaller plants radiate out, down toward the front of the border, giving a graduated, tiered effect. But such arrangements are not strictly necessary. You might prefer, instead, to give a more informal look by gently mixing heights, creating undulations. When doing this, the most important point to remember is that no plant should be hidden by its neighbor, or cast in total shade, and that all should be visible from some vantage point so that you can appreciate their color and shape.

A number of plants, such as mulleins and red hot pokers, give very strong vertical accents that contrast well with lower, more variably shaped plants. And striking foliage plants, such as cardoon and *Melianthus major*, are grown more for their strong structural shape than for their flowers. (Note that the latter is tender for the first two years, but once it has a shrubby base it can be left outside all-year around in milder areas, provided it is given some frost protection.) These big plants must be sited carefully and probably not used to excess. A contrast in leaf color, shape, and texture will also add considerable interest to the perennial garden. If you have the luxury of being able to create a very large or long perennial border, you will need to think about repeating some of the shapes and colors to tie the planting together. The other great advantage of growing perennials is that you can move them around when they are dormant, or semi-dormant, if you are not totally satisfied with their appearance or performance. They allow you to modify the design.

Everyone would love to have a yard that is in full flower for months at a time. Planning to ensure a succession of blooms over many months is the hard part of designing a garden. Even if you consult the best reference books by the best writers, reliable local nurseries, and experienced friends, you will find that plants behave differently in different situations; in the end, what counts is personal experience. Prior research is essential, providing vital guidance, and it is worth walking around your neighborhood to see exactly which plants are being grown successfully.

USING COLOR

Color is, of course, a most important consideration. If you are making a large perennial garden it is a good idea to put your planting suggestions on paper, even using colored pencils or paints to help you see how the colors work together. You do not need to be an artist—rough shapes or blobs of color will do. You would not want or expect to have all the plants in flower at the one time, but you need to think about overlapping flowering times.

If you want a cool-looking yard you could restrict yourself to white, blue, cream, or pale pink flowers, with some silver foliage plants as accents. Red, yellow, and orange flowering plants will give you a hot and vibrant look. Sometimes the addition of an area of very strong color lifts the yard out of the ordinary. Some very famous long perennial borders cover a wide color range, starting with very soft pastel colors, ending with strong, hot colors. Another idea is to position clumps of the same plant at intervals along a border, as the repetition will add to the effect of the design. Even if you have only a small space to work with, you will find the repetition gives more form to the garden.

BLUE LUPINS and white poppies provide a cool contrast with the bright reds and yellows in the extensive borders behind.

PERENNIALS FOR ALL SEASONS

At every season of the year there is some perennial plant in flower. Winter brings the delicate and subtle beauty of the winter or Lenten rose (*Helleborus* spp.), and also bergenia in mild areas. Spring brings a succession of flowers in both mild and cold districts. Columbines, armeria, Solomon's seal, candelabra primula, geum, pinks, and heuchera are just a few of the beautiful spring-flowering perennials. Summer brings bergamot, achillea, platycodon, and rudbeckias, some of which flower well into the fall. Fall perennials include chrysanthemums, favored for their garden display and cut flowers, while red hot pokers, sedum, and asters provide color and interest at a time when annuals are either being pulled out or planted for the next season. These fall-flowering perennials, along with some fall-flowering bulbs such as colchicums and nerines, will carry your yard beautifully into winter.

Perennials also generally combine well with spring bulbs. While the perennials are still dormant, or are just beginning to put on new growth, the bulbs produce flowers, providing a combination of foliage and blooms. Then, when the bulbs have finished performing and the foliage is beginning to look untidy and start dying, the perennials begin to take over, becoming the dominant garden feature.

ACANTHUS MOLLIS
Bear's breeches

LITTLE FLOWERS in purple and white open along tall spikes above the foliage.

THE BEAR'S BREECHES in this Scottish garden are thriving in the open. The masses of handsome foliage suit a large yard where you can stand back and see the plants in perspective.

FEATURES

HERBACEOUS

Also known as bear's breeches, this handsome foliage plant grows from 28 to 39in high, and can make a clump close to 39in wide. The dark, glossy leaves provided the inspiration and model for the decoration on Corinthian columns. This striking feature plant is at its best when mass-planted, although one generous clump can be extremely effective in quite a small area. It enjoys full sunlight, but also tolerates shade. The stiff flower spikes of purple-and-white flowers appear among the foliage from the spring into summer. It can be quite a vigorous grower, although it dies back after flowering. It can multiply quickly once established, but is rarely troublesome.

ACANTHUS AT A GLANCE

A. mollis is a vigorous Mediterranean perennial liking dry, stoney ground. Hardy to 5°F (zone 7), with bold, shapely foliage.

Jan	/	Recommended Varieties
Feb	sow	*Acanthus mollis* "Fielding Gold"
Mar	divide	
Apr	transplant	*A.m.* "Hollard's Gold"
May	flowering	*A.m.* Latifolius Group
Jun	flowering	
July	/	Companion Plants
Aug	/	*Bergenia* x "Ballawley"
Sept	/	Forsythia
Oct	divide	Gypsophila
Nov	/	*Syringa vulgaris*
Dec	/	

CONDITIONS

Aspect It flowers best in full sun, but also grows in light shade.

Site Needs well-drained soil that contains plenty of organic matter to aid water retention. Give plants a deep layer of mulch with compost in the spring, and then a second application in mid-summer, if necessary.

GROWING METHOD

Propagation Grows from seed sown in spring, or divide clumps in the spring or fall. Plant new divisions 12–16in apart. Young plants must be given ample water in dry weather during the spring and summer. After flowering, cut back on the watering.

Feeding Apply a complete plant food as growth starts during the spring.

Problems Since slugs and snails can cause a lot of damage to young growth, badly disfiguring it, take precautions. No other problems are known.

FLOWERING

Season The tall spikes of purple-and-white flowers appear in late spring and summer.

Cutting It is possible to use this as a cut flower; the dried spikes make good indoor decoration.

AFTER FLOWERING

Requirements Protect young plants with straw over winter. Cut off the flowering stems once faded.

ACHILLEA
Yarrow

LONG-FLOWERING and not as invasive as the species, the new hybrid achilleas will give great pleasure for months.

ACHILLEA IS ALSO KNOWN *as soldier's woundwort, nosebleed, and sanguinary, which reflects its value in herbal medicine.*

FEATURES

SUMMER AUTUMN WINTER SPRING

HERBACEOUS

Yarrow are vigorous perennials offering heights from 2in to 4ft. The species has flattish heads of white flowers and feathery foliage, but cultivars have flowers in a lovely range of shades, including yellow, pink, apricot, and crimson. Flowers are long-lasting. Yarrow is quick and easy to establish, and may need to be controlled; however, the runners are quite easy to pull out. Some of the cultivars are less invasive than the species.

A. filipendulina has flat heads of bright yellow flowers that last all summer. Selected forms have deep or pale yellow blooms. Best planted in large drifts, yarrow is ideal for the back of borders or among annuals.

ACHILLEA AT A GLANCE

Mainly deciduous perennials grown for their attractive, daisy-like summer and fall flowers. Hardy to 5°F (zone 7).

		Recommended Varieties
Jan	/	*Achillea* "Coronation Gold"
Feb	sow	*Achillea filipendulina*
Mar	sow	"Cloth of Gold"
Apr	transplant	*A. f.* "Gold Plate"
May	divide	*A.* x *lewisii* "King Edward"
Jun	flowering	*A. millefolium*
July	flowering	"Cerise Queen"
Aug	flowering	*A. m.* "Lilac Beauty"
Sept	flowering	*A. m.* "White Queen"
Oct	/	*A.* "Moonshine"
Nov	/	*A. tomentosa*
Dec	/	

CONDITIONS

Aspect Needs full sunlight for the best results, but will tolerate some shade for part of the day.
Site Any well-drained soil is suitable.

GROWING METHOD

Propagation Grows easily if established clumps are lifted and divided in the spring. Plant the vigorous new divisions 8–12in apart, and discard the old ones. New, young plants need regular watering in prolonged dry spells, but once established achillea is remarkably drought-tolerant, and needs only an occasional deep drink.
Feeding Apply a complete plant food as growth commences in the spring.
Problems No specific pest or disease problems are known to attack achillea.

FLOWERING

Season The long flowering period lasts throughout the summer into early fall. Regular removal of the spent, fading flower stems will significantly prolong blooming.
Cutting The flowers are good for cutting because they have a reasonably long vase life. Take handfuls of cut flowers for the vase as soon as the heads are fully open. Also excellent for drying.

AFTER FLOWERING

Requirements Cut off any spent flower stalks that remain on the plant in late fall.

AGAPANTHUS
African blue lily

THE BLUE AND WHITE flowering heads of agapanthus are composed of numerous flowers. They make a striking feature.

THIS DENSE PLANTING of agapanthus needs little attention and rewards the gardener with its wonderful summer flowers.

FEATURES

SUMMER AUTUMN WINTER SPRING

HERBACEOUS

Agapanthus has dark green, strap-shaped leaves that grow to about 20in long. It produces rounded heads of blue or white flowers on top of stems 39in or more tall, but even without the flowers it makes a great foliage accent. It is hardy in moderate areas, but in colder regions needs winter protection. The Headbourne hybrids are particularly hardy. It can be grown in containers, and looks excellent in eye-catching tubs. Several attractive dwarf forms have foliage that rarely exceed 8in.

CONDITIONS

Aspect   Tolerates some shade, but the flowering will be poor. Full sunlight is ideal.

AGAPANTHUS AT A GLANCE

A vigorous perennial, forming bold, eye-catching flowering clumps, from southern Africa. Many hardy to 23°F (zone 9).

Jan	/	Recommended Varieties
Feb	sow	*Agapanthus africanus*
Mar	sow	*A. a.* "Albus"
Apr	divide	*A. caulescens*
May	transplant	"Lilliput"
Jun	/	"Loch Hope"
July	flowering	"Peter Pan"
Aug	flowering	*A. praecox* "Variegatus"
Sept	flowering	
Oct	/	
Nov	/	
Dec	/	

Site   Grows in almost any soil, but well-drained ground with organic matter is perfect. In colder yards, grow near a south-facing wall.

GROWING METHOD

Propagation   Divide clumps in the spring, ensuring that each division has a crown and a good batch of healthy roots. The latter can be shortened and some outer leaves removed, if necessary. Plant approximately 10in apart. Also grows from seed sown in the spring. It needs regular watering to establish, but once settled it can cope with long, dry periods. However, for the best growth and flowering, do not let new, young plants dry out.

Feeding   Apply complete plant food in the early spring. Potted plants will perform better with an application of slow-release granules, or a monthly liquid feed, carefully following the manufacturer's recommended rate.

Problems   There are no particular problems, but clumps will harbor groups of snails. Pick off.

FLOWERING

Season   Blooms appear in mid- to late summer, depending on the conditions.

Cutting   Agapanthus can be used as a cut flower if the stems are plunged into boiling water for 15 seconds immediately after cutting.

AFTER FLOWERING

Requirements   No pruning needed, other than cutting off spent flower stems and dead leaves. Protect crowns over winter with a thick mulch of straw or dry leaves.

ALCHEMILLA MOLLIS

Lady's mantle

LONG USED as a folk medicine to help heal wounds and gynecological problems, lady's mantle is today usually grown for its decorative value and ability to self-seed. The pure lime-green flowers brighten the yard, making a marvellous contrast against the wide, lobed leaves.

FEATURES

HERBACEOUS

This is a quick-growing herbaceous perennial mostly used as a border plant to edge paths and beds. An abundant self-seeder, it is good for suppressing weeds, filling any free spaces, often popping up in cracks in paths. Growing anywhere between 8 and 16in high, one plant may spread to 11–16in. The rounded, slightly hairy leaves overlap one another, and the plant produces trusses of bright lime-green flowers through summer. It provides a lovely contrast with other, stronger colors. The leaves tend to trap raindrops or dew, adding to the effect.

ALCHEMILLA AT A GLANCE

A. mollis is a hardy perennial grown for its prolific self-seeding and attractive lime-green foliage. Hardy to 5°F (zone 7).

		Companion Plants
Jan	/	
Feb	sow	Delphinium
Mar	sow	Dicentra
Apr	transplant	Eremurus
May	transplant	Eucomis
Jun	flowering	Euonymus
July	flowering	Geranium
Aug	flowering	Gladiolus
Sept	flowering	Lupin
Oct	divide	Rose
Nov	/	
Dec	/	

CONDITIONS

Aspect Thrives in full sun, although it tolerates a degree of light shade.

Site Needs well-drained soil that has a high organic content.

GROWING METHOD

Propagation Self-sown seedlings can be easily transplanted to other positions. Clumps can be divided in the spring or fall with the divisions spaced 8–10in apart. Newly planted specimens may need watering, but mature plants tolerate dry periods. Justifiably known as a great survivor and spreader.

Feeding Apply a complete plant food as the new growth begins.

Problems No specific problems are known.

FLOWERING

Season Masses of lime-green flowers appear from late spring through the summer.

Cutting A great favorite with flower arrangements.

AFTER FLOWERING

Requirements If you do not want plants to self-seed, trim spent flowers as soon as they fade. Once flowering has finished and growth begins to die down, the plants can be cut back hard with shears, or even a trimmer if you want to be ruthless.

ALSTROEMERIA
Peruvian Lily

ALSO KNOWN AS THE LILY of the Incas, the Peruvian lily can be placed in a mixed perennial border as here, or planted between shrubs. Bold groupings are best. Gardeners can choose from a colorful range of species and cultivars, but may be unable to obtain some of the varieties sold by florists.

FEATURES

HERBACEOUS

The Peruvian lily is grown commercially on a large scale, since the flowers are long lasting when cut. In the garden it is a herbaceous perennial with flower spikes growing mostly 12–24in high, although there are dwarf forms and very tall ones. The flowers are beautifully marked with streaks and spots of color, contrasting with a wide range of base colors of cream, yellow, orange, pink, and red. If conditions are suitable, these plants spread by means of fleshy rhizomes (roots) to form large clumps. Also excellent when grown in pots.

ALSTROEMERIA AT A GLANCE

A hardy perennial surviving 14°F (zone 8). Grown for their excellent showy flowers—many make unbeatable cut flowers.

Jan	/	Recommended Varieties
Feb	/	
Mar	/	*Alstroemeria ligtu* hybrids
Apr	sow	"Orange Gem"
May	/	"Orange Glory"
Jun	transplant	"Princess Mira" (and all
July	flowering	"Princess" varieties)
Aug	flowering	"Solent Crest"
Sept	flowering	"Solent Rose"
Oct	divide	"Stamoli"
Nov	/	"Strapripur"
Dec	/	"Staroko"
		"Stasilva"

CONDITIONS

Aspect　Needs full sunlight and shelter to thrive, especially in colder areas. Also requires shelter from strong wind. Makes an excellent potted greenhouse plant.

Site　Must have very free-draining soil containing plenty of decayed organic matter.

GROWING METHOD

Propagation　Many grow readily from seed sown in the spring, but division of established clumps is easiest; spring is generally considered the best time. Bare-root plants can be hard to establish; pot-grown plants, available in the summer, are better. Plant the roots 2in deep and about 6in apart. In a prolonged dry period, water the bedded plants regularly in the spring and summer, but restrict watering after flowering.

Feeding　Apply slow-release granular fertilizer in spring.

Problems　No specific problems are known.

FLOWERING

Season　Most species and their cultivars flower from the spring into summer, some into fall.

Cutting　This is a first-class cut flower.

AFTER FLOWERING

Requirements　Cut off spent flower stems at ground level. Protect crowns with straw during cold winters.

AQUILEGIA
Columbine

WIDELY CONTRASTING COLORS *successfully combine in the flowers of this modern, long-spurred hybrid columbine.*

AN OPEN WOODLAND SETTING *is ideal for columbines, letting them freely self-seed forming, bold, distinctive groups.*

FEATURES

HERBACEOUS

These old-fashioned favorites, also called granny's bonnets, give a fine display in the garden and make decorative cut flowers. The foliage is often blue-green, and the flowers come in single colors—white, pink, crimson, yellow, and blue—and combinations of pastel and brighter shades. There are also excellent black and whites ("Magpie"). The older forms have short-spurred flowers that resemble old-fashioned bonnets, especially "Nora Barlow," a good double which is a mix of red, pink, and green. Modern hybrids are long spurred, and available in many single colors and bicolors. Plants may be 16–28in high. Columbines are not long lived but are easily seed grown. Ideal for the dappled garden, grow them under deciduous trees and in borders.

CONDITIONS

Aspect	Prefers semi-shade, and thrives in woodland gardens, but full sun is not a problem.
Site	Needs well-drained soil that contains plenty of organic matter.

GROWING METHOD

Propagation	Clumps are actually quite hard to divide, but it can be done, the fall being the best time. Columbine also grows from seed sown in early spring, or in the fall. Self-sown plants are hardy, but note that they may not always be true to type. Space plants about 12in apart. New young plants must not be allowed to dry out in prolonged dry spells in the spring and summer months. Keep a careful watch.
Feeding	Apply complete plant food in the spring as the new growth begins to emerge.
Problems	No particular pest or disease problems are known for this plant.

FLOWERING

Season	There is a long flowering period from mid-spring to mid-summer.
Cutting	Flower stems can be cut for the vase, and they make an attractive display, but the garden show lasts considerably longer.

AFTER FLOWERING

Requirements	Spent flower stems can either be removed or left on the plants enabling the seeds to mature. Cut back the old growth to ground level as it dies off.

AQUILEGIA AT A GLANCE

A clump-forming perennial, happy in semi-shade, perfect for the cottage garden where it freely self-seeds. Hardy to 5°F (zone 7).

		Recommended Varieties
Jan	/	
Feb	/	*Aquilegia bertolonii*
Mar	sow	*A. canadensis*
Apr	transplant	*A. flabellata*
May	flowering	*A. f.* var. *pumila*
Jun	flowering	*A. f.* var. *f. alba*
July	/	"Henson Harebell"
Aug	/	"Magpie"
Sept	divide	Music series
Oct	sow	*A. vulgaris* "Nora Barlow"
Nov	/	
Dec	/	

ARMERIA MARITIMA
Sea thrift

EACH FLOWERHEAD resembles a tiny posy, which is why thrift makes a fine cut flower, alone or in a composition with other flowers.

POOR STONY GROUND, which resembles thrift's natural habitat, provides ideal conditions for growing this plant.

FEATURES

Also known as sea thrift, this evergreen perennial grows in little grassy mounds 2–5in high. It occurs naturally in northern Europe and around the Mediterranean, often in very exposed situations, including cliff tops. The rounded flowerheads are carried above the foliage on stems 6–12in high. Flowers vary in color in the species and may be white, pink, or almost red, and there are a number of named cultivars available. Thrift can be used as a groundcover or edging plant, or can be planted in rockeries, on dry walls, or in poor soil where few other plants will survive. It also makes a good container plant.

ARMERIA AT A GLANCE

A. maritima is an attractive evergreen, clump-forming perennial which colonizes inhospitable areas. Hardy to 0°F (zone 7).

Jan	/	
Feb	/	**Recommended Varieties**
Mar	division	*Armeria maritima* "Alba"
Apr	/	*A. m.* "Corsica"
May	transplant	*A. m.* "Launcheana"
Jun	flowering	*A. m.* "Ruby Glow"
July	flowering	*A. m.* "Splendens"
Aug	flowering	*A. m.* "Vindictive"
Sept	/	
Oct	/	
Nov	/	
Dec	/	

CONDITIONS

Aspect Needs full sun all day. Thrift tolerates dry, windy conditions and salt spray, and is an excellent choice for coastal gardens.

Site Grows in any kind of soil so long as it is very well drained. Adding sharp sand will improve the drainage.

GROWING METHOD

Propagation Divide established clumps in the spring and replant about 6–8in apart. The species can be grown from seed sown in the spring, or from semi-ripe cuttings taken in the summer

Feeding Give a light dressing of complete fertilizer in early spring.

Problems Thrift has a tendency to rot if soils are in any way too heavy, poorly drained, or overwatered. In humid weather and in sheltered positions it may also be susceptible to the fungal disease which is called rust. Use a fungicide to attack the problem.

FLOWERING

Season Thrift has a long flowering period through spring and summer, provided the plants are deadheaded regularly.

Cutting Makes a good cut flower.

AFTER FLOWERING

Requirements Regularly remove spent flower stems to give a prolonged flowering period.

ASTER
Michaelmas daisy

RICH MAUVE flowers virtually obscure the foliage on a mature plant.

THE ATTRACTIVE Aster ericoides, which has produced many excellent cultivars.

ONE OF the best of the reds is the low-growing "Winston Churchill."

FEATURES

HERBACEOUS

There is a wide variety of asters, and all of them flower in late summer and the fall. The most commonly grown is *A. novi-belgii*, which has a range of cultivars from dwarf forms 10in high to tall varieties reaching 39in. Flowers are blue, violet, pink, red, or white, and all are good for cutting. *A. ericoides* has very small leaves and produces stems of white flowers up to 39in high. *A.* x *frikartii* grows about 30in tall and has violet-blue flowers. All of these plants are extremely easy to grow and tolerate a wide range of conditions. They multiply readily. Taller varieties need staking.

ASTER AT A GLANCE

Hardy perennials creating large clumps, giving strong fall color in most situations. Hardy to 5°F (zone 7).

Jan	/		Recommended Varieties
Feb	sow		
Mar	sow		*Aster alpinus*
Apr	divide		*A. amellus* "Framfieldii"
May	transplant		*A. a.* "Jacqueline Genebrier"
Jun	/		"Coombe Fishacre"
July	flowering		*A. ericoides* "Golden Spray"
Aug	flowering		*A.* x *frikartii* "Monch"
Sept	flowering		*A. novae-angliae*
Oct	divide		*A. novi-belgii* "Audrey"
Nov	/		
Dec	/		

CONDITIONS

Aspect	Grows best in full sun. Tolerates light shade, but blooming may not be so prolific and growth will be less compact.
Site	Add well-rotted organic matter to the soil. Feed and water well to counter disease.

GROWING METHOD

Propagation	Divide clumps in late winter. These plants are prolific growers—one plant will multiply itself tenfold in a season. Replant divisions 8in apart. The best results are from regular watering during the spring and summer, especially in long, dry periods.
Feeding	Apply complete plant food in early spring.
Problems	Powdery mildew can be a major problem, especially with varieties of *A. novi-belgii*. Mildew-resistant varieties include *A.* x *frikartii* and varieties of *A. amellus*.

FLOWERING

Season	The long flowering display lasts from late summer into the fall.
Cutting	Cut flowers last very well if given a frequent change of water.

AFTER FLOWERING

Requirements	Cut off spent flower stems close to ground level after blooming. Plants will gradually die back, but should not need more close attention until new growth appears in the next spring.

ASTILBE HYBRIDS
Astilbe

SOFT AND FEATHERY, the pale pink plumes on this astilbe will provide a long display of bright flowers and fern-like foliage.

UPRIGHT SIDE BRANCHES are an unusual feature of this deep pink astilbe cultivar. They give an eye-catching, stiff appearance.

FEATURES

HERBACEOUS

These perennial hybrids revel in moist soil and light shade, although they can be grown in an open, sunny position if well watered. The shiny, compound leaves are quite attractive, with astilbe also bearing tall plumes of soft flowers 20in or more tall, in shades of pink, red, mauve, or white. They look best when mass-planted, and are ideal for surrounding ponds, or naturalizing in a wild garden. They can be used as cut flowers, but they are probably best left in the yard where their big, theatrical effect can be enjoyed for much longer. They can quickly flag in a heat wave; water at the first sign of wilting.

ASTILBE AT A GLANCE

A rhizomatous perennial that enjoys damp soil. Striking, tall flowerheads can reach 4ft tall. Hardy to 5°F (zone 7).

Jan	/	Recommended Varieties
Feb	sow	*Astilbe x arendsii*
Mar	divide	"Brautschleier"
Apr	transplant	A. x *a.*"Bronce Elegans"
May	flowering	A. x *a.*"Fanal"
Jun	flowering	A. x *a.* "Irrlicht"
July	flowering	A. x *a* "Snowdrift"
Aug	flowering	A. x *crispa* "Perkeo"
Sept	flowering	"Rheinland"
Oct	/	A. *simplicifolia*
Nov	divide	"Sprite"
Dec	/	

CONDITIONS

Aspect These are versatile plants, performing equally well in bright sunlight and dappled shade.

Site The ideal soil is rich in organic matter and retains plenty of moisture. Regular, heavy applications of mulch are essential.

GROWING METHOD

Propagation Divide clumps in late fall, ensuring that each division has a crown and a decent set of roots. Plant at 8–10in spacings. New, young plants need plenty of water in prolonged dry spells in the spring and summer months. Do not let them dry out.

Feeding Apply a general fertilizer as growth starts in the spring, and repeat 6–8 weeks later.

Problems No specific problems are known.

FLOWERING

Season Flowers from late spring through the summer. The flower display is longer lasting in a cooler summer.

Cutting Flowers can be cut for indoor decoration.

AFTER FLOWERING

Requirements Spent flowerheads will turn a pleasant rich brown color, and are quite attractive through the winter months. They add considerable interest to the yard. Do not cut back spent flower stems to ground level until the following spring.

ASTRANTIA MAJOR
Masterwort

ASTRANTIA MAJOR *"HADSPEN BLOOD"* *is a striking, vibrant red, more of an eye-catcher than the species, which is much whiter. Both can be used to link and soften more permanent shrubby features, or as part of a free-flowing, flowery display for late spring and early summer.*

FEATURES

HERBACEOUS

Also known as masterwort, *Astrantia major* is a "must-have" for the "cottage garden," a clump-forming perennial that produces delightful sprays of green or pink, sometimes reddish flowers, surrounded by green-veined white bracts. A native of central Europe, it grows about 24in tall, forming clumps 18in wide. Flowering in early and mid-summer, it can be left to colonize areas of dappled shade, though it also enjoys full sunlight. There are some excellent cultivars, including the new "Hadspen Blood," a striking blood red, "Shaggy" with long bracts, and "Sunningdale Variegated," with pale pink bracts and yellow/ cream leaves. Best in large clumps.

ASTRANTIA AT A GLANCE

A. major is a clump-forming perennial grown for its abundant, attractive flowers. Excellent cultivars. Hardy to 0°F (zones 6–7).

Jan	/	Recommended Varieties
Feb	/	*Astrantia major alba*
Mar	divide	*A. m.* "Claret"
Apr	divide	*A. m.* "Hadspen Blood"
May	transplant	*A. m. involucrata* "Shaggy"
Jun	flowering	*A. m. rosea*
July	flowering	*A. m. rubra*
Aug	sowing	*A. m.* "Sunningdale
Sept	/	Variegated"
Oct	/	
Nov	/	
Dec	/	

CONDITIONS

Aspect Thrives in either dappled shade or a more open, sunny position.

Soil Likes compost-rich, moist, fertile soil, though it will tolerate drier conditions. Woodland gardens and streamsides are ideal.

GROWING METHOD

Propagation Can either be grown from seed sown in late summer, once ripe, or by division in the spring. Plant out at least 18in apart, or closer for an immediate covering. Do not let young plants begin to dry out in a prolonged dry spring or summer spell. The variants do not require such moist conditions, and will tolerate drier soil.

Feeding Lay a mulch around the plants in the spring. This has two advantages: it enriches the soil and also prevents moisture loss.

Problems Slugs can be a major problem, attacking the stems and foliage. Pick off when seen. Powdery mildew can also strike; spray against attacks.

FLOWERING

Season The one flowering spell is in early and mid-summer.

Cutting Makes good cut flowers, which can be used to soften a stiff, structural arrangement, or as part of a more flowery display.

AFTER FLOWERING

Requirements Cut down the spent flower stems, and tidy up the foliage.

AURINIA SAXATILIS
Golden dust

A SHARP, ATTRACTIVE CONTRAST, with the bright yellow flowers of golden dust against clusters of green, spoon-shape foliage.

YELLOW AND BLUE always make a lively color combination, as this wonderful planting of golden dust and Italian lavender proves.

FEATURES

EVERGREEN

This is a little, rounded, evergreen perennial that can grow from 4 to 12in high, forming a mound up to 16–20in across. In the species the flowers are a clear yellow, but the various cultivars produce flowers in white, cream, lemon, or rich gold. Since its natural habitat is rocky, mountainous country, it is ideal for a rock garden, for dry, sloping ground, or for edging garden beds, provided the drainage is excellent. It is also ideally suited to troughs and the edges of large pots, perhaps containing a shrub. Although golden dust is a perennial, some gardeners grow it as part of an annual spring display.

AURINIA AT A GLANCE

A. saxatilis is an evergreen, hardy perennial that forms thick clumps topped by yellow flowers. Hardy to 0°F (zone 6–7).

Jan	/	Recommended Varieties
Feb	/	*Aurinia saxatilis* "Citrina"
Mar	transplant	*A. s.* "Compacta"
Apr	/	*A. s.* "Dudley Nevill"
May	flowering	*A. s.* "Goldkugel"
Jun	flowering	*A. s.* "Silver Queen"
July	/	
Aug	/	Companion Plants
Sept	/	*Aurinia corymbosa*
Oct	sow	Aubrieta
Nov	/	
Dec	/	

CONDITIONS

Aspect   Needs an open position in full sunlight.
Site   Soil must contain plenty of chalk, sand, or grit, and be free-draining but not rich.

GROWING METHOD

Propagation   Grows readily from seed sown in the fall. Cultivars can be grown from tip cuttings taken in late spring and early summer. Space the plants about 4in apart, giving them plenty of growing room. Aurinia is sold among the alpines at garden centers.

Feeding   Small amounts only of complete plant food may be given in early spring as a boost, but feeding is not essential.

Problems   No specific problems are known besides poor drainage. Overwatering pot-grown specimens can quickly rot and kill the plants.

FLOWERING

Season   Flowers appear from mid- to late spring, the flowers completely covering the plant and hiding the foliage.

Cutting   The flowers are not suitable for picking.

AFTER FLOWERING

Requirements   It is probably easiest to shear radically over the whole plant with clippers, unless you are waiting for the seed to ripen. Shearing the plants also helps to keep a compact, neatly rounded shape.

BERGENIA
Elephant's ears

THE WELL-DEFINED, SOLID SHAPE of bergenias makes them ideal edging plants, as this neat row beside a path demonstrates. Bergenias have other advantages, too, in that they flower in the shade and from late winter onward, both features that are not common among perennials.

FEATURES

EVERGREEN

An excellent evergreen, groundcover plant, it is also known as elephant's ears, because of the large, rounded leaves approximately 8–12in long. They are often leathery and glossy, generally green, many turning reddish in the fall. The flowers are held on short stems, from mid-spring to early summer, some, such as "Morgenrote," repeat-flowering in cool conditions. The color range is invariably shades of pink, with some white forms. Bergenia is not a fussy plant, and enjoys a wide range of conditions, from bright sun to shade, and from moist to dry ground. Long-living and easy to propagate, it can colonize areas beneath trees, edge paths, or front a border.

BERGENIA AT A GLANCE

A versatile evergreen with large, ornamental foliage that thrives in a range of conditions. Hardy to 0°F (zones 6–7).

Jan	/	Recommended Varieties
Feb	flowering	
Mar	flowering	*Bergenia* "Abendglut"
Apr	flowering	B. "Baby Doll"
May	flowering	B. "Bressingham Salmon"
Jun	/	B. "Bressingham White"
July	/	B. *cordifolia* "Purpurea"
Aug	/	B. "Morgenrote"
Sept	/	B. *purpurescens*
Oct	divide	B. "Silberlicht"
Nov	divide	
Dec	/	

CONDITIONS

Aspect   Grows in either full sunlight or shady areas, but avoid extremes of the latter.

Site   Likes well-composted, moist soil with good drainage, but it will also tolerate much poorer conditions that bring out a richer winter leaf color. Provide a late fall mulch.

GROWING METHOD

Propagation   Grows from seed sown in spring, producing hybrids, or divide in the spring or fall every five years to rejuvenate a declining plant. Plant up to 24in apart, depending on the variety, or closer for immediate coverage.

Feeding   Feed generously in early spring with a complete plant food, especially on poorer ground, and give a generous layer of mulch later in the fall.

Problems   Slugs and snails can be a major problem to the new, young foliage, ruining its shapely appearance. Pick off, or treat with chemicals. Spray with a fungicide if leaf spot occurs.

FLOWERING

Season   The flowers appear from late winter or early spring, depending on the variety, for a few weeks.

Cutting   Though the flowers are useful in cut flower arrangements, the foliage, especially when red in winter, makes a particularly attractive foil.

AFTER FLOWERING

Requirements Remove the spent flower stems and foliage.

CAMPANULA
Bellflower

CAMPANULA PERSICIFOLIA ALBA makes a valuable addition to a white border, flowering prolifically in early and mid-summer.

CAMPANULAS ARE THE MAINSTAY of the cottage or woodland garden, freely spreading, adding plenty of color and charm.

FEATURES

HERBACEOUS

Also known as the bellflower, campanula contains about 300 species of annuals, biennials, and perennials. Generally easy to grow in either full sunlight or dappled shade, on walls, banks, and in borders, it has a wide range of flowers, from the tubular to the saucer-shaped. They also vary considerably in height, from the low, 3in-high spreaders, like *C. betulifolia,* to the 5ft-tall *C. lactiflora.* The former are excellent at the front of a border, the latter need staking at the rear. There are many excellent forms: *C. glomerata* "Superba" is a vigorous grower, reaching 24 x 24in, while *C. burghaltii* produces pale lavender tubular bells around the same time.

CAMPANULA AT A GLANCE

A near 300-strong genus, thriving in a wide variety of conditions, grown for their abundant flowers. Hardy to 5°F (zone 7).

Jan	/	Recommended Varieties
Feb	/	
Mar	sow	*Campanula arvatica*
Apr	transplant	
May	flowering	**C. carpatica**
Jun	flowering	C. garganica
July	flowering	C. latiloba
Aug	flowering	C. medium
Sept	flowering	C. persicifolia
Oct	divide	C. thyrsoides
Nov	/	C. trachelium
Dec	/	

CONDITIONS

Aspect   Campanula thrive in both sunny yards and those with dappled shade.

Site   There are three broad types of campanula, each requiring different conditions: well-drained, fertile soil for border plants; moist, fast-draining ground for the rock garden species; and a gritty scree bed for the alpines that dislike being wet over winter.

GROWING METHOD

Propagation   Grow the species from seed in spring in a cold frame, or from cuttings, and sow alpines in a frame in the fall. Varieties must be propagated by spring cuttings, or spring or fall division if they are to grow true to the parent.

Feeding   Apply a complete plant food in the spring, especially on poorer soils, or plenty of dug-in, organic material.

Problems   Slugs and snails are the major problem, and if not kept under control they can ruin a border display. In some areas *C. persicifolia* is prone to rust.

FLOWERING

Season   The long-lasting flowers appear from midwinter to the spring.

Cutting   Makes an excellent display of cut flowers, especially the taller plants.

AFTER FLOWERING

Requirements Cut back to the ground in late fall.

CENTRANTHUS RUBER
Red valerian

TRUSSES of rich crimson and softer pink valerian provide months of bright color in the yard, rivalling the display of annuals.

RED VALERIAN flourishing in the conditions that suit it best—the fence provides shelter, and the raised bed warmth and good drainage.

FEATURES

SUMMER AUTUMN WINTER SPRING

HERBACEOUS

This evergreen perennial is very easy to grow, but it often exceeds its allotted space by self-seeding (seedlings are easy to pull out). It has a long flowering period and can survive in poor, dry soil. It generally reaches 16in tall, but in good soil tops 28in. Flowers are a deep pink to red, and there is a white form, too. Ideal for a low-maintenance yard, it is often planted in mixed borders for its long display. It is also grown in large rock gardens and on dry, fast-draining slopes. Self-sown plants can be found in almost no soil on rocky outcrops, and thrive in chalky ground.

CENTRANTHUS AT A GLANCE

C. ruber is a hardy, herbaceous perennial, a favorite in "cottage gardens" with tall, red summer flowers. Hardy to 10°F (zones 7–8).

		Companion Plants
Jan	/	
Feb	sow	*Argyranthemum foeniculaceum*
Mar	sow	*A. frutescens*
Apr	transplant	Cytisus
May	transplant	*Geranium robertianum*
Jun	flowering	*Hedera colchica* "Dentata Variegata"
July	flowering	*Helleborus orientalis*
Aug	flowering	Stipa
Sept	flowering	Yucca
Oct	/	
Nov	/	
Dec	/	

CONDITIONS

Aspect   Likes full sunlight all day.
Soil   Needs very well-drained soil, but it need not be particularly rich.

GROWING METHOD

Propagation   Grows readily from tip cuttings taken in late spring and summer, or from seed sown in the spring. Space the plants 8in apart.
Feeding   Fertilizer is generally not necessary, but you may give a little complete plant food in the spring, as new growth begins. Needs regular watering to establish, after which plants are extremely drought-tolerant.
Problems   No specific problems are known.

FLOWERING

Season   The very long flowering period extends from the spring until early fall, especially if plants are cut back after each flowering flush to encourage plenty of new buds.
Cutting   Does not make a good cut flower.

AFTER FLOWERING

Requirements   No attention is needed, beyond removing the spent flower stems. This has a double advantage: it keeps the plant looking neat, and prevents abundant self-seeding.

CHRYSANTHEMUM HYBRIDS
Dendranthema

CASCADING OVER *the fence onto the massed erigeron below, this wonderful garden chrysanthemum gives a prolific display.*

THE QUILLED PETALS *are characteristic of this open "spider" style of chrysanthemum, as is the shading of color.*

HYBRID CHRYSANTHEMUMS *are justifiably highly popular in the cut flower trade, and are available for most of the year.*

FEATURES

HERBACEOUS

Chrysanthemums probably originated in China, but were introduced into Japan a very long time ago. A big favorite in garden and florists' displays, they are the highlight of the late summer and fall border. They are also widely used as a long-lasting cut flower. Chrysanthemums have been renamed and moved to the genus *Dendranthema*, though the name has yet to catch on. Four kinds to look out for include: the Korean (e.g. "Yellow Starlet"), which give a long flowering performance but dislike excessive winter wet (store inside in severe conditions); the thigh-high, dwarf, bushy pompons ("Mei Kyo") with a sea of rounded flowers; the clump-forming rubellums (named hybrids of *C. rubellum*) which are hardiest, have a woody base, but again dislike extreme damp; and the sprays ("Pennine") which are grown both for the border and cutting.

Color
The color range is wide, covering white, cream, yellow, many shades of pink and lilac, burgundy, pale apricot, and deep mahogany.

Types
There are many forms of chrysanthemums, and they have been classified by specialist societies and nurseries according to floral type. Some of the types are decorative, anemone centered, spider, pompon, single, exhibition, and Korean spray. There is virtually a shape for every taste.

Staking
Many of the taller varieties need staking, which needs to be carefully thought out if the display is to avoid looking too structured. One reliable, traditional method is to insert bamboo canes at intervals around and through the planting, and thread twine from cane to cane in a criss-cross fashion, perhaps 20–24in above the ground.

CONDITIONS

Aspect
Grows best in full sun with protection from strong winds.

Site
Needs well-drained soil that has been heavily enriched with organic matter before planting. Plants should also be mulched with decayed compost or manure.

THIS UNUSUAL chrysanthemum has the central petals incurved like those of the Korean spray, while the outer ones are widespread.

THE RUSSET COLORS of these flowers seem appropriate to their fall flowering season, when the leaves are turning.

GROWING METHOD

Propagation — In spring lift and divide the new suckering growth so that each new plant has its own roots and shoots. Cuttings of the new growth can be taken. Space plants 16in apart.

Feeding — Once the plants are well established you can fertilize them every four to six weeks with a soluble liquid fertilizer.

Problems — • You can spot chrysanthemum leaf miners by the wavy white or brown lines in the foliage. Furthermore, hold up the leaf to the light and you might see the pupa or grub. Control by immediately removing the affected leaves and crushing the grubs, or better still by regular spraying with a systemic insecticide.

• Chrysanthemum eelworm is evident by browning, drying leaves. Immediately destroy all infected plants. There is no available remedy.

• A number of fungal diseases can attack these plants, including leaf spot, powdery mildew, rust, and white rust. Avoid overhead watering or watering late in the day, and ensure that residue from previous plantings is cleared away. You may need to spray with a registered fungicide. White rust is a particularly serious disease, and affected plants are probably best removed and destroyed.

• Watch for aphids clustering on new growth. Pick them off by hand, wash them off, or use an insecticidal spray.

CHRYSANTHEMUM AT A GLANCE

Chrysanthemums are the colorful mainstay of the the end-of-season border. The hardy forms will tolerate 5°F (zone 7).

Jan	/		Recommended Varieties
Feb	sow		"Anna Marie"
Mar	sow		"Bronze Elegance"
Apr	divide		"Cappa"
May	transplant		"Faust"
Jun	/		"Lord Butler"
July	/		"Mrs Jessie Cooper"
Aug	flowering		"Poppet"
Sept	flowering		"Salmon Fairie"
Oct	/		
Nov	/		
Dec	/		

FLOWERING

Season — Flowering time is mid to late fall. The exciting new race of Yoder or cushion chrysanthemums from America are dwarf, hardy, free-flowering (starting in late summer), and perfect for the front of the border. Those to look out for include "Lynn," "Robin," and "Radiant Lynn."

Cutting — Cut flowers will last two to three weeks with frequent water changes, as long as the foliage is removed from the parts of the stems that are under water.

AFTER FLOWERING

Requirements Once flowering has finished, cut off plants 5–6in above the ground.

CONVALLARIA
Lily-of-the-valley

LILY-OF-THE-VALLEY makes a vivid display because of the strong contrast between the shapely oval leaves and the small, bright white flowers. It can be left to naturalize in woodland conditions, or allowed to spread through a shady border. Though invasive, it is quite easily controlled.

FEATURES

HERBACEOUS

Lily-of-the-valley is a one-species (sometimes considered three) genus, featuring the bell-shaped, fragrant *Convallaria majalis*. A native of Europe, it grows in woods and meadows, and produces 8in-tall stems of nodding white flowers shortly after the foliage has unfurled. Given the correct conditions—specifically, a cool, moist area—it can spread extremely quickly by means of underground shoots, but it is easily controlled. There are several attractive forms, "Albostriata" having cream striped foliage, and "Fortin's Giant" has flowers up to $\frac{1}{2}$in across. Lily-of-the-valley is essential in a woodland area, or in a damp shady spot where little else of note will grow.

CONVALLARIA AT A GLANCE

Basically a one-species genus with wonderful, waxy, scented spring flowers. Hardy to 5°F (zone 7). Good cultivars available.

Jan	/	Companion Plants
Feb	/	
Mar	/	Bergenia
		Euphorbia robbiae
Apr	transplant	Galanthus
May	flowering	Primula
Jun	/	Pulmonaria
July	/	Rodgersia
Aug	sow	
Sept	division	
Oct	division	
Nov	/	
Dec	/	

CONDITIONS

Aspect   Shade is essential.

Site   The soil must be damp, rich, and leafy. For an impressive, vigorous display, apply a thick mulch of leaf mold around the clumps of plants every fall.

GROWING METHOD

Propagation   When the seed is ripe, remove the fleshy covering, and raise in a cold frame. Alternatively, divide the rhizomes in the fall. A 6in piece will provide approximately six new plants. The success rate is generally high. Make sure that young plants are not allowed to dry out. Mulch them to guarantee against moisture loss.

Feeding   Every other year, apply a scattering of complete fertilizer in the spring.

Problems   *Botrytis* can be a problem, but is rarely anything to worry about.

FLOWERING

Season   One brief display in late spring.

Cutting   Lily-of-the-valley makes excellent cut flowers, providing a striking spring display, while emitting a gentle sweet scent. They can also be lifted and grown indoors in a pot to flower the following spring. When finished, replace in the garden.

AFTER FLOWERING

Requirements   Remove the spent flower stems, but leave the foliage intact to provide the energy for next year's display.

COREOPSIS
Coreopsis

COREOPSIS ARE wonderful plants which can quickly colonize a space, say between shrubs, producing striking, bright yellow flowers.

THIS DOUBLE-FLOWERED FORM of golden coreopsis provides many weeks of marvelous color throughout the summer.

FEATURES

HERBACEOUS

Perennial coreopsis carries a profusion of bright yellow daisy-like flowers over a long period, generally through summer into the fall, though some do flower in spring. Regular deadheading will ensure a long display. *C. lanceolata*, known as calliopsis, has become naturalized in many parts of the world. The strong-growing *C. grandiflora* may grow 24–36in high, with *C. verticillata* about 8in shorter. There are several species worth trying, some with dwarf form or flowers displaying a dark eye. The foliage is variable too. The plants are easy to grow. Plant in bold clumps in a mixed border.

COREOPSIS AT A GLANCE

A genus with well over 100 species that make a big contribution to the summer and early fall display. Hardy to 5°F (zone 7).

Jan	/	Recommended Varieties
Feb	/	
Mar	/	*Coreopsis auriculata*
		"Schnittgold"
Apr	sow	*C.* "Goldfink"
May	divide	*C. grandiflora* "Early Sunrise"
Jun	flowering	*C. g.* "Mayfield Giant"
July	flowering	"Sunray"
Aug	flowering	*C. verticillata*
Sept	flowering	*C. v.* "Grandiflora"
Oct	/	*C. v.* "Zagreb"
Nov	/	
Dec	/	

CONDITIONS

Aspect	Prefers an open, sunny position right through the day, with little shade.
Site	Performs best in well-drained soil enriched with organic matter, but it will grow in poor soils too. Over-rich soil may produce a profusion of foliage with poor flowering.

GROWING METHOD

Propagation	Grows most easily from divisions of existing clumps lifted in the spring. Space new plants at about 12in intervals. Species can be grown from seed sown in mid-spring. Since cultivars of *C. grandiflora* can be ephemeral, sow seed for continuity.
Feeding	Apply complete plant food as growth begins in the spring. However, no further feeding should be needed.
Problems	No pest or disease problems are known.

FLOWERING

Season	The long flowering period extends through summer and the fall. *C.* "Early Sunrise," *C. lanceolata*, and "Sunray" flower in their first year from an early sowing.
Cutting	Flowers can be cut for indoor decoration.

AFTER FLOWERING

Requirements	Cut off spent flower stems and tidy up the foliage as it dies back. In mild, frost-free winters, coreopsis may not totally die back.

CORYDALIS
Corydalis

THE FOLIAGE and flowers of Corydalis ochroleuca *are dainty and highly decorative. It looks good in walls and ornamental pots.*

THE BLUE SPECIES and forms of corydalis are highly prized. This is Corydalis flexuosa*, with long, upcurving spurs on its flowers.*

FEATURES

HERBACEOUS

Pretty, fern-like foliage and tubular, spurred flowers are characteristic of the 300 or so species of corydalis. Only a small number of species are grown in cultivation, and they mainly flower in shades of yellow or blue, but there are some in pink or crimson. Some of the brilliant blues make a distinctive feature, and a recent cultivar with electric blue flowers, known as *C. flexuosa* "China Blue," is now widely available. It mixes well with *C. solida* "George Baker," salmon-pink, and *C. ochroleuca*, white. Heights vary from 6 to 24in. Many corydalis are excellent rock garden plants, while others are suitable for mixed borders or planting under deciduous trees. Many varieties may be available only from specialist nurseries that grow alpine plants.

CORYDALIS AT A GLANCE

A large group of annuals, biennials, and perennials, growing in a wide range of moist and dry conditions. Hardy to 5°F (zone 7).

Month	Activity	Recommended Varieties
Jan	/	
Feb	/	*Corydalis cashmeriana*
Mar	/	*C. cava*
Apr	divide	*C. cheilanthifolia*
May	transplant	*C. elata*
Jun	flowering	*C.lutea*
July	flowering	*C.sempervirens*
Aug	flowering	*C. solida*
Sept	divide	*C. s.* "Beth Evans"
Oct	sow	*C. s. f. transsylvanica*
Nov	/	*C. s. f.* "George Baker"
Dec	/	

CONDITIONS

Aspect   The preferred aspect varies with the species. Some tolerate an open, sunny position, while others need degrees of dappled sunlight. Species grown in "hot spots" should be given plenty of shade.

Site   Needs very well-drained soil that is able to retain some moisture in the summer.

GROWING METHOD

Propagation   Grows from seed sown as soon as it is ripe, in the fall. The seed is ripe when the small elongated capsules, which form after the flowers have fallen, turn brown and dry. Some species can be divided, while others produce tubers from which offsets can be taken. Plant at 4–6in intervals. New young plants need regular watering in prolonged, dry weather during the spring and summer months.

Feeding   Apply a sprinkling of slow-release fertilizer when growth commences in the spring.

Problems   There are no specific pest or disease problems.

FLOWERING

Season   Most species flower in the spring, or from spring into summer. *C. flexuosa* dies down in the summer.

Cutting   The flowers are unsuitable for cutting.

AFTER FLOWERING

Requirements   Remove spent flower stems, unless you are waiting for seed to set. Tidy up the foliage as it dies back.

CYNARA CARDUNCULUS
Cardoon

CARDOON LOOKS *similar to a Scotch thistle. Its purple flowers can be left to dry, and then used for a striking indoor arrangement.*

THE SILVERY LEAVES *of cardoon are distinctive, large, and shapely, and a big clump forms a geometric, sculptural feature.*

FEATURES

HERBACEOUS

A close relative of the globe artichoke, the cardoon is generally grown for its arching, 39in-long, silver-gray foliage. Growing up to 78in tall and almost 78in wide, it is a terrific accent plant for the back of a border, or it can be combined with low-growing green plants in an open position. Both the color and form stand out against most other plants. The purple, thistle-like flowers develop in the summer, and the dried heads left on the plant make a decorative fall feature. Cardoon is edible, being grown for the tasty, fleshy base of each leaf. It is difficult to place in a small yard, since you need room to stand back and appreciate its startling form.

CYNARA AT A GLANCE

C. cardunculus is a clump-forming perennial grown for its long, striking foliage and purple flowers. Hardy to 0°F (zones 6–7).

Jan	/	Companion Plants
Feb	/	
Mar	sow	Brugmansia
Apr	divide	Centranthus
May	transplant	Echinops
Jun	flowering	Geranium
July	flowering	Miscanthus
Aug	flowering	Rose
Sept	flowering	Salvia
Oct	/	Yucca
Nov	/	
Dec	/	

CONDITIONS

Aspect	Needs full sun all day for best results. Also requires shelter from strong, leaf-tearing winds.
Soil	Needs rich, well-drained soil. Before planting, dig in large amounts of manure or compost.

GROWING METHOD

Propagation	Propagate in late spring, or grow from seed. Position plants at least 4ft apart. Seed-grown plants vary in quality, and do not normally reach maturity in their first year. During the growing season, regular, deep watering is essential for new, young plants in prolonged dry spells.
Feeding	Apply a complete plant food as growth commences in the spring, and repeat in mid-summer. When cardoon is grown as a vegetable it is given a weekly liquid feed.
Problems	Beware of the sharp points on the flowerheads.

FLOWERING

Season	The purple, thistle-like flowers appear during summer on stems 6½–10ft high.
Cutting	If the flowers are allowed to dry on the plant, they can be cut and used as part of a big, bold indoor decoration.

AFTER FLOWERING

Requirements	Once the flowers have lost their decorative value, cut off the whole stem low down. As the plant starts to die off and look untidy, cut it back just above the ground.

DELPHINIUM
Delphinium

DOZENS OF individual flowers make up the striking spires of the delphinium. Blue shades, from pale to purple, predominate.

THESE STAKED DELPHINIUMS, growing in the shelter of a house, should remain stately and upright through the flowering season.

FEATURES

HERBACEOUS

Tall, handsome, and stately, delphiniums make an outstanding feature in perennial borders. Growing 39–78in high, the long-lasting spires of blooms, originally were in a rich blue only, but now offer shades of pink, lavender, white, and red. Delphiniums should be mass-planted at the back of a border for the best effect, but they can also be placed as accent plants at intervals across a border. They mix well with climbers like clematis. Tall-growing varieties may need staking unless they are in a very sheltered spot. Colors can be mixed, but the best effect comes from massing plants of the same color.

DELPHINIUM AT A GLANCE

A hardy annual, biennial, and perennial, it is grown for its striking, vertical spires, thick with flowers. Hardy to 5°F (zone 7).

		Recommended Varieties
Jan	/	
Feb	sow	*Delphinium* "Bruce"
Mar	sow	"Cassius"
Apr	transplant	"Emily Hawkins"
May	transplant	"Lord Butler"
Jun	flowering	"Our Deb"
July	flowering	"Rosemary Brock"
Aug	flowering	"Sandpiper"
Sept	/	"Sungleam"
Oct	divide	"Walton Gemstone"
Nov	/	
Dec	/	

CONDITIONS

Aspect   Needs full sun and shelter from strong winds, and staking if it is not well sheltered.

Soil   Needs well-drained soil enriched with copious amounts of decayed manure or compost before planting. Water regularly and mulch.

GROWING METHOD

Propagation   Divide established clumps in the fall, ensuring each division has a crown and its own roots. Place them about 12in apart. Grows from seed sown in the spring, but the results are variable. Take 3in basal cuttings in mid-spring.

Feeding   Apply complete plant food once growth begins in the spring, and each month until flowering.

Problems   Watch for aphids on new growth, and hose off or spray with pyrethrum or insecticidal soap. In humid conditions a bad attack of powdery mildew may need to be tackled by spraying with a fungicide. Beware of slugs.

FLOWERING

Season   Blooms for a long season through early and late summer.

Cutting   Flowers make a good display, and can be dried.

AFTER FLOWERING

Requirements   Remove the flower stems when the main blooms fade and small spikes may flower in late summer and early fall.

DIANTHUS CARYOPHYLLUS
Wild carnation

FRINGED PINK FLOWERS and silver-gray buds and stems make this a classic.

UPWARD-ANGLED CANES are one way of making sure that top-heavy blooms do not tumble onto a path. The other, more discrete method is to employ a series of small twiggy sticks.

FEATURES

EVERGREEN

Carnations are very popular, both as cut flowers and as a garden subject. Flowers are carried singly or in groups on stems 12–20in high, although florists' carnations may be taller. *Dianthus caryophyllus* from the Mediterranean, a woody perennial with elegant stiff stems, bears richly scented, purple-pink flowers that grow taller than the average, reaching 32in under perfect conditions. It has given rise to several excellent series. The Floristan Series comes in a wide color range, and makes good cut flowers, the Knight Series is shorter and bushier, and includes yellow, white, and orange blooms, and the Lilliput Series, shorter still at 8in, includes a rich scarlet.

DIANTHUS AT A GLANCE

D. caryophyllus is a colorful woody perennial, part of the large dianthus family of over 300 species. Hardy to 5°F (zone 7).

		Companion Plants
Jan	/	
Feb	/	Campanula
Mar	sow	Cistus
Apr	/	Crepis
May	transplant	Eryngium
Jun	flowering	Helianthemum
July	flowering	Portulaca
Aug	flowering	Sedum
Sept	/	Tulip
Oct	/	
Nov	/	
Dec	sow	

CONDITIONS

Aspect Needs full sunlight all day. Protect from very strong winds.

Soil Needs very well-drained soil, with plenty of additional, well-decayed organic matter. Unless the soil is alkaline, apply a light dressing of lime before each planting.

GROWING METHOD

Propagation Grows easily from cuttings taken at almost any time. Use leafy side shoots and strip off all but the top leaves. Roots form in 3–5 weeks. Set newly rooted plants 8in apart. Water regularly to establish, then occasionally in dry weather. Carnations tolerate dry conditions well.

Feeding Little fertilizer is needed if the soil contains plenty of organic matter, but you may give a complete feed twice, in the spring and again in mid-summer.

Problems Carnation rust, a fungal disease, is common in warm, humid conditions. Grayish spots appear on leaves or stems, and the foliage may curl and yellow. Take prompt action by immediately spraying with a fungicide. Remove caterpillars when seen.

FLOWERING

Season The crop of flowers appears in the summer, but it can be forced for other times. Remove any excess buds to produce good-sized, main blooms.

Cutting An excellent cut flower. Recut stems between nodes (joints) to aid water uptake.

DIANTHUS CULTIVARS
Pinks

DIANTHUS CULTIVARS make reliable, popular edging plants with bright colors and, in many cases, a rich, pervasive scent.

ONE OF THE BEST pinks for the garden, or as a cut flower, "Doris" is vigorous, long-flowering, and sweetly scented. A "must-have."

FEATURES

Pinks are crosses of *D. caryophyllus* (wild carnation) and *D. plumarius* (cottage pink). Allwood Brothers nursery in West Sussex, England, has bred an enormous range of cultivars that are free-flowering, given the correct conditions. The gray-green foliage grows in a tufted mat and flowering stems are 4–12in tall. Most flowers are heavily scented and may be single or bicolored, some with a clear margin of contrasting color. Most are white, pink, red, deep crimson, or salmon, with cultivars ideally suited for the rock garden.

CONDITIONS

Aspect   Needs full sunlight all day, and protection from strong winds.

Site   Needs very free-draining soil, enriched with

additional decayed organic matter, well ahead of planting. Use a soil-testing kit to determine whether your soil is acid—if so, add quantities of lime according to the manufacturer's instructions. Beware of exceeding the recommended rate—it will simply do more harm than good.

GROWING METHOD

Propagation   Grows easily from cuttings taken in late summer and the fall. Start fresh plants every three or four years to keep vigorous, compact growth. Space the plant approximately 6–12in apart, depending on the variety. Water until the plants are well established.

Feeding   Apply complete plant food in the early spring, when active spring growth begins.

Problems   Aphids and slugs are the two major problems. The former can be tackled by a regular spraying program with, for example, malathion. The latter can be seen late at night or early in the morning. Either treat chemically, or pick off by hand and drown.

FLOWERING

Season   Some pinks only flower during the spring, others have a long flowering period from the spring to early fall.

Cutting   Pinks make excellent cut flowers, providing indoor decoration and scent.

AFTER FLOWERING

Requirements   Cut off any spent flower stems to the ground as they fade. No other pruning action is necessary.

DIANTHUS AT A GLANCE

The cultivars include perennials in a wide color range, many richly scented. Generally hardy to 5°F (zone 7).

Month	Activity	Recommended Varieties
Jan	/	
Feb	/	*Dianthus alpinus*
Mar	sow	"Bovey Belle"
Apr	transplant	"Devon Glow"
May	transplant	*D. deltoides*
Jun	flowering	"La Bourboule"
July	flowering	"Monica Wyatt"
Aug	flowering	"Sam Barlow"
Sept	/	"Whitehill"
Oct	sow	"Widecombe Fair"
Nov	/	
Dec	/	

DIASCIA
Twinspur

ONE OF THE MOST USEFUL *garden plants, twinspur produces flowers throughout the growing season, from the spring to fall, and at 12in tall, it makes the perfect front-of-border filler, tolerating a sunny position, and one with a degree of shade. Despite a short lifespan, it is easily propagated.*

FEATURES

Twinspur has an extremely long flowering season, lasting from the spring until the first frosts. Though there is a large number of forms available, ranging from "Lilac Mist" to "Salmon Supreme," the color range is quite limited, essentially only including shades of pink. Diascia requires moist, rich soil, but over-feeding results in fewer flowers. The height ranges from 6 to 12in, which means the taller plants can be given free reign to burst through their neighbors, adding to the display. "Salmon Supreme" is an attractive low-spreader, being

6in high. *D. vigilis* is twice as tall, hardier, and even more free-flowering.

CONDITIONS

Aspect Enjoys full sun; though it tolerates some shade, it will not flower as long or as prolifically.
Soil Moisture-retentive, well-drained ground.

GROWING METHOD

Propagation This is essential, since diascias are short-lived, but propagation is easily managed. Success rates are high by all methods, though cuttings are particularly easy. Either sow the seed when ripe or in the following spring, take cuttings during the growing season, or divide in the spring. Since young plants might die in severe winters, keep indoor cuttings as possible replacements.
Feeding Mulch well in the spring to enrich the soil.
Problems Slugs and snails are the main enemies. Pick them off or use a chemical treatment.

FLOWERING

Season An unusually long season from the spring, beyond the end of summer, to the first frosts.
Cutting Diascias cut well, and although they do not last particularly long in water, replacements are quickly available from the parent plant.

AFTER FLOWERING

Requirements Cut ruthlessly to the ground after flowering to promote a second flush of flowers.

DIASCIA AT A GLANCE

A near 50-strong genus of annuals and perennials, with a pink color and a long flowering season. Hardy to 23°F (zone 9).

Jan	/	
Feb	sow	
Mar	divide	
Apr	transplant	
May	flowering	
Jun	flowering	
July	flowering	
Aug	flowering	
Sept	flowering	
Oct	/	
Nov	/	
Dec	/	

Recommended Varieties

Diascia barberae "Ruby Field"
D. "Dark Eyes"
D. "Hector's Hardy"
D. integerrima
D. "Lilac Mist"
D. "Rupert Lambert"
D. vigilis

DICENTRA SPECTABILIS
Bleeding heart

THE ARCHING STEMS *of this bleeding heart carry masses of bright pink, heart-shaped flowers resembling tiny lockets.*

THE BLEEDING HEART *is well worth growing for its foliage alone, since the delicate, fern-like leaves are very decorative.*

FEATURES

HERBACEOUS

With fern-like foliage and curving stems bearing pretty pink-and-white, heart-shaped flowers, bleeding heart is an all-time favorite perennial. It appeals to children and adults alike. There is a cultivar, "Alba," which has pure white flowers. Another species less commonly grown is *D. formosa*, which has very ferny foliage, but its flowers are not so completely heart-shaped. Bleeding heart can be grown in a mixed border or in the filtered shade of trees. Plants may reach 16–24in tall in good conditions, and form a clump approximately 20in wide.

DICENTRA AT A GLANCE

D. spectabilis is a clump-forming perennial, with arching stems and decorative deep pink flowers. Hardy to 0°F (zones 6–7).

Jan	/	Recommended Varieties
Feb	/	
Mar	sow	*D.* "Adrian Bloom"
Apr	transplant	"Bountiful"
May	transplant	*D. cucularia*
Jun	flowering	*D. f. alba*
July	flowering	"Langtrees"
Aug	/	"Ruby Slippers"
Sept	/	*D. macrantha*
Oct	division	*D. spectabilis*
Nov	sow	*D. s.* "Alba"
Dec	/	"Stuart Boothman"

CONDITIONS

Aspect   Dicentra grows best in filtered sunlight. Strong, hot, drying winds make it shrivel up. A sheltered position protects against late frosts.

Site   Needs well-drained soil rich in organic matter. Dig in copious quantities of decayed manure or compost several weeks before planting.

GROWING METHOD

Propagation   Divide large established clumps in the fall, and plant divisions 10–12in apart. Also grows from seed sown in the spring or fall. Needs regular, deep watering during dry periods in the spring and summer.

Feeding   Apply a sprinkling of a complete plant food whenever growth begins in the spring.

Problems   There are no specific pest or disease problems known for this plant.

FLOWERING

Season   Blooms for several weeks during late spring and early summer.

Cutting   Flowers are not suitable for cutting.

AFTER FLOWERING

Requirements   Cut out spent flower stems. As the foliage yellows and dies off, cut it off just above the ground.

ECHINACEA PURPUREA
Purple coneflower

BOLDER THAN *many perennials, coneflowers are sometimes slow to appear in the spring but they are definitely worth the wait.*

THIS FINE STAND *of bright purple coneflowers adds a striking touch to this scheme. The flowers fade as they age, but petals don't fall.*

FEATURES

Native to the prairie States of America, the coneflower is a hardy, drought-resistant plant. Its dark, cone-shaped center is surrounded by rich pink ray petals, and there are cultivars available in shades of pink-purple and white. They make excellent cut flowers. Coneflowers often grow over 39in tall, and are a great addition to a perennial border because they bloom over a long period, from mid-summer into the fall, when many other plants have finished. Echinacea should be mass-planted to get the best effect. Excellent varieties include *E. purpurea* Bressingham Hybrids, "Magnus," and "White Swan."

ECHINACEA AT A GLANCE

E. purpurea is an attractive, daisy-like perennial with purple flowers, ideal for naturalizing or borders. Hardy to 5°F (zone 7).

Month	Activity	Companion Plants
Jan	/	
Feb	sow	Allium
Mar	sow	Delphinium
Apr	transplant	Geranium
May	transplant	Gladiolus
Jun	/	Iris
July	flowering	Lavandula
Aug	flowering	Rosemary
Sept	flowering	Yucca
Oct	divide	Delphinium
Nov	/	Rose
Dec	/	

CONDITIONS

Aspect   Prefers full sunlight all day. Although it is tolerant of windy conditions, the blooms will have a better appearance if the plants are sheltered from strong winds.

Site   Needs well-drained, rich soil. Poor or sandy soils can be improved by digging in large quantities of compost or manure before planting.

GROWING METHOD

Propagation   Divide existing clumps in the early spring or fall, and replant divisions 8–10in apart. It can be grown from seeds sown in early spring, which may produce color variations. Echinacea needs regular watering to establish itself in prolonged dry spells, but occasional deep soakings in dry weather are enough, as it tolerates dry conditions well.

Feeding   Apply complete plant food in early spring and again in mid-summer.

Problems   No specific problems are known.

FLOWERING

Season   There is a long flowering period from late summer into the fall.

Cutting   Cut flowers for the vase when they are fully open, but before the petals separate.

AFTER FLOWERING

Requirements   Remove spent flower stems. The whole plant can be cut back to ground level in winter.

ECHINOPS
Globe thistle

THESE METALLIC BLUE *globe thistles form an elegant picture against a stone wall.*

EARLY MORNING LIGHT *accentuates the rounded, slightly spiky heads of these globe thistle flowers, planted here in a bold drift in a countryside yard.*

FEATURES

HERBACEOUS

This plant's very distinctive appearance makes a good accent in a mixed planting. Taller species need to be placed at the rear of a border, but others can be planted in bold groups through the bed. Most have foliage that is stiff, prickly, and finely divided, with silvery stems growing from 12in to 6½ft tall. Some of the species have foliage that has fine white hairs on the underside. The flowerheads are usually white or metallic blue, and are highly prized for their decorative value when cut and dried. The most commonly grown is *E. ritro* and its cultivars, some of which have deep blue flowers. *E. sphaerocephalus* has pale gray-to-silvery flowers.

ECHINOPS AT A GLANCE

A group of annuals, biennials, and perennials grown for their geometric shapes and blue flowers. Hardy to 23–50°F (zones 9–11).

Jan	divide	Recommended Varieties
Feb	divide	
Mar	sow	*Echinops bannaticus* "Blue Globe"
Apr	/	*E. b.* "Taplow Blue"
May	transplant	*E. ritro ruthenicus*
Jun	/	*E. r.* "Veitch's Blue"
July	flowering	
Aug	flowering	Companion Plants
Sept	flowering	Buddleja
Oct	divide	Kniphofia
Nov	divide	Perovskia
Dec	divide	

CONDITIONS

Aspect Prefers full sunlight all day.
Site Soil must be very well drained but need not be rich. The globe thistle can be grown in poor, gravel-like, or sandy soils.

GROWING METHOD

Propagation It can either be grown from seed, from division of existing clumps, or from root cuttings. All propagation is done from the fall to winter. Plant out about 16in apart and water regularly to establish. Although drought-tolerant, this plant benefits from occasional deep watering during prolonged dry spring and summer periods.
Feeding Apply a complete plant food or poultry manure in early spring.
Problems There are no known pest or disease problems, but plants will rot on sticky clay or poorly drained soil.

FLOWERING

Season Each species or variety will flower for approximately two months.
Cutting Flowerheads required for drying should be cut before the blooms are fully open.

AFTER FLOWERING

Requirements Cut off any remaining spent flowerheads, unless you want the seed to ripen. As the plant dies down, clean away dead foliage, wearing gloves to protect yourself against the foliage.

EPIMEDIUM
Barrenwort / Bishop's miter

NEW GROWTH on the bishop's miter bears attractive bronze or pink shadings, but the older foliage is plain green.

A DENSE CARPET of bishop's miter makes wonderful groundcover under a grove of shapely Japanese maples.

FEATURES

HERBACEOUS

EVERGREEN

This low-growing perennial is grown more for its attractive foliage than its flowers, although the blooms are quite attractive. The shape resembles a bishop's miter, giving rise to its common name. Many species have small, starry flowers in white, cream, or yellow, although there are pale and rose-pink varieties, too. This is a woodland plant that makes a good groundcover or filler for shady parts of the yard. Some die down completely in winter, while others remain evergreen. Plants are rarely more than 12in tall. Combine it with plants such as Solomon's seal, primrose, or lenten rose, which enjoy similar woodland-type conditions.

EPIMEDIUM AT A GLANCE

An evergreen, deciduous perennial making excellent groundcover in shady situations. Small flowers. Hardy to 5°F (zone 7).

		Recommended Varieties
Jan	/	
Feb	sow	*Epimedium cantabrigiense*
Mar	/	*E. grandiflorum*
Apr	transplant	*E. g.* "Nanum"
May	flowering	*E. g.* "Rose Queen"
Jun	/	*E. perralderianum*
July	/	*E. pinnatum colchicum*
Aug	/	*E.* x *rubrum*
Sept	sow	*E.* x *versicolor* "Sulphureum"
Oct	divide	
Nov	/	
Dec	/	

CONDITIONS

Aspect   Epimedium needs dappled shade and protection from strong winds.

Site   Requires well-drained soil, heavily enriched with organic matter. Regular mulching is beneficial to retain moisture.

GROWING METHOD

Propagation   Clumps can be divided in the fall, although with some varieties this is not easy. Pull apart or cut away sections of plant, keeping both roots and a bud or shoot on each piece. Plant 6–8in apart. Some species seed readily. Keep young plants well watered until they are well established.

Feeding   Apply a slow-release fertilizer in the spring.

Problems   Snails may attack soft new growth when it appears, so take precautions.

FLOWERING

Season   The small flowers appear in spring, along with the leaves. But shear off the foliage of all varieties in winter, even when green (except *E. perralderianum*), to prevent the flowers being obscured. Fresh leaves will quickly follow.

Cutting   Flowers can be cut for the vase and last quite well in water.

AFTER FLOWERING

Requirements   Spent flower stems can be clipped off. Old, dead foliage should be tidied up and removed by the end of the fall.

ERYNGIUM
Sea holly

AN OUTSTANDING PLANT for the Mediterranean-style garden is Eryngium maritimum. *It has strong architectural features with a stiff, branching habit, and mid- to late summer flowers. It can be grown in the border, or better still, in a gravel bed to highlight the shape.*

FEATURES

HERBACEOUS

EVERGREEN

Sea holly is a 230-species strong genus, with annuals, biennials, and perennials. Although they are related to cow parsley, they bear no resemblance, being grown for their marvellous, attractive, spiky appearance, blue flowers (though some are white or green), and ability to thrive in poor, rocky, sunny ground. Heights can vary considerably, from *E. alpinum*, 28in tall, which as its name suggests grows in the Alps, to *E. eburneum* from South America, which can reach 5ft, and *E. pandanifolium*, which is much taller at 10ft. One of the most attractive is the Moroccan *E. variifolium*, which has rounded, white-veined foliage setting off the pale blue flowers. It is also more manageable at 14in high—good for the front of a border.

ERYNGIUM AT A GLANCE

Annuals, and deciduous/evergreen perennials grown for their shape. Hardiness varies from 13°F (zone 8) to 0°F (zones 6–7).

Jan	/	
Feb	sow 🌱	**Recommended Varieties**
Mar	division	*Eryngium alpinum*
Apr	transplant ✋	*E. a.* "Blue Star"
May	transplant ✋	*E. bourgatii*
Jun	flowering 🌼	*E. b.* "Oxford Blue"
July	flowering 🌼	*E. giganteum*
Aug	flowering 🌼	*E. x oliverianum*
Sept	flowering 🌼	*E. x tripartitum*
Oct	sow 🌱	
Nov	/	
Dec	/	

CONDITIONS

Aspect   Grow in full sunlight, well out of the shade.
Site   There are two types of sea holly, with different growing needs. Most prefer fast-draining, fertile ground (e.g. *E. alpinum* and *E. bourgatii*), and some (e.g. *E. eburneum*) poor stony ground, out of the winter wet.

GROWING METHOD

Propagation   Sow the seed when ripe; alternatively, take root cuttings in late winter, or divide in the spring.
Feeding   Only for the first kind of sea holly, which benefits from a spring feed and some well-rotted manure. Good drainage is important.
Problems   Slugs and snails are the main problem when sea holly is grown in the border, damaging the new, young leaves. Promptly remove when seen, or use a chemical treatment.

FLOWERING

Season   The earliest sea hollies begin flowering in early summer, while others last from mid- to early or mid-fall in dry weather.
Cutting   Sea holly makes an invaluable cut flower. They also make exceptional dried arrangements, combining with other architectural plants and softer, flowery ones.

AFTER FLOWERING

Requirements   Cut back the spent flowering stems to the ground.

GERANIUM
Cranesbill

THE FOLIAGE on this clump-forming, North American Geranium macrorrhizum *is as attractive as its pink-white or pink flowers. The leaves are scented and quickly form a dense carpet.*

GERANIUM PRATENSE, *with its deep violet flowers that bloom over a long period.*

FEATURES

HERBACEOUS

EVERGREEN

There are a great many perennial species of the true, hardy geranium, and many are reliable, long-flowering plants. Most cranesbill geraniums (not to be confused with tender, pot-plant pelargoniums) are easy to grow and are ideal in perennial borders, as edging plants, or as an infill between shrubs. Some species self-sow freely, but unwanted seedlings are easily removed. Cranesbills range from about 6 to 39in tall. Most have attractive, deeply divided leaves, and the flowers cover a range of shades, mostly in violet, blue, pink, rose, and cerise. Species worth seeking out include *G. endressii* and its cultivars, especially "Wargrave Pink," *G. pratense*, *G. psilostemon*, *G. himalayense*, and *G. sanguineum*. A variety of *G. sanguineum*, "Lancastriense," is a dwarf-growing type that can be used as groundcover.

GERANIUM AT A GLANCE

A genus of some 300 annuals, biennials, and perennials grown for their big flowering clumps. Most are hardy to 5°F (zone 7).

Jan	/	Recommended Varieties
Feb	sow	*Geranium himalayense*
Mar	sow	"Gravetye"
Apr	divide	"Johnson's Blue"
May	transplant	*G. x oxonianum* "Wargrave
Jun	flowering	Pink"
July	flowering	*G. palmatum*
Aug	flowering	*G. pratense* "Mrs Kendall
Sept	flowering	Clark"
Oct	sow	*G. psilostemon*
Nov	/	
Dec	/	

CONDITIONS

Aspect   Most like sunlight; others prefer shade.
Site   Needs open, well-drained soil, but it need not be rich. Very acid ground should be limed before planting; use a soil-testing kit to ascertain the quantity required.

GROWING METHOD

Propagation   Most cranesbills are easily grown from seed sown in the fall, but note that the results will be variable. They can also be grown from cuttings taken in the growing season. Established clumps can be lifted and divided in the spring. The exact spacing depends on the variety, but it is usually within the range of 8–16in. Established plants tolerate dry conditions and rarely need watering, except in prolonged droughts.
Feeding   Apply a little complete plant food when growth starts in the spring.
Problems   No specific pest or disease problems are known for these plants.

FLOWERING

Season   Cranesbills flower through the spring, into late summer.
Cutting   Flowers do not cut well.

AFTER FLOWERING

Requirements   Remove spent flower stems, unless you want the plants to seed. Some pruning may be needed through the growing season if growth becomes too rampant. Prune to maintain shape.

GEUM CHILOENSE
Avens

THE BRIGHT RED double geum "Mrs J Bradshaw," a justifiably popular perennial.

LIKE MOST PERENNIALS, geums look best when planted together in large numbers. Here a mass of deep red flowers looks wonderful against a background of green foliage.

FEATURES

HERBACEOUS

Although there are many species of geum, the two most commonly grown are cultivars. "Lady Stratheden" has double yellow flowers, and "Mrs J Bradshaw" bright scarlet double flowers. Flowers appear on stems 12–20in tall high that emerge from large rosettes of slightly hairy, lobed compound leaves. Foliage is generally evergreen, but may be herbaceous in some areas. Geums can be planted as accent plants, preferably in groups, in the wild garden or near the front of a mixed border. While flowers are not very suitable for cutting, they give a long, vibrant display in the yard if they are regularly deadheaded.

GEUM AT A GLANCE

A brightly colored perennial, essential for the spring border, with plenty of attractive cultivars. All hardy to 0°F (zones 6–7).

Jan	/	Recommended Varieties
Feb	sow	"Borisii"
Mar	divide	"Fire Opal"
Apr	transplant	"Lady Stratheden"
May	flowering	*G. montanum*
Jun	flowering	"Mrs J Bradshaw"
July	/	*G. rivale*
Aug	/	*G. urbanum*
Sept	/	
Oct	divide	
Nov	/	
Dec	/	

CONDITIONS

Aspect   Prefers full sunlight, but it can also be grown successfully in dappled shade.

Site   Needs well-drained soil. Plants will benefit from the addition of plenty of decayed manure or compost before planting.

GROWING METHOD

Propagation   Clumps can be divided in the spring or fall. Cut back foliage to reduce moisture loss while divisions re-establish. It also grows from seed sown in spring, but plants may not be true to type. Plant about 10–12in apart. Since most popular varieties tend to be short-lived, propagate often for a regular supply.

Feeding   Apply complete plant food in early spring and again in mid-summer.

Problems   No particular problems are known.

FLOWERING

Season   There is a long flowering display, through late spring and mid-summer. Young vigorous plants will keep going to the fall.

Cutting   Regular cutting (or deadheading) is essential to prolong the display.

AFTER FLOWERING

Requirements   None, apart from the removal of spent flower stems and any dead foliage that may accumulate under the rosette.

GUNNERA MANICATA
Gunnera

THE HUGE, *theatrical, eye-catching leaves of* Gunnera manicata.

DAMP GROUND *at the bottom of this steep bank allows the clump of gunnera to thrive in its favorite conditions. The attractive pink-flowering shrub beside it is a hawthorn (*Crataegus *species).*

FEATURES

HERBACEOUS

This is not a plant for small yards. Growing to 8½ft high, clumps grow 10–13ft wide. The huge rhubarb-like leaves can be well over 42in in diameter, and are supported by long, stout, hairy stems. This is a magnificent feature plant from Africa, Australasia, and South America. It needs a damp or wet yard area, beside a pond or stream, or to the edge of a lawn. In summer it produces a dramatic tall spike of greenish flowers, often completely concealed by the foliage, but this plant is grown for the impact of its giant, architectural foliage. It is herbaceous, dying right back to the ground in winter. This is not a difficult plant to grow in the correct conditions, but it must be carefully sited. It needs space to grow, and gardeners need space to stand back and admire it.

GUNNERA AT A GLANCE

One of the largest, most spectacular perennials, it produces huge, often lobed, leaves. Spectacular flower spike. Hardy to 5°F (zone 7).

Jan	/	Recommended Varieties
Feb	/	*Gunnera arenaria*
Mar	/	*G. flavida* (groundcover)
Apr	transplant 🌱	*G. hamiltonii*
May	transplant 🌱	*G. magellanica*
Jun	/	(groundcover)
July	flowering 🌼	*G. manicata*
Aug	/	*G. prorepens*
Sept	sow 🖐	*G. tinctoria*
Oct	/	
Nov	/	
Dec	/	

CONDITIONS

Aspect Grows both in semi-shade and sunlight in cool, damp areas.

Site Likes a rich, moist soil. Dig plenty of organic matter into the ground before planting, and mulch crowns heavily with decayed compost or manure for protection.

GROWING METHOD

Propagation Divide small clumps in the spring, replanting them no less than 6½ft apart. Cuttings can be taken from new growth, too. Pot them up and nurture them until they are well rooted. Plants can be raised from seed, but this is slow and difficult. Keep moist throughout the spring and summer.

Feeding Apply pelleted poultry manure as new growth commences in the early spring to give the plant a boost. Add a fresh mulch of rotted manure at the same time.

Problems No specific pest or disease problems are known for gunnera.

FLOWERING

Season Heavy spikes of greenish flowers are produced in early summer.

Fruits The inflorescence is followed by fleshy red-green fruits, which can be ornamental.

AFTER FLOWERING

Requirements As the weather becomes cold in the fall and leaves begin to brown, cut off the foliage and cover the crown of the plant with a thick layer of straw. Use a large leaf as a hat to keep it dry.

GYPSOPHILA PANICULATA
Baby's breath

THE WONDERFUL, MASSED DISPLAY OF Gypsophila paniculata *"Pink Star" in full bloom. The rippling, airy mound of flowers justifiably led to its common name, baby's breath. It makes a stunning sight in its native habitats, spreading across the sandy steppes of the Far East and eastern Europe.*

FEATURES

HERBACEOUS

Baby's breath is an eye-catching border perennial that grows to 4ft high, and produces a summer flower display that looks like a puffy aerial cloud. The flowers appear in mid- and late summer, and are white on the species, though there are gently colored cultivars. "Compacta Plena" is soft pink, "Flamingo" is lilac-pink, and "Rosenschleier" pale pink. The latter is also quite short, at 1ft tall, and is worth repeat-planting in a long border. "Bristol Fairy" has the advantage of large, white flowers, ½in across, but it is not as vigorous as the rest and is relatively short-lived, needing to be propagated every few years. *G. paniculata* mixes well with contrasting, vertical plants.

CONDITIONS

Aspect   Full sunlight is required for it to thrive.
Site   Free-draining soil is essential, since the plant's native habitat is sandy steppes and stony sites in eastern Europe, Central Asia, and China.

GROWING METHOD

Propagation   Sow seed in a cold frame in spring, or in pots in a gently heated greenhouse in winter. Species can be propagated by root cuttings, again in late winter. Though adult plants tolerate some dryness, the young plants must not be allowed to dry out. Water regularly in the growing season. Plant out in its final position, since it dislikes disturbance.
Feeding   A scattering of complete plant food in the spring.
Problems   Generally problem-free.

FLOWERING

Season   The one flowering period is mid- and late summer; an unmissable sight.
Cutting   Makes excellent cut flowers—the light sprays of white-to-pink flowers add considerably to any arrangement, formal or flowery.

AFTER FLOWERING

Requirements   Cut back to ground level in the fall.

GYPSOPHILA AT A GLANCE

A striking, tallish herbaceous perennial that gives an impactful, flowery mid-summer display. Hardy to 0°F (zones 6–7).

Month		Companion Plants
Jan	/	
Feb	/	*Agapanthus africanus*
Mar	sow	*Geranium himalayense*
Apr	transplant	*Iris* "Magic Man"
May	/	*Osteospermum* "Whirligig"
Jun	/	*Salvia cacaliifolia*
July	flowering	*Silene coeli-rosa*
Aug	flowering	*Solanum crispum*
Sept	/	
Oct	/	
Nov	/	
Dec	/	

HELENIUM AUTUMNALE
Sneezeweed

STILL ONE OF THE BEST *and most popular cultivars of sneeze-weed, "Moerheim Beauty" has been a favorite since the 1930s.*

ORANGE AND TAWNY COLORS *are a feature of sneezeweed, a reliable perennial that brightens the fall garden.*

FEATURES

HERBACEOUS

As its Latin name suggests, this herbaceous perennial flowers from late summer to mid-fall. The straight species has bright golden, daisy-like flowers with dark centers, but many of the most popular cultivars have flowers in rich tones of orange-red or copper-red. "Butterpat," "Moerheim Beauty," and "Waldtraut," are among the most popular varieties. Sneezeweed can grow 39–60in or more high, eventually forming large clumps over 20in across. Flowers cut well, but the plant is probably more valuable for its contribution to the fall garden. Place at the back of a perennial border or among shrubs. Easy to grow.

HELENIUM AT A GLANCE

A group of annuals, biennials and perennials. Grown for their prolific, bright flowering display. Hardy to 5°F (zone 7).

Jan	/	
Feb	sow	
Mar	sow	**Recommended Varieties**
Apr	transplant	"Butterpat"
May	transplant	"Chipperfield Orange"
Jun	/	"Crimson Beauty"
July	flowering	"Moerheim Beauty"
Aug	flowering	"Rotgold"
Sept	flowering	"The Bishop"
Oct	/	
Nov	/	
Dec	/	

CONDITIONS

Aspect Needs to be grown in full sun right through the day. Avoid shade.

Site Needs a moisture-retentive soil heavily enriched with organic matter. It will not thrive in dry soil. Mulch around clumps to help keep soil moist.

GROWING METHOD

Propagation Established clumps can be lifted and divided about every three years. Discard the oldest central sections and replant the divisions about 12in apart in spring or fall. Give new young plants a regular watering right through the growing season.

Feeding Apply complete plant food as new growth commences in spring.

Problems Sneezeweed is generally free from problems, although slugs and snails can damage newly emerging growth in damp weather.

FLOWERING

Season The flowering season starts in mid-summer and continues into the fall.

Cutting Flowers cut well for indoor decoration.

AFTER FLOWERING

Requirements Spent flower stems should be removed. As the plant dies down, cut off and remove dead foliage. It can be chopped and left on the ground as a mulch. With flowers blooming into the fall, the foliage remains in good condition until attacked by frost.

HELLEBORUS
Lenten rose

PRETTY SHADINGS of color are shown on the Lenten rose. Seedlings often produce unexpected colors, which can be maintained if the plants are then propagated by division.

NATIVE to Corsica and Sardinia, this is the green-flowered Helleborus argutifolius.

FEATURES

Various species of hellebores are known as the Christmas or Lenten rose because of their flowering times—mid-winter or early spring. *H. niger*, which has pure white flowers with green centers, can be difficult to grow to perfection; *H. argutifolius* (syn. *H. corsicus*) and *H. orientalis* are more resilient. *H. argutifolius* has lovely lime-green flowers and spiny-toothed leaf margins, while *H. orientalis* is more variable and may have white, green, pink, or mottled flowers. Cultivars include a deep crimson variety. These perennials are mostly evergreen and are best planted under deciduous trees, where they can remain undisturbed. Some are fairly short-lived, but they tend to self-seed freely so that numbers readily increase, creating an impressive sight.

HELLEBORUS AT A GLANCE

A free-spreading, attractively flowering perennial in a wide range of colors. Excellent in woodland. Hardy to 23–59°F (zones 9–11).

		Recommended Varieties
Jan	flowering	
Feb	flowering	*Helleborus argutifolius* (syn.
Mar	flowering	*H. corsicus*)
Apr	divide	*H. foetidus*
May	transplant	*H. lividus*
Jun	/	*H. niger*
July	/	*H. x nigercors*
Aug	/	*H. orientalis* Cultivars
Sept	/	*H. x sternii* Blackthorn
Oct	/	Group
Nov	/	*H. viridis*
Dec	/	

CONDITIONS

Aspect Prefers dappled sunlight under trees, or in other partially shaded spots.

Site Soil must be well enriched with organic matter, and able to retain moisture. Excellent in winter containers.

GROWING METHOD

Propagation Divide clumps in the spring or summer, directly after flowering, replanting the divisions about 8–12in apart. Seed can be sown when ripe, but seedlings will take about three years to flower. Seedlings often produce interesting shades. Recently planted hellebores need plenty of water in prolonged, dry spells in the spring and summer.

Feeding Apply a little complete plant food in the spring. Mulch each spring with manure or compost to aid moisture retention.

Problems Leaf blotch can disfigure and weaken plants. Spray with a fungicide. Beware aphids, particularly after flowering. Slugs attack the flowers and foliage.

FLOWERING

Season From mid-winter to early spring.

Cutting Lenten roses provide attractive cut flowers at the time of year when supply is short.

AFTER FLOWERING

Requirements Prune off the dead flower stems and any dead leaves. Do not disturb.

HEMEROCALLIS
Daylily

MAHOGANY RED is one of the many strong colors available in the huge range of daylily cultivars now available from specialist growers.

THE MASS PLANTING of this creamy yellow daylily increases its impact. Blooms will appear one after the other for many weeks.

FEATURES

HERBACEOUS

EVERGREEN

Easily grown in a wide range of conditions, the daylily is a trouble-free plant with single or double flowers. As its name suggests, individual flowers last only one day, but they are produced over a long period. They come in a wide range of colors, the main ones being shades of yellow, orange, red, magenta, and purple. There is an enormous number of exciting, attractive hybrids available from specialist growers. The clumps of grassy foliage may be from 10–39in high; some are evergreen while others die down in winter. While straight species are not as readily available as the hybrids, they are important in hybridizing new varieties and several species are worth seeking out. They include *H. altissima* from China, which has pale yellow fragrant flowers on stems 5ft or so high, and *H. lilio-asphodelus*, which has pale yellow fragrant flowers above leaves 22in high.

Categories Daylilies have been divided into five categories which list them according to flower type. The divisions are circular, double, spider-shaped, star-shaped, and triangular. Most are single; hot weather can produce extra petals and stamens.

Dwarf forms The number of dwarf forms available is steadily increasing and they may be better suited to today's smaller gardens. Those with a reliable reflowering habit can also be successfully grown in pots. Use a good quality potting mix and crowd three plants into a 8in pot for good effect. "Little Grapette," "Little Gypsy Vagabond," "Penny's Worth," and "Stella d'Oro" are good ones to try, all growing about 12 x 18in.

Uses Mass plantings of dwarf or tall forms create the best effect. Daylilies are not plants that should be dotted about in the garden. Use large numbers of either the one variety or use varieties of similar color; it is clearly preferable to planting a mixture of types or colors. In a mixed border they give a very pleasing effect as the foliage is very full.

"BURNING DAYLIGHT," one of the top daylilies, blooms prolifically in sun or semi-shade.

MANY OF the finest daylily cultivars are in creamy yellow or orange tones, not surprisingly as these are the colors of many of the species.

CONDITIONS

Aspect   Grows best in full sun but tolerates semi-shade. Can be mass planted on banks or sloping ground as the roots are very efficient soil binders.

Site   Grows in any type of soil, wet or dry, but to get maximum growth from the newer hybrids the soil should be enriched with manure or compost before planting.

HEMEROCALLIS AT A GLANCE

A genus of semi-, evergreen, and herbaceous perennials; 30,000 cultivars that give a long summer show. Hardy to 5°F (zone 7).

		Recommended Varieties
Jan	/	
Feb	sow 🖐	"Burning Daylight"
Mar	sow 🖐	"Cartwheels"
Apr	transplant 🖐	"Golden Chimes"
May	transplant 🖐	"Neyron Rose"
Jun	flowering 🌸	"Pink Damask"
July	flowering 🌸	"Red Precious"
Aug	flowering 🌸	"Stafford"
Sept	flowering 🌸	"Whichford"
Oct	divide 🖐	"Zara"
Nov	/	
Dec	/	

GROWING METHOD

Propagation   Divide established clumps in spring or fall. Cut back foliage before or straight after division. Spacing may be from 6–12in, depending on variety.
New plants need regular watering to establish. Once established, plants are very drought tolerant, but better sized blooms can be expected if deep waterings are given every week or two.

Feeding   Grows without supplementary fertilizer, but an application of complete plant food in early spring encourages stronger, more vigorous growth.

Problems   Daylilies growing in very soggy ground tend to survive quite well but produce few flowers. Otherwise no problems.

FLOWERING

Season   Depending on variety, plants may be in bloom any time from late spring until the fall. Most flowers only last one day.

Cutting   Single flowers can be cut for the vase. Attractive and well worth using.

AFTER FLOWERING

Requirements   Cut off any spent flower stems. Herbaceous types that die down in the fall can have their foliage cut back too.

HEUCHERA SANGUINEA
Coral flower

DAINTY LITTLE PINK FLOWERS are massed above the attractive foliage, making the North American coral flower an excellent choice for the front of a border or a garden bed. Here they are planted to provide an excellent foil for the abundant blooms of white roses behind.

FEATURES

EVERGREEN

This perennial forms a low rosette of lobed leaves that make a neat plant for edging, or for mass-planting at the front of the border. The foliage is evergreen. Established plantings produce a striking display of blooms. The flower stems, which stand above the foliage, are from 12 to 18in tall. The species has red flowers; cultivars are available with pink, white, or deeper crimson blooms. Note the superb foliage varieties ("Palace Purple"—chocolate-colored; "Pewter Moon"—gray; and "Snow Storm"—white flecked). New American varieties include "Pewter Veil."

HEUCHERA AT A GLANCE

H. sanguinea is a red-flowering, summer perennial forming low, wide clumps, 6 x 12in. Hardy to 5°F (zone 7).

		Recommended Plants
Jan	/	
Feb	sow	*Heuchera americana*
Mar	sow	"Chocolate Ruffles"
Apr	divide	*H. cylindrica*
May	transplant	"Green Ivory"
Jun	flowering	"Helen Dillon"
July	flowering	"Persian Carpet"
Aug	flowering	"Pewter Moon"
Sept	/	"Rachel"
Oct	divide	"Red Spangles"
Nov	/	"Scintillation"
Dec	/	

CONDITIONS

Aspect   Prefers full sun but tolerates light shade.
Site   Needs very well-drained, open-textured soil. Permanently wet soil will kill this plant.

GROWING METHOD

Propagation   Clumps can be divided in the spring or in the fall, but ensure that each division has its own set of healthy roots. It can also be grown from seed sown in the spring; cuttings will also root quite freely. Plant at approximately 8–10in intervals for a good effect.
Feeding   Apply a complete plant food when growth commences in the spring.
Problems   Vine weevil grubs may devour roots and stems. Destroy the infected clump, and use severed shoots as cuttings.

FLOWERING

Season   It flowers well through most of the summer, with a few spikes hanging on until the early fall.
Cutting   Flowers do not last well as cut blooms.

AFTER FLOWERING

Requirements   Promptly remove any spent flower stems once they begin to look untidy. Apart from the removal of any dead leaves, this is all that is necessary.

HOSTA
Plantain lily

LEAVES PATTERNED VARIOUSLY *in lime-green and blue make this* Hosta *"Frances Williams" an outstanding garden feature. Here it lights up a dull area under a tree, the little available light being reflected outward by the lime-green. In shady areas where few flowers bloom, it is a real bonus.*

FEATURES

HERBACEOUS

Also known as the plantain lily, this herbaceous perennial is grown for its attractive, decorative foliage. It is long-lived, and foliage may be tiny or up to 18in wide and 36in high. There are hundreds of cultivars with leaves that may be light or dark green, chartreuse or yellow, gray-green or blue. Many are variegated. Leaf texture also varies: it can be smooth or shiny, matt or powdery, puckered or corrugated. Hostas are excellent at forming big, bold clumps that keep down the weeds, but until they emerge in late spring some weeding will be necessary; they also benefit from heavy mulching. Hostas look best mass-planted near water features, or when allowed to multiply in shady areas under trees.

Variegations Cultivars with cream, white, or yellow variegations will brighten a shady part of the yard, and so long as the tree or shrub canopy is high enough to let sufficient light reach the hostas, they will maintain their variegation. Likewise, plants with sharp chartreuse or acid-lime-colored foliage can be used to give a lift to shady areas. Types can be mixed to create a wealth of different effects.

Flowers The bell-shape flowers, mostly in mauve shades, appear in the summer and are held high above the foliage. Some species, such as *H. plantaginea* and its cultivar "Grandiflora," produce pure white, lightly fragrant flowers. However, few gardeners plant hostas just for the flowers; the leaves alone are good enough.

HOSTA AT A GLANCE

A mainly clump-forming perennial from the Far East. Grow in pots or the garden for the foliage. Hardy to 0°F (zones 6–7).

		Recommended Varieties
Jan	/	
Feb	/	"Aureomarginata"
Mar	sow	"Blue Angel"
Apr	divide	"Francee"
May	transplant	"Frances Williams"
Jun	flowering	"Golden Tiara"
July	flowering	"Love Pat"
Aug	divide	*H. lancifolia*
Sept	flowering	"Shade Fanfare"
Oct	/	"Wide Brim"
Nov	/	
Dec	/	

PURE WHITE FLOWERS appear on some species of hosta, such as Hosta plantaginea *and some of its cultivars.*

HOSTAS, RODGERSIAS, and ferns revel in the light shade and constant damp soil prevalent in woodlands.

Companions Since hostas do not come into leaf early in the spring, the early-flowering bulbs, such as snowdrops and snowflakes, or early perennials, such as corydalis, can be planted among them. They make a bright, successful show.

CONDITIONS

Aspect Most hostas grow in full sunlight if well watered. They thrive in shade or dappled light. Blue-leaved forms can be the hardest of all to place because they turn green with either too much sun or too heavy shade. Yellow or gold forms are best with direct sunlight in the early morning or late in the afternoon.

Site Needs rich, moisture-retentive soil. Large amounts of decayed manure or compost should be dug into the ground before planting. Mulch plants after planting. Superb in tubs, getting bigger and better each year.

GROWING METHOD

Propagation Divide the fleshy underground rhizomes in early spring. Most hostas are best divided every four to five years. Plant the dwarf cultivars 6in

apart, the larger ones at intervals of 36in. Several species can be raised from seed, though they may not be true to type.

Feeding Apply pelletted poultry manure in the spring.

Problems Slugs and snails can be a major problem. Pick off snails, and avoid watering in the evening. Place slug pellets or sharp sand around the leaves.

FLOWERING

Season Flowers are produced in the summer. The color range varies from white to purple.

Cutting Hosta provides cut flowers; the foliage is also attractive.

AFTER FLOWERING

Requirements Cut off any spent flower stems in the spring. Continue watering the plants until the foliage begins to die down, and then tidy up the clumps, which can look unsightly. Mulch the area with supplies of compost or manure. Some hostas (*sieboldiana*) produce good fall tints. The seedheads can be left on for winter decoration.

KNIPHOFIA
Red hot poker

FLAME-COLORED *pokers and soft purple perovskia both tolerate dry conditions.*

THE COLORS *in this generous planting of red hot pokers reflect both the yellow achillea behind and the red plants in the foreground. The abundant grassy foliage provides a valuable contrast.*

FEATURES

SUMMER AUTUMN WINTER SPRING
EVERGREEN

These evergreen perennials, also known as torch lilies, make great feature plants, with their bright flower spikes in cream, orange, red, yellow, and many shadings of these colors. Flower stems stand high above the grassy foliage, which may be anywhere from 24in to 6½ft tall. Even out of flower, the distinctive foliage makes red hot poker a good accent plant. Since clumps should remain undisturbed for many years, plant red hot pokers in their final position.

CONDITIONS

Aspect Needs full sunlight all day. A valuable plant because it tolerates a wide range of exposed windy or coastal areas.

KNIPHOFIA AT A GLANCE

A genus of some 70 species of evergreen and deciduous perennials, grown for their flowering spires. Hardy to 5°F (zone 7).

Jan	/	Recommended Varieties
Feb	/	
Mar	sow	"Bees Sunset"
		"Brimstone"
Apr	divide	"Buttercup"
May	transplant	*K. caulescens*
Jun	flowering	"Little Maid"
July	flowering	"Royal Standard"
Aug	flowering	"Samuel's Sensation"
Sept	flowering	"Sunningdale Yellow"
Oct	flowering	*K. triangularis*
Nov	/	
Dec	/	

Site Needs well-drained soil. Although it tolerates poorer soils, especially sandy ones, you will get better results if the soil is enriched with manure or compost.

GROWING METHOD

Propagation Well-established clumps can be divided in late spring. Foliage on new divisions must be reduced by half to allow successful root regrowth to take place. The smaller-growing forms can be planted at 20in spacings, but the large growers may need up to 30in or more. Needs regular watering to establish in prolonged dry spells, after which it is very drought-tolerant.

Feeding Grows without supplementary fertilizer, but complete plant food applied in the spring should noticeably increase the quantity and quality of the flowers.

Problems No specific problems are known.

FLOWERING

Season Flowering times can vary slightly with species and cultivar. Generally, red hot pokers flower in late summer and early fall.

Cutting The flowers last well when cut if the stems are scalded for approximately 10 seconds. They make an invaluable tall, stiff background for a display of smaller, flowery cuttings.

AFTER FLOWERING

Requirements Spent flower stalks should be promptly cut off. Any dead leaves should be pulled away to give the clump a clean look. Protect the crown with straw or leaves in cold areas.

LEUCANTHEMUM

Shasta daisy

LONG-STEMMED *shasta daisies are an ideal component of flower arrangements.*

A CONTINUOUS PLANTING *of shasta daisies fills this awkward narrow space between a path and a low brick wall. The cheerful white flowers appear throughout the summer.*

FEATURES

HERBACEOUS

Leucanthemum x *superbum* (Shasta daisy) looks wonderful when planted in a mixed border, where the large white flowers mix with more brightly colored flowers. Despite being easy to grow and multiplying rapidly, the daisies do not become a menace. Flower stalks can grow 24–36in tall, while the dark green leaves are only 4–6in high. Shasta daisies make striking cut flowers, livening up any arrangement. There are a number of named cultivars, some, such as "Esther Read," "Wirral Supreme," and "Cobham Gold," with double flowers. (Despite its name, the flowers on "Cobham Gold" are cream, not gold.) "Everest" is probably the largest of the single cultivars, though it is rarely available.

LEUCANTHEMUM AT A GLANCE

L. x *superbum* is a vigorous, clump-forming perennial with many attractive cultivars, mainly in white. Hardy to 23°F (zone 9).

Jan	/	Recommended Varieties
Feb	/	
Mar	divide	*Leucanthemum* x *superbum*
Apr	transplant	"Aglaia"
May	transplant	"Alaska"
Jun	flowering	"Bishopstone"
July	flowering	"Cobham Gold"
Aug	flowering	"Horace Read"
Sept	flowering	"Phyllis Smith"
Oct	divide	"Snowcap"
Nov	/	
Dec	/	

CONDITIONS

Aspect   Prefers full sunlight all day and wind protection.
Site   The soil should be well drained, and improved by the addition of decayed compost or manure.

GROWING METHOD

Propagation   Divide the clumps in early spring or late summer, replanting only the younger, vigorous, outer growths, each with its own set of roots and shoots. Plant the divisions approximately 10in apart. Cuttings of young, short shoots can also be taken in early spring.

Feeding   Apply complete plant food as growth begins in the spring. Liquid fertilizer applied in late spring should help produce better blooms.

Problems   The main problems are aphids, slugs, earwigs, and chrysanthemum eelworm. The first can be tackled with a proprietary spray, and the second and third by traps (saucers filled with beer, and inverted flower pots filled with straw placed on bamboo canes). In the case of eelworm, evident from browning/blackening, drying foliage from the base upward, the whole plant must be destroyed.

FLOWERING

Season   Flowering is all summer long.
Cutting   Cut flowers regularly for indoor decoration, which will also prolong the garden display.

AFTER FLOWERING

Requirements Cut back spent flower stems to the ground.

LIGULARIA
Ligularia

A MARVELLOUS ligularia display—spikes of bright yellow, eye-catching flowers. No matter what size your border, there is a suitable ligularia. They vary from the medium to tall, at 6ft high. Big groupings invariably succeed much better than a few individual flowers.

FEATURES

HERBACEOUS

Ligularia, with its bright yellow daisies, has four key advantages. It mainly flowers in mid- and late summer, and tolerates dappled shade, making it invaluable for the border. It often has interesting, well-displayed foliage; it can be shaped like a kidney, a five-pointed star, or be oval, held on tallish stems. The fourth advantage is that these are tall plants, adding height to schemes, being from 36in to 6ft tall. They can be used in small groups to punctuate arrangements of smaller plants, or form an impressive massed display. The flowers are yellow or orange. *L. dentata* "Othello" has purple-tinged leaves with a red underside, and "Desdemona" has brownish-green leaves, similarly colored beneath. With room for only one ligularia, "The Rocket" offers height, yellow flowers, black stems, and interesting, big-toothed foliage.

LIGULARIA AT A GLANCE

A genus of 150 species of perennials grown for their tall flower spikes and large, architectural foliage. Hardy to 0°F (zones 6–7).

Jan	/	Recommended Varieties
Feb	sow 🖐	
Mar	sow 🖐	*Ligularia dentata*
Apr	transplant 🖐	*L. d.* "Desdemona"
May	transplant 🖐	*L. d.* "Othello"
Jun	/	"Gregynog Gold"
July	flowering 🌼	*L. przewalskii*
Aug	flowering 🌼	"The Rocket"
Sept	/	*L. wilsoniana*
Oct	divide 🖐	
Nov	/	
Dec	/	

CONDITIONS

Aspect Tolerates full sun and some light shade. Also requires shelter from cutting winds.

Site The soil must be moist—ligularias grow well beside ponds and streams—for a big performance. If the soil begins to dry out to any degree, the plants quickly show signs of distress by wilting.

GROWING METHOD

Propagation Increase the species by sowing seed or division in the spring or fall. Cultivars can only be raised by division. Make sure that the emerging new growth is well-watered, and never allowed to dry out. Set out from 24in to 4ft apart.

Feeding Border plants need plenty of well-rotted manure or compost, and a deep mulch to guard against moisture loss.

Problems Slugs and snails can be a major problem, especially as the leaves emerge. Pick off or treat chemically.

FLOWERING

Season Generally from late summer into the fall, but some flower in mid-summer, and *L. stenocephala* in early summer.

Cutting It is not advisable to strip the plants of their impressive flowering stems, especially when you only have room for a few plants.

AFTER FLOWERING

Requirements Cut back to the ground.

LIMONIUM LATIFOLIUM
Sea lavender

THE MOST FAMILIAR *annual statice is*
Limonium sinuatum *"Blue Peter."*

SEA LAVENDER *has broad, slightly fleshy leaves, and flowers for several months. It is equally successful as part of a free-flowing design or, as shown, as a segregated, eye-catching feature.*

FEATURES

EVERGREEN

HERBACEOUS

Limonium latifolium (sea lavender) is a perennial type of statice often grown for its tall, finely branched stems of tiny white and pale lavender flowers, which are widely used both in fresh and dried floral arrangements. Flower stems may be over 20in high, and the cultivar "Violetta" has deep violet flowers. The plant forms a basal rosette of broad, rounded, slightly fleshy leaves growing around 10in high. Clumps may ultimately spread 18in or more wide. This is a good plant for rockeries because it is quite drought tolerant. Sea lavender is native to parts of south-east and central Europe, thriving in dry summers and cold winters.

LIMONIUM AT A GLANCE

L. latifolium is a perennial grown in windy coastal areas for its abundant, late summer flowers. Hardy to 0°F (zones 6–7).

Jan	/	Companion Plants
Feb	/	Eremurus
Mar	divide	Escallonia
Apr	transplant	Linum
May	/	Kniphofia
Jun	/	Olearia
July	/	Perovskia
Aug	flowering	Scabiosa
Sept	flowering	
Oct	sow	
Nov	/	
Dec	/	

CONDITIONS

Aspect   Prefers full sun all day, and tolerates exposed windy or coastal sites.

Site   The soil must be very well drained, but need not be rich. In fact, sea lavender tolerates very poor soil.

GROWING METHOD

Propagation   Grows from seed sown as soon as it is ripe, when the flowers have dried and turned brown, or from root cuttings taken in spring. New plantings should be spaced about 10–12in apart. Water regularly to establish new plants, and then give an occasional deep soaking during prolonged dry spring and summer weather.

Feeding   Does not need feeding, but a little complete plant food may be applied in early spring, giving a decent boost.

Problems   Heavy, poorly drained soils or overwatering may cause the plant to rot and collapse.

FLOWERING

Season   Sea lavender flowers in late summer, when its spikelets of lavender flowers with white calyces begin to appear.

Cutting   Flowers can be cut for drying when most of the flowers on the stem have fully opened.

AFTER FLOWERING

Requirements Cut off any remaining flower stems when they are past their best.

LIRIOPE MUSCARI
Lilyturf

STRIKING FLOWER SPIKES in deep violet add to the attraction of this variegated form of liriope.

AMONG ITS MANY USES, liriope makes an excellent edging for garden beds. Here it accentuates the circular form of the fountain.

FEATURES

HERBACEOUS

This plant, known as lilyturf, is sometimes confused with *Ophiopogon jaburan* which is called white lilyturf. The two are similar but *Ophiopogon* has white flowers. Liriope grows in early summer about 12–14in high. The species has dark green leaves, but there are variegated forms as well. A spike of deep violet flowers stands well above the leaves. A tough and useful Far Eastern plant for the garden, especially as it flowers in the fall.

LIRIOPE AT A GLANCE

L. muscari is a stout perennial ideal for difficult places, which also provides good ground cover. Hardy to 0°F(zones 6–7).

Jan	/	Recommended Varieties
Feb	/	
Mar	sow	*Liriope muscari* "Big Blue"
Apr	divide	*L. m.* "Gold Banded"
May	transplant	*L. m.* "Majestic"
Jun	/	*L. m.* "Monroe White"
July	/	Companion Plants
Aug	/	Dicentra
Sept	flowering	Dryopteris
Oct	flowering	*Euphorbia robbiae*
Nov	flowering	Polypodium
Dec	/	Ribes
		Vinca major and *minor*

CONDITIONS

Aspect Will grow in shade or dappled sunlight, but flowers best in full sun.
Site Tolerates most soils but acid is preferred; grows best in well-drained soil enriched with plenty of organic matter.

GROWING METHOD

Propagation The easiest method of increase is to lift and divide the clumps in the spring. Replant the divisions approximately 3–4in apart. Water young plants regularly during prolonged dry spring and summer weather. Plants tolerate drought but prefer some regular water.
Feeding Apply complete plant food in the spring.
Problems No specific problems are known.

FLOWERING

Season The flowering begins in the early fall, and continues until the end of the season.
Cutting Lasts quite well in water.

AFTER FLOWERING

Requirements Cut off spent flowerheads once the flowers have dropped. As growth dies down toward winter, cut it off cleanly.

LOBELIA CARDINALIS
Cardinal flower

THIS LOBELIA is also known as cardinal flower, an apt description, since the tall spikes of flowers are the same scarlet as a cardinal's robes.

IN ITS NATURAL HABITAT in North America this lobelia grows on wet meadows and river banks. It thrives on plenty of moisture.

FEATURES

HERBACEOUS

To most people, lobelia is a small edging plant with bright blue flowers. There are, however, about 400 species of lobelia, many of them perennials. This herbaceous species with bright scarlet flowers is also known as the cardinal flower and grows to about 36in tall. With its dark green leaves and bright flowers, it really stands out—it is sometimes used as a feature plant. It can also be used in a mixed border or mass-planted among shrubs, so long as the ground retains plenty of moisture.

LOBELIA AT A GLANCE

L. cardinalis is a clump-forming, short-lived perennial, grown for its striking, vivid red flowers. Hardy to 5°F (zone 7).

		Recommended Varieties
Jan	/	
Feb	/	*Lobelia* "Cherry Ripe"
Mar	sow	"Dark Crusader"
Apr	divide	"Kompliment Scharlach"
May	transplant	"Queen Victoria"
Jun	/	*L. siphilitica*
July	flowering	*L. tupa*
Aug	flowering	
Sept	flowering	
Oct	/	
Nov	/	
Dec	/	

CONDITIONS

Aspect Grows in full sunlight or semi-shade.

Site Needs rich and moisture-retentive soil, as these plants are not tolerant of drought. A streamside setting is ideal.

GROWING METHOD

Propagation Plants are usually divided every two or three years, in the spring. Plant the divisions about 12in apart. Lobelia must be kept moist and well watered while it is in active growth, especially during prolonged dry spells in the spring and summer.

Feeding Apply a complete plant food, and a mulch of compost or manure in the spring.

Problems Slugs and snails will attack the flower spikes. Put down slug pellets or beer traps.

FLOWERING

Season There is a long flowering period through the summer and fall period when the brilliant scarlet blooms appear.

Cutting Flowers are not suitable for cutting.

AFTER FLOWERING

Requirements Cut off spent flower stems. The dark-leaved hybrids ("Cherry Ripe") are not fully hardy and need a thick, protective winter mulch.

LUPINUS POLYPHYLLUS
Lupins

RUSSELL LUPINS *are noteworthy for their rich colors, including this pinky-red.*

LUPINS ARE *traditional favorites for perennial borders, where they provide vertical interest. Here they are growing among oriental poppies, campion, and gray-leaved germander.*

FEATURES

SUMMER AUTUMN WINTER SPRING

HERBACEOUS

This herbaceous perennial lupin is generally known as the Russell lupin, named after the hybridizer who began developing many fine strains of this plant early this century. It produces tall, densely packed spires of blooms in myriad colors. Growing well over 42in tall, these are plants for a massed display. They flower in early to mid-summer and can look unsightly after flowering; placed at the rear of a border the problem is solved. Although they can be cut for indoor use they give much more value in the yard, with several spikes per plant. The only irritation is that plants can be short-lived, and should therefore be divided regularly.

LUPINUS AT A GLANCE

L. polyphyllus is an attractive, summer-flowering perennial with striking vertical spires of purple flowers. Hardy to 5°F (zone 7).

Jan	/	
Feb	/	
Mar	sow	Recommended Varieties
Apr	transplant	Band of Noble Series
May	transplant	"Esmerelder"
Jun	flowering	"Helen Sharman"
July	flowering	"Kayleigh Ann Savage"
Aug	/	"Olive Tolley"
Sept	/	"Pope John Paul"
Oct	sow	"The Page"
Nov	/	"The Chatelaine"
Dec	/	

CONDITIONS

Aspect   Grows in full sunlight or semi-shade, but it does need wind protection.

Site   Soil need not be rich—moderate fertility will suffice—but it must be well drained. Light, slightly sandy, acidic soil is ideal.

GROWING METHOD

Propagation   Division of these plants may be difficult. Many strains come true from seed, which should be soaked in warm water before planting in the spring or fall. Cuttings can be taken from new shoots emerging from the crown in early spring. Set plants approximately 12–16in apart. Give ample water to young plants to help them establish.

Feeding   Needs little fertilizer, as lupins fix nitrogen in nodules on their roots. High potash fertilizer may be applied as buds begin to form.

Problems   Powdery mildew may be a problem in humid conditions; if necessary, spray with a fungicide. Control lupin aphids with an appropriate spray. Virus may cause stunting and discoloration. Destroy affected plants.

FLOWERING

Season   Early and mid-summer.
Cutting   Flowers may be cut for the vase.

AFTER FLOWERING

Requirements   Cut off the spent flower stems before they manage to set seed. This will encourage smaller spikes to follow.

LYCHNIS CORONARIA
Rose campion

THE DISTINCTIVE ARRANGEMENT of petals on Lychnis chalcedonica *has given rise to its common name, Maltese cross. The bright red flowers show up well against white or blue flowers.*

TRUE CAMPION, Lychnis coronaria, *has abundant, bright cerise flowers.*

FEATURES

HERBACEOUS

Rosettes of soft, silver-gray foliage make *Lychnis coronaria* a very useful plant in the garden, and they contrast with the deep cerise or magenta flowers that appear on stems 12–16in high. There is also a white-flowered form. Easily grown in a sunny, well-drained position, rose campion tends to be short-lived, but it self-seeds prolifically to provide a fresh supply. It can be grown as a border plant or as part of a mixed perennial display. *L. flos-jovis* is another species where silvery foliage effectively combines with purple-red blooms. Another popular species of lychnis is the Maltese cross, *L. chalcedonica*, which has mid-green leaves and produces a rounded head of bright scarlet flowers. Pink and white forms, and a double, "Flore Plena," are also available.

LYCHNIS AT A GLANCE

L. coronaria is a flowery, short-lived purple-red perennial that gives a prolific late summer display. Hardy to 5°F (zone 7).

Jan	/	
Feb	/	Recommended Varieties
Mar	sow	*Lychnis alpina*
Apr	division	*L. chalcedonica*
May	transplant	*L. coronaria* Alba Group
Jun	/	*L. c.* Atrosanguinea Group
July	flowering	*L. flos-cuculi*
Aug	flowering	*L. viscaria* subsp.
Sept	flowering	"Splendens Plena"
Oct	sow	*L. yunnanensis*
Nov	/	
Dec	/	

CONDITIONS

Aspect   Grows best in full sunlight, but it tolerates shade for part of the day.

Site   Needs very well-drained soil, but the soil need not be especially rich.

GROWING METHOD

Propagation   Tends to self-seed. These plants may show variation from the parent plant. Divide clumps in spring, discard the oldest, lackluster sections, and space the new vigorous ones about 8in apart. There are some beautiful strains to be raised from seed, with mixtures of white, deep violet, carmine, and rose-pink flowers, and a pastel eye.

Feeding   Needs little fertilizer. A little complete plant food may be given in early spring.

Problems   No pest or disease problems are known, but overwatering or prolonged summer rain in heavy ground may cause rotting.

FLOWERING

Season   Flowers in mid- to late summer, but it is well worth the wait, with a big showy display that maintains interest in the border at a time when many other plants are flagging.

Cutting   Flowers are unsuitable for cutting.

AFTER FLOWERING

Requirements   If you do not want plants to self-seed, deadhead with vigilance as the flowers fade. This should also prolong blooming. Completely spent stems should be cut off as low to the ground as possible.

LYSIMACHIA PUNCTATA
Loosestrife

A STRONG, MASSED DISPLAY of loosestrife. Individually unremarkable, a clump makes a splendid feature beside a pond or stream.

FEATURES

EVERGREEN

HERBACEOUS

Loosestrife, which is widely naturalized in Europe and northeast North America, has stalks of bright yellow flowers in summer. It thrives in damp, boggy ground and can easily become invasive. The flowering stems reach 3ft high, bearing slightly coarse foliage. Other species offer white flowers on stiff, blue-green stems (*L. ephemerum*), while *L. nummularia* "Aurea" is a complete contrast. It grows 2in high, but spreads indefinitely, with evergreen, bright yellow leaves and summer flowers in a matching color. With room for only one, try *L. clethroides*, which has attractive white flowers (36 x 24in). The new variegated form, *L. p.* "Alexander" is a great success.

LYSIMACHIA AT A GLANCE

L. punctata is an erect, herbaceous perennial grown for its yellow flowers and ability to colonize damp areas. Hardy to 0°F (zones 6–7).

Jan	/	Recommended Varieties
Feb	/	
Mar	/	*Lysimachia atropurpurea*
Apr	divide 🐌	*L. ciliata*
May	/	*L. clethroides*
Jun	flowering 🌼	*L. minoricensis*
July	flowering 🌼	*L. nummularia* "Aurea"
Aug	flowering 🌼	*L. thyrsiflora*
Sept	/	*L. vulgaris*
Oct	divide 🐌	
Nov	/	
Dec	/	

CONDITIONS

Aspect	Loosestrife tolerates both full sun and light, dappled shade, but growing in the former gives by far the best results.
Site	Moist ground is essential. Add plenty of organic matter to border plants, and mulch well to guard against moisture loss.

GROWING METHOD

Propagation	Seed can be difficult. The most reliable method is by spring or fall division.
Feeding	Humus-rich ground produces the best display. Fork plenty of well-rotted manure and compost around the plants in the spring.
Problems	Colonies of slugs and snails can be a major problem, attacking and disfiguring the new, emerging foliage. Either pick off by hand or treat chemically. Plants grown in areas cut by strong winds may need to be staked.

FLOWERING

Season	Flowers appear in the summer, their timing depending on your chosen variety.
Cutting	They make unremarkable cut flowers, given the enormous competition in summer, but are nonetheless very useful when bulking out large displays with their flowering spires.

AFTER FLOWERING

Requirements	Cut back the old, spent flowering stems down to the ground.

MACLEAYA CORDATA
Plume poppy

THE PLUME POPPY starts inauspiciously, but quickly puts out tall, white summer flowers, making it an indispensable feature plant. It is a key ingredient for the rear of the border, where its lobed, olive-green foliage makes a lovely background for smaller plants. The plume poppy does not need staking.

FEATURES

HERBACEOUS

The plume poppy is an essential plant for the rear of the border, tall, graceful, and showy. Growing 8ft tall, it sports long, thin stems with mid- and late summer panicles of pale white flowers. "Flamingo" has pinkish flowers. The large, lobed foliage is equally attractive. With more room in the border, *M. microcarpa* can be grown. It is slightly invasive and has pink flowers, while "Kelway's Coral Plume" produces coral-pink flowers opening from pure pink buds. The plume poppy's natural habitat is Chinese and Japanese meadows, where it makes large impressive colonies, spreading quickly through the damp soil by underground rhizomes and flowering all summer long.

MACLEAYA AT A GLANCE

M. cordata is a rhizomatous perennial with gray-green foliage, grown for its tall flower spikes. Hardy to 0°F (zones 6–7).

Jan	/	Companion Plants
Feb	/	
Mar	/	Clematis Gypsophila
Apr	division 🖐	Hibiscus
May	/	Miscanthus
Jun	/	Lobelia
July	flowering 🖐	Osteospermum
Aug	flowering 🖐	Rose
Sept	/	Salvia
Oct	division 🖐	
Nov	/	
Dec	/	

CONDITIONS

Aspect   Macleaya likes full sun and light shade, although the former produces a longer, better display. Avoid dark areas and open, windy sites; shelter is required.

Site   Light, well-drained soil is ideal.

GROWING METHOD

Propagation   The quickest, easiest results are either by making spring or fall divisions, or by separating lengths of rhizome when the plant is dormant. Make sure each has its own root system. Water new plants well, and space out at 3ft intervals.

Feeding   Provide moderate applications of compost and well-rotted manure in the spring as a mulch.

Problems   Colonies of slugs can be a severe problem, badly attacking the new, vigorous growth. Either pick off by hand or treat accordingly with chemicals.

FLOWERING

Season   Flowers appear in mid- and late summer, on long, thin stems, producing an airy display.

Cutting   Macleaya make very attractive cut flowers, requiring a regular change of water, their airy panicles adding considerably to both formal and flowery arrangements.

AFTER FLOWERING

Requirements   Cut back old growth to the ground.

MECONOPSIS
Himalayan blue poppy

NO OTHER blue flower has quite the same startlingly clear color as the amazing blue poppy, a true delight whenever it can be grown.

WOODLAND CONDITIONS where the soil never dries out are essential for the Himalayan or Tibetan blue poppy.

FEATURES

HERBACEOUS

Meconopsis betonicifolia is the beautiful blue poppy everyone loves. There is probably no other plant that produces such an intense sky-blue flower. Its natural habitat is very high altitude alpine meadows in China. Plants do not flower the first year, and they die down in winter, growing and blooming in the second year. If meconopsis is prevented from blooming the first time it sets buds, it is more likely to become perennial. Growing to almost 6½ft in its native habitat, in cultivation it is more likely to be 20–28in tall. Looks best when grown as part of a massed display, or threaded through a border.

MECONOPSIS AT A GLANCE

M. betonicifolia is a deciduous perennial, making a strong show, with blue or white early summer flowers. Hardy to 0°F (zones 6–7).

Jan	/	Recommended Varieties
Feb	/	
Mar	sow	*Meconopsis cambrica*
Apr	transplant	*M. betonicifolia*
May	transplant	*M. grandis*
Jun	flowering	*M. napaulensis*
July	flowering	*M. quintuplinervia*
Aug	flowering	*M. x sheldonii*
Sept	flowering	*M. x s. "Slieve Donard"*
Oct	sow	*M. superba*
Nov	/	
Dec	/	

CONDITIONS

Aspect   Needs partial, dappled shade; also provide some protection from strong, cutting, drying winds.

Site   Needs well-drained soil that is rich in organic matter. In colder regions it grows best in acid soil.

GROWING METHOD

Propagation   Grows from fresh ripe seed sown in the fall, or in spring. Give winter seedlings frost protection in a greenhouse, but beware of damping off, and plant out in late spring or early summer. Initially, water well. Do not waterlog or the crowns will rot.

Feeding   Apply a little general fertilizer in the spring.

Problems   Overwet soil, especially during winter, will rot the crown. Downy mildew may be a problem in some seasons. Spray plants with a fungicide at the first sign of an attack.

FLOWERING

Season   Abundant flowers begin appearing at the start of summer.

Cutting   While they make extremely good cut flowers, they do not last long.

AFTER FLOWERING

Requirements   Remove spent flower stems, unless you are waiting for seed to ripen. Once growth dies down, cut it off at ground level.

MELIANTHUS MAJOR
Honey bush

NECTAR-RICH, *these dark red flowers are very attractive to insects. The foliage too is unusual, with its distinctive color and form.*

THE BLUE-GREEN FOLIAGE *of honey flower is a feature in itself. Only in a large yard will you appreciate the full effect.*

FEATURES

EVERGREEN

This very striking evergreen plant, with its unusual blue-green foliage, really stands out. It is grown as a feature in a mixed border or as a focal point in an annual or perennial display. In a large yard it could be repeat-planted to tie together various arrangements. Honey bush can grow to 6ft in height, and it spreads by suckers, forming a large clump if left undivided. The dark mahogany-red flowers contain copious quantities of nectar, attractive to bees. Although native to South Africa, and initially tender here, after two years the base becomes woody and it can survive outside if given good frost protection in mild areas. It can also be grown in a large pot.

MELIANTHUS AT A GLANCE

M. major is a tender, southern African plant with wonderful, architectural foliage. It is damaged below 41°F (zone 11).

Jan	/	Companion Plants
Feb	/	
Mar	sow	Canna
Apr	divide	Choisya
May	transplant	*Hosta* "Krossa Regal"
Jun	flowering	Philadelphus
July	flowering	Pinus
Aug	flowering	Pseudopanax
Sept	/	Salvia
Oct	/	
Nov	/	
Dec	/	

CONDITIONS

Aspect Needs full sun all day (i.e. a south-facing wall).
Site Soil must be well drained but it need not be specially rich—in fact over-rich soils will produce good foliage effects but poor flowering. However, the outstanding architectural foliage is the main reason for growing this striking plant.

GROWING METHOD

Propagation Grows from seed sown in the spring or from division of suckers from an existing plant, also in spring. Plant at least 39in apart. For best growth, give deep watering every week or two in hot, dry spells during the growing season. It will, however, tolerate drought well.
Feeding Apply a complete plant food in the spring.
Problems Red spider mites may strike. Use an appropriate insecticide.

FLOWERING

Season Dark crimson flowers may appear in late summer or earlier on long stems that survive the winter.
Cutting Flowers are probably best left on the plant, as they do not smell particularly pleasant.

AFTER FLOWERING

Requirements Cut off the spent flower stems, unless you are waiting for seed to set and ripen. Protect the base and roots with straw or bracken against frost. The older and woodier the plant, the better its chance of survival.

MISCANTHUS SINENSIS
Miscanthus

FINE STRIPES *in cream and green make "Variegatus" a popular form of miscanthus.*

ZEBRA GRASS *is the common name given to "Zebrinus," with its yellow-spotted horizontal markings. Ornamental grasses can provide useful contrast in the perennial garden.*

FEATURES

SUMMER AUTUMN WINTER SPRING

HERBACEOUS

This is a group of large, ornamental, herbaceous perennial grasses. The plain green species is not often grown as the many cultivars with striped or banded foliage are much more decorative. Cultivars range in height from about 32in to 6½ft. Clumps spread from short, thick rhizomes and become very wide after a few years if not divided. Commonly grown cultivars include "Zebrinus" with distinct, horizontal gold banding, and "Variegatus" with long cream or white stripes, while other varieties such as "Silberfeder," "Morning Light" and var. *purpurascens* are worth seeking out. All produce pale, creamy beige feathery plumes of flowers in late summer, and fall, often accompanied by good fall color. The tall growers look good crested with frost.

MISCANTHUS AT A GLANCE

M. sinensis is a deciduous, large perennial, growing 6ft x 6ft. Produces blue-green foliage. Hardy to 0°F (zones 6–7).

		Recommended Varieties
Jan	/	
Feb	sow	"Ferne Osten"
Mar	sow	"Flamingo"
Apr	transplant	"Gracillimus"
May	divide	"Kleine Fontane"
Jun	/	"Kleine Silberspinne"
July	/	"Morning Light"
Aug	flowering	"Strictus"
Sept	flowering	"Undine"
Oct	flowering	
Nov	/	
Dec	/	

CONDITIONS

Aspect   Grows best in full sun, but tolerates shade for part of the day.

Site   Prefers a soil that has been heavily enriched with organic matter to aid moisture retention. Avoid any damp or boggy ground. Good drainage really is essential for a massed, architectural display.

GROWING METHOD

Propagation   Clumps can be lifted and divided in spring. This can require considerable muscle and effort because the roots are extremely tenacious. Replant the divisions approximately 12in apart, or closer if you want quicker, immediate coverage. Water well until established.

Feeding   Complete plant food can be applied in the spring, when new growth begins, but it is not essential if the soil contains plenty of manure or compost.

Problems   No specific pest or disease problems are known to attack this plant.

FLOWERING

Season   Flowering plumes appear well above the foliage in the fall.

Cutting   Plumes can be cut and dried like pampas grass.

AFTER FLOWERING

Requirements   Once foliage starts to die off and become unsightly, cut it off at ground level. If the foliage is left uncut to provide winter shapes and outlines, especially when frosted, it must be cut back by early spring.

MONARDA DIDYMA
Bergamot

THE HOT-PINK FLOWERS on this bergamot are easy to place in the yard. They combine well with blue or white schemes.

FOR COLOR over a long period, this brilliant red variety of bergamot, "Cambridge Scarlet," is hard to beat. It requires little care.

FEATURES

HERBACEOUS

This aromatic herbaceous perennial is also known as bee balm and Oswego tea. The name "bee balm" refers to its nectar-rich flowers, which are very attractive to bees, and "Oswego tea" to its use by the Oswego Indians and early colonists of North America as a tea substitute. Growing approximately 36in tall, bergamot flowers from mid- to late summer. The heads of tubular flowers are red, pink, white, or purple, with some outstandingly named cultivars, including "Cambridge Scarlet" and "Croftway Pink." It is easy to grow—being a member of the mint family, its roots spread vigorously. It makes a lively addition to a mixed planting for its bright scarlet or pink flowers.

MONARDA AT A GLANCE

M. didyma is a clump-forming perennial with lance-shape leaves, and bright, late summer flowers. Hardy to 0°F (zones 6–7).

Jan	/	Recommended Varieties
Feb	sow	"Aquarius"
Mar	sow	"Beauty of Cobham"
Apr	transplant	"Cambridge Scarlet"
May	transplant	"Croftway Pink"
Jun	/	"Fishes"
July	flowering	"Mahogany"
Aug	flowering	"Prarienacht"
Sept	/	"Sagittarius"
Oct	sow	"Scorpion"
Nov	/	
Dec	/	

CONDITIONS

Aspect   Grows in either full sunlight or semi-shade, but flowering will be best in the open.

Site   Needs well-drained soil that is made moisture-retentive by the addition of large amounts of decayed organic matter.

GROWING METHOD

Propagation   Lift and divide clumps in the spring before new growth begins. Replant the young, vigorous outer growths 8–12in apart. Plants usually need dividing every two or three years. Bergamot may be also be grown from seed sown in the early spring or fall, but this does not develop true to type. It needs regular, deep watering through prolonged dry spells in the heat of summer.

Feeding   If the soil is well supplied with humus, but a little fertilizer is needed. Apply some complete plant food in the spring.

Problems   Since snails love to eat the new growth as it appears, take precautions. Mildew can be a problem at times. You may need a fungicide spray or it might become severe. Remove all dead and diseased leaves.

FLOWERING

Season   Flowers in mid- and late summer.

Cutting   Makes a decent cut flower. Use the scented leaves in a pot pourri.

AFTER FLOWERING

Requirements   Prune off spent flower stems. Cut plants back to ground level once growth begins to die off.

OENOTHERA
Evening primrose

THOUGH EVENING PRIMROSE is thought of as yellow, the flowers of Oenothera speciosa *"Rosea" are pink-and-white, with yellow.*

O. SPECIOSA *"ROSEA" is doubly attractive because it grows 12in high, mixes well with argyranthemum, and forms large clumps.*

FEATURES

Evening primrose is an essential plant for formal and cottage-style yards. While each flower (white, yellow, or pink, depending on the variety) opens and fades fast, barely lasting 24 hours, there is an abundance of new buds developing through the summer and early fall. The plant has two extra advantages. Often fragrant, and often tall, it can make an eye-catching addition to the border. *O. biennis*, the traditional favorite, is actually an annual or biennial. *O. fruticosa*, a biennial or perennial, has two fine forms, "Fyrverkeri" ("Fireworks"), which has red buds opening to yellow flowers and purple-tinged leaves, and subsp. *glauca*, with yellow flowers and purple leaves.

CONDITIONS

Aspect   Grow in an open, sunny position.
Site   Moderately rich soil will suffice, although evening primrose can self-seed and appear in even the stoniest ground.

GROWING METHOD

Propagation   Sow seed or divide in early spring, or take cuttings of non-flowering shoots. Keep in a frost-free place in winter, plant out in spring.
Feeding   Not necessary, although moderate quantities of manure will suffice in especially poor soil.
Problems   Slugs tend to be the main problem, attacking tender new growth. Pick off or treat with chemicals. The sturdy kinds of evening primrose are free-standing, but others (*O. macrocarpa*) may require support.

FLOWERING

Season   Lasts from late spring to late summer, with flowers tending to open in early evening, when they release their scent.
Cutting   Short-lived but attractive flowers.

AFTER FLOWERING

Requirements   Collect seed when ripe, if required, and then cut spent stems to the ground.

OENOTHERA AT A GLANCE

A genus of mainly annuals and biennials, with excellent perennials. Scented and yellow flowering, they are hardy to 5°F (zone 7).

		Recommended Varieties
Jan	/	
Feb	sow	*Oenothera biennis*
Mar	divide	*O. fruticosa*
Apr	transplant	*O. f.* "Fyrverkeri"
May	flowering	*O. f.* subsp. *glauca*
Jun	flowering	*O. macrocarpa*
July	flowering	*O. speciosa* "Rosea"
Aug	flowering	*O. stricta* "Sulphurea"
Sept	/	
Oct	/	
Nov	/	
Dec	/	

PAEONIA
Paeony species and cultivars

GLORIOUS COLOR and perfume combine in this extensive planting of peony cultivars to produce a spectacular result.

THIS HALF-OPENED peony flower gives a hint of delights to come, with a touch of white against the bright pink.

FLUTED PETALS give extra interest to this single white peony. The large mass of central stamens adds a touch of color.

FEATURES

SUMMER AUTUMN WINTER SPRING

HERBACEOUS

Beautiful to look at and fragrant, too, peonies are among the aristocrats of the plant world, and although there are only 33 wild species, there are many hundreds of cultivars. Peonies were prized by the Chinese for many hundreds of years, and by the early 18th century they had developed the garden peonies from which the forms of *P. lactiflora* (often referred to as Chinese peonies) are generally descended. Peonies were first introduced into Europe at the end of the 18th century. Peonies are divided into two groups: the tree peonies, which are shrubby and derived from *P. suffruticosa*, and the herbaceous peonies, of which the cultivars of *P. lactiflora* are most commonly grown. Although the name "tree peony" is used, this is an exaggeration—they rarely grow more than 6½ft tall. Herbaceous peonies grow about 39in high and wide. Plants are long-lived.

Flowers Flowers may be single or double and come in every shade of pink, red, purple, white, and cream, many with a delicious light perfume. Some flowers have a large central boss of golden stamens, and some have fringed or crimped edges on the petals. Among the categories of flowers recognized are: small, 2–4in across; medium, 4–6in across; large, 6–8in across; and very large, over 8in across. Tree peonies are generally 2–12in. Other categories have been developed in the United States where a great deal of hybridizing is practiced.

CONDITIONS

Aspect Needs full sunlight or semi-shade, with protection from strong winds.
Site Soil must be well drained, but heavily enriched with manure or compost. Dig it over deeply to allow the free spread of roots.

THE ATTRACTIVE FOLIAGE greatly adds to the value of peonies and often emerges with lovely rich red and bronze tints.

THE VERY POPULAR double cultivar "Rubra Plena" is a rich crimson anemone-centered peony that looks very like a camellia.

GROWING METHOD

Propagation Divide plants in the spring or fall, taking care not to break the brittle roots. Each division must have roots and dormant growth buds. Crowns should be replanted 1in below the surface, and spaced about 20in apart. Plants can be raised from seed but they will take four to five years to reach flowering size, and only the species will be true to type. Peony seeds generally need two periods of chilling with a warm period between, and care should be taken not to disturb the seeds during this time. Most seeds germinate during the second spring after sowing.

Feeding Apply a general fertilizer in early spring. At the same time, mulch but avoid the crown.

PAEONIA AT A GLANCE

A genus of over 30 species of clump-forming perennials and sub-shrubs, often with highly scented flowers. Hardy to 5°F (zone 7).

Month	Activity	Recommended Varieties
Jan	/	
Feb	/	*P. cambessedesii*
Mar	/	"Defender"
Apr	divide	*P. lactiflora* "Bowl of
May	transplant	Beauty"
Jun	flowering	*P. l.* "Festiva Maxima"
July	/	*P. l.* "Sarah Bernhardt"
Aug	/	*P. mlokosewitschii*
Sept	/	*P. obovata*
Oct	sow	
Nov	sow	
Dec	sow	

Problems Botrytis or gray mold is the main problem with peonies. It can cause rotting of stems and leaf bases. Destroy affected foliage, improve drainage and air circulation, and spray with a fungicide. Replace the top layer of soil carefully around the plants.

FLOWERING

Season The flowering period is invariably in early summer. Some peonies bloom for only a short time, but the flowers on other types are much longer lasting.

Cutting Cut flowers for indoor use when the blooms are opening. Peonies are excellent cut flowers, which will last longer if kept in a cool part of the home and given frequent water changes.

AFTER FLOWERING

Requirements Remove spent flower stems, but allow the foliage to die down naturally before trimming it back. Some varieties produce lovely fall color. Do not cut down the flowering stems of varieties such as *P. mlokosewitschii* that produce handsome berries.

HINT

Disturbance Peonies may flower poorly, if at all, in the first year after planting, but this should improve year by year. Generally speaking, peonies are best left undisturbed; even 50-year-old clumps can be seen flowering profusely. It may be wiser to increase your stock by buying young container-grown plants than split a precious specimen.

PAPAVER ORIENTALE
Oriental poppy

THIS FRINGED red flower indicates the wide range of colors within P. orientale. *No border should be without one.*

THE STRIKING SHAPE of Papaver orientale. *Note the straight, slightly furry stem with, here, pink flowers and a black basal mark.*

FEATURES

HERBACEOUS

The oriental poppy is a clump-forming perennial with a variety of different forms, and colors ranging from soft hues to sharp red. They all bear the hallmarks of the species *P. orientalis* from northeast Turkey and Iran, which has a large cupped bowl of a flower with paper-thin petals. Growing up to 36in tall, with a similar spread, they self-seed freely, creating attractive colonies. They look the part in both wild or natural gardens, and large mixed borders. "Black and White" is a striking contrast of white petals and a black mark at its base. "Cedric Morris" is soft pink with a black base. "Indian Chief" is reddish-brown.

PAPAVER AT A GLANCE

P. orientalis is a perennial with 12in-long leaves, and big, cupped flowers in a range of colors. Hardy to 0°F (zones 6–7).

Jan	/	
Feb	/	Recommended Varieties
Mar	/	*Papaver orientale* "Allegro"
Apr	division	*P. o.* "Beauty of Livermere"
May	flowering	*P. o.* "Black and White"
Jun	flowering	*P. o.* Goliath Group
July	flowering	*P. o.* "Mrs Perry"
Aug	/	*P. o.* "Patty's Plum"
Sept	/	*P. o.* "Perry's White"
Oct	sow	*P. o.* "Picotee"
Nov	/	*P. o.* "Turkish Delight"
Dec	/	

CONDITIONS

Aspect   Provide full sunlight, the conditions it receives in its natural habitat.

Site   Rich soil and good drainage bring out the best in these plants.

GROWING METHOD

Propagation   Since they self-seed freely, propagation may not be necessary. Slicing off sections of root in late fall or early winter will provide abundant new plants. The success rate is invariably high. Alternatively, divide clumps in the spring, or sow seed in pots in the fall in a cold frame. Plant out the following spring, 9in apart.

Feeding   Add plenty of rich, friable compost in spring to add fertility to poor soils. This also improves the drainage, which needs to be quite good.

Problems   Fungal wilt and downy mildew can be problems; spray at the first sign.

FLOWERING

Season   The flowers appear from late spring to mid-summer.

Cutting   Poppies do not make good cut flowers.

AFTER FLOWERING

Requirements   When the flowers have died down, severely cut back the foliage to the ground. This will produce a second showing of attractive summer leaves.

PENSTEMON
Beard tongue

MANY MONTHS of fine bloom can be expected from this fine red cultivar—well into the fall, if it is regularly deadheaded.

A GENEROUS PLANTING of these attractive white cultivars makes a perfect surround for this small ornamental fountain.

FEATURES

EVERGREEN

This very large group of perennials consists of 250 species and countless cultivars, all originating in a wide variety of habitats in the southern and western United States. Their tubular or funnel-shaped flowers come in a range of shades of pink, red, purple, lavender, blue, and white, some with a contrasting throat. There is a large range of cultivars in many of these shades. Collections of young rooted cuttings can also be bought. Penstemons have a long flowering period, through the summer to mid-fall, especially if the spent blooms are regularly cut, but many plants can be short-lived. Take cuttings regularly. The various species and hybrids grow anything from 4 to 24in tall.

PENSTEMON AT A GLANCE

A large genus of perennials grown for their late-season flower display. Hardiness varies from the frost-tender to 5°F (zones 10–7).

		Recommended Varieties
Jan	/	
Feb	sow ✍	"Alice Hindley"
Mar	sow ✍	"Beech Park"
Apr	transplant ✍	"Chester Scarlet"
May	transplant ✍	"Evelyn"
Jun	flowering ❀	"Garnet"
July	flowering ❀	"Margery Fish"
Aug	flowering ❀	"Osprey"
Sept	flowering ❀	"Pennington Gem"
Oct	flowering ❀	"Rubicundus"
Nov	/	
Dec	/	

CONDITIONS

Aspect   Grows best in full sunlight with some protection from strong, cutting winds. Since most varieties are not fully hardy, warmth and shelter are essential.

Site   Needs very open and well-drained soil.

GROWING METHOD

Propagation   They grow well from cuttings taken in mid-summer, then overwintered in a greenhouse frame. A wide range of penstemons can be grown from seed, which is widely available. They need a cold period before germination; sow in the fall or refrigerate the seed for three weeks before sowing in the spring.

Feeding   Apply a general fertilizer as new growth commences in the spring.

Problems   No specific pest or disease problems, but root rot may occur on sticky clay soil.

FLOWERING

Season   Most have a fairly long flowering period, from the summer to mid-fall. However, many can only be seen as true perennials in milder parts of the country, being killed by winter frosts; raise new stock to replace any losses. "Garnet" is the hardiest.

Cutting   This is not a satisfactory cut flower.

AFTER FLOWERING

Requirements   Either cut entirely to the ground, or leave some stems as frost protection. Protect clumps with a mulch of straw or bracken.

PHLOX PANICULATA
Perennial phlox

THE ATTRACTIVE, *individual flowers on the heads of perennial phlox last right through the season, making it essential in any border.*

A GREAT STANDBY *for the summer yard, perennial phlox fills the whole of the back of this border with two shades of pink.*

FEATURES

HERBACEOUS

Easy to grow and producing a summer-long display of flowers, perennial phlox has a place in any perennial collection. Plants may grow from 16 to 36in tall, and the clumps spread rapidly; position new plantings 12in apart. The large heads of flowers, some with a contrasting eye, come in shades of red, pink, orange, mauve, purple, and white. This plant looks best mass-planted, either in solid blocks of one color or in mixed colors. Also note the highly popular, new variegated cultivars. With mixed plantings, ensure that the taller forms do not obscure the shorter ones.

PHLOX AT A GLANCE

P. paniculata is an erect, herbaceous perennial with scented flowers, and many excellent cultivars. Hardy to 5°F (zone 7).

Jan	/	Recommended Varieties
Feb	sow	*Phlox paniculata* "Alba
Mar	sow	Grandiflora"
Apr	transplant	*P. p.* "Blue Ice"
May	transplant	*P. p.* "Bumble's Delight"
Jun		*P. p.* "Eventide"
July	flowering	*P. p.* "Le Mahdi"
Aug	flowering	*P. p.* "Prince of Orange"
Sept	flowering	*P. p.* "Prospero"
Oct	divide	*P. p.* "White Admiral"
Nov	/	
Dec	/	

CONDITIONS

Aspect   Prefers full sunlight with some protection from strong wind.
Site   Needs a well-drained soil enriched with organic matter.

GROWING METHOD

Propagation   Divide clumps in the fall every three or four years, making sure that each division has a crown and a good set of roots. Replant only the younger, vigorous outer growths, discarding the rest. Plants propagated from root cuttings will be free of eelworm.
Feeding   Apply a complete plant food in spring and mulch well with rotted manure or compost, but do not cover the crowns.
Problems   Powdery mildew can be a problem. Spray with a fungicide. Phlox eelworm causes leaves to shrivel, and shrubs distort. Plants must be destroyed.

FLOWERING

Season   From the summer into early fall.
Cutting   It makes a good cut flower.

AFTER FLOWERING

Requirements   Remove spent flower stems as they fade. In late fall, cut off any remaining growth. Give the plants a thorough tidy-up for the winter.

PHYSOSTEGIA VIRGINIANA
Obedient plant

THE SHORT SPIKES of flowers are attached to the obedient plant by a joint, so they can be rearranged as you please.

OBEDIENT PLANT looks best in large plantings. It is well worth devoting yard space to it, since the flowers last for several months.

FEATURES

HERBACEOUS

This is an easy-care, fast-growing perennial. Since it spreads by stolons (runners) and seed, large clumps can develop in one season. Excess plants are quite easily removed. The dark green leaves are only 4–6in long, but flowering stems bring the height up to 4ft. The flowers in the species are pinky-mauve, but there are cultivars with flowers in various shades of pink, red, and white. It looks best when planted in large drifts in a border, or among shrubs. The common name refers to the fact that flowers remain fixed the way they are turned. It is also sometimes known as "false dragon's head."

PHYSOSTEGIA AT A GLANCE

P. virginiana is a spreading, tall perennial with purple or lilac-tinged flowers lasting into the fall. Hardy to 32°F (zone 10).

		Recommended Varieties
Jan	/	
Feb	/	*Physostegia virginiana* "Alba"
Mar	divide	*P. v.* "Crown of Snow"
Apr	transplant	*P. v.* "Red Beauty"
May	transplant	*P. v.* "Summer Snow"
Jun	/	*P. v.* "Vivid"
July	flowering	*P. v.* subsp. *speciosa*
Aug	flowering	"Bouquet Rose"
Sept	flowering	
Oct	sow	
Nov	/	
Dec	/	

CONDITIONS

Aspect Grows well in both full sunlight and semi-shade. However, some form of protection from strong winds is desirable. The taller varieties may need staking.

Site Tolerates a wide range of soils, but the best results occur when it's grown in well-drained soil, rich in organic matter.

GROWING METHOD

Propagation Divide old clumps in the spring, planting new divisions in groups for the best effect. The oldest sections can be discarded. Because of its vigorous habit, you need to divide it every couple of years. Physostegia tolerates dry periods well, but you must water young plants regularly until they are established.

Feeding Apply a complete plant food in spring. Mulch with decayed organic matter at the same time.

Problems No specific problems are known.

FLOWERING

Season Flowers appear from mid- to late summer into the fall.

Cutting Frequent cutting of blooms should produce a second flush of flowers. Scald-cut the stems to prolong their vase life.

AFTER FLOWERING

Requirements Remove spent flower stems and tidy up growth as it dies down.

PLATYCODON
Balloon flower

THE BUDS *of platycodon swell into a balloon shape, hence the common name, then pop open to reveal these beautiful flowers.*

THIS WELL-ESTABLISHED CLUMP *of balloon flower is supported by stakes guaranteeing height, as well as color.*

FEATURES

HERBACEOUS

Also known as Chinese bellflower, this herbaceous perennial grows approximately 20in high, slightly taller in perfect conditions. It has a shortish flowering period in late summer, and the open, bell-shape flowers come in a range of blue shades, but also in white and pale pink. Flowers last well when cut. There are several named cultivars available, including double and semi-double examples. Since clumps are compact and spread slowly, they are best planted where they can remain undisturbed for some years. The new growth appears in late spring; mark its position to avoid hauling it out as a weed.

PLATYCODON AT A GLANCE

P. grandiflorus is a one-specie genus grown for its beautiful purple-blue flowers. Several fine cultivars. Hardy to 5°F (zone 7).

Jan	/	Companion Plants
Feb	/	Aster
Mar	sow	Clematis
Apr	divide	Dahlia
May	transplant	Fuchsia
Jun	/	Osteospermum
July	/	Phygelius
Aug	flowering	*Rhodochiton atrosanguineus*
Sept	flowering	Rose
Oct	/	
Nov	/	
Dec	/	

CONDITIONS

Aspect Grows in sun or dappled sunlight.
Site Grows best in a well-drained soil enriched with plenty of organic matter.

GROWING METHOD

Propagation Seed is the best means of propagation; sow in the spring. Young shoots can be taken as cuttings, and the double forms must be grown from cuttings. Also, clumps can be lifted and divided in the spring; replant the divisions approximately 8–10in apart. Give newly bedded plants a regular watering during prolonged dry spells in the spring and summer.

Feeding Apply a complete plant food when new growth begins to appear in the spring.

Problems Slugs can be a major problem devouring new growth. Either pick off by hand or treat chemically.

FLOWERING

Season A relatively short display, which is more than compensated for by the nature of the exquisite flowers.

Cutting Flowers can be cut for the vase.

AFTER FLOWERING

Requirements Cut all spent flower stems right back to the ground, and then the whole plant as the growth dies off.

POLYGONATUM
Solomon's seal

A HORIZONTAL STEM of pretty white Solomon's seal flowers is suspended above a groundcover of lungwort and dead nettle.

SOLOMON'S SEAL grows tall in the dappled shade of this yard, where it is teamed with hostas, lady's mantle, and foxgloves.

FEATURES

HERBACEOUS

This lovely herbaceous perennial is ideal for naturalizing in the dappled shade of a yard. The plant has a graceful, arching habit with stems 24–36in long. The finely veined foliage tends to stand up on the stem, while the tubular white bell flowers hang down. It grows from a creeping rhizome and will spread to form a colony of plants, given the correct conditions. If space is no problem, plant several to start your display, letting them form large colonies. A number of other species are grown, some, such as *P. odoratum*, with scented flowers; "Flore Pleno" has double flowers. There are two variegated, eye-catching forms.

POLYGONATUM AT A GLANCE

P. x hybridum (multiflorum) is a rhizomatous perennial with green-tipped white flowers and black fruit. Hardy to 0°F (zones 6–7).

		Recommended Varieties
Jan	/	
Feb	/	
Mar	divide	*P. biflorum*
Apr	transplant	*P. falcatum*
May	flowering	*P. f.* "Variegatum"
Jun	/	*P. hookeri*
July	/	*P. odoratum* "Flore Pleno"
Aug	/	*P. verticillatum*
Sept	/	
Oct	sow	
Nov	/	
Dec	/	

CONDITIONS

Aspect Needs a sheltered spot in part or full shade.
Site The soil should drain well but be heavily enriched with organic matter to retain some moisture at all times. The plants benefit from an early spring mulch.

GROWING METHOD

Propagation Established clumps can be divided in early spring; new divisions should be positioned 8–10in apart. This plant is best left undisturbed for several years, if possible. Young plants need to be watered regularly during the growing season; do not let them dry out.
Feeding Apply complete plant food as new growth commences in the spring.
Problems Plants can be severely devastated by attacks of sawfly larvae, which reduce them to skeletons. Either treat with a spray, or pick off the caterpillars.

FLOWERING

Season Flowers appear in late spring.
Cutting Flowers can be cut for indoor decoration. They last fairly well and make a good display.

AFTER FLOWERING

Requirements Do not cut down the flower stems or you will end up weakening the plant, and consequently losing the attractive, yellow fall tints.

POTENTILLA
Cinquefoil

A SMART RED AND WHITE MIX of cinquefoil with annual heartsease, or Viola tricolor, *growing through it.*

DESPITE THE SMALL FLOWERS, these bright little plants are difficult to overlook in any perennial yard.

FEATURES

HERBACEOUS

There are over 500 species of cinquefoil, including annuals, perennials, and small shrubs. All have the characteristic five-lobed leaf, and the single or double flowers may be white or in shades of yellow, red, or pink. Cinquefoil belongs to the rose family, and the foliage can be attractive, even when plants are not in flower. They may be from 2–20in or more high. The short types make good edging plants, while the taller ones can be used successfully in a mixed planting. Since flower stems tend to flop over, they may need light support. Many red cinquefoils are hybrids of *P. atrosanguinea*, while some yellows derive from *P. argyrophylla* and *P. recta*. Some cinquefoils tend to self-seed.

POTENTILLA AT A GLANCE

A 500-species genus, mainly of herbaceous perennials and shrubs. An excellent color range. Hardy to 0°F (zones 6–7).

Jan	/	**Recommended Varieties**
Feb	/	
Mar	sow 🌱	*Potentilla cuneata*
Apr	transplant 🌿	"Gibson's Scarlet"
May	transplant 🌿	*P. megalantha*
Jun	flowering 🌸	*P. nepalensis* "Miss Willmott"
July	flowering 🌸	"William Rollison"
Aug	flowering 🌸	
Sept	flowering 🌸	
Oct	sow 🌱	
Nov	/	
Dec	/	

CONDITIONS

Aspect   While it needs full sunshine, cinquefoil will also tolerate some dappled shade.

Site   Needs well-drained soil enriched with some organic matter.

GROWING METHOD

Propagation   Species and single-flowered varieties grow from both seed and cuttings. Sow the seed in early to mid-spring. The hybrid doubles must be grown from divisions taken during the spring or fall, or you can use spring cuttings. The plant spacing depends on ultimate size, and may be anywhere from 6 to 16in.

Feeding   Apply a complete plant food as new growth commences in the spring.

Problems   Since these plants can easily flower themselves to death, propagate regularly to ensure you always have a good supply.

FLOWERING

Season   Flowers may begin in late spring in warm spells, but the main flowering period is during the summer months. Give the plant a light trim in early spring to force plenty of new growth and buds.

Cutting   Flowers do not last well when cut.

AFTER FLOWERING

Requirements   Cut off spent flower stems at ground level, and tidy up the plants as the growth dies off. In milder areas the foliage may hang on.

PRIMULA VULGARIS
Primrose

A CARPET OF PALE YELLOW PRIMROSES is one of the finest ways to announce the arrival of spring in the yard. Given a cool, sheltered spot, they will thrive and multiply year by year, even if they receive little attention.

FEATURES

HERBACEOUS

This is the true primrose of European woodlands. The species generally has soft, pale yellow flowers tucked in among the leaves on very short stalks, although white or pale pink forms are occasionally found. Cultivars come in a huge range of colors, with single or double flowers, some on short stalks, others on quite tall ones. Primroses look their best when mass-planted under deciduous trees, or in drifts at the front of a lightly shaded bed or border. They can also be grown well in pots. Plants grow from about 4 to 6in high, with flowering stems about the same height.

PRIMULA AT A GLANCE

P. vulgaris is an evergreen or semi-evergreen with scented, spring, generally pale yellow flowers. Hardy to 5°F (zone 7).

Jan	/	
Feb	sow	
Mar	flowering	
Apr	flowering	
May	flowering	
Jun	/	
July	/	
Aug	/	
Sept	sow	
Oct	divide	
Nov	/	
Dec	/	

Recommended Varieties

"Ken Dearman"

"Miss Indigo"

Primula vulgaris "Lilacina Plena"

P. v. subsp. *sibthorpii*

"Wanda"

CONDITIONS

Aspect   Prefers to grow in semi-shade, and must have protection from the summer sun.

Site   Grows best in a medium-to-heavy moisture-retentive soil, heavily enriched with organic matter. Mulch around the plants in spring.

GROWING METHOD

Propagation   Lift and divide the crowns after flowering, in late fall, and replant about 4–6in apart. Sow your plant's own seed when ripe (from late spring to early fall); sow bought seed in early spring. Do not let young plants dry out.

Feeding   Little fertilizer is needed if the soil is well enriched with plenty of humus, but a little general fertilizer in early spring gives an extra boost.

Problems   Generally trouble-free.

FLOWERING

Season   Flowering usually lasts for several weeks during the spring. Deadheading prolongs the blooming. Massed displays look best.

Cutting   Makes a fine small bouquet, mixed with a range of other early spring miniatures.

AFTER FLOWERING

Requirements   In suitable conditions, plants may self-seed. Remove dead leaves around the plant base.

PRIMULA SPECIES
Candelabra primulas

PRIMULA PULVERULENTA *happily combine here with hostas, both enjoying the damp conditions of a bog garden.*

THE CHARACTERISTIC TIERS *of flowers are well displayed in this healthy clump of white perennial primulas.*

FEATURES

HERBACEOUS

EVERGREEN

Candelabra primulas, which produce their flowers in distinct whorls or tiers up the stems, form one group among the several hundred species of primula. Most are herbaceous, but *P. helodoxa*, which has clear yellow flowers, is evergreen. Other species in this group include *P. aurantiaca*, *P. bulleyana*, *P. japonica*, and *P. pulverulenta*. Flowers may be white, or in shades of yellow, orange, pink, red, or purple. Plant heights vary from 24 to 39in. These are plants that need to be placed in large groups for maximum impact. They need damp soil, often being planted around ponds and water features. Given the right conditions, these plants give a great show every year.

PRIMULA AT A GLANCE

Candelabra primulas are deciduous or semi-evergreen, flower on tall stems, and brighten up damp areas. Hardy to 5°F (zone 7).

		Recommended Varieties
Jan	/	
Feb	sow	*Primula beesiana*
Mar	sow	*P. bulleyana*
Apr	flowering	"Inverewe"
May	flowering	*P. japonica*
Jun	/	Pagoda Hybrids
July	/	*P. japonica*
Aug	/	*P. pulverulenta*
Sept	sow	
Oct	divide	
Nov	/	
Dec	/	

CONDITIONS

Aspect   Candelabra primulas thrive in dappled shade.
Site   Needs deep, moisture-retentive soil that is heavily enriched with organic matter, but it clearly dislikes being waterlogged over the winter months.

GROWING METHOD

Propagation   Lift and divide the crowns after flowering, in late fall, and replant about 4–6in apart. Sow your plant's own seed when ripe (from late spring to early fall); sow bought seed in early spring. Do not let young plants dry out.
Feeding   Little fertilizer is needed if the soil is well enriched with plenty of humus, but a scattering of general fertilizer in early spring gives an extra boost.
Problems   Generally trouble-free.

FLOWERING

Season   This charming, essential primula flowers during the spring.
Cutting   Flowers probably last a few days in the vase, and they add considerable charm to any arrangement, but the massed garden display is more rewarding.

AFTER FLOWERING

Requirements Spent flower stems can be cut off, unless you are waiting for seed to set. In good conditions many of the species will self-seed.

PULMONARIA
Lungwort

FLOWERING PULMONARIA are an essential feature of the spring yard.

THE SPOTTED FOLIAGE of lungwort makes dense and attractive groundcover under trees. It is a reliable grower, so long as it gets regular water in the spring and summer.

FEATURES

HERBACEOUS

EVERGREEN

Lungwort is well suited to planting under trees, between shrubs, or at the front of a shady border. The abundant flowers appear before the leaves have fully developed, and are mostly in shades of blue, pink, and white. The foliage is very handsome, often silver-spotted, and if sheared over after flowering, produces a second, fresh mound of leaves. The whole plant is rarely more than 10–12in high, and when established is very decorative, even out of flower. The plant gets its common name from the similarity between a spotted leaf and a diseased lung.

PULMONARIA AT A GLANCE

A genus of 14 species of deciduous and evergreen perennials. A flowering spreader for damp shade. Hardy to 0°F (zones 6–7).

Jan	/	
Feb	/	
Mar	flowering	
Apr	flowering	
May	flowering	
Jun	divide	
July	/	
Aug	/	
Sept	/	
Oct	divide	
Nov	/	
Dec	/	

Recommended Varieties

Pulmonaria angustifolia
P. a. "Munstead Blue"
P. longifolia "Bertram Anderson"
P. officinalis Cambridge Blue Group
P. o. "Sissinghurst White"
P. rubra
P. saccharata Argentea Group

CONDITIONS

Aspect Grows best in light shade, or in borders that are shady during the hottest part of the day. The leaves quickly wilt under a hot sun.

Site The soil should be heavily enriched with decayed organic matter, but it also needs to drain quite well.

GROWING METHOD

Propagation Grows from ripe seed, or by division of clumps, either after flowering or in the fall. Replant divisions approximately 6in apart. Better still, let plants freely hybridize. Young and established plants need moist soil during the growing season.

Feeding Apply a little complete fertilizer in early spring and mulch well.

Problems No specific problems are known.

FLOWERING

Season Lungworts flower in the spring.

Cutting Flowers last quite well in a vase.

AFTER FLOWERING

Requirements Spent flowers can be cut off if you do not want seeding to occur. After the flowers have finished, the foliage can be cut back to produce new fresh growth for the summer. Otherwise, little attention is required until the fall, when the foliage can be tidied as it fades.

PULSATILLA VULGARIS
Pasque flower

FOLK MEDICINE *makes use of the pasque flower, but it should be treated with caution, since it can be fatal if used incorrectly.*

LIGHT FROST *here coats buds of the pasque flower, showing up its silky hairs. They will be more obvious on the seedheads.*

FEATURES

HERBACEOUS

The soft purple flowers appear before the leaves on this small, spring-flowering perennial. The whole plant is covered with silky hairs, giving it a delicate appearance that belies its hardy nature. After the petals have fallen, a decorative seedhead forms. The finely divided leaves grow from 4 to 6in long, while the flowers may be on stems 4–12in tall. Pasque flower should be planted in groups or drifts to get the best effect. There are now pink, white, and red forms available. Since the leaves and flowers may cause skin irritation, wear gloves when handling if you have sensitive skin.

PULSATILLA AT A GLANCE

P. vulgaris is an attractive, clump-forming perennial, with bell-like, silky flowers in shades of purple. Hardy to 0°F (zones 6–7).

Month		Recommended Varieties
Jan	/	
Feb	/	*Pulsatilla alpina subsp.*
Mar	/	*apiifolia*
Apr	flowering	*P.halleri*
May	flowering	*P. halleri subsp. slavica*
Jun	flowering	*P. vernalis*
July	sow	*P. vulgaris*
Aug	sow	*P. v.* "Eva Constance"
Sept	/	*P. v.* var. *rubra*
Oct	divide	
Nov	/	
Dec	/	

CONDITIONS

Aspect Prefers full sun but tolerates semi-shade.
Site Needs very well-drained, gritty soil, rich in organic matter. They thrive on lime.

GROWING METHOD

Propagation Divide existing clumps after the foliage has died down, and then replant the divisions approximately 6–8in apart. Named varieties must be divided, but the species can also be grown from seed sown as soon as it is ripe in July. Overwinter the seedlings in a greenhouse or frame. Pot up when the new leaves begin to show in the spring.

Feeding Apply a little general fertilizer when growth commences in the spring.

Problems No specific pest or disease problems are known for this plant.

FLOWERING

Season Flowers appear in the spring and early summer, generally before the leaves. They last well and the display is prolonged by the pretty, silky seedheads.

Cutting The flowers are unsuitable for cutting, but the seedheads add to an attractive display.

AFTER FLOWERING

Requirements Plants should be left alone until the seedheads have faded or fallen. Cut off spent stems, and trim off the foliage as the plant dies.

RANUNCULUS
Buttercup

A STRONG, vivid display of ranunculus showing how they can enliven a border. By mixing two or three different varieties you will certainly get extra impact. However, since some types of ranunculus can rapidly multiply and spread, you must take great care when selecting a particular variety.

FEATURES

EVERGREEN

HERBACEOUS

Buttercups basically divide into the invasive and the less-so. Take care which you chose for the border. The genus contains about 400 species of annuals, biennials, and perennials, with a wide range of demands, which vary from free-draining alpine slopes to ponds.

R. ficaria, lesser celandine, is a woodland type with early spring, yellow flowers that can become a weed. There are several cultivars; "Brazen Hussy" has dark brown foliage and yellow flowers, while "Salmon's White" is cream with a blue tint on the reverse.

R. aconitifolius "Flore Pleno," fair maids of France, likes full sun and has white, long-lasting flowers. And *R. flammula,* lesser spearwort, is a marginal aquatic for early summer with yellow flowers.

RANUNCULUS AT A GLANCE

A large genus of over 400 species with many annuals, biennials, and perennials, hardy to 5°F (zone 7) for all kinds of garden.

Jan	/	
Feb	/	Recommended Varieties
Mar	sow	
		Ranunculus aconitifolius
Apr	transplant	"Flore Pleno"
May	flowering	*R. calandrinioides*
Jun	flowering	*R. ficaria* "Brazen Hussy"
July	flowering	*R. f.* "Picton's Double"
		R. f. "Salmon's White"
Aug	/	*R. flammula*
Sept	/	*R. gramineus*
Oct	divide	*R. montanus* "Molten Gold"
Nov	/	
Dec	/	

CONDITIONS

Aspect   It tolerates a wide range of conditions from medium to dappled shade, to full sun. When buying a ranunculus do carefully check its specific needs.

Site   This too varies considerably from moist, rich soil, to fertile, free-draining ground, to gritty, fast-draining soil for the alpine types, to ponds and pond margins for the aquatics.

GROWING METHOD

Propagation   Divide in the spring or fall, or sow fresh, ripe seed in the fall.

Feeding   This depends entirely on the natural habitat and growing needs of the plant. Border perennials need reasonable applications of well-rotted manure in the spring, as new growth appears, while the woodland types need plenty of leafy compost dug in around the clumps.

Problems   Slugs and snails are a particular nuisance; pick off or use chemical treatment.

FLOWERING

Season   From late spring to mid-summer, depending on the chosen variety.

Cutting   All ranunculus make excellent cut flowers, being especially useful in spring before the main flush of garden flowers.

AFTER FLOWERING

Requirements Cut back all spent stems.

RODGERSIA
Rodgersia

NO GARDEN IS COMPLETE without rodgersia. They can be grown apart from other plants, perhaps surrounded by gravel, highlighting the shapely, distinctive leaves, which on R. pinnata *grow 10in long. Or grow them in a mixed border, where they add strength and structure.*

FEATURES

HERBACEOUS

A six-species genus with particularly interesting foliage, and flowers, ideal for the border or shady woodland garden. The three most commonly grown types are *R. aesculifolia, R. pinnata,* and *R. podophylla* (the last two having handsome, bronze new foliage). All form big, bold clumps in the right conditions. The first has crinkled leaves like those of a horse-chestnut, up to 10in long, with tall panicles of creamy white flowers; height 6½ft. *R. pinnata* "Superba," 4ft, has purple-bronze foliage and white, pink, or red flowers. And *R. podophylla,* 5ft, with creamy green flowers, also has horse-chestnut-type leaves, reddish in the fall.

RODGERSIA AT A GLANCE

These tall, clump-forming perennials add structure to any damp-ish garden. Whitish summer flowers; hardy to 0°F (zone 7).

		Recommended Varieties
Jan	/	
Feb	/	*Rodgersia aesculifolia*
Mar	sow	*R. pinnata*
Apr	dvide	*R. p.* "Elegans"
May	transplant	*R. p.* "Superba"
Jun	/	*R. podophylla*
July	flowering	*R. sambucifolia*
Aug	flowering	
Sept	/	
Oct	/	
Nov	/	
Dec	/	

CONDITIONS

Aspect   Rodgersia, from the mountaineous Far East, like full sun or partial shade. They thrive in both conditions.

Site   Grow in rich, damp ground; they grow by streams in the wild, and also in woodland settings.

GROWING METHOD

Propagation   Either divide, which is the easiest method, or grow from seed in the spring, raising the plants in a cold frame. Water the new young plants well, and do not let them dry out in prolonged, dry spells. They quickly wilt and lose energy, and their performance is badly affected.

Feeding   Add plenty of well-rotted manure or compost to the soil. The shadier the conditions, the less rich the soil need be.

Problems   Vine weevil grubs can demolish the roots of container-grown perennials. While slugs rarely attack the new emerging growth, when they do strike they can ruin a potentially impressive display with tall, astilbe-like flowers. Pick off any offenders or treat with a chemical.

FLOWERING

Season   Flowers appear in mid- and late summer, and in early summer in the case of *R. sambucifolia.*

Cutting   Rodgersia make good cut flowers, helping create an impressive display.

AFTER FLOWERING

Requirements   Cut the spent stems to the ground, and promptly remove all debris.

ROMNEYA COULTERI
Californian tree poppy

CRIMPED WHITE PETALS around a mass of golden stamens make the matilija poppy as effective in close-up as in a group.

THE BLUE-GREEN FOLIAGE and splendid white flowers of the matilija poppy make an eye-catching display in the garden.

FEATURES

SUMMER AUTUMN WINTER SPRING

EVERGREEN

Also known as the matilija poppy, this lovely perennial is not always easy to accommodate. It is native to the canyons and dry riverbeds in parts of California where there is generally rain only in winter, and where summers are hot and dry. When conditions are suitable, this plant can spread via underground roots. The large, white, summer flowers have beautiful crinkled petals that look like silk. Plants grow from 3 to 6½ft tall, and the blue-green foliage is deeply cut and attractive. Place these perennials in groups among shrubs or mixed perennials. Most plants available are likely to be hybrids of the standard species and *R. coulteri* var. *trichocalyx.*

ROMNEYA AT A GLANCE

This is a deciduous sub-shrub with gray-green leaves and highly attractive white summer flowers. Hardy to 0°F (zones 6–7).

		Companion Plants
Jan	/	
Feb	/	Ceanothus
Mar	sow	Clematis
Apr	division	Delphinium
May	transplant	Helenium
Jun	flowering	Hemerocallis
July	flowering	Pelargonium
Aug	flowering	Pennisetum
Sept	/	Philadelphus
Oct	/	
Nov	/	
Dec	/	

CONDITIONS

Aspect   Romneya needs bright, full sunlight all day.
Site   Needs well-drained, preferably sandy or gravelly loam; avoid thick, heavy, wet clay. They can be tricky and slow to establish, but thereafter thrive, given the correct conditions.

GROWING METHOD

Propagation   Grows from seed sown in the spring, but it is easiest propagated from root cuttings or suckers growing away from the main plant in spring. Wait until plants are very well established before attempting to disturb the roots—something they do not react well to. Position plants approximately 16in apart. Water regularly in the spring, when the foliage is growing and buds are appearing; thereafter, water occasionally in prolonged, dry spells.
Feeding   Give a little complete plant food in early spring.
Problems   Poor drainage can kill Californian tree poppies. Can become invasive.

FLOWERING

Season   Right through the summer.
Cutting   Like all poppies they make lovely cut flowers. Scald or burn the stems before arranging.

AFTER FLOWERING

Requirements   Cut off spent flowers. As the plant flowers on new growth, it is best to cut it down to the ground in winter. Protect the crown with straw or bracken in cold areas.

RUDBECKIA
Coneflower

THE DAISY-LIKE flower shape of the coneflower, a bright color, and a central dark marking. It looks best in a bold group display.

A VALUABLE, forceful, late summer display from a mass planting of coneflowers, especially useful when many borders are starting to fade.

FEATURES

HERBACEOUS

The coneflower rewards a bright, sunny position with a bold display of daisy-like flowers. The genus consists of annuals, biennials, and perennials, with some traditional garden favorites. *R. fulgida*, Black-eyed Susan, grows 36 x 18in, producing yellow-orange flowers at the end of summer, into the fall. "Goldsturm" has bigger flowers but only grows two-thirds as tall. For a powerful, vigorous display at the back of the border, try *R. lacinata*. It has thin, wiry stems, lemon-yellow flowers, and puts on a mid-summer to mid-fall display that can reach 8ft high, while its spread is relatively contained at just 3ft.

RUDBECKIA AT A GLANCE

A near 20-species genus with annuals, biennials, and perennials, often with striking, yellowish flowers. Hardy to 0°F (zones 6–7).

Month		Recommended Varieties
Jan	/	
Feb	/	"Goldquelle"
Mar	sow	"Herbstonne"
Apr	divide	*Rudbeckia fulgida* var. *deamii*
May	transplant	*R. f.* var. *sullivantii*
Jun	/	"Goldsturm"
July	flowering	*R. laciniata*
Aug	flowering	*R. maxima*
Sept	flowering	
Oct	flowering	
Nov	divide	
Dec	/	

CONDITIONS

Aspect   A bright, open sunny position is essential. Avoid shady areas. The plant's natural habitat is North American meadows and big, open woods.

Site   Do not plant in over-dry, Mediterranean-style yards. The soil must remain heavy and lightly damp. In the wild *R. fulgida* grows in marshy valleys.

GROWING METHOD

Propagation   Either divide in the spring or fall, or sow seeds in the spring in a cold frame. Do not let the new, young plants dry out.

Feeding   Fertility must be quite high. Dig large quantities of well-rotted manure and compost into poor soil.

Problems   Slugs can be a major problem. Keep watch, and pick them off by hand or treat chemically. A potentially good flowering display can be quickly ruined if they take control.

FLOWERING

Season   A long flowering season from the summer to late fall.

Cutting   Rudbeckia make good cut flowers, adding height and color to any arrangement. They are especially useful, having a dark-colored central disk (black, brown, or green) in the center of the flower.

AFTER FLOWERING

Requirements   Cut back to the ground, although some stems can be left to provide interesting shapes over winter, especially when frosted.

SALVIA
Sage

SALVIA X SYLVESTRIS "MAINACHT" ("MAY NIGHT") is a wonderful, clumpy perennial that sends up spires of rich blue flowers. It can be guaranteed to soften even the most rigid landscaped yard, flowering in early and mid-summer. "Blauhugel" ("Blue Mound") is very similar.

FEATURES

HERBACEOUS

EVERGREEN

Salvias are a huge plant group of over 700 species, comprising shrubs, herbaceous perennials, and annuals. Most people associate salvias with red or purple flowers, but there are also species with cream, yellow, white, blue, and pink flowers. Many have highly aromatic foliage, with scents ranging from the delicious to the outright unpleasant: the foliage of pineapple sage, *S. elegans* (syn. *S. rutilans*) has a delicious perfume, while the bog sage (*S. uliginosa*) smells rather unpleasant. Most salvias are extremely easy to grow and once established need little attention, beyond occasional deep watering in hot weather and some cutting back after flowering. The tall salvias are ideal for the rear of the border or as fillers between shrubs. There are many others of varying heights that are suitable as edging plants or for planting among annuals, bulbs, and other perennials. *Salvia* x *sylvestris* "Mainacht" ("May Night"), shown above, is an exceptionally good border perennial, but if it is unavailable there are plenty of fine alternatives, including "Rose Queen."
Common sage, *S. officinalis*, is a highly popular salvia. It has gray, wrinkly foliage and flowers that are usually pale violet. The one problem is that, in certain conditions, it spreads like a weed. Coming from the Mediterranean, it demands sharp drainage and dislikes a soaking wet summer.

Others
For spring–summer flowers in a range of colors, from cream to lilac and blue, try *S. sclarea*. It is perfectly hardy, and grows up to 3ft high. *S. bulleyana* is equally easy, and grows approximately 16in–3ft high. It has yellow flowers with a brownish lower lip appearing from the middle to the end of summer, and is also fully hardy, coming from western China. For an early summer–fall flower show, use *S. forsskaolii* from the Black Sea coast. It grows 3ft tall high, and bears white flowers with lips in violet and faint yellow. Alternatively, try *S.* x *superba*. It has violet flowers from mid-summer to the fall, and reaches the same height. For mild areas where you can grow half-hardy plants, there are plenty more salvias, including *S. microphylla*, and the bog sage, *S. uliginosa*. The former has rich green leaves and magenta flowers at the end of summer to early fall. Bog sage has bright blue flowers with a touch of white, and blooms from late summer to the fall. Both reach 3ft high.

CONDITIONS

Aspect
Provide full sunlight, perhaps in a scree bed, and, in the case of half-hardy plants, a position against a south-facing wall.

Site
Any well-drained soil is suitable. Mulching with decayed manure in the early spring improves the soil condition.

SALVIA SCLAREA *VAR.* TURKESTANICA *can be grown as a perennial or biennial. It produces wonderful pink stems of pinky-white flowers, and is perfectly hardy.*

THE ELECTRIC BLUE *Salvia transsylvanica contrasting with a "Star Gazer" lily.*

GROWING METHOD

Propagation
Salvias grow from seed that has been sown in the spring, or from cuttings that have been taken in late summer through to the fall. Many species can also be propagated from rooted divisions of an established clump. Simply lift such a clump and you will find numerous pieces with both roots and shoots. The divisions are best taken in the spring months. Set each division approximately 10in apart. Salvias need regular watering to establish. Once established, plants can be drought-tolerant.

Feeding
A complete plant food or pelleted poultry manure can be applied in the spring, in poor soil, as the new growth commences. However, note that too much fertilizer will be counter-

productive, merely resulting in all foliage and very few flowers.

Problems
The worst problems tend to occur when you provide a certain species with the wrong conditions. Carefully check the notes invariably supplied with plants when buying from a garden center or specialist nursery. As a general rule, avoid damp ground and any shady areas.

FLOWERING

Season
Many salvias have a very long flowering period, extending into the fall before being cut down by frost.

Cutting
None of the salvias mentioned makes a particularly good cut flower, but their long, dependable flowering season makes them a great asset in any part of the yard.

AFTER FLOWERING

Requirements
Borderline, half-hardy species will need plenty of protection in cold areas over winter. Provide a thick, protective layer of straw or bracken, held in place with sticks. As a precaution against any losses, keep a stock of new, young plants. The tender salvias must be kept indoors in winter, in a frost-free place. Plants can be tip-pruned after each flowering flush to promote further blooming. In late fall plants can be cut back to just above ground level. If you do not want to lift and divide a clump you can wait until new growth starts in the spring, and simply divide any growth that is becoming too crowded. A number of perennial salvias are extremely vigorous, but they can be kept in control by pulling out the new plants or the running roots when they are getting invasive.

SALVIA AT A GLANCE

A large genus with fine perennials. The color range is mainly blue. Hardy plants to 0°F (zones 6–7); half-hardy 23°F (zone 9).

Jan	/	Recommended Varieties
Feb	/	
Mar	sow	*Salvia argentea*
Apr	divide	*S. bulleyana*
May	transplant	*S. forsskaolii*
Jun	flowering	*S. involucrata* (half-hardy)
July	flowering	*S. microphylla* (half-hardy)
Aug	flowering	*S. patens* (half-hardy)
Sept	flowering	*S. sclarea*
Oct	flowering	*S.* x *superba*
Nov	/	*S. uliginosa* (half-hardy)
Dec	/	

SCABIOSA
Scabious

*SCABIOSA CAUCASICA "CLIVE GREAVES" is a wonderful laven-
der blue and looks especially impressive when planted in thick clusters.*

*SCABIOUS ARE VERSATILE PLANTS. They make a wonderful
addition to most yards, whether schematic or cottage-style.*

FEATURES

SUMMER AUTUMN WINTER SPRING

HERBACEOUS

Scabious is a vital ingredient of cottage-style,
flowery gardens, rock gardens, and mixed
borders. From hot, dry, stony sites, mainly in
the Mediterranean, it provides pale hues in
blue, pink, yellow, or white. The flowers are
held above long, thin stems, many attracting
bees and butterflies. Heights generally range
from 12 to 36in. There are plenty of
interesting choices, and top of the list are the
dwarf forms "Butterfly Blue" and "Pink Mist,"
both relatively new and proving extremely
popular. On the plus side, they flower for six
months; the down side is they are short-lived.
Take cuttings to maintain the display.

CONDITIONS

Aspect   Full sunlight is essential.
Site   Dryish, free-draining soil is important, so that
                the roots are not plunged in soaking wet ground
                over the winter months. The soil must also veer
                from the neutral toward the slightly alkaline.

GROWING METHOD

Propagation Scabious is not long-lived, and begins to lose its
                 vigor and impact after three years. It is therefore
                 vital to replenish the garden with spring
                 divisions, or to sow fresh, ripe seed in pots in a
                 cold frame to maintain a good supply.
Feeding   Do not over-feed the soil, which will be
                 counter-productive, producing leaf growth at
                 the expense of flowers. Very poor soils,
                 however, may need some additions of compost
                 in the early spring.
Problems   Spray at the first sign of powdery mildew.

FLOWERING

Season   The flowers appear right through the summer,
                 in some cases not until mid-summer, often
                 into early fall.
Cutting   Scabious make excellent sprays of cut flowers,
                 and are indispensable for indoor arrangements,
                 either adding to flowery schemes or softening
                 more rigid, structured ones.

AFTER FLOWERING

Requirements Cut all spent stems down to the ground.

SCABIOSA AT A GLANCE

A genus of annuals, biennials, and perennials, providing abundant
soft colors. Good for romantic displays. Hardy to 0°F (zones 6–7).

Jan	/	Recommended Varieties
Feb	/	
Mar	sow 🖙	*Scabiosa caucasica*
Apr	divide 🖙	"Clive Greaves"
May	transplant 🖙	*S. c.* "Miss Willmott"
Jun	flowering 🌼	"Chile Black"
July	flowering 🌼	*S. columbaria* var. *ochroleuca*
Aug	flowering 🌼	*S. lucida*
Sept	flowering 🌼	"Pink Mist"
Oct	sow 🖙	
Nov	/	
Dec	/	

SEDUM SPECTABILE
Ice plant

DENSE FLOWERHEADS of Sedum spectabile "Brilliant" provide a rich source of nectar, attracting butterflies and other insects.

BILLOWING HEADS of sedum add color to the fall yard. Here they edge a mixed border, with white beard tongue behind.

FEATURES

HERBACEOUS

One of over 600 species of succulent sedums, spectabile is unusual because it is frequently used in perennial plantings where many succulents look out of place. It has fleshy, soft green leaves on stems that can reach 24in tall. Similar varieties are available with purple and variegated leaves. Since the new growth appears at the base of older stems, dividing plants is easy. The large heads of flowers are a soft mauve-pink in the species, but there are cultivars with colors ranging from bright hot pinks to rosy red, and the brick red of "Herbstfreude" ("Autumn Joy"). The plants flower from late summer into the fall. This is an easy-care plant that accepts a wide range of conditions.

SEDUM AT A GLANCE

S. spectabile is a clump-forming, late season perennial with pink flowers. Many excellent forms. Hardy to 5°F (zone 7).

Jan	/	Recommended Varieties
Feb	/	
Mar	/	*Sedum alboroseum*
Apr	divide	"Mediovariegatum"
May	/	*S. cauticola*
Jun	/	"Herbstfreude" ("Autumn Joy")
July	/	"Ruby Glow"
Aug	flowering	*S. spectabile* "Brilliant"
Sept	flowering	*S. telephium maximum*
Oct	divide	"Atropurpureum"
Nov	sow	
Dec	/	

CONDITIONS

Aspect   Prefers full sun, but tolerates some light shade for part of the day.

Site   While it can grow in a sandy, well-drained soil, it will tolerate a heavier soil, which gives it an advantage over other sedums.

GROWING METHOD

Propagation   Clumps of plants are easily pulled apart or sliced apart with a spade in the spring or late fall. The divisions are best replanted at approximately 6 8in intervals. Division gives very high success rates. It is also possible to propagate sedum by striking from stem cuttings. Water regularly to establish new young plants.

Feeding   Slow-release fertilizer can be applied in the spring, as new growth commences. Avoid overfeeding, because this may result in plenty of sappy leaf growth at the expense of a display of flowers.

Problems   Plants in containers may rot at the base if overwatered. Vine weevil grubs may devour both bases and roots with devastating effect.

FLOWERING

Season   The late, highly rewarding display occurs at the end of summer, running through the fall.

Cutting   A long-lasting cut flower.

AFTER FLOWERING

Requirements   Leave the skeletal flowerheads over winter to provide attractive, burnished tints.

SISYRINCHIUM
Sisyrinchium

SISYRINCHIUM IDAHOENSE "ALBUM" *is a clump-forming white flower that at 5in tall is ideal for edging borders.*

SISYRINCHIUM MACROCARPON *is 30in tall, has eye-catching vertical foliage, and gentle yellow flowers in early summer.*

FEATURES

EVERGREEN

This is a star plant for the border, with spires of pale yellow flowers over summer, 36in high, and iris-like, strap-shaped foliage. The only problem is that it can self-seed too much for the liking of some, although with vigilance the seedlings are easily removed. The genus also offers blue, mauve, and white flowers. *S. idahoense* is a lovely violet-blue, with a yellow throat, growing 12in high, while *S. graminoides* is slightly taller at 20in, with a deeper blue flower, although it self-seeds more prolifically. For a dwarfish, low-growing white, try "Pole Star," good for the rock garden, where it can best be seen and appreciated. It grows to just 1 x 2½in, and is perfectly hardy.

SISYRINCHIUM AT A GLANCE

S. striatum is an evergreen perennial with spires of pale yellow flowers and long, stiff, pointed leaves. Hardy to 5°F (zone 7).

Jan	/	Recommended Varieties
Feb	/	
Mar	sow	*Sisyrinchium angustifolium*
		"Biscutella"
Apr	transplant	"Californian Skies"
May	/	*S. californicum*
Jun	flowering	"E. K. Balls"
July	flowering	*S. idahoense*
Aug	/	*S. macrocarpon*
Sept	divide	"Quaint and Queer"
Oct	/	*S. striatum* "Aunt May"
Nov	/	
Dec	/	

CONDITIONS

Aspect Full sun is required, well away from the shade.
Site Relatively poor soil is adequate, but free-draining ground is essential. Do not let the plants stand out in damp, wet soil over the winter months.

GROWING METHOD

Propagation Divide in late summer to guarantee a supply of vigorous plants, since mature ones become quite lackluster after three years. Alternatively, sow seed in the spring. To prevent any established plants from self-seeding, cut off the flowers the moment they begin to fade.
Feeding Some enriching with well-rotted manure or compost will provide a boost to poor areas of ground. High levels of fertility, however, are not necessary.
Problems Generally trouble-free.

FLOWERING

Season Flowers in early and mid-summer.
Cutting They make unusual, striking cut flowers, adding smart verticals to any arrangement, forming a basic structure. Use both flowering stems and foliage.

AFTER FLOWERING

Requirements Cut back the flowering stems to the ground, either promptly to prevent large-scale self-seeding, or later to increase numbers, especially when established plants are past their best.

SOLIDAGO
Golden rod

THE HIGHLY DISTINCTIVE *sight of golden rod: a bright spray of yellow flowers, and long, thin, dark green leaves.*

A PERFECT EXAMPLE OF HOW *an invasive plant, such as golden rod, can be reined in and controlled by hard landscaping.*

FEATURES

HERBACEOUS

Golden rod forms large colonies of sometimes quite tall yellow plants, reaching 6ft high. The small flowers in themselves are nothing special, but they appear in such profusion that they make quite an impact. There are plenty of varieties to choose from. The key differences are more to do with height than color. "Crown of Rays" grows to 24in high, and as its name suggests has bright yellow flowers. "Goldenmosa" is almost as bright and grows slightly taller, and has yellow-green foliage. But if you need a golden rod for the rear of the border, especially one where the soil is quite poor, the best choice is "Golden Wings." It can reach 6ft tall, topping smaller plants

with its late summer and early fall show. The best choice of golden rod for growing at the front of the border is the 8in-high "Queenie" or *S. virgaurea minuta*.

CONDITIONS

Aspect	Grow in full sunlight in the border. Avoid borders that are in the shade.
Site	Free-draining soil, preferably quite sandy or gritty, is ideal.

GROWING METHOD

Propagation	Golden rod self-seeds, but to be sure of getting new plants that are true to type, spring or fall division invariably give successful results.
Feeding	High soil fertility is not in any way essential. Very poor ground can be improved in the spring, however, by digging in some quantities of well-rotted manure.
Problems	Powdery mildew can strike quite severely; treat with a fungicide at the first sight of an attack. Repeat sprayings are necessary to control major outbreaks.

FLOWERING

Season	Generally mid- to late summer, though sometimes slightly before and after.
Cutting	Not the best cut flowers—there are better alternatives—but they effectively bulk up any arrangement.

AFTER FLOWERING

Requirements	Cut back spent flower stems.

SOLIDAGO AT A GLANCE

Varieties of golden rod create mainly big, bold, clumps of bright yellow flowers. Can be invasive. Hardy to 0°F (zones 6–7).

Jan	/	Recommended Varieties
Feb	/	
Mar	/	*Solidago cutleri*
Apr	divide	*S. flexicaulis* "Variegata"
May	transplant	"Golden Baby"
Jun	/	"Goldenmosa"
July	flowering	"Queenie"
Aug	flowering	*S. virgaurea minuta*
Sept	/	
Oct	/	
Nov	/	
Dec	/	

STACHYS BYZANTINA
Lamb's ears

SINCE LAMB'S EARS, or lamb's tails, needs good drainage, grow it in an attractive container if your soil is relentlessly heavy and damp.

MORE TRADITIONAL is this planting, where lamb's ears edge a garden bed. The plants will multiply rapidly, given the right situation.

FEATURES

HERBACEOUS

Lamb's ears is a low-growing, evergreen perennial most often used as an edging plant. It could also be used to edge rose beds, but wherever it is planted it must have excellent drainage and full exposure to the sun. The leaves are densely covered with hairs, giving them a white, or pale gray, woolly appearance, hence its common name. It produces pink-purple flowers on spikes that stand above the foliage, but they are not especially attractive; it is grown for its foliage, not the flowers (*S. macrantha* "Robusta" and *S. officinalis* are the exceptions). "Cotton Boll" has woolly flowers good for dried flower arrangements if they are cut when fully open. Plants grow 6–8in tall, but spread a good distance.

STACHYS AT A GLANCE

S. byzantina is a valuable garden plant, noted for its front-of-the border color and soft, silky foliage. Hardy to 0°F (zones 6–7).

		Recommended Varieties
Jan	/	
Feb	/	*S. coccinea*
Mar	sow	*Stachys byzantina* "Big Ears"
Apr	divide	*S. b.* "Cotton Boll"
May	transplant	*S. b.* "Primrose Heron"
Jun	flowering	*S. macrantha*
July	flowering	*S. m.* "Robusta"
Aug	flowering	*S. officinalis*
Sept	flowering	
Oct	divide	
Nov	/	
Dec	/	

CONDITIONS

Aspect Full sunlight is essential all day for the plants to thrive and perform well.

Site Needs very fast-draining soil. It grows well in poor, sandy, or gravelly soil. Avoid thick, wet, heavy clay at all costs.

GROWING METHOD

Propagation Grows readily from cuttings that are taken in the spring or fall. The new divisions must be planted out approximately 8in apart. Water new plants regularly. Once they are established, they need only be watered very occasionally.

Feeding Grows without supplementary fertilizer, but a little complete plant food can be applied in the early spring.

Problems There are no specific problems, but container plants will quickly fail if they are overwatered, and border plants rot if waterlogged.

FLOWERING

Season Flowers are produced in the summer, sometimes into the fall, but the tactile gray foliage is by far the chief attraction.

Cutting Use the foliage in an arrangement; the flower spikes can be cut and dried for later use.

AFTER FLOWERING

Requirements Cut spent flower stems at the base. Trailing growth can be shortened at any time, but plants may need to be cut back hard in the early spring.

STOKESIA LAEVIS
Stokes' aster

THE FLOWERING HEADS *of Stokes' aster are quite complex, made up from many "petals" (more properly bracts or ray florets).*

IT IS HARD *to understand why the pretty Stokes' aster should go out of fashion, but it is certainly grown less often than before.*

FEATURES

HERBACEOUS

Stokes' aster is an easily grown plant that provides great decorative value throughout its long flowering period from mid-summer to early fall. It makes excellent cut flowers, too. Flower stems 12–20in tall rise from a cluster of dark green basal leaves. Although this plant is completely herbaceous in cold areas, the basal growth remains evergreen in mild winters. Its flowers are reminiscent of large cornflowers or asters, and come in shades of blue, white, and mauve. This plant can look outstanding in mass plantings, but is equally at home in a mixed border, or when grown in wooden tubs or pots.

STOKESIA AT A GLANCE

S. laevis is an evergreen, perennial, sprawling plant with large, purple, flat, late summer flowers. Hardy to 5°F (zone 7).

		Companion Plants
Jan	/	
Feb	sow	Aster
Mar	divide	Box
Apr	transplant	Dahlia
May	transplant	Fuchsia
Jun	/	Miscanthus
July	/	Penstemon
Aug	flowering	Potentilla
Sept	flowering	Stipa
Oct	flowering	
Nov	divide	
Dec	/	

CONDITIONS

Aspect   While Stokes' aster prefers full sunlight, it barely tolerates dappled shade. Provide a shelter to protect from strong winds.

Site   Needs well-drained soil enriched with compost or manure.

GROWING METHOD

Propagation   Divide established clumps in the spring or fall, replanting divisions approximately 10in apart. The plant can also be grown from root cuttings taken in the early spring, and from fall seed. It tolerates dry periods, but looks best if given an occasional deep watering during prolonged, dry spells. Provide young plants with twiggy support.

Feeding   Apply some complete plant food in the spring.

Problems   Poorly drained, heavy soils induce root or crown rot, which kills plants.

FLOWERING

Season   The long flowering period is from late summer into the fall.

Cutting   Cut flowers regularly for the vase. This both gives a good ornamental display and prolongs the garden show, inducing plenty of new flower buds.

AFTER FLOWERING

Requirements   Prune all spent flower stems. As the growth dies back, promptly clear away all of the dead foliage.

THALICTRUM
Meadow rue

THE FLUFFY PINK FLOWERS of meadow rue do not last long, but the pretty foliage persists well until the fall.

FINER FOLIAGE, smaller starry flowers and very full growth are features of the related Thalictrum delavayi *and its cultivars.*

FEATURES

HERBACEOUS

Thalictrum aquilegiifolium is easy and quick to grow, a herbaceous perennial reaching about 42in tall. The rather fern-like, blue-green foliage is attractively lobed, and the flowers are mauve-pink in dense, fluffy heads. While the floral display does not last long, the foliage adds months of charm. Meadow rue can be planted in mixed borders or in light shade under trees. There are a number of cultivars, including a white form and one with violet blooms. Also try *T. delavayi* (syn. *T. dipterocarpum*) and its cultivars "Album" and "Hewitt's Double." This has finer foliage and the pink-mauve flowers are star shaped.

THALICTRUM AT A GLANCE

T. aquilegiifolium is a clump-forming, rhizomatous perennial with gorgeous sprays of purple flowers. Hardy to 5°F (zone 7).

		Recommended Varieties
Jan	/	
Feb	/	*Thalictrum aquilegiifolium*
Mar	divide	var. *album*
Apr	transplant	*T. a.* "Thundercloud"
May	/	*T. delavayi*
Jun	flowering	*T. flavum* subsp. *glaucum*
July	flowering	*T. kiusianum*
Aug	/	*T. minus*
Sept	/	*T. rochebruneanum*
Oct	sow	
Nov	/	
Dec	/	

CONDITIONS

Aspect   Grow in either light shade, or in a border with morning sun followed by plenty of afternoon shade.

Soil   Likes well-drained soil that has been enriched with organic matter.

GROWING METHOD

Propagation   Grows from seed sown in the spring or fall, or by divisions of a clump made in spring. Plant the new divisions approximately 10–12in apart. Do not let the young plants dry out— give regular, deep waterings through dry springs and summers.

Feeding   As growth begins in the spring, apply complete plant food and mulch around the plants with well-decayed manure or compost.

Problems   No specific pest or disease problems are known to attack this plant. Generally trouble-free. Note that growth begins late in spring, so avoid damaging new growth while weeding.

FLOWERING

Season   Flowers appear during early summer, depending on temperatures.

Cutting   Both the foliage and flowers can be cut for the vase.

AFTER FLOWERING

Requirements   Cut off any spent flower stems, unless you want to save seed. When the plants die down in the fall, cut off the foliage at ground level.

TIARELLA
Foam flower

THE FOAM FLOWER *produces both a fine early summer bloom display, and often burnt-red-colored fall foliage.*

GIVEN A FREE RUN, Tiarella polyphylla *produces a large, spreading clump with wonderful spires of white flowers.*

FEATURES

HERBACEOUS

Tiarella trifoliata is a North American clump-forming rhizomatous perennial, making excellent groundcover in light shade. From late spring to mid-summer it produces light airy sprays of white flowers, on 12in-long panicles, held above the foliage. A more invasive plant is *T. cordifolia*, foam flower, from east North America, where it grows in mountainside woods, forming extensive colonies, remorselessly spreading by underground stolons. *T. wherryi*, also from North America, is more compact and less invasive—the better choice for a smaller, shady area. Its natural habitat is shady ravines and rocky woods. The white flowers are tinged pink. "Bronze Beauty"

is a popular choice, benefiting from contrasting white flowers and bronze-red foliage.

CONDITIONS

Aspect	Thrives in both dappled and darkish shade, which is its natural habitat.
Site	It tolerates a wide range of soils, but naturally prefers rich, fertile ground, damp but definitely not boggy.

GROWING METHOD

Propagation	Division is the simplest method, although ripe seed can also be sown. Sow in pots in the fall in a cold frame, and keep young plants well watered. Do not let them dry out.
Feeding	The ground needs to be quite rich. Fork in leaf mold and compost in the early spring, and again in the fall, between plants.
Problems	Slugs can strike, but given the situation, out of the way in the shade, and the plant's vigor, it is rarely a major problem. Treat with slug pellets if matters get out of hand.

HARVESTING

Season	A profusion of white flowers appear from late spring to mid-summer.
Cutting	There are better choices for airy white sprays in the summer, but nonetheless they make good cut flowers.

AFTER FLOWERING

Requirements	Cut back to the ground.

TIARELLA AT A GLANCE

T. trifoliata is a North American white perennial, ideal for spreading quickly through shady sites. Hardy to 5°F (zone 7).

Jan	/	Recommended Varieties
Feb	/	
Mar	sow	*Tiarella cordifolia*
Apr	divide	"Elizabeth Oliver"
May	flowering	*T. polyphylla*
Jun	flowering	*T. p.* pink
July	flowering	*T. wherryi*
Aug	/	*T. w.* "Bronze Beauty"
Sept	sow	
Oct	/	
Nov	/	
Dec	/	

TRADESCANTIA
Tradescantia / spiderwort

SPIDERWORT FLOWERS look like small purple irises but each lasts only a day. The surrounding buds are waiting their turn to open.

DENSE PLANTINGS of spiderwort produce plenty of flowers that thrive in filtered sunlight, ideal for a mixed or herbaceous border.

FEATURES

SUMMER AUTUMN WINTER SPRING

HERBACEOUS

This North American herbaceous perennial is a spreading plant with tapering, strap-like leaves and showy, triangular flowers in rich purple, rose-pink, or white. The flowers generally last only one day but they appear in succession over a long period. There are several named cultivars available. Spiderwort grows from 12 to 24in high, and is multi-stemmed. It is easy to grow in the correct conditions and can make a tall groundcover in filtered sunlight under trees. In a mild winter it may not die down completely.

TRADESCANTIA AT A GLANCE

T. virginiana is a purple, repeat-flowerer in a genus of largely tender indoor plants. Ideal for the border. Hardy to 5°F (zone 7).

Jan	/	Recommended Varieties
Feb	/	
Mar	divide 🖐	*Tradescantia* x *andersoniana*
Apr	/	"Bilberry Ice"
May	/	*T.* x *a.* "Isis"
Jun	flowering 🌸	*T.* x *a.* "Osprey"
July	flowering 🌸	*T.* x *a.* "Purple Dome"
Aug	flowering 🌸	*T.* x *a.* "Red Cloud"
Sept	flowering 🌸	*T.* x *a.* "Zwanenburg Blue"
Oct	divide 🖐	
Nov	divide 🖐	
Dec	/	

CONDITIONS

Aspect It requires full sunlight or partial shade.
Site It grows best in soil that is well drained, but is also heavily enriched with plenty of decayed, organic matter.

GROWING METHOD

Propagation Clumps can be lifted and divided in the spring and fall. The species can be grown from seed sown in the fall. It is occasionally self-sown. New plantings should be approximately 12–18in apart, depending on how rapidly you need cover. Needs regular watering during a prolonged, dry growing period.
Feeding Apply a complete plant food when growth starts in the spring.
Problems No specific problems are known.

FLOWERING

Season The long succession of flowers starts in early summer and continues through to mid-fall.
Cutting The buds continue to open when cut.

AFTER FLOWERING

Requirements Growth starts to yellow and die back after flowering. Clean away dead foliage, and tidy up for the winter.

TRILLIUM
Wake robin

THE WAKE ROBIN is the perfect plant for a moist shady area, whether it be light or deep shade. The plants are quickly identified by their three leaves, three calyces, and three petals.

FEATURES

HERBACEOUS

Trilliums are deciduous perennials that make excellent groundcover in partial or full shade, with spring and early summer flowers. The color range includes white, maroon, pink, yellow, bronze-green, and red-purple. *T. grandiflorum*, the North American wake robin, has 3in-long white flowers and veined petals. It is long-lived and easy to grow, requiring little attention. *T. sessile* "Rubrum" has claret petals and attractively mottled foliage. Several clones bear this name and there is little to choose between them. At the front of a shady, slightly acidic border, try *T. rivale*. It grows 6in tall and wide, has pointed ovate petals, white or pale pink, with purple speckling toward the base. *T. luteum* has scented yellowish flowers and mottled, pale and dark leaves. It grows 16in tall, spreading by almost the same amount.

CONDITIONS

Aspect
Mottled or deep shade is required. Avoid open areas with full sunlight.

Site
The soil should be the acid side of neutral, although some trilliums will tolerate low levels of alkalinity.

GROWING METHOD

Propagation
Preferably divide the rhizomes when dormant, ensuring each section has one strong growing point. Note that they are slow to establish. It is quite possible to sow ripe, late summer seed in a cold frame, but the 5–7 years to flower is prohibitively long.

Feeding
The soil needs to be rich, with plenty of well-rotted leaf mold and compost, being damp and free-draining. Where necessary, provide a thick mulch every spring and fall.

Problems
Both slugs and snails feed on the tender new foliage. Pick off by hand when this becomes a problem, or use a chemical treatment.

FLOWERING

Season
The flowers appear in spring and summer.

Cutting
They make attractive cut flowers, especially *T. grandiflorum*, with its near diamond-shaped white flowers.

AFTER FLOWERING

Requirements Cut spent stems to the ground.

TRILLIUM AT A GLANCE

A 30-species strong genus with rhizomatous perennials, excellent for flowering ground cover in shade. Hardy to 5°F (zone 7).

		Recommended Varieties
Jan	/	
Feb	/	*Trillium cernuum*
Mar	/	*T. chloropetalum*
Apr	transplant	*T. cuneatum*
May	flowering	*T. erectum*
Jun	flowering	*T. grandiflorum*
July	/	*T. g. flore-pleno*
Aug	/	*T. luteum*
Sept	sow	*T. rivale*
Oct	divide	*T. viride*
Nov	/	
Dec	/	

VERBASCUM
Mullein

MULLEINS ARE FAMED for their striking shape and bright flowers, but as seen here they can blend with the gentlest design.

MULLEINS HAVE few equals as accent plants, since they are tough and adaptable, capable of tolerating many climates and conditions.

FEATURES

EVERGREEN

HERBACEOUS

Not all mulleins are reliably perennial—some are best treated as biennials and replaced after two years. However, most are easy to raise. They are grown for their large rosettes of foliage, often silver or gray, from which emerges a tall, striking spike of flowers up to 6ft high. They make eye-catching accent plants in any sunny part of the yard. The various species and their cultivars have flowers in a range of colors, including white and gentler shades of yellow, pink, and purple. The common mullein, *V. thapsus*, also known as Aaron's rod, freely self-seeds. Mullein has a long folk history, first as a candle, then as a medical treatment.

VERBASCUM AT A GLANCE

A 360-species genus, famed for its dramatic, colored spires in summer. Heights 12in–6ft. Hardy to 5°F (zone 7).

Month	Activity	Recommended Varieties
Jan	/	
Feb	/	*Verbascum bombyciferum*
Mar	/	*V. chaixii* "Album"
Apr	sow ✍	*V. c.* "Cotswold Beauty"
May	transplant ✍	*V. c.* "Gainsborough"
Jun	flowering ✿	*V. dumulosum*
July	flowering ✿	"Golden Wings"
Aug	flowering ✿	"Helen Johnson"
Sept	sow ✍	"Letitia"
Oct	/	*V. phoeniceum*
Nov	/	
Dec	/	

CONDITIONS

Aspect Grows best in full sunlight all day.
Site Grows in any kind of well-drained soil, even poor and alkaline ones.

GROWING METHOD

Propagation Grows from seed sown as soon as it is ripe, or from root cuttings taken in late fall or winter. The seed forms on the spike after the flowers have fallen, and is ripe when it has changed color, becoming brown or black. Sow in pots in a cold frame in either the spring or fall. Plants of the larger mullein species need to be planted out approximately 39in apart.
Feeding Apply a complete plant food in early spring, when new growth commences.
Problems No specific problems are known.

FLOWERING

Season Mullein produces flowers right through the summer, but its amazing spire of a stem remains a big architectural feature long after the flowers have finished.
Cutting A nipped-off section of the flowering spire considerably adds to a formal, architectural display.

AFTER FLOWERING

Requirements Cut off the spent flower spike, unless you want seed to set.

VIOLA ODORATA

English violet

DESPITE the range of cultivars available, the violet species is still a big favorite.

VIOLETS PROVIDE great groundcover under deciduous trees or in other shaded, sheltered spots. They do, however, need high levels of sunlight to put on a good flowering display.

FEATURES

EVERGREEN

Violets have been in cultivation since ancient times, and were highly valued by the ancient Greeks. In Victorian period an enormous number of varieties was grown, including a wide range of the double Parma violets. The violet's sweet fragrance and elegant flowers make them big favorites with gardeners and florists alike. The plants have a creeping habit, spreading up to 12in, and are rarely more than 6–8in tall. There are cultivars with single or double flowers in purple, pink, white, or bicolors, but the deep purple is probably the best loved. There are other violet species to grow in the garden, from the summer-flowering *V. cornuta*, fine under hybrid tea roses, to the spring/summer *V. sororia* and its form, "Freckles."

VIOLA AT A GLANCE

V. odorata is a rhizomatous, semi-evergreen perennial with blue or white flowers. A good self-seeder. Hardy to 0°F (zone 6–7).

Jan	/	Recommended Varieties
Feb	/	
Mar	flowering	*Viola cornuta*
Apr	flowering	*V. c.* Alba Group
May	flowering	*V. c.* Lilacina Group
Jun	/	*V. c.* "Minor"
July	/	*V. odorata* "Alba"
Aug	/	*V. o.* "Rosea"
Sept	divide	*V. sororia* "Freckles"
Oct	/	*V. s.* "Priceana"
Nov	/	
Dec	/	

CONDITIONS

Aspect	It needs either shade, or light dappled sunshine.
Site	For the best results it needs well-drained, moisture-retentive soil, heavily enriched with organic matter.

GROWING METHOD

Propagation	Clumps can be lifted and divided, or runners can be dug up and replanted every couple of years, in the spring or fall. Set out at 8in spacings, with the plant crowns kept just above soil level. Violets self-seed, too. Keep young plants well watered during the first growing season.
Feeding	Apply complete plant food in spring after flowering ceases.
Problems	Slugs and snails can be a major nuisance, devouring tasty new growth. Pick off by hand, or treat chemically.

FLOWERING

Season	Violets flower from late winter into early spring.
Cutting	Scalding the stems of cut violets before arranging them will certainly increase their vase life.

AFTER FLOWERING

Requirements	No special treatment is needed, but excess runners can be removed during the growing season if they are invasive. This has the added benefit of channeling vigor back to the main crown.

Growing Roses

GROWING ROSES

A favorite of many, roses, with their single, semi-double or fully double flowers, and their bicolored, multicolored, striped or "hand-painted" blooms, are often richly scented and deck bushy stems.

FEATURES

Plant roses to color beds, borders, patio pots, hanging baskets and rocky yards. Position them so that they form a canopy over pergolas, obelisks, arches, trees, walls and fences.

There are seven distinct groups of roses:

Large-flowered roses (hybrid tea):
These form shapely double blooms on long stems and are good for cutting. They are usually grown as bushes to 3ft high. Choice varieties are soft peachy-pink "Scent-Sation," golden-yellow "Lions International," and white "Polar Star."

Cluster-Flowered (floribunda)
Sumptuous heads adorn stems from 2–3ft. Plant tangerine-orange "Razzle Dazzle," sparkling yellow "Charter 700," and scarlet "Invincible" to fringe a path or driveway.

English roses
They combine the scent and cupped- or rosette-shaped flower of an old-fashioned rose with the color range and repeat-flowering qualities of a cluster flowered variety. Forming plants from 3–6ft, newcomers include warm-pink "Anne Boleyn," yellow and spray-flowered "Blythe Spirit," and scarlet "Falstaff."

Miniature and patio
Small cluster-flowered roses that reach 15–24in—they flower all summer and spill from patio pots. Look out for peachy-apricot "Sweet Dream" and vermilion "Top Marks."

Shrub roses
Some varieties treat us to a succession of flowers, others to a billowing surge of bloom in mid-summer. Outstanding varieties included repeat-flowering, creamy white "Sally Holmes," and single pink and white "Ballerina."

Carpeters
Also known as ground-cover roses — they spread and suppress weeds — the famed County Series yields a spectacular display of flush upon flush of blossom. Riveting are single, scarlet and golden-centerd "Hampshire" and semi-double, bright yellow "Gwent."

LEFT: The shape of rose flowers vary considerably, from high and split-centered, globular, open cup-shaped and quartered to flat, rosette and pompon. Most are grafted onto rootstocks in order to charge them with vigor.

Climbers and ramblers
Thrusting skywards to cloak walls, fences, arches, pergolas and trees with a welter of blossom, climbers, such as honey-colored "Penny Lane," delight us with a succession of perfumed blooms.
Ramblers (including cream "Bobbie James") usually flower once in a midsummer.

CONDITIONS

Aspect	Roses need bright sunlight to excel. Some, such as "Canary Bird" and "Flower Carpet" also flower magnificently in light shade.
Site	Though a few kinds thrive in light sandy or stony soils, most benefit from humus-rich loam. Drainage must be good.

GROWING METHOD

Planting	Garden-center bushes can be planted throughout the year, provided the soil is "open." Mail-order plants are delivered bare rooted and dispatched from November to March.
Feeding	Sprinkle a high-potash and magnesium rich granular fertilizer over the root area in April and prick it into the surface. Follow with a 3in mulch. Repeat feeding in June.
Dead heading	Nip off faded blooms at the "knuckle" to channel energy into new flowering shoots.
Propagation	Take 9in cuttings of ramblers, climbers, miniatures and vigorous cluster-flowered varieties from the fully mature middle part of a pencil-thick side shoot in September. Remove all but two leaves at the top. Make a horizontal cut below the bottom bud and a sloping cut above the top bud. Nip off thorns. Insert cuttings 6in deep in a straight-backed trench lined with sharp sand. Firm soil around them. Roots will form within eight weeks.
Pruning	Prune with pruning shears from March to early April. *Large Flowered and Cluster Flowered bushes and standards:* Shorten main stems by half their height, cutting to a bud. Reduce side shoots to two buds. to two buds. *Miniature and shrub roses:* Shorten dead and broken stems to live wood. *Climbers:* Cut back flowered shoots to within 3in of the main stem. *Ramblers:* Prune in September. Remove flowered shoots at ground level and replace with current-year stems.
Problems	Control black spot, mildew and rust disease, together with greenfly and other sap-sucking insects, by spraying with a pesticide containing pirimicarb, bupirimate and triforine. Wearing gloves, remove the suckers, which are more thorny, with paler green leaves than varietal shoots. Twist them from the stock.

SCEPTERED ISLE

GRAHAM THOMAS

Raised by David Austin Roses, "Sceptered Isle" is an English Rose whose cupped and perfumed soft pink blooms grow freely above the foliage on stems to 3ft. Blooming continuously from early summer to mid-fall, it needs full sun to form a stocky bush. Dead-head regularly.
Create an arresting feature by inter-planting it with silver- and fern-leaved Artemisia "Powis Castle." Grown as a standard, it rewards you with a large head of blossom which makes a stunning focal point in a bed or border.

A glorious English Rose, "Graham Thomas," (named after the famed rosarian and writer), sports unusually rich golden yellow flowers. This color is missing from old-fashioned roses from which the variety was born. Forming a rounded bush to 4ft high and across, its branches elegantly arch. Interestingly, it can also be trained as a climber to 6–8ft. If you plant it to cover a wall, set the root system at least 15in from the brickwork to avoid moisture being sucked from the root area. Fan-train shoots as low as possible to trigger an abundance of blossom.

SCEPTERED ISLE AT A GLANCE

Must have full sunlight in order to thrive and bloom freely. Fully hardy to frost hardy.

JAN	rest		deadheading
FEB	rest	OCT	light pruning
MAR	planting, pruning	NOV	planting
APR	feeding	DEC	rest
MAY	mulching		
JUN	flowering		OTHER ENGLISH ROSES:
JULY	flowering, deadheading		"The Countryman"
AUG	flowering, deadheading		"Port Meirion"
SEPT	flowering,		"Barbara Austin"
			"Dr Herbert Gray"

GRAHAM THOMAS AT A GLANCE

Flowers best when grown in full sunlight. Fully hardy to frost hardy.

JAN	rest	SEPT	flowering, deadheading
FEB	rest	OCT	light pruning
MAR	planting, pruning	NOV	planting
APR	feeding	DEC	rest
MAY	mulching		
JUN	flowering, deadheading		
JULY	flowering, feeding		
AUG	flowering, deadheading		

FELICIA

A prized Hybrid Musk — the family bears large trusses of bloom in early summer and intermittently later—"Felicia" is a joy. Yielding aromatically fragrant silver-pink blooms amid dark green leaves on sturdy shoots to 5ft long, it's very healthy and seldom suffers from pests and diseases. If there's room, encourage it to flower bounteously by pegging down shoots so they radiate from the center of the bush. Alternatively, set "Felicia" to cover a trellis-clad sunny wall or fence.

FELICIA MOON AT A GLANCE

Performs best when grown in full sunlight. Fully hardy to frost hardy.

JAN	rest	SEPT	flowering, deadheading
FEB	rest		
MAR	planting, pruning	OCT	light pruning
		NOV	planting
APR	feeding	DEC	rest
MAY	mulching		
JUN	flowering, deadheading		OTHER HYBRID MUSKS:
JULY	flowering, feeding		"Pax"
			"Penelope"
AUG	flowering, deadheading		"Camelia"
			"Francesca"

FLOWER CARPET

Spreading enthusiastically to 4ft "Flower Carpet," which grows to 2ft high, treats us to an almost non-stop parade of huge trusses of semi-double bright pink flowers from June to November. Unlike many varieties, it romps in light shade and flowers as well there as in full sun. Its shining, glossy leaves appear to be fully resistant to black spot, mildew and rust.

It is even more alluring when trained as a standard. It's such a profuse performer that flower-bowed branches are liable to snap, so support them with strings tied to a cane fastened to the main stem. Its cousins, "White Flower Carpet" and "Sunshine," a new yellow form, are equally healthy and spirited.

FLOWER CARPET AT A GLANCE

Flowers freely in full sunlight or light shade. Fully hardy to frost hardy.

JAN	rest	SEPT	flowering, deadheading
FEB	rest		
MAR	planting, light pruning	OCT	light pruning
		NOV	planting
APR	feeding	DEC	rest
MAY	mulching		
JUN	flowering, deadheading		OTHER FLOWER CARPET FORMS:
JULY	flowering, feeding		"White Flower Carpet"
AUG	flowering, deadheading		"Sunshine"

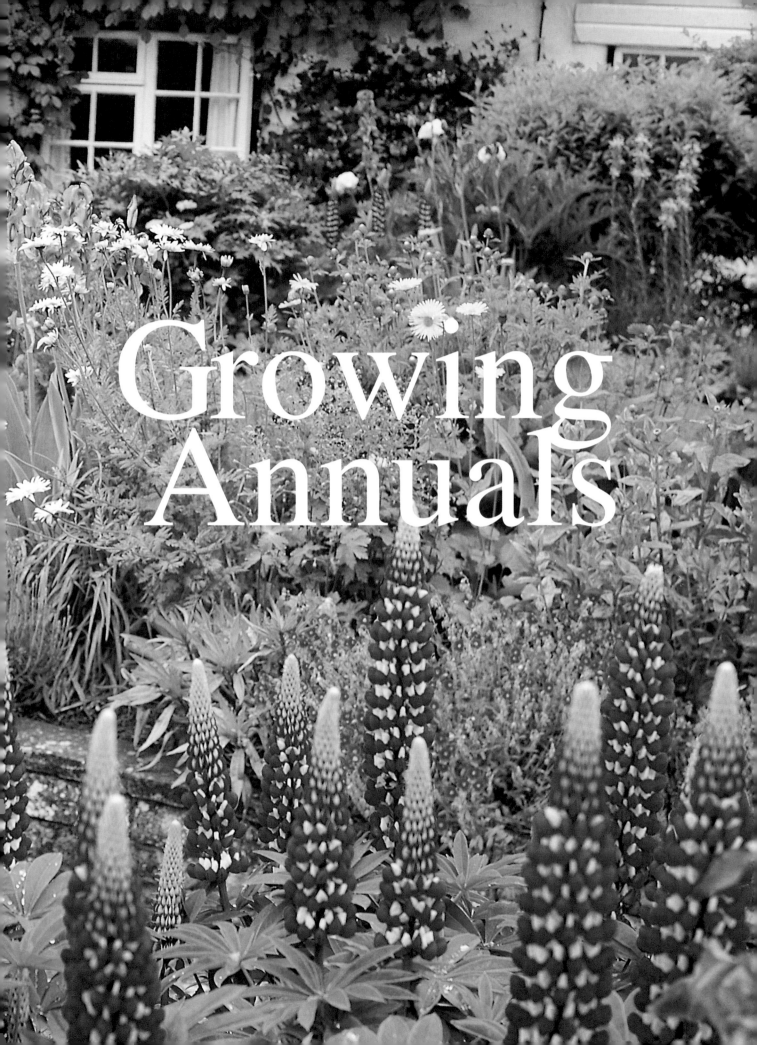

Growing Annuals

GROWING ANNUALS

Annuals are perhaps the easiest plants you will ever grow. Yet their ease of growth in no way detracts from their ability to provide color in the yard, in some cases virtually all year around. Whether your yard is large, small, or you work within the confines of just a small courtyard, annuals are the plants for you.

Miracles are happening in our gardens every day, but perhaps the greatest "miracle" in which we can take part is growing plants from seeds. Nothing is quite as amazing, or as humbling, as seeing a fully grown plant, that started life as a tiny seed, burst into flower and create a riot of color just a few months after it was sown. Some annuals need no more care than simply scattering the seeds over the surface of the ground and "raking" them in using your fingertips; others only demand that they are sown to the correct depth and then given space to grow as they develop. By their very nature, many annuals produce brilliant results, even in the poorest of soils. So get some seed catalogs, visit the local garden center, and start performing your own gardening miracles with the easiest plants on earth!

LEFT: Annuals like these purple violas and white-flowered lobularia (alyssum) can be sown directly into the soil where you want them to flower, in criss-crossing patterns as here.

ABOVE: Rudbeckia or coneflower is available in a wide range of sizes, and provides valuable color in late summer.

MANY ANNUALS THRIVE in some of the most inhospitable parts of the yard. These portulacas, or sun flowers, are perfectly at home growing on a rock garden with very little soil for their roots—and are just as suited to light, sandy soils and make good summer bedding plants.

WHAT ARE ANNUALS?

Virtually all annuals are raised by sowing seeds, either in the early spring under cover (in a heated greenhouse, conservatory, or on the kitchen windowsill), or directly into prepared soil outdoors. Some annuals are so adaptable that you only need sow them once—from then onward these so-called "self-seeders" regularly drop seeds into the soil which then "come up," or germinate, of their own accord. In many ways, these "hardy annuals" do a better job of sowing than we do, finding just the right spot for perfect growth, often in places we might never dream of sowing seeds, such as in cracks in the sidewalk and in the gravel of driveways.

At the other extreme are annuals that need to be started into growth long before the warmer days of spring arrive outdoors. The so-called "half-hardy" annuals are those plants that are damaged by frosts, but perform brilliantly during the summer months. For these you must be able to provide suitable growing conditions, especially at sowing time, when temperature is all-important for getting the seeds to come up. In some cases, such as with ricinus, the castor oil plant, it is grown as a half-hardy annual, even though it is by nature a shrub, which in its native habitat would, like the shrubs in our gardens, eventually form a large plant. Petunias are another example of a half-hardy annual that is really a perennial plant, and quite capable of surviving the winter if potted-up and kept protected in a cold but frost-free place over winter. It helps to understand what the terms mean when growing annuals, since you will come across them all the time in catalogs and on the back of seed packets.

HARDY ANNUALS

The easiest of all annuals to grow, sow hardy annuals exactly where you want the plants to flower. Many hardy annuals do not like root disturbance, so bear this in mind.

They are given their ideal planting distances by gradually "thinning out" as the young plants grow—all this means is carefully removing a few plants every few weeks in the spring, to give those left behind more room to develop. By early summer this thinning should be complete, and plants can be left to produce flowers. Hardy annuals are not affected by low temperatures, and many, like calendula, the pot marigold, are sown and germinate outdoors in September, for strong plants with earlier flowers the following spring. Most self-seeders belong to this group.

HALF-HARDY ANNUALS

As already mentioned, these plants are not able to withstand frost or freezing temperatures and must be raised from seed every season, often starting in late winter and very early spring. Many half-hardy annuals are actually perennials—plants that keep growing year after year, but which are better suited to our needs when grown as strong, young plants every season. Half-hardy annuals are only planted (or moved outdoors if grown in containers) when spring frosts are finished. The exact timing of this depends on the area you garden in, but this book gives sowing/planting times for average conditions. At the other end of the season, the first fall frosts will flatten most half-hardy annuals, and they can be removed for composting.

HARDY BIENNIALS

A biennial is simply a plant that straddles two growing seasons before it produces its show of flowers or foliage. A good example is cheiranthus, or wallflower, which is sown outdoors in early summer. The young leafy plants are grown on, then lifted and planted in October where you want the flowers to grow the following spring. Think of hardy biennials as annuals with a foot in two seasons—instead of producing their flowers or leaves all within what we think of as "summer," they get going in one season, spend the winter building up speed, then go all-out for flowering the next spring and summer. Biennials are especially useful for filling any gaps between late spring and early summer, and many, such as Sweet William, are easy and worthwhile plants for cut flowers.

BUYING SEEDS

Growing from seed is addictive—once you have sampled one seed catalog, you will certainly want more. You can buy annual seeds by sending for them via post or a home delivery service, by visiting garden centers or the gardening section of hardware stores, or, increasingly, by buying them with your other shopping at the supermarket.

The choice will always be greater in catalogs, but the more limited range that you may find in garden centers can actually be more helpful. The seed packets are guaranteed to be colorful, giving encouragement to the beginner. Some mail order seed companies pack their products in plain, information-only packets—this is no reflection on the quality of the seeds, but they do lack inspiration! Bright, colorful packets are a great help when planning a color-themed display with annuals, so do not be afraid to play around with a handful of packets until you get a good balance or contrast of colors just to your liking.

If you do buy seeds from garden centers and similar outlets, always avoid any packets that are faded, yellow, and have obviously been exposed to the sun, as the results are likely to be disappointing.

SEED PACKETS

Remember that seeds are alive, and need looking after to keep them in tiptop condition until sowing. Inside most seed packets you will find another, smaller packet made of foil. Seeds are sealed inside this inner packet in a kind of suspended animation that preserves them until the foil seal is broken. This is when the normal ageing process of the seed begins. Where this type of storage is not vital for success, seeds are simply found sealed within the outer paper packet. Foil packets should not be opened until the time of sowing, for best results. On most packets the inspiration on the front is backed by full growing instructions on the reverse. The better packets give sowing times, expected flowering period, and alternative sowing times in the fall. Keep seed packets after sowing—along with catalogs, they build up into an invaluable library that you can refer to as and when necessary. Always keep seeds in a cool, dry, frost-free place.

YOUNG PLANTS

Many half-hardy annuals included in this book can also be bought in the spring and summer as "young plants," and this is stated, where relevant, in the "features" paragraph for each of the 90 annuals covered. The term "young plant" covers anything from ready-germinated trays of small seedlings to a large plant, perhaps in flower, growing in a 3½in pot that you can find for sale in garden centers. Buying young plants simply means that a lot of the work in raising the plants from seed has been done for you by the grower—which has advantages and disadvantages. Young plants are a great help if you do not have facilities for raising seeds or enough space, and they are often delivered ready to go directly into containers. The range compared to the number of varieties available from seed is limited, although this is always improving. You pay for convenience: seed-raising is usually cheaper than buying in young plants.

WHAT CAN GO WRONG?

Yellow leaves
● Seedlings are being grown too cold in the early stages, or plants may have been planted outdoors too early.
● Plants may need feeding—water thoroughly with an all-purpose liquid or soluble plant food, wetting the leaves at the same time to act as a foliar feed.

Curled or distorted leaves
● Look for clusters of aphids attacking flower buds and the youngest leaves at the shoot tips. Rub them off with your fingers or use a spray containing permethrin.
● Drift from weedkillers can cause this problem, so take great care if you are treating a lawn for weeds using a hormone-based weedkiller. Avoid days when there is any breeze, and keep well away from bedding displays.

Holes and silvery trails on/in leaves
● Slugs and snails will eat most annual plants and are a particular threat in late spring and early summer, especially after rain, when the air is warm and moist. They leave silver slime trails on the soil and on plants where they have been feeding. Chemical slug pellets can be scattered sparingly among plants, or an unbroken ring of sharp grit 2in wide can be used as a physical deterrent on smaller areas. Another option is to check plants at night and pick off slugs and snails while they feed, dropping them into salty water.

White "powder" on leaves
● Powdery mildew affects many annuals, but usually not until late summer. This disease is not a serious threat and treatment is not needed.

Seedlings indoors suddenly collapse
● "Damping off" disease can attack annual seedlings, and is a particular problem if the compost becomes too wet. Always use clean pots for sowing and fresh compost. If it does attack, water lightly with a copper-based fungicide and resow to play safe.

Leaf edges chewed
● Various caterpillars will attack annuals and can soon strip leaves bare. Pick them off by hand or use a spray containing permethrin, wetting both sides of the leaves with a strong jet from a sprayer.

Plants cut off at ground level
● Cutworms can sever newly planted bedding plants outdoors, causing a sudden wilting and yellowing of plants under attack. Search around in the soil and the greenish-brown caterpillars are easily found and destroyed.

Creamy-white grubs eating roots
● Vine weevil grubs can cause severe damage to container plants. Never re-use old compost, and if you find grubs, treat all pots with biological control or a chemical based on phenols as a drench.

ORANGE MARIGOLDS, red and orange nasturtiums, asters, and brown-coned rudbeckia intermingle to form a color-coordinated annual border.

One of the wisest approaches is to decide carefully just what you feel you can achieve with your existing facilities. If your propagator (somewhere that plants are raised from seeds in the early stages) is just the kitchen windowsill, buying half-hardy annuals as young plants may be the best option. These small plug plants are delivered in mid-spring and can be potted up and grown on placed on the windowsill, or even next to the glass in an unheated conservatory. This eliminates the often tricky job of germinating the seeds to begin with, but means you can still grow the plants you really want. And of course, there is nothing to stop you sowing hardy annuals directly into the soil outdoors at the correct time.

If you are more restricted, say to just a small courtyard or balcony, young plants may be the whole solution—larger plants are delivered (or can be bought) in late spring and early summer, and these can be planted directly into containers and hanging baskets without growing on. Even then there is nothing to stop you scattering a few seeds of malcolmia, Virginian stock, in the top of your courtyard pots for some quick and scented flowers!

Most seed catalogs and specialist young plant suppliers carry extensive and informative sections on young plants, and they are well worth getting. Pay particular attention to "last order dates"—these are the cut-off points for placing your order for young plants and many start to appear as early as January and February.

ANNUALS IN CONTAINERS
A container in the broadest gardening sense is anything capable of holding compost and supporting plant growth—this could be anything from a 3½in-diameter plastic plant pot to a large terracotta trough or tub. Whatever you use, it must have some form of drainage, and this is usually through holes in the base. Molded plastic containers often have no preformed holes, so you must drill these before planting up. Waterlogged compost kills plant roots and the whole plant will soon die.

For most uses, a good "multipurpose" compost serves all of an annual plant's needs—from sowing to growing on, and finally being planted up. Most multipurpose composts are based on peat, with plant nutrients and other materials, such as water-storing granules and "wetters" (allowing dried-out compost to be re-wetted), already added. An increasing number of composts available are based on recycled materials, and the coir-based ones are improving constantly. A few specific plants prefer a soil-based compost, such as the "John Innes" types, both for sowing and growing—details of these are given under "growing method" sections of this book, where relevant. Always buy fresh bags of compost in spring, avoiding any that are over-heavy and wet, or split, with green algae growing in them, or faded and past their use-by date.

There is no reason why hardy annuals cannot be used for container growing—the fact that many are usually sown directly into the soil is not a problem. Simply sow them in small pots or multi-cell trays (plastic trays where the area is divided into individual units or "cells") at the same times as recommended for outdoor sowing, and plant into your containers during the spring. Where appropriate under each plant entry, varieties suited to containers are given—these are usually dwarf versions of taller varieties, and the range is increasing all the time. Half-hardy annuals offer great scope for container growing, for the reasons already discussed.

SOWING ANNUALS
Annual seeds are sown indoors or outdoors. Those sown outdoors are the easiest—they need no extra warmth or heat, just sow them in a patch of well-prepared ground and thin them out to give space as they grow. Sowing depth will depend on the size of the seed, but it is essential to work the soil using a rake (or your fingers in a small area) so it is fine and crumbly to at least 1in deep.

Seed can then be simply scattered over the soil and raked in, or sown in seed drills—these are simply grooves made in the soil with the head of a rake, the edge of a piece of wood, a length of bamboo cane, or even the side of your hand. Whichever you use, just press the edge into the soil to make a groove of the correct depth. Then sprinkle the seeds thinly along the drill, by rubbing them between your finger and thumb. Once finished, soil is moved back over the seeds with a rake or by lightly brushing the flat of your hand over the sown area. Take care not to disturb the sown seeds, and label with the variety and date sown. If you are sowing a large area with a variety of hardy annuals, or planning a mixture of hardy and half-hardy varieties, mark the sown patches with boundaries of light-colored sand—a traditional but still effective way of seeing just where you have been! By sowing in short drills within these marked areas it is easy to tell the annuals from the weeds, because they come up in rows.

Indoors, half-hardy annuals are sown ideally in a heated propagator with temperature control, and this piece of equipment is virtually essential when raising plants like pelargoniums (bedding geraniums) and begonias, both of which need high, constant temperatures. Otherwise, a brightly lit windowsill in a warm kitchen will work miracles—many half-hardy annuals are very undemanding once they have come up, and if not kept over-wet will grow steadily, even in quite cool conditions.

Narrow "windowsill propagators" are available that have a heated base and allow you to move pots on and off as seedlings appear—these are invaluable if you plan to do a lot of seed-raising. For all the plants in this book, a 3½in-diameter pot is sufficient for the germination of an average packet of half-hardy annual seeds. If you raise half-hardy annuals, remember that they will not be able to go out until after the last spring frosts. You can sow many plants later than the ideal times—this book describes the optimum sowing times unless otherwise stated—and plan for a later display of flowers, with the advantage of them being easier to raise and care for a little later in the spring season.

SOIL PREPARATION
All that annuals need to grow well is soil that has had plenty of "organic matter" added before sowing or planting, and this is best done by digging it in thoroughly the previous fall or in early spring. Suppliers of manure take some tracking down these days, so using home-made compost (or leaf mold) is a better option.

Whatever you use, it must be dark, well-rotted, and thoroughly broken down. Organic matter is vital for improving the soil's ability to hold onto moisture at the height of summer, and also supplies some plant foods. To take proper care of feeding, scatter pelleted poultry manure over the area 2–3 weeks before sowing/planting and rake it in. This should provide ample nutrients for the rest of the summer.

THINNING OUT
"Thinning out" or "thinning" means allowing sufficient room for plants to develop fully. This is most important with hardy annuals—as young seedlings grow larger, some are gradually removed to leave room for those left behind. Make sure you put your fingers on the soil when pulling plants out, or there is a risk the plants you leave behind will be uprooted. Water well after thinning, to settle seedlings back in. Thinning can start when plants are just 1in tall and is usually finished by early summer. Fall-sown annuals should be thinned in the spring, in case some plants are lost during the winter months.

GROWING ON
Once seedlings have been transplanted (moved) to either individual pots or cell trays, they are "grown on." This stage lasts until they are finally hardened off before planting outdoors or in pots. During growing on, make sure plants do not dry out, spread them out (if pot-grown) as they develop, and keep a look out for pests and diseases. Some plants (like thunbergia, Black-eyed Susan) benefit from being potted on when their roots fill the pot.

HARDENING OFF
Toughening plants raised indoors ready for outdoor conditions is vital if they are not to suffer a growth check when you put them out. Few of us have (or have the room for) the traditional "cold frame," which was the classic way of hardening off. These days we can make use of garden fleece, which is much easier, and just as effective. From mid-May onward, plants can be stood outside on warm days, in a sunny spot. For the first week, bring them in at night, then leave them out, but covered with fleece at night. Gradually, unless frost is forecast, the fleece can be left off even at night, but replaced during frosty spells. By early June, plants will be hardened off and ready to plant.

PLANTING
Whether you are planting in beds or containers, water the pots/trays the previous night to soak the roots. Planting can be done with a trowel—or even by hand in light soils. Using your hands is certainly the best way of planting up containers and hanging baskets. Never plant the base of plants deeper than they were growing originally. Firm well, and water. Keep labels with the plants for future reference, and note the planting date on the label, too.

WATERING
Lack of water causes many hardy annuals to flower and then quickly die. When the soil feels dry, enough water should be given so that it gets down to the roots—the soil should feel moist at least 6in down. Use a trowel and check that this is happening. Containers need much more care, since they rely solely on you for their water. Choosing a compost that contains water-storing crystals provides the best insurance. Do not overwater early on or roots may rot, but check them at least every other day and never allow them to dry out.

FEEDING
By mixing slow-release fertilizer granules with the compost before planting, you can take care of feeding for the whole season—you just need to water the plants. Outdoors, bedding displays will benefit from liquid feeding every 2–4 weeks. Many hardy annuals need no extra feeding and actually thrive on poor, hungry soils.

USING ANNUALS IN YOUR GARDEN

With annuals, the sky really is the limit. You can choose to grow just hardy or half-hardy annuals, a mixture of both, or you can be more adventurous and put them to work for you in a wide range of yard situations. Or, of course, you could just leave them to do their own thing!

Once you have annuals in your yard, you will never want to be without them. Self-seeding annuals, like limnanthes and nigella, will want to do their own thing and grow where they fall, while others such as lavatera and ricinus are put to much better use by carefully planning where they will grow. You can find a spot for annuals in every yard, and sometimes they can even help you out of a tight corner! What better plants could you ask for?

ABOVE: The delicately veined flower of agrostemma, the corncockle, an easily grown hardy annual that is sown outdoors in spring where you want it to flower.

AS EDGING PLANTS these Begonia semperflorens *are a good choice. Being of even height, they are good for growing in line.*

BEDDING SCHEMES

We see annuals used in bedding schemes almost every day of our lives, on traffic islands, in public parks, and in each other's yards. The "scheme" part of the phrase comes from the fact that many of these impressive colorful displays are pre-planned, and in many ways made-to-measure. If that is the effect you are after, you must do your homework. The structure of a basic bedding scheme is quite simple—you have tall plants in the center of the bed, and the shortest plants around the edge. In between are plants in a range of sizes and with varying growth habits, which fill the space between the tallest and the shortest. Bedding schemes can be as simple, or as elaborate, as you choose. The key points to remember are to decide which plants are going where, how many you need, and of course, whether they are suited to being grown together.

HARDY ANNUAL SCHEMES

Creating a show using just hardy annuals is both very easy and tremendous fun. The sheer range of hardy annual varieties is enormous and it is easy to be spoiled for choice. You can go out and sow an entire bed with hardy annuals at one go, then sit back and wait for the seedlings to come up. Then all you need to do is keep down annual weeds (all perennial weeds should be removed before sowing), thin out every few weeks until early summer, push in twiggy supports for taller, straggly plants, and enjoy the show.

THIS SUMMER BEDDING SCHEME features zinnias in the center of the bed (with variegated tradescantia creeping through) then scarlet salvias, dropping down to the pink fluffy heads of ageratum, the floss flower, below.

The best effect is from bold groups of color, so sow in patches at least 2ft across. Sow roughly circular areas as a foolproof guide, although interweaving shapes can create some dramatic effects, with different plants merging as they grow into each other. Take a tip from the traditions of the past and mark out the sown areas with sand, just so you know what is where, and label each patch, or mark the varieties clearly on a sketch plan, if you have one. Using just hardy annuals means there is no need for heating early in the season, and no crisis when growing space runs short. Many hardy annuals can also be sown in the fall, usually September, to grow through the winter and then give an early performance the following spring.

CARE-FREE HARDY ANNUALS
What could be better than a plant you only buy once, but will then always have many of? It sounds too good to be true, but that is just what you get with a great many hardy annuals—the self-seeders that arrive in a packet and then spread to all their favorite spots. We have to thank the origins of many of these plants for their valuable qualities. Agrostemma (corncockle), for example, was once a common weed of cornfields, and many other care-free annuals like it thrive on the poorest and hungriest of soils. These plants will tell you where they prefer growing by seeding themselves there, and they will need no more attention, other than being pulled out when they get too

dominant or invasive in areas set aside for more carefully planned activities. Calendula, centaurea, eschscholzia, papaver, and tropaeolum are all good examples of care-free annuals.

BORDER FILLERS
With the sudden loss of a favorite plant, your dreams of a "perfect" border can soon evaporate, and this is where annuals can get you out of a tight spot. Any spare patch of ground can be sown, or planted, with annuals, which will grow quickly to fill any gaps. You might even scatter seeds among perennial plants and let them get on with things. Lunaria (honesty), is quite at home growing among spring-flowering perennial euphorbias; the purple lunaria flowers make a good contrast with the pale yellow-green euphorbias. For a touch of the tropical, ricinus, the castor oil plant, is unbeatable, with its large, exotic-looking leaves in a range of colors. Sunflowers (helianthus) are always a good choice for some instant color when it's needed, and the newer dwarf varieties like "Pacino" are easy to grow in pots for planting out whenever their bright flowers are needed to perk up flagging borders.

AGERATUM

Floss flower

AGERATUM FLOWERS are carried on neat-growing plants and are good for "cooling down" other plants with bright flowers.

MODERN VARIETIES of ageratum for bedding produce masses of flowers which gradually rise above the leaves as they open.

FEATURES

Ageratum, a half-hardy annual, has fluffy long-lived flowers in blue, pink, white and bicolors such as blue-white. Use dwarf varieties for edging, as they grow up to 6in. Tall varieties are used in borders and for cutting, growing to 2½ft. Use for bedding/containers. Available as young plants.

CONDITIONS

Aspect Needs full sun and a sheltered position.

AGERATUM AT A GLANCE

A half-hardy annual grown for its fluffy flowers, ideal for edging, bedding, containers, and cutting. Frost hardy to 32°F (zone 10).

JAN	/	**RECOMMENDED VARIETIES**
FEB	sow	*Ageratum houstonianum:*
MAR	sow	**For bedding**
APR	grow on	"Adriatic"
MAY	plant	"Bavaria"
JUN	flowering	"Blue Champion"
JULY	flowering	"Blue Mink"
AUG	flowering	"Pink Powderpuffs"
SEPT	flowering	"White Blue"
OCT	/	"Capri"
NOV	/	"White Hawaii"
DEC	/	**For cutting**
		"Blue Horizon"

Site Prefers well-drained soil enriched with rotted manure or compost well ahead of planting. In containers use multipurpose compost and ensure that there is good drainage.

GROWING METHOD

Sowing Sow seeds in 3½in pots in February/March and just cover, and keep at 70°F. Seedlings appear after a week and can be moved to cell trays of multipurpose compost when two leaves are developed. Harden off and plant outside after frosts, spacing tall varieties 12–16in apart, dwarf varieties 4–6in apart.

Feeding Apply liquid feed fortnightly to maintain strong growth, or mix slow-release fertilizer with compost before planting up.

Problems Ageratum can suffer from root rot so grow in well-drained containers on heavy clay soils, and avoid getting the compost too wet.

FLOWERING

Season Flowers appear all summer until the first frosts. Regular dead-heading, especially after heavy rain, will prolong flowering and often encourage a second "flush" of color.

Cutting Tall varieties are suitable for cutting.

AFTER FLOWERING

General Remove plants when past their best, usually after the first sharp frosts of fall.

AGROSTEMMA

Corncockle

SOFT PINK "Milas" is one of the best known of the corncockle varieties. Pink and white varieties are also available.

GROW AGROSTEMMA in bold clumps in borders where the tall lanky, swaying plants help to give each other support.

FEATURES

A very easily grown hardy annual for use in cottage gardens and borders where it self-seeds year after year. Plants are tall, growing 2–3ft tall, and carry pink, purple, or white trumpet-like blooms. The seeds are poisonous. Commonly known as corncockle.

CONDITIONS

Aspect   Grow in full sun.

AGROSTEMMA AT A GLANCE

A tall hardy annual grown for its pink, purple, or white flowers which are ideal for cottage borders. Frost hardy to 5°F (zone 7).

Jan	/	Recommended Varieties
Feb	/	*Agrostemma githago:*
Mar	sow 🌱	"Milas"
Apr	thin out 🌱	"Ocean Pearl"
May	flowering 🌸	"Purple Queen"
Jun	flowering 🌸	"Rose of Heaven"
July	flowering 🌸	
Aug	flowering 🌸	
Sept	flowering 🌸	
Oct	sow 🌱	
Nov	/	
Dec	/	

Site

Succeeds on well-drained and even light, sandy soils that are quite "hungry" (it used to grow as a weed in cornfields). Excessive feeding may actually reduce the number of flowers.

GROWING METHOD

Sowing   Sow outdoors from March onward when the soil is warming up, in patches or drills ½in deep where you want the plants to flower. Thin seedlings so they are eventually 6–12in apart. Do not transplant. Can also be sown in pots in the fall, overwintered in a sheltered spot then potted up in spring for flowers in early summer.

Feeding   Extra feeding is unnecessary, but water occasionally but thoroughly in dry spells.

Problems   Agrostemma is a floppy plant and twiggy supports can be useful.

FLOWERING

Season   Summer onward, but earlier flowers are produced by sowing in the fall.

Cutting   Short-lived as a cut flower, and rather floppy.

AFTER FLOWERING

General   Dead-heading throughout summer will keep flowers coming but always leave a few to ripen and set seeds. Plants will self-sow and germinate the following spring. Alternatively, collect seedheads in paper bags and store.

ALCEA
Hollyhock

FLOWERS OF ALCEA *come in a wide range of colors and are carried along the entire length of the tall leafy stems.*

THE TALL STEMS *of hollyhocks tend to lean over as they mature, so support them at the base with short lengths of bamboo cane.*

FEATURES

Alcea is also known as althaea, and is the familiar "hollyhock" found in cottage borders. Flowers are single or double in a range of colors, and carried on stems which can be up to 8ft tall depending on variety. Tall varieties are best at the back of borders. Alcea is grown as an annual sown in spring, or as a biennial sown in summer. Spring-sown plants suffer less with rust disease. Fully hardy.

CONDITIONS

Aspect   Needs full sun.
Site   Plants can often be found growing in cracks between paving slabs and in walls but the tallest spikes are produced by adding generous amounts of rotted manure or compost to the soil before planting. Soil must have good drainage. In windy spots stake tall varieties.

GROWING METHOD

Sowing   To grow as an annual sow seed in 3½in pots of multipurpose compost in February. Just cover the seeds and keep at 68°F. Seedlings appear in about two weeks and can be transplanted to individual 3½in pots of compost. Grow on and plant in May after hardening off. Seeds can also be sown outdoors in April. To grow as biennials, sow seed in midsummer but germinate outdoors in a shaded spot. Plant in September.

Feeding   A monthly liquid feed encourages growth.
Problems   Rust disease spoils the look of and weakens growth and is worse in wet summers. Control is difficult but for a few plants pick off leaves and try a spray containing mancozeb.

FLOWERING

Season   Early spring-sown plants grow rapidly and flower from early summer. Those planted in fall will overwinter in the ground and flower in early summer the following season.
Cutting   Striking as cut flowers—take them when there are plenty of flowerbuds still to open.

AFTER FLOWERING

General   Leave a few spikes to set self-sown seeds, but remove dead plants to reduce rust problems.

ALCEA AT A GLANCE

A hardy biennial grown as an annual or biennial for its tall spikes of flowers suited to cottage gardens. Frost hardy to 5°F (zone 7).

Jan	/	Recommended Varieties
Feb	sow	*Alcea rosea:*
Mar	grow on	**Single flowered**
Apr	sow outdoors	"Nigra"
May	plant	"Single Mixed"
Jun	flowers/sow	**Double flowered**
July	flowering	"Chater's Double Mixed"
Aug	flowering	"Majorette Mixed"
Sept	flowers/plant	"Peaches 'n' Dreams"
Oct	/	"Powder Puffs Mixed"
Nov	/	"Summer Carnival
Dec	/	Mixed"

AMARANTHUS

Love-lies-bleeding

SOME AMARANTHUS produce masses of copper-crimson leaves in summer and red flower spikes. They make good pot plants.

"JOSEPH'S COAT," 2ft tall, has striking gold-and-crimson upper leaves and green-yellow lower leaves marked with brown.

FEATURES

Amaranthus is grown for its colorful, exotic-looking foliage and its spiky, erect or drooping tassels of blood-red, green, golden-brown, purple, or multi-colored flowers up to 18in long. Leaves can be red, bronze, yellow, brown, or green, depending on the variety grown. Size ranges from 15in to 4ft tall. Use plants as potted plants, in courtyard containers, and as dramatic centerpieces in summer bedding displays. Superb when used cut for fresh or dried flower arrangements indoors.

CONDITIONS

Aspect Full sun and shelter is essential for success.
Site Soil should be well-drained, with plenty of

rotted compost or manure added. Varieties of *Amaranthus caudatus* will also succeed on thin, dry soils. Use multipurpose compost in containers and pots. In northern areas grow in 8–10in diameter pots in the greenhouse or conservatory. Tall-growing varieties may need staking.

GROWING METHOD

Sowing Sow seeds in March at 70°F in 3½in-diameter pots of multipurpose compost, just covering the seed. Seeds germinate in 7–14 days or sooner, and should be transplanted into cell trays or 3½in-diameter pots of multipurpose compost. Plant outside after the last frosts in late May/early June, 1–3ft apart, and water.

Feeding Feed weekly from early summer onward with general-purpose liquid feed. In containers, mix slow-release fertilizer with compost before planting, and also feed every two weeks with half-strength liquid feed.

Problems Aphids can feed on the colorful leaves and build up into large colonies, unless caught early. Use a spray containing permethrin.

FLOWERING

Season Foliage is colorful from early summer onward, and is joined by flowerheads and then colorful seedheads later on.

Cutting Varieties grown for their flowers can be cut and used fresh, while seedheads can be left to develop, then cut and dried for indoor use.

AFTER FLOWERING

General Remove plants when past their best.

AMARANTHUS AT A GLANCE

A half-hardy annual grown for its leaves and flowers for bedding, containers, and for drying. Frost hardy to 32°F (zone 10).

Month	Activity	Recommended Varieties
Jan	/	
Feb	/	*Amaranthus caudatus:*
Mar	sow 🖐	"Green Thumb"
Apr	transplant 🖐	"Viridis"
May	transplant 🖐	*Amaranthus cruentus:*
Jun	flowering	"Golden Giant"
July	flowering	"Split Personality"
Aug	flowering	"Ruby Slippers"
Sept	flowering	*Amaranthus hybridus:*
Oct	flowering	"Intense Purple"
Nov	/	*Amaranthus tricolor:*
Dec	/	"Aurora Yellow"
		"Joseph's Coat"

ANTIRRHINUM
Snapdragon

OLDER VARIETIES of snapdragon like this have flowers that "snap" when squeezed. This trick is not found in newer types.

DWARF VARIETIES reaching just 6in are colorful for bed edges and have bushy growth without the need for pinching out.

FEATURES

Antirrhinums fall into three groups: tall varieties up to 4ft for cutting; intermediates for bedding, 18in; dwarf varieties for edging/containers, 12in. Color range is wide, and includes bicolors and doubles. Flowers of older varieties open when squeezed at the sides, hence the name "snapdragon." Grow as a half-hardy annual. Available as young plants.

CONDITIONS

Aspect   Must be in full sunlight all day.
Site   Soil must be very well-drained but have plenty

ANTIRRHINUM AT A GLANCE

A half-hardy annual grown for tubular flowers, used for containers, bedding displays, and cutting. Frost hardy to 32°F (zone 10).

Jan	/	Recommended Varieties
Feb	sow	
Mar	sow	*Antirrhinum majus:*
Apr	grow on	**For containers**
May	plant	"Lipstick Silver"
Jun	flowering	"Magic Carpet Mixed"
July	flowering	"Tom Thumb Mixed"
Aug	flowering	**For bedding**
Sept	flowering	"Brighton Rock Mixed"
Oct	/	"Corona Mixed"
Nov	/	"Sonnet Mixed"
Dec	/	**For cutting**
		"Liberty Mixed"

of rotted compost or manure dug in before planting. In containers, use multipurpose compost and ensure good, free drainage.

GROWING METHOD

Sowing   Sow in February/March and barely cover the very fine seed. Use 3½in pots of multipurpose compost and keep in light at 64°F. Seedlings appear after a week and can be transplanted to cell trays when two young leaves have developed. Plant outside after hardening off, following the last frosts, 6–18in apart, depending upon the variety. Those grown for bedding purposes should have the growing tip pinched out when 6in tall to encourage bushy growth.

Feeding   Liquid-feed plants in beds with a handheld feeder fortnightly. Mix slow-release fertilizer with container compost before planting up.

Problems   Seedlings are prone to "damping off," so water the pots with a copper-based fungicide. Plants suffer with rust disease. Grow a resistant variety such as "Monarch Mixed" or use a spray containing penconazole at regular intervals.

FLOWERING

Season   Flowers appear all summer and should be removed as they fade to keep buds coming.

Cutting   Tall varieties are excellent as cut spikes.

AFTER FLOWERING

General   Pull plants up when they are over.

ARCTOTIS
African daisy

AFRICAN DAISIES should be pinched out when they are 5in tall to encourage branching and masses of summer flowers.

WHEN PLANTED in groups of 3–6 plants, arctotis will form spreading clumps in sunny, south-facing borders and on banks.

FEATURES

African daisy is a perennial grown as a half-hardy annual for its flowers in shades of pink, red, yellow, gold, white, and even blue, often with darker center. Plants reach 18in in height and have attractive silvery leaves. Use in bedding or as a container plant. Flowers are good for cutting.

CONDITIONS

Aspect   Must have full sun all day long for the flowers to stay open and give the best display, so

Site   choose a south-facing border, patio or bank. Soil must be well-drained but moisture-retentive, so work in rotted compost before planting. In containers use multipurpose compost and ensure drainage by adding a 2in layer of gravel or polystyrene chunks.

GROWING METHOD

Sowing   Sow in February/March in small pots of multipurpose compost, just covering the seed, and keep at 64°F. Seedlings appear in 2–3 weeks and are transplanted individually into 3½in pots. Grow on, harden off at the end of May before planting after frosts, spacing plants 12–18in apart.

Feeding   Extra feeding is rarely necessary but container-grown plants benefit from liquid feed every two weeks. Avoid getting the compost too wet, especially in cooler, wet spells.

Problems   Grows poorly on heavy, badly drained soils. Plants in containers must receive full sun.

FLOWERING

Season   Flowers from early summer onwards.
Cutting   A useful but short-lived cut flower.

AFTER FLOWERING

General   Pot up before frosts and keep dry and frost-free over winter. Take and root cuttings in spring.

ARCTOTIS AT A GLANCE

A half-hardy annual grown for its flowers, used in bedding, containers and as a cut flower. Frost hardy to 32°F (zone 10).

Month	Activity	Recommended Varieties
Jan	/	
Feb	sow	*Arctotis hybrida:*
Mar	sow	"Harlequin"
Apr	transplant	"Special Hybrids Mixed"
May	transplant	"Treasure Chest"
Jun	flowering	"T&M Hybrids"
July	flowering	
Aug	flowering	*Arctotis hirsuta*
Sept	flowering	
Oct	/	*Arctotis venusta*
Nov	/	
Dec	/	

BEGONIA
Begonia

FOR BEDDING DISPLAYS *in partial shade few plants can equal the mixed varieties of* Begonia semperflorens, *seen here.*

IN CONTAINERS *begonias give a show from early summer, and you can choose dark-leaved types for specific color schemes.*

FEATURES

Excellent for bedding and containers, begonias have fleshy green or bronze leaves and flowers in many colors, and are grown as half-hardy annuals. "Fibrous" rooted varieties of *Begonia semperflorens* grow up to 8in, have many small flowers and do well in shaded spots. "Tuberous" rooted types reach 10in tall with fewer but larger flowers up to 4in across. Trailing varieties are also available for hanging baskets, reaching 1–2ft. Flowers are in mixed or single colors. A wide range of all types are available as young plants.

CONDITIONS

Aspect   Will succeed best in partial shade with at least

BEGONIA AT A GLANCE	
A half-hardy annual grown for its flowers and green/bronze foliage, useful for bedding/containers. Frost hardy to 32°F (zone 10).	
Jan sow	Recommended Varieties
Feb sow	*Begonia semperflorens:*
Mar transplant	"Ambassador Mixed"
Apr grow on	"Cocktail Mixed"
May harden off	"Pink Sundae"
Jun flowering	**Tuberous varieties**
July flowering	"Non-Stop Mixed"
Aug flowering	"Non-Stop Appleblossom"
Sept flowering	"Pin-Up"
Oct /	**Trailing varieties**
Nov /	"Illumination Mixed"
Dec /	"Show Angels Mixed"

Site   some protection from direct hot sun.
Soil should be very well prepared with plenty of rotted manure or compost mixed in. Begonias produce masses of fine feeding roots. Plants do not like very heavy clay soils that stay wet for long periods, so grow in containers if necessary, using multipurpose compost when potting up in spring.

GROWING METHOD

Sowing   Sow January/February. Seed is as fine as dust, so mix with a little dry silver sand and sow on the surface of 3½in pots of seed compost based on peat or coir. Stand the pot in tepid water until the compost looks moist. Keep at 70°F in a heated propagator in a light spot, and carefully transplant seedlings to cell trays when they have produced several tiny leaves. Seed raising is a challenge so consider growing from young plants. Plant outdoors after the last frosts in early June, 6–8in apart depending on variety.

Feeding   Water regularly in dry spells and liquid feed bedding displays every 2–3 weeks, or mix slow-release fertilizer with compost first.

Problems   Overwatering causes root rot and death. Remove faded flowers, especially in wet spells.

FLOWERING

Season   Flowers from early summer until frost.
Cutting   Not suitable as a cut flower.

AFTER FLOWERING

General   Varieties that form round tubers can be potted up in the fall, dried off and then grown again the following spring.

BELLIS
Daisy

VARIETIES OF BELLIS differ greatly. Some have small flowers with yellow centers, or the whole flower is a mass of fine petals.

AFTER THE SPRING SHOW is over bellis can be replanted on rock gardens where it will grow as a perennial in spreading clumps.

FEATURES

All varieties of bellis are related to garden daisies, and are perennials grown as hardy biennials. Use in spring bedding and containers, with bulbs like tulips. Plants are spreading, 4–8in high, with white, pink, red, or bicolored double or "eyed" flowers. Petals can be tubular, or fine and needle-like. Available as young plants.

CONDITIONS

Aspect   Needs a sunny, warm spot to encourage early

BELLIS AT A GLANCE

A perennial grown as a biennial for spring bedding displays and used with bulbs in yard containers. Frost hardy to 5°F (zone 7).

		Recommended Varieties
Jan	/	
Feb	flowering	*Bellis perennis:*
Mar	flowering	**Small flowers**
Apr	flowering	"Carpet Mixed"
May	flowers/sow	"Medici Mixed"
Jun	sow	"Pomponette Mixed"
July	grow on	"Pomponette Pink"
Aug	grow on	"Buttons"
Sept	grow on	**Large flowers**
Oct	plant	"Blush"
Nov	/	"Giant Flowered Mixed"
Dec	/	"Goliath Mixed"
		"Habanera Mixed"

Site   flowers when grown for spring displays. Most soils are suitable, but adding well-rotted manure or compost before planting increases plant vigor and flower size. In containers, use multipurpose compost and make sure the container is very free-draining.

GROWING METHOD

Sowing   Sow seed outdoors in May/June in fine soil in drills ½in deep. Keep well-watered and when plants are large enough, space small clumps out in rows, 4–6in apart. Alternatively, pot up into 3½in pots. Grow on during the summer, then water, lift carefully, and plant out in beds or containers in the fall, spacing 6–8in apart.

Feeding   Liquid feed can be given every 2–3 weeks in the spring when growth starts, but avoid feeding in winter, and take special care not to overwater containers or plants will rot off.

Problems   Bellis is trouble-free.

FLOWERING

Season   Flowers appear from early spring into the summer. Removal of faded flowers helps prolong flowering and reduces self-seeding.

Cutting   Can be used in small spring posies.

AFTER FLOWERING

General   Plants are removed to make way for summer bedding and can either be discarded or replanted and left to grow as perennials.

BRACHYSCOME
Swan river daisy

SWAN RIVER DAISIES *produce mounds of small, daisy-like flowers in profusion throughout the summer months.*

FOR MIXED SHADES *and "eyes" of different colors, choose an up-to-date variety of* Brachyscome iberidifolia *such as "Bravo Mixed."*

FEATURES

Brachyscome is covered in mounds of daisy flowers, and is good in beds and in hanging baskets and courtyard containers. It makes an effective edging plant, where it can develop unhindered without being crowded out by more vigorous plants. Leaves are light green and feathery, with a delicate appearance. Plants grow 9in tall with a similar spread. Choose single colors or mixtures. Brachyscome can be planted in May before the last frosts, and will tolerate short dry spells. A half-hardy annual, also seen as "brachycome."

CONDITIONS

Aspect   Choose a south-facing position in full sunlight.

BRACHYSCOME AT A GLANCE

A half-hardy annual grown for its daisy-like flowers, useful for bedding, baskets, and containers. Frost hardy to 32°F (zone 10)

Jan	/
Feb	/
Mar	sow
Apr	sow/transplant
May	plant outdoors
Jun	flowering
July	flowering
Aug	flowering
Sept	flowering
Oct	/
Nov	/
Dec	/

Recommended Varieties

Brachyscome iberidifolia:
  "Blue Star"
  "Bravo Mixed"
  "Mixed"
  "Purple Splendor"
  "White Splendor"

Site   Choose a warm, sheltered spot away from wind. Brachyscome likes rich, well-drained soil, with plenty of rotted compost or manure added. Use multipurpose potting compost in containers.

GROWING METHOD

Sowing   Sow in March and April in 3½in diameter pots, just covering the seeds, and germinate at 64°F. Seedlings emerge within three weeks. Transplant into cell trays of multipurpose compost, and plant out in beds, 9–12in apart.

Feeding   Liquid-feed each week outdoors. Add slow-release fertilizer granules to container compost, and also liquid-feed every two weeks in the summer. Avoid overwatering, especially in dull, wet spells, or plants may rot off.

Problems   Support floppy plants with small twigs. Avoid planting among large, vigorous container plants that will swamp low growers and cast them in shade at the height of summer. Control slugs with pellets or set slug traps in bedding displays.

FLOWERING

Season   Flowers appear all summer and are faintly scented—this is best appreciated by growing them at nose height in hanging baskets, flower bags, and windowboxes.

Cutting   Not suitable.

AFTER FLOWERING

General   Remove when flowers are over and add to the compost heap or bin.

BRASSICA
Ornamental cabbage and kale

ORNAMENTAL KALES help pack a punch in the yard during the fall, with their bright leaves that deepen in color when the temperature falls below 50°F. Plants grown in containers should be kept in a sheltered spot during spells of severe winter weather.

FEATURES

Ornamental cabbages and kales are grown for colorful fall and winter foliage, growing 12–18in tall and wide. Use for bedding or large pots. Leaf color is pink, rose, or white, and improves with temperatures below 50°F. Damage is caused by severe frost. Available as young plants.

CONDITIONS

Aspect   Needs full sunlight to develop good color.

BRASSICA AT A GLANCE

A hardy annual grown for its brightly colored leaves that last from the fall until spring. Frost hardy to 5°F (zone 7).

		Recommended Varieties
Jan	leaves	
Feb	leaves	**Cabbages**
Mar	leaves	"Delight Mixed"
Apr	leaves	"Northern Lights"
May	leaves	"Ornamental Mixed"
Jun	sow	"Tokyo Mixed"
July	sow	
Aug	grow-on	**Kales**
Sept	plant	"Nagoya Mixed"
Oct	leaves	"Red & White Peacock"
Nov	leaves	"Red Chidori"
Dec	leaves	

Site   Enrich soil with rotted compost or manure ahead of planting. Adding lime will improve results in acid soils. Avoid places exposed to driving winter winds. Plant up containers using multipurpose compost, making sure pots and tubs are free-draining.

GROWING METHOD

Sowing   Seed is sown in June/July in 3½in pots of multipurpose compost and kept out of the sun. Large seedlings appear after a week and are transplanted to individual 3½in pots. Grow these on outdoors, watering frequently, and then plant out in beds or in containers in the early fall where the display is required.

Feeding   Give a high-potash liquid feed fortnightly throughout the summer months. Tomato food is suitable and encourages leaf color.

Problems   Cabbage caterpillars will also attack ornamental varieties and kales. Pick off by hand or use a spray containing permethrin.

FLOWERING

Season   Plants are at their best in the fall and early winter. Any surviving the winter will produce tall clusters of yellow flowers during spring.

Cutting   Whole heads makes a striking, unusual element in winter flower arrangements.

AFTER FLOWERING

General   Remove in the spring or if killed by frosts.

BROWALLIA
Bush violet

BROWALLIA FLOWERS have an almost crystalline texture when lit by the sun. They appear in masses on rounded plants, and at the height of summer can almost completely hide the leaves. Seen here are the varieties "Blue Troll" and "White Troll."

FEATURES

Browallia takes its common name from its violet-blue flowers, which have a pale "eye." White flowered varieties and mixtures are available. Plants grow up to 12in and are suitable for containers and baskets, and in warmer areas, bedding. Varieties of *Browallia speciosa* are grown as half-hardy annuals and can also be used as indoor potted plants.

CONDITIONS

Aspect   Needs a warm, sheltered spot in sunlight.

BROWALLIA AT A GLANCE

A half-hardy annual grown for its blue, white, or pink flowers, useful for bedding/container planting. Frost hardy to 32°F (zone 10).

Jan	/	Recommended Varieties
Feb	sow	*Browallia speciosa:*
Mar	sow	**Blue flowers**
Apr	grow on	"Blue Troll"
May	plant	"Blue Bells"
Jun	flowering	"Starlight Blue"
July	flowering	
Aug	flowering	**White flowers**
Sept	flowering	"White Troll"
Oct	/	
Nov	/	**Blue/pink/white flowers**
Dec	/	"Jingle Bells"

Site   Browallia does not tolerate poor drainage, and on heavy soils should only be grown as a container plant, using multipurpose compost. Otherwise, mix in well-rotted compost or manure several weeks before planting out.

GROWING METHOD

Sowing   For summer bedding, sow the seed on the surface of 3½in pots of multipurpose compost in February/March. Keep at 64°F and do not let the surface dry out. Seedlings appear in 2–3 weeks and should be transplanted to individual cell trays or 3in pots. Harden off at the end of May and plant in early June. For flowering potted plants, seed can be sown in the same way until June.

Feeding   Give plants a liquid feed fortnightly or, in containers and windowboxes, mix slow-release fertilizer with the compost first.

Problems   Aphids sometimes attack the soft leaves, so use a spray containing permethrin if they appear.

FLOWERING

Season   Flowers appear from early summer onward and continue until the first frosts. Take off faded flowers regularly to encourage buds.

Cutting   Not suitable as a cut flower.

AFTER FLOWERING

General   Plants die when frosts arrive. Potted plants indoors can be kept alive indefinitely.

CALCEOLARIA
Slipper flower

THE HOT COLORS OF THE "SUNSET" strain of calceolaria excel outdoors and combine well with marigolds.

FEATURES

Only a few varieties of calceolaria are suitable for outdoors; these are different to the indoor pot type. By nature shrubs, they are grown from seed each year as hardy annuals and are useful for bedding and containers. None grow more than 16in tall and wide.

CONDITIONS

Aspect   Needs full sun or part shade.

CALCEOLARIA AT A GLANCE

A half-hardy annual, calceolaria is used for bedding and containers, with bright flowers. Frost hardy to 32°F (zone 10).

Jan	sow	
Feb	sow	
Mar	transplant	
Apr	grow on	
May	harden off	
Jun	flowering	
July	flowering	
Aug	flowering	
Sept	flowering	
Oct	/	
Nov	/	
Dec	/	

Recommended Varieties
Calceolaria hybrids:
   "Little Sweeties Mixed"
   "Midas"
   "Sunshine"
   "Sunset Mixed"

Site   Slipper flowers thrive in moist soil where their roots stay as cool as possible. Mix in well-rotted compost or manure before planting and use a peat- or coir-based multipurpose compost for filling containers.

GROWING METHOD

Sowing   The fine seed can be sown on the surface of peat- or coir-based multipurpose compost in a 3½in pot, January–March, at a temperature of 64°F. Keep in a bright place. Seedlings appear in 2–3 weeks and can be transplanted to cell trays, then hardened off and planted after frosts, 6–12in apart, or used with other plants in containers.

Feeding   Liquid feed every 3–4 weeks or mix slow-release fertilizer with compost before planting.

Problems   Slugs will eat the leaves of young plants in wet spells during early summer. Protect plants with a barrier of grit or eggshell or scatter slug pellets sparingly around plants.

FLOWERING

Season   Plants will flower from early summer until frosts. Take off dead flowers weekly.

Cutting   A few stems can be taken but avoid damaging the overall shape and appearance of the plant.

AFTER FLOWERING

General   Remove plants in fall when finished.

CALENDULA
Pot marigold

MIXED VARIETIES of calendula offer a wide color range, most commonly shades of orange and yellow, as seen here.

CALENDULA is a bushy plant producing masses of summer flowers —the edible petals can be scattered on summer salads.

FEATURES

Also known as English marigold, calendula is a fast-growing, hardy annual with daisy-type flowers in shades of yellow, orange, red, pinkish, and even green. Flowers can be fully double, while others have a distinct darker "eye." The edible petals can be used in salads. Perfect for a "cottage garden" bed or border, and very easy to grow, the large curled seeds are sown straight into the soil outdoors. Plant size ranges from 12 to 28in tall and wide.

CONDITIONS

Aspect Needs full sunlight to succeed.
Site Does well even in poor soil, which can increase the number of flowers. Add rotted organic matter to the soil ahead of planting time to improve results. Calendula does not do well on heavy, badly drained soils, so grow in containers under these conditions.

GROWING METHOD

Sowing March to May or August/September are the sowing periods. Sow the large seeds direct into finely raked moist soil where you want plants to flower, in drills ½in deep, and cover. Thin out as seedlings grow so that plants are eventually spaced 10–12in apart. Fall-sown plants flower earlier the following year. If flowers for cutting are required, sow seed thinly in long rows.

Feeding Liquid feed once a month to encourage larger blooms. Use a feed high in potash to encourage flowers rather than leafy growth—tomato fertilizers are a good choice.

Problems The leaves are prone to attack by aphids, causing twisting and damage. Use a spray containing permethrin, but avoid eating flowers. Powdery mildew can affect leaves in late summer, but is not worth treating—pick off the worst affected leaves and compost them.

FLOWERING

Season Flowers appear in late spring on plants sown the previous fall, and from early summer on spring-sown plants. Removal of faded blooms will keep up a succession of flowers.

Cutting Good as a cut flower—cutting helps to keep flowers coming. Cut when flowers are well formed but before petals open too far.

AFTER FLOWERING

General Pull up after flowering. Will self-seed if a few heads are left to ripen fully and shed seeds.

CALENDULA AT A GLANCE

A hardy annual for growing in beds and borders and a useful cut flower in many shades. Frost hardy to 5°F (zone 7).

		Recommended Varieties
Jan	/	*Calendula officinalis:*
Feb	/	"Art Shades Mixed"
Mar	sow	"Fiesta Gitana Mixed"
Apr	sow	"Greenheart Orange"
May	thin out	"Kablouna Lemon Cream"
Jun	flowering	"Kablouna Mixed"
July	flowering	"Orange King"
Aug	flowers/sow	"Pacific Beauty"
Sept	flowers/sow	"Pink Surprise"
Oct	/	"Princess Mixed"
Nov	/	"Radio"
Dec	/	"Touch of Red Mixed"

CALLISTEPHUS
China aster

CHINA ASTERS, with their large, showy, and often double flowers, can be used as summer bedding plants for massed displays.

AS A CUT FLOWER, callistephus is unrivalled for producing long-lasting blooms in late summer when other flowers are past their best.

FEATURES

China asters are half-hardy annuals and are not to be confused with the perennial asters or Michaelmas daisies. Grow as bedding, as cut flowers, and in large pots. Flowers come in a wide range, from narrow, quill-like petals to bicolors, and also single shades. Size ranges from 8 to 36in tall, depending on the variety. Available as young plants.

CONDITIONS

Aspect   Must have a warm spot in full sunlight all day.

CALLISTEPHUS AT A GLANCE

A half-hardy annual grown for its flowers, used in bedding, container,s and as a cut flower. Frost hardy to 32ºF (zone 10).

Jan	/	Recommended Varieties
Feb	/	*Callistephus chinensis:*
Mar	sow	"Apricot Giant"
Apr	sow	"Dwarf Comet Mixed"
May	plant	"Matsumoto Mixcd"
Jun	flowering	"Moraketa"
July	flowering	"Milady Mixed"
Aug	flowering	"Ostrich Plume Mixed"
Sept	flowering	"Red Ribbon"
Oct	flowering	"Teisa Stars Mixed"
Nov	/	
Dec	/	

Site

Site   Plants need well-drained soil with added organic matter, such as rotted manure or compost, dug in before planting. If grown in containers, use multipurpose compost mixed with slow-release fertilizer granules.

GROWING METHOD

Sowing   Sow in March/April in 3½in pots of compost and keep at 61ºF. Seedlings appear after a week and can be transplanted to cell trays and grown on. Planted in late May, plants are not damaged by the last frosts. Seed can also be sown direct into the ground in late April and May. Plant 8–24in apart.

Feeding   Water regularly and give plants in containers a general liquid feed every two weeks. In beds, feed when you water with a handheld feeder.

Problems   Aphids cause the leaves to distort, which can affect flowering. Use a spray containing dimethoate. If plants suddenly collapse and die, they are suffering from aster wilt and should be removed with the soil around their roots and put in the trashcan. Avoid growing asters in that spot and try "resistant" varieties.

FLOWERING

Season   Early summer to early fall.
Cutting   An excellent and long-lasting cut flower.

AFTER FLOWERING

General   Remove plants after flowering and compost any that do not show signs of wilt disease.

CATHARANTHUS
Madagascar periwinkle

THE FAMILIAR FLOWERS of Catharanthus roseus *look similar to those of its close relative, the hardy vinca.*

FOR BEDDING DISPLAYS, catharanthus is available in mixed colors that often contain flowers with darker "eyes," as seen here.

FEATURES

Varieties of *Catharanthus roseus* have pink/rose, mauve, or white flowers, often with a deeper center. These plants quickly spread, growing to 10–16in, and are suitable for massed bedding displays or pots indoors. Grow as a half-hardy annual.

CONDITIONS

Aspect Needs full sunlight to succeed outdoors.

CATHARANTHUS AT A GLANCE

A half-hardy annual grown for its bright flowers and ideal for use in containers on a warm sunny yard. Frost hardy to 32°F (zone 10).

		Recommended Varieties
Jan	/	
Feb	/	*Catharanthus roseus:*
Mar	sow	"Apricot Delight"
Apr	transplant	"Pacifica Red"
May	harden off/plant	"Peppermint Cooler"
Jun	flowering	"Pretty In… Mixed"
July	flowering	"Tropicana Mixed"
Aug	flowering	"Terrace Vermillion"
Sept	flowering	
Oct	/	
Nov	/	
Dec	/	

Site Needs good drainage, but enrich the soil with well-rotted manure or compost before planting. For containers, use multipurpose compost mixed with extra slow-release fertilizer before planting up.

GROWING METHOD

Sowing Sow seed in March/April in 3½in pots of multipurpose compost and lightly cover. Keep at 64°F in a light spot and transplant seedlings when they are 1in tall, into cell trays. Keep in a warm greenhouse or warm spot indoors and do not get the compost too wet. Harden off in late May and plant 8–12in apart in their final positions or use in containers.

Feeding In bedding displays, apply a liquid plant food monthly to keep plants growing vigorously throughout the summer months.

Problems Overwatering and wet soil/compost can lead to rotting. If red spider mite attacks the leaves, use a spray containing bifenthrin.

FLOWERING

Season Flowers appear throughout the summer.
Cutting Not suitable for cutting.

AFTER FLOWERING

General Remove plants after the first fall frosts and use for composting.

CELOSIA
Prince of Wales' feathers

THE FEATHERY FLOWERS *of celosia are made up of masses of smaller flowers, and have a distinctive, plume-like shape.*

THE BRILLIANT PLUMES *of cockscomb always look best in patio pots and containers when planted together in groups of 4–6 plants.*

FEATURES

Also known as Prince of Wales' feathers, celosia, or cockscomb has plume-like or crested flowers (shown left) ranging in color from deep crimson to scarlet, orange, and yellow. Tall forms grow to 30in, the dwarf forms to 10–12in. Grow it as a half-hardy annual and use in bedding or as a striking plant for containers. Good for cutting.

CONDITIONS

Aspect   Must have a sunny, warm spot to do well.

CELOSIA AT A GLANCE	
A half-hardy annual grown for its feathery, plume-like flowerheads in a range of colors. Frost hardy to 32°F (zone 10).	
Jan /	Recommended Varieties
Feb sow	**Plumed**
Mar sow	*Celosia argentea:*
Apr pot on	"Kimono Mixed"
May harden off/plant	"Dwarf Geisha"
Jun flowering	"Century Mixed"
July flowering	"New Look"
Aug flowering	*Celosia spicata:*
Sept flowering	"Flamingo Feather"
Oct /	**Crested**
Nov /	*Celosia cristata:*
Dec /	"Jewel Box Mixed"

Site   Needs well-drained soil that has been enriched with well-rotted manure or compost. Good soil preparation is essential to ensure strong plants and large flowerheads. Plant up containers using multipurpose compost

GROWING METHOD

Sowing   Celosias dislike having their roots disturbed so sow 2–3 seeds per cell in a multi-cell tray using multipurpose compost, in February/March. Keep at 64°F and when the seedlings appear after 2–3 weeks, remove all but the strongest. Carefully pot the young plants on into 3½in pots, then harden off for two weeks before planting after the last frosts. Plant without damaging the roots, 6–12in apart, and water.

Feeding   Feed bedding monthly with liquid feed. Mix slow-release fertilizer with the compost before planting up containers.

Problems   Wet, cold soil/compost can cause rotting of the roots, so avoid heavy soils and grow in pots.

FLOWERING

Season   Flowers appear throughout summer.

Cutting   May be used as a cut flower for unusual indoor decoration. Cut some plumes and hang them upside down in a dry, airy place for later use in dried flower arrangements.

AFTER FLOWERING

General   Remove plants after the first frosts of fall.

CENTAUREA
Cornflower

CORNFLOWERS should have pale, fading flowers removed regularly. For indoor use, cut the stems when the buds are still closed.

GROWN IN GROUPS like this, cornflowers will support each other quite naturally. In windy spots, push twigs in between plants.

FEATURES

Cornflower, *Centaurea cyanus*, is one of the easiest hardy annuals to grow and can be used in bedding, containers, and for cut flowers. Other than blue, there are mixtures available and single colors such as the "Florence" types in red, pink, and white, reaching 14in tall. Taller varieties like "Blue Diadem" are best for cutting. Regular removal of dead flowers is essential to prolong flowering and to stop plants from becoming shabby.

CENTAUREA AT A GLANCE

A hardy annual grown for its "cottage garden"-style flowers in various colors, useful for cutting. Frost hardy to 5°F (zone 7).

		Recommended Varieties
Jan	/	
Feb	/	*Centaurea cyanus:*
Mar	sow	**Short varieties**
Apr	thin out	"Florence Blue"
May	flowering	"Florence Mixed"
Jun	flowering	"Florence Pink"
July	flowering	"Florence Red"
Aug	flowering	"Florence White"
Sept	flowers/sow	"Midget Mixed"
Oct	/	**Tall varieties**
Nov	/	"Blue Diadem"
Dec	/	"Black Ball"

CONDITIONS

Aspect Needs full sunlight all day.
Site Must have very well-drained soil, but no special soil preparation is necessary. Staking is necessary when grown in windy situations, but the plants are self-supporting when they are planted in groups. For container growing, use multipurpose compost.

GROWING METHOD

Sowing Sow seed in the spring where plants are to flower in short rows ½in deep and approximately 12in apart. Thin out so the plants are finally 3–6in apart. This can also be done in late September for stronger plants and earlier flowers, but leave thinning out until the following spring. Can also be sown in pots and transplanted to cell trays for plants to use in courtyard containers.
Feeding Extra feeding is usually unnecessary.
Problems White mildew affects leaves but is not serious.

FLOWERING

Season Summer until early fall.
Cutting Cut before the petals open too far.

AFTER FLOWERING

General Remove plants once flowering is finished. Plants self-seed if they are left in the ground.

CHEIRANTHUS
Wallflower

THE INTENSE COLORS of wallflowers are only matched by their strong, lingering scent that is best on warm, still days.

"IVORY WHITE" is a useful single-colored variety of Cheiranthus cheiri *for bedding schemes that are color-themed.*

FEATURES

Wallflowers have fragrant flowers of yellow, brown, cream, red, and orange and are grown for their sweet spring scent. These hardy biennials grow between 8 and 18in, depending on the variety, and are available as mixed or single colors. Plants are used for bedding but may also be used in courtyard containers, where they can be moved near doors and windows when in bloom. Ready-grown plants can be bought in early fall.

CHEIRANTHUS AT A GLANCE

With its bright flowers and strong scent, this biennial is useful for spring bedding and for containers. Frost hardy to 5°F (zone 7).

		Recommended Varieties
Jan	/	
Feb	flowering	*Cheiranthus cheiri:*
Mar	flowering	**Tall**
Apr	flowering	"Blood Red"
May	sow	"Cloth of Gold"
Jun	sow	"Harlequin"
July	thin out	**Medium**
Aug	grow on	"My Fair Lady Mixed"
Sept	grow on	"Vulcan Improved"
Oct	plant	**Dwarf**
Nov	/	"Prince Mixed"
Dec	/	"Tom Thumb Mixed"

CONDITIONS

Aspect   Grow in full sunlight for the best scent.
Site   Must have very well-drained soil. Add lime before planting to reduce the effect of clubroot disease. Use multipurpose compost in containers and windowboxes. Avoid places exposed to winter winds and move containers to shelter during severe winter weather.

GROWING METHOD

Sowing   Sow May/June outdoors in rows 12in apart and ½in deep. As plants grow, thin them to 12in apart, and pinch when 3in tall to make growth bushy. Can also be sown in pots and transplanted into 3½in pots. Plant in October in beds or containers. When lifting plants, keep as much soil on the roots as possible.
Feeding   Give a liquid feed monthly during summer.
Problems   Avoid growing in soil known to be infected with clubroot disease, or raise plants in pots using multipurpose compost.

FLOWERING

Season   Late winter through to the spring.
Cutting   Cut stems last well in water.

AFTER FLOWERING

General   Remove plants in late spring after flowering.

CLEOME
Spider flower

SPIDER FLOWERS *are available as single colors or mixed. The* popular "Color Fountains Mixed" *is seen here in a summer border.*

THE EXOTIC FEEL *that cleome adds to the yard can be used to best effect on a warm courtyard where their scent lingers in still air.*

FEATURES

The spider-like flowers of *Cleome spinosa*, in pink, white, or rose, have narrow petals with long stamens. They appear all summer up and down the length of the stem. These large half-hardy annuals grow to 5ft tall with a single stem, and with lobed leaves. Plant at the back of borders or use them as central "dot" plants in large tubs for an "exotic" feel. Look out for the thorny stems and pungent leaves.

CONDITIONS

Aspect   Needs full sunlight and a sheltered position to achieve maximum height during the summer.

CLEOME AT A GLANCE

A half-hardy annual grown for its exotic flowers and ideal as a centerpiece for bedding/containers. Frost hardy to 32°F (zone 10).

Jan	/	Recommended Varieties
Feb	sow	*Cleome spinosa:*
Mar	sow	**Mixed colors**
Apr	grow on	"Color Fountain Mixed"
May	harden off/plant	
Jun	flowering	**Single colors**
July	flowering	"Cherry Queen"
Aug	flowering	"Helen Campbell"
Sept	flowering	"Pink Queen"
Oct	/	"Violet Queen"
Nov	/	
Dec	/	

Site   Needs good drainage but tolerates a wide range of soils. For best results, improve soil by digging in rotted manure or compost, and use multipurpose compost with slow-release fertilizer added when planting containers. Stems are generally strong enough that they can be grow without extra support.

GROWING METHOD

Sowing   Sow seeds in 3½in pots of multipurpose compost in February/March and keep at 64°F. Seedlings appear after two weeks and are transplanted to 3½in pots, grown on in a warm greenhouse or conservatory. Pot on into 5in containers in early May, and harden off before planting after the last frosts.

Feeding   Feed plants in beds fortnightly with liquid feed from a handheld applicator. Don't allow the compost in containers to become over-wet.

Problems   Aphids attack young plants and cause twisted growth. Check under the leaves regularly and use a spray with permethrin if necessary, making sure the spray gets under the leaves.

FLOWERING

Season   The long flowering period extends throughout summer and well into mild falls. The long thin seed pods give it a real "spidery" look.

Cutting   Useful as a cut flower, but watch the spines.

AFTER FLOWERING

General   Remove plants after flowering, but wear gloves for protection, since the stems are spiny.

CONSOLIDA
Larkspur

LARKSPUR IS DOUBLY useful as a cut flower, because the spikes can be dried and used for dried flower arrangements.

FINELY DIVIDED LEAVES are characteristic of Consolida ajacis, while flowers can be single, as here, or double, in various colors.

FEATURES

Consolida ajacis, larkspur, is related to delphinium but is not as tall and is grown as a hardy annual. Ideal for a "cottage garden" border, larkspur grows up to 3ft tall and has spikes of pink, white, red, blue, and violet single or double flowers, with finely cut leaves. Good for cutting. Seeds are poisonous.

CONDITIONS

Aspect   Grow in a sunny, open spot.

CONSOLIDA AT A GLANCE

A hardy annual grown for its spikes of bright flowers that are useful for borders and cutting. Frost hardy to 5°F (zone 7).

Jan	/	Recommended Varieties
Feb	/	
Mar	sow	*Consolida ajacis:*
Apr	thin out	**Tall, for cutting**
May	thin/flowers	"Earl Grey"
Jun	flowering	"Frosted Skies"
July	flowering	"Giant Imperial Mixed"
Aug	flowering	"Hyacinth Flowered Mixed"
Sept	flowers/sow	
Oct	/	**Short, for bedding**
Nov	/	"Dwarf Hyacinth Flowered Mixed"
Dec	/	"Dwarf Rocket Mixed"

Site

Soil can be enriched with manure or compost well ahead of planting, but it must be well-drained. Plants will also grow well on thin and hungry soils. Plants should support each other as they grow and not need artificial support. Use taller varieties at the rear of borders.

GROWING METHOD

Sowing   Sow direct where the plants are to grow for best results, in short rows ½in deep, in either March or September. Expect seedlings to appear in 2–3 weeks. Thin plants out as they grow so they are eventually 3–6in apart, depending on the variety.

Feeding   Extra feeding is not necessary.

Problems   Slugs eat young seedlings so scatter slug pellets around plants or protect them with a 2in wide barrier of sharp grit.

FLOWERING

Season   Flowers appear from spring onward on fall-sown plants, June onward from spring sowings. Removing faded flower spikes will encourage more flowers.

Cutting   An excellent cut flower. Cut long stems and scald ends before soaking in cool water.

AFTER FLOWERING

General   Leave a few plants to die down naturally and self-seed into the soil, otherwise pull up when finished and use for composting.

COSMOS
Cosmos

"SENSATION MIXED" is a tall-growing (3ft) cosmos with single flowers of red, pink, white, and shades in between.

DURING THE SUMMER, varieties of Cosmos bipinnatus *grown in borders form masses of feathery leaves topped by flowers.*

FEATURES

Cosmos, with their finely cut, feathery foliage and large daisy-type flowers grow up to 5ft tall, but shorter varieties are available and can be used in containers. Varieties of *Cosmos bipinnatus* have red, pink, purple, or white flowers, while yellow, orange, and scarlet are available in varieties of *Cosmos sulphureus*. Cosmos is grown as either a hardy or a half-hardy annual, and is an excellent choice for a cottage yard-style border. "Seashells" has tubular "fluted" petals, and the taller varieties such as "Sensation Mixed" are good for cutting.

COSMOS AT A GLANCE

A hardy or half-hardy annual grown for its large daisy-like flowers. For borders, pots, and cutting. Frost hardy to 32°F (zone 10).

		Recommended Varieties
Jan	/	
Feb	/	*Cosmos bipinnatus:*
Mar	sow 🖐	"Daydream"
Apr	sow/transplant 🖐	"Gazebo"
May	sow/plant 🖐	"Picotee"
Jun	flowering 🌸	"Seashells/Sea Shells"
July	flowering 🌸	"Sensation Mixed"
Aug	flowering 🌸	"Sonata Mixed"
Sept	flowering 🌸	*Cosmos favorureus:*
Oct	/	"Ladybird Mixed"
Nov	/	"Ladybird Scarlet"
Dec	/	"Sunny Red"

CONDITIONS

Aspect   Needs full sunlight to flourish.
Site   Well-drained soil is essential for success, and good results are guaranteed on light and slightly hungry soils. Pea sticks or twiggy shoots may be needed for support in exposed spots. Any multipurpose compost will give good results in courtyard pots and containers.

GROWING METHOD

Sowing   Raise plants by sowing in March at 61°F. Sow the long thin seeds in 3½in pots of multipurpose compost, then transplant to cell trays and grow on. Harden off at the end of May before planting after frosts, or sow in April/May directly into the ground where the plants are to grow. Final spacing between plants should be 6–18in, depending on the variety grown.
Feeding   Generally not necessary.
Problems   Slugs will eat young seedlings outdoors, so protect with slug pellets.

FLOWERING

Season   Flowers appear from the early summer onward.
Cutting   The taller varieties are ideal as cut flowers. Ensure regular removal of faded flowers.

AFTER FLOWERING

General   Pull up plants when frosted, but leaving a few to die off will ensure some self-sown seedlings.

DIANTHUS BARBATUS

Sweet William

THE IMPACT OF SWEET WILLIAMS comes from their massed heads of small flowers, which often have attractive "picotee" edges.

STRONG SCENT is a characteristic of Dianthus barbatus *varieties and makes this an ideal plant for cutting in bunches in early summer.*

FEATURES

Sweet Williams are varieties of *Dianthus barbatus* and have flowers in pink, white, red, burgundy, and bicolors, on large rounded heads. Individual flowers often have darker central "eyes." Plants have clumping growth up to 18in, while dwarf forms grow to just 6in. The flowers appear from the spring into early summer and are scented and ideal for cutting. They are easily grown from seed as a hardy biennial, and useful for bedding schemes and as blocks of spring color in mixed borders. Some less common varieties, like "Sooty," have dark, almost black flowers.

DIANTHUS AT A GLANCE

A summer-sown biennial grown for its large heads of scented flowers in spring and early summer. Frost hardy to 5°F (zone 7).

Jan	/	Recommended Varieties
Feb	/	*Dianthus barbatus:*
Mar	/	**Tall varieties**
Apr	flowering	"Auricula-Eyed Mixed"
May	flowers/sow	"Forerunner Mixed"
Jun	flowers/sow	"Gemstones"
		"Harlequin"
July	flowering	"Monarch Mixed"
Aug	grow on	**Dwarf varieties**
Sept	grow on	"Dwarf Mixed"
Oct	plant	"Indian Carpet Mixed"
Nov	/	
Dec	/	

CONDITIONS

Aspect Grow Sweet Williams in full sunlight.
Site Needs well-drained soil that has been limed before planting, and has had plenty of rotted compost mixed in several weeks before.

GROWING METHOD

Sowing Sow the fine seed in rows outdoors, ½in deep and just cover, in May/June. Transplant the seedlings so they are in rows 6in apart and pinch out the growing tips to make them bushy. Water regularly throughout the summer months, and then lift and plant into their flowering positions in October, keeping the roots intact. For cut flowers only, the plants can be left growing in rows.
Feeding Liquid-feed monthly during the summer.
Problems Poor drainage during winter can kill plants. If leaves are attacked by rust disease, try a spray containing the fungicide penconazole.

FLOWERING

Season Flowers appear from late spring to early summer, and it is possible to get a second "flush" if all the stalks are cut hard back after the first flowers have faded.
Cutting An excellent cut flower, and ideal for making into a small, rounded bouquet.

AFTER FLOWERING

General Pull plants up when they are past their best, or leave some to develop into bigger clumps.

DIANTHUS CHINENSIS
Chinese pink

AS CONTAINER PLANTS, Chinese pinks are perfect as tidy edging plants, all growing to the same height. They are also valuable as colorful fillers and effectively bridge the gap between taller plants in the center of large tubs and trailing plants falling over the edges.

FEATURES

Growing 8–12in high, varieties of *Dianthus chinensis* are suitable for massed planting, edging garden beds, or for use in troughs or pots. Chinese pink is grown as a half-hardy annual, although it is fully hardy outdoors. Flower are red, pink, or white, with only slight scent. Available as young plants.

CONDITIONS

Aspect   Needs full sunlight to flower at its best.

DIANTHUS AT A GLANCE

A hardy annual grown for its small brightly colored pink-type flowers, used in bedding/pots. Frost hardy to 5°F (zone 7).

		Recommended Varieties
Jan	/	
Feb	/	*Dianthus chinensis:*
Mar	sow 🖏	"Baby Doll Mixed"
Apr	transplant 🖏	"Black & White
May	harden off/plant 🖏	Minstrels"
Jun	flowering 🌼	"Double Gaiety Mixed"
July	flowering 🌼	"Princess Mixed"
Aug	flowering 🌼	"Raspberry Parfait"
Sept	flowering 🌼	"Snowfire"
Oct	/	"Strawberry Parfait"
Nov	/	"T&M Frosty Mixed"
Dec	/	

Site   Needs well-drained soil, but dig in plenty of well-rotted manure or compost when preparing beds. Lime can be added to the soil before planting and raked in. Containers must have very good drainage.

GROWING METHOD

Sowing   Sow seeds in 3½in pots of multipurpose compost in March, just cover, and keep at 60°F in a light place. When seedlings are 1in tall, transplant to cell trays and grow on with some protection (a cold frame is suitable). Harden off at the end of May and plant out in beds or containers.

Feeding   Do not overwater—a good weekly watering should be sufficient—and add liquid feed every 2–3 weeks. Plants in containers need no extra feeding if slow-release fertilizer is added.

Problems   Overwatering will cause yellowing of the leaves and rotting off at soil/compost level.

FLOWERING

Season   Plants come into flower from early summer onward and will continue until the fall if dead flowerheads are removed regularly.

Cutting   Taller varieties can be used as cut flowers, but choose a variety known for its scent such as "Double Gaiety Mixed."

AFTER FLOWERING

General   Remove plants when finished and compost.

DIGITALIS
Foxglove

FOXGLOVES *are perfect for cottage-style borders and make good companions for the red poppies and white lavatera.*

WHITE FOXGLOVES *are useful for a specific color scheme—this is a white-flowered plant of the "Excelsior Hybrids".*

FEATURES

Varieties of *Digitalis purpurea* grow up to 6ft tall with spikes of tubular pink, white, magenta, cream, or purple flowers, each with a spotted lip. Plant in groups in borders or in a partly-shaded spot under trees. All parts of the plant are poisonous, including the seeds. Grow as a hardy biennial, although the variety "Foxy" can be treated as an annual and sown in spring.

CONDITIONS

Aspect   Succeeds in part or dappled shade, or in sun.

DIGITALIS AT A GLANCE

A hardy biennial grown for tall spikes of flowers appearing in early summer. Useful for shade. Frost hardy to 5°F (zone 7).

		Recommended Varieties
Jan	/	
Feb	/	*Digitalis purpurea:*
Mar	/	"Alba"
Apr	sow	"Excelsior Hybrids"
May	sow/transplant	"Foxy Mixed"
Jun	sow/flowers	"Giant Spotted Mixed"
July	flowering	"Glittering Prizes Mixed"
Aug	grow	"Selected Mixed"
Sept	grow	"Suttons Apricot"
Oct	plant	
Nov	/	
Dec	/	

Site   Soil needs to be free-draining and enriched with organic matter well ahead of planting—use rotted compost or manure in generous amounts. Staking is necessary when plants are grown in a position exposed to winds.

GROWING METHOD

Sowing   Sow the very small seed in a 3½in pot and barely cover, from April–June. Keep outside in a coldframe or sheltered spot, and transplant seedlings individually to 3½in pots. Grow on through the summer, potting on into 5in pots when roots fill the smaller pots. Plant out in October where you want the plants to flower. The variety "Foxy" can be sown in February in warmth and planted in May for flowers the same summer. Treat as a half-hardy annual.

Feeding   Feed fortnightly with liquid feed while plants are in pots and do not allow to dry out. Water in spring during dry spells as growth begins.

Problems   No special problems affect foxgloves.

FLOWERING

Season   Flowers appear in early summer.

Cutting   Not particularly good as a cut flower.

AFTER FLOWERING

General   Once stems have flowered, cut them off just above the leaves and plants may then produce several shorter flowering stems. Leave a few spikes to set seed pods which will self-seed.

DOROTHEANTHUS

Mesembryanthemum or Livingstone daisy

LIVINGSTONE DAISIES set beds alight with color on bright sunny days when the flowers open fully. Planted 6in apart they soon knit together to create a tapestry of color, and look especially at home when creeping among pieces of stone on a sunny rock garden.

FEATURES

Mesembryanthemum, also known as Livingstone daisy, is ideal for planting on dry, sunny banks, on rock gardens, and in pots of free-draining compost. It has a spreading habit, but is only 6in tall at most. The fleshy leaves have a crystalline texture with bright, daisy-like flowers in many shades. Grow as a half-hardy annual. All varieties of *Dorotheanthus bellidiformis* have the habit of closing their flowers in dull and wet spells of weather, opening again in bright sunshine.

DOROTHEANTHUS AT A GLANCE

A half-hardy, spreading annual grown for its daisy-like flowers that open fully in sunshine. Frost hardy to 32°F (zone 10).

Jan	/	**Recommended Varieties**
Feb	/	*Dorotheanthus bellidiformis:*
Mar	sow	"Gelato Pink"
Apr	sow/transplant	"Harlequin Mixed"
May	plant/harden off	"Lunette" ("Yellow Ice")
Jun	flowering	"Magic Carpet Mixed"
July	flowering	"Sparkles"
Aug	flowering	
Sept	flowering	
Oct	/	
Nov	/	
Dec	/	

CONDITIONS

Aspect   Needs full direct sun all day and will perform even better on a south-facing sloping bank.

Site   Needs very well drained soil, with no special soil preparation necessary, since plants grow better on light, sandy, and hungry soils. If grown in containers, used soil-based compost and mix with fifty percent grit for good drainage.

GROWING METHOD

Sowing   Sow seed in a 3½in pot of soil-based seed compost in March and barely cover. Keep at 64°F in a light place. When seedlings are large enough, transplant to cell trays of soil-based potting compost and grow on. Harden off at the end of May for two weeks and plant after the last frosts 6in apart.

Feeding   Extra feeding is unnecessary and produces leaves at the expense of flowers. Take care not to overwater in beds or pots, else plants will rot.

Problems   Slugs will attack the fleshy young leaves so scatter slug pellets after planting out.

FLOWERING

Season   Flowers appear from midsummer onward. Remove faded flowers to encourage more.

Cutting   Not suitable for cutting.

AFTER FLOWERING

General   Pull up and compost when finished.

Eschscholzia

California poppy

FALL SOWING of eschscholzia will produce early spring flowers around the same time as this bright green Euphorbia polychroma.

DRY, HOT, SUN-BAKED banks are perfect for California poppies, where conditions are very like those of their native State.

FEATURES

The bright flowers and finely divided blue-green foliage of the California poppy are best in large drifts, although it grows well even in cracks in paving slabs and in gravel, and thrives on dry soils in full sun. Varieties of *Eschscholzia californica* have flowers in yellow, cream, pink/beige, apricot, and scarlet. They grow 12in tall and wide. Grow as a hardy annual, sowing where plants are to flower. Very easy to grow and quickly self-seeds.

CONDITIONS

Aspect Eschscholzia thrives in hot, sun-baked spots

ESCHSCHOLZIA AT A GLANCE	
A hardy annual grown for its bright poppy-like flowers and ideal for light, dry soils and along paths. Frost hardy to 5°F (zone 7).	
Jan /	Recommended Varieties
Feb /	*Eschscholzia californica:*
Mar sow	"Apricot Bush"
Apr thin out	"Apricot Chiffon"
May thin out	"Apricot Flambeau"
Jun flowering	"Dalli"
July flowering	"Mission Bells Mixed"
Aug flowering	"Prima Ballerina"
Sept flowers/sow	"Rose Bush"
Oct /	"Thai Silk Mixed"
Nov /	*Eschscholzia lobbii:*
Dec /	"Moonlight"

Site where other annuals struggle to grow. Must have full sunlight and likes it hot.
Poor, light soil often gives the best results, so long as drainage is good. No special soil preparation is necessary, and avoid adding compost or manure, which encourages leafy growth at the expense of flowers.

GROWING METHOD

Sowing Sow in March or September outdoors where the plants are to flower, since it dislikes being transplanted. Spread seed thinly in short drills ½in deep and cover. Thin out the seedlings as they grow to allow 3–6in between plants. Water thoroughly after thinning to settle plants back in.

Feeding Except in spells of drought, watering is not necessary, and extra feed is not required.

Problems No particular problems.

FLOWERING

Season Long flowering period through the spring and summer months if faded flowers are removed.

Cutting Use as a cut flower, although flowers close at night. Cut long stems and place in water immediately to just below the flower buds.

AFTER FLOWERING

General Often self-seeds, so seedlings can be expected the following season. These will appear in cracks in the sidewalk, along paths and drives, and in gravel, where they are perfectly at home in dry, poor soil conditions.

EUPHORBIA

Snow-on-the-mountain

THE COLOR *of snow-on-the-mountain comes from its white-edged leaves; this becomes more intense near the tops of the plants.*

WHEN GROWN IN POTS, Euphorbia marginata *can be planted in mixed borders in groups of 3–5 plants for cool splashes of color.*

FEATURES

Commonly known as snow-on-the-mountain, *Euphorbia marginata* is grown for its attractive leaves. The flowers are insignificant, but the leaves have an edging of white. Plants grow 2–3ft tall and are used in annual or mixed borders. Grow as a hardy annual. The milky sap is poisonous.

CONDITIONS

Aspect   Needs to be grown in the open in full sun.

EUPHORBIA AT A GLANCE

A hardy annual grown for its attractive leaves, which are streaked and edged with white. Frost hardy to 23°F (zone 9).

Jan	/	Recommended Varieties
Feb	/	
Mar	sow	*Euphorbia marginata:*
Apr	thin out	"Summer Icicle"
May	thin out	
Jun	flowering	
July	flowering	
Aug	flowering	
Sept	flowering	
Oct	/	
Nov	/	
Dec	/	

Site   Does not tolerate poor drainage and succeeds best in light and slightly hungry soils—sandy soils give good results. Add very well-rotted organic matter before planting to help retain soil moisture.

GROWING METHOD

Sowing   Sow seed during March direct into the ground, where plants are to grow, which avoids root disturbance as they develop. Make short drills ½in deep and scatter seed thinly, then cover. Plants are gradually thinned out so that final spacing is 6–12in by early summer. In exposed yards, short twigs can be used as supports. Alternatively, sow in pots in a cold frame and transplant to cell trays, planting out in May.

Feeding   Grows well without extra feeding.

Problems   Trouble-free.

FLOWERING

Season   From early summer onward.

Cutting   Foliage may be used in arrangements but stems must be burnt or scalded to stop the milky sap bleeding. Wear gloves to avoid getting the irritant sap on skin.

AFTER FLOWERING

General   Remove plants in late summer and fall when they are past their best, but leave a few to die down and self-seed into the soil.

GAZANIA
Gazania

GAZANIA flowers often have striking darker markings toward their centers.

IN MILD COASTAL YARDS it is worth leaving gazanias out during the winter months, since they often survive unharmed and will give an early show of flowers in the following spring.

FEATURES

Gazanias come in an amazing range of brilliant colors, from pastel pinks to cream, strong reds, and mahogany. Modern varieties with striped petals are very eye-catching. All have contrasting "eyes" to their flowers. Gazanias are grown as half-hardy annuals from spring-sown seeds and used in beds and courtyard pots. Flowers tend to close up in dull weather, but newer varieties like "Daybreak Bright Orange" stay open for longer. They grow up to 12in tall and wide and thrive in coastal yards.

CONDITIONS

Aspect   For the flowers to open reliably, gazanias must be grown where they get roasting sun all day.

GAZANIA AT A GLANCE

A half-hardy annual grown for its bright flowers that open fully in sun. Use in beds and containers. Frost hardy to 23°F (zone 9).

Jan	/	Recommended Varieties
Feb	/	
Mar	sow ✎	*Gazania rigens:*
Apr	transplant ✎	"Chansonette"
May	harden off/plant ✎	"Chansonette Pink Shades"
Jun	flowering ❀	"Daybreak Bright Orange"
July	flowering ❀	"Daybreak Red Stripe"
Aug	flowering ❀	"Harlequin Hybrids"
Sept	flowering ❀	"Mini Star Mixed"
Oct	/	"Sundance Mixed"
Nov	/	"Talent"
Dec	/	

Site   Needs well-drained soil that is not too rich or leafy growth is the result. Light sandy soils give the best results. If growing in courtyard containers, choose clay pots or troughs and use a soil-based compost with extra sharp grit mixed in to ensure good drainage at all times.

GROWING METHOD

Sowing   Seed is sown in March at 68°F in a heated propagator, in 3½in pots. Just cover the seeds and keep in a light place. Seedlings appear in 1–2 weeks and can be transplanted into cell trays, when large enough. Grow on in a greenhouse or conservatory, then harden off and plant in late May, spacing plants 12in apart. In mixed containers, make sure they are not shaded out by other plants growing nearby.

Feeding   Only water gazanias when the soil or compost is dry, and stand courtyard pots undercover during prolonged spells of summer rain.

Problems   No real problems, but slugs may attack leaves in wet weather, so protect with slug pellets.

FLOWERING

Season   The flowering period lasts throughout summer if dead flowers and their stalks are removed.

Cutting   Flowers are not suitable for cutting.

AFTER FLOWERING

General   Favorite plants can be lifted, potted up, and kept dry in a frost-free greenhouse over winter. Cuttings can be taken in the spring and new plants grown on for planting out.

GODETIA
Godetia

FOR A RAINBOW of summer color, sow a mixed variety of godetia that includes shades of rose, pink, and white flowers.

AT ITS PEAK, godetia is smothered in masses of bright flowers with large petals that have a texture similar to crepe paper.

FEATURES

Godetia is available in a wide range of varieties and many colors. This hardy annual can be spring- or fall-sown, the latter giving earlier flowers on bigger plants. Size ranges from 8 to 36in; the taller varieties are ideal for cutting. Don't labor over godetia—the best flowers are produced on slightly hungry, dry soils.

GODETIA AT A GLANCE

Grown for its bright single or double flowers, this hardy annual can be spring- or fall-sown. Frost hardy to 5°F (zone 7).

Jan	/	Recommended Varieties
Feb	/	*Godetia hybrids:*
Mar	sow	**Tall varieties**
Apr	sow	"Duke of York"
May	thin out	"Grace Mixed"
Jun	flowering	"Schamini Carmine"
July	flowering	"Sybil Sherwood"
Aug	flowering	**Dwarf varieties**
Sept	flowers/sow	"Charivari"
Oct	/	"Lilac Pixie"
Nov	/	"Precious Gems"
Dec	/	"Salmon Princess"

CONDITIONS

Aspect	Needs an open position in full sunlight.
Site	Needs perfect drainage, but not rich soil.

GROWING METHOD

Sowing	Sow where plants are to grow, just covering the seeds in shallow drills 6in apart during March/April, or during September. Thin out seedlings until they are 6–12in apart, depending on the variety. Do not thin fall-sown plants until the following spring, to allow for winter losses.
Feeding	Not needed, or excessive leafy growth results.
Problems	Overwatering quickly causes root rot, followed by collapse and death of plants.

FLOWERING

Season	Flowers appear from May onward on plants sown the previous fall. Spring-sown plants start flowering from June.
Cutting	An excellent cut flower, especially if the taller varieties such as "Schamini Carmine" and "Grace Mixed" are grown in rows.

AFTER FLOWERING

General	Remove plants when flowering is over. A few can be left to self-seed onto the soil.

GOMPHRENA
Globe amaranth

"STRAWBERRY FIELDS" is a large-growing variety of gomphrena with red flowers 2in across, on stems 30in tall.

GLOBE AMARANTH makes a good edging for paths—choose one of the lower-growing varieties such as "Gemini Mixed" at 2ft.

FEATURES

Also commonly known as bachelor's buttons, gomphrena is a half-hardy annual growing 12–30in tall, depending on the variety. Its rounded heads of purple, pink, white, red, and mauve flowers are used in bedding displays and for cutting and drying. "Strawberry Fields" has bright red flowers.

GOMPHRENA AT A GLANCE

A half-hardy annual grown for its clover-like flowerheads, used in bedding and for cutting. Frost hardy to 32°F (zone 10).

		Recommended Varieties
Jan	/	
Feb	/	**Gomphrena globosa:**
Mar	sow	"Buddy"
Apr	transplant	"Full Series"
May	harden off/plant	"Gemini Mixed"
Jun	flowering	"Globe Amaranth"
July	flowering	"Qis Mixed"
Aug	flowering	
Sept	flowering	**Gomphrena hybrid:**
Oct	/	"Strawberry Fields"
Nov	/	
Dec	/	

CONDITIONS

Aspect	Must have a sunny spot.
Site	Needs well-drained soil enriched with rotted manure or compost.

GROWING METHOD

Sowing	Sow in March in 3½in pots of multipurpose compost, just covering the seeds (soaking for a few days before helps germination). Keep at 64°F in a warm, dark place such as an airing cupboard and check regularly—seedlings appear in approximately two weeks. Transplant into cell trays, grow on under cover, harden off in late May, and plant out after frosts, 10–12in apart.
Feeding	Give an all-purpose liquid feed monthly.
Problems	No special problems affect gomphrena.

FLOWERING

Season	Flowers appear from midsummer to fall.
Cutting	Used fresh as a cut flower, but can also be dried in late summer by hanging upside-down in a warm, dry, airy place.

AFTER FLOWERING

General	Pull up in the fall and use for composting.

GYPSOPHILA
Baby's breath

CLOUDS OF SMALL FLOWERS are produced on annual gypsophila all summer if a few seeds are sown at two-week intervals from April until early June. For cut flowers, grow plants in a spare corner because they look bare once you begin to regularly remove stems.

FEATURES

Hardy annual varieties of *Gypsophila elegans* grow up to 2ft tall and wide, with many-divided stems bearing small, dainty pink, white, or rose flowers. It is widely used in flower arranging and as a "foil" for other plants in summer bedding schemes. The dwarf-growing *Gypsophila muralis* "Garden Bride," at 6in, is ideal for baskets and containers.

CONDITIONS

Aspect   Grow gypsophila in full sunlight.
Site   Rotted compost or manure should be dug in before planting, for strong plants and better flowers, but the soil must also be well-drained. Varieties grown in baskets and containers will succeed in any multipurpose compost.

GROWING METHOD

Sowing   Seeds can go directly into the ground, where plants will grow and flower. Sow in short drills ½in deep in April, then thin to finally leave plants 4–6in apart to give each other support and allow room to grow. September sowing produces stronger plants with earlier flowers the following spring—do not thin out until after winter.
Feeding   Feeding is not generally necessary if the soil has been well prepared beforehand. In dry spells, give the soil a thorough soaking, and do not let containers dry out.
Problems   Gypsophila is trouble-free, but young plants are prone to rotting off in heavy soils.

FLOWERING

Season   Flowers appear from June onward on spring-sown plants, several weeks earlier on those sown the previous fall.
Cutting   Excellent when cut and an ideal "filler" to marry together other flowers in a wide range of floral arrangements.

AFTER FLOWERING

General   Pull up plants and use for composting.

GYPSOPHILA AT A GLANCE

Gypsophila is a hardy annual grown for tall, much-branching stems of flowers, for beds/cutting. Frost hardy to 5°F (zone 7).

		Recommended Varieties
Jan	/	
Feb	/	Gypsophila elegans:
Mar	/	"Bright Rose"
Apr	sow	"Color Blend"
May	thin out	"Covent Garden"
Jun	flowering	"Kermesina"
July	flowering	"Monarch White"
Aug	flowering	"Rosea"
Sept	flowers/sow	"Snow Fountain"
Oct	/	"White Elephant"
Nov	/	Gypsophila muralis:
Dec	/	"Garden Bride"

HELIANTHUS
Sunflower

SUNFLOWERS have a central "disc" which eventually becomes the fat seedhead in fall and makes useful food for the birds.

"PACINO" is a modern variety of Helianthus annuus, small enough to be used in patio pots, growing to only 18in tall.

FEATURES

Sunflowers range in height from 18in up to 15ft depending on the variety grown. They can be used in bedding, in patio containers, as cut flowers, or can be grown as traditional "giants" to several feet tall. Plants produce single or multi-flowered heads and the color range is enormous. "Teddy Bear" has furry, double flowers. Annual sunflowers are fully hardy and flower from mid-summer onward. Certain varieties such as "Prado Sun & Fire" have been bred to be pollen-free and these are ideal for use as indoor cut flowers. Seedheads left in the yard in the fall provide food for birds.

CONDITIONS

Aspect   Must have an open position in full sun.

HELIANTHUS AT A GLANCE

A hardy annual grown for its large flowers on both dwarf and tall plants; some are ideal for cutting. Frost hardy to 5°F (zone 7).

		Recommended Varieties
Jan	/	*Helianthus annuus:*
Feb	/	**Tall varieties**
Mar	sow	"Italian White"
Apr	thin out	"Pastiche"
May	support	"Velvet Queen"
Jun	flowering	**For containers**
July	flowering	"Big Smile"
Aug	flowering	"Pacino"
Sept	flowering	**Double flowers**
Oct	/	"Orange Sun"
Nov	/	"Sungold Double"
Dec	/	"Teddy Bear"

Site   Tolerates most soil conditions but soil enriched with plenty of manure or compost makes growth both rapid and vigorous, producing the largest flowerheads. Plants grown in groups in borders tend to support each other, but in exposed spots tie tall varieties to a cane. Use multipurpose compost mixed with slow-release fertilizer for planting up patio containers and windowboxes.

GROWING METHOD

Sowing   Seeds are large and easy to handle—sow three seeds outdoors where plants are to grow in March, removing all but the strongest when 6in tall. Can also be sown three seeds to a 3½in pot of compost and treated in the same way. Pot-grown plants can be kept outdoors and planted when the roots fill the pot. Spacing depends on the variety grown.

Feeding   Extra feeding is not usually needed but keep plants well watered in long dry spells.

Problems   Slugs and snails can attack young plants cutting them off at ground level, so protect with slug pellets or a barrier of sharp grit.

FLOWERING

Season   Throughout summer and early fall.

Cutting   A very good cut flower but use a heavy vase or add some weight to the bottom of it to prevent it toppling over. Pollen-free varieties should be grown if allergies are a known problem.

AFTER FLOWERING

General   Leave the seedheads as bird food during fall and winter, and then dig out the extensive roots. Sunflower roots can help break-up and loosen heavy, compacted soils.

HELICHRYSUM
Strawflower

FOR DRYING cut helichrysum before the flowers reach this stage, while the petals are still curved inward (bottom right).

PAPER DAISIES ARE APT to be rather leggy, but the range of flower colors can be stunning, as shown here.

FEATURES

Varieties of strawflower come from *Helichrysum bracteatum*, with plants growing 6–24in tall. They are among the easiest annuals to grow for dried flowers, with double blooms in many colors, and petals that feel straw-like. Dwarf varieties make long-lasting container plants. A half-hardy annual.

CONDITIONS

Aspect   Must have a warm spot in full sun.

HELICHRYSUM AT A GLANCE

A half-hardy annual grown for its long-lasting dried flowers, and also used in bedding and containers. Frost hardy to 32°F (zone10).

Jan	/	Recommended Varieties
Feb	/	
Mar	sow	*Helichrysum bracteatum:*
Apr	transplant/grow	**Tall varieties**
May	harden off/plant	"Drakkar Pastel Mixed"
Jun	flowering	"Monstrosum Double Mixed"
July	flowering	"Pastel Mixed"
Aug	flowering	"Swiss Giants"
Sept	flowers/cutting	**Dwarf varieties**
Oct	flowers/cutting	"Bright Bikini"
Nov	/	"Chico Mixed"
Dec	/	"Hot Bikini"

Site   Needs very well-drained soil that has been enriched with rotted compost or manure. If growing in containers use multipurpose compost and add slow-release fertilizer. Tall varieties will need staking as they develop.

GROWING METHOD

Sowing   Sow seeds in March in 3½in pots of multipurpose compost and germinate at 64°F. Transplant seedlings to cell trays when large enough and grow on, then harden off at the end of May, and plant 6–24in apart depending on the variety. Seed can also be sown direct into short drills in the soil during May and the young plants gradually thinned to the planting distances above. In containers pack 2–3 plants together in groups to get a good block of flower color.

Feeding   Helichrysum grows well without extra feeding, but water container-grown plants regularly.

Problems   By late summer the leaves are often attacked by mildew, but it is not worth treating.

FLOWERING

Season   Flowers appear from early to midsummer.

Cutting   Pick the flowers when the petals are still incurved. Hang the bunches upside down in a dry, airy place to dry out. Long-lasting.

AFTER FLOWERING

General   Cut what you want and then pull up.

HELIPTERUM

Everlasting daisy

WHEN PLANTS REACH this stage of growth the entire plant can be harvested and hung up to dry. Individual stems are then cut off.

THINNING PLANTS to 6–12in apart helps them support each other. The flowers have a distinct rustle in a breeze.

FEATURES

The papery flowers of everlasting daisies come mainly in pinks and white. They grow 12–18in tall, and can be used in bedding or cut for dried flower arrangements. In catalogs they are also found listed under acrolinium and rhodanthe. Hardy annual.

CONDITIONS

Aspect   These Australian natives need full sun.
Site   Helipterum must have perfectly drained soil

and does not require special preparation—the best results are obtained on thin and hungry soils that mimic the plant's natural growing conditions. Sheltered hot-spots are best.

GROWING METHOD

Sowing   Sow seeds direct into the soil in short drills ½in deep and 6in apart in April and May. Thin the seedlings as they grow, so plants are eventually 6–12in apart by early summer. Water only during long dry spells, but this is not necessary when flower buds begin to appear.
Feeding   Do not feed.
Problems   Plants fail on heavy, wet soils that are slow to warm up in spring, so try growing them in raised beds which have better drainage.

FLOWERING

Season   Although the plants flower for only a brief spell the effect is long-lasting because of their "everlasting" nature.
Cutting   Ideal as cut, dried flower. For the best results cut off whole plants when most of the flowers are still just opening out, and hang upside down in a dry, airy place.

AFTER FLOWERING

General   Plants sometimes self-seed. Any plants not lifted for drying are pulled up in fall and added to the compost heap.

HELIPTERUM AT A GLANCE

A half-hardy annual grown for its pinkish, "papery" flowers that are good for cutting and drying. Frost hardy to 32°F (zone 10).

		Recommended Varieties
Jan	/	
Feb	/	**Helipterum hybrids:**
Mar	/	"Bonny"
Apr	sow	"Double Mixed"
May	sow/thin	"Goliath"
Jun	flowering	"Pierrot"
July	flowering	"Special Mixed"
Aug	flowers/cutting	
Sept	flowers/cutting	
Oct	/	
Nov	/	
Dec	/	

IBERIS
Candytuft

CANDYTUFT *is available in a wide range of colorful mixtures.*
Each 2in-wide "flower" is actually a mass of smaller flowers.

ALL SORTS OF COLORS *appear in varieties of* Iberis umbellata, *including white as seen here. The flowers have a sweet fragrance.*

FEATURES

Very decorative plants that grow no more than 12in tall, varieties of *Iberis umbellata,* a hardy annual, have sweet-scented flowers in white, pink, mauve, red, and purple. They produce good results even in poor soils and quickly self-seed so you get new plants springing up every year, which are at home growing in-between paving and in gravel drives. The best plants with the most flowers come from sowing in early spring.

CONDITIONS

Aspect
Site

Iberis prefers an open spot in full sun. Although it is happy in poor soil, adding rotted manure or compost before planting will help keep moisture in and reduce the need for extra watering during summer.

IBERIS AT A GLANCE

Iberis is a hardy annual grown for its heads of bright, scented flowers which are used in bedding. Frost hardy to 5°F (zone 7).

Jan	/	
Feb	/	
Mar	sow	
Apr	sow	
May	thin out	
Jun	flowering	
July	flowering	
Aug	flowering	
Sept	sow	
Oct	/	
Nov	/	
Dec	/	

Recommended Varieties

Iberis umbellata:
"Dwarf Fairy Mixed"
"Fantasia Mixed"
"Flash Mixed"
"Spangles"

GROWING METHOD

Sowing

Seed is sown outdoors in March/April where the plants are to flower. Mark out circular patches of ground with sand and make short parallel drills ½in deep inside the circle, spaced 6in apart. Sow the seeds thinly in these drills and cover with fine, raked soil. Seedlings appear in 2–3 weeks and should be thinned out so they are eventually 3–6in apart by early summer. Can also be sown in September for earlier flowers.

Feeding

Extra feeding is not necessary. Watering in early summer will stop plants flowering prematurely before they achieve a good size.

Problems

Being relatives of brassicas like cabbage, they can suffer from clubroot disease. Treatment is not worthwhile, but to continue to enjoy candytuft where clubroot is present, sow a pinch of seed in 3½in pots of multi-purpose compost in early spring and plant out clumps in early summer. Disease-free roots will support the plants and let them flower.

FLOWERING

Season
Cutting

Flowers will appear from early summer. Good cut flower. Flowers that are well-formed but not over-mature should last well if picked early in the day and immediately plunged into water to soak before arranging.

AFTER FLOWERING

General

Plants can be cut down after flowering, given a good soak with liquid feed, and they will usually produce a second "flush" of flowerheads several weeks later. Candytuft self-seeds very easily so leave a few plants to die away naturally and scatter their seeds. Seed can also be collected for sowing the following spring.

IMPATIENS
Busy lizzie

VIGOROUS AND LARGE-FLOWERED, "Accent Mixed" will carpet the ground in borders or fill containers in sun or shade.

NEW GUINEA busy lizzies can be successfully combined with smaller flowered varieties like this delightful "Mosaic Lilac."

FEATURES

Impatiens perform well in sun or shade and a huge range is available. Use in bedding, tubs, windowboxes, hanging baskets, and flower bags. As well as busy lizzies, there are also the larger "New Guinea" types (12in), and the "balsams," with bushy growth (10in). Busy lizzies grow from 6–12in tall and wide depending on variety. All impatiens are half-hardy annuals, and raising from seed requires some care. Widely available as young plants by mail order, they can also be bought ready-grown in spring. Flowers can be single or double in mixed or various colors.

IMPATIENS AT A GLANCE

A half-hardy annual grown for its flowers for bedding, containers, and hanging planters. Frost hardy to 32°F (zone 10).

Jan	/	Recommended Varieties
Feb	sow 🖐	**Busy lizzies:**
Mar	sow 🖐	"Accent Mixed"
Apr	grow on 🖐	"Bruno"
May	harden/plant 🖐	"Mosaic Rose"
Jun	flowering ✻	"Super Elfin Mixed"
July	flowering ✻	**New Guinea impatiens:**
Aug	flowering ✻	"Firelake Mixed"
Sept	flowering ✻	"Spectra"
Oct	flowering ✻	"Tango"
Nov	/	**Impatiens balsamifera:**
Dec	/	"Tom Thumb Mixed"

CONDITIONS

Aspect Will succeed in full sun or moderate shade.

Site Soil should have rotted manure or compost mixed in before planting, and should be well-drained. Avoid planting in windy spots. In containers and baskets use multipurpose compost with slow-release fertilizer added.

GROWING METHOD

Sowing In late February/March sow seeds onto a fine layer of vermiculite in 3½in pots of seed compost. Tap to settle but do not cover. Seal in a clear plastic bag or put in a heated propagator, in a bright place at 70–75°F. Seedlings appear in 2–3 weeks and are transplanted to cell trays when 1in tall. Grow on, then harden off and plant out after frosts, 6–12in apart.

Feeding Apply liquid feed weekly to beds or containers using a hand-held feeder.

Problems Damping off disease attacks seedlings. Use clean pots, fresh compost, and treat with a copper-based fungicide if seedlings collapse.

FLOWERING

Season Flowers appear on young plants before planting and then throughout summer. Take off dead flowers to keep new ones coming.

Cutting Not suitable as a cut flower.

AFTER FLOWERING

General Remove when plants are past their best.

IPOMOEA
Morning glory

"HEAVENLY BLUE" morning glory never looks better than when scrambling through a host plant like this apple.

FEATURES

Look under ipomoea or morning glory in seed catalogs to find varieties of this stunning climber. Most familiar is sky-blue flowered "Heavenly Blue," others are red, pink, white, mauve, chocolate, one is striped, and "Murasaki Jishi" is double-flowered. Average height is 10–12ft. Plants will climb fences and other plants. For patios grow 3–4 plants in a 12in pot up a wigwam of 5ft canes. A half-hardy annual with flowers mostly 3in across. Seeds are poisonous.

IPOMOEA AT A GLANCE

A half-hardy annual climber grown for its trumpet-shaped flowers that open in the morning. Frost hardy to 32°F (zone 10).

		Recommended Varieties
Jan	/	
Feb	/	Ipomoea hybrids:
Mar	/	"Cardinal"
Apr	sow	"Chocolate"
May	grow on	"Early Call Mixed"
Jun	plant	"Flying Saucers"
July	flowering	"Grandpa Otts"
Aug	flowering	"Heavenly Blue"
Sept	flowering	"Mini Sky-Blue"
Oct	/	"Murasaki Jishi"
Nov	/	"Platycodon Flowered White"
Dec	/	

CONDITIONS

Aspect Must have full sun all day.
Site Mix rotted compost with soil before planting. In containers use multipurpose compost with slow-release fertilizer added. All ipomoeas must have shelter from wind, and must have support for their twining stems.

GROWING METHOD

Sowing Soak the seeds in warm water the night before sowing, then sow one to a 3½in pot, 1in deep, in April. Keep in a temperature of at least 70°F and put in bright light when the big pink seedlings come up 1–2 weeks later. Keep warm and grow on, potting on into 5in pots when the roots fill the pot. Support shoots with short stakes. Gradually harden-off in late May, planting out or into containers in early June.

Feeding Feed monthly with a high-potash tomato food.
Problems Seedlings will turn yellow if they are kept too cold in the early stages. Red spider mite feeds on leaves—use a spray containing bifenthrin.

FLOWERING

Season Summer.
Cutting Unsuitable for cutting.

AFTER FLOWERING

General Use for composting when finished.

KOCHIA

Summer cypress

SUMMER CYPRESS is so-called because it resembles a dwarf conifer in color and shape. In early fall plants turn bright red.

KOCHIA MAKES a bold plant for the focus of a bedding display— seen here with pink nicotianas and silver-leaved senecio.

FEATURES

Summer cypress is a bushy half-hardy foliage annual that grows up to 3ft high with soft, light-green feathery foliage forming an upright cone- or dome-shape. "Trichophylla" has narrow leaves and looks similar to a dwarf conifer in summer, turning to a fiery bronze red in fall, hence its other common name of burning bush. Grow in groups of 2–3 or singly as the centerpiece of a bedding scheme.

KOCHIA AT A GLANCE

A half-hardy annual grown for its light-green leaves on bushy plants which turn red in fall. Frost hardy to 32°F (zone 10).

Jan	/	Recommended Varieties
Feb	sow 🖑	
Mar	sow 🖑	**Kochia scoparia:**
Apr	grow on 🖑	"Trichophylla"
May	harden off/plant 🖑	
Jun	leaves 🌿	**For all-green leaves**
July	leaves 🌿	"Evergreen"
Aug	leaves 🌿	
Sept	leaves 🌿	
Oct	leaves 🌿	
Nov	/	
Dec	/	

CONDITIONS

Aspect   Needs full sun to get the best leaf color.
Site   Grows on most soils but must be well-drained. Add manure/compost before planting.

GROWING METHOD

Sowing   Sow February/March on the surface of a 3½in pot of moist multipurpose compost but do not cover. Keep at 61°F in a bright spot, and expect seedlings in 2–3 weeks. When large enough, transplant to 3½in pots of multipurpose compost and grow on, hardening off in late May and planting outdoors after the last frosts. Space plants at least 2ft apart to allow room for development. They can also be planted in rows as a temporary and unusual summer "hedge."

Feeding   Water thoroughly in early summer for 2–3 weeks after planting. Extra feeding is not essential to get good results.

Problems   No particular problems.

FLOWERING

Season   Not grown for flowers but leaves.
Cutting   Unsuitable for cutting.

AFTER FLOWERING

General   Pull up and compost in fall.

LATHYRUS
Sweet pea

SWEET PEAS are perhaps the easiest and most rewarding of cut flowers you can grow. Choose a variety known for its fragrance.

CLIMBING VARIETIES of Lathyrus odoratus *make useful "living screens" in summer with the added benefits of color and scent.*

FEATURES

Varieties of *Lathyrus odoratus*, or sweet pea, occupy several pages in seed catalogs, but there are two basic groups—the tall climbers reaching 6–8ft, used as cut flowers and for screening, and dwarf "patio" varieties reaching up to 3ft which are used in bedding, baskets, and containers. Not all sweet peas have good scent, so check before buying seeds, and choose a fragrant mixed variety for a range of flower colors, which can be white, pink, red, mauve, orange, or blue, as well as many with picotee and other patterns. Sweet peas are easily-grown hardy annuals.

CONDITIONS

Aspect   Grow in full sun.

LATHYRUS AT A GLANCE

A hardy annual climber producing often strongly-scented flowers which are ideal for cutting. Frost hardy to 5°F (zone 7).

Jan	/	
Feb	/	
Mar	sow 🌱	
Apr	grow on 🌱	
May	plant 🌱	
Jun	flowering 🌸	
July	flowering 🌸	
Aug	flowering 🌸	
Sept	flowering 🌸	
Oct	sow 🌱	
Nov	/	
Dec	/	

Recommended Varieties

Lathyrus odoratus:
Tall, fragrant varieties
  "Bouquet Mixed"
  "Great Expectations"
  "Old Fashioned Mixed"
  "Old Spice Mixed"
Dwarf/patio varieties
  "Explorer"
  "Fantasia Mixed"
  "Jet-Set Mixed"
  "Knee-High"

SITE

Site   Needs well-drained soil packed with organic matter. Add compost or rotted manure the fall before sowing or planting. Climbing varieties need canes, bean netting, fences, or other supports to grow through. Use multipurpose compost for planting up baskets and patio containers.

GROWING METHOD

Sowing   Seeds can be sown individually in 3⅓in pots in February/March and germinated in a coldframe, cold porch, or even outdoors in a spot sheltered from rain. Nick or file the tough seed coat until a pale "spot" appears, then sow 1in-deep in soil-based seed compost. Pinch out the growing tips when plants are 3in tall to encourage sideshoots to grow. Grow outside, then plant out in May, 12in apart for climbers, and 6–12in apart for patio varieties used in baskets and containers.

Feeding   Plants benefit from a monthly feed with liquid tomato food. Water thoroughly in dry spells.

Problems   Mice will dig young seedlings up so set traps. Powdery mildew can attack leaves in the summer—use a spray containing sulfur.

FLOWERING

Season   Seed can also be sown in October, and plants overwintered for flowers from early summer. Spring-sown plants flower from June.

Cutting   Cut when the first few flowers on the stalk are opening and stand up to their necks in water.

AFTER FLOWERING

General   Cut off at ground level in fall so the nitrogen-rich roots rot down in the soil.

LAVATERA
Annual mallow

"SILVER CUP" is one of the most popular varieties of annual mallow, with rose-pink flowers up to 5in across.

IN MIXED BORDERS annual mallow can be sown direct into open patches of soil, for mounds of color from mid to late summer.

FEATURES

White, rose, pink, and red flowers with a silky sheen are characteristic of annual mallow. Plants grow between 2–4ft depending on variety, and bloom continuously from mid-June onward. Use them as the centerpiece in summer bedding schemes or grow in large blocks in annual borders. An easily-grown hardy annual that is also useful as a cut flower.

LAVATERA AT A GLANCE

A hardy annual grown for its large, colorful summer flowers on bushy plants 2–4ft tall. Frost hardy to 5°F (zone 7).

Month		Recommended Varieties
Jan	/	
Feb	/	
Mar	sow	*Lavatera trimestris:*
Apr	sow/thin out	"Beauty Mixed"
May	sow/thin out	"Dwarf White Cherub"
Jun	flowering	"Loveliness"
July	flowering	"Mont Blanc"
Aug	flowering	"Mont Rose"
Sept	flowering	"Parade Mixed"
Oct	/	"Pink Beauty"
Nov	/	"Ruby Regis"
Dec	/	"Silver Cup"

CONDITIONS

Aspect   Must have full sun all day.
Site   Lavatera needs good drainage but not rich soil —plants flower better if the ground is hungry, making them good plants for light sandy soils. They do well in seaside gardens.

GROWING METHOD

Sowing   Seed is sown outdoors March–May, and earlier sowings mean earlier flowers. Mark out circles 2ft or more across, then sow seed in short drills ½in deep. When seedlings appear thin them out gradually so they are 1–2ft apart by early summer. Growing this way creates a roughly circular block of color, which can be used as the centerpiece of a bedding scheme using annuals.
Feeding   Feeding is not necessary. Water thoroughly in early summer during long dry spells.
Problems   Sometimes killed suddenly by soil fungal diseases–grow in a new spot the next season.

FLOWERING

Season   Summer.
Cutting   Grow a few plants just for cut stems.

AFTER FLOWERING

General   Leave a few plants to self-seed, then pull up.

LIMNANTHES
Poached egg flower

POACHED EGG FLOWER has 1in-wide flowers like tiny eggs in early summer, and attractive, divided, fern-like leaves.

THE SEEDS OF LIMNANTHES go everywhere after flowering and seem to enjoy spreading along path edges in particular.

FEATURES

Limnanthes douglasii has cup-shaped white flowers with bright yellow centers, which explains its common name of poached egg flower. Plants grow to 6–9in in height and have a spreading habit. A hardy annual, it self-seeds very easily and keeps on coming. Grow in annual beds, along path edges and among other plants in borders.

LIMNANTHES AT A GLANCE

A hardy annual that quickly self-seeds, producing masses of yellow/white flowers in summer. Frost hardy to 5°F (zone 7).

Jan	/	Recommended Varieties
Feb	/	**Limnanthes douglasii**
Mar	sow 🖐	
Apr	sow/thin 🖐	
May	sow/thin 🖐	
Jun	flowering 🌼	
July	flowering 🌼	
Aug	/	
Sept	sow 🖐	
Oct	/	
Nov	/	
Dec	/	

CONDITIONS

Aspect Prefers full sun and an open situation.
Site Needs moisture-retentive soil with rotted organic matter mixed in well ahead of sowing.

GROWING METHOD

Sowing Spring or fall are the sowing times. Sow from March to May or in September. Either sow seed in short drills ½in deep or mark areas of soil, scatter the seed over the surface, and rake in. Seedlings appear after 1–2 weeks and should be thinned out so they are about 3–6in apart, although this is not too critical. If sowing in fall do not thin until spring in case of winter losses.
Feeding Feeding is not necessary, but water thoroughly in dry spells during early summer.
Problems No special problems.

FLOWERING

Season Overwintered plants flower from late spring depending on the weather, and are very attractive to bees and beneficial garden insects.
Cutting Not suitable for cutting.

AFTER FLOWERING

General Pull plants up as soon as they are over.

LIMONIUM
Statice

LONG AFTER *the small pale flowers have faded the colorful papery bracts are still going strong, and they keep their color when dried.*

"PURPLE MONARCH" *is a classic strain of statice for cutting and drying. It grows to 24in.*

FEATURES

Annual varieties of *Limonium sinuatum* grow up to 3ft tall and have peculiar winged stems. The actual flowers are small, but statice is grown for its papery bracts of purple, white, pink, apricot, yellow, rose, or blue, which persist all summer, and can be used as a cut and dried flower. A half-hardy annual that is used solely for cutting, or in the case of the short varieties as a bedding/container plant.

CONDITIONS

Aspect   Grow in full sun in an open position.

LIMONIUM AT A GLANCE

A half-hardy annual grown for its heads of brightly colored bracts used for bedding and drying. Frost hardy to 23°F (zone 9).

Jan	/	Recommended Varieties
Feb	sow	*Limonium sinuatum:*
Mar	sow/transplant	**Tall varieties**
Apr	grow on	"Art Shades Mixed"
May	grow on/harden	"Forever Mixed"
Jun	plant/grow	"Forever Moonlight"
July	flowering	"Sunburst Mixed"
Aug	flowers/cutting	"Sunset Mixed"
Sept	flowers/cutting	**Short varieties**
Oct	/	"Biedermeier Mixed"
Nov	/	"Petite Bouquet"
Dec	/	

Site   Must have very well-drained soil, and is quite happy in sandy, light soils that are on the "hungry" side. If growing dwarf varieties for containers use multipurpose compost. Statice does exceedingly well in seaside gardens.

GROWING METHOD

Sowing   Sow seed in February/March in a 3½in pot of multipurpose compost and keep at 64°F. Transplant to cell trays, grow on, then harden off in late May and plant after the last frosts 6–18in apart. If growing for cut flowers, seed can be sown outdoors in rows from early May, ½in deep and thinned to similar spacings.

Feeding   Does not need regular feeding, but water well if dry straight after planting out.

Problems   Plants may rot on heavy, wet soils, and powdery mildew can attack the leaves in late summer, but this is rarely serious.

FLOWERING

Season   Long flowering period throughout summer.

Cutting   Ideal cut flower. Can be used fresh, or cut and dried by hanging bunches upside down in a dry airy place. Cut when the flowerheads are showing maximum color. Dried flowers retain their color well over a long period.

AFTER FLOWERING

General   Pull plants up and compost when all the flowers have been cut or have gone over.

LINARIA
Toadflax

WHEN SOWN IN BOLD PATCHES varieties of Linaria maroccana *soon knit together to produce a tapestry of color if one of the mixtures such as "Fairy Bouquet" is grown. Clumps can also be carefully lifted and planted into patio pots in late spring and early summer.*

FEATURES

Linaria is commonly known as toadflax and has dainty little flowers like tiny snapdragons in a wide color range including white, cream, yellow, red, blue, and pink. Plants grow 9–24in and are good massed in drifts in annual borders, or used as fillers in mixed border plantings. Most annual toadflax are varieties of *Linaria maroccana*. A hardy annual that can be sown direct outdoors.

LINARIA AT A GLANCE

A hardy annual grown for its spikes of pretty flowers like small snapdragons appearing in summer. Frost hardy to 5°F (zone 7).

Jan	/	Recommended Varieties
Feb	/	
Mar	sow	*Linaria anticaria*
Apr	sow/thin out	
May	sow/thin out	*Linaria maroccana:*
Jun	thin/flowers	"Fairy Bouquet"
		"Fantasia Blue"
July	flowering	"Fantasia Mixed"
Aug	flowering	"Fantasia Pink"
Sept	flowering	"Northern Lights"
Oct	/	
Nov	/	*Linaria reticulata:*
Dec	/	"Crown Jewels"

CONDITIONS

Aspect Needs a warm, sunny spot.
Site Well-drained soil enriched with manure or compost ahead of planting is essential. Very good plants can be grown on light, sandy soils.

GROWING METHOD

Sowing Seeds are best sown in short drills ½in deep March–May. Mark the sowing areas with a ring of light-colored sand and label if sowing more than one annual in the same bed. The seedlings will appear in rows and can be told from nearby weed seedlings quite easily. Thin the seedlings out so they are finally 4–6in apart by early summer. Alternatively, leave them to grow as small clumps of 4–6 plants every 12in or so.
Feeding Feeding is rarely needed but water well after the final thinning if the soil is dry.
Problems No special problems.

FLOWERING

Season Flowers appear early to mid summer.
Cutting Not usually used for cutting.

AFTER FLOWERING

General Leave a few plants to die down and self-seed. Others can be pulled up and composted.

LOBELIA
Lobelia

LOBELIA FLOWERS *are tubular with a large lower "lip" divided into three rounded lobes. Dark flowers have pale throats.*

IN THIS HANGING BASKET lobelias mingle with begonias and brachyscome, and bright red nasturtiums creep up from below.

FEATURES

Choose the bushier "edging" varieties for bedding schemes and the "trailers" for hanging baskets, flower bags, and containers. Flower color ranges from white through pink, mauve and white to blue, and striking two-toned varieties like "Riviera Blue Splash" are also available. Edgers grow 4–6in tall, trailers up to 18in long when well-fed, and plants have a similar spread. Varieties of *Lobelia erinus* are available as single or mixed colors, and modern coated seed makes sowing much easier. A range of varieties are available as young plants by mail order. Half-hardy.

LOBELIA AT A GLANCE

A half-hardy annual used as an edging plant or a trailing plant for baskets, with many small flowers. Frost hardy to 32°F (zone 10).

Jan	sow	Recommended Varieties
Feb	sow/transplant	*Lobelia erinus:*
Mar	sow/transplant	**Edging varieties**
Apr	grow on	"Cambridge Blue"
May	harden off/plant	"Crystal Palace"
Jun	flowering	"Mrs Clibran Improved"
July	flowering	"Riviera Lilac"
Aug	flowering	**Trailing varieties**
Sept	flowering	"Cascade Mixed"
Oct	/	"Fountains Mixed"
Nov	/	"Regatta Mixed"
Dec	/	"String of Pearls Mixed"

CONDITIONS

Aspect Flowers best when grown in full sun.
Site Enrich soil with rotted compost or manure before planting. Drainage must be good, but lobelia must also have adequate moisture all through the season. For baskets and containers use multipurpose compost and add slow-release fertilizer granules before planting up.

GROWING METHOD

Sowing Sow January–March in a 3½in pot of multipurpose compost. Sow the tiny seeds evenly over the surface but do not cover, and put in a well-lit spot at 64°F. When the seedlings form a green "mat," carefully tease them apart into small clumps of 4–6, and transplant each clump to one unit of a multi-cell tray. Grow on, harden off in late May and plant after frosts.
Feeding Feed fortnightly with high-potash liquid feed, and never allow the plants to dry out.
Problems Trouble-free, but if seedlings keel over in spring water with copper-based fungicide.

FLOWERING

Season Flowers appear from June onward.
Cutting Not suitable for cutting.

AFTER FLOWERING

General Go over plants with shears when they look untidy and water with liquid feed—this encourages more flowers. Compost in fall.

LOBULARIA
Alyssum

ALYSSUM IS COMPACT and this makes it the ideal edging plant to fill in between other summer bedders. Flowers smell of honey.

"CARPET OF SNOW" is used here in a bed to create living lines and patterns around slightly taller plants like these violas.

FEATURES

Lobularia maritima, alyssum, has masses of tiny flowers in various colors in round heads; white, pink, lavender, and purple. All varieties smell sweetly of honey, although you need to get up close. None grow more than 6in high, making alyssum ideal as an edging plant, but it is also useful for planting in pots, troughs, and hanging baskets.

CONDITIONS

Aspect Grow alyssum in a spot receiving full sun.
Site Must have well-drained soil and adding rotted

LOBULARIA AT A GLANCE

A low-growing hardy annual for edging summer bedding schemes, with honey-scented flowers. Frost hardy to 5°F (zone 7).

Jan	/	Recommended Varieties
Feb	sow	
Mar	sow/transplant	*Lobularia maritima* :
Apr	sow/grow on	"Aphrodite"
May	sow/harden off	"Creamery"
Jun	flowering	"Easter Basket Mixed"
July	flowering	"Easter Bonnet"
Aug	flowering	"Golf Mixed"
Sept	flowering	"Golf Rose"
Oct	/	"Little Dorrit"
Nov	/	"Rosie O'Day"
Dec	/	"Snow Carpet"
		"Snow Crystals"

organic matter helps retain soil moisture. For baskets and patio containers plant using multipurpose potting compost.

GROWING METHOD

Sowing Alyssum grown for bedding and containers is best raised in early spring. Sow a whole packet of seeds in February/March in a 3½in pot of multipurpose compost, and just cover. When seedlings are ½in tall split up into small clumps of 4–6 seedlings and transplant each to individual units of a multi-cell tray. This is especially useful to get a good spread of different flower colors when growing a mixed variety. Grow on and harden off in late May before planting out. Seeds can also be sown direct into the soil in an annual border during April/May ½in deep.

Feeding Extra feeding is unnecessary.
Problems Look out for slugs—they will attack newly-planted alyssum, especially after rain.

FLOWERING

Season Flowers often appear before planting and until late summer—clip them over with shears and water well to encourage a second flush.
Cutting Not suitable as a cut flower.

AFTER FLOWERING

General Seeds will self-sow very easily, and come up the following spring. Compost when finished.

LUNARIA
Honesty

THE SEEDHEADS of Lunaria annua *are sought after for dried flower arrangements. Here they are still in the green stages of growth.*

"ALBA VARIEGATA" has leaves splashed with creamy-white and also white flowers. It adds easy and quick color to spring borders.

FEATURES

Honesty, *Lunaria annua*, a hardy biennial is also known as the money plant because of its large circular, smooth, silvery seedheads that resemble coins. It grows up to 3ft tall and is a plant that is best left to do its own thing, self-seeding very quickly, and thriving under dry hedges where most plants will not grow, and will seed into mixed borders. Flowers are purple or white and appear in early spring, and variegated varieties are available.

LUNARIA AT A GLANCE

A hardy biennial grown for its pretty purple/white flowers followed by large silvery seedheads. Frost hardy to 5°F (zone 7).

Jan	/	Recommended Varieties
Feb	/	
Mar	sow/flowers	*Lunaria annua:*
		"Fine Mixed"
Apr	thin/flowers	"Mixed"
May	thin/flowers	
Jun	flowering	**Variegated leaves**
July	/	"Variegata"
Aug	/	
Sept	/	**White flowers**
Oct	/	"Alba Variegata"
Nov	/	
Dec	/	

CONDITIONS

Aspect   Succeeds in sun or the shade cast by hedges and large shrubs.

Site   Thriving in poor soils, plants grow larger still if they are sown into soil that has been improved with rotted manure or compost, and produce the best seedheads for drying.

GROWING METHOD

Sowing   Mark out patches using sand and sow the large seeds 1in deep in short drills, with 2–3in between each seed in March. Seedlings are quick to appear and can be thinned or left to develop as they are. Next spring look out for seedlings and move them when small to where you want plants to grow.

Feeding   Needs no extra feeding or watering.

FLOWERING

Season   Flowers from early spring to early summer.

Cutting   Can be cut for flowers but some must be left to set seed if you want the large, silvery heads.

AFTER FLOWERING

General   Cut when the seedheads are mature and dry, on a warm day, and hang upside-down in a dry, airy place until you can carefully remove the outer skin of the pod. Leave a few plants to die down naturally and self-seed.

LUPINUS

Annual lupin

SHORTER AND SQUATTER than their perennial cousins, annual lupins can create a sea of color when sown in large drifts like this. As the flowers fade the spikes should be removed completely with pruning shears to divert energy into new flowers rather than seed pods.

FEATURES

By growing annual lupins from seed you can enjoy the features of their perennial relatives without giving up too much space in the yard. Annual lupins are smaller, growing between 1–3ft tall, but have very colorful spikes in mixed shades and also striking single colors such as the blue-flowered *Lupinus texensis*. Hardy annuals. Seeds and plants are poisonous if eaten.

LUPINUS AT A GLANCE

A hardy annual grown for its spikes of colorful and spicey-scented flowers during summer. Frost hardy to 5°F (zone 7).

Jan	/	Recommended Varieties
Feb	/	**Lupinus hybrids:**
Mar	/	"Biancaneve"
Apr	sow 🖐	"New White"
May	thin out 🖐	"Pink Javelin"
Jun	flowering 🌿	"Pixie Delight"
July	flowering 🌿	"Sunrise"
Aug	flowering 🌿	**Yellow flowers**
Sept	flowering 🌿	*Lupinus luteus*
Oct	/	**Blue flowers**
Nov	/	*Lupinus texensis*
Dec	/	*Lupinus varius*

CONDITIONS

Aspect   Needs full sun.
Site   Well-drained, light soil is best for annual lupins, but mix in rotted manure or compost.

GROWING METHOD

Sowing   The large seeds can go straight into the ground in April, but to ensure germination the tough seed coat must be nicked with a sharp knife or rubbed down with a file until the pale inside just shows. Next, soak the seeds on wet tissue paper and sow when they have swollen up, 3–6in apart and 2in deep, where you want plants to grow. Thin seedlings to 6in apart when well established. To grow in pots do the same, sowing one seed to a 3½in pot, then plant out.

Feeding   Lupins need no extra feeding.
Problems   Fat green lupin aphids can kill entire plants, so use a spray containing permethrin.

FLOWERING

Season   Flowers appear from midsummer.
Cutting   Cut when some buds at the base of the flower spike are fully open.

AFTER FLOWERING

General   Cut off to leave the nitrogen-rich roots to rot in the ground, and compost the tops.

MALCOLMIA
Virginian stock

PINK IS JUST one of the colors found in Virginian stocks. Expect reds, yellows, and whites from a variety like "Fine Mixed."

JUST FOUR WEEKS after sowing plants will be in flower. Malcolmia maritima *thrives in the thin light soils of seaside gardens.*

FEATURES

Keep a packet of Virginian stock, *Malcolmia maritima* seed to hand at all times and sow a pinch of seeds every two weeks in gaps and under windows—plants will flower just a month later. They grow 6–8in high with small, single, four-petalled, sweetly scented flowers in red, mauve, pink, yellow, and white from June–September. They can also be sown into patio tubs. Hardy annual.

MALCOLMIA AT A GLANCE

Hardy annual grown for its pink, red, yellow, or white flowers. Flowers a month after sowing. Frost hardy to 5°F (zone 7).

Month		Recommended Varieties
Jan	/	
Feb	/	
Mar	sow 🖐	*Malcolmia maritima:*
Apr	sow/flowers 🖐🌱	"Fine Mixed"
May	sow/flowers 🖐🌱	"Mixed"
Jun	sow/flowers 🖐🌱	
July	sow/flowers 🖐🌱	
Aug	sow/flowers 🖐🌱	
Sept	sow/flowers 🖐🌱	
Oct	sow 🖐	
Nov	/	
Dec	/	

CONDITIONS

Aspect	Prefers full sun but tolerates some shade.
Site	Will grow on most soils but needs good drainage to do well.

GROWING METHOD

Sowing	Seed can be scattered in small patches 12in across on the soil where you want flowers, and mixed in using your fingertips, or it is simply scattered along the cracks in paths and driveways, from March onward, and repeated every few weeks all through the summer. Mark sown areas in borders with a label or circle of light-colored sand. Seedlings soon come up and there is no need to bother with thinning. For early flowers the following spring sow in October.
Feeding	Not necessary.
Problems	Trouble-free.

FLOWERING

Season	Expect flowers all summer long with repeat sowings.
Cutting	Unsuitable as a cut flower.

AFTER FLOWERING

General	Pull up as soon as the plants are over, and resow. Self-sown seedlings soon appear.

MATTHIOLA
Brompton stock

WHEN BEDDED-OUT *in spring Brompton stocks provide an early splash of color and fill the air with scent on warm days.*

FLOWER COLOR *varies, and it should be possible to see the color in the flower buds before you plant, ensuring an even display.*

FEATURES

The sweetly scented flowers of Brompton stocks are held above the gray-green leaves on plants up to 18in tall. There is a full range of pastel colors with some stronger purples, crimson and magenta as well; the flowers are double. Derived from *Matthiola incana*, Brompton stocks are beautiful in massed spring plantings, giving off a delicious strong fragrance. They are grown as biennials.

CONDITIONS

Aspect Need full sun and a sheltered position.
Site Must have well-drained soil. Incorporate rotted manure or compost into the soil a few weeks before planting. Tall varieties will need short stakes to prevent their flowers flopping.

MATTHIOLA AT A GLANCE

A hardy biennial sown in summer for strongly-scented pink flowers the following spring. Frost hardy to 5°F (zone 7).

Jan	grow on 🖐	**Recommended Varieties**
Feb	plant 🖐	*Matthiola incana:*
Mar	plant 🖐	"Brompton Mixed"
Apr	flowering 🌸	"Brompton Dwarf Mixed"
May	flowering 🌸	"Spring Flowering Mixed"
Jun	sow 🖐	
July	sow/transplant 🖐	
Aug	transplant 🖐	
Sept	grow on 🖐	
Oct	grow on 🖐	
Nov	grow on 🖐	
Dec	grow on 🖐	

GROWING METHOD

Sowing June/July is the time to sow seed, in a 3½in pot of multipurpose compost. When the seedlings are large enough, transplant one seedling to a 3½in pot of multipurpose compost, water well and grow on. Later, pot on into 5in pots. When the first frosts arrive take the young plants into a coldframe, cold greenhouse or porch, standing them outside during mild spells all through the winter months. Keep on the dry side and only water when they wilt. Plant out from February onward when the soil is workable, or pot on into large pots and grow in a cool conservatory or porch with canes for support.

Feeding Do not feed until 2–3 weeks before planting out, then give a general purpose liquid feed.

Problems Cabbage butterflies will lay eggs on the young plants in late summer and the caterpillars can strip leaves, so use a spray containing permethrin, or pick them off by hand.

FLOWERING

Season Brompton stocks will fill beds and borders with color and scent during April and May, weather permitting. They perform best in calm, mild spells with plenty of sunshine. While most plants will have double flowers, there may be singles that can be put to one side, planted separately, and used for cutting.

Cutting A good cut flower. Scald stems after picking and change vase water every couple of days.

AFTER FLOWERING

General Dig plants up when the show is over and prepare the ground for summer bedding plants. Add to the compost heap/bin.

MIMULUS
Monkey flower

MONKEY FLOWERS have blooms that are face-like and marked with intricate patterns and spotting. They are good for shade.

PLANT MIMULUS along the edges of a path. Monkey flowers will bloom in just nine weeks.

FEATURES

Mimulus or monkey flower is grown as a half-hardy annual and is useful for summer bedding and containers, with bright flowers in a range of colors, mainly red and orange, on plants 12–18in tall and wide. It is very useful for growing in shaded and wet spots.

CONDITIONS

Aspect   Will grow in sun or shade.

MIMULUS AT A GLANCE

Grown as a half-hardy annual for bedding, windowboxes, and hanging baskets. Colorful flowers. Frost hardy to 5°F (zone 7).

Jan	/	Recommended Varieties
Feb	sow	**Mimulus hybrids:**
Mar	sow/transplant	"Calypso"
Apr	grow on	"Extra Choice Mixed"
May	grow on/harden	"Magic Ivory"
Jun	flowering	"Magic Pastels Mixed"
July	flowering	"Malibu"
Aug	flowering	"Malibu Orange"
Sept	flowering	"Malibu Sunshine"
Oct	/	"Queen's Prize Mixed"
Nov	/	"Sparkles"
Dec	/	"Viva"

Site   Needs moist soil so dig in plenty of rotted organic matter well-ahead of planting. Use a peat- or coir-based multipurpose compost for growing mimulus in containers. Add slow-release fertilizer granules when planting.

GROWING METHOD

Sowing   Sow in 3½in pots in February/March, barely covering the fine seed. Keep at 54°F in bright light and expect seedlings after about two weeks. When large enough transplant to cell trays and grow on until the end of May, then harden off and plant from mid-May onward, 6–12in apart, or in groups of 2–3 in troughs and pots.

Feeding   Feed monthly with liquid feed and ensure that containers never dry out or flowering will be reduced and plants damaged.

Problems   If slugs attack plants growing in shaded areas protect with slug pellets or scatter sharp grit to make a physical barrier. Container-grown plants suffer in excessive heat so move them to a position where they are out of midday sun.

FLOWERING

Season   Summer, from June onward.
Cutting   Not suitable for cutting.

AFTER FLOWERING

General   Pull up and compost when finished.

MOLUCCELLA
Bells of Ireland

THE FLOWERS OF Moluccella laevis *are actually small, pale, and found in the center of each of the showier bell-like bracts.*

MOLUCCELLA *is ideal for use in mixed borders to add a welcome touch of vivid green. Sow in patches 2ft across.*

FEATURES

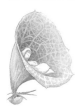

A half-hardy annual, also known as shell flower, moluccella is very lightly scented, and produces 2–3ft tall spikes in summer. It has small flowers surrounded by the more obvious and showy bell- or shell-like apple-green bracts. You can grow moluccella in flower beds and mixed borders, but its main value is as a cut flower, either fresh or dried. It is long-lasting when dried in late summer, the green spikes gradually fade from green to pale brown through fall and into winter.

CONDITIONS

Aspect   Needs an open spot in full sun.

MOLUCCELLA AT A GLANCE

A half-hardy annual grown for its tall spikes of green bracts that are used for drying. Frost hardy to 32°F (zone 10).

Jan	/	Recommended Varieties
Feb	sow 🖐	*Moluccella laevis*
Mar	sow 🖐	
Apr	transplant/grow 🖐	
May	plant/sow 🖐	
Jun	flowering 🌿	
July	flowering 🌿	
Aug	flowering 🌿	
Sept	flowers/cutting 🌿	
Oct	/	
Nov	/	
Dec	/	

Site   Must have good drainage, and working rotted manure or compost into the ground before sowing or planting helps. Avoid exposed, windy spots or the tall stems may be flattened.

GROWING METHOD

Sowing   Either sow seed in 3½in pots of multipurpose compost in February/March at 64°F, or sow directly in the soil where they are to grow in late April and May. Gradually thin out so plants are spaced 12–16in apart. Plants raised under cover are hardened off before being planted.

Feeding   If organic matter has already been added to the soil, extra feeding is not necessary, but keep plants well-watered during long dry spells.

Problems   Seeds can sometimes be slow and difficult to germinate, so put them in the bottom of a refrigerator for two weeks before you sow, to "chill" them, then sow in pots as described above and expect seedlings in 2–3 weeks.

FLOWERING

Season   Even after the actual flowers have faded the green bracts go on providing color and interest until they are cut for drying.

Cutting   Ideal as a cut flower, used fresh or dried. Cut when flowers are well-formed. Leaves can be removed to display the green bracts better. The stems dry to a light brown color.

AFTER FLOWERING

General   Remove roots when stems have been harvested, but leave a few behind to develop on the plant and finally shed seeds, which will self-sow.

MYOSOTIS

Forget-me-not

FORGET-ME-NOTS flower from early spring after growing slowly during the winter months. Flowers often have yellow "eyes."

"MONTE CARLO" early double tulips rising up through a haze of forget-me-nots is a springtime classic that is seldom bettered.

FEATURES

Forget-me-nots are useful spring bedding plants, producing swathes of pink, blue, or white flowers from April onward. They go well with bulbs like tulips which push up through the myosotis flowers. Grow as a hardy biennial and use shorter varieties such as "Blue Ball," reaching 6in, in winter and spring patio containers. None grow more than 12in tall, and these are the ideal choice for spring bedding displays. Available by mail order in fall as ready-grown young plants.

MYOSOTIS AT A GLANCE

A hardy biennial grown for its small flowers which appear in masses from early spring. Frost hardy to 5°F (zone 7).

		Recommended Varieties
Jan	/	
Feb	/	*Myosotis sylvatica:*
Mar	/	"Blue Ball"
Apr	flowering	"Carmine King"
May	flowers/sow	"Compindi"
Jun	sow	"Indigo"
July	grow on	"Light Blue"
Aug	grow on	"Music"
Sept	grow on	"Rosylva"
Oct	plant	"Royal Blue"
Nov	/	"Spring Symphony Mxd"
Dec	/	"Victoria Mixed"

CONDITIONS

Aspect — Full or dappled sunlight is suitable.

Site — Responds well to soil with plenty of rotted compost or manure mixed in that holds plenty of moisture. When planting containers in fall ensure good drainage and use a multipurpose compost.

GROWING METHOD

Sowing — Seed is sown direct into the ground May–July, in drills ½in deep. Thin seedlings as they develop so plants are eventually 3–6in apart, keep weed free and water copiously in dry spells. Plant into their flowering positions/containers in October and water to settle in.

Feeding — Do not feed after planting in fall, but scatter a general granular fertilizer around plants in spring as they show signs of growth.

Problems — Powdery mildew can affect leaves but this is generally not worth treating.

FLOWERING

Season — From late winter to early summer.

Cutting — Not suitable for cutting.

AFTER FLOWERING

General — Remove plants to make way for summer bedding, but if you leave a few to die down they will self-sow into the soil.

NEMESIA
Nemesia

THE TWO-LIPPED FLOWERS *of nemesias come in an array of colors and they all have patterns deep in the flower's "throat."*

NEMESIAS CARRY THEIR *flowers in large, almost flat heads with individual flowers pointing off in all directions.*

FEATURES

No varieties of *Nemesia strumosa* grow more than 12in high making them ideal for beds and containers. Grown as a half-hardy annual, flowers can be single colors or bright and varied mixtures. Good as edging for troughs and windowboxes. Very easy to grow.

CONDITIONS

Aspect   Must have full sun to grow successfully.

NEMESIA AT A GLANCE

A half-hardy annual grown for its pretty lipped flowers, used for bedding and patio containers. Frost hardy to 32°F (zone 10).

		Recommended Varieties
Jan	/	
Feb	/	*Nemesia strumosa:*
Mar	sow	**Mixed colors**
Apr	sow/transplant	"Carnival Mixed"
May	harden off/plant	"Pastel Mixed"
Jun	flowering	"Sparklers"
July	flowering	"Tapestry"
Aug	flowering	**Single colors**
Sept	flowering	"Blue Gem"
Oct	/	"Fire King"
Nov	/	"KLM"
Dec	/	"National Ensign"

Site   In containers use multipurpose compost with slow-release fertilizer mixed well in. Soil with plenty of organic matter dug in well-ahead of planting gives good results, and must be well-drained.

GROWING METHOD

Sowing   Raise plants by sowing in small pots of soil-based seed compost starting in March/April (and repeating every few weeks for a succession of flowers), just covering the seeds. Keep at 60°F in a light place, and transplant to cell trays when seedlings are large enough to handle. Grow on and harden off in late May before planting after the last frosts, 6–12in apart. In containers make sure they are not swamped.

Feeding   Give a liquid feed to plants grown as bedding every two weeks, with a hand-held feeder. Regular watering in dry spells is vital.

Problems   Plants may rot off in heavy, wet soils.

FLOWERING

Season   For more flowerheads, pinch out growing tips of plants when they are 4in high.

Cutting   Not suited to cutting.

AFTER FLOWERING

General   Pull plants up when finished—this is quite often as they have a short flowering period.

NEMOPHILA

Baby blue eyes

NEMOPHILA MENZIESII flowers are a brilliant sky-blue with a distinctive paler "eye," carried over bright green feathery leaves.

NEMOPHILA can be grown with other hardy annuals such as limnanthes, the poached egg flower, for a striking color combination.

FEATURES

Nemophila is an easy annual sown in fall or spring. Flowers are sky-blue, white, or black/white. Plants grow to 8in high, with feathery leaves and a carpeting habit. Use them in borders, on rockeries, and around the edge of containers and windowboxes.

CONDITIONS

Aspect   Needs full sun or part shade to succeed.

NEMOPHILA AT A GLANCE

A hardy spreading annual grown for its flowers for beds, rockeries and container edges. Frost hardy to 5°F (zone 7).

Jan	/	Recommended Varieties
Feb	/	*Nemophila menziesii:*
Mar	/	(Also listed as *N. insignis*)
Apr	sow 🖐	"Baby Blue Eyes"
May	flowers/sow 🌱🖐	"Penny Black"
Jun	flowering 🌱	"Snowstorm"
July	flowering 🌱	
Aug	flowering 🌱	*Nemophila maculata:*
Sept	flowers/sow 🌱🖐	"Five Spot"
Oct	/	
Nov	/	
Dec	/	

Site   Needs well-drained soil, but mix in well-rotted organic matter before sowing to retain moisture. Nemophila will thrive in most multipurpose composts used in containers.

GROWING METHOD

Sowing   Sow seeds straight into the soil in fall or spring, in drills ½in deep. Seeds sown in fall will produce young plants that survive the winter and flower earlier. Gradually thin plants out so they are 3–6in apart as flowers appear.

Feeding   On well-prepared soil feeding is unnecessary, although large beds can be fed monthly with a general liquid feed applied through a hand-held feeder. Keep plants watered in dry spells or they may quickly die off.

Problems   Aphids can attack the soft leaves, so use a spray containing permethrin.

FLOWERING

Season   On fall-sown plants flowers appear from early spring to the first frosts, but appear slightly later on spring-sown plants.

Cutting   Not suitable for use as a cut flower.

AFTER FLOWERING

General   Leave plants to set seed and die back before removing—nemophila self-seeds and plants will appear on their own each spring.

NICOTIANA
Tobacco plant

"DOMINO SALMON PINK" is a popular variety of nicotiana because of its striking color and sheer flower power. Here in a bedding display it covers the ground and produces tubular, salmon-pink flowers non-stop through the summer. It is also useful for containers.

FEATURES

Not grown for tobacco but for their tubular flowers. Choose from dwarf modern varieties growing 1ft tall with upward-facing flowers, for bedding and containers, to *Nicotiana sylvestris* at 5ft for large borders—plant it behind other plants and especially against a dark evergreen background so that the large leaves as well as the flowers are shown off to best effect. Some release scent in the evening, so plant near doors and windows, or grow a few in large tubs that can be moved into the house or conservatory on a warm summer evening. Flowers can be pink to lime-green. A half-hardy annual. Widely available as young plants in a good selection of varieties.

NICOTIANA AT A GLANCE

A half-hardy annual grown for it colorful and often scented flowers, used in bedding/containers. Frost hardy to 32°F (zone 10).

		Recommended Varieties
Jan	/	
Feb	/	*Nicotiana sanderae:*
Mar	sow	"Domino Mixed"
Apr	transplant/grow on	"Domino Salmon Pink"
May	harden off/plant	"Havana Appleblossom"
		"Hippy Mixed"
Jun	flowering	"Lime Green"
July	flowering	"Merlin Peach"
Aug	flowering	
Sept	flowering	*Nicotiana langsdorfii*
Oct	/	
Nov	/	*Nicotiana sylvestris*
Dec	/	

CONDITIONS

Aspect Full sun or light shade. The flowers stay open longer in sun.

Site Grow in well-drained, moisture-retentive soil with rotted manure/compost mixed in. For container growing use multipurpose compost.

GROWING METHOD

Sowing Use 3½in diameter pots of multipurpose compost, sow the fine seed on the surface in March, but do not cover, and keep in a light place at 70°F. Tiny seedlings emerge within three weeks. Transplant to cell trays of multipurpose compost or into 3½in diameter pots when each young plant has developed 3–4 small leaves. Grow on and harden off in late May, then plant after the last frosts in your area, 12–18in apart depending on the variety grown.

Feeding Liquid feed weekly outdoors. Add slow-release fertilizer granules to container compost before planting.

Problems Use a spray containing pirimicarb for aphids. Destroy plants attacked by virus, showing any puckered and mottled leaves

FLOWERING

Season Flowers all summer. Nip off dead flowers.

Cutting Not suitable.

AFTER FLOWERING

General Remove plants after first frosts. It is possible to collect seed from *Nicotiana sylvestris* that can then be sown the following spring.

NIGELLA
Love-in-a-mist

"MISS JEKYLL" with semi-double blue flowers is a reliable variety of Nigella damascena. *Each flower has a feathery "collar."*

AFTER THE FLOWERS come the curiously attractive seedheads that give the plant its other common name, devil-in-a-bush.

FEATURES

Love-in-a-mist has fine, feathery leaves, with a fringe of foliage surrounding and slightly veiling each of the flowers, hence its common name. When the spiky seed pods appear it is also called devil-in-a-bush. Flowers are blue, pale and deep pink, white, or purple. Nigella grows 18in tall and is good for big drifts in beds or for cutting. Hardy annual. The variety "Transformer" has novel seed pods.

CONDITIONS

Aspect   Give it a sunny spot in an open position.

NIGELLA AT A GLANCE

A hardy annual grown for its flowers and its attractive, inflated seed pods which can be dried. Frost hardy to 5°F (zone 7).

Month		Recommended Varieties
Jan	/	
Feb	/	*Nigella damascena:*
Mar	sow	"Dwarf Moody Blue"
Apr	flowers/thin	"Miss Jekyll"
May	flowering	"Miss Jekyll Alba"
Jun	flowering	"Mulberry Rose"
July	flowering	"Oxford Blue"
Aug	flowering	"Persian Jewels"
Sept	flowers/sow	"Shorty Blue"
Oct	/	
Nov	/	*Nigella orientalis:*
Dec	/	"Transformer"

Site

Needs good drainage but isn't too fussy about soils—rotted organic matter may be dug in ahead of planting, but this is not essential, and good results can be had on quite thin, poor soils as long as it is grown in full sun.

GROWING METHOD

Sowing   Sow in March or September, in short drills ½in deep. Thin plants as they grow so there is about 6–8in between them as they begin to produce flower buds. Leave thinning of fall-sown plants until spring in case there are winter losses. Plants can also be raised in cell trays, sowing 2–3 seeds per tray and removing all but the strongest seedling—nigella does not like disturbance.

Feeding   Does not need extra feeding during summer.
Problems   Plants are trouble free.

FLOWERING

Season   Fall-sown plants flower from late spring, spring-sown from early summer.
Cutting   Delightful cut flower. Remove foliage from lower part of stalk to prolong flower life.

AFTER FLOWERING

General   The inflated seed pods that form are useful in dried flower arrangements. Pick stems after pods have dried on the plant and hang upside-down in a warm, airy place. Nigella self-seeds prolifically and will produce masses of seedlings the following spring. Dead plants can be pulled up and composted.

OSTEOSPERMUM
Osteospermum

OSTEOSPERMUM flowers are at their best in full sun in an open situation.

CREATE A CARPET OF OSTEOSPERMUM BEDDING in early summer that will continue to flower in flushes until the first frosts. Remember to propagate fresh plants each year.

FEATURES

Many varieties of osteospermum can be bought in spring as young plants, but others can be grown from seed and treated as half-hardy annuals. Growing from seed is a cost-effective way of raising large numbers of plants quickly. Favorite plants can be potted-up in fall and kept in a well-lit frost-free place over winter, then increased by cuttings in spring. In mild areas plants will often survive the winter outdoors and carry on producing a few flowers except in severe spells. In some catalogs it is listed as dimorphotheca. Plants can grow 12–30in tall.

CONDITIONS

Aspect   Must have full, baking sun for best results.

OSTEOSPERMUM AT A GLANCE

A hardy/half-hardy annual grown for its brightly-colored daisy-like flowers that appear all summer. Frost hardy to 23°F (zone 9).

Jan	/	Recommended Varieties
Feb	/	**Osteospermum hybrids:**
Mar	sow	"Gaiety"
Apr	sow/transplant	"Giant Mixed"
May	harden off/plant	"Glistening White"
Jun	flowering	"Ink Spot"
July	flowering	"Potpourri"
Aug	flowering	"Salmon Queen"
Sept	flowering	"Starshine"
Oct	flowering	"Tetra Pole Star"
Nov	/	
Dec	/	

Site   Is not fussy about soil but it must be very well-drained. A sheltered spot with the sun beating down all day is ideal. Plants also perform well in containers and these should be sited in full sun facing south if possible. Use multipurpose compost.

GROWING METHOD

Sowing   March/April is the time to sow, sowing seed thinly in 3½in diameter pots of soil-based seed compost, and just covering. Germinate at 64°F in a bright spot. Seedlings are transplanted to cell trays or individual 3½in pots when large enough to handle. Harden off for two weeks and start planting from mid-May onward.

Feeding   Water well to establish and then water only in long spells of hot, dry weather. Extra feeding is unnecessary, but container-grown plants will benefit from occasional liquid feeds given for the benefit of other plants.

Problems   Aphids can attack the leaves, flower stalks and buds so choose a spray containing permethrin and wet both sides of the leaves.

FLOWERING

Season   Flowers appear from early summer onward with a peak later on when temperatures reach their highest.

Cutting   Flowers are unsuitable for cutting.

AFTER FLOWERING

General   After the main flowering give plants an overall clipping to tidy them up and maintain compact growth. Lift and pot favorite plants and keep frost-free over winter.

PAPAVER NUDICAULE
Iceland poppy

ICELAND POPPY has petals with the texture of crepe paper and a velvety sheen. The center of the flower is a mass of yellow stamens.

THEIR TALL STEMS mean the flowers of Papaver nudicaule waft gently in the breeze, and look good like this, massed in bedding.

FEATURES

Varieties of *Papaver nudicaule* are available in a wide range of colors and range from 10–30in tall depending on variety. They can be treated as either half-hardy annuals or hardy biennials sown in summer or fall. Tall varieties are used for cutting. Plants sown early flower from April onward.

CONDITIONS

Aspect Can be grown in cool and warm areas.
Site Poppies need well-drained but moisture-retentive soil with plenty of rotted organic matter added ahead of planting or sowing.

GROWING METHOD

Sowing Sow seed outdoors April-June or in September. Scatter the seed thinly along shallow drills ½in deep, and rake over with fine soil. Thin out when seedlings are 2in high, so that the spacing is ultimately at about 6–12in intervals by October. Do not disturb the fine roots when thinning out, and always water when finished to settle plants back in. Thin fall-sown poppies in spring in case of winter losses. For earlier flowers sow in pots at 60°F in February and grow in cell-trays, planting in late May.
Feeding Extra feeding not needed.
Problems Fall-sown plants may rot off in heavy soils, so sow in cell trays and keep dry in a coldframe over winter, planting out in spring.

FLOWERING

Season Flowers appear during early summer and should be picked off as they fade.
Cutting Excellent cut flower. Pick when buds are just opening. Singe stem ends before arranging.

AFTER FLOWERING

General Leave a few plants to self-seed, but otherwise pull up after the flowers are finished.

PAPAVER AT A GLANCE

A hardy biennial (or half-hardy annual) grown for its large showy flowers that appear in summer. Frost hardy to 5°F (zone 7).

Month		Recommended Varieties
Jan	/	
Feb	/	*Papaver nudicaule:*
Mar	/	**Biennials**
Apr	sow	"Large Flowered Special Mixture"
May	flowers/sow	"Meadow Pastels"
Jun	flowers/sow	"Red Sails"
July	flowering	"Wonderland Mixed"
Aug	flowering	
Sept	flowers/sow	**Half-hardy annuals**
Oct	plant	"Summer Breeze"
Nov	/	
Dec	/	

PAPAVER RHOEAS
Shirley poppy

THE UNOPENED BUDS of Shirley poppies gradually rise up from among the leaves before bursting open as the petals unfurl.

WHEN ALLOWED TO self-seed, poppies will come up among other plants. Unwanted plants are very easily pulled out.

FEATURES

Shirley poppies, varieties of *Papaver rhoeas*, generally grow to about 2ft high, have a very delicate appearance, and come in a wide range of colors including pastels. There are single or double varieties and they look effective in large drifts, but can also be sown in patches 1–2ft across and used as fillers in mixed borders. Each flower can be 3in across. A hardy annual.

PAPAVER AT A GLANCE

Shirley poppies are hardy annuals sown in spring or fall and grown for their large flowers. Frost hardy to 5°F (zone 7).

		Recommended Varieties
Jan	/	
Feb	/	*Papaver rhoeas:*
Mar	sow	"Angels Choir Mixed"
Apr	sow/thin	"Angel Wings Mixed"
May	flowers/sow	"Mother of Pearl"
Jun	flowering	"Selected Single Mixed"
July	flowering	"Shirley Double Mixed"
Aug	flowering	"Shirley Single Mixed"
Sept	flowers/sow	
Oct	/	
Nov	/	
Dec	/	

CONDITIONS

Aspect Avoid any shade and grow in full sun.
Site Must have very well-drained soil. Rotted compost or manure should be added to the soil a few weeks before sowing.

GROWING METHOD

Sowing The fine seed can either be scattered on the soil and simply raked in, and the area marked with a circle of sand, or it can be sown in short ½in deep drills. March–May and September are the sowing times. Gradually thin out the seedlings until they are 12in apart, but avoid transplanting as they dislike disturbance. If sowing in fall leave thinning until the following spring in case of winter losses.
Feeding Extra summer feeding is not required, but water thoroughly should plants start to wilt.
Problems Trouble-free.

FLOWERING

Season Fall-sown plants flower from late spring onward, while spring-sown flower in summer.
Cutting Suitable as a cut flower if stems are scalded before arranging.

AFTER FLOWERING

General Leave a few plants to die down and self-seed.

PELARGONIUM

Bedding geranium

DARK ZONED LEAVES and an enticing range of single and two-tone flower colors are characteristic of "Avanti Mixed."

YOU MAY BE SURPRISED to see an ivy-leaved geranium as good as "Summertime Lilac" coming true from seed.

FEATURES

Better known as geraniums, seed-raised pelargoniums are available with large bright flowerheads for bedding, and also as trailing "ivy-leaved" types. Seeds are sown January/February and need warmth to succeed, so consider buying them as young plants delivered ready-grown in spring. Varieties for bedding and patio containers grow no more than 1ft, while ivy-leaved types can spread and trail up to 2ft. Flowers may be single colors or mixtures—the new "ripple" varieties are eye-catching. Plant 1–2ft apart. All are half-hardy annuals.

PELARGONIUM AT A GLANCE

Half-hardy annuals grown for their flowers and also the attractive ivy-like foliage of some varieties. Frost hardy to 32°F (zone 10).

Jan	sow	Recommended Varieties
Feb	sow	**Pelargonium hybrids:**
Mar	transplant	**For bedding**
Apr	pot on	"Avanti Mixed"
May	harden off/plant	"Raspberry Ripple"
Jun	flowering	"Ripple Mixed"
July	flowering	"Sensation Mixed"
Aug	flowering	"Stardust Mixed"
Sept	flowering	"Video Mixed"
Oct	/	**Ivy-leaved varieties**
Nov	/	"Summertime Lilac"
Dec	/	"Summer Showers"

CONDITIONS

Aspect   Must be grown in full sun.

Site   Well-prepared soil with rotted compost or manure mixed in gives best results. Soil must be well-drained, and when planting up containers use multipurpose compost with slow-release fertilizer mixed in. Bedding geraniums do well in terracotta containers.

GROWING METHOD

Sowing   Sow January/February in a heated propagator in a guaranteed temperature of 64°F. Seedlings appear in 2–3 weeks and can be transplanted to 3in pots or cell trays of multipurpose compost. Plants must have good light and a temperature of 61–64°F to grow well. Pot on into 4–5in diameter pots, harden off in late May, and plant out after the last frosts.

Feeding   Liquid feed bedding plants every 2–3 weeks.

Problems   Heavy wet soils can lead to rotting of the stems, so grow in containers. Snap off faded flowerheads to avoid gray mold.

FLOWERING

Season   Flowers appear from early summer onward.

Cutting   Not suitable.

AFTER FLOWERING

General   Pull up and compost. Favorite plants can be kept dry and frost-free over winter.

PETUNIA
Petunia

"FANTASY MIXED" is the latest in a new range of "milliflora" petunias with 1in flowers, ideal for containers and baskets.

MULTIFLORA PETUNIAS such as "Summer Morn Mixed" have 2in flowers and are suited to large patio tubs and bedding.

FEATURES

Petunias come in a wide range of different types depending on whether they are raised from seed or bought as young plants. Most petunias are perennials grown as half-hardy annuals. Seed-raised varieties fall into the following groups: Millifloras—small flowers 1in across on compact mounds, for containers and hanging baskets; Multifloras—plenty of 2in-wide flowers on bushy plants. For bedding and patio containers, with good weather resistance; Floribundas—intermediate in size between multifloras and grandifloras with 3in flowers; Grandifloras—large trumpet-like 5in flowers that can bruise in heavy rain and are best for containers in a sheltered position. These all grow 9–12in tall and can spread up to 2ft, and are also available as double-flowered varieties. Plant 9–12in apart. Flower color varies from single shades to striped, picotee, and other variations. Many seed-raised varieties are also widely available as young plants. An increasing number of petunias are only available as young plants, setting no seed. These are suited to container growing, and include many large double-flowered "patio" varieties such as "Able Mabel" and the vigorous Surfinias which can trail to 4–5ft—see page 194.

PETUNIA AT A GLANCE

A half-hardy annual grown for all-round use in summer bedding, hanging baskets and containers. Frost hardy to 5°F (zone 7).

Jan	sow	
Feb	sow	
Mar	sow/transplant	
Apr	pot on/grow on	
May	harden off/plant	
Jun	flowering	
July	flowering	
Aug	flowering	
Sept	flowering	
Oct	/	
Nov	/	
Dec	/	

Recommended Varieties

Petunia hybrida:

Millifloras
　"Fantasy Mixed"
Multifloras
　"Celebrity Bunting"
　"Summer Morn Mixed"
Floribundas
　"Mirage Mixed"
　"Niagara Mixture"
Grandifloras
　"Daddy Mixed"
　"Lavender Storm"

CONDITIONS

Aspect	Choose a sunny, south-facing situation for petunias in beds and containers.
Site	Avoid spots exposed to wind (which damages the flowers). Light, free-draining soil with rotted compost/manure mixed in is best.

PETUNIA "ABLE MABEL" is the first of a revolutionary new type of double-flowered "patio" petunia available only as young plants.

In containers use multipurpose compost.

GROWING METHOD

Sowing   Sowing can take place January–March where a temperature of 70°F is possible. Sow onto the level surface of a 3½in pot of multipurpose compost, but do not cover seeds, and keep in the light. Seedlings will appear inside two weeks, and should be transplanted to cell trays of multipurpose compost when large enough. Pot on into 3½in diameter pots, grow-on and harden off before planting out in early June.

Feeding   Give a weekly liquid feed with a high-potash fertilizer to encourage flowers. Mix slow-release fertilizer granules with container compost.

Problems   Slugs eat leaves in wet weather–use pellets or slug traps. Plants with mottled, crinkled leaves affected by virus should be destroyed.

FLOWERING

Season   Flowers appear all summer. Pick off dead flowers regularly.

Cutting   Not suitable.

AFTER FLOWERING

General   Remove when flowers end.

FOR A TOUCH OF the patriotic, "Celebrity Bunting" is a stunning multiflora variety with blend of red, white, and blue flowers.

PHLOX
Annual phlox

"TWINKLE MIXED" is a striking variety of annual phlox growing about 6in tall with star-like flowers in various shades.

THE FLOWERS OF annual phlox open at their peak to make rounded heads of color that can completely fill summer containers.

FEATURES

Annual phlox are versatile plants that can be used for bedding, containers, and as unique cut flowers. They are half-hardy annuals, growing between 4–18in tall depending on the variety –taller are better for cutting. Flower color ranges from the blue of "Bobby Sox" to the varied shades of "Tapestry" which is also scented. Several varieties are now available as young plants by mail order. Flowers are long-lived and plants are easy to care for.

PHLOX AT A GLANCE

A half-hardy annual grown for its heads of colorful flowers, for bedding, containers, and for cutting. Frost hardy to 23°F (zone 9).

		Recommended Varieties
Jan	/	
Feb	sow	*Phlox drummondii:*
Mar	sow/transplant	"African Sunset"
Apr	grow on	"Bobby Sox"
May	harden off/plant	"Bright Eyes"
Jun	flowering	"Brilliant"
July	flowering	"Cecily Old & New Shades"
Aug	flowering	"Double Chanel"
Sept	flowering	"Phlox of Sheep"
Oct	/	"Tapestry"
Nov	/	"Tutti-Frutti"
Dec	/	"Twinkle Mixed"

CONDITIONS

Aspect Needs full sun.
Site Needs well-drained soil with manure or compost mixed in to improve moisture holding. Phlox grow well in multipurpose compost used to fill summer containers.

GROWING METHOD

Sowing Sow seed in February/March in 3½in pots of multipurpose compost, keep at 64°F, and expect seedlings in 1–3 weeks. Transplant to cell trays or 3½in pots, pinch out the tips when 3in high, and grow on until late May, then harden off and plant after the last frosts in your area.

Feeding Add slow-release fertilizer granules to compost before planting containers, which should be sufficient. Plants in beds can be given a liquid feed every 2–3 weeks in summer.

Problems Plants will struggle on heavy soils in a cold spring so delay planting until warmer weather.

FLOWERING

Season Flowers appear all summer until frosts.
Cutting Tall varieties are good for cutting and some like "Tapestry" have a strong, sweet scent.

AFTER FLOWERING

General Pull up after flowering and compost them.

PORTULACA

Sun plant

DOUBLE-FLOWERED *mixed varieties of portulaca come in a wide range of colors, but attractive single colors are also available.*

SUN PLANTS *can survive the winter in mild seaside gardens, and thrive in the well-drained soil of rockeries.*

FEATURES

Commonly known as sun plant, portulaca grows 6in high with a spreading habit and succulent leaves. The 2in flowers open in sun, although modern varieties open even on dull days. It thrives in poor, dry soils and is easily ruined by too much coddling. A half-hardy annual, for beds, pots, and rockeries.

CONDITIONS

Aspect   A hot, sunny position gives the best plants.

PORTULACA AT A GLANCE

Portulaca is a half-hardy annual grown for summer flowers, and gives good results even on thin soils. Frost hardy to 32°F (zone 10).

		Recommended Varieties
Jan	/	
Feb	/	*Portulaca grandiflora:*
Mar	sow	"Cloudbeater Mixed"
Apr	sow	"Double Mixed"
May	harden off/plant	"Kariba Mixed"
Jun	flowering	"Patio Gems"
July	flowering	"Sundance"
Aug	flowering	"Sundial Mango"
Sept	flowering	"Sundial Mixed"
Oct	/	"Sundial Peppermint"
Nov	/	"Swanlake"
Dec	/	

Site   Unless soil is very well-drained plants are prone to rotting. Otherwise plants grow and flower well even where the soil is quite poor—particularly in seaside gardens—as they are adapted to live on little water. Grow them on their own in patio containers, using soil-based potting compost mixed fifty-fifty with sharp grit. Do not feed, and water only when plants start to wilt. Place pots in blazing sunshine.

GROWING METHOD

Sowing   Sow seeds in March/April in 3½in pots of soil-based seed compost and germinate at 64°F in good light. Keep the seedlings on the dry side and transplant to cell trays of soil-based compost with grit added. Grow on, harden off in late May, and plant after frosts, watering in well, then only when plants wilt.

Feeding   Feeding portulaca is not necessary.

Problems   Seedlings will "damp off" if the compost is kept too wet. If they do fall over, water the pots lightly with a copper-based fungicide.

FLOWERING

Season   Flowers appear throughout summer and into early fall.

Cutting   Not suitable.

AFTER FLOWERING

General   Pull plants up after the first fall frosts and add their fleshy remains to the compost heap.

PRIMULA
Polyanthus

NOT AN F1 HYBRID STRAIN, but "Giant Superb Mixed" polyanthus are tough, large-flowered, and full of character.

F1 "CRESCENDO MIXED" exhibit the clearer, more uniform colors of a highly bred strain, but seed is more expensive.

FEATURES

Polyanthus, a hybrid type of primula, is perfect in patio pots or mass-planted in the garden for a stunning spring display. Its very brightly-colored flowers up to 2in across, on stems 6–12in tall, rise from neat clumps of bright green, crinkled leaves. A hardy perennial, it is grown as a hardy biennial for spring bedding and containers. Widely available as young plants.

CONDITIONS

Aspect Grows in full sun or light shade under trees.
Site Needs well-drained soil but with plenty of

organic matter mixed in to help retain moisture—plants do not like to be bone dry at any stage while growing. For containers use multipurpose compost with gravel or chunks of styrofoam put in the base.

GROWING METHOD

Sowing Polyanthus seed can be tricky to germinate, and the most important rule is not to keep it too warm. Sow in 3½in pots of peat-based seed compost from March–July, barely cover, then stand outside in a covered, shaded spot out of the sun. Seedlings will appear 2–3 weeks later. Transplant to cell trays or 3½in pots of peat-based potting compost, and pot on into 5in pots when roots are well-developed. Grow during the summer in a shaded spot and do not let them dry out. Plant out in October where flowers are required the following spring, in beds or containers with bulbs and other plants.
Feeding Feed fortnightly with liquid feed in summer.
Problems Slugs can devour leaves so use slug pellets. Never bury the crowns or plants may rot.

FLOWERING

Season Flowers appear earlier in mild winters and carry on throughout spring.
Cutting Charming in spring posies.

AFTER FLOWERING

General Polyanthus taken from spring displays can be planted in borders where they will form large clumps and flower regularly every spring.

PRIMULA AT A GLANCE

A hardy biennial grown for its bright spring flowers for use in bedding and containers. Frost hardy to 5°F (zone 7).

Jan	/	Recommended Varieties
Feb	flowering	**Primula hybrids:**
Mar	flowers/sow	"Crescendo Mixed"
Apr	flowers/sow	"Dobies Superb Mixed"
May	flowers/sow	"Giant Superb Mixed"
Jun	sow/grow	"Gold Lace"
July	sow/grow	"Harlequin Mixed"
Aug	grow	"Heritage Mixed"
Sept	grow	"Large Flowered Mixed"
Oct	plant	"Pacific Giants Mixed"
Nov	/	"Spring Rainbow Mixed"
Dec	/	"Unwins Superb Mixed"

RANUNCULUS

Persian buttercup

DOUBLE FLOWERS are characteristic of Ranunculus asiaticus *varieties, and are all clear and bright as in this yellow-flowered plant.*

YOU CAN PLANT ranunculus in beds in spring when the worst of the winter is over, where they will give a bright show of color.

FEATURES

Hardy varieties of *Ranunculus asiaticus* are sown in late summer and fall for flowers during winter and spring. Seed-raised plants reach about 8–10in tall. Flowers are double. Young plants are sometimes offered in spring catalogs for delivery in late summer/fall ready for potting up. Add them to your spring containers as they come into flower—they will grow happily in a cold greenhouse or porch.

RANUNCULUS AT A GLANCE

A half-hardy annual grown for its large, double, buttercup-like flowers that appear in spring. Frost hardy to 23°F (zone 9).

		Recommended Varieties
Jan	grow	
Feb	grow	**Ranunculus hybrids:**
Mar	flowering	"Bloomingdale Mixture"
Apr	flowering	
May	flowering	
Jun	/	
July	/	
Aug	sow	
Sept	sow/transplant	
Oct	sow/grow	
Nov	grow	
Dec	grow	

CONDITIONS

Aspect Give as much sun as possible, and move containers into shelter during stormy or very frosty weather to stop damage to the flowers.

Site Use a multipurpose compost for potting up and potting on, and for filling containers if you are creating an "instant" display as the plants come into flower from early spring.

GROWING METHOD

Sowing Sow seed August–October in 3½in pots of peat-based compost, just covering the seeds. Stand outdoors in shade and keep moist—if they get too hot the seeds will not come up. When seedlings appear, bring them into full light and transplant when large enough into 4in pots. Grow outdoors until frosts start, then move under protection at night and out during the day. A cool porch is useful. In winter keep plants dry under cover.

Feeding Feeding is not usually required.

Problems No special problems.

FLOWERING

Season Late winter and throughout spring.

Cutting Cut when the buds are just unfurling.

AFTER FLOWERING

General Plants will survive most winters in a sheltered spot and can be planted out in borders.

RESEDA
Mignonette

MIGNONETTE FLOWERS individually are insignificant, but the strong sweet fragrance is striking and well worth the effort of sowing.

THE FLOWERHEADS of Reseda odorata branch out as they develop. Sow along path edges so the fragrance can be enjoyed.

FEATURES

Mignonette has greenish, pink, red, yellow, or coppery flowers and grows to 12in. It is not particularly striking but is grown mainly for its strong, fruity fragrance—grow it near doors, windows, in patio pots, and near sitting areas to appreciate the qualities of this easily- grown hardy annual. It makes a good addition to cottage-style borders.

RESEDA AT A GLANCE

An easily grown hardy annual grown for its highly fragrant spikes of summer flowers. Frost hardy to 5°F (zone 7).

Jan	/	Recommended Varieties
Feb	/	
Mar	sow	*Reseda odorata:*
Apr	sow/thin out	"Crown Mixture"
May	thin out	"Fragrant Beauty"
Jun	flowering	"Machet"
July	flowering	"Sweet Scented"
Aug	flowering	
Sept	flowers/sow	
Oct	sow	
Nov	/	
Dec	/	

CONDITIONS

Aspect	Needs full sun.
Site	Needs well-drained soil—dig in organic matter and add lime to acid soils.

GROWING METHOD

Sowing	Seed is sown directly into the ground in short drills ½in deep, 6in apart. Thin seedlings to 6in apart. Sowing can take place in March/April or September/October. Fall-sown plants need protecting with cloches during cold spells, and should not be thinned until spring. For pots, sow a pinch of seeds in each unit of a cell tray and thin to 2–3 seedlings, grow on and plant up when ready—reseda does not like root disturbance.
Feeding	Extra feeding is not usually necessary
Problems	Free of troubles.

FLOWERING

Season	Flowers appear from late spring on fall-sown plants, later on spring-sown.
Cutting	Cut when just a few flowers are opening. Dried flowers retain their fragrance.

AFTER FLOWERING

General	Pull plants up when they are past their best, but leave a few to produce seeds and self-sow.

RICINUS
Castor oil plant

THE VARIETY "IMPALA" is an excellent choice if you want bold, dark leaves for a dramatic show, growing 4ft tall.

BY MIDSUMMER the leaves of ricinus will have formed a dense canopy when grown in beds and planted 2–3ft apart.

FEATURES

A striking and memorable plant grown for its large, lobed, exotic-looking leaves, which are used for bedding, borders, and large tubs and containers. The often brightly-colored summer flowers are followed by spiny seed clusters. By nature an evergreen shrub, ricinus is fast growing and plants are raised fresh from seed each year—in long hot summers they can reach 6ft by 3ft tall and wide. Annual flowering climbers like thunbergia or ipomoea will climb its stems, their bright orange/blue flowers contrasting with the often deeply colored ricinus foliage. All parts of the plant are poisonous, especially the seeds. Treat as a half-hardy annual and scrap plants at the end of the summer.

RICINUS AT A GLANCE

A half-hardy annual with large, exotic leaves in a range of colors, and prized as bold bedder. Frost hardy to 32°F (zone 10).

Jan	/	Recommended Varieties
Feb	/	*Ricinus communis:*
Mar	sow	"Carmencita"
Apr	pot on	"Carmencita Pink"
May	harden/plant	"Impala"
Jun	leaves	"Gibbsonii"
July	leaves	"Red Spire"
Aug	leaves	"Zanzibarensis"
Sept	leaves	
Oct	/	
Nov	/	
Dec	/	

CONDITIONS

Aspect Must have full sun. In northern areas choose a sheltered, south-facing spot.

Site Soil should be well-drained with plenty of rotted compost or manure dug in. Use loam-based or multipurpose potting compost in containers. In windy spots, stake plants.

GROWING METHOD

Sowing Soak the hard seeds overnight in warm water, then sow individually in 3½in diameter pots of soil-based compost, 2in deep in March, and keep at 70°F. Seedlings appear within three weeks. Pot on into 5in diameter pots when 6in tall. In beds plant 3–6ft apart after the last frosts.

Feeding Apply liquid feed weekly from early summer, or mix slow-release fertilizer with the potting compost before planting.

Problems Red spider mite attacks leaves. Wetting the leaves thoroughly every day can help, or use a spray containing bifenthrin.

FLOWERING

Season The large leaves keep coming all summer long and are joined later by clusters of flowers that rise up above them.

Cutting Leaves are useful for flower arranging, but avoid getting the sap on skin.

AFTER FLOWERING

General Plants are usually killed by the first frosts of fall. Ripe seeds can be saved for sowing again the following spring.

SALPIGLOSSIS
Salpiglossis

PETAL VEINING in salpiglossis is intricate and gives rise to the common name of painted tongue. Many different colors are available.

THE EXOTIC LOOK can be had by growing mixed salpiglossis in large bold drifts. Choose a variety like "Casino" at just 18in.

FEATURES

Salpiglossis blooms are trumpet-shaped and come in a range of colors, all with patterned veins. They must have shelter and warmth to do well, so for guaranteed success use them in containers on sunny patios or in south-facing beds protected from the wind. Choose mixed colors or try dark brown "Chocolate Pot," striking "Kew Blue" or even the blue/yellow mix Chili Blue." Half-hardy, growing up to 2ft. Available as young plants.

CONDITIONS

Aspect   Must be in full sun and protected from wind.

SALPIGLOSSIS AT A GLANCE

Half-hardy annual grown for its exotic flowers but needing a sheltered spot in the yard to do well. Frost hardy to 32°F (zone 10).

		Recommended Varieties
Jan	/	
Feb	sow	*Salpiglossis sinuata:*
Mar	transplant/sow	"Batik"
Apr	grow on	"Bolero"
May	harden off/plant	"Carnival"
Jun	flowering	"Casino"
July	flowering	"Chili Blue"
Aug	flowering	"Chocolate Pot"
Sept	flowering	"Chocolate Royale"
Oct	/	"Festival Mixed"
Nov	/	"Flamenco Mixed"
Dec	/	"Kew Blue"
		"Triumph Mixed"

Site   Drainage must be good or plants will rot—prepare soil by digging in plenty of rotted manure or compost well before planting. Use multipurpose compost in containers and make sure there is a 2in layer of gravel in the base to guarantee good drainage. Support plants with twigs or short canes as they get taller and begin to flower.

GROWING METHOD

Sowing   Sow in a 3½in pot in February/March and just cover the fine seed. Keep at a temperature of 75°F in a light place, and when seedlings are large enough transplant to cell trays or 3½in pots. Grow on and then harden off in late May before planting after frosts in early June. Plants are quite brittle so handle carefully.

Feeding   Little additional feeding should be needed for plants in bedding displays, but containers can be liquid-fed every two weeks if slow-release fertilizer is not used; otherwise just water well.

Problems   The flowers are very prone to bruising and damage by wind and heavy rain, so pick off casualties after unsettled spells to avoid an attack by gray mold which can cause rotting.

FLOWERING

Season   Flowers appear throughout the summer.
Cutting   Weak-stemmed as a cut flower.

AFTER FLOWERING

General   Pull up after fall frosts and compost.

SCHIZANTHUS

Poor man's orchid

THE EXOTIC APPEAL of schizanthus earns it the common name of poor man's orchid. Each flower has a network of darker veining.

THE FINELY DIVIDED leaves are the perfect foil for the large heads of flowers. Varieties like "Pierrot" are distinctly dome-shaped.

FEATURES

Also known as butterfly flower, schizanthus is stunning when used in bedding or in large pots and troughs. It has fern-like foliage and brilliantly colored, trumpet-shaped flowers in rich tones of pink, purple, magenta, pastels, or white. The flower throats are intricately patterned. Only the dwarf varieties reaching 8–12in are worth growing outdoors, and they must have shelter from strong winds and the hot midday sun. Schizanthus is a half-hardy annual and very sensitive to even slight frost.

SCHIZANTHUS AT A GLANCE

A half-hardy annual grown in containers on patios or in south-facing borders for summer flowers. Frost hardy to 32°F (zone 10).

		Recommended Varieties
Jan	/	
Feb	/	*Schizanthus pinnatus:*
Mar	sow	"Angel Wings Mixed"
Apr	transplant	"Disco"
May	harden off	"My Lovely"
Jun	plant/flowers	"Pierrot"
July	flowering	"Star Parade"
Aug	flowering	
Sept	flowering	
Oct	/	
Nov	/	
Dec	/	

CONDITIONS

Aspect Must be sheltered and have full sun.

Site Well-drained soil that has been enriched before planting with rotted manure or compost produces strong plants. Peat- or coir-based potting compost guarantees good results when containers are used.

GROWING METHOD

Sowing Seeds are sown in March at 61°F in small pots of peat- or coir-based seed compost, and seedlings appear after 1–2 weeks. Transplant to cell trays or 3½in pots, grow through spring and plant after hardening off, in early June. Space plants 6–12in apart. Pinch out growing tips when 4in high to make bushy plants.

Feeding Liquid feed monthly, and water containers regularly—if slow-release fertilizer is added to the compost extra feeding is not necessary.

Problems No special problems.

FLOWERING

Season Flowers reach a peak in mid to late summer and keep coming if faded stems are removed.

Cutting Not usually used as a cut flower.

AFTER FLOWERING

General The soft leafy plants soon break down when put on the compost heap.

SENECIO
Dusty miller

A WHITE WOOLLY LAYER covering the otherwise green leaves gives Senecio cineraria *its attractive silvery-gray appearance.*

OVERWINTERED PLANTS will keep on growing the following season, get larger, and also produce heads of bright yellow flowers.

FEATURES

Grown for its attractive silver-gray foliage, *Senecio cineraria* is often found listed under "cineraria" in seed catalogs. Use in bedding schemes and as a foliage container plant. Plants grow up to 12in tall and wide in summer, but if left outdoors over winter can be twice that if the yellow flowerheads are allowed to develop. Usually grown as a half-hardy annual, senecio is naturally an evergreen, eventually developing a tough woody base.

SENECIO AT A GLANCE

Prized for its silver-gray leaves and grown as a foliage bedding plant and for using in containers. Frost hardy to 23°F (zone 9).

Jan	/	Recommended Varieties
Feb	sow 🖐	
		Senecio cineraria:
Mar	sow 🖐	**Fine, divided leaves**
Apr	transplant 🖐	"Dwarf Silver"
May	harden off/plant 🖐	"Silver Dust"
Jun	leaves 🌿	
July	leaves 🌿	**Rounded leaves**
Aug	leaves 🌿	"Cirrus"
Sept	leaves 🌿	
Oct	leaves 🌿	
Nov	/	
Dec	/	

CONDITIONS

Aspect   Must have full sun.
Site   Well-drained soil is needed, but plants do well in light, sandy soils, especially in seaside gardens. Use multipurpose compost in pots.

GROWING METHOD

Sowing   Start plants in February/March at 68°F, by sowing seed in a small pot of compost and just covering. Expect seedlings after 1–2 weeks and keep in good light. Keep compost slightly on the dry side to avoid "damping off." Transplant to cell trays or 3½in pots, grow on, then harden off at the end of April and plant in May, 12in apart.

Feeding   Planted containers need liquid feed every two weeks, and regular watering. Plants stand dry spells outside but water them if they wilt.

Problems   If seedlings collapse, give a light watering with a copper-based fungicide.

FLOWERING

Season   The silvery leaves are attractive all summer.
Cutting   Foliage can be used in arrangements.

AFTER FLOWERING

General   Pull up and compost in fall. In many areas plants will survive the winter if left and produce bigger clumps of leaves and flowers.

SOLENOSTEMON

Coleus or flame nettle

"BLACK DRAGON" is a modern variety of coleus with black-edged, pinkish-red leaves, and is useful for specific color themes.

LEAF COLOR is apparent from an early age with solenostemon, making it possible to group the different colors when planting.

FEATURES

Look under "coleus" in seed catalogs for a wide range of varieties of this striking foliage plant. A half-hardy annual, solenostemon is a valuable bedding and container plant with large multicolored leaves that add a certain "tropical" and eccentric element to summer gardens. As well as mixtures, dark-leaved varieties like "Black Dragon" can be put to use in color-themed displays. Size range is 8–18in depending on variety, and it is important to remove all flowerheads as they appear or the plant will stop producing leaves. Varieties are available as young plants.

CONDITIONS

Aspect   Flame nettles need full sun to really thrive and also need shelter from persistent winds.

Site   Well-drained soil that has had plenty of rotted

SOLENOSTEMON AT A GLANCE

A half-hardy annual grown for its brightly-colored leaves which are used in bedding and for patio pots. Frost hardy to 32°F (zone 10).

		Recommended Varieties
Jan	/	
Feb	/	*Solenostemon scutellarioides:*
Mar	sow	"Black Dragon"
Apr	transplant	"Camelot Mixed"
May	harden off/plant	"Dragon Sunset & Volcano, Mixed"
Jun	leaves	"Fairway"
July	leaves	"Flame Dancers"
Aug	leaves	"Magic Lace"
Sept	leaves	"Salmon Lace"
Oct	/	"Top Crown"
Nov	/	"Wizard Mixed"
Dec	/	

manure or compost mixed in before planting produces strong plants with good color. Where they are grown in patio containers use multipurpose compost with slow-release fertilizer granules added at planting time.

GROWING METHOD

Sowing   March is the time to sow seed, in 3½in pots of multipurpose compost, just scattering the seed on the surface—don't cover. Keep at 75°F where they get bright light. Seedlings grow slowly but when they are large enough, transplant to 3½in pots or large cell trays. Pinch out the growing tip when plants are 3in tall to encourage bushy growth and the maximum number of leaves. Harden off in late May and plant after frosts, 6–12in apart.

Feeding   Liquid feeding every two weeks during summer maintains vigorous leaf growth. If slow-release fertilizer has been used, feed only monthly with half-strength liquid feed.

Problems   Slugs and snails attack young plants, so protect with slug pellets or a barrier of sharp grit around each plant.

FLOWERING

Season   All flowers should be removed as soon as they appear to encourage maximum leaf growth. Plants generally stay colorful until frosts.

Cutting   Not suitable.

AFTER FLOWERING

General   Favorite plants can be lifted and potted up in fall, and kept dry over winter in a frost-free greenhouse or cool room. Take cuttings from these plants in spring.

TAGETES
Marigold

THESE SINGLE-FLOWERED French marigolds are much daintier than their loud cousins with larger double flowers.

SINGLE FLOWER COLORS are useful in color-themed displays and this double-flowered French marigold would go well with blues.

FEATURES

The marigold "family" is made up of African and French types, and tagetes. All are easily grown half-hardy annuals and their flowers are among some of the loudest available—bright oranges, reds, yellows, and bronzes that set borders and containers alight. Plant size varies from 6in dwarfs to 3ft giants, and there are unusual flower colors such as "Vanilla" and even bright stripey-petalled varieties such as "Mr Majestic." Use them for bold bedding or as reliable patio container plants. Flowers can be single, semi or fully double and up to 3in across. Many varieties are also available as young plants.

TAGETES AT A GLANCE

A half-hardy annual grown for its bright flowers which are ideal for bedding and patio pots/troughs. Frost hardy to 32°F (zone 10).

Jan	/	
Feb	sow 🖐	
Mar	sow 🖐	
Apr	sow/transplant 🖐	
May	harden off/plant 🖐	
Jun	flowering 🌸	
July	flowering 🌸	
Aug	flowering 🌸	
Sept	flowering 🌸	
Oct	/	
Nov	/	
Dec	/	

Recommended Varieties

African marigolds
  "Inca Mixed"
  "Shaggy Maggy"
  "Vanilla"
French marigolds
  "Boy O'Boy Mixed"
  "Mischief Mixed"
  "Mr Majestic"
Tagetes tenuifolia:
  "Lemon Gem"
  "Red Gem"

CONDITIONS

Aspect — Must have a sunny position.
Site — Marigolds are not too fussy about soils, but mixing in rotted compost before planting helps keep soil moist. For container growing use multipurpose compost with slow-release fertilizer granules mixed well in. Tall varieties of African marigold need shelter from wind.

GROWING METHOD

Sowing — All marigolds can be sown February–April, but a May sowing on a windowsill will also be successful as they are fast growers and soon catch up. Just cover the large seeds with compost and keep at 70°F. Seedlings will appear in a week and can be transplanted to cell trays. Grow on, harden off in late May and plant after frosts. Nip off any flower buds that appear before and two weeks after planting.
Feeding — Fortnightly liquid feeding keeps plants in beds going strong. Keep containers well watered.
Problems — Slugs and snails can strip plants overnight so protect with slug pellets in wet/warm spells.

FLOWERING

Season — Early sowings produce earlier flowers and vice-versa. Late sowings provide handy color in late summer and if grown in pots, plants can be used to revive flagging summer containers.
Cutting — African marigolds are useful for cutting.

AFTER FLOWERING

General — Pull plants up when finished and compost.

THUNBERGIA
Black-eyed Susan

BLACK-EYED SUSAN is one of the brightest and showiest of all the annual climbers, and readily entwines the stems of other plants. It hates having its roots disturbed so sow seeds straight into small pots, and pot 2 3 plants on together when necessary. Plant out after frosts.

FEATURES

The flowers of thunbergia can be orange, yellow, or white, and sometimes the black eye is missing altogether. Grow as a half-hardy annual for indoors and out. Outdoors, grow up wigwams of 5ft canes, either in borders, or large tubs for a moveable display of color. In hanging baskets thunbergia soon entwines the chains, making an effective camouflage. In patio tubs train plants up through other tall annuals like ricinus and sunflowers, or plant them around the base of outdoor plants in early summer. In colder areas grow plants in the conservatory or porch to guarantee a good show of flowers. Seed pods tend to set very easily which reduces the ability of the plant to keep flowering, so nip these off regularly.

THUNBERGIA AT A GLANCE

A half-hardy annual climber flowering in summer for patio containers, baskets, and bedding. Frost hardy to 32°F (zone 10).

Jan	/	
Feb	/	
Mar	sow	*Recommended Varieties*
Apr	pot on/grow on	
May	harden/plant out	*Thunbergia alata:* "Susie Mixed"
Jun	flowers	
July	flowers	
Aug	flowers	
Sept	flowers	
Oct	/	
Nov	/	
Dec	/	

CONDITIONS

Aspect   A south-facing spot in full sun is essential. In conservatories direct hot sun should be avoided or the leaves may be scorched.

Site   In containers use multipurpose compost with slow-release fertilizer added. Well-drained, moisture retentive soil, with rotted manure or compost is needed outdoors.

GROWING METHOD

Sowing   Soak seeds overnight then sow three to a 3½in diameter pot in March. Germinate at 64°F. Germination is erratic and seedlings may take a month to emerge. A small wigwam of canes will support the shoots. Grow several plants on in large pots during May, then harden off and plant after the last frosts. They dislike root disturbance.

Feeding   Liquid feed once a week in summer.

Problems   Red spider mite attacks leaves. Wet the leaves daily or use a spray containing pirimiphos-methyl. Indoors use the predator phytoseiulus. Whitefly will feed on the leaves and cause sticky "honeydew." Use a spray containing permethrin or the natural encarsia indoors.

FLOWERING

Season   Flowers appear all summer and the flowering period is extended when plants are grown under some form of protection.

Cutting   Not suitable.

AFTER FLOWERING

General   Nip off faded flowers. Remove outdoor plants after frosts and add to the compost heap.

TITHONIA
Mexican sunflower

THE DAHLIA-LIKE FLOWERS of tithonia have an "exotic" feel to them and each one can be up to 3in across, on strong stems.

THE HEART-SHAPED LEAVES of Mexican sunflower are an added bonus, and each flower also has a distinct swollen "neck."

FEATURES

Tithonia, as its common name suggests, comes from warmer areas, so does well when there is plenty of sun. Grow as a half-hardy annual. "Fiesta del Sol" is just 1ft tall, while "Torch" can reach 4ft. Flowers are large, exotic-looking and dahlia-like, red-orange, and have a distinct swollen "neck."

CONDITIONS

Aspect   Must have full sun or plants will suffer.

TITHONIA AT A GLANCE

A half-hardy annual grown for its large orange flowers on strong stems. Use in bedding and pots. Frost hardy to 32°F (zone 10).

Jan	/	Recommended Varieties
Feb	sow	*Tithonia rotundifolia:*
Mar	sow	**Tall varieties**
Apr	sow/transplant	"Goldfinger"
May	harden off/plant	"Torch"
Jun	flowering	
July	flowering	**Short varieties**
Aug	flowering	"Fiesta del Sol"
Sept	flowering	
Oct	/	
Nov	/	
Dec	/	

Site   Not fussy about soil, but needs good drainage. Plant in a fairly sheltered spot away from cold driving winds. Tithonia has a tendency to go pale and yellow when growing conditions are poor. Grow plants in containers if the soil is heavy, using multipurpose compost.

GROWING METHOD

Sowing   Sow seeds February to April in 3½in pots of multipurpose compost, just covering them, and germinate at 64°F in a warm place or heated propagator. Transplant to individual 3½in pots or large cell trays and grow on. Harden off for 2–3 weeks and plant in early summer when the soil warms up. If seedlings or young plants turn yellow they are being kept too cold. Can also be sown outdoors in early June where plants are to flower.

Feeding   Feed container-grown plants twice a month with liquid feed.

Problems   Slugs may attack the leaves after early summer rains so protect with slug pellets.

FLOWERING

Season   Flowers appear from midsummer and later sowings continue to give color into fall.

Cutting   Suitable for use as a cut flower.

AFTER FLOWERING

General   Pull up after flowering. May self-seed.

TORENIA

Wishbone flower

WISHBONE FLOWER gets its common name from the dark markings found on the lower lip of the flowers of some varieties.

SHELTER IS ESSENTIAL for success with torenia, which can also be potted up and grown on as a flowering plant for indoors.

FEATURES

Wishbone flower needs to be in the "front row" of a summer bedding scheme, or used around the edge of pots and troughs. The variety "Susie Wong" has bright yellow flowers with black throats, and a spreading habit making it ideal for baskets. Half-hardy annuals, torenias grow no more than 1ft in height.

CONDITIONS

Aspect   Choose a sheltered spot with sun.

TORENIA AT A GLANCE

A low growing half-hardy annual grown for its colorful lipped flowers, for edging in beds and pots. Frost hardy to 32ºF (zone 10).

Jan	/	Recommended Varieties
Feb	/	
Mar	sow 🖑	*Torenia fournieri:*
Apr	sow/transplant 🖑	"Clown Mixed"
May	grow/harden off 🖑	"Susie Wong"
Jun	plant/flowers 🖑🌼	
July	flowering 🌼	
Aug	flowering 🌼	
Sept	flowering 🌼	
Oct	/	
Nov	/	
Dec	/	

Site   Dig in rotted manure or compost a few weeks ahead of planting out, or use multipurpose compost for container growing. Soil and compost used must be free-draining. Avoid planting where winds are persistent.

GROWING METHOD

Sowing   Sow the very small seeds in pots or trays in March/April, barely cover and keep at 64ºF in a well-lit place. When large enough the seedlings can be transplanted to cell trays and grown on until late May, then hardened off and planted well after the last frosts, 6in apart, or in groups in patio pots. Plant five plants to a 16in diameter hanging basket, four around the sides and one in the center. "Susie Wong" will creep in and out of other plants.

Feeding   Feed regularly every 2–3 weeks with a balanced liquid plant food.

Problems   Trouble free.

FLOWERING

Season   Throughout summer.
Cutting   Not used as a cut flower.

AFTER FLOWERING

General   Pull or dig out the plants when flowering has stopped. They will sometimes self-seed, and they will then produce seedlings in the following year.

TROPAEOLUM
Nasturtium

"MOONLIGHT" is a climbing variety of nasturtium reaching 6ft with soft yellow flowers against light green leaves.

FOR DOUBLE VALUE grow "Alaska Mixed" with light green leaves speckled with creamy-white, plus red and yellow flowers.

FEATURES

With big seeds and quick growth, tropaeolum, better known as nasturtium, is one of the easiest of all hardy annuals to grow. Plants just 9in tall are perfect for bedding and patio planters, while others will scramble up throughout a dull hedge. The color range is huge, and single and mixed colors are available. For pretty leaves too, grow "Alaska Mixed," which is speckled with white.

TROPAEOLUM AT A GLANCE

A hardy annual grown for its colorful flowers and often variegated leaves. For beds and containers. Frost hardy to 32°F (zone 10).

Jan	/	Recommended Varieties
Feb	sow	*Tropaeolum majus:*
Mar	sow	**Tall climbers**
Apr	transplant	"Climbing Mixed"
May	transplant	"Jewel of Africa"
Jun	flowering	**Short, mixed colors**
July	flowering	"Alaska Mixed"
Aug	flowering	"Gleam Mixed"
Sept	flowering	"Tip Top Mixed"
Oct	/	**Single colors**
Nov	/	"Empress of India"
Dec	/	"Gleaming Mahogany"
		"Moonlight"

CONDITIONS

Aspect   Needs full sun.
Site   Poor, thin soil gives excellent results when grown under hedges or in bedding displays.

GROWING METHOD

Sowing   Simply push the large seeds 1–2in into the soil in April, in groups of 3–5 where plants are to flower. Fleshy seedlings appear 2–3 weeks later and they can all be left to develop and form a large clump. If needed for containers, sow three seeds to a 3½in pot at the same time and keep warm until seedlings appear, then keep outdoors.

Feeding   Feeding encourages leaves at the expense of flowers, although if other plants are growing in a container or basket, some extra feeding is unavoidable. Don't feed plants growing in soil.

Problems   Aphids and caterpillars feed under the leaves, so check regularly and squash if seen.

FLOWERING

Season   Flowering is all summer long.
Cutting   Not used cut, but flowers and the peppery leaves can be used raw in summer salads.

AFTER FLOWERING

General   Pull up and compost. Self-seeds very easily.

VERBENA
Verbena

SOFTER PASTEL SHADES can be found in modern varieties of verbena—these are just a few flowers of the variety "Romance Pastels."

"PEACHES & CREAM" has a unique color that makes it a real winner, at 8in, for patio containers and hanging baskets.

FEATURES

Most verbenas grow 6–12in tall and are prized for their heads of bright flowers. Mixtures or single shades like "Peaches & Cream" are used for planting containers or for bedding. Raise from seed—although this is tricky—or grow them from mail order plants. Most trailing verbenas are not seed raised but bought as ready-grown plants from garden centers and mail order catalogs in spring.

VERBENA AT A GLANCE

A half-hardy annual used in bedding and containers. Masses of bright flowers appear during summer. Frost hardy to 32°F (zone 10).

		Recommended Varieties
Jan	/	
Feb	/	*Verbena hybrida:*
Mar	sow	**Mixed colors**
Apr	transplant	"Crown Jewels"
May	grow/harden off	"Novalis Mixed"
Jun	flowering	"Raspberry Crush"
July	flowering	"Romance Pastels"
Aug	flowering	**Single colors**
Sept	flowering	"Adonis Blue"
Oct	/	"Apple Blossom"
Nov	/	"Peaches & Cream"
Dec	/	**Spreading/trailing**
		"Misty"

CONDITIONS

Aspect	Needs full sun for best results.
Site	Use multipurpose compost in containers, and mix rotted compost with soil outdoors.

GROWING METHOD

Sowing	To succeed with verbena seed, sow on the surface of peat-based seed compost in March and cover the seeds with a thin layer of fine vermiculite. Water and keep at 70°F. Seedlings appear 2–3 weeks later, and should be kept slightly on the dry side. When large enough, transplant seedlings to cell trays or individual 3in pots, and grow on. Plant after hardening off in late spring/early summer.
Feeding	Feed monthly with balanced liquid feed.
Problems	Powdery mildew can attack leaves—use a spray containing sulfur at the first signs.

FLOWERING

Season	Flowers appear all summer.
Cutting	Not used for cutting.

AFTER FLOWERING

General	Pull up when finished and use for compost.

VIOLA CORNUTA
Viola

DIMINUITIVE "Bambini" violas are guaranteed to steal your heart with their inquisitive whiskery faces.

FOR A TOUCH OF DRAMA try combining the moody "Blackjack" with a clear yellow variety in a hanging basket.

FEATURES

Violas are smaller than pansies but they are no less prolific, and what they lack in size they make up for in sheer character. Most are varieties of *Viola cornuta*, and all are quite hardy, being sown in spring or summer. Grow single colors, mixtures like "Bambini," or trailing yellow "Sunbeam" for hanging baskets. Violas grow to around 6in, making bushy little plants for bedding or containers. Try planting them in cottage style wicker baskets. Available as young plants.

VIOLA AT A GLANCE	
A hardy annual grown for its pretty little pansy flowers which appear on branching plants. Frost hardy to 5°F (zone 7).	
Jan /	Recommended Varieties
Feb sow	**Viola hybrids:**
Mar sow	"Bambini Mixed"
Apr sow/flower	"Blackjack"
May sow/flower	"Blue Moon"
Jun sow/flower	"Cuty"
July sow/flower	"Juliette Mixed"
Aug grow on/flowers	"Midnight Runner"
Sept grow on/flowers	"Princess Mixed"
Oct plant	"Sorbet Yesterday, Today & Tomorrow"
Nov /	"Sunbeam"
Dec /	

CONDITIONS

Aspect   Grows well in sun or dappled, light shade.
Site   Soil does not need to be over prepared, but must be well-drained. For container growing use multipurpose compost.

GROWING METHOD

Sowing   Sow from February under cover for flowers the same summer, or outside May–July for flowers the following spring. Either way, sow in a 3½in pot of multipurpose compost and barely cover seeds. In early spring keep at 60°F and transplant seedlings when large enough to cell trays, grow, harden off, and plant in late May. When summer sowing, stand the pot outside in shade to germinate then treat seedlings the same, planting out in October where you want the plants to flower.

Feeding   Extra feeding is not usually necessary.
Problems   Use slug pellets if the leaves are attacked.

FLOWERING

Season   Spring-sown plants flower during summer, summer-sown the following spring/summer.
Cutting   The delicate cut stems of "Queen Charlotte" are sometimes used for making scented posies.

AFTER FLOWERING

General   Plants often carry on as short-lived perennials, and also self-seed freely.

VIOLA TRICOLOR
Wild pansy

EACH FLOWER of wild pansy is like a tiny whiskered "face" and individual plants all vary from each other very slightly.

ONE PLANT left in the ground to mature through the summer will shed hundreds of seeds which will germinate the next spring.

FEATURES

Viola tricolor is the wild pansy, also known commonly as heartsease or Johnny-jump-up. It is usually grown as a hardy annual but can also be treated as a biennial. Much daintier than its relatives the pansies, these plants are at home in cottage-style beds and as pot edging. A few single colored varieties are available, such as the unusual "Bowles' Black," having black flowers with a small central yellow "eye".

VIOLA AT A GLANCE

A hardy annual grown for its pretty little pansy flowers which appear on branching plants. Frost hardy to 5°F. (zone 7)

Jan	/
Feb	sow
Mar	sow
Apr	sow/flower
May	sow/flower
Jun	sow/flower
July	sow/flower
Aug	grow on/flowers
Sept	grow on/flowers
Oct	plant
Nov	/
Dec	/

Recommended Varieties

Viola tricolor

Single colors:

Blue
"Prince Henry"

Yellow
"Prince John"

CONDITIONS

Aspect Grows well in sun or dappled, light shade.

Site Soil does not need to be over prepared, but must be well-drained. Multipurpose compost is best for growing *Viola tricolor* in containers.

GROWING METHOD

Sowing Sow from February under cover for flowers the same summer, or outside May–July for flowers the following spring. Either way, sow in a 3½in pot of multipurpose compost and barely cover seeds. In early spring keep at 60°F and transplant seedlings when large enough to cell trays, grow, harden off, and plant in late May. When summer sowing, stand the pot outside in shade to germinate, treat seedlings the same, and plant in October.

Feeding Extra feeding is not usually necessary.

Problems Use slug pellets if the leaves are attacked.

FLOWERING

Season Spring-sown plants flower during summer, summer-sown the following spring/summer.

Cutting Not suitable for cutting.

AFTER FLOWERING

General Pull plants up and compost, or leave a few to shed seeds. They will sometimes grow as perennials and last for several years.

VIOLA WITTROCKIANA
Pansy

PANSY FLOWERS have "faces" that tend to face the sun, especially in early spring. Use them in patio pots with bulbs like tulips.

"JOLLY JOKER" is a unique and prolific variety of summer-flowering pansy with orange and rich royal purple two-tone flowers.

FEATURES

Pansies are hardy and will flower almost all year around. There are two groups, summer flowering, and fall/winter flowering. None grow more than 8in tall. Flowers are like large flat "faces" up to 3in across. Colors vary enormously from single, pastel shades to striking bicolors, and are available in mixtures or as single colors. Many varieties are available as young plants by mail order. Most are varieties of *Viola wittrockiana*.

VIOLA AT A GLANCE

Hardy and grown either as an annual or a biennial for flowers in summer and fall/winter. Frost hardy to 5°F (zone 7).

Month		Recommended Varieties
Jan	/	*Viola wittrockiana:*
Feb	sow	**Summer flowers**
Mar	sow	"Antique Shades"
Apr	sow/flower	"Padparadja"
May	sow/flower	"Romeo & Juliet"
Jun	sow/flower	"Watercolors"
July	sow/flower	**Fall/winter flowers**
Aug	grow on/flowers	"Homefires"
Sept	grow on/flowers	"Ultima Pastel Mixed"
Oct	plant	"Universal Mixed"
Nov	/	"Velour Mixed"
Dec	/	

CONDITIONS

Aspect	Fall/winter pansies need full sun. Summer flowering varieties like dappled shade.
Site	Add plenty of manure to the soil. Winter pansies need excellent drainage. Use multipurpose compost for containers.

GROWING METHOD

Sowing	Sow from February under cover for flowers the same summer, or outside May–July for flowers the following spring. Either way, sow in a 3½in pot of multipurpose compost and barely cover seeds. In early spring keep at 60°F and transplant seedlings when large enough to cell trays, grow, harden off, and plant in late May. When summer-sowing, stand the pot outside in shade to germinate then treat seedlings the same, planting out in October where you want the plants to flower.
Feeding	Liquid feed summer plants every two weeks.
Problems	Spray with permethrin if aphids attack.

FLOWERING

Season	Spring-sown plants flower in summer, fall-sown from October onward.
Cutting	Pansies last a few days in water.

AFTER FLOWERING

General	Pull up and compost when finished.

ZINNIA
Zinnia

ZINNIA FLOWERS tend to come as doubles but plants sometimes appear that are single like this. Zinnias are good bee plants.

IF PINCHED WHEN YOUNG zinnias make bushy, branching plants that fill gaps in mixed borders quickly. Take dead flowers off.

FEATURES

There is a zinnia for every garden. Dwarf varieties at 6in tall are suited to beds and containers, while "Dahlia-Flowered Mixed" has big heads on stems 2ft high, and is useful for mixed borders. Modern varieties have fully double flowers, and some like "Zebra Mixed" are stripey. "Starbright Mixed" is an unusual variety with masses of small orange and gold flowers. Red, yellow, pink, scarlet, orange, lavender, purple, white, and even green are typical flower colors. Half-hardy annual.

ZINNIA AT A GLANCE

A half-hardy annual grown for its bright flowers in a wide range of colors, for bedding and cutting. Frost hardy to 32°F (zone 10).

		Recommended Varieties
Jan	/	
Feb	/	**Zinnia hybrids:**
Mar	/	**Tall varieties**
Apr	/	"Allsorts"
May	sow 🖐	"Dahlia-Flowered Mixed"
Jun	thin out	"Zebra Mixed"
July	flowering	**Short varieties**
Aug	flowering	"Belvedere"
Sept	flowering	"Fairyland"
Oct	flowering	"Persian Carpet Mixed"
Nov	/	"Starbright Mixed"
Dec	/	"Thumbelina"

CONDITIONS

Aspect   Zinnias enjoy heat and need sun and shelter.
Site   Must have well-drained soil, previously improved with rotted organic matter. For containers use multipurpose compost.

GROWING METHOD

Sowing   Although half-hardy, zinnias grow best when sown direct where they are to flower, in short drills ½in deep. Do this in May and cover seedlings with a piece of garden fleece on frosty nights. Thin out seedlings so the young plants are eventually 6–24in apart, depending on their final size. To grow dwarf varieties in containers sow 2–3 seeds to a 3in pot at the same time, leave just the strongest, grow on, and plant when ready, not disturbing the roots.
Feeding   Extra feeding is usually not necessary.
Problems   Powdery mildew can be a problem, so avoid planting too close—sulfur sprays can help. Stem rots cause plants to collapse suddenly.

FLOWERING

Season   Flowers appear from midsummer onward.
Cutting   Very good cut flower. "Envy Double" is a striking plant with double green flowers.

AFTER FLOWERING

General   Pull up in fall and compost.

Growing Bulbs

GROWING BULBS

Bulbs are the easiest of plants to grow—probably no other plant group gives as much variety and pleasure to the gardener with so little effort. Even people without yards can enjoy bulbs as there are so many that make excellent container plants.

Most people think of bulbs as an essential part of spring, but spring is by no means their only season—there are bulbs that flower through the summer, fall, and even through the depths of the winter. They are usually very easy to look after, and many types will go on giving pleasure for years with the minimum of attention.

ABOVE: These parrot tulips just breaking from their buds already show the typical ruffled petals and color streaking.

LEFT: Deepest blue hyacinths make a wonderful foil for the bright yellow tulips in this landscape planting.

BULBS, CORMS, TUBERS, AND RHIZOMES

What most people know as bulbs covers a whole range of plants with some kind of underground storage organ that allows their survival over their dormant season, which may be winter or summer. They include true bulbs and plants with corms, tubers, and rhizomes.

• True bulbs are made up of a bud enclosed by modified leaves or fleshy scales from which roots and shoots emerge. The shoots grow out of the pointed top and the roots from the other end. Most, such as onions, daffodils, and hyacinths, have an outer papery cover or tunic: lilies, which are bulbs, too, have a bulb of swollen leaf bases but lack the protective tunic.

• Corms are bulb-like structures formed by the enlargement of an underground stem base. They do not have the "rings" of true bulbs, but stems grow out of the top and roots from the base in the same way. Freesias, gladioli, and crocuses all grow from corms.

• Tubers are swollen underground parts of roots or stems. Dahlias grow from buds at the ends of tubers.

• Rhizomes may grow underground or along the soil surface. They are fleshy, tuberous roots with new growth emerging from the end. Some irises grow from rhizomes (other irises are bulbs). Some bulbous plants described as having rhizomes or tubers appear to have little more than a small crown from which the roots emerge.

For convenience, all the above groups are discussed throughout this book as bulbs.

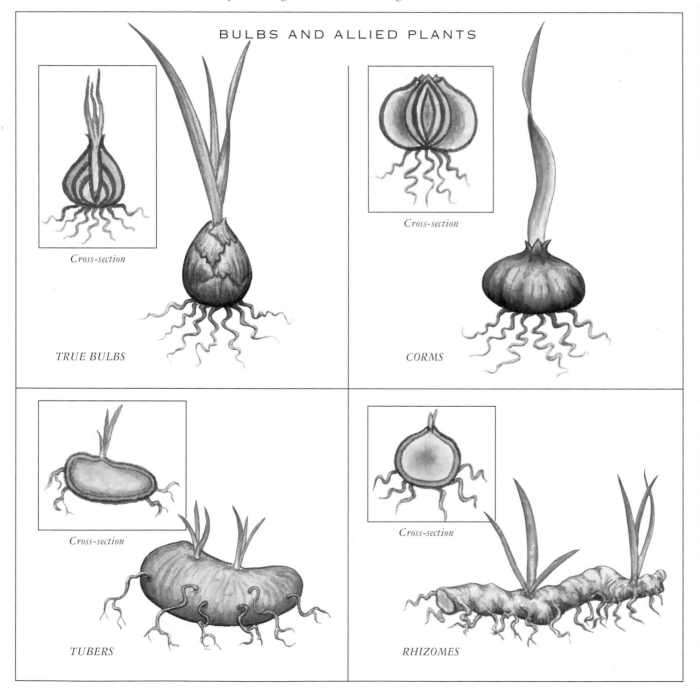

BULBS AND ALLIED PLANTS

Cross-section

Cross-section

TRUE BULBS

CORMS

Cross-section

Cross-section

TUBERS

RHIZOMES

TENDER BULBS

Indoors or out?

Some bulbs are not suitable for growing outdoors, and must be grown in a greenhouse or conservatory, or in the home, to produce good results. In many cases, bulbs can be started into growth under protection and brought outside later in the season when the weather has warmed up: when grown in containers, these look good on patios or even positioned amongst other flowering plants in borders so that the container is hidden. Other bulbs, however, need to be grown under protection throughout their lives, as their flowers would be spoiled outdoors.

Which bulbs must be considered tender enough for indoor cultivation often depends on the area in which you live, and the situation of your own garden. Species that can be grown successfully outside in mild areas would often fail in cold, exposed gardens, but even in mild regions a garden may be exposed to cold, windy weather that makes it unsuitable for the more tender plants.

Experience is often the only way to gain an accurate picture of which plants are hardy enough for your conditions, but when growing dubiously hardy bulbs, always play safe and overwinter one or two specimens under cover in case an unexpectedly cold winter destroys your outdoor stock. Protect slightly tender bulbs by heaping straw, dry leaves, or bracken over the planting site once the foliage has died down in the fall: this helps to prevent frost penetrating to the bulbs below ground. Deep planting is also recommended for extra protection.

The table below gives a guide to the plants that need indoor conditions, and those that are risky outdoors in all but the most favored areas of the country. It is often adequate to bring tender bulbs under cover for the winter only: the information under each bulb entry gives further details.

THE TUBEROUS ROOTS of dahlias can be left in the ground in some areas, but are better lifted and stored in a frost-free place.

TENDER BULBS

BULBS FOR THE HOUSE, GREENHOUSE, OR CONSERVATORY ONLY

- Achimenes
- Clivia
- Gloriosa
- Hippeastrum
- Lachenalia
- Sinningia

BULBS NEEDING PROTECTION OR OVERWINTERING UNDER COVER IN COLD AREAS

- Agapanthus
- Amaryllis
- Canna
- Crinum
- Cyrtanthus
- Dierama
- Eremurus
- Eucomis
- Gladiolus callianthus
- Hedychium
- Hymenocallis
- Ixia
- Nerine
- Polianthes
- Romulea
- Schizostylis
- Sparaxis
- Sprekelia
- Tigridia
- Tritonia
- Zantedeschia
- Zephyranthes

AGAPANTHUS PLANTS are suitable for leaving outdoors over winter in warmer areas of the country only.

STRONGLY CONTRASTING white and rich crimson tulips are mass planted under a silver birch tree in this lovely garden. The tulip planting is brilliantly set off by the wide, sweeping border of purple Virginian stock.

CHOOSING BULBS

What do you want from your plants?

There are so many bulbs, in such a range of colors, sizes, and forms, that it is all too easy to get carried away when buying them. Their appeal is instantaneous: here they are, ready packaged, just needing to be popped into the soil—and within a short time, with no further effort, you can expect to be enjoying the brilliant flowers pictured on the display units at garden centers.

Perhaps one of their greatest virtues is that the bulk of bulbs appear for sale at just the time when summer is finally drawing to a close. The summer flowers are nearly over, trees will soon be shedding their leaves, and the days growing shorter and more gloomy; the cold, wet, miserable weeks of winter stretch out ahead. No wonder we are so pleased to see the arrival of bulbs, with their promise of the spring to come!

But in order to achieve the best possible results from your bulbs, you should plan for them more carefully. Consider the type of garden in which they are to be grown; whether it is mild and sheltered or cold and exposed. Where in the garden are the bulbs to grow? Is there space on a rock garden or in a border? Do you have an area of lawn where bulbs could be naturalized, and if so, are you prepared for the grass to be untidy while the bulb foliage is dying down? Do you want all your bulbs to flower in spring, or would a longer flowering season be more appropriate? Do you want bulbs in pots for growing on the patio, or varieties that will flower out of season to brighten up the home in the middle of winter? If you have a good idea of what you want from your bulbs *before* you go out to buy them, it could save you making some expensive mistakes.

Choose for color

Consider the color schemes of your bulb planting as you would any other item, either inside your home or outside it. Do you want strong contrasts in color, gradations of a single color, or colors that complement each other? Do you want to create a bright, warm, active look or do you want to give a cooler, calmer impression? Warm, active colors are red, yellow, orange, and bright pink, while blue, lavender, white, cream, pale pink, and pale yellow are cooler colors.

Blue and white spring-flowering bulbs include spring star flower, grape hyacinth, bluebell, and hyacinth, all of which would team well with white or cream daffodils. Some of the brightest bulbs in the "hot" color range are ranunculus and harlequin flowers (sparaxis). Both these are more commonly available in mixed colors but sometimes you can find a supplier who is able to sell them as single colors. Anemones also come in strong colors and these too can be purchased in single colors. Greater impact is generally achieved by planting blocks of single colors rather than mixtures. Try bulbs in blocks of red, orange, and yellow for a tremendous impact, or if you want a quieter look, plant groups of two shades of pink and white.

Many bulbous plants, such as daffodils, come in a wide range of varieties but a fairly limited color range: they also look their best if planted in groups of one variety. Corn lily is another good example. Although there is a wide color range available, and corn lilies can be purchased in mixtures, these flowers look best if planted in blocks of one color. They can, of course, be planted as mixtures, especially in an informal garden setting, but in nature they would be more likely to grow in blocks of one color.

Consider flowering time

Some gardeners prefer one huge display over three or four weeks in spring while others may find more interest in spreading the season over several months of the year. For instance, with crocus alone, different varieties provide blooms from late fall right through to mid-spring. There is some form of bulbous plant to give a display in every month of the year if that is what you require.

It can be hard to give precise information on exactly when different species will be in bloom, as the time can vary from one district to another and even from one garden to another because of variation in microclimates. However, if you spend some time noting the times when bulbs flower in your garden, in future seasons you will be able to plan to have a succession of bulbs in flower during many months of the year.

BUYING BULBS

There are several different ways in which you can buy bulbs. Most garden centers, and several other stores, sell bulbs in perforated plastic bags backed by a card giving planting details, along with a picture of the bulb in flower. Bulbs are also available in small netting sacks with attached pictures and growing instructions. Most garden centers and nurseries sell bulbs in bulk in the main planting season, and you can make your own selection from large bins. Another option is to send away for catalogs from bulb-growing nurseries and order bulbs by mail—these growers advertise in popular gardening magazines. The range of bulbs available from specialist nurseries is generally very much more extensive than what is on offer at your local garden center. Mail order is a good option if you want some of the more unusual varieties, and if you want to order a lot of bulbs as it can be a good deal cheaper, though you need to take postal charges into account. When planning to buy by mail order, remember that you need to order well in advance of the planting date; if you leave it until bulbs are starting to appear in stores, the specialist suppliers are likely to have sold out of many of the less common varieties. Once you are on the mailing list of mail order suppliers, they will send you their catalogues in plenty of time in future years.

When buying bulbs at a garden center, try to buy them as soon as possible after they have been delivered, as they tend to deteriorate in the warm conditions, and will soon become bruised as other buyers sort through them to make their choice. Select plump, firm, well-rounded bulbs and make sure there are no soft spots or patches of mould. Especially avoid buying any bulbs that are starting to shoot and showing signs

HYACINTH BULBS will be on sale from early fall. Select yours early to be sure of getting the best available.

GOLDEN DAFFODILS planted in sweeping drifts beneath a fine magnolia tree show to advantage against an old stone wall.

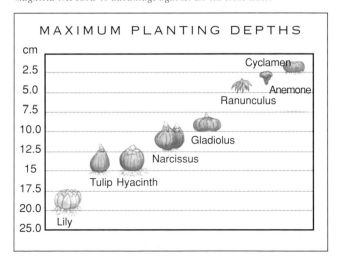

MAXIMUM PLANTING DEPTHS

cm
2.5 — Cyclamen
5.0 — Anemone
— Ranunculus
7.5
10.0 — Gladiolus
12.5 — Narcissus
15
— Tulip Hyacinth
17.5
20.0
— Lily
25.0

GROUPS OF BRIGHT PINK, fall-flowering nerines provide showy splashes of color as summer flowers fade.

BLUEBELLS, TULIPS, and daffodils are here planted informally in a lovely woodland setting beside a tiny stream.

of growth. Unless there is just the tiniest shoot appearing and you know you can plant the bulbs at once, these bulbs will be a bad buy as they will not thrive. Some chain stores and supermarkets sell bulbs and continue to display them long after they should have been planted out or discarded. If you see long pale shoots emerging from bulbs definitely don't buy them. These bulbs have been stored for too long in poor conditions. They are badly stressed and have used up a great deal of their stored reserves of energy and growing capacity so that they may fail completely or do very poorly. Try to make your selection early in the season so that you have a choice of the best on offer.

Bulbs are best planted as soon as possible once you get them home, but if you are forced to delay planting for a short while, store the bulbs in paper bags or nets—not plastic bags—and keep them in a cool, dry, airy place. If the weather is very warm, the crisper drawer of a refrigerator can be a good place to keep bulbs in good condition, but do not put them in the main part of the refrigerator as this will dry them out.

PLANTING BULBS

Choosing a site

For the majority of bulbs, choose an open planting site where they will receive sun for at least half a day. There are a few bulbs that will grow well in shade but most like at least some sun. Even woodland species such as bluebell and wood anemone grow as understorey plants in deciduous woodlands and so receive some sun during their early growing and flowering period, before the trees are fully in leaf.

The vast majority of bulbs need well-drained soil or they will rot. If there is any doubt about the drainage, plant bulbs

in raised beds or mix sharp sand or grit with the soil in the planting area. Bulbs like a fairly rich, fertile soil. At least a month before planting, incorporate a generous amount of well-rotted manure or garden compost into the planting area.

Positioning the bulbs

Your bulbs will look more natural if you plant them in clumps or groups, not in straight lines. The depth depends on the size of the bulb but it is usually two or three times its diameter (see diagram on page 11). Details of planting depths are given in the individual entries for each bulb, and refer to the depth of soil above the tip of the bulb. Spacing between bulbs is also dependent on size. Larger bulbs are usually set out about 3in apart and smaller ones 1–2in apart, but they can be crowded together for effect.

Be sure to plant the bulbs the right way up. Usually the pointed part points upwards, but there are exceptions to this rule: ranunculus and anemone have the claws or points facing down into the soil and some lilies and crown imperials are sometimes planted on their sides to avoid moisture collecting between the scales, which can lead to rotting.

In dry conditions, bulbs may need to be watered in after planting, but it is usually not necessary to water again at least until leaf shoots have appeared.

Planting under trees

Mass planting of bulbs that flower through winter and early spring under deciduous trees can turn what might otherwise be a somewhat dull area of the garden into a lovely feature. Although it is sometimes difficult to dig and plant in these areas as the soil is hard and full of matted roots, the result can be well worth the effort. The leaves that fall from the trees in fall break down into leafmould which provides ideal growing conditions for the bulbs.

MAJESTIC WHITE LILIES grown in a large ceramic container make a stunning decoration for a courtyard.

INCREASING YOUR STOCK OF BULBS

Left to themselves, many bulbs will multiply of their own accord, but there are a number of ways in which you can help the process along.

Separation

Many bulbs produce offsets or bulblets that can be gently broken away from the mother bulb when the bulbs are lifted, and planted separately. Most first-year bulblets will reach flowering size in two or three years if they are planted separately, but some are slower to flower. When separating clumps of dahlia tubers, make sure each tuber has an "eye" attached or it will not sprout and flower.

PROPAGATING DAHLIAS

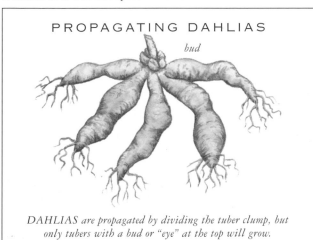

bud

DAHLIAS are propagated by dividing the tuber clump, but only tubers with a bud or "eye" at the top will grow.

THREE WAYS TO PROPAGATE LILIES

1. DETACHING SCALES

THE LILY BULB consists of lots of scales. Remove the outer scales.

PUSH the individual scales, right way up, into a box of moist peat.

BULBLETS will appear at the base of each scale.

POT UP the scales when the new bulblets appear.

2. DETACHING AERIAL BULBILS

BULBILS grow in the leaf axis of some species. Collect them and pot them up.

3. DETACHING BULBLETS

OFFSETS on the base of some lilies can be detached and planted out.

LIFTING BULBS

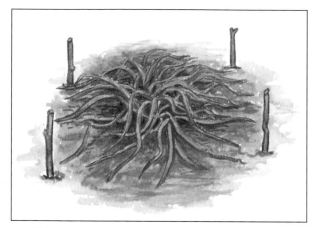

1. PUT A FEW STAKES around the edge of the clump so that you know where to dig when the leaves have died down.

2. AFTER THE LEAVES have died down, use a spade to outline the area of the clump.

3. LIFT THE CLUMP UP with a fork and shake off as much soil as possible.

4. SEPARATE THE BULBS from the clump, clean them and then store them in a dry, airy place or replant them.

Scoring and scooping

Cut a V-shape into the base plate of a mature bulb at planting time, taking care not to damage the growth bud of the bulb. This should result in many small offsets being produced by the end of the growing season. Or score through the basal plate of the bulb at right angles with a sharp knife to produce the same result. Depending on species these small offsets should produce bulbs of flowering size in two to four years.

With a sharp-sided teaspoon or curved knife, you can scoop out the entire basal plate and bulblets will form around the rim of the scooped out area. Wear gloves if you are treating hyacinths as the sap can sometimes irritate the skin.

Lilies

These techniques are not suitable for lilies, which are propagated by other methods (see page 13).
• A mature lily bulb is composed of numerous individual scales. The individual scales can be carefully removed and planted upright in a coarse, free-draining mixture such as three parts coarse washed sand and one part peatmoss or peat substitute. The scales should produce bulblets at their bases.

• Some lilies produce aerial bulbils in the axis of the leaf and these can be collected as they are about to fall. Potted into pots or trays they should produce leaves by the following spring and reach flowering size in two or three years.
• Other lilies produce bulblets just below the soil surface, around the base of the stem. If these are carefully dug out from among the roots they can be potted up and will form flowering plants in two or three years.

CARING FOR GROWING BULBS

Once planted, bulbs need little maintenance. Once the plants are actively growing, the soil should be kept moist, but never soggy. Bulbs do not usually need feeding before they flower. They are fed after blooming, when they are storing food for the following season's growth. Special instructions for feeding and watering are included in the entries for individual plants where appropriate.

AFTER FLOWERING

• After flowers have finished, cut off the spent flower stems but do not cut back the foliage. If you cut off the leaves before they have died down naturally, the bulb will not have the reserves to grow and flower the following season.

• After flowering, feed the plants with a liquid or granular balanced fertilizer and continue to water in dry conditions until the leaves begin to die off naturally. This may take about two or three months.

• If bulbs have been planted in clumps, you may be able to plant annuals between the clumps, using either seed or seedlings. Quick growers such as Virginian stock will provide a pretty distraction from the dying bulb foliage. You could also put in summer-flowering annuals or perennials that will be ready to take over the display once the bulbs have truly died down. Or you can, of course, purchase some "potted color"—annuals that are already in bloom.

• Bulbs do not usually need to be lifted every season. Most are left in the ground and lifted only every two or three years, or in a number of cases only every four or five years. Many bulbs flower well when they are crowded and then it is only necessary to lift and divide clumps when the flower numbers or quality drop off.

• Take care when you lift bulbs that you do not cut or

TALL WHITE RANUNCULUS dominate this white border, formed of plants with contrasting shapes, textures, and sizes.

A CARPET OF COLOR has been created in this garden bed by combining white tulips with violas and anemones in a range of colors. To achieve such a pleasing effect, careful planning before planting is necessary.

TALL BEARDED IRIS make an elegant border for this attractive garden path. Irises come in a rich array of colors.

ZEPHYR LILY, with its starry white flowers and deep green glossy foliage, makes an ideal edging plant. Here it grows with portulacas.

damage them—it is easy to slice into them with a spade or spear them with a fork. Discard damaged, soft, or rotted bulbs immediately. Place the sound bulbs to dry in a cool, airy spot, brush off excess soil and then store them in nets, old stockings, or in single layers in cardboard boxes. Ideally, bulbs should be stored so that they do not touch each other: they can be kept separate with shredded paper or something similar.

• Because lilies have no protective outer sheath on their bulbs, they must be lifted, the clumps divided if necessary, and the bulbs replanted at once. They can be stored for short periods in damp sphagnum moss but take care that they don't dry out.

• Some bulbous plants, such as freesias, produce quite a lot of seed if the spent flower stems are not cut off. You can collect these seeds when they are ripe or allow them to self-sow. Seedlings may take two to five years to reach flowering size, depending on the type of bulb, and they will probably not be true to type. The results can, however, be interesting as you never know quite what to expect. Particularly good seedlings should be marked at flowering time so that the bulbs can be propagated at the end of the season.

MAKING THE MOST OF BULBS IN THE GARDEN

You may wish to plant groups of bulbs under deciduous trees or in other permanent places in the garden but there are many other options. Bulbs mix well with many herbaceous perennials as the new growth of the perennials tends to camouflage the not-so-attractive foliage of the bulbs as it yellows and dies off. Bulbs in this situation can usually be left in the ground for several years before they need to be lifted and divided.

Many bulbs can be treated like annuals for a seasonal display, then lifted, and stored for use the following season. This, of course, creates more work but the results can be well worth the effort, allowing you to create different displays each year. You can have a delightful show of bulbs on their own but consider the possibility of planting bulbs and spring bedding plants together for a really stunning spring display. As well as forming an attractive association, the bedding plants help to mask the dying foliage of the bulbs, which must be left to die down naturally if the bulbs are to flower well next season. Hardy annuals sown in the fall will also serve the same purpose. Plant your bulbs and bedding plants at the same time, placing a bulb between each of the plants. For best effect, planting should be quite dense. You can experiment with color combinations or opt for tried and tested associations such as yellow lily-flowered tulips and blue forget-me-nots.

• An early-flowering bedding plant such as white primula could be interplanted with cream or yellow narcissi, or deep blue anemones for a vivid contrast.

• White, yellow-centerd primulas would team well with blue *Anemone blanda* and the dwarf narcissus "Tête-à-Tête."

• Other spring-flowering plants to combine with bulbs include polyanthus, wallflowers, and forget-me-nots.

Dwarf bulbs are ideal for growing on a rockery, usually providing color and interest before the other alpine plants come into their own. Suitable bulbs include alliums, chionodoxa, crocus, cyclamen, iris, muscari, narcissus, oxalis, and rhodohypoxis, among others.

IF YOU WANT show quality tuberous begonias, grow them under cover. Here they grow in a conservatory, where they can also be placed on raised benches so the flowers are more easily admired.

NATURALIZING BULBS IN GRASS

Bulbs naturalized in grass make a very attractive feature in gardens. However, you need to remember that the bulb foliage must be allowed to die down naturally if the bulbs are to perform well in future years, and that means that the grass cannot be mown for several weeks after the bulbs have finished flowering. This can look rather untidy, so a position for naturalized bulbs needs to be chosen with some care. Popular sites are the perimeters of lawns or under deciduous trees. In a small garden with a limited area of lawn used for many purposes, naturalizing in turf may not be a practical idea.

Choose bulbs that will flower at an appropriate period; early spring is convenient because the grass can then be mown from late spring onward. Some summer-flowering bulbs are good in a wildflower meadow, and autumn-flowering bulbs such as colchicum also grow well in grass. You can either lift a square of turf, plant a group of bulbs, and replace the cut turf, or you can plant larger bulbs individually, using a trowel or bulb-planting tool to cut a hole in the turf. Place the bulb in the bottom of the hole and replace the plug of soil and turf. Give a good watering after planting, both to settle the bulbs and to help the turf re-establish.

After the bulbs have bloomed, give the plants an application of balanced fertilizer and water the area regularly if conditions are dry. Once the bulb foliage has yellowed and died off mowing can be resumed—this usually takes some six weeks after flowering.

MINIATURE PINK NERINES and other small bulbous plants grow between paving stones where they benefit from the sharp drainage.

GROWING BULBS IN CONTAINERS

Many bulbs make lovely container plants. Pots full of bulbs are ideal for balcony gardens and patios, and for instant color, pots of bulbs in bud or in flower can be plunged into garden beds throughout the growing season.

Use a good quality potting compost, and make sure the base of the container is crocked for good drainage. Plant the bulbs at the same depth as you would in the soil, crowding them into the container for a good flowering display. Keep the compost moist at all times; regular watering will be needed.

Growing bulbs indoors

"Prepared" bulbs are specially treated to flower early—often in time for Christmas. Plant them in a shallow pot or bowl of moist potting compost and put them in a cold place such as a garden shed, keeping them dark by placing them in a black plastic bag. Leave them for 8–12 weeks; when shoots begin to appear, move them into a bright, cool room. Once flower buds begin to show color, move the bulbs to their flowering position in the home.

The bunch-flowered narcissus "Paperwhite" is unusual in that it doesn't need a cold, dark period after planting; bulbs can be left on a cool, light

Continued on page 234

A POT OF JACOBEAN LILIES can be brought to the fore when they flower.

POTTING NARCISSI FOR INDOOR USE

1. CHOOSE A POT at least twice as tall as the bulbs.

2. HALF FILL the pot with a good soil-less potting compost.

3. POSITION THE BULBS with their tops level with the top of the pot and a small gap between each and around the edge of the pot.

4. COVER THE BULBS with the compost and gently firm it down. Water, drain and place in a cold—40°F—position in total darkness. A cold, dark period of 8–12 weeks is necessary.

5. WHEN SHOOTS appear, move the pot into a bright, cool position at about 50°F.

6. WHEN BUDS appear, move the pot into its flowering position, still in bright light.

WHAT CAN GO WRONG?

There are relatively few pest and disease problems that regularly beset the home gardener growing bulbs. Bulbs that fail to come up at all have usually been planted too deep or have rotted through disease or waterlogging, especially in clay based soils. Yellowing foliage early in the growing season may also be caused by waterlogging. More serious pests of bulbs are often associated with storage conditions and it is wise to examine bulbs for damage, decay or insect pests such as aphids before planting. Diseases specific to certain bulbs are mentioned in the text under individual entries.

Failure to flower
This may be due to a number of reasons, including:
• natural offsets are not sufficiently mature to flower.
• foliage has been cut off prematurely the previous season.
• insufficient sunlight or lack of water while the foliage is still green.
• congestion of bulbs.
• "blindness"—a condition that occurs especially with daffodils and tulips. The flower bud forms but gives up trying to continue on to bloom. It may be due to incorrect storage temperature, lack of chilling or fluctuating temperatures as the flower bud emerges from the bulb.

Leaf scorch
• This fungal disease affects bulbs of daffodils and narcissi, and others including hippeastrum, crinum and belladonna lilies. It is worse in wet seasons, and occurs at the top of the bulb scales so that emerging leaves are infected. The leaf tips are reddish and scorched, and later on brown spots appear further down the leaf. Eventually the tissue around these damaged areas goes yellow. Remove and destroy the worst affected leaves and spray with a suitable fungicide if symptoms persist.

Bulb rots
• These may be caused by a number of bacteria or fungi, and lead to rotting and decay of the bulbs either in store or in the ground. They are made worse by poor drainage and overwet soil conditions. Damaged bulbs are particularly prone to infection, so take care when handling or lifting bulbs and discard damaged ones.

Grey mould (botrytis species)
• Grey mould attacks an enormous range of plants. It may manifest itself initially by spotting on leaves or stems, followed by breakdown of the tissue and the typical furry grey growth. Poor air circulation, overcrowding, overwatering and cool, humid weather conditions are favorable to its spread. Improve growing conditions and spray if necessary with a suitable fungicide.

Bulb flies
• Bulb flies lay their eggs in the soil near the bulb neck; the maggots tunnel into the bulb to feed. Affected plants produce sparse, yellow foliage and fail to flower. If you are not lifting the bulbs in the fall, pull soil up round their necks to fill the holes left by the leaves dying down.

Thrips
• Gladioli are very susceptible to attack by thrips, or thunderflies. These tiny winged insects cause silver streaking and flecking of both foliage and flowers; in a bad attack, the display can be ruined. The pest is worst in hot, dry conditions. Affected plants can be sprayed with a contact insecticide. Thrips overwinter on the corms, so after an attack, dust the corms with HCH dust after lifting and again before planting out in spring.

Lily beetle
• These small, scarlet beetles can be a serious pest of lilies and other plants such as fritillaries. Both larvae and adults feed on the leaves and stems of plants, often causing considerable damage. They are quite conspicuous and should be picked off by hand and destroyed whenever they are noticed; bad infestations can be sprayed with a contact insecticide. Beetles overwinter on weeds and plant debris, so clean up round the planting area in the fall.

Aphids
• These may attack a range of bulbous plants and should be sprayed or hosed off as they can carry virus diseases. A bad infestation disfigures flowers and foliage.

MULTI-COLORED RANUNCULUS and anemone are crowded together to produce this bright springtime scene.

Continued from page 232

windowsill directly after planting and flowers will appear in about six weeks. Plant mid-November for Christmas blooms.

Normally, non-prepared bulbs will flower at their normal period. They should be planted and left out in a sheltered position in the garden in their containers until flower buds are showing, when they can be brought into the house.

After flowering

If after flowering the whole plant and bulb are planted out into the garden, there is some chance of the bulb flowering the following year. Bulbs that stay in their pots until they have died down will in most cases not reflower the following year. When the foliage on these bulbs has died down, lift the bulbs, store them and replant them in the garden at the right time the following season. They may not flower that year but should do so the next. They are not suitable for growing as indoor-flowering plants again.

BULBS AS CUT FLOWERS

Many bulbous plants produce flowers that are ideal for cutting for the house. Most are best picked before they are fully open. For longer vase life, change the water daily or add a few drops of household bleach, or a proprietary cut flower food to the water.

FRAGRANT FREESIAS come in a glorious range of colors to epitomize the joy of the spring garden.

THIS RUSTIC BASKET of choice hyacinth blooms could not fail to lift the spirits, appearing as they do just when winter draws to a close.

TULIPS MAKE ideal cut flowers and several colorful bunches are here shown to perfection against the terracotta of the containers.

ACHIMENES
Hot water plant

HOT CERISE PINK flowers decorate this pretty little plant throughout summer. Hot water plants come in a range of colors.

THE LARGE, delicate purple-blue flowers of Achimenes "Paul Arnold" help to make this one of the most popular varieties.

FEATURES

Achimenes are easy to grow and undemanding; they are raised from small rhizomes that look a little like miniature fir cones. Leaves are toothed, elongated, and slightly furry in texture, and the colorful, trumpet-shaped flowers are carried in profusion on short stems above the foliage. The plants often assume a semi-trailing habit, making them good for growing in a basket, or in a raised pot where the stems can cascade.

Flowers are available in a wide range of shades including cream, pink, red, purple, and blue; some varieties have attractively veined throats. Although individual flowers are quite short lived, they are quickly replaced by a profusion of others throughout the season. The plants grow to about 10in.

ACHIMENES AT A GLANCE

A colorful house and greenhouse plant, flowering throughout the summer. Minimum temperature 50°F (zone 11).

Jan	/	
Feb	plant 🖐	
Mar	plant 🖐	**Recommended Varieties**
Apr	/	"Little Beauty"
May	/	"Paul Arnold"
Jun	flowering 🌸	"Peach Blossom"
July	flowering 🌸	"Queen of Sheba"
Aug	flowering 🌸	
Sept	flowering 🌸	
Oct	/	
Nov	/	
Dec	/	

CONDITIONS

Aspect Bright light is necessary, but not direct sun, which may scorch the foliage and flowers.

Site House plant, preferring cool to moderately warm conditions without marked temperature fluctuations. Use soil-less potting compost, based on peat or peat substitute.

GROWING METHOD

Planting Bury the rhizomes shallowly—about ¾in deep—in a pot of moist compost, spacing them about ½in apart, in early spring. Keep the pot in a warm room.

Feeding Feed with a high potash liquid fertilizer every 10 days or so from when the flower buds appear. Keep the compost just moist when the rhizomes start to grow, increasing the watering slightly as flowers start to form, but ensure the compost is never saturated. Tepid water is preferred, hence their common name. Stop watering when the flowers have faded.

Problems No specific problems, though aphids may attack the new growth.

FLOWERING

Season Flowers profusely throughout the summer.

Cutting Flowers are not suitable for cutting.

AFTER FLOWERING

Requirements Stop watering once the flowers have faded and allow the plants to dry off. Remove the dead top growth and keep the rhizomes in the pot of dry compost over winter in a frost-free place. The following spring, tip them out, pot them up carefully in fresh compost, and water to start them into growth again.

ALLIUM
Ornamental onion

LARGE ROUNDED HEADS are typical of alliums and the star-burst effect of this one looks stunning in the yard.

THE PURPLE-PINK FLOWERS of Allium oreophilum (also known as A. ostrowskianum) brighten up the early summer garden.

FEATURES

There are a large number of *Allium* species, including edible onions, garlic, and chives as well as many ornamental plants. Typically, they produce rounded heads of flowers, often in rosy purple shades, but there are also yellow- and white-flowered species. Some are small-growing and suitable for the rock garden, while others make excellent plants for the middle or back of borders. *A. giganteum* produces its eye-catching heads of mauve-pink, starry flowers on stems 3ft or more high, while *A. moly* grows to only 8in and has loose clusters of golden yellow blooms. Many alliums make excellent cut flowers. They are usually long lasting in water, and the dried inflorescence that remains after the blooms have fallen can be used successfully in dried arrangements, too.

ALLIUM AT A GLANCE

Versatile and varied bulbs with usually rounded heads of starry flowers in spring and early summer.

		Recommended species
Jan	/	
Feb	/	*Allium albopilosum*
Mar	/	*A. beesianum*
Apr	flowering	*A. caeruleum*
May	flowering	*A. giganteum*
Jun	flowering	*A. karataviense*
July	flowering	*A. moly* "Jeannine"
Aug	/	*A. neapolitanum*
Sept	plant	*A. oreophilum*
Oct	plant	*A. schubertii*
Nov	/	*A. siculum*
Dec	/	

CONDITIONS

Aspect Best in full sun but will tolerate light shade.
Site Alliums in borders should be positioned where other plants will help to hide their often untidy foliage. Smaller species are suitable for rock gardens. The soil must be well-drained and should contain plenty of well-decayed manure or compost. Add a dressing of lime to acid soils before planting.

GROWING METHOD

Planting Plant in fall. Planting depth varies according to the size of the bulb: cover bulbs with soil to three times their height.
Feeding Apply a high potash liquid fertilizer as buds form. Water during dry spells, but never allow the soil to become sodden. After flowering, stop watering altogether.
Problems Plants may suffer from the fungal disease rust, causing orange pustules on the foliage: destroy affected specimens. Feeding with high potash fertilizer may increase resistance to attacks.

FLOWERING

Season Flowers in late spring and summer.
Cutting Cut alliums when about half the flowers are fully open.

AFTER FLOWERING

Requirements Foliage starts to die down before blooming is complete. Cut off the spent flower stems if required. Overcrowded clumps can be divided in fall, replanting immediately.

AMARYLLIS BELLADONNA
Belladonna lily

THESE TALL FLOWER STEMS appear before the leaves, which is why belladonna lilies are also known as "naked ladies."

BRIGHT PINK BELLADONNA LILIES brighten the late summer and fall garden. The foliage here is from a clump of daylilies.

FEATURES

This beautiful South African bulb produces its multiple and sweetly perfumed blooms on sturdy purple-green stems 24in or more high. The funnel-shaped flowers may be various shades of pink or white and the flowering stem appears before the leaves, giving the plant its alternative common name of naked lady. This bulb is a great asset in the garden as the flowering period is fall, while the glossy strap-like leaves look good throughout winter and early spring. It makes an excellent cut flower. Best flowering comes from clumps that are left undisturbed for several years.

AMARYLLIS AT A GLANCE

A tall plant producing its stems of fragrant, funnel-shaped flowers in fall. Needs a warm, sheltered, sunny position.

Jan	/	Recommended Varieties
Feb	/	
Mar	/	"Johannesburg"
Apr	/	"Kimberley"
May	/	"Major"
Jun	plant 🖐	
July	plant 🖐	
Aug	/	
Sept	flowering 🌺	
Oct	flowering 🌺	
Nov	/	
Dec	/	

CONDITIONS

Aspect   Prefers a warm, sheltered spot in full sun—the bulbs need a good summer baking to produce the best flowers.

Site   A good plant for a flower bed under a south-facing wall. *Amaryllis belladonna* can also be grown in containers, planting the large bulbs singly in 8in pots. Well-drained soil is required: poor soil is tolerated but best results are achieved by digging in decayed organic matter a month or more before planting.

GROWING METHOD

Planting   Plant bulbs with their necks just at ground level and 8–12in apart in early to mid-summer.

Feeding   Apply a balanced fertilizer after flowering, as the leaves appear. Water in dry periods while the plant is in growth.

Problems   It is rarely troubled by any problems.

FLOWERING

Season   Flowers in very late summer and fall.

Cutting   A good cut flower for large arrangements.

AFTER FLOWERING

Requirements   Remove spent flower stems. Protect the crowns with a mulch of peat over winter. Leave bulbs undisturbed for several years. If lifting and dividing, do so in early summer.

ANEMONE
Windflower

THE DARK CENTERS, *deep blue or black, of* Anemone coronaria *make a stunning contrast to the rich colors of the petals.*

THIS MIXED PLANTING *of* Anemone coronaria *shows some of the range of color and form available from this lovely plant.*

FEATURES

Anemones, also known as windflowers, form a large and versatile group of plants, the most commonly grown species being *A. coronaria*, *A. blanda* and *A. nemorosa*. *Anemone coronaria* grows from a hard little tuber, *A. blanda* from hard tuberous roots, and *A. nemorosa* from very brittle, creeping rhizomes. The flowers are often very colorful, and can be daisy-like with lots of petals, or cup-shaped, rather like poppies. Anemones flower in spring; *A. coronaria* will also flower in summer, depending on the planting time. They are excellent for cutting.

ANEMONE AT A GLANCE

Low-growing, hardy plants which form a colorful carpet of spring or summer flowers.

		Recommended Varieties
Jan	/	
Feb	flowering	*Anemone blanda:*
Mar	flower /plant *	"Atrocaerulea"
Apr	flower /plant *	"White Splendor"
May	/	"Radar"
Jun	flowering	*Anemone coronaria:*
July	flowering	"Mona Lisa"
Aug	flowering	"Mister Fokker"
Sept	plant **	*Anemone nemorosa:*
Oct	plant **	"Alba Plena"
Nov	/	"Purity"
Dec	/	"Robinsoniana"
		"Vestal"

* summer flowering   **spring flowering

TYPES

A. coronaria Reaching 6–8in high, *A. coronaria* is available in a lovely range of clear colors including red, white, blue, violet, cerise, and pink, all with a black to deep navy blue center. The most popular strains are "de Caen," with single poppy-like flowers, and "St Brigid," with semi-double to double flowers. There are many named cultivars in both these strains. They can be planted in single blocks of color or mixed at random, and they can be grown in containers as well as making an excellent garden display.

A. blanda This native of Greece and Turkey bears daisy-like flowers, usually in shades of blue, although white and pink forms are available. One of spring's early bloomers, its flowers are carried on stems some 6–10in high above ferny, divided leaves. A variety of cultivars is available now and some of these are grown as potted plants. This species seeds readily and can be naturalized under trees.

A. nemorosa The wood anemone, *A. nemorosa*, likes a cool, moist climate and is often grown massed under deciduous trees, imitating its natural habitat. Here, its starry, white (sometimes lavender blue), single flowers, with their central boss of golden stamens, make a glorious showing in late spring and into early summer. The wood anemone's mid-green foliage is deeply cut. Growth may be from 4–8in high. This species increases rapidly where it finds the growing conditions suitable, and plants will eventually increase to carpet the ground.

THE BRIGHT, DAISY-LIKE flowers of Anemone blanda *brighten up the garden in late winter or very early spring.*

*WOODLAND ANEMONE (*Anemone nemorosa*) makes a pretty groundcover in a cool, moist climate, where it naturalizes readily.*

CONDITIONS

Aspect   All anemones prefer some protection from strong wind. *A. coronaria* is best in full sun, while *A. nemorosa* prefers to be grown in dappled sunlight or with morning sun and afternoon shade. *A. blanda* comes from exposed sites in mountainous districts and so will tolerate full sun or part shade.

Site   *A. blanda* and *A. nemorosa* grow well under deciduous trees, or on a rock garden, while *A. coronaria* provides bright color toward the front of beds and borders. Soil must be well drained or tubers and roots will rot. All anemone species prefer a soil rich in organic matter although *A. blanda* is happy to grow in quite poor soils as long as drainage is good. Plenty of well-decayed compost or manure should be dug into the ground about a month before planting the bulbs.

GROWING METHOD

Planting   Plant tubers of *A. coronaria* 2in deep and 4–6in apart in September and October for spring flowers, or in March and April to bloom in summer. *A. blanda* and *A. nemorosa* should be planted 2–3in deep and 4in apart in early fall. Take care not to damage brittle roots; soaking the tubers or rhizomes overnight before planting will help them to get established quickly. After planting, mulch soil with bark chips or leafmold.

Feeding   A balanced fertilizer can be applied after flowering, but feeding is not usually necessary in reasonably fertile soils.

Water in after planting if the soil is dry, and ensure the soil is kept moist but not waterlogged when the flower buds start to form.

Problems   Mosaic virus can cause distortion and mottling of the leaves and eventual death of plants. Control aphids, which spread the virus.

FLOWERING

Season   *A. coronaria* will bloom from late winter until mid-spring, or in mid-summer, depending on planting time. *A. blanda* flowers in early spring while *A. nemorosa* flowers later in spring and into early summer.

Cutting   *A. coronaria* makes an excellent cut flower. Cut rather than pull flowers from the plant. The flowers of *A. blanda* and *A. nemorosa* may last a few days in the vase but these anemones make a much better showing in the ground. Leaving the flowers on the plants allows seed to form to increase your stock.

AFTER FLOWERING

Requirements   If dry, continue to water plants until the foliage dies down. Cut off spent flowerheads unless you require seeds to form. Tubers of *A. coronaria* can be lifted, cleaned, and stored in a dry, airy place until the following fall, or left in the ground as long as drainage is good. The other species are best left in the ground to form large colonies. Lift, divide, and replant in fall if required.

ANOMATHECA
Syn. *Lapeirousia laxa*

THE OPEN-FACED, trumpet-shaped flowers resemble those of freesias, and are carried on slender spikes above the foliage.

THESE PLANTS may well be quite small, but the bright color of the flowers really stands out in the garden, even when seen from a distance.

FEATURES

Occasionally known as scarlet freesia, this pretty little plant is trouble-free and most rewarding in the garden. It multiplies readily from seed sown in spring. The trumpet-shaped flowers are pale scarlet with darker markings. They appear in mid-summer and are followed by seed pods which split open to expose red seeds. The slightly stiff, ribbed, sword-shaped leaves grow about 6–8in high while the flowers are held on spikes which extend well above the foliage. There is a pure white cultivar, "Alba," but this is not nearly as vigorous as the species. *Anomatheca viridis* has unusual green flowers and is normally grown as an indoor plant, flowering in early spring.

ANOMATHECA AT A GLANCE

A graceful, pretty bulb with sprays of trumpet-shaped flowers. Reasonably hardy in most areas.

		Recommended Varieties
Jan	/	
Feb	/	
Mar	/	
Apr	plant 👆	*Anomatheca laxa:*
May	/	"Alba"
Jun	/	"Joan Evans"
July	flowering 🌱	
Aug	flowering 🌱	*Anomatheca viridis*
Sept	flowering 🌱	
Oct	/	
Nov	/	
Dec	/	

CONDITIONS

Aspect Grows happily in full sun or partial shade.
Site This bulb is very useful for the front of borders, or for growing in pots for the patio or in the house or conservatory. Ideally, soil should be well drained but it need not be rich.

GROWING METHOD

Planting Plant corms about 2in deep and 4in apart in spring.
Feeding Supplementary feeding is generally not needed, but on poor soils a balanced fertilizer can be applied after planting. Plants in containers should be given a liquid feed every 14 days throughout the growing season. In very dry springs, water occasionally once plants have started into growth.
Problems No specific pest or disease problems are known for this plant.

FLOWERING

Season Flowers generally appear in mid-summer.
Cutting This is not a good choice as a cut flower.

AFTER FLOWERING

Requirements Cut off faded flower stems immediately after flowering if you do not want seed to set. In warm gardens the corms can be left in the ground, but in cooler areas they are better lifted in the fall and stored for replanting next spring.

CAMASSIA
Quamash

THE INTENSE BLUE flower spikes of Camassia leichtlinii *make a striking group among other border plants. A moisture-retentive soil is needed for best results—regular watering is likely to be necessary if the weather is dry. Camassias can cope with heavier soil conditions than many other bulbs.*

FEATURES

The botanical name of this plant is derived from that given to it by Native Americans, who grew the bulbs for food. It is relatively unusual among bulbous plants in preferring moist, heavy soils. The tall, graceful flower stems carry dense spires of starry blue flowers. *Camassia leichtlinii* is very reliable, with 3ft flowering stems: *C. quamash (C. esculenta)* is a little shorter and has flowers varying from white, through pale blue to deep purple. *C. cusickii* produces its 4ft pale lavender flower spikes in late spring.

CAMASSIA AT A GLANCE

Tall, stately spikes of blue, starry flowers provide valuable color in the perennial border in early summer.

Jan	/	
Feb	/	Recommended Varieties
Mar	/	
		Camassia cusickii
Apr	/	
May	flowering	*Camassia leichtlinii:*
		"Electra"
Jun	flowering	"Blue Danube"
July	flowering	"Semiplena"
Aug	flowering	
		Camassia quamash
Sept	plant	
Oct	plant	
Nov	/	
Dec	/	

CONDITIONS

Aspect Full sun or light, dappled shade will suit these bulbs.

Site Camassias make excellent border plants, valuable for early summer color. A moisture-retentive, fertile soil is preferred, though they will also grow adequately in free-draining conditions.

GROWING METHOD

Planting Plant the bulbs in early to mid-fall, 3–4in deep. Space them about 6in apart.

Feeding Feeding is not usually necessary, but an application of a balanced, granular fertilizer can be made in spring, especially on poor soils. Water thoroughly in dry conditions and on free-draining soil.

Problems Camassias are usually trouble free.

FLOWERING

Season Flowers from late spring through early summer.

Cutting Stems can be cut as the lowest buds on the spike begin to open.

AFTER FLOWERING

Requirements Cut down the flowering spikes when the flowers have faded. Do not disturb the bulbs until they become overcrowded, when they can be lifted and divided in fall.

CANNA
Indian shot

THE APRICOT-ORANGE FLOWERS of these cannas will contribute a rich, flamboyant color to the garden for many months.

THE COLOR of these scarlet cannas is highlighted by the darker green, slightly bronzed foliage that surrounds them.

FEATURES

Canna is an exotic-looking plant with bold, brilliantly colored flowers carried on tall stems, up to 4ft, above large, paddle-shaped leaves. The large blooms form an impressive spike; colors available are mainly shades of yellow, orange, and red. Sometimes the flowers are bi-colored, or spotted, streaked, or splashed with a contrasting shade. The foliage is also attractive, and in some varieties is tinged with bronze or purple. There are a number of varieties with attractively variegated foliage, which has yellow or pink veins.

Cannas are not hardy and must be protected from frost. *Canna indica* is the best known species, but most varieties generally available are hybrids, often sold as *Canna hybrida*. A wide range of named varieties is available from specialist suppliers.

CANNA AT A GLANCE

An impressive, exotic-looking plant with tall stems of brightly colored flowers and lush, attractive foliage.

		Recommended Varieties
Jan	/	
Feb	/	"Durban"
Mar	plant (indoors)	"Lucifer"
Apr	plant (indoors)	"Oiseau de Feu" ("Firebird")
May	plant (outdoors)	"Picasso"
Jun	plant (outdoors)	"Wyoming"
July	flowering	
Aug	flowering	
Sept	flowering	
Oct	/	
Nov	/	
Dec	/	

CONDITIONS

Aspect These plants must have an open but sheltered position in full sun.

Site Cannas make an impressive focal point in a bedding display, in mixed or herbaceous borders, or grow well in tubs and large containers. Soil should be free draining but rich in organic matter. In cold areas, the plants are best grown in a greenhouse or conservatory.

GROWING METHOD

Planting Set the rhizomes about 3in deep in fertile soil in late spring, once the risk of frosts is over. Better plants will be obtained by starting the rhizomes off in pots in a frost-free greenhouse in April, and planting them outide in early summer, once all risk of frost is over and the weather is suitably warm.

Feeding Give an occasional high potash liquid feed as the flower buds develop. Keep the soil moist at all times but make sure that it is never waterlogged.

Problems No specific problems are generally experienced.

FLOWERING

Season Flowers in mid to late summer, until the first frosts.

Cutting Flowers are not suitable for cutting—they are best enjoyed on the plants.

AFTER FLOWERING

Requirements Lift and dry the rhizomes in early fall, before the first frosts. Store them in a cool, frost-free place in just-moist peat or sand through the winter. If kept bone dry, the rhizomes will shrivel.

CHIONODOXA
Glory of the snow

"PINK GIANT," a variety of Chionodoxa siehei, *has relatively large blooms in a pale, purplish-pink shade.*

THE BRIGHT BLUE flowers of chionodoxa, with their prominent central white eye, make a cheerful sight in the early spring months.

FEATURES

This dainty little bulb is ideal for rock gardens or raised beds, with its mass of open, star-shaped blue flowers with white centers. They are carried on short spikes of up to a dozen or so flowers per spike. The strap-shaped leaves form loose, rather untidy rosettes.

Chionodoxa luciliae (C. gigantea) grows to 4in tall with clear blue, white-eyed flowers some 1½in or more across. *Chionodoxa siehei,* which used to be known as *C. luciliae,* and is sometimes listed as *C. forbesii,* reaches 4–10in, with slightly smaller flowers that are available in pale blue, white, or purplish-pink forms. The flowers have a distinct white eye and a central boss of stamens, tipped with gold. *C. sardensis* has flowers of a striking gentian blue

with a tiny white center that is almost unnoticeable.

CONDITIONS

Aspect Full sun or dappled shade is suitable, though they grow best in an open, sunny position.

Site Chionodoxa is suitable for window boxes, rock gardens, raised beds, the front of borders, or naturalized in grass. Soil should be free-draining, but otherwise these bulbs are not fussy about their growing conditions.

GROWING METHOD

Planting Plant the bulbs in groups about 3in deep and 3in apart in early fall.

Feeding A balanced granular fertilizer can be sprinkled over the soil surface in spring, but plants usually grow well without supplementary feeding, except in very poor, thin soils. Watering is necessary only in very dry conditions.

Problems Apart from occasional slug damage, plants are generally trouble-free.

FLOWERING

Season Chionodoxa flowers in early spring, sometimes appearing as the snow is thawing to live up to its common name.

Cutting Flowers can be cut when they begin to open. They are valuable for cutting when few other flowers are available in the garden.

AFTER FLOWERING

Requirements Lift and divide overcrowded plants when the foliage dies down in early summer after flowering, otherwise little attention is needed.

CHIONODOXA AT A GLANCE

A low-growing bulb producing plenty of bright blue flowers in early spring.

Jan	/	
Feb	flowering	
Mar	flowering	
Apr	flowering	
May	/	
Jun	/	
July	/	
Aug	/	
Sept	plant	
Oct	/	
Nov	/	
Dec	/	

Recommended Varieties

Chionodoxa siehei:
"Alba"
"Pink Giant"
"Rosea"

CLIVIA MINIATA
Kaffir lily

CLIVIAS MAKE SHOWY and colorful house plants, and will bloom for many years if they are given a winter rest.

THE PALE creamy yellow flowers of Clivia miniata citrina *make this unusual plant worth seeking out.*

FEATURES

This evergreen forms a striking house or conservatory plant, with long, deep green, strap-shaped leaves that overlap at the base rather like a leek. In spring or summer, a stout stem pushes between the leaf bases and grows to about 18in, carrying a head of 20 or so bright orange, bell-shaped flowers. These are marked with yellow in the throat and have prominent golden anthers.

Selected hybrids have larger flowers in various rich orange shades: a beautiful yellow-flowered variety, *C. miniata citrina*, has been developed but to date these plants are scarce and expensive, as are cultivars with cream-striped foliage.

CLIVIA AT A GLANCE

A striking house plant with large heads of orange, bell-shaped flowers on stout stems. Minimum temperature 50°F (zone 11).

Month		Recommended Varieties
Jan	/	
Feb	flowering ❀	*Clivia miniata citrina*
Mar	flowering ❀	"Striata"
Apr	flowering ❀	
May	transplant ✍	
Jun	/	
July	/	
Aug	/	
Sept	/	
Oct	/	
Nov	/	
Dec	/	

CONDITIONS

Aspect   Clivia prefers a reasonably bright position in the home, but not one in direct sun, which will scorch the foliage. Provide shading in a greenhouse or conservatory.

Site   Grow as a room plant while it is flowering; during the summer the container can be placed in a sheltered position outdoors. Use a loam-based or soil-less potting compost.

GROWING METHOD

Planting   Clivias are usually bought as house plants in growth.

Feeding   Give a high potash liquid feed every two or three weeks from early spring through the summer. Keep the compost thoroughly moist from spring to fall, then keep the plant cool and water it very sparingly in winter.

Problems   Mealy bugs can appear as fluffy white blobs between the leaf bases; use a systemic insecticide to control them.

FLOWERING

Season   Flowers may be carried any time between late winter and early summer.

Cutting   Not suitable for cutting.

AFTER FLOWERING

Requirements   Remove spent flower stalks. Repot only when essential; crowded plants tend to flower more reliably.

COLCHICUM AUTUMNALE
Fall crocus, meadow saffron

THE DELICATE COLOR and form of meadow saffron flowers are particularly prominent, as they appear long before the leaves. They are very welcome as they appear in fall when the yard is often looking rather untidy and faded after its summer exuberance.

FEATURES

This is another beautiful plant to brighten and lift the garden in fall. It is unusual in that the 6–9in-high flowers emerge directly from the neck of the corm, the leaves not appearing until months later, in spring. Although the flowers look similar to crocuses, the plants are not related. Up to a dozen rose pink to pale lilac, goblet-shaped flowers emerge from each corm. There is a pure white form, "Alba," and a glorious double form known as "Waterlily," that has a profusion of rose-lilac petals. Always plant in quite large groups for the best effect.

This easy-care bulb gives great rewards. It has a long history of use in herbal medicine but all parts of the plant are poisonous.

COLCHICUM AT A GLANCE

A crocus-like plant valuable for its fall flowers held on delicate stems.

		Recommended Varieties
Jan	/	
Feb	/	
Mar	/	"Alboplenum"
Apr	/	"Album"
May	/	"Pleniflorum"
Jun	/	"The Giant"
July	plant 🖐	"Waterlily"
Aug	plant 🖐	
Sept	flowering 🌸	
Oct	flowering 🌸	
Nov	flowering 🌸	
Dec	/	

CONDITIONS

Aspect Colchicum grows in full sun or very light shade.

Site Suitable for rock gardens, borders, or for naturalizing in grassed areas or in light shade under trees. For best results grow this plant in well-drained soil to which organic matter has been added.

GROWING METHOD

Planting Corms should be planted in late summer, 3in deep and 4–6in apart, in groups. Established clumps are best divided at this time, too.

Feeding Apply a generous mulch of decayed organic matter in winter. Further feeding is not usually necessary. Water in dry spells when the leaves appear in spring, and throughout their growing period.

Problems No specific pest or disease problems are common for this plant.

FLOWERING

Season Flowers spring out of the ground in fall.

Cutting Cut flowers for the vase when the goblet shape is fully formed but before it opens out. Flowers last about a week in the vase.

AFTER FLOWERING

Requirements Spent flowers may be cut off or left on the ground. Dead foliage may need tidying up at the end of the season.

CRINUM
Swamp lily

LIGHT PERFUME is an added reason to grow these pretty pink crinums. They are a good choice for a sheltered border.

VERY TALL STEMS carry the white flowers of Crinum x powellii *well-clear of the leaves so that the blooms are always well-displayed.*

FEATURES

There are more than 100 species of crinum, but *C.* x *powellii* and the more tender *C. moorei* are the two most commonly grown. Both bear large, scented, lily-like flowers in pale pink or white on stems up to 3ft high; plants have long, strap-shaped, light-green leaves. The flowers appear from middle to late summer and sometimes into fall.

The bulbs can grow very large indeed, up to 6in or more across, and can be very weighty. In time very large clumps are formed and they require considerable physical effort to lift and divide. Crinums need a sheltered position to do well. In cool areas they can also be grown quite successfully in containers that can be moved under cover in fall.

CRINUM AT A GLANCE

Large, scented, lily-like flowers in late summer and fall. This plant needs a sheltered, sunny position to thrive.

Jan	/	Recommended Varieties
Feb	/	
Mar	/	*Crinum* x *powellii*:
Apr	plant 🌱	"Album"
May	plant 🌱	"Roseum"
Jun	/	
July	/	*Crinum moorei*
Aug	flowering 🌼	
Sept	flowering 🌼	*Crinum bulbispermum*:
Oct	/	"Album"
Nov	/	
Dec	/	

CONDITIONS

Aspect   Grow crinum in a sunny, south-facing, sheltered position. *C. moorei* is best grown in a pot in a conservatory.

Site   Suitable for borders or as a specimen plant in a container on a patio or similar. Soil must be free-draining but moisture-retentive.

GROWING METHOD

Planting   Plant in spring, which is also the best time to divide existing clumps. *C.* x *powellii* should have the neck of the bulb above soil level, while *C. moorei* should be planted with the nose of the bulb at the level of the soil.

Feeding   Balanced fertilizer may be applied as new growth starts in spring. Keep the soil moist while the plants are in growth. Water plants in containers regularly.

Problems   Not generally susceptible to disease or pests but snails love to eat the foliage and flowers.

FLOWERING

Season   Flowers appear during summer and into the fall months.

Cutting   It is possible to cut blooms for the house but they last longer on the plant.

AFTER FLOWERING

Requirements   Cut off the flowering stalk when the flowers are over. Protect the crowns with a mulch of peat over winter, or move plants under cover. Disturb established plants as little as possible.

CROCOSMIA
Montbretia

THE VIBRANT COLOR of crocosmia flowers gives great decorative value but is matched by vigorous growth that may need to be controlled.

THE CLEAR, GOLDEN YELLOW flowers of "Citronella" make a pleasant change from the intense orange-reds of other varieties.

FEATURES

Also known as montbretia, some types of crocosmia are extremely vigorous and can become invasive in warm areas. It will often survive in old, neglected yards where virtually everything else has disappeared. The foliage is slender, sword-shaped, and upright or slightly arching. The flowers are carried on double-sided spikes that also arch gracefully, reaching some 2–3ft tall. Most types have eye-catching bright reddish-orange flowers that open progressively from the base of the spike. In cold areas, plants should be protected with a mulch of dry leaves over winter, and should be planted in a reasonably sheltered position.

CROCOSMIA AT A GLANCE

A vigorous plant with sword-shaped leaves and brightly colored spikes of flowers through the summer.

		Recommended Varieties
Jan	/	
Feb	/	"Bressingham Blaze"
Mar	plant	"Canary Bird"
Apr	plant	"Citronella"
May	/	"Emily McKenzie"
Jun	/	"Jackanapes"
July	flowering	"Lucifer"
Aug	flowering	"Solfaterre"
Sept	flowering	
Oct	/	
Nov	/	
Dec	/	

CONDITIONS

Aspect   Grows best in a fully open, sunny position.
Site   Good in beds or borders in well-drained soil.

GROWING METHOD

Planting   Plant corms in spring, 3in deep and about 6in apart. Pot-grown specimens can be planted throughout the spring and summer, even when in flower. It usually becomes necessary to thin out clumps every few years.
Feeding   A balanced fertilizer can be applied in early summer, but feeding is not generally necessary.
Problems   There are no pests or diseases that commonly attack crocosmia.

FLOWERING

Season   There is a long flowering period all through summer. Congested clumps often seem to produce more blooms.
Cutting   Flowers are not suitable for cutting and are better appreciated in the garden.

AFTER FLOWERING

Requirements   Cut off spent flower stems as soon as the blooms have faded to avoid seed setting and plants spreading. When the leaves have died down, protect the corms with a mulch of straw or dry leaves in all but very warm, sheltered yards.

CROCUS
Crocus

SAFFRON CROCUS (Crocus sativus) *displays branched bright orange stigmas, the source of saffron, the costly spice used in cooking.*

CROCUS CHRYSANTHUS "ARD SCHENK"—one of the most popular species—pushes up white goblet-shaped flowers in spring.

FEATURES

There are more than 80 species of crocus, mainly late winter and spring flowering, but there are some fall bloomers, too. Crocus are among the earliest flowers to appear in spring, often pushing their flowers up through the snow. In some species flowers appear some weeks before the leaves. Crocus are mostly native to the countries around the Mediterranean Sea where they usually grow at high altitudes. They do, however, extend as far east as Afghanistan.

Appearance Crocus foliage is short, rather sparse, and looks like a broad-leaf grass. The gorgeous little goblet-shaped flowers are borne on short stems 2–5in high. Most are blue, violet, white, yellow, or cream but some species have pink flowers. Many have deeper colored stripes or feathering on the petals.

Uses Although unsuitable for cutting, these little bulbous plants are one of the greatest delights of the yard. They are often mass-planted in garden beds, especially at the front of borders. They can be naturalized in lawns or grouped together under deciduous trees. Crocuses are excellent plants for rock gardens and they make good container plants, being especially suitable for winter and early spring window-boxes. The floral display of some individual species in the yard can be short, but by growing a selection of species you can enjoy these charming flowers over an extended period, from early fall right through to late spring.

POPULAR SPECIES

Spring Some of the most popular spring-flowering species are *C. biflorus*, *C. chrysanthus*, *C. flavus*, *C. minimus*, *C. tommasinianus* and *C. vernus*. Cultivars of a number of these species are available, with the many and varied cultivars of *C. chrysanthus* being especially popular, although each of these species have their admirers. *C. ancyrensis* is particularly early flowering, appearing in January and February.

Autumn Fall-flowering species include *C. kotschyanus*, *C. niveus*, *C. laevigatus*, *C. longiflorus*, *C. nudiflorus*, *C. sativus* (the saffron crocus), *C. serotinus* (also known as *C. salzmannii*) and *C. speciosus*. *Crocus sativus* is well known as the source of the costliest of all herbs and spices. Native to temperate Eurasia and widely grown in Mediterranean regions, saffron crocus needs a very specific climate to flourish and is an extremely labor-intensive crop to harvest. Saffron comes only from the stigmas of the flowers and 75,000 flowers are needed to make up a pound of pure saffron.

CONDITIONS

Aspect Prefers an open, sunny position but may be grown in light shade.

Site Good for rock gardens, raised beds, the fronts of borders or naturalized in grass. Soil must be well-drained, preferably containing plenty of well-rotted organic matter.

FALL-BLOOMING Crocus serotinus here displays its beautiful pale lilac flowers and stiff, grass-like foliage. All crocus look best when planted like this, in a random fashion that mimics their natural growth.

GROWING METHOD

Planting   Plant new corms about 2in deep and 2–4in apart. Spring-flowering varieties should be planted in fall, from September to November, while fall-flowering species should be planted in July and August. The corms of some species become quite large over time; lift and plant them further apart as it becomes necessary.

Feeding   Apply a light dressing of balanced fertilizer after flowering, particularly in poor soil conditions. Watering is necessary only if conditions are very dry: however, fall-flowering types are likely to need watering after planting in summer.

Problems   Few problems are encountered when crocuses are grown in the right aspect and soil. However, birds can sometimes damage flowers. Some birds, particularly sparrows, seem to be attracted by the shape or color of flowers and can peck them to pieces. If this occurs you will have to place a frame covered in wire netting over the plants.

FLOWERING

Season   Flowering depends on the species; some varieties begin flowering in late winter to very early spring, others slightly later in spring. Fall-flowering species flower between September and early December, and may overlap with the earliest of the winter-flowering species growing against a warm wall.

Cutting   Crocuses are not good cut flowers although they may last a few days in the vase.

AFTER FLOWERING

Requirements It is essential not to remove crocus leaves before they have yellowed as they are important in building up the corms and, therefore, next season's flowering potential. Plantings may need lifting and dividing every 3–4 years, but they can be left until corms start to push their way to the surface.

CROCUS AT A GLANCE

Low-growing bulbs valuable for their early spring flowers in a range of colors. Good for containers.

		Recommended Varieties
Jan	flowering*	
Feb	flowering*	*Crocus chrysanthus:*
Mar	flowering*	"Cream Beauty"
Apr	flowering*	"Ladykiller"
May	/	"Snow Bunting"
Jun	/	*Crocus tommasinianus:*
July	plant**	"Ruby Giant"
Aug	plant**	*Crocus vernus:*
Sept	**/ *	"Little Dorrit"
Oct	**/ *	"Queen of the Blues"
Nov	**/ *	"Vanguard"
Dec	flowering **	

* spring flowering species   ** fall flowering species

CYCLAMEN
Cyclamen

GORGEOUS UPSWEPT PETALS and a range of glorious colors ensure the lasting popularity of florist's cyclamen as house plants.

NEAPOLITAN CYCLAMEN (Cyclamen hederifolium) provides weeks of flowers and many months of decorative foliage.

FEATURES

Cyclamen form an enchanting group of plants admired for their attractive, mostly marbled foliage and distinctive flowers with swept back, slightly twisted petals. Some, such as the florists' cyclamen, have large showy flowers, while many of the species have small flowers growing only 3–4in high. Some cyclamen flower in fall or winter, while others flower in late winter and spring. Native to parts of Europe and countries around the Mediterranean, all share a similar need to be kept rather dry during their dormant period. Plants growing in good conditions can remain undisturbed for many years. The original tubers will increase greatly in size and many new plants will come from self-sown seed.

Uses
The smaller varieties make a great show when planted in masses or drifts. The floral display is quite long-lasting and even out of flower the marbled leaves make a good groundcover for many months of the year. Cyclamen can be grown in light shade under trees, in rock gardens, and in containers.

Potted plants of *C. persicum* hybrids in bloom make excellent house plants and are available from late summer right through the winter. The flowers may be delicately scented. In warm rooms in the home it can be difficult to keep these plants in good condition, and they are sometimes best considered as short-term floral decoration.

TYPES

Florists'
Florists' cyclamen (*C. persicum*) is usually seen as a flowering potted plant for indoor use, and many hybrids are available, including very fragrant miniature types. The beautifully marbled foliage and spectacular flowers make this a very showy plant. The flowers with their swept back petals come in every shade of pink and red, purple, cerise, white, and bicolors, and there are some fancy frilled or ruffled kinds. This species came originally from the eastern Mediterranean but many of the modern hybrids grown bear little resemblance to the original species.

Garden
The most easily-grown garden cyclamen is the Neapolitan cyclamen (*C. hederifolium*) which flowers during fall. It can be grown more successfully in warmer areas than most of the other species. *C. hederifolium* has beautifully marbled foliage about 3–4in high, with the small, clear pink flowers held above the leaves. There is also a pure white form of this species. *C. coum* flowers from late winter into spring and has larger, very deep pink flowers on short stems. Again, there is a white form of this species available. *C. repandum*, another spring bloomer, has probably the largest flowers of all the species cyclamens but none of these have flowers that are the size of the florists' cyclamen. The foliage on *C. repandum* is noted for its reddish undersides.

THESE CYCLAMEN COUM are thriving in an alpine-type sink garden: when they are allowed to self-seed, they soon form dense colonies. The marbled leaves are attractive, as well as the dainty, pale pink and purple flowers with their upswept petals.

CONDITIONS

Aspect   The ideal situation for hardy cyclamen is beneath deciduous trees where there is some winter sun but dappled sunlight for the rest of the year. In the home, florists' cyclamen need a cool, bright position.

Site   Hardy cyclamen can be grown on rock gardens, under trees and shrubs, and in borders. The soil must be well-drained with a high organic content. Indoors, choose a bright, cool windowsill or a conservatory.

GROWING METHOD

Planting   The flattened tubers (often wrongly referred to as corms) should be planted with their tops just below the soil surface. Plant in late summer and early fall at about 6in intervals. Pot-grown seedlings are easier to establish than dry tubers, and can be obtained from garden centers and specialist nurseries.

Feeding   If soil is poor, a sprinkling of balanced fertilizer can be given when growth begins and again after flowering. Florists' cyclamen should be given high potash liquid fertilizer every 14 days from when the flower buds appear until flowering is over. Water carefully from the base to avoid splashing the top of the tuber; never leave the pots standing in water.

Problems   Florists' cyclamen grown indoors often succumb to overwatering, drying out, and a dry, overwarm atmosphere. Vine weevils are attracted to the tubers and may cause the sudden collapse of the plant: use a soil insecticide if they are caught in time.

CYCLAMEN AT A GLANCE

Characteristic, upswept petals on a mound-forming plant with attractive marbled foliage. Suitable for outdoors or as pot plants.

		Recommended Varieties
Jan	flowering	
Feb	flowering	*Cyclamen cilicium album*
Mar	flowering	*Cyclamen coum album*
Apr	flowering	*Cyclamen hederifolium*
May	/	"Bowles' Apollo"
Jun	/	"Silver Cloud"
July	plant	*Cyclamen libanoticum*
Aug	plant	*Cyclamen pseudibericum*
Sept	flowering	*Cyclamen purpurascens*
Oct	flowering	*Cyclamen repandum*
Nov	flowering	*Cyclamen persicum:* many
Dec	flowering	hybrids available

FLOWERING

Season   *C. persicum* flowers through winter into spring. *C. hederifolium* has a long flowering period in fall, while *C. coum* and *C. repandum* flower betwen late winter and spring.

Cutting   Pull flowers from the plant with a rolling motion and cut off the thin base of the stalk.

AFTER FLOWERING

Requirements   Outdoors, leave spent flowering stems to set seed and do not disturb tubers. After flowering, allow pot plants to die down and keep dry over summer. Start into growth again in August.

CYRTANTHUS ELATUS
Vallota, Scarborough lily

SCARLET FLOWERS with a flared, trumpet-like shape make Scarborough lily a most striking plant.

IN WARM AREAS Scarborough lily can be grown outdoors, but it is more reliable as a pot plant for the conservatory or greenhouse.

FEATURES

Still more commonly known under its earlier botanical name of *Vallota*, this old favorite should be more widely grown. Four or more brilliant scarlet, open trumpet-shaped blooms are held on a sturdy stem some 18in tall among dark green, strappy leaves. The plant originates from South Africa, and unfortunately, is not hardy enough to try outdoors except in the most favored, warmest areas of the country. However, it makes a good pot plant for a cool greenhouse or conservatory, or it can be grown indoors on a sunny windowsill. During the summer, the pots can be taken outside to decorate the patio. The Scarborough lily is not difficult to cultivate, and deserves to be more popular.

CYRTANTHUS AT A GLANCE

A tender bulb with large, trumpet-shaped flowers in summer—an excellent house or greenhouse plant. Min 45°F (zone 11).

Month		Recommended Varieties
Jan	/	
Feb	/	"Pink Diamond"
Mar	/	
Apr	/	
May	/	
Jun	plant	
July	flowering	
Aug	flowering	
Sept	flowering	
Oct	/	
Nov	/	
Dec	/	

CONDITIONS

Aspect   Grows best in a bright, sunny position.
Site   Must be grown as a house or greenhouse plant in all but the very warmest areas of the country.

GROWING METHOD

Planting   Plant bulbs in summer with the tip of the bulb just at or above soil level. Set one bulb in a 5in pot.
Feeding   Apply liquid fertilizer every 14 days as soon as growth appears. Keep the plant well-watered throughout the spring and summer, but reduce watering after flowering.
Problems   No specific pest or disease problems are known for this plant.

FLOWERING

Season   Flowers usually appear in midsummer.
Cutting   Flowers will last well when cut but probably give better decorative value if they are left on the plant.

AFTER FLOWERING

Requirements   Cut off the spent flower stems. Reduce watering and allow the compost to dry out completely between late winter and mid-spring. Do not repot for several years as the plants flower best when the pot is crowded. Offsets are produced freely, and some of these may be removed to pot up and grow on to flowering size in two or three years.

Dahlia
Dahlia

THE RICH PINK of this freshly opened dahlia will gradually lighten to a delicate pale pink as the flower ages.

BICOLORED DAHLIAS have always had a strong following, whether in small, neat forms or dinner-plate sized blooms.

FEATURES

Dahlias come in many different flower forms and in a huge range of colors. Flower sizes range from tiny pompoms less than 2in across to huge blooms 12in or more wide, and they may be single, double, or semi-double. Most home gardeners are content to have a beautiful garden display but there are many enthusiasts who grow dahlias for showing.

Dahlias are grouped into different classes according to the shape and form of their flowers, and classes include single, anemone-flowered, collerette, waterlily, decorative, ball, pompon, cactus, and semi-cactus. There is also a miscellaneous group for any other type not covered by these classes. Plants can be anywhere from 12in to nearly 5ft high. They have a long flowering season from mid to late summer right through the fall. An ever-increasing range of bedding dahlias can be grown from seed; they form tubers which can be lifted and stored in the normal way in fall. Bedding varieties can also be bought as growing plants in spring.

CONDITIONS

Aspect   Dahlias prefer full sun all day with protection from strong wind. The taller varieties need staking.

Site   Dahlias are especially suitable for the herbaceous or mixed border, where they provide very welcome late summer color, but they can also be grown as bedding plants or the smaller varieties can be grown in containers. Soil must be well-drained and heavily enriched with manure or compost. Dahlias give best results in rich soil and are heavy feeders.

GROWING METHOD

Planting   The tuberous roots should be planted 4–6in deep with the neck containing the sprouting eyes pointing up, in middle to late spring. Spacing between plants depends on variety—set small growers about 12in apart, very large growers 30–40in apart. The stakes and labels should be put in at planting time to avoid damaging tubers later.

Dahlia tubers can also be potted up in moist compost in a warm greenhouse in early spring, and cuttings taken of the shoots that arise from the tubers. These can be potted up individually and planted out in the yard when the risk of frost has passed. This is a good way to increase your stock of a particularly prized variety.

Feeding   When flowering has begun, feed dahlias monthly with balanced fertilizer, or apply a high potash liquid feed every 14 days from when the flower buds begin to form. Applying a mulch of well-rotted garden compost will also help to retain soil moisture. Water well after planting tubers if the soil is dry, but further watering is usually unnecessary until after growth begins. During the growing and flowering season, it is important to make sure the plants never go short of water.

Problems   Dahlias are affected by a number of viruses, notably dahlia mosaic virus, which causes

THIS SHRUB-LIKE DAHLIA with its clear, scarlet flowers will give many months of color in the garden if dead blooms are regularly removed. Dahlias prefer a sunny corner of the yard where they are protected from the wind.

yellowing foliage and sometimes stunted plants. It is transmitted by aphids. Spotted wilt virus causes spots and rings on leaves; it is carried by thrips and affects a range of plants. Watch for thrips and aphids early in the season and spray if necessary. Snails love dahlia foliage and flowers so take care to control them. They will climb up into the plant and stay there: if plants are being damaged, search for snails on and under the leaves and destroy them, or use slug bait, making sure it is positioned out of the reach of pets and wildlife. Earwigs can also damage blooms, feeding mainly at night and causing ragged holes in petals or distorted blooms. During the day they can be trapped in upturned pots stuffed with straw positioned on stakes among the plants.

FLOWERING

Season	The long flowering period lasts from midsummer to the first frosts. Deadhead the plants regularly to prolong blooming.
Cutting	Cut flowers early in the day, remove lower leaves, and scald stems for 10–15 seconds before arranging them. They are very long lasting in a vase.

AFTER FLOWERING

Requirements Tubers may survive in the ground for several years if the soil is well-drained, but in heavy soils and in cold areas, they are better lifted in late fall. Cut off the stem 6–8in above ground, dig up the clump carefully, and shake off excess soil. Stand upside-down to drain moisture from the stem, then store in a cool, airy place such as a garden shed, lightly covered with sand, soil, or peat, for replanting next spring. Tubers can be divided, but make sure that each section has a portion of stem with a visible bud or "eye"—the tuberous root portion on its own cannot grow.

DAHLIAS AT A GLANCE		

Spectacular flowering plants giving four months of bloom. Perfect for cutting, showing, or garden decoration.

Month		Recommended Varieties
Jan	/	
Feb	/	
Mar	/	"Bishop of Llandaff"
Apr	plant	"Daleko Jupiter"
May	plant	"Firebird"
Jun	/	"Glorie van Heemstede"
July	flowering	"Grenidor Pastelle"
Aug	flowering	"Hamari Gold"
Sept	flowering	"Jescot Julie"
Oct	flowering	"Kenora Fireball"
Nov	/	"Wootton Cupid"
Dec	/	

DIERAMA PULCHERRIMUM
Fairy fishing rods, wandflower

SILKY FLOWERS in two shades of pink are suspended from the fine stems of this lovely South African plant.

AN ESTABLISHED CLUMP of fairy fishing rods produces many flowering stems. It is easy to see how the plant gained its common name.

FEATURES

The slender, arching stems of this highly desirable South African plant carry numerous bell-shaped, pendulous flowers and rise out of stiff, evergreen, sword-shaped leaves. Flowers are a rich silvery-pink in the species but there are a number of named cultivars in shades of pink, lilac, and even white.

Dense clumps of established plants produce many flowering stems, which sway in the slightest breeze to give a delightful effect. A mass planting creates a striking feature in the garden and it is often placed near water where the reflections increase its impact. Foliage grows 20in or so high but the flowering stems may be almost 6ft long in the right conditions.

DIERAMA AT A GLANCE

A perennial with graceful, slender, arching stems carrying dainty pink blooms in summer. Needs moist soil to thrive.

Jan	/	Recommended Varieties
Feb	/	
Mar	/	"Blackbird"
Apr	/	"Peregrine"
May	/	"Slieve Donard Hybrids"
Jun	/	
July	flowering	
Aug	flowering	
Sept	flowering	
Oct	plant	
Nov	plant	
Dec	/	

CONDITIONS

Aspect Needs full sun all day.

Site Dierama fits well in the herbaceous border. This plant needs well-drained but moisture-retentive, fertile soil containing plenty of well-rotted organic matter such as garden compost or animal manure.

GROWING METHOD

Planting Plant in mid to late fall, 3in deep and 12in apart.

Feeding A balanced fertilizer can be applied annually in early spring or after flowering. Water during late spring and summer if conditions are dry; the soil should remain moist throughout the growing season.

Problems There are no specific pest or disease problems normally experienced with this plant.

FLOWERING

Season Dierama bears its flowers from mid to late summer.

Cutting Not suitable for cutting.

AFTER FLOWERING

Requirements When spent, flower stems can be cut off at ground level, although they can be left to set seed if required. Dierama resents root disturbance, so corms should not be lifted unless it is essential. Self-sown seedlings can often be transplanted successfully to increase your stock of this plant.

ERANTHIS
Winter aconite

THE GLOSSY, golden buttercups of winter aconites, backed by their green leafy ruffs, give a welcome show of color in early spring.

"GUINEA GOLD," a variety of Eranthis x tubergenii, *has particularly large, showy flowers.*

FEATURES

The glossy yellow flowers of this tuber are a welcome sight in early spring. They are backed by a bract that forms a green leafy ruff, giving the flowers a Jack-in-the-green appearance. The true winter aconite is *Eranthis hyemalis*, with divided, pale green leaves and buttercup-yellow blooms: it seeds itself freely and soon spreads to form a carpet. *Eranthis* x *tubergenii* is a more vigorous hybrid, with larger, slightly later flowers. Both types grow to about 4in. Another type is sometimes sold as the Cilicica form of *E. hyemalis*, sometimes as a separate species, *E. cilicica*. It has deep yellow flowers, carried in March, backed by bronzy green, very finely cut foliage, and it grows to 2–3in tall.

CONDITIONS

Aspect	Full sun or light shade are acceptable.
Site	Winter aconites are perfect for rock gardens, the fronts of borders, or beneath deciduous trees, which allow sufficient light to the plants during their spring growing period. They prefer a free-draining but moisture-retentive soil.

GROWING METHOD

Planting	Plant the tubers in September, as soon as they are obtained—if they dry out before planting they are difficult to establish. They should be planted 1–2in deep and 3–4in apart. Eranthis are also available freshly lifted, like snowdrops, in spring, when they establish more readily.
Feeding	Ensure the soil is kept moist during the spring, especially where the plants are growing under trees or shrubs. Supplementary feeding is not normally necessary.
Problems	Plants can become invasive where conditions suit them as they seed freely; otherwise no specific problems are generally experienced.

ERANTHIS AT A GLANCE

A low-growing plant, welcome for its bright golden-yellow flowers in late winter and early spring.

Jan	/	Recommended Varieties
Feb	flowering	"Guinea Gold"
Mar	flowering	
Apr	plant flowering	
May	/	
Jun	/	
July	/	
Aug	/	
Sept	plant (tubers)	
Oct	/	
Nov	/	
Dec	/	

FLOWERING

Season	Flowers from early February to mid-March or into April.
Cutting	Flowers can be cut just as the buds are opening.

AFTER FLOWERING

Requirements	Divide crowded clumps after flowering, replanting the tubers immediately.

EREMURUS
Foxtail lily

THE STATELY yellow spikes of bloom of Eremurus stenophyllus *make this border plant certain to attract attention.*

THE TALLEST member of the group is Eremurus robustus, *its salmon-pink flower spikes towering up to 10ft.*

FEATURES

These stately plants produce tall spires of numerous, star-shaped flowers, giving a very impressive display and making good focal points in the garden. Their foliage is pale green and strap shaped; the flowering spikes tower above the leaves, reaching as much as 10ft or more in some species.

Eremurus robustus is among the tallest, with 8–10ft spikes of salmon-pink blooms: *E. stenophyllus (E. bungei)* grows to about 4ft with orange-yellow flowers. Probably most popular are some of the hybrid varieties at about 6ft, which bear flowers in a range of yellow, orange, and pink shades. Because of their height, plants need a position sheltered from wind.

EREMURUS AT A GLANCE

Tall, stately plants with large, showy flower spikes made up of masses of individual starry flowers.

		Recommended Varieties
Jan	/	
Feb	/	"Shelford Hybrids"
Mar	/	"Ruiter Hybrids"
Apr	/	"Moneymaker"
May	/	
Jun	flowering	
July	flowering	
Aug	/	
Sept	plant	
Oct	plant	
Nov	/	
Dec	/	

CONDITIONS

Aspect   Eremurus are reasonably hardy but demand a sheltered position in full sun.

Site   These are excellent plants for a place at the back of a border, or plant a foxtail lily at the end of a path for a dramatic focal point. Taller varieties usually need staking. Soil must be rich and fertile but free-draining; dig some sharp sand into the site at planting time to improve drainage if necessary.

GROWING METHOD

Planting   In early to mid-fall, set the roots 4–6in deep and 2–3ft apart.

Feeding   Keep the soil moist at all times. A dressing of balanced granular fertilizer can be made over the site in early spring, or high potash liquid feed can be given occasionally during the growing season.

Problems   Usually, no problems are experienced. The young foliage is vulnerable to frost damage and may need protection in early spring when shoots first appear through the soil.

FLOWERING

Season   Flowers in early to mid summer.

Cutting   Flower spikes may be cut as the first flowers are opening. They last well in water.

AFTER FLOWERING

Requirements   Cut down flower stems when the flowers fade. Protect the crowns from frost with a mulch of sand or dry leaves over winter. When overcrowded, divide the clumps in fall.

ERYTHRONIUM
Dog's tooth violet

"PAGODA" IS DESERVEDLY one of the most popular erythronium hybrids, with its tall stems of graceful, nodding, yellow flowers.

THE DOG'S TOOTH VIOLET, E. dens-canis, *has beautifully mottled foliage as well as attractive little rose-pink flowers.*

FEATURES

Plants of the dappled shade of woodlands, erythroniums have attractive spring flowers, star-shaped and generally nodding, with swept-back petals.

The dog's tooth violet (named after the shape of its tuber) is *E. dens-canis*, with pinkish-purple flowers carried about 6in above the attractively mottled leaves. Slightly taller is *Erythronium californicum*, with lush, mid-green, lightly mottled leaves and creamy flowers with bronze backs to the petals. *Erythronium revolutum* grows to 12in, with white, pink, or purple mottled flowers, and has given rise to the popular hybrid "Pagoda," with 6–10 pendent, graceful yellow flowers on a slender, 16in flower stalk.

CONDITIONS

ERYTHRONIUM AT A GLANCE

Spring-flowering tubers with appealing, pendulous flowers in a range of heights and colors. Many also have attractive foliage.

Jan	/	Recommended Varieties
Feb	/	"Pagoda"
Mar	/	"Citronella"
Apr	flowering ❊	
May	flowering ❊	*Erythronium californicum:*
Jun	/	"White Beauty"
July	/	
Aug	plant ✍	*Erythronium dens-canis*
Sept	plant ✍	"Lilac Wonder"
Oct	/	"Rose Queen"
Nov	/	
Dec	/	

Aspect	As a woodland plant, erythronium thrives in cool conditions and light shade.
Site	Excellent under trees or among shrubs in beds and borders or on rock gardens. Fertile, moisture-retentive soil with plenty of organic matter will ensure good growth.

GROWING METHOD

Planting	Plant the tubers in groups, 3–6in deep and 4–6in apart in late summer or early fall. Do not let the tubers dry out before planting or you will find it difficult to get the plants established: plant them as soon as possible after purchase.
Feeding	Feeding is not usually necessary. Moist soil is essential during the growing season, but the tubers must never become waterlogged. Water carefully during dry spells.
Problems	No specific pest or disease problems are usually experienced with this plant. Plants resent disturbance and may be difficult to re-establish if lifted and replanted.

FLOWERING

Season	Flowers in mid-spring.
Cutting	The taller species can be cut successfully when the buds have opened.

AFTER FLOWERING

Requirements	Disturb the roots as little as possible. If clumps become so overcrowded that flowering is adversely affected, they can be lifted and divided in late summer, replanting the tubers immediately.

EUCOMIS COMOSA
Pineapple lily

THE TUFT on top of the flower spike does resemble a pineapple, but the pretty individual flowers below give a softer impression.

THE ROBUST GROWTH of this clump of pineapple lilies shows that the growing conditions in this spot are ideal.

FEATURES

This South African plant gets its common name from the pineapple-like flower spike with its topknot of tufted leaves. The greenish-white or white flowers, sometimes tinged with pink, are scented and packed tightly onto the spike; their weight can sometimes cause the stem to flop over. The broad, sword-shaped leaves are light green and attractively spotted with purple on the underside. This flower is always of interest, whether in the yard or as a potted plant: blooms are extremely long-lasting when cut. Another species in cultivation is *E. bicolor,* with attractive green and purple flowers. Both species grow to about 24in. Pineapple lily grows from a fleshy bulbous rootstock and is dormant in winter.

EUCOMIS AT A GLANCE

A tall, striking bulb with a pineapple-like flower stem. A sunny, sheltered spot is required.

		Recommended Varieties
Jan	/	
Feb	/	
Mar	plant	*Eucomis bicolor*
Apr	plant	*E. b.* "Alba"
May	/	*E. comosa*
Jun	/	*E. pole-evansii*
July	flowering	*E. zambesiaca*
Aug	flowering	
Sept	/	
Oct	/	
Nov	/	
Dec	/	

CONDITIONS

Aspect Prefers full sun but tolerates light shade. Grows best in warm, sheltered areas, but can also be grown in colder gardens if the rootstock is protected or lifted for winter.

Site Eucomis is good for the middle or back of the flower border. Needs well-drained soil enriched with decayed organic matter before planting time.

GROWING METHOD

Planting Plant in spring, 2–4in deep and 8–12in apart.

Feeding Apply complete plant food as new growth begins. Mulch around plants in summer with well-decayed compost or manure. Keep the soil moist while the plant is actively growing.

Problems No specific problems are known.

FLOWERING

Season Flowers during midsummer.

Cutting The pineapple lily is usually enjoyed as a specimen garden plant, but if there are enough blooms, or if the stems are broken by wind, the cut flowers may last for several weeks if the vase water is changed regularly.

AFTER FLOWERING

Requirements Cut down the flowering stem when the flowers have passed their best. Either dig up the bulb and overwinter in a frost-free place, or in mild districts, mulch the planting area with peat or dry leaves to protect the bulb over winter.

FREESIA
Freesia species and hybrids

THE SPECIES Freesia alba (also known as F. refracta*) is the most heavily scented of all freesias, but can be difficult to find.*

THERE ARE MANY hybrid varieties of freesia, some with strikingly bicolored flowers like these. Most, but not all, are sweetly scented.

FEATURES

Freesias are loved for their strong perfume as well as their appearance. The wild species have yellow or white flowers and may grow about 12in high: modern hybrids grow 18in or more high and are available in a wide range of colors which includes blue, mauve, pink, red, and purple. However, some of these large-flowered hybrids have no scent. The white-flowered *F. alba* (*F. refracta*) is generally considered to have the best perfume.

For growing outdoors, buy specially prepared freesias and plant them in a sheltered position; they will flower in summer. Other freesias should be planted in containers that are brought into the house and greenhouse in fall for winter flowering.

FREESIA AT A GLANCE

Fragrant, tubular flowers in a wide range of colors are held on delicate spikes. Grow indoors or outside in a sheltered position.

		Recommended Varieties
Jan	flowering**	
Feb	flowering**	"Diana"
Mar	flowering**	"Fantasy"
Apr	plant *	"Obcron"
May	/	"Romany"
Jun	/	"White Swan"
July	plant **	"Yellow River"
Aug	plant **/flowering	
Sept	flowering*	
Oct	flowering*	
Nov	/	
Dec	/	

** indoors   *outdoors

CONDITIONS

Aspect   Freesias prefer full sun but tolerate very light shade for part of the day.

Site   Grow outdoors in a sheltered border. For winter flowers, plant in pots in summer, standing the pots in a sheltered position outside until fall, then bring them into a cool greenhouse or conservatory to flower. Use free-draining, John Innes, or soiless potting compost.

GROWING METHOD

Planting   Outdoors, plant 2in deep and the same distance apart in mid-spring. For pot culture, plant 2in deep, six to a 5in pot in July.

Feeding   Apply a high potash liquid fertilizer every 14 days through the growing season. Keep the compost just moist at all times.

Problems   Aphids may attack the flower stems. Control with a contact insecticide when necessary.

FLOWERING

Season   From middle to late winter through to mid-spring indoors, late summer outside.

Cutting   Cut when the lowest flower on the spike is fully open and other buds are well-developed.

AFTER FLOWERING

Requirements Remove spent flower stems. When the foliage dies down, lift corms and store them in dry peat until it is time for replanting.

FRITILLARIA
Crown imperial, snake's head fritillary

THE FLOWERS *of snake's head fritillary bear a distinctive, intricately checkered pattern that looks a bit like a game board.*

SNAKE'S HEAD FRITILLARY *is probably the easiest fritillary to grow and is ideal for damp meadows or woodlands.*

FEATURES

The name fritillary comes from the Latin word *fritillus*, meaning "dice-box," as the checkered patterns on the flowers of some of the species resemble the checkerboards associated with many games played with dice. There are about 100 species of this striking bulbous plant, which is related to the lilies, but only a relatively small number are in general cultivation. The form and color of the flowers varies considerably from one species to another, and some are fascinating rather than beautiful. The flowers are generally pendent and bell-shaped, carried on leafy stems; their height varies considerably, from low-growing rock garden plants such as the 4–6in *Fritillaria michailovskyi*, to the stately and imposing crown imperials (*F. imperialis*), which can reach well over 3ft tall. Many fritillaries, especially crown imperial, have a strong "foxy" scent to them which some people find unpleasant. All parts of the plant, including the bulbs, possess this scent, which can be quite penetrating.

Uses These plants, especially crown imperial, deserve a prominent place in the spring garden. They are sometimes seen taking pride of place in a bulb garden but are more often included in a mixed border planting with other bulbs and perennials. To show them to their best advantage, plant several of the same type together as individual plants will not have the same impact. Those that multiply readily, such as the snake's head fritillary, can be naturalized in dappled shade. All species can be grown in containers but most are easier to grow in the open ground.

Availability Crown imperials and snake's head fritillaries are readily available from garden centers, but some of the other species may have to be obtained from mail order bulb specialists.

TYPES

F. imperialis The best known fritillary is the majestic crown imperial, *F. imperialis*, which has a cluster of orange, yellow, or red bell-shaped flowers hanging below a crown of green leaves on a stem 20–39in high.

F. meleagris The snake's head fritillary or checkered lily, *F. meleagris*, occurs in the wild in meadows throughout Europe and is one of the easiest to cultivate. The checkered flowers occur in shades of green, purple, magenta, or white.

Others Among the many other species worth growing are *F. acmopetala*, with bell-shaped green and brown flowers; *F. biflora* "Martha Roderick," with brown-streaked cream flowers, *F. camschatcensis*, with very deep purple, almost black flowers; *F. michailovskyi*, with yellow-tipped purple bells, *F. pallidiflora*, with soft yellow flowers veined lime-green or burgundy; *F. persica* with deep purple flowers; *F. pontica* with greenish bells; and *F. pyrenaica*, a deep burgundy purple, spotted green outside while the inside is purple-checked green.

CROWN IMPERIAL (Fritillaria imperialis) is an exciting fritillary that takes pride of place in many keen bulb growers' yards. The "crown" referred to in the common name is the topknot of leaves from which the bell-shaped flowers are suspended.

CONDITIONS

Aspect Fritillary grows best in light shade or with morning sun and afternoon shade. Some species take full sun. All are best with protection from strong wind.

Site Fritillaries can be grown in beds and borders, on rockeries, or in containers, according to species. *F. meleagris* can be naturalized in grass. Soil for fritillaries must be well-drained but should contain plenty of well-rotted compost or manure. The area around the plants should be well-mulched, too. *F. meleagris* prefers a more moisture-retentive soil than some of the other species.

FRITILLARIA AT A GLANCE

Unusual bulbs in a wide range of sizes and flower forms, with striking, pendent, bell-shaped blooms.

		Recommended Varieties
Jan	/	
Feb	/	*Fritillaria biflora:*
Mar	/	"Martha Roderick"
Apr	flowering	
May	flowering	*Fritillaria imperialis:*
Jun	/	"Lutea"
July	/	"Rubra Maxima"
Aug	/	"Prolifera"
Sept	plant	"The Premier"
Oct	plant	
Nov	plant	*Fritillaria persica:*
Dec	/	"Adiyaman"

GROWING METHOD

Planting The lily-like bulbs can dry out quickly and should be planted as soon as they are available. Planting depth varies between 2–8in depending on species. Plant the large bulbs of crown imperials on their sides on a layer of sand so that water does not collect in the hollow center.

Feeding Apply a general fertilizer after flowering or a high potash fertilizer in early spring as growth starts. Water in dry spells during the growing season, especially before flowering.

Problems Bulbs may rot in badly drained soil.

FLOWERING

Season Flowers appear from mid-spring to early summer.

Cutting Despite being quite long-lasting as a cut flower, blooms are rarely used this way because of the unpleasant smell of some flowers. Unfortunately crown imperial is one of these. However, they are so striking in the garden that they are best enjoyed there.

AFTER FLOWERING

Requirements When flowers have faded, flowering stems can be cut down, but leave the flowerheads on snake's head fritillaries to set seed. Bulbs are best left undisturbed, but if necessary clumps can be divided in summer and replanted immediately.

GALANTHUS
Snowdrop

TRUE HARBINGERS of spring, snowdrops are among the first bulbs to appear in late winter, often pushing up through the snow.

THE DOUBLE SNOWDROP, Galanthus nivalis "Flore Pleno," is an easily grown, vigorous, and reliable variety.

FEATURES

The snowdrop (*G. nivalis*) is well-loved for flowering in late winter while conditions are still very bleak. Most of the dozen or so species flower in late winter to early spring although there is one fall-flowering species (*G. reginae-olgae*). *G. elwesii* and *G. caucasicus* are also very early bloomers. There are named varieties of several species available. *G. nivalis* grows only 4–5in high, but taller varieties such as *G. elwesii* can grow up to 10in. The nodding flowers have three long, pure white petals and three shorter ones marked with a bright green horseshoe shape. The dark green foliage may be matt or glossy but is usually shorter than the flowers.

GALANTHUS AT A GLANCE

A small, dainty bulb popular for its late winter and early spring flowers. Very hardy.

		Recommended Varieties
Jan	flowering	"Atkinsii"
Feb	flowering	"Cordelia"
Mar	flowering / plant "in the green"	"Sam Arnott"
Apr	/	*Galanthus lutescens:*
May	/	"Magnet"
Jun	/	*Galanthus nivalis:*
July	/	"Flore Pleno"
Aug	/	"Lady Elphinstone"
Sept	plant	"Lutescens"
Oct	plant	"Pusey Green Tip"
Nov	/	"Scharlockii"
Dec	flowering	"Viridapicis"

CONDITIONS

Aspect   Grows best in shade or dappled sunlight.
Site   Ideal for rockeries, the fronts of beds, and borders or naturalizing under deciduous trees. Soil must contain plenty of decayed organic matter to prevent excessive drying out in summer. Mulching in fall with old manure, compost, or leafmold is beneficial.

GROWING METHOD

Planting   Plant bulbs in fall 3–4in deep (deeper in light soils) and about the same apart. Do not allow the bulbs to dry out before planting. Snowdrops are much more reliable when transplanted while in growth, after flowering—known as planting "in the green." Plants are available from specialist suppliers in late winter or early spring.
Feeding   Mulch during fall with decayed organic matter. Watering is not usually necessary.
Problems   No specific problems are known.

FLOWERING

Season   Flowering is from winter through to spring, depending on species.
Cutting   Flowers can be cut for indoor decoration.

AFTER FLOWERING

Requirements   Existing clumps can be lifted, divided, and replanted as soon as the flowers have faded. Do not leave the plants out of the soil any longer than necessary.

GLADIOLUS CALLIANTHUS
Acidanthera

EACH BLOOM *carries an attractive central, deep purple blotch, and has a slightly uneven, star-like shape.*

THE SWEETLY-SCENTED *white blooms of acidanthera appear late in the summer, when many other bulbs are over.*

FEATURES

Although this plant is now classified as a species of gladiolus, many gardeners still know it better under its previous botanical name of *Acidanthera murielae*. The pure white, slightly drooping blooms have a dark purple central blotch, and are sweetly scented; their similarity to a gladiolus flower is obvious, but they are more delicate and graceful. The leaves are erect and sword shaped, growing to about 2ft. The flowers—up to a dozen per corm—are held on slender stems above the tips of the leaves, and appear in late summer.

This is not a plant for cold, exposed yards, requiring a warm, sunny position to do well. In cold regions it can be grown successfully as a conservatory or cool greenhouse plant.

G. CALLIANTHUS AT A GLANCE

A late summer flowering plant with attractive, white, scented blooms. Suitable for growing outdoors in mild areas only.

		Recommended Varieties
Jan	/	
Feb	/	"Murieliae"
Mar	plant (indoors) 🗝	
Apr	plant (outdoors) 🗝	
May	/	
Jun	/	
July	/	
Aug	flowering 🌸	
Sept	flowering 🌸	
Oct	/	
Nov	/	
Dec	/	

CONDITIONS

Aspect	These plants require full sun.
Site	Acidantheras can be grown in a sheltered, sunny spot outside in mild areas: otherwise grow the corms in pots in a greenhouse or conservatory, moving the pots onto a sheltered patio or similar position in midsummer. Light, free-draining soil is required. In pots, use soiless or John Innes potting compost.

GROWING METHOD

Planting	Plant in late spring, 4in deep and 8–10in apart.
Feeding	Give an occasional application of high potash liquid fertilizer (such as rose or tomato feed) during the growing season. Pot-grown plants should be fed every 10–14 days. Watering is not necessary for plants in the open ground except in very dry conditions; water pot-grown plants sufficiently to keep the compost just moist.
Problems	Plants may fail to flower in cold, exposed yards. Corms may rot in heavy, clay soils.

FLOWERING

Season	Flowers in late summer; mid-August through September.
Cutting	Pick the stems when the buds are showing white at their tips.

AFTER FLOWERING

Requirements	Allow the foliage to die down, then lift the corms before the first frosts. Allow them to dry, brush off soil and store in dry, cool, frost-free conditions until the following spring.

GLADIOLUS HYBRIDS
Gladiolus, sword lily

THE STRIKING *red and yellow flowers of* Gladiolus dalenii *ensure this species will always stand out in a crowd.*

A POPULAR *hybrid gladiolus, "Green Woodpecker" is much sought after by flower arrangers because of its unusual coloring.*

FEATURES

The gladiolus with which we are most familiar comes from South Africa as do many other species, but other species originated in the Mediterranean regions and western Asia. There are about 300 species of gladiolus, many of them well worth seeking out for your garden, but the modern garden gladiolus is a hybrid. The stiff, sword-shaped leaves surround a flower spike that appears in spring and may be 39in or more high, but there are dwarf forms less than half this height. Flower spikes carry numerous individual blooms, usually densely packed on the stem and of a characteristic, irregular trumpet shape. The color range is extensive, including various shades of pink, red, yellow, orange, mauve, maroon, white, and green: flowers are often bicolored.

Special types   A great range of species and cultivars is now available to add to the familiar hybrids. Baby gladiolus or painted ladies, *G.* x *colvillei*, (sometimes wrongly known as *G. nanus*) grows 12–16in high and comes in a range of colors, including many with contrasting markings. Green and white "The Bride" is perhaps the best known. Other species worth seeking out include *G. tristis*, with pale creamy yellow flowers; *G. dalenii* (syn. *G. natalensis*) with red to yellow flowers; *G. carneus*, with pink flowers; *G. cardinalis*, with rich red flowers marked in white; and *G. communis byzantinus*,

hardy in warmer parts of the country and producing spikes of purple-pink flowers in early summer.

Uses   Gladiolus makes a great garden display and cut flower. Dwarf forms make good pot plants.

CONDITIONS

Aspect   Grows best in full sun with some shelter from strong wind.

Site   Gladiolus can be difficult to place, as their stiff, upright form, which usually requires staking, is very formal. They are often grown in the vegetable garden and used as cut flowers, but with care they can be grown in beds and borders. Soil should be well-drained with a high organic content. Dig in well-rotted manure or compost a month or more before planting.

GROWING METHOD

Planting   Corms should be planted 3–4in deep and about 6in apart. Plant hybrid varieties in spring; stagger planting between March and May to give a succession of blooms. Spring-flowering species should be planted in fall; in colder areas of the country they are best overwintered in a cool greenhouse.

Feeding   In soils enriched with organic matter

THE GLOWING red blooms of "Victor Borge" make a brilliant splash of color in any garden setting.

THE PURE WHITE of these gladiolus appears even whiter against the blue forget-me-nots. The blooms will last longer in cool areas.

supplementary feeding should not be necessary. In poor soils apply a balanced fertilizer to the soil before planting. In dry weather, water regularly throughout the growing season.

Problems Thrips, which rasp and suck sap from foliage and flowers, are a perennial problem in some areas. Deep colored flowers, such as reds and maroons, show their damage more readily than paler ones, with light-colored flecks spoiling their appearance. The summer months are the worst time for attacks, but the pest may overwinter on corms in store. Dust the corms with a suitable insecticide before storing and again before planting. At planting time, discard corms with dark or soft spots, which may be infected with various fungal rots.

FLOWERING

Season Hybrids planted in spring will produce flowers through summer into early fall. Fall-planted species will flower in early summer.

Cutting Cut spikes for indoor decoration when the second flower on the spike is opening. Cut the flower stem without removing the leaves if that is possible. Change the water in the vase daily and remove lower blooms from the spike as they fade.

AFTER FLOWERING

Requirements Lift corms carefully as soon as foliage begins to yellow. Cut off old leaves close to the corm. Dry corms in a warm, airy place for 2–3 weeks and clean them by removing old roots and the outer sheath of corm. To increase your stock of gladiolus, remove the small cormlets from the parent bulb and store them separately. These cormlets should produce full flowering size corms in the second year. If you have had problems with thrips in previous seasons, treat corms with insecticide dust before storing.

GLADIOLUS AT A GLANCE

Popular hybrid varieties have tall, stiff spikes, packed with large, colorful flowers; more delicate species flower in spring.

		Recommended Varieties
Jan	/	
Feb	/	*Hybrids:*
Mar	plant	"Amsterdam"
Apr	plant	"Christabel"
May	flowering */plant	"Esta Bonita"
Jun	flowering *	"Green Woodpecker"
July	flowering	"Hunting Song"
Aug	flowering	"Lady Godiva"
Sept	flowering plant *	"Victor Borge"
Oct	/	
Nov	/	*G. x colvillei:*
Dec	/	"Amanda Mahy"
		"The Bride"

*fall planted species

GLORIOSA
Glory lily

FLUTED RECURVED PETALS give these flowers an airy, floating effect. Plants grow rapidly in warm, humid conditions.

THESE GLORIOSA LILIES at various stages of development display a fascinating range of colors and shapes.

FEATURES

This climber is always sure to attract attention. It grows from elongated, finger-like tubers, and needs greenhouse or conservatory conditions. A plant will grow up to 8ft in the right conditions, its long, slender stems twining their way through netting or wooden trellis supports by means of tendrils at the tips of the lance-shaped leaves. The unusual lily-like flowers are crimson and yellow, with their wavy-edged petals strongly recurved to show the prominent, curving stamens.

Gloriosa has a long flowering period through summer and fall and usually gives a spectacular display. It is worth growing in a prominent position where it can be admired, but it is not hardy enough to grow outdoors.

GLORIOSA AT A GLANCE

A greenhouse climber with spectacular summer flowers. Minimum temperature 50°F (zone 11).

Jan	plant	
Feb	plant	
Mar	plant	
Apr	/	
May	/	
Jun	/	
July	flowering	
Aug	flowering	
Sept	flowering	
Oct	/	
Nov	/	
Dec	/	

Recommended Varieties

Gloriosa superba:
  "Rothschildiana"
  "Lutea"

CONDITIONS

Aspect   Grow in a greenhouse or conservatory, in bright light but shaded from direct summer sun.

Site   Use either soilless or John Innes potting compost.

GROWING METHOD

Planting   The tubers are planted out in late winter or early spring about 2in deep, placing one tuber in a 6in pot of moist compost. Take care not to injure the tips of the tubers.

Feeding   Apply high potash liquid fertilizer every 14 days during the growing season. Water sparingly until growth commences, more freely during active growth but never allow the soil to become waterlogged.

Problems   Slugs may attack the tubers, and poor drainage or overwatering will rot them.

FLOWERING

Season   Flowers throughout the summer.
Cutting   Flowers last well when picked.

AFTER FLOWERING

Requirements   Snap off flowers as they fade. Reduce watering when flowering has finished and allow the tubers to dry out for the winter. Store them dry in their pots or in dry peat in a minimum temperature of 50°F and replant in spring.

HEDYCHIUM
Ginger lily

LONG RED STAMENS contrast nicely with the clear yellow flowers on this kahili ginger. The flowers have a strong perfume.

THIS GINGER LILY needs room to spread out and show off its strong lines. It is a useful landscaping plant.

FEATURES

There are over 40 species of ginger lily although not many species are in cultivation. These plants are strong growers, mostly to about 6ft, their growth originating from sturdy rhizomes. They can be bedded out in borders for the summer, or grown in tubs as a patio or greenhouse and conservatory plant. Mid-green leaves are lance shaped.

The tall, showy heads of flowers are carried in late summer. White ginger or garland flower, *H. coronarium*, has white and yellow, very fragrant flowers while scarlet or red ginger lily, *H. coccineum*, has faintly scented but most attractive blooms in various shades of red, pink, or salmon. Also heavily scented is kahili ginger, *H. gardnerianum*, with large, clear yellow flowers and prominent red stamens.

HEDYCHIUM AT A GLANCE

Large, showy leaves are topped by striking heads of many flowers, often scented. Needs a minimum temperature of 45°F (zone 11).

Jan	/	Recommended Varieties
Feb	/	
Mar	plant	*Hedychium coccineum*
Apr	plant	*aurantiacum*
May	/	*Hedychium coccineum:*
Jun	/	"Tara"
July	flowering	*H. coronarium*
Aug	flowering	*H. densiflorum:*
Sept	flowering	"Assam Orange"
Oct	/	*H. gardnerianum*
Nov	/	
Dec	/	

CONDITIONS

Aspect	Needs a bright, sunny spot.
Site	In cold areas, grow in a greenhouse or conservatory; otherwise grow in a sheltered border outside. Rich, moisture-retentive soil is necessary; add well-rotted organic matter before planting time.

GROWING METHOD

Planting	Plant in spring, with the tip of the rhizome just buried below the soil surface. Space rhizomes about 24in apart.
Feeding	A balanced fertilizer can be applied as growth begins in spring. Keep the soil moist throughout the growing season.
Problems	There are generally no particular problems experienced.

FLOWERING

Season	Flowers in mid to late summer and early fall.
Cutting	Flowers can be cut for indoor decoration but they will last very much longer on the plant.

AFTER FLOWERING

Requirements	Cut flower stems down to the ground when the flowers have faded. Lift the rhizomes when the foliage has died down and overwinter in dry peat in a frost-free place, replanting the following spring. Pot plants can be left in their pots over winter. Rhizomes may be divided in spring to increase your stock.

HIPPEASTRUM
Hippeastrum, amaryllis

"APPLE BLOSSOM" is a cultivar with unusual soft, pastel flowers. Most hippeastrums have very strongly colored flowers in the red range.

BIG, SHOWY TRUMPET FLOWERS on stout stems are a feature of hippeastrums.

FEATURES

There are many species of hippeastrum but the most familiar plants, with their very large, trumpet-shaped flowers, are cultivars or hybrids of a number of species. They are popular winter-flowering house plants; between two and six large flowers are carried on thick stems that are generally over 20in high. Blooms appear all the more spectacular because they appear ahead of the leaves or just as the leaves are emerging. There are many cultivars available but most flowers are in various shades of red, pink, or white, separately or in combination. Because of the very large size of the bulb it is normal to use only one bulb per 7in pot. The bulbs should be allowed to rest during summer if they are to be brought into bloom again.

HIPPEASTRUM AT A GLANCE

A windowsill plant with very showy, large, trumpet-shaped flowers on tall stems in winter and spring. Minimum 56°F (zone 11).

Jan	flowering	
Feb	flowering	
Mar	flowering	
Apr	flowering	
May	/	**Recommended Varieties**
Jun	/	"Apple Blossom"
July	/	"Bouquet"
Aug	/	"Lady Jane"
Sept	/	"Lucky Strike"
Oct	plant	"Mont Blanc"
Nov	plant	"Flower Record"
Dec	plant	"Oscar"
		"Picotee"
		"Star of Holland"

CONDITIONS

Aspect   Needs full sun and bright conditions.
Site   Grow as a pot plant in the home or greenhouse. Use soilless potting compost.

GROWING METHOD

Planting   Plant with about half to one-third of the bulb above soil level in a pot just large enough to hold the bulb comfortably. Bulbs can be planted any time between October and March. Use "prepared" bulbs for Christmas and early winter flowers.

Feeding   Apply a high potash liquid feed every 10–14 days when the bulb starts into growth. Water sparingly until the bud appears, then more freely until the foliage begins to die down.

Problems   No problems usually, but overwatering can cause the bulb to rot.

FLOWERING

Season   Showy flowers appear in about eight weeks after planting, between late December and late spring.

Cutting   With frequent water changes flowers can last well, but are usually best left on the plant.

AFTER FLOWERING

Requirements   Remove spent flower stems, continue to water and feed until foliage starts to yellow and die down. Allow the bulbs to dry off in a cool place, repot in fresh compost and resume watering in fall to start them into growth.

HYACINTHOIDES
Bluebell

AN ALL-TIME FAVORITE, clear sky-blue bluebells don't need a lot of attention to produce a beautiful display year after year.

NATURALIZED UNDER TREES, these Spanish bluebells revel in the moist soil formed from the decaying leaf litter.

FEATURES

This is the ideal bulb for naturalizing under deciduous trees or for planting in large drifts in the yard. The delicately scented blue flowers are a great foil for many spring-flowering shrubs which have pink or white flowers: there is a white and a pink form but the blue is undoubtedly the most popular. The botanical names of these plants have undergone several changes in recent years, and they are sometimes listed under endymion and scilla as well as hyacinthoides. The Spanish bluebell (*H. hispanica*) is a little larger, up to 12in high, and more upright in growth than the English bluebell (*H. non-scripta*). Bluebells multiply rapidly and can be very invasive. They can also be grown in containers.

HYACINTHOIDES AT A GLANCE

Well-known and loved blue flowers in mid to late spring, ideal for naturalizing under deciduous trees.

Jan	/	**Recommended Varieties**
Feb	/	
Mar	/	*Hyacinthoides hispanica:*
Apr	flowering	"Danube"
May	flowering	"Queen of the Pinks"
		"White City"
Jun	/	
July	/	*Hyacinthoides non-scripta:*
Aug	plant	"Pink Form"
Sept	plant	"White Form"
Oct	plant	
Nov	/	
Dec	/	

CONDITIONS

Aspect These woodland plants prefer dappled sunlight or places where they receive some morning sun with shade later in the day.

Site Perfect when naturalized under deciduous trees; bluebells also grow well in borders but don't let them smother delicate plants. A moisture-retentive soil with plenty of organic matter suits them best.

GROWING METHOD

Planting Plant bulbs 2in deep and about 3–4in apart in late summer or early fall. The white bulbs are fleshy and brittle; take care not to damage them when planting.

Feeding Not usually required.

Problems No specific problems are usually experienced.

FLOWERING

Season Flowers from middle to late spring, with a long display in cool seasons. Flowers do not last as well if sudden high spring temperatures are experienced.

Cutting Not suitable for cutting.

AFTER FLOWERING

Requirements Remove spent flower stems unless you require plants to seed themselves. Keep the soil moist until the foliage dies down. The bulbs are best left undisturbed, but overcrowded clumps can be lifted and divided in late summer and replanted immediately.

HYACINTHUS ORIENTALIS
Hyacinth

WELL-ROUNDED FLOWER SPIKES are characteristic of the fine hyacinth cultivars available today. They make excellent pot plants.

HYACINTHS, with cool white flowers and dark green foliage, combine with a silvery groundcover to make a pretty garden picture.

FEATURES

Sweet-scented hyacinths are favorites in the garden or as potted plants. In the garden they look their best mass-planted in blocks of one color. They are widely grown commercially both for cut flowers and as potted flowering plants. Flower stems may be from 6–12in high and the color range includes various shades of blue, pink, and rose, and white, cream and yellow. Individual flowers are densely crowded onto the stem, making a solid-looking flowerhead. Bulbs usually flower best in their first year, the second and subsequent years producing fewer, looser blooms. Some people with sensitive skin can get a reaction from handling hyacinth bulbs, so wear gloves if you think you may be affected.

Types The most popular hyacinths are the so-called Dutch hybrids; many varieties are available from garden centers and mail order bulb suppliers. Blues range from deep violet to pale china blue: the rose range includes deep rosy red, salmon, and light pink. As well as white varieties, there are those with cream and clear yellow flowers. Some varieties have flowers with a lighter eye or a deeper colored stripe on the petals, giving a two-tone effect.
Roman hyacinths—*H. orientalis albulus*—have smaller flowers loosely arranged on the stems: Multiflora varieties have been treated so that they produce several loosely packed flower spikes from each bulb, and have a delicate appearance that makes them ideal for growing in pots.
Cynthella hyacinths are miniatures growing to about 6in, usually sold in color mixtures.

CONDITIONS

Aspect Does well in sun or partial shade but does not like heavy shade.
Site Grow hyacinths in pots and bowls indoors; pots and tubs outside and in flower borders. Soil must be well-drained.

GROWING METHOD

Planting Plant bulbs 6in deep and 8in apart in early to mid-fall. Apply compost or rotted manure as a mulch after planting.
Feeding Apply a balanced general fertilizer after flowering. Watering is not usually necessary in beds and borders, but bulbs in containers must be kept just moist during the growing season.
Problems Hyacinths are not generally susceptible to pest and disease problems, though bulbs will rot if soil conditions are too wet. Forced bulbs indoors often fail to flower if they have not had the correct cold, dark period after planting.

FLOWERING

Season Flowers appear from late winter to mid-spring. "Prepared" bulbs should be used for Christmas flowering, and must be planted in September.
Cutting Blooms may be cut for the vase where they will last about a week if the water is changed daily.

AFTER FLOWERING

Requirements Remove spent flower stems and continue to water and feed the plants until the foliage starts to yellow and die down.

BLUE AND WHITE are always an effective combination, a proposition amply demonstrated by this formal garden in which deep violet-blue hyacinths stud a bed of white pansies. Although they are often grown in pots, hyacinths are at their most beautiful in a setting such as this.

POTTED HYACINTHS

Features   Potted hyacinths in bloom make a lovely cut flower substitute and are ideal as gifts. They can be grown to flower in midwinter when their color and fragrance are most welcome.

Outdoors   If growing hyacinths outdoors choose a container at least 6in deep so that you can place a layer of potting compost in the base of the pot before planting. Bury the bulbs 4in below the surface of the compost. Water to moisten the compost thoroughly after planting and place the pot where it will receive sun for at least half a day. Don't water again until the compost is feeling dry or until the shoots appear. When the flower buds are showing color, move the pots indoors. When blooms have faded, cut off spent stems and water as needed until the foliage dies down.

Indoors   If growing hyacinths indoors, choose a container 4–6in deep but plant the bulbs just below the surface of the compost. (In pots without drainage holes, bulb fiber can be used intead of compost.) Water after planting, allow to drain and then transfer the pot to a cool, dark position. The pots can be placed inside a black plastic bag and put into a shed, cold frame or similar place with a temperature of about 40°F. Check from time to time to see if shoots have emerged. When shoots emerge (this usually takes about 10–12 weeks) and reach 1–2in in height, bring the pot into the light, gradually increasing the amount of light as the shoots green up. As buds appear, give them as much sunlight as possible.

In glass   Hyacinths can also be grown in a glass or ceramic container that has a narrow neck. Sometimes you can buy a purpose-built container, usually plastic, that has the top cut into segments so that the bulb sits neatly on it. Fill the container with water to just below the rim. Choose a good-sized bulb, then rest it on top of the rim of the container so that the base of the bulb is in water. Place the container in a cool, dark place and leave it there until large numbers of roots have formed and the flower bud is starting to emerge, when they can be brought into the light. These bulbs are unlikely to regrow and may be discarded after flowering.

HYACINTHUS AT A GLANCE

Sweetly scented, densely packed flower spikes, ideal for growing indoors or outside. Frost hardy.

Month		Recommended Varieties
Jan	flowering	"Amsterdam"
Feb	flowering	"Anna Marie"
Mar	flowering	"Blue Giant"
Apr	flowering	"City of Haarlem"
May	/	"Delft Blue"
Jun	/	"Gipsy Queen"
July	/	"Jan Bos"
Aug	/	"L'Innocence"
Sept	plant	"Lord Balfour"
Oct	plant	"Mont Blanc"
Nov	/	"Queen of the Pinks"
Dec	flowering	

HYMENOCALLIS
Spider lily, Peruvian daffodil

THE WHITE *or cream flowers of spider lilies are something like an exotic daffodil, with an attractive fragrance.*

HYMENOCALLIS CAN *be grown outside in reasonably sheltered yards, but the bulbs should be lifted in fall to ensure survival.*

FEATURES

Spider lilies are native to various parts of North and South America. They produce broad, strap-shaped, deep green leaves and fascinating, lightly fragrant flowers that are carried on a stout stem. The flower has a trumpet-shaped central cup with long, narrow, petal-like segments surrounding it; flowers are usually white but can be yellow or cream. Hymenocallis can be grown in a sheltered, sunny position outside, but is often treated as a greenhouse or conservatory plant. All spider lilies can be container grown. *H.* x *festalis, H. narcissiflora* and the cultivar "Sulfur Queen" are the deciduous varieties most often grown, while the more difficult to find *H. littoralis* and *H. speciosa* are the most popular of the evergreen species. Hymenocallis is sometimes also listed as ismene.

HYMENOCALLIS AT A GLANCE

A rather tender bulb bearing unusual fragrant blooms like exotic daffodils. Can also be grown as a conservatory plant.

Jan	/	
Feb	/	
Mar	plant (indoors) 🌱	**Recommended Varieties**
Apr	/	"Advance"
May	🌱(outdoors)/flowering 🌸	"Sulfur Queen"
Jun	flowering 🌸	
July	/	*Hymenocallis* x *festalis:*
Aug	flowering 🌸	"Zwanenburg"
Sept	/	
Oct	/	
Nov	/	
Dec	/	

CONDITIONS

Aspect   Grows in full sun or light shade with shelter from strong wind.

Site   In sheltered yards hymenocallis can be grown outside in beds and borders or containers. In cold areas, it is best grown as a greenhouse or conservatory plant. Soil must be free-draining. Use soil-less potting compost for pots.

GROWING METHOD

Planting   For growing in containers, plant bulbs in spring with the neck of the bulb just below the soil surface, using one of the large bulbs per 6in pot. Outdoors, plant in May, burying the bulbs 5in deep.

Feeding   High potash liquid fertilizer can be applied as buds form. Mulching around plants with well-rotted organic matter also supplies nutrients. Water sparingly until the shoots show, then water regularly through the growing season.

Problems   No specific problems are usually experienced.

FLOWERING

Season   The fragrant spider lilies are produced in early summer indoors, mid to late summer outside.

Cutting   Makes a delightful and unusual cut flower.

AFTER FLOWERING

Requirements   Allow the foliage to die down after flowering; lift outdoor bulbs and store in dry peat in a frost-free place over winter. Leave potted plants dry in their containers over winter and repot the following spring.

IPHEION UNIFLORUM
Spring star flower

SPRING STAR FLOWER is an ideal edging plant for a sunny yard and it can be left undisturbed for several years.

THE SOFT LILAC of the flowers makes spring star flower very versatile as it blends into most garden color schemes.

FEATURES

This low-growing plant makes an ideal edging but should be planted in large drifts wherever it is grown to produce its best effect. Tolerant of rather tough growing conditions, it is most suitable for filling pockets in a rockery or growing toward the front of a herbaceous border. It also makes a good container plant. It has grey-green, narrow, strappy leaves that smell strongly of onions when crushed; the pale blue, starry, lightly scented flowers are carried on stems 6in or so high.

There are several varieties available with flowers ranging in color from white to deep violet-blue.

IPHEION AT A GLANCE

A low-growing bulb with a profusion of starry blue or white flowers in spring.

		Recommended Varieties
Jan	/	
Feb	/	
Mar	flowering	"Album"
Apr	flowering	"Alberto Castello"
May	flowering	"Froyle Mill"
Jun	/	"Rolf Fiedler"
July	/	"Wisley Blue"
Aug	/	
Sept	plant	
Oct	plant	
Nov	/	
Dec	/	

CONDITIONS

Aspect   Grows best in full sun but tolerates light shade for part of the day.

Site   Good for a rockery, border, or container. Ipheion needs well-drained soil. It will grow on quite poor soils but growth will be better on soils enriched with organic matter.

GROWING METHOD

Planting   Plant bulbs 2in deep and the same distance apart in fall.

Feeding   Apply some balanced fertilizer after flowers have finished. Water regularly during dry spells while plants are in leaf and bloom.

Problems   No specific problems are usually experienced with this bulb.

FLOWERING

Season   The starry flowers appear from early spring to mid-spring.

Cutting   Flowers are too short to cut for all but a miniature vase but they may last a few days in water.

AFTER FLOWERING

Requirements   Shear off spent flower stems and remove the old foliage when it has died down. If clumps become overcrowded and fail to flower well, they can be lifted in fall, divided, and replanted immediately.

IRIS—BULBOUS TYPES
Irises

THE LOW-GROWING flowers of Iris danfordiae *appear very early in the year—usually February or March.*

SEVERAL DIFFERENT cultivars of Iris reticulata *are available, in varying shades of blue with yellow markings.*

FEATURES

There are many species of these irises, which have true bulbs as storage organs, unlike the creeping rhizomes of their larger cousins. The leaves are not arranged in the typical fan of sword shapes like rhizomatous irises, but are usually narrow and lance shaped, or rolled. The flowers have the typical iris form with six petals, three inner ones (standards), and three outer ones (falls). The falls are often brightly marked or veined. Many species and varieties are blue with yellow markings on the falls; some types are yellow with brown or green speckling on the falls and others are white with yellow markings. The blue varieties come in many shades, from deep violet and purple through to pale China blue.

Many bulbous irises are early-flowering dwarf forms suitable for growing on rockeries or at the front of beds: they are also excellent for shallow pots ("pans") in the greenhouse or alpine house. Other types are taller and flower in summer; they are valuable for herbaceous and mixed borders, and are particularly good for cutting for flower arrangements. There are also some spring-flowering irises that are far less commonly grown than the other groups.

POPULAR SPECIES

Bulbous irises can be split into three main groups: Reticulata irises, Xiphium irises and Juno irises.

Reticulata These irises have bulbs with a netted tunic around them which gives them their group name. They are dwarf, growing to about 6in high, and the flowers appear early in the year, usually in February and March. *I. danfordiae* has lightly fragrant flowers whose yellow petals are speckled with greenish brown. *I. reticulata* also has fragrant flowers: the petals are thinner than those of *I. danfordiae* and are blue or purple with yellow markings. Several different cultivars are available. The flowers of *I. histriodes* and its cultivars are larger and have short stems; they are deep to light blue, with dark blue, white, and yellow markings. The flowers open before the leaves reach their full height.

Xiphium This group of summer-flowering irises is popular and easily grown. It consists of Dutch irises, flowering in early summer, in white, yellow, or blue with contrasting markings; English irises, flowering in early to mid-summer in shades of white, blue, or purple; and Spanish irises, flowering in midsummer in various shades of white, blue, purple, and yellow.

Juno The Juno irises are not as well-known as the other bulbous types, probably because they are more difficult to grow well. The group includes *I. bucharica*, bearing yellow or white flowers with yellow falls, and *I. graeberiana*, which has lavender flowers with a white crest on the falls. These two are among the easiest Juno irises to grow: others include *I. fosteriana*, *I. magnifica*, and *I. rosenbachiana*, which do best in an alpine house.

WHEN EXAMINED closely, the lightly fragrant flowers of Iris danfordiae *can be seen to have attractive freckling in the throat.*

"KATHERINE HODGKIN," a cultivar of Iris histrioides*, is perhaps the most sought-after of all the dwarf irises.*

CONDITIONS

Aspect All bulbous irises like open, sunny, positions.
Site Reticulatas are good for rock gardens, raised beds, or containers: Xiphiums and Junos for sunny, sheltered borders. Soil needs to be well-drained; Juno irises require a soil containing plenty of well-rotted organic matter.

GROWING METHOD

Planting Plant Reticulatas 3in deep and 4in apart. Xiphiums are planted 4-6in deep and 6in apart, and Juno irises are planted 2in deep and 8in apart, taking care not to damage the brittle, fleshy roots. They are all planted in fall, in September or October.
Feeding Supplementary feeding is not usually necessary.
Problems Bulbs may rot in overwet soil. Bulbous irises in warmer areas of the country may be affected by iris ink disease, causing black streaks on the bulb and yellow blotches on the leaves. Destroy affected bulbs.

FLOWERING

Season Reticulata irises flower in February and March, Junos in April and May, and Xiphiums in June and July.
Cutting The Xiphiums make excellent, long-lasting cut flowers.

AFTER FLOWERING

Requirements Remove faded flowers. Most bulbous irises are best left undisturbed for as long as possible; they can be increased by lifting and dividing the bulbs after flowering when necessary. Juno irises should not be divided until the foliage has died down, and must be handled very carefully. Spanish irises of the Xiphium group benefit from being lifted when the foliage has died down and replanted in September; this helps the bulbs to ripen.

BULBOUS IRIS AT A GLANCE

A varied group of plants with colorful flowers in early spring or in summer. Good for a range of situations.

Month		Recommended Varieties
Jan	flowering	
Feb	flowering	Reticulata group:
Mar	flowering	*I. danfordiae*
Apr	flowering	*I. reticulata* "Katharine Hodgkin"
May	flowering	*I. histrioides* "Major"
Jun	flowering	Xiphium group:
July	flowering	"Bronze Queen"
Aug	/	"Excelsior"
Sept	plant	"Ideal"
Oct	plant	Juno group:
Nov	/	*I. bucharica*
Dec	/	*I. graeberiana*

Iris—rhizomatous types
Iris

IRIS WAS THE Greek god of the the rainbow, and this plant is aptly named as there are irises in every color of the spectrum.

WATER IRIS (Iris pseudoacorus) is a tall grower that needs to be planted in water or permanently wet soil.

FEATURES

Irises comprise a very large plant group of more than 200 species. Some grow from bulbs (see the previous two pages): those covered here grow from rhizomes. They have stiff, sword-shaped leaves and carry their colorful flowers on tall, stiff stems in spring and early summer. Iris flowers have six petals; three inner, vertical ones, (standards), and three outer ones, which curve outward (falls). The color range is very varied, covering blue, purple, lavender, yellow, rose, and white; many of the flowers are bicolored, and attractively marked. Rhizomatous irises contain several different groups, the most popular of which are bearded, Japanese and Siberian irises. **Bearded irises** have large, very showy flowers with a short, bristly "beard" on the falls; dwarf cultivars are also available. **Japanese irises** have unusual flat-faced flowers, and **Siberian irises** have delicate flowers with finer petals.

CONDITIONS

Aspect Rhizomatous irises like a position in full sun, but with protection from strong winds.

Site Excellent plants for the middle to back of a mixed or herbaceous border. Bearded irises like a slightly alkaline, well-drained soil: Japanese and Siberian irises need moisture-retentive, humus-rich loam.

GROWING METHOD

Planting Usually sold as container-grown plants in growth. Plant shallowly, with the rhizome barely covered, in late summer.

Feeding Supplementary feeding is rarely necessary. Ensure moisture-loving types are never allowed to dry out during the growing season.

Problems Slugs and snails can be troublesome. Use covered slug bait where necessary, or hand pick the pests after dark.

FLOWERING

Season Flowers are carried in early summer.

Cutting Make beautiful cut flowers.

AFTER FLOWERING

Requirements Cut off spent flower stems. Every few years, lift the rhizomes after flowering, cut them into sections each containing a strong, healthy fan of leaves, and replant, discarding the old, woody, worn out portions of rhizome.

RHIZOMATOUS IRIS AT A GLANCE

Stately border plants with fans of sword-shaped leaves and tall, attractively marked flowers in summer.

Month		Recommended Varieties
Jan	/	
Feb	/	
Mar	/	*Bearded irises:*
Apr	/	"Black Swan"
May	flowering	"Rocket"
Jun	flowering	"White City"
July	flowering	*Siberian irises:*
Aug	/	"Sparkling Rose"
Sept	plant	"Caesar"
Oct	/	"Perry's Blue"
Nov	/	*Japanese irises:*
Dec	/	"Rose Queen"
		"Moonlight Waves"

IRIS UNGUICULARIS
Winter iris, Algerian iris

THE FULL BEAUTY of this iris can be seen in close up. Many iris have fine veining or feathering on their petals.

A LARGE PATCH of Algerian iris gives a great lift to the garden in winter. Even if flowers come singly their appearance is still a joy.

FEATURES

This beardless, rhizomatous iris is different to all others in its group because it flowers throughout the winter. The beautiful little fragrant flowers rarely exceed 8in in height and may be hidden by the stiff, grassy foliage. They are ideal for cutting and taking indoors, where their sweet scent may be almost overpowering at times.

The flowers of the species are deep lavender with creamy yellow centers deeply veined in violet. There are some cultivars available, including a white form, one or two varieties in particularly deep shades of blue, one in a pale silvery lilac, and a dwarf form. A large single clump of this iris is effective but in the right position it could be mass-planted to good effect.

I. UNGUICULARIS AT A GLANCE

A low-growing iris valuable for its sweetly scented flowers which appear throughout the winter.

		Recommended Varieties
Jan	flowering	
Feb	flowering	"Abington Purple"
Mar	plant	"Alba"
Apr	/	"Bob Thompson"
May	/	"Mary Barnard"
Jun	/	"Oxford Dwarf"
July	/	"Walter Butt"
Aug	/	
Sept	/	
Oct	/	
Nov	flowering	
Dec	flowering	

CONDITIONS

Aspect   Needs a reasonably sheltered position because of its flowering time. The rhizomes must be exposed to a summer baking if plants are to flower well, so a position in full sun is essential.

Site   Grow in beds or borders where it will be able to spread—plants can be invasive. Soil must be well-drained. If it is very poor, dig in quantities of well-decayed manure or compost ahead of planting time.

GROWING METHOD

Planting   Plant rhizomes in spring with the top at or just below soil level. Container-grown plants in growth can also be bought and planted virtually year-round in suitable weather.

Feeding   Supplementary feeding is generally unnecessary. Water the plants in spring and fall if conditions are dry, but do not water in summer.

Problems   Slugs and snails will often attack the flowers. Use slug pellets if necessary.

FLOWERING

Season   Flowers are produced any time from late fall through winter.

Cutting   The flowers make a lovely indoor decoration.

AFTER FLOWERING

Requirements   Cut off spent flowers and tidy up foliage when necessary. Little other attention is required. Crowded plants can be divided in spring.

IXIA
Corn lily

EACH TALL SPIKE of corn lily produces dozens of flowers. These are still producing blooms despite the many fading and falling ones.

PALEST TURQUOISE FLOWERS make this lovely corn lily (Ixia viridiflora) a favorite although its corms are not always easy to buy.

FEATURES

This plant produces starry flowers in a stunning range of colors including white, cream, yellow, orange, red, cerise, and magenta. Hybrid varieties are the most popular, but the sought-after *I. viridiflora* has duck-egg blue flowers with a dark center. The narrow, grass-like foliage may be 12–20in high while the wiry-stemmed flower spikes stand clear of the leaves. Corn lilies are a great addition to the garden. Being quite tall they should be planted toward the back of a bed or among other bulbs and perennials. Although colors can be mixed, a better effect is obtained by planting blocks of one color.

IXIA AT A GLANCE

A rather tender plant with masses of colorful, starry flowers on slender stems.

		Recommended Varieties
Jan	/	
Feb	/	"Blue Bird"
Mar	plant	"Mabel"
Apr	plant	"Rose Emperor"
May	flowering	"Venus"
Jun	flowering	
July	flowering	
Aug	/	
Sept	/	
Oct	plant (indoors)	
Nov	/	
Dec	/	

CONDITIONS

Aspect   Prefers full sun all day but with shelter from strong wind.

Site   A good border plant in reasonably mild districts. In colder areas it can be grown in containers on a sheltered patio or in a conservatory. Needs well-drained soil.

GROWING METHOD

Planting   Plant corms in the open garden in spring, about 2in deep and 3–4in apart. Plant in pots for the conservatory in fall.

Fertilizing   Apply balanced liquid fertilizer in early spring to increase the size of the blooms. In dry conditions, water if necessary in spring when the shoots are growing strong.

Problems   No specific pest or disease problems are usually experienced, though corms may rot in overwet soil.

FLOWERING

Season   Flowers from late spring to mid-summer.

Cutting   Flowers can be cut for the vase but will probably give better value in the garden.

AFTER FLOWERING

Requirements   In all but the mildest gardens, lift the corms when the foliage has died down and store them in a dry place for replanting in spring.

LACHENALIA ALOIDES
Cape cowslip

STIFF FLOWER SPIKES of yellow and red tubular bells are the feature of Lachenalia aloides.

CAPE COWSLIPS need a cool room to grow well. In the right conditions they make excellent winter-flowering house plants.

FEATURES

Also known as "soldier boys" because of their upright, neat and orderly habit, this bulb is grown as a house plant to produce its colorful bell-like flowers in midwinter. The rather stiff leaves grow to about 6in high and are dark green, often spotted with purple. The 8–12in spikes of 20 or so tubular flowers stand well above the foliage and remain colorful for several weeks. Individual blooms are yellow or orange-red, marked with red, green, or purple; they are often a deeper color in bud, becoming paler as the flowers open. There are several different varieties with subtly varying shades to the flowers.

LACHENALIA AT A GLANCE

A tender bulb grown as a house or greenhouse plant for its spikes of yellow or orange tubular flowers in winter.

		Recommended Varieties
Jan	flowering	
Feb	flowering	*Lachenalia aloides:*
Mar	flowering	"Aurea"
Apr	/	"Lutea"
May	/	"Nelsonii"
Jun	/	"Quadricolor"
July	/	
Aug	plant	*Lachenalia bulbifera:*
Sept	plant	"George"
Oct	/	
Nov	/	
Dec	/	

CONDITIONS

Aspect Needs a very brightly lit spot; will stand direct sun for part of the day.

Site Grow on a bright windowsill in a cool room, or in a cool greenhouse or conservatory. Lachenalia does not like dry heat.

GROWING METHOD

Planting Plant bulbs in late summer or early fall, growing six to a 5in pot. Set them just below the surface of the compost.

Feeding Apply high potash liquid fertilizer every 14 days or so from when the buds appear. Water regularly while plants are in flower.

Problems Overwatering or poorly drained compost will cause the bulbs to rot.

FLOWERING

Season Flowers appear between midwinter and early spring.

Cutting Not suitable for cutting.

AFTER FLOWERING

Requirements Cut off spent lachenalia flower stems. Continue to water until early summer, then gradually stop watering and allow the pot to dry out until the following fall, when the bulbs can be shaken out and repotted in fresh compost.

LEUCOJUM
Snowflake

THE WHITE BELLS *with their fresh green dots at the end of each petal make* Leucojum vernum *particularly evocative of spring.*

PREFERING SHADE *and moist soil, spring snowflake is one of the easiest bulbs to grow. This plant is typical of an established clump.*

FEATURES

Easily grown snowflakes have clusters of white, bell-shaped flowers, each petal bearing a bright green spot on its tip. Foliage is a rich, deep green and bulbs multiply readily to form good sized clumps in a few years.

There are three types of snowflake; spring snowflake (*Leucojum vernum*), summer snowflake (*L. aestivum*), and fall snowflake (*L. autumnale*). The spring snowflake flowers in February or March, while the summer snowflake, despite its name, usually flowers in late spring. Spring snowflake reaches a height of about 8in; summer snowflake up to 24in, and fall snowflake 6in, with very fine, narrow foliage. The flowers have a passing resemblance to snowdrops, but are easily distinguished by their rounded, bell shape and taller growth.

LEUCOJUM AT A GLANCE

Delicate looking plants with white bells tipped with green, appearing in spring or early fall. Hardy.

Jan	/	Recommended Varieties
Feb	flowering	
Mar	flowering	*Leucojum aestivum:*
Apr	flowering	"Gravetye Giant"
May	flowering	
Jun	/	*Leucojum autumnale:*
July	/	"Cobb's Variety"
Aug	/	"Pulchellum"
Sept	plant / flower	
Oct	plant	*Leucojum vernum:*
Nov	/	"Carpathicum"
Dec	/	"Vagneri"

CONDITIONS

Aspect Grows well in sun but also happy in shade or in dappled sunlight. Fall snowflakes prefer an open, sunny position.

Site Low-growing species are excellent for rock gardens or the front of borders; taller summer snowflakes toward the middle of a border. Spring and summer snowflakes prefer a moisture-retentive soil enriched with organic matter: fall snowflake needs light, free-draining soil.

GROWING METHOD

Planting Plant bulbs 3in deep and 4–8in apart in late summer or early fall.

Feeding An annual mulching with decayed manure or compost after bulbs have died down should provide adequate nutrients. Keep the soil for spring and summer snowflakes moist throughout the growing season.

Problems No specific problems are known.

FLOWERING

Season Spring snowflake flowers between midwinter and early spring; summer snowflake mid to late spring; and fall snowflake in September.

Cutting Best enjoyed in the garden.

AFTER FLOWERING

Requirements Remove spent flower stems. Divide crowded clumps when the foliage dies down, and replant immediately.

LILIUM
Lily

THIS BURNED ORANGE HYBRID shows the characteristic dark spotting in its throat. Lilies make excellent cut flowers.

WHITE LILIES are traditionally symbols of purity. Lilium regale is one of the most popular species, and its flowers are very strongly scented.

FEATURES

Lilies are tall, stately plants that carry a number of large, trumpet-shaped blooms on each flowering stem. Flowering stems may be anywhere from about 2ft to over 6ft high. There are 80–90 species of lily and many hundreds of cultivars, so it is difficult to outline their requirements concisely. Lily flowers are often fragrant and the main color range includes white, yellow, pink, red, and orange—many have spotted or streaked petals. A quite small range of lily bulbs is usually available in garden centers in fall and these should be planted as soon as possible after their arrival: lily bulbs have no tunic or outer covering and so can dry out unless they are carefully handled. For a greater range of species and hybrids you will need to contact specialist growers and mail order suppliers. Many lily enthusiasts belong to societies devoted to learning more about the enormous range of types available and their cultivation.

Types Some of the more popular species grown are *L. auratum*, golden-rayed lily, which has white petals with gold bands; *L. candidum*, Madonna lily, which is pure white; *L. martagon*, Turk's cap lily, with fully recurved, dark red petals with dark spots; *L. regale,* the regal lily, with white flowers that have purple backs to the petals and a yellow base; *L. speciosum* which has white petals with a deep pink center and reddish spots; and *L. tigrinum*, tiger lily, dark orange with black spots and revurving petals. As well as the species, many hybrid varieties are grown, which are classified into a number of groups. Among the most popular are the Asiatic hybrids, short to medium height, with upward-facing flowers produced early in the season; and the Oriental hybrids, which are taller and more refined, with nodding, strongly scented blooms. Asiatic hybrids are ideal for pots and are available pot-grown throughout the summer.

CONDITIONS

Aspect The ideal situation is a sunny position with a little dappled shade during part of the day. They need protection from strong wind.

Site Lilies grow well when mixed with other plants that will shade their roots, in a bed or border, or in containers. Plant them where their perfume can be appreciated. Soil must be well-drained with a high organic content. Dig in copious amounts of well-rotted manure or compost a month or so before planting.

GROWING METHOD

Planting Plant 4–9in deep and 9–15in or so apart in fall or early spring. Bulbs must not be bruised or allowed to dry out, and they should be planted as soon as possible after purchase. Apply a layer of compost or manure to the soil surface as a mulch after planting. Your stock of lilies can be increased by bulb scales, bulbils or offsets, according to type: see page 11 for more details on propagation.

THE GOLDEN-RAYED lily of Japan, Lilium auratum, *carries its attractively speckled, reflexing flowers late in the summer.*

MASSES OF BLOOMS, with buds still to open, make this yellow lily a great asset for the summer garden.

Feeding If the soil contains plenty of organic matter these plants should not need a lot of feeding. Apply a slow-release granular fertilizer as growth starts and after flowering. Water regularly during dry spells but avoid overwatering which may rot the bulbs.

Problems Most problems with lilies result from poor cultivation or unsuitable growing conditions. Gray mold (botrytis) can be a problem in cool, humid conditions, especially if plants are overwatered or if air circulation is poor. The small, bright red lily beetle and their larvae can cause a lot of damage in some areas:

control them with a contact insecticide and clear away plant debris in which the adults overwinter.

FLOWERING

Season Lilies flower some time between early summer and fall with many flowering in middle to late summer. Flowering time depends on the species and, to some extent, the conditions.

Cutting Lilies make wonderful and very long-lasting cut flowers. Cut them when flowers are just open or all buds are rounded and fully colored. Don't cut right to the bottom of the stem—retain some leaves on the lower part. Change water frequently and cut off spent flowers from the cluster to allow the other buds to develop fully.

AFTER FLOWERING

Requirements Remove spent flower stems as they finish blooming. Remove only the flowering stem and leave as much foliage as possible. Don't be in a hurry to cut back yellowing growth too soon: allow the plant to die back naturally and mulch with chipped bark for the winter. Bulbs are best left in the ground for several years. When they are lifted they must be divided and replanted at once, as having no tunic on the bulb means they dry out very quickly. If they can't be planted at once, store them in damp sphagnum moss or peat.

LILIUM AT A GLANCE

Stately plants with trumpet-shaped, usually intensely fragrant flowers on tall spikes.

		Recommended Varieties
Jan	/	
Feb	/	"Apollo"
Mar	/	"Barcelona"
Apr	/	"Casa Blanca"
May	/	"Corsage"
Jun	flowering	"Enchantment"
July	flowering	"Green Dragon"
Aug	flowering /plant	"Mrs R. O. Backhouse"
Sept	flowering /plant	"Orange Triumph"
Oct	plant	"Shuksan"
Nov	plant	"Tamara"
Dec	/	

MORAEA
Peacock iris, butterfly iris

IT IS EASY to see how this pretty bulb got its common name of peacock iris. Iridescent blue spots are sharply defined against the white petals.

THE FOLIAGE of peacock iris looks unpromising, as it is sparse and grass-like, but the "floating" flowers are worth waiting for.

FEATURES

Of the 120 species of *Moraea*, most come from South Africa with others native to tropical Africa and Madagascar. Few are in cultivation but it is worth seeking out this unusual plant from specialist bulb growers. All grow from corms and some, such as *M. spathulata*, grow only a single leaf, which may be 8–20in high. Flowers are like those of irises, with three showy outer petals and three smaller, rather insignificant inner ones. The commonest species is *M. spathulata*, with bright yellow, summer flowers on 2ft stems. *Moraea aristata* has white flowers with a large blue blotch at the base of the outer petals, while *M. villosa* bears flowers in a range of colors with a blue blotch on the petals. Plant peacock iris in groups for the best effect.

MORAEA AT A GLANCE

An uncommon bulb with iris-like flowers, often strikingly marked. Needs a warm, sunny position.

Month		Recommended Species
Jan	/	
Feb	/	
Mar	/	*Moraea aristata*
Apr	plant 🖑	*M. bellendenii*
May	/	*M. gawleri*
Jun	flowering ❄	*M. spathulata*
July	flowering ❄	
Aug	flowering ❄	
Sept	/	
Oct	/	
Nov	/	
Dec	/	

CONDITIONS

Aspect   Moraea needs full sun all day.

Site   A warm, sunny, and sheltered position is necessary. This corm needs well-drained soil with plenty of decayed organic matter incorporated into it before planting. Moraea also makes an attractive plant for the conservatory or home when grown in containers. Use John Innes or soilless potting compost.

GROWING METHOD

Planting   Plant corms 2in deep and 8in apart in spring.

Feeding   Performance is improved by applying a balanced fertilizer as flower buds appear. Container-grown plants should be liquid-fed every three weeks or so through the growing season. Water in dry conditions, but take care not to make the soil too wet or the corms will be liable to rot.

Problems   No specific pest or disease problems are known for this plant.

FLOWERING

Season   Flowers throughout the summer.

Cutting   Not suitable for cutting.

AFTER FLOWERING

Requirements   Cut off spent flower stems unless you want to obtain seed from them. In fall, lift the corms and store them in a dry place over winter, ready for replanting the following spring.

MUSCARI
Grape hyacinth

THE FEATHERY violet heads of Muscari comosum *"Plumosum"
make this showy variety quite different from other grape hyacinths.*

*ROYAL BLUE grape hyacinths here border a garden of daffodils and
pop up from among the groundcover of snow-in-summer.*

FEATURES

Vigorous and easy to grow, grape hyacinths have blue flowers of varying intensity. There are several species and named varieties available, including the double "Blue Spike" and the feathery "Plumosum." *Muscari aucheri* (*M. tubergenianum*) is known as "Oxford and Cambridge" because it has pale blue flowers at the top of the spike and is dark blue at the base, reminiscent of the English universities' uniform colors. Grape hyacinths are a great foil for other bright spring-flowering bulbs such as tulips or ranunculus. Flowers are lightly scented and are carried on a stem about 4–8in tall. This plant gives the most impact when planted in drifts: in large yards where there is space it can easily be naturalized in grass or under deciduous trees.

MUSCARI AT A GLANCE

Pretty, easy-to-grow, little bulbs with short spikes of intense blue bells in spring.

		Recommended Varieties
Jan	/	
Feb	/	*Muscari armeniacum:*
Mar	flowering	"Blue Spike"
Apr	flowering	"Early Giant"
May	flowering	
Jun	/	*Muscari azureum:*
July	/	"Album"
Aug	/	
Sept	plant	*Muscari comosum:*
Oct	plant	"Plumosum"
Nov	/	
Dec	/	

CONDITIONS

Aspect Best in full sun or dappled sunlight such as is found under deciduous trees.

Site Useful on rockeries, in the front of borders, and for naturalizing under trees, but the plants can be invasive. Muscari needs well-drained soil, preferably with plenty of organic matter incorporated before planting.

GROWING METHOD

Planting Plant the bulbs about 3in deep and 4in apart in late summer or early fall.

Feeding Supplementary feeding is not usually necessary, but a light sprinkling of general fertilizer after flowering helps to ensure good growth. Watering is not normally necessary unless the weather is exceptionally dry.

Problems No specific problems are known.

FLOWERING

Season Flowers appear in early to mid-spring.

Cutting Although not often used as a cut flower, it lasts in water quite well if picked when half the flowers on the stem are open.

AFTER FLOWERING

Requirements Remove spent flower stems if required. Bulbs can be divided every 3–4 years in fall, replanting immediately. The foliage appears in the winter, long before the flowers.

NARCISSUS
Daffodil and narcissus

MODERN HYBRID DAFFODILS come in a wide range of forms, including double-flowered varieties and varieties with split coronas.

SUNSHINE YELLOW, this group of smaller growing daffodil cultivars lights up the late winter garden.

FEATURES

Daffodils are probably the best known and most widely grown of all bulbs and to many they are the true indicator of spring. They look wonderful mass-planted in the garden or naturalized in grass, but they also make great pot plants and excellent cut flowers. The best-known color is yellow, but there are also flowers in shades of white, cream, orange, and pink. The trumpet, or cup, is often a different color to the petals and may be bicolored. There are many species and cultivars and the genus *Narcissus* has been divided into 12 different groups, depending on the form and size of the flowers. The height varies from 3–20in, depending on variety.

Trumpet   The trumpet (cup) is at least as long as the petals, and there is one flower per stem.

Large cupped   Cup is shorter than, but at least one-third of, the length of the petals. One flower per stem.

Small cupped   The cup is less than one-third of the length of the petals; flowers usually carried singly.

Double   Double or semi-double flowers carried single or in small groups. The whole flower may be double, or just the cup.

Triandrus   Two to six pendant flowers with reflexed petals per stem.

Cyclamineus   Slightly pendant flowers with long trumpets and strongly reflexed petals, usually one per stem.

Jonquilla   Several flowers per stem, with short cups. Sweetly scented.

Tazetta   Half hardy. Very fragrant flowers in clusters of 10 or more per stem. Early flowering.

Poeticus   Small red or orange cup and broad white petals, usually one or two per stem. Often strongly fragrant. Late flowering.

Wild   A varied group containing the species and natural varieties found in the wild.

Split cupped   The cup is split to varying degrees for at least one-third to half its length.

Miscellaneous   Hybrids that do not fit into any of the other divisions.

CONDITIONS

Aspect   These bulbs grow best in a sunny spot or under deciduous trees where they will receive sun in the early spring.

Site   Grow narcissi in beds and borders, on rockeries, or in containers for the patio or in the home. Soil must be well-drained, ideally with some well-rotted organic matter dug in a month or so before planting.

GROWING METHOD

Planting   Planting depth will vary greatly according to the size of the bulb. Plant so that the nose is covered to twice the height of the bulb, in September or October. Plant as early as possible for the best results.
Continued on page 298

THE ESSENCE OF SPRING BEAUTY is captured in this drift of mixed daffodils and delicate white blossom. As the planting has been kept to the edge of the lawn, the grass can be mown while still allowing the bulb foliage to die down naturally.

Continued from page 293

Feeding   Feed with a balanced fertilizer in early spring. Plants can be given a liquid feed after the flowers have faded. Watering may be necessary in very dry spells, particularly once flowering has finished.

Problems   Basal rot can occur in storage; destroy bulbs with any sign of softening or rot at planting time. Similar symptoms can be caused by stem eelworm; these bulbs should also be destroyed by burning. Narcissus fly lays eggs near the necks of the bulbs; these hatch into larvae that tunnel into the bulb and weaken or destroy it. Bulbs in light shade are less susceptible to attack. Pull soil up round the necks of the bulbs after flowering to discourage egg laying.

FLOWERING

Season   Depending on area and variety, flowers may be carried anywhere from midwinter to early summer. Bulbs indoors may be brought into flower for Christmas or earlier; specially treated bulbs are available to ensure early flowering.

Cutting   This excellent cut flower should last a week with frequent water changes, or with the use of proprietary cut flower additives. For longest vase life pick daffodils when the buds are about to burst open or as soon as they are fully open. Cut, don't pull, the stems as low as possible. Cut off any white section at the base of the stem. Don't mix daffodils with other flowers until they have spent a day in a vase on their own as their slimy sap may reduce the vase life of other blooms.

AFTER FLOWERING

Requirements   Spent flowers should be removed before they set seed. Allow foliage to die down naturally; do not tie the leaves in clumps. Where bulbs are naturalised in grass, do not mow the grass until at least six weeks after the flowers have faded. Premature removal of leaves will have a detrimental effect on growth and flowering the following season.

If drainage is good, bulbs may be left in the ground and clumps can be divided after flowering every three years or so. Bulbs grown indoors in pots can be planted out in the garden after flowering, where they should recover in a season or two.

NARCISSUS AT A GLANCE

Well-known spring-flowering bulbs in a wide variety of flower forms and sizes. Most types are very hardy.

Month		Recommended Varieties
Jan	flowering	"Carlton"
Feb	flowering	"Cheerfulness"
Mar	flowering	"February Gold"
Apr	flowering	"Irene Copeland"
May	flowering	"King Alfred"
Jun	/	"Minnow"
July	/	"Peeping Tom"
Aug	plant	"Pipit"
Sept	plant	"Thalia"
Oct	plant	N. *bulbocodium*
Nov	/	N. *canaliculatus*
Dec	/	

NERINE
Nerine, Guernsey lily

THE GUERNSEY LILY, Nerine sarniensis, *needs to be grown in a conservatory or greenhouse except in very mild areas.*

TALL AND ELEGANT, these bright pink nerines appear as the summer garden fades away in fall.

FEATURES

Nerine bowdenii brightens the fall garden, producing its heads of bright pink flowers before the leaves appear. It is easy to grow and flowers last well when cut. Bulbs should be planted where they can be left undisturbed for several years; they flower best when crowded and after a dry summer. They can also be grown in containers. Flower stems grow 12–18in high and the deep green, strappy leaves from 8–12in long.

The Guernsey lily (*N. sarniensis*) has bright red flowers, and other species and cultivars of nerines may be red, white, pink or apricot, but only *N. bowdenii* is hardy enough to grow outdoors in this country.

NERINE AT A GLANCE

Heads of funnel-shaped pink flowers appear on leafless stalks in fall. Needs a warm, sheltered position.

Jan	/	
Feb	sow	
Mar	sow	
Apr	plant	
May	/	
Jun	/	
July	/	
Aug	plant	
Sept	flowering	
Oct	flowering	
Nov	flowering	
Dec	/	

Recommended Varieties

Nerine bowdenii alba
Nerine bowdenii:
　　"Mark Fenwick"
　　"Pink Triumph"
　　"Wellsii"

N. "Corusca Major"
N. "Fothergillii Major"
N. *undulata*

CONDITIONS

Aspect　　Nerines require full sun and a warm, sheltered spot.

Site　　A useful plant for borders, especially under the shelter of a south-facing wall. The soil should be free-draining and moderately fertile. In cold areas and with the more tender species, grow bulbs in pots of John Innes potting compost.

GROWING METHOD

Planting　　Plant in middle to late summer or in mid-spring, 4in deep and 6in apart. In containers, plant with the neck of the bulb at or just below soil level.

Feeding　　Can be grown successfully without supplementary fertilizer. However, if you wish, you can give weak liquid fertilizer every couple of weeks once flower buds appear until growth slows down. Water regularly while in active growth but keep the bulbs dry during the dormant period.

Problems　　No specific problems are known.

FLOWERING

Season　　Flowers appear during early fall.

Cutting　　Nerines last well as cut flowers with frequent water changes.

AFTER FLOWERING

Requirements　　Cut off spent flower stems. Outdoors, mulch the planting site for winter protection.

ORNITHOGALUM
Chincherinchee, star of Bethlehem

CHINCHERINCHEE gives a long and pretty floral display, as the flowers open slowly from the bottom up to the top of the cone.

A BILLOWING CLOUD of white flowers makes this mass planting a striking feature. Close inspection reveals the pretty green centers.

FEATURES

There are around 100 species of *Ornithogalum* originating in Africa, Asia and parts of Europe, but the chincherinchee, *O. thyrsoides*, is perhaps the best known, with its imposing spikes of white summer flowers growing up to 18in. The leaves are narrow and sword-shaped. Other commonly grown species are *O.arabicum*, whose scented white flowers have a striking black eye, *O. nutans*, with delicate spikes of dangling white flowers, and *O. umbellatum*, or star of Bethlehem, which forms clumps of grassy foliage studded with pure white, upward-facing white blooms: these are all spring flowering. Chincherinchee and *O. arabicum* are frost tender.

ORNITHOGALUM AT A GLANCE

Half-hardy and hardy bulbs producing attractive white flowers in spring or early summer.

		Recommended Species
Jan	/	
Feb	/	*Ornithogalum arabicum*
Mar	/	*O. longibracteatum*
Apr	plant / flower	*O. montanum*
May	flowering	*O. nutans*
Jun	flowering	*O. oligophyllum*
July	flowering	*O. thyrsoides*
Aug	/	*O. umbellatum*
Sept	/	
Oct	plant	
Nov	/	
Dec	/	

CONDITIONS

Aspect Prefers an open position in full sun but will grow in light shade. *O. thyrsoides* can be grown outside in summer though it will not survive the winter; in cold areas it can be grown as a pot plant in the home or greenhouse.

Site Good for mixed borders, rockeries or naturalising in grass. The bulbs need well-drained but not very rich soil.

GROWING METHOD

Planting Plant bulbs in spring or fall, 2in deep and about 8–12in apart.

Feeding Not usually essential, but an application of balanced or high potash fertilizer given as the plants start into growth may improve flowering. Watering is not necessary unless the season is exceptionally dry; for container-grown plants, keep the compost just moist.

Problems This bulb is generally trouble-free.

FLOWERING

Season Flowers will appear spring and early summer.

Cutting This is a first class cut flower.

AFTER FLOWERING

Requirements Cut spent flower stems at ground level. Non-hardy species should be lifted in fall and stored in a dry, cool place for replanting the following spring. Hardy species can be divided after flowering and replanted immediately.

OXALIS
Wood sorrel

THE SATINY WHITE FLOWERS on Oxalis purpurea *"Alba" are a far cry from the weedy forms of oxalis that invade our yards.*

THIS PRETTY PINK OXALIS makes a charming groundcover here on the edge of a paved area.

FEATURES

A number of species of oxalis are very invasive, but others are very decorative and well worth growing. Most have clover-like leaves and five-petalled, satiny flowers which are furled in bud. The usual color is pink or white; there are also purple, yellow, orange, or red varieties. Some species need greenhouse cultivation in this country. Height varies from 2–8in.
O. adenophylla is the most popular species, with grayish leaves and silvery flowers;
O. enneaphylla has white flowers and attractive, folded, silvery leaves. *O. laciniata* has narrow leaflets and purple, veined flowers. Once known as *O. deppei*, *O. tetraphylla* has brown-marked leaves and pink flowers.

OXALIS AT A GLANCE

A low-growing, clump-forming plant with clover-like leaves and attractive, satiny flowers. Can be invasive.

Month		Recommended Varieties
Jan	/	
Feb	/	"Beatrice Anderson"
Mar	/	"Bowles' White"
Apr	/	"Ione Hecker"
May	/	"Royal Velvet"
Jun	flowering	
July	flowering	*O. enneaphylla:*
Aug	/	"Alba"
Sept	planting	"Minutifolia"
Oct	planting	"Rosea"
Nov	/	
Dec	/	*O. tetraphylla:*
		"Iron Cross"

CONDITIONS

Aspect   Grow in full sun for good flowering and compact leaf growth.
Site   Grow on a rockery or near the front of a border, preferably in a confined bed where growth can be controlled. The more invasive varieties are best grown in pots. Free-draining soil is preferred.

GROWING METHOD

Planting   Plant in early fall, 3in deep and 4in apart. It is usual to plant clumps in growth rather than the tiny tubers or rhizomes.
Feeding   Supplementary fertilizer is rarely needed.
Problems   Few problems are usually encountered although some oxalis do suffer from the fungal leaf disease rust. Pick off the worst affected leaves and avoid overhead watering.

FLOWERING

Season   Most species flower through early and mid-summer.
Cutting   Flowers are unsuitable for cutting.

AFTER FLOWERING

Requirements   Plants can be divided after flowering in summer. Clear away dead foliage once the leaves have died down; beware of putting plant debris from invasive varieties on the compost heap.

POLIANTHES TUBEROSA
Tuberose

"THE PEARL," a double-flowered cultivar, is the variety most often available to home gardeners.

PINK-TINGED BUDS open to the heavy-textured cream flowers, so prized for their characteristic strong perfume.

FEATURES

Tuberose is known for its heavily perfumed flowers—tuberose oil is used in perfume production. A double form known as "The Pearl" is the most widely grown. It can be grown in a sunny, sheltered border, but is often more reliable when grown as a conservatory or house plant, especially in cooler areas. The scent can more easily be appreciated under cover.

A flower spike 2ft or more high appears from the basal leaves in summer and early fall. The waxy flowers have a heavy texture and are white with a pinkish tinge at the base. Tubers that have bloomed once will not reflower the following season—new tubers must be planted each year.

POLIANTHES AT A GLANCE

Valued for its intensely fragrant, creamy white flowers that are carried on tall spikes in late summer.

Jan	/	Recommended Varieties
Feb	/	
Mar	plant 🤏	*Polianthes tuberosa:*
Apr	/	"The Pearl"
May	/	
Jun	/	
July	/	
Aug	flowering 🌿	
Sept	flowering 🌿	
Oct	flowering 🌿	
Nov	/	
Dec	/	

CONDITIONS

Aspect   Prefers full sun and shelter from strong wind.
Site   Grow in a warm, sheltered border, or in containers for the conservatory, house, or greenhouse. Use either John Innes or soil-less potting compost.

GROWING METHOD

Planting   Plant 2in deep, or 1in deep in containers.
Feeding   When growth appears, liquid feed with a balanced fertiliser every 14 days through the growing season. Water sparingly to start with, but keep the plant moist at all times when in growth.
Problems   No particular problems are known.

FLOWERING

Season   Flowers should appear during late summer or in early fall.
Cutting   Makes an excellent cut flower. Cut spikes for the vase when two or three of the lower blooms are fully open. Removing spent flowers from the spike as they fade will help to prolong the vase life.

AFTER FLOWERING

Requirements   Tubers are usually discarded at the end of the season. Offsets are produced, and these may sometimes be grown on to flower in two years or so, but they are often disappointing.

RHODOHYPOXIS BAURII
Rose grass

TINY MAGENTA CENTERS emphasise the stark white of this pretty rose grass. The unusual flower form is clearly seen here.

DEEP ROSE-PINK in color, this form of rose grass is sometimes sold as "Rosy Posy." It gives a long flowering display.

FEATURES

This enchanting little plant, which comes from high altitude areas of South Africa, is ideally suited to growing in a rock garden, on the edge of a border or in pots. The slightly hairy leaves, similar to those of a broad-leaf grass, grow to around 4in high. The flowers, which are white or pink through to deep rosy crimson, are about the same height. As they have become better known several varieties with deeper color or larger flowers have become available. They have six petals with one set of three appearing to be set on top of the other, so the flower has no visible eye. The floral display is long lasting, from late spring through to late summer.

If grown in the garden the positions of these plants should be marked in some way as they are completely dormant during winter.

RHODOHYPOXIS AT A GLANCE

A tuberous alpine with mounds of attractive pink or white flowers carried for a very long season.

Month		Recommended Varieties
Jan	/	
Feb	/	"Alba"
Mar	plant	"Dulcie"
Apr	plant	"Dawn"
May	flowering	"Douglas"
Jun	flowering	"Eva-Kate"
July	flowering	"Fred Broome"
Aug	flowering	"Garnett"
Sept	flowering	"Harlequin"
Oct	/	"Picta"
Nov	/	"Ruth"
Dec	/	"Stella"

CONDITIONS

Aspect Grows best in full sun in a sheltered spot.
Site Suitable for rockeries, scree gardens, or containers. The soil must be well drained but enriched with decayed organic matter. It needs to be lime free, as rose grass is not tolerant of alkaline soils. Good quality potting compost mixed with a little extra sharp sand should be adequate for containers.

GROWING METHOD

Planting Tubers should be planted in late spring about 2in deep and 4in apart. Lift and divide offsets in the fall.
Feeding Mulch garden plants with decayed manure or compost in late winter or early spring. Potted plants that have not been repotted will benefit from slow-release fertilizer in early spring. Water regularly during the growing period in dry spells, but keep dry through winter.
Problems No specific problems are known.

FLOWERING

Season The long flowering period runs from late spring through to late summer.
Cutting Flowers are unsuitable for picking.

AFTER FLOWERING

Requirements Spent blooms can be snipped off or ignored. Protect plants from excess winter rainfall; a sheet of glass supported horizontally over the plants on four wooden stakes should prevent the crowns rotting off in wet weather.

ROMULEA
Romulea

THE CHARMING FLOWERS of little Romulea rosea *may be best appreciated when it is grown in a container.*

PALE LAVENDER PETALS and a recessed deep gold throat make Romulea bulbocodium *worth growing. It tolerates cool conditions.*

FEATURES

These small plants have grassy leaves and brightly colored, crocus-like flowers. There are 75 species native to parts of Africa, the Mediterranean and Europe, most in cultivation being South African.

Growing 3–6in high, depending on species, they are ideal for rock gardens and pots where their neat growth can be admired. The color range includes cream and yellow, many shades of blue and violet, and also pinks and reds: many flowers have a very attractive "eye" of contrasting color in the center of the flower. The most popular type, *R. bulbocodium*, has pale lavender flowers with a yellow throat, and is hardier than some of the other species. Flowers remain closed in dull weather.

ROMULEA AT A GLANCE

A low-growing plant with crocus-like flowers which open wide in full sun. Needs a protected position.

Jan	/	
Feb	/	Recommended Species
Mar	flowering 🌱	*Romulea bulbocodium clusiana*
Apr	flowering 🌱	*Romulea flava*
May	flowering 🌱	*Romulea sabulosa*
Jun	/	
July	/	
Aug	/	
Sept	plant ✍	
Oct	plant ✍	
Nov	/	
Dec	/	

CONDITIONS

Aspect	Needs full sun all day. The flowers will not open in shady conditions.
Site	Grows best when grown in a sharply draining, rather sandy soil. Good for scree beds, rockeries and containers.

GROWING METHOD

Planting	The small corms should be planted some 2in deep and 2–3in apart in the fall.
Feeding	Feeding is not normally necessary for this plant, but in poor soils some balanced fertilizer may be applied as growth begins. Water freely to keep the soil moist through the growing season but keep plants dry during the summer, when they die down.
Problems	No specific pest or disease problems are known for romulea.

FLOWERING

Season	Flowers are carried throughout the spring months.
Cutting	None of the species has flowers that are suitable for cutting.

AFTER FLOWERING

Requirements	Protect the crowns with a mulch of peat or similar material for the winter months. Overcrowded clumps can be lifted and divided when the flowers have faded.

SCHIZOSTYLIS COCCINEA
Kaffir lily

THE EXTENDED FLOWER spikes give the appearance of a small gladiolus, though the individual flowers are more delicate.

THE RICH ROSE flowers of Schizostylis "Tambara" are displayed to great effect against evergreen shrubs in the late fall garden.

FEATURES

The beautiful, scarlet or pink, gladiolus-like flowers of schizostylis add a very welcome splash of color to fall borders, coming as they do right at the end of the season. The tall, grassy leaves form a clump from which 2–3ft spikes of flowers rise, bearing some 8–10 open, star-shaped blooms. There are several named varieties in a range of pink and red shades: "Major" has large, deep red flowers, "Viscountess Byng" is a delicate pink, and "Tambara" is a rich, rosy pink. "November Cheer" is one of the latest-flowering varieties. Schizostylis is not suitable for cold, exposed yards, but grows and spreads rapidly where conditions suit it.

SCHIZOSTYLIS AT A GLANCE

A valuable late fall-flowering plant for the border, with colorful scarlet or pink, gladiolus-like flower spikes.

Jan	/	Recommended Varieties
Feb	/	
Mar	plant	"Jennifer"
Apr	plant	"Mrs Hegarty"
May	/	"November Cheer"
Jun	/	"Sunrise"
July	/	"Tambara"
Aug	/	"Viscountess Byng"
Sept	flowering	
Oct	flowering	
Nov	flowering	
Dec	/	

CONDITIONS

Aspect A sheltered spot in full sun or light shade suits this plant.

Site Suitable for the middle of the flower border; in cold districts they do well as pot plants in a conservatory or greenhouse. Moisture-retentive, fertile soil is required.

GROWING METHOD

Planting Plant in spring, 2in deep and 12in apart. Pot-grown plants are available for planting in summer and fall. Rhizomes can also be planted in 8in pots of soil-less or John Innes compost in a sheltered position outdoors, being brought into a cool conservatory or greenhouse before the first frosts for flowering inside.

Feeding Keep the soil moist at all times. Feed pot-grown plants with high potash liquid fertiliszer every 14 days from early summer until flower buds form.

Problems No specific problems are generally experienced.

FLOWERING

Season Flowers from late September into November.

Cutting The flower spikes are excellent for cutting, lasting well in water. Pick them when the buds start to show color.

AFTER FLOWERING

Requirements Cut down faded flower stems. Protect the crowns with a mulch of chipped bark, straw, or dry leaves over winter. Overcrowded plants can be divided in fall.

SCILLA
Squill

A STARBURST of bright blue flowers topped with golden stamens makes up the pretty inflorescence of Scilla peruviana, *the Cuban lily.*

THE SIBERIAN SQUILL, Scilla siberica, *makes its appearance in early spring. "Atrocoerulea" has particularly rich blue flowers.*

FEATURES

The most familiar scillas are the dwarf varieties that flower in early spring. They include *Scilla siberica* (Siberian squill), which has clusters of nodding blue bells about 6in high, and *Scilla mischtschenkoana* (*S. tubergeniana*), which has starry, pale blue flowers with a deeper blue stripe on the petals. This species grows only 2–4in high. *S. bifolia* grows to 2–6in, with a spike of 15 or more star-shaped flowers in blue, pink, or white. Leaves of all these species are elongated and strap shaped. *Scilla peruviana*, the Cuban lily, is quite different—a tall, early summer-flowering bulb with densely packed, conical heads of purple-blue flowers.

SCILLA AT A GLANCE

Mainly dwarf bulbs with starry or bell-shaped blue or white flowers in early spring.

		Recommended Varieties
Jan	/	
Feb	flowering	*Scilla bifolia:*
Mar	flowering	"Rosea"
Apr	flowering	*Scilla siberica:*
May	flowering	"Alba"
Jun	flowering	"Spring Beauty"
July	/	*Scilla peruviana:*
Aug	plant	"Alba"
Sept	plant	*Scilla peruviana elegans*
Oct	plant	*S. p. venusta*
Nov	/	
Dec	/	

CONDITIONS

Aspect Tolerates full sun but the flowers will have better, longer lasting color if they are grown in semi-shade.

Site Grow in beds and borders, in almost any kind of soil as long as it drains well. Soils enriched with organic matter will give better results.

GROWING METHOD

Planting Plant the bulbs about 2–4in deep and 6–8in apart in late summer or early fall.

Feeding Apply a balanced fertiliser after flowering in early summer. Water during dry spells before and during the flowering season.

Problems No specific pest or disease problems are known for this plant.

FLOWERING

Season The flower spikes appear during late spring and early summer.

Cutting Flowers can be cut successfully for indoor decoration.

AFTER FLOWERING

Requirements Faded flower spikes should be cut off just above ground level. Clumps will usually need to be lifted only every 4–5 years unless they are very congested. Divide crowded clumps in late summer, replanting immediately to avoid drying out of the bulbs.

SINNINGIA
Gloxinia

THE VELVETY texture of trumpet-shaped gloxinia flowers shows up well here on the variety "Blanche de Meru".

"GREGOR MENDEL" is one of several fully double-flowered varieties. The heavy heads of bloom may need supporting with thin canes.

FEATURES

Gloxinias are tender plants suitable for growing in the home, greenhouse or conservatory, where they will make an impressive, colorful display. The large, showy, brilliantly colored flowers are trumpet shaped, often with speckled throats. Both flowers and leaves have a velvety feel and appearance: the large leaves are mid-green and oval.

Flowers are produced in abundance on well-grown plants, and are available in many colors, from white through pink and red to deepest blue and violet. The edges of the petals may be ruffled, or frilled with a contrasting color; there are several double-flowered varieties.

SINNINGIA AT A GLANCE

A showy house plant with colorful, velvety-textured flowers. Minimum temperature 60°F (zone 11).

		Recommended Varieties
Jan	plant	
Feb	plant	"Blanche de Meru"
Mar	plant	"Mont Blanc"
Apr	/	"Princess Elizabeth"
May	/	"Gregor Mendel"
Jun	flowering	
July	flowering	
Aug	flowering	
Sept	/	
Oct	/	
Nov	/	
Dec	/	

CONDITIONS

Aspect Choose a bright position, but not one which is in direct sun or the foliage will be scorched.

Site Gloxinias are house plants requiring average warmth; they dislike hot, dry air and benefit from standing on a dish of moist pebbles for increased humidity. Moisture-retentive soil-less potting compost should be used.

GROWING METHOD

Planting Start the tubers off in moist peat or compost in a frost-free position in spring, potting them up individually once the shoots start to grow. Tubers must be planted with the dished side up, level with the surface of the compost—not buried.

Feeding Apply high potash liquid fertilizer every 14 days during the growing season. Keep the compost only just moist until growth has started, then water more freely. Take care to keep water splashes off the leaves and flowers, and never waterlog the compost.

Problems Hot, dry air causes the leaves to shrivel and flower buds to fall before opening. Overwatering leads to rotting of the roots.

FLOWERING

Season Flowers throughout the summer.
Cutting Not suitable for cutting

AFTER FLOWERING

Requirements Gradually reduce watering until the leaves have died back, then store the tubers in dry compost in a cool but frost-free place. Repot in fresh potting compost in spring.

SPARAXIS TRICOLOR
Harlequin flower

HARLEQUIN FLOWERS come in a veritable kaleidoscope of colors, with the patterned throat revealing yet more colors and patterns.

THE STRONG, BRIGHT COLORS of harlequin flowers are shown to best advantage when they are planted in an open, sunny spot.

FEATURES

This showy, easy-care plant has bright flowers of yellow, red, pink, orange, or purple carried on stems that can be anywhere from 6–18in high. Many of the brightly colored flowers have a darker purple or deep red area in the center and a yellow throat. Harlequin flowers hybridise readily, often producing seedlings that have interesting color variations. These are bulbs that thrive in dry, warm areas of the yard. They look their best when mass-planted but can also be grown in containers, where they should be crowded together for best effect. The flowers cut well for indoor decoration. Harlequin flower bulbs increase rapidly by offsets.

SPARAXIS AT A GLANCE

Very brightly colored, star-shaped flowers are carried on slender stems in early summer. Not suitable for cold, exposed yards.

Jan	/	Recommended Varieties
Feb	/	
Mar	/	Usually supplied as a
Apr	/	color mixture
May	flowering	
Jun	flowering	
July	/	
Aug	/	
Sept	/	
Oct	/	
Nov	plant	
Dec	/	

CONDITIONS

Aspect Needs full sun all day for best results.
Site Sparaxis needs a sheltered spot in a reasonably mild area to do well; in cold gardens it is best grown in containers under cover. Soil must be well-drained and moderately fertile.

GROWING METHOD

Planting Corms should be planted 3in deep and 3–4in apart in mid-fall. Mulch the planting area with chipped bark or leafmold for winter protection.
Feeding In very poor soil apply a balanced fertiliser in early summer after flowering. Mulch the soil in late winter with well-rotted organic matter. In dry seasons, water when the foliage emerges and as buds and flowers develop if necessary.
Problems No specific problems are known.

FLOWERING

Season Flowering should be abundant in late spring and early summer.
Cutting Sparaxis makes a good cut flower for the home and should last well in water.

AFTER FLOWERING

Requirements Allow foliage to die down naturally, then lift the corms and dry them off until it is time to replant in fall. Any cormlets that have formed can be removed when the corms are lifted and replanted separately.

SPREKELIA FORMOSISSIMA
Jacobean lily

THE SCULPTURED LINES of Jacobean lilies need to be appreciated at close quarters. Growing them in containers is a perfect solution.

THE DARK CRIMSON of the flowers tends to recede into the deep green foliage but still gives a lovely rich glow.

FEATURES

The rich crimson flowers of Jacobean lily are carried singly on stems 12–18in high and the foliage, which is about the same height, appears with or just before the flowers. This plant is sometimes called the Aztec lily and is in fact native to Mexico where it occurs in open, sunny places, often in poor soil. The unusual shape of the flower gives rise to another common name, orchid amaryllis, and the exotic-looking flower could easily be mistaken for an orchid. Unfortunately it is suitable for gardens in mild areas only; in less favored climates it must be grown as a greenhouse or conservatory plant. Formerly much more widely grown than it is today, it deserves to become more popular.

SPREKELIA AT A GLANCE

An exotic-looking, rather tender plant that needs greenhouse conditions in cooler areas. Minimum temperature 45°F (zone 11).

		Recommended Varieties
Jan	/	
Feb	/	Only the straight species
Mar	/	is grown—no cultivars or
Apr	plant	varieties of this plant are
May	/	available.
Jun	flowering	
July	/	
Aug	/	
Sept	/	
Oct	/	
Nov	/	
Dec	/	

CONDITIONS

Aspect Grows best in full sun with wind protection. Indoors it likes a bright position.

Site Suitable for a sheltered border in mild areas, or containers in a greenhouse or conservatory. Outdoors, soil must be well-drained and enriched with compost or manure. Use John Innes potting compost for containers.

GROWING METHOD

Planting Plant bulbs in spring, 2in deep and 8in apart. In containers, plant with the neck of the bulb just above the compost surface.

Feeding Give a high potash liquid feed every two or three weeks throughout the growing season. Water container plants regularly until the foliage starts to die down.

Problems No specific problems are known.

FLOWERING

Season The showy flowers appear in early summer.

Cutting Can be cut for the vase but usually better enjoyed on the plant.

AFTER FLOWERING

Requirements When the leaves die down, lift outdoor bulbs and keep them in a cool, dry place. For container-grown plants, allow the compost to dry out when the leaves die down, then keep the bulb dry in its pot until spring when watering will start it into growth again.

STERNBERGIA LUTEA
Fall daffodil, lily-of-the-field

MOST SCHOLARS today believe Sternbergia lutea *is the plant referred to in the Bible as "the lily of the field."*

SHORT IN STATURE but big on impact, lily-of-the-field is one of the most delightful of bulbs, especially as it blooms in fall.

FEATURES

Clear, bright yellow flowers, rather like crocuses, appear on 6in stems from their surround of shorter, dark green, strappy leaves. The foliage persists until spring when it dies down to remain dormant until the following fall. Ideal for the rock garden, these plants also show to advantage when planted in the yard in good-sized groups where they can be left to multiply. This is a bulb that could be naturalized in turf but the area would have to be well-marked to avoid cutting off the emerging growth in fall, and the grass could not be mown for several months. Lily-of-the-field can be grown in containers but they are more successful in the open ground.

STERNBERGIA AT A GLANCE

A crocus-like bulb with flowers appearing in late summer and fall. Needs very well-drained soil to thrive.

Month		Recommended Varieties
Jan	/	
Feb	/	*Sternbergia lutea:*
Mar	/	Angustifolia Group
Apr	/	
May	/	*Sternbergia clusiana*
Jun	/	
July	plant ✍	*Sternbergia sicula*
Aug	plant ✍	
Sept	flowering ✿	
Oct	flowering ✿	
Nov	/	
Dec	/	

CONDITIONS

Aspect Prefers full sun: a summer baking of the dormant bulbs is necessary for good flowering in the fall.

Site Suitable for a rockery, raised bed, or a sunny, reasonably sheltered border. Very well-drained soil is essential for this plant. Well-rotted organic matter can be dug into the bed ahead of planting.

GROWING METHOD

Planting Plant bulbs in summer about 5in deep and the same distance apart.

Feeding Supplementary fertiliser is generally not needed.

Problems The main problem encountered is rotting of bulbs due to heavy or poorly drained soil. Improve drainage by incorporating sharp sand into the planting area.

FLOWERING

Season The small, bright golden flowers appear in fall.

Cutting These flowers are not suitable for cutting.

AFTER FLOWERING

Requirements Ensure the plants are allowed to remain dry once the foliage has died down in early summer. The site may need protection from excessive summer rain with a cloche or similar. Do not disturb established plants unless it is essential.

TIGRIDIA PAVONIA
Tiger flower, peacock flower

THE SHOWY FLOWERS *of* Tigridia pavonia *often have colorful spotting in the center, making it worth studying them closely.*

EACH EXOTIC *bloom lasts only a day, but is swiftly followed by others to give a succession of flowers over several weeks.*

FEATURES

Although each flower of the tiger or peacock flower lasts only a day, there is a succession of spectacular blooms over a long period. Flowers have six petals; the outer petals are large and broad, the inner ones smaller and thinner, usually spotted with a contrasting color. The species is red with a spotted yellow and purple center but there is a large range of colors available, in combinations of white, cream, yellow, orange, pink, mauve, and red, with contrasting spotting around the center of each flower. The tiger flower is also called jockey's cap lily in some parts of the world. Plants usually grow to around 18in. They are often included in mixed borders of summer-flowering shrubs and perennials.

TIGRIDIA AT A GLANCE

Spectacularly colorful but short-lived flowers are produced in succession from mid to late summer. Best in warmer areas.

Jan	/	Recommended Varieties
Feb	/	
Mar	/	Generally available only as color mixtures.
Apr	plant	
May	plant	
Jun	/	
July	/	
Aug	flowering	
Sept	flowering	
Oct	/	
Nov	/	
Dec	/	

CONDITIONS

Aspect　Prefers full sun with some wind protection. Grows best in warm, sheltered gardens.
Site　Grow the plants towards the front of beds and borders, where their flamoyant flowers can be appreciated close at hand. They need well-drained but not particularly rich soil.

GROWING METHOD

Planting　Plant in mid to late spring 4in deep and about 6–8in apart.
Feeding　Growth is usually improved by the application of a balanced fertilizer in spring. Occasional liquid feeds of a high potash fertilizer can be given through the growing season. Water during spring and summer in dry spells.
Problems　No specific problems are usually experienced with this plant.

FLOWERING

Season　Blooms appear from middle to late summer into the early fall.
Cutting　Flowers are not suitable for cutting.

AFTER FLOWERING

Requirements　Remove spent flower stems. In sheltered, mild areas and in free-draining soil the bulbs can be left in the ground over winter, but more reliable results are obtained by lifting before the first frosts, and storing bulbs in a frost-free place until the following spring.

TRITELEIA
syn. *Brodiaea laxa*

"QUEEN FABIOLA" is probably the most widely planted of the triteleias. The paler center gives definition to the flower form.

BLUE FLOWERS are always a favorite, and the violet-blue, starry flowers of these triteleias fill a sheltered pocket in the garden.

FEATURES

These pretty bulbous plants are native to Oregon and California. There is some confusion over their correct name; they are often listed as brodiaea, with some species as dichelostemma. *T. laxa* is the most popular form. Flower stems may be 18–24in or so high with the strappy leaves growing to about 12in. The starry flowers are carried in loose clusters and are pale or violet blue with the most popular cultivar, "Queen Fabiola," producing deeper violet-blue blooms with a pale center. The foliage dies back in spring while the plant is in bloom, and the corm remains dormant from midsummer until winter.

TRITELEIA AT A GLANCE

Dainty clusters of tubular blue blooms are carried on slender stems in midsummer. Well-drained soil is essential.

		Recommended Varieties
Jan	/	
Feb	/	*Triteleia hyacinthina*
Mar	/	
Apr	/	*Triteleia ixioides*
May	flowering	
Jun	flowering	*Triteleia laxa:*
July	flowering	"Queen Fabiola"
Aug	/	
Sept	plant	*Triteleia peduncularis*
Oct	/	
Nov	/	
Dec	/	

CONDITIONS

Aspect An open, sunny but sheltered site is necessary.
Site Grow this plant in the flower border or in containers. The soil must be light and very well-drained; triteleia cannot stand waterlogging. It can be grown in containers of sandy potting compost where the garden soil is heavy.

GROWING METHOD

Planting Plant corms 3–4in deep and 4–6in apart in fall.
Feeding A balanced or high potash fertiliser can be given when the flower buds appear, but normally no feeding is necessary. Plants in containers can be liquid-fed every two weeks. Watering is not normally necessary; the soil should be allowed to dry out while the corm is dormant during the summer.
Problems There are no specific pest or disease problems known for this plant.

FLOWERING

Season Flowers appear from early to mid-summer.
Cutting Blooms last particularly well as a cut flower.

AFTER FLOWERING

Requirements Flowering stems can be cut off when they are past their peak, or left to set seed. Plants resent disturbance, so should be left alone once planted.

TRITONIA
Tritonia

THIS ORANGE TRITONIA (Tritonia crocata) is planted beside a path where it revels in the reflected heat and somewhat dry conditions. Like most tritonias, it will increase rapidly if it is happy with the growing conditions.

FEATURES

This is a most undemanding little plant that will give great value in containers or as a cut flower. Tritonias are not fully hardy and in colder areas need to be grown indoors, but in sheltered gardens in milder parts of the country they can be grown outside successfully as long as they have full sun and a well-drained soil.

Most species flower from middle to late spring or in early summer on spikes that are around 12in high. *T. crocata* usually has bright orange flowers with darker markings in the throat but there are other forms with bright pink, salmon, or scarlet flowers. *T. disticha rubrolucens* has rose pink flowers and is hardier; it is often listed as *T. rosea*.

TRITONIA AT A GLANCE

Colorful, freesia-like flowers in late spring and early summer. Not suitable for growing outdoors in colder areas.

Month		Recommended Varieties
Jan	/	Usually available only as color mixtures.
Feb	/	
Mar	/	
Apr	/	
May	flowering	
Jun	flowering	
July	/	
Aug	/	
Sept	plant	
Oct	/	
Nov	/	
Dec	/	

CONDITIONS

Aspect Grows best in full sun, preferably with shelter from strong wind.

Site In mild areas, tritonias do well in pockets of a rockery or planted in generous clumps in a garden bed. Soil must be well drained but it need not be very rich. In cold gardens, grow the corms in pots of John Innes or soil-less potting compost.

GROWING METHOD

Planting Plant the corms about 2in deep and 4–6in apart in autumn. Five corms can be grown in a 6in pot.

Feeding A light application of balanced fertilizer can be given as growth starts. In containers, liquid feed every 14–21 days. Begin watering container plants when the leaves appear but allow the compost to dry out once the leaves start to turn yellow.

Problems No specific problems are known.

FLOWERING

Season Flowers are carried from mid-spring to early summer.

Cutting Flowers will last in the vase for up to a week.

AFTER FLOWERING

Requirements Cut off spent flower stems. Mulch plants growing outdoors for winter protection: allow container plants to remain dry in their pots until planting time.

TULBAGHIA VIOLACEA
Wild garlic

THE PALE PURPLE *flowers of wild garlic are pleasantly fragrant, though the crushed foliage has a distinctive onion smell.*

THE FLOWERS APPEAR *throughout the summer above the clumps of vigorous, gray-green foliage.*

FEATURES

This is another plant which needs warm, sheltered gardens to do well when left outdoors, though it can be grown as a container plant very successfully in cooler areas. The strappy leaves grow to about 12in with the flowering stems standing 4in or more above the foliage. The individual rosy-violet flowers form a rounded head of bloom. Society garlic flowers through the summer, and stems can be cut for the vase.
Tulbaghia natalensis grows to 6in high and has fragrant white flowers with a yellow center that gives them a narcissus-like appearance. This is a hardier species which is usually more successful in colder gardens, though it is not as common as *T. violacea*.

TULBAGHIA AT A GLANCE

A slightly tender plant with mounds of grassy foliage and heads of pretty pink summer flowers.

Jan	/	Recommended Varieties
Feb	/	*Tulbaghia violacea pallida*
Mar	/	
Apr	plant 👈	*Tulbaghia violacea:*
May	/	"Silver Lace"
Jun	flowering	
July	flowering	
Aug	flowering	
Sept	/	
Oct	/	
Nov	/	
Dec	/	

CONDITIONS

Aspect Prefers a position in full sun.
Site Tulbaghia is a good plant for seaside gardens, and can be included in a mixed border of annuals and perennials or grown in containers. Soil should be well drained and contain plenty of well-rotted organic matter.

GROWING METHOD

Planting Plant in spring about 1in deep and 8in or so apart. Congested clumps can be lifted and divided in spring.
Feeding If the organic content of the soil is high little extra feeding is needed. However, a light dressing of balanced fertilizer may be given as growth becomes active. Keep the soil moist during the growing season, watering in dry spells as necessary.
Problems No specific problems are known.

FLOWERING

Season Flowers are carried all through summer.
Cutting Flowers are very decorative when cut for the vase, although the smell of the foliage may discourage some people.

AFTER FLOWERING

Requirements Tidy up the foliage and apply a mulch of chipped bark, leafmould or dry leaves for winter protection. Container plants should be allowed to dry out and moved under cover for the winter.

TULIPA
Tulip

THE POINTED PETALS of these goblet-shaped, bright lipstick-pink tulips will open to form a starry shape.

A NATIVE of Crete, pale pink Tulipa saxatilis *needs a sunny, warm position with perfectly drained soil in which to grow.*

FEATURES

There are over 100 species of tulips and many hundreds of hybrids. Most modern garden tulips are the result of extensive breeding programmes that began in the late sixteenth century in Europe and are continuing to this day. Tulips were all the rage at that time as more and more species were introduced to Europe from Turkey, Iran, and central Asia. Tulip species range in height from about 6–24in but the greatest number of hybrids are probably in the range of 12–16in. Tulips look their best in mass plantings of one color but they can, of course, be mixed. They make very good container plants and are delightful cut flowers. Some of the most charming are the dwarf types which do particularly well in rock gardens and are also very suitable for containers.

Tulip bulbs are widely available in garden centers in late summer and early fall, but to get a wider choice it is often best to obtain catalogues from specialist bulb growers who run mail-order businesses. Many of the species tulips are only available from specialist growers. With careful selection it is possible to have a tulip in flower from early to very late spring.

Like daffodils, tulips are split into a number of divisions according to their flower form and time of flowering.

Single early	Cup-shaped single flowers, up to 16in in early to mid-spring.
Double early	Fully double flowers up to 16in in early to mid-spring.
Triumph	Conical then rounded, single flowers up to 20in in mid to late spring.
Darwin hybrid	Large, single flowers of varying shape, up to 24in in mid to late spring.
Single late	Single, blocky or square shaped flowers up to 30in in late spring and early summer.
Lily-flowered	Single, waisted flowers with pointed petals, up to 24in in late spring.
Fringed	Single flowers with very finely cut petal edges, up to 24in in late spring.
Viridiflora	Single flowers with green bands or streaks on the outside, up to 20in in late spring.
Rembrandt	Single flowers with a broken pattern of feathering or streaking caused by a virus. Up to 30in in late spring.
Parrot	Single flowers with very strongly frilled and curled petals, up to 24in in late spring.
Double late	Large, fully double flowers up to 24in in late spring.
Kaufmanniana	Single, often bi-colored flowers of a waterlily shape, up to 10in in late spring. Leaves may be mottled.
Fosteriana	Large, single, wide-opening flowers up to 20in in early to mid-spring.
Greigii	Large, single flowers up to 14in in mid to late spring. Leaves streaked and mottled.
Miscellaneous	Any other species, varieties, and hybrids.

THE BIZARRE FORM of parrot tulips is exemplified by this dark crimson flower. People either love these forms or hate them.

THE BURGUNDY of these full-blown tulips will appeal to lovers of the unusual but they may be hard to incorporate into the garden scheme.

CONDITIONS

Aspect   Tulips need full sun for at least half the day, with some wind protection.

Site   Grow tulips in beds and borders, on rockeries or in containers. Soil should be well drained with a high organic content. Add lime to acid soils.

GROWING METHOD

Planting   Bulbs should be planted in late fall. Planting depth varies according to the size of the bulbs; usually 6–8in for the larger types and 4in for the smaller species. Space them 4–8in apart.

Feeding   Apply liquid fertilizer as soon as buds appear and again after flowers have faded. Water regularly in dry spells, especially once the buds have appeared.

Problems   Tulip breaking virus, causing streaking of the flowers, is carried by aphids. Remove affected plants and keep aphids under control. Tulip fire disease is a type of botrytis or gray mould. It causes small brown spots on flowers and leaves; stems may rot and gray furry growth may develop on the damaged areas. Destroy plants infected with this disease and avoid planting tulips in the same spot for a couple of years. Spraying with a general fungicide may control early infection.

FLOWERING

Season   Tulips flower somewhere between late winter and late spring, depending on variety.

Cutting   If cutting blooms for the house, choose those that are not fully open and cut them early in the morning. Change vase water frequently.

AFTER FLOWERING

Requirements   Remove spent flower stems and dead foliage. Tulips may be left in the ground for two or three years, or the bulbs can be lifted once the foliage has died down, cleaned and stored in a cool, dry, airy place. Dwarf tulips tend to be left in the ground, but other varieties usually perform better if they are lifted and replanted every year. If you do not want to lift them annually, make sure the bulbs are planted deeply.

TULIPA AT A GLANCE		
Well-known flowers in a very wide range of colors, sizes, and forms, flowering between late winter and late spring.		
Jan	/	
Feb	flowering	Recommended Varieties
Mar	flowering	"Peach Blossom"
Apr	flowering	"Apeldoorn"
May	flowering	"Clara Butt"
Jun	/	"China Pink"
July	/	"Burgundy Lace"
Aug	/	"Spring Green"
Sept	/	"Texas Gold"
Oct	/	"Angelique"
Nov	plant	"Ancilla"
Dec	plant	*Tulipa fosteriana*
		Tulipa greigii
		Tulipa tarda

WATSONIA
Watsonia

THE VIVID PINK FLOWERS of watsonia make it a most desirable plant, but it is not commonly grown in gardens.

WATSONIA FLOWERS are displayed well clear of the upright foliage and so are ideal for planting at the back of a border.

FEATURES

Although there are many species of watsonias in the wild, they are not commonly cultivated plants. The stiff, sword-shaped leaves are similar to those of a gladiolus: the flower spike, growing to over 39in carries tubular flowers in various shades of pink and red, violet, magenta and orange. Watsonia is ideally placed towards the back of a mixed border. In all but very warm districts the corms should be lifted in fall and stored in a dry place until it is time to replant them the following spring. The usual species offered is *W. pillansii* (also known as *W. beatricis*), which has orange-red flowers. The slightly more tender *W. borbonica* (*W. pyrimidata*) has rich pink blooms.

WATSONIA AT A GLANCE

An unusual bulb with tall, stately spikes of pink or red flowers, good for the back of the border.

Jan	/	Recommended Varieties
Feb	/	
Mar	/	
Apr	plant ✍	"Stanford Scarlet"
May	plant ✍	"Tresco Dwarf Pink"
Jun	flowering ✿	
July	flowering ✿	*Watsonia borbonica ardernei*
Aug	flowering ✿	
Sept	plant ✍ (warm areas)	
Oct	/	
Nov	/	
Dec	/	

CONDITIONS

Aspect Watsonia needs full sun and a warm, sheltered position.

Site These tall plants are good for the back of a border. They can also be grown in pots in a greenhouse. Any well-drained soil is acceptable, but growth will be better if well-rotted organic matter is dug in before planting.

GROWING METHOD

Planting Plant corms in mid to late spring, 4in deep and 12in apart. In warm, sheltered areas, corms can be planted in fall 6in deep and mulched with chipped bark or dry leaves.

Feeding Apply a long-acting fertilizer such as general fertilizer in early summer. Watering is necessary only in prolonged dry spells.

Problems Generally free from pest or disease problems when grown in an open, sunny position.

FLOWERING

Season Watsonias flower in mid-summer.

Cutting Stems can be cut for the vase. They should last well with frequent water changes.

AFTER FLOWERING

Requirements Except in very warm areas, lift the corms after flowering, when the foliage starts to die down. Clean them, allow them to dry, and store in a cool, airy place until the following spring.

ZANTEDESCHIA
Arum lily, calla lily

ARUM LILIES have long been favorites with flower arrangers for their texture and sculptural shape which adds form to an arrangement.

PURE WHITE FLOWERS and decorative leaves are features of arum, which are quite easy to grow in a variety of conditions.

FEATURES

Arum lilies are greatly prized for their beautiful waxy flowers, pure white with a golden central spadix. The arrow-shaped leaves are deep green, and the whole plant can grow up to 39in high. Several species are suitable for growing only in a greenhouse or conservatory, but *Z. aethiopica* can be grown outside in reasonably sheltered gardens. It likes moist, boggy conditions, and often grows best beside a pond or water feature: it can be grown as a marginal plant in up to 12in of water. *Z. elliottiana*, the golden arum, and *Z. rehmannii*, the pink arum, are good greenhouse or conservatory plants.

ZANTEDESCHIA AT A GLANCE

A rhizomatous plant grown for its beautiful waxy white flower spathes. Needs greenhouse conditions in some areas.

Jan	/	
Feb	/	
Mar	/	
Apr	plant 🖐	
May	/	
Jun	flowering 🌸	
July	flowering 🌸	
Aug	/	
Sept	/	
Oct	/	
Nov	/	
Dec	/	

Recommended Varieties

Zantedeschia aethiopica:
"Crowborough"
"Green Goddess"

CONDITIONS

Aspect Can be grown in full sun or light shade. It should be sheltered from strong wind.

Site *Z. aethiopica* can be grown on the fringe of a pool or in a border in moist, humus-rich soil. Other arum species need rich but free-draining soil and are grown in a greenhouse or conservatory in containers.

GROWING METHOD

Planting Plant rhizomes 6in deep and 18in apart in spring.

Feeding Apply liquid fertilizer as buds appear and continue to feed every 14–21 days while plants are in bloom. Keep the soil moist at all times while the plants are in active growth during spring and summer.

Problems Leaf spot can cause dark blotches on all parts of the plant and may cause premature leaf drop. It often occurs where conditions are too cool and damp. Destroy affected parts and spray with a suitable fungicide.

FLOWERING

Season Flowers in early summer.

Cutting Flowers are excellent for cutting.

AFTER FLOWERING

Requirements Remove flower stems as they fade. Mulch outdoor plants with dry leaves for winter.

ZEPHYRANTHES

Zephyr lily, rainflower

ZEPHYR LILY shows how even the simplest of flowers can be very beautiful. The green throat and yellow stamens emphasise the purity.

A BROAD BORDER of zephyr lily gives a star-studded performance in the fall garden.

FEATURES

With its starry white flowers and shiny green, grass-like foliage, zephyr lily is a bulb for mass planting in sheltered gardens. It is quite easy to grow and can remain undisturbed for years where conditions suit it. It can be planted in borders or on a rockery, and it can also be grown very successfully in containers. The crocus-like flowers are carried in late summer or fall, especially after showers of rain, which accounts for its common name of rainflower. *Zephyranthes candida* is the species suitable for growing outdoors in Britain; it generally reaches a height of 8–10in. *Z. grandiflora* (also called *Z. rosea*) has lovely rosy pink flowers but is only suitable for cultivation in a greenhouse or conservatory, as is the yellow flowered *Z. citrina*.

ZEPHYRANTHES AT A GLANCE

An attractive, low-growing plant with crocus-like flowers in the fall.

Jan	/
Feb	/
Mar	/
Apr	plant
May	/
Jun	flowering *
July	flowering *
Aug	/
Sept	flowering
Oct	flowering
Nov	/
Dec	/

Recommended Species

Zephyranthes candida

Z. citrina

Z. flavissima

Z. grandiflora

CONDITIONS

Aspect Grows best in full sun.

Site Grow in beds or borders or in pockets in a rockery. Needs a well-drained but moisture-retentive soil. Growth will be improved if soils contain some humus.

GROWING METHOD

Planting Plant in spring, 2in deep and 4in apart. For greenhouse cultivation, plant 5 bulbs in a 5in pot in loam-based potting compost.

Feeding Supplementary fertilizer is generally not needed. Spread a mulch of well-decayed manure or compost around the bulbs in spring. Water in dry spells during spring, but stop watering when the foliage starts to die down.

Problems No specific problems are usually experienced with this plant.

FLOWERING

Season Flowers appear from late summer into fall, or in mid-summer in the greenhouse.

Cutting Flowers are not suitable for cutting.

AFTER FLOWERING

Requirements Spent flower stems may be cut off but this is not essential. No special treatment is needed as the bulbs are best left undisturbed for several years. If you wish to lift and divide a clump this is best done in spring. Greenhouse plants should be allowed to dry out when the leaves die down, and started into growth again by plentiful watering the following spring.

Growing Shrubs

GROWING FLOWERING SHRUBS

Beautiful borders can be created almost entirely from shrubs—the bones of a garden. They impart form and character and complement trees and herbaceous perennials. All shrubs flower— and many that have small, modest flowers produce bright berries that ornament the late summer, fall, and winter garden.

Shrubs are usually defined as perennial woody plants. They are frequently multi-stemmed, but not always, and the line between tall shrubs and small trees is rather vague. Indeed, gardeners and professional horticulturists do not always agree. Shrubs may be evergreen or deciduous, leaves are small or large, glossy or matt, and come in a huge range of shapes. Some shrubs, such as hibiscus, have showy flowers. Others, such as box, have tiny, insignificant ones. Cotton lavender (*santolina*) and rosemary, among others, have aromatic foliage. A few— such as syringa, mock orange, and choisya—are prized for their sweetly perfumed blooms.

Shrubs come in every shape and size. There is a species or variety to suit virtually every situation. When you are planning a garden, select kinds that favour a particular position. Will the shrub thrive in full sun, or does it prefer shade? Consider how high and wide it will grow. Some shrubs can take up to 5–10 years to mature, become well established, and assume their final shape. Never buy a large-growing shrub for a small space, thinking you can prune it to keep it small. Repeated cutting back will spoil its natural symmetry and you will eventually come to hate it and thus remove it.

ABOVE: Brilliant red "Royal William"—a bounteous large-flowered rose.

LEFT: A sculpturally appealing symphony of golden pansies, box hedging, and green bottlebrush blooms of Euphorbia wulfenii.

PROPAGATION

Most shrubs are raised from stem cuttings. They may be grown from soft-tip cuttings (of, for example, hydrangea or fuchsia) taken in late spring and early summer; semi-ripe nodal cuttings of side shoots, or heel cuttings of shoots tugged from the main stem in midsummer—most shrubs being propagated this way; or from dormant hardwood cuttings of deciduous shrubs.

Soft-tip, semi-ripe nodal, and heel cuttings should be 2–4in long and taken from strong, healthy plants, preferably from stems that have not flowered. Hardwood cuttings of mature, dormant shoots, 10–12in long, are rooted in the fall, in a slit trench in the garden. Layering, that is, pegging down young, flexible stems close to the soil any time between spring and fall, is another easy way to multiply shrubs.

Soft-tip and semi-ripe nodal cuttings

Take these early in the day, when plump and dew-fresh. If you are not able to insert them into pots of compost immediately, enclose them in a plastic bag and keep them in a cool, shady place.

Use a very sharp knife or razor blade to remove all but the topmost two or three leaves. If the leaves are large, as in hydrangeas, it is best to shorten them by half their length. At the base of the cutting make a clean, horizontal cut, just below a node (joint) from which leaves appear. Encourage rapid rooting by dipping the cutting in hormone rooting compound. Prepare a rooting mix of three parts, by volume, of coarse, washed sand or Perlite and one part of peat or loam-based seed compost. Alternatively, use proprietary, peat-based cutting compost. Place the compost mix in a small, 4in pot and gently firm it. Make holes with a pencil where the cuttings are to go and insert them to a third of their length, about 2in apart.

Firm compost around the stems. You can place several cuttings in one pot. Water them in, allow compost to drain, then transfer them to a propagator or garden frame, or enclose them in an inflated plastic bag and place them on a windowsill. In warm conditions, soft-tip cuttings will root within 2–4 weeks. You can tell if a cutting has rooted if new leaves have formed and a gentle pull on the stem meets with resistance. A few weeks later, move the plant into a small pot of potting compost.

HARDWOOD CUTTINGS

They usually take many weeks or months to root. Leaves may form long before roots develop. They should be about 12in long and ¼–½in thick. Take them from the middle of well-ripened, current-year shoots. Prepare them by making a gently sloping cut just above the topmost bud and a horizontal cut immediately below the bottom node (joint). Next, in a sunny, well-drained area of deeply dug and friable soil, use a spade to take out a 6–8in deep trench with one vertical wall. Trickle a 1inch layer of sharp sand into it.

Insert cuttings to two-thirds their depth, 6in apart, pressing them into the sand. Tread soil firmly around them, hoe out footprints and water copiously.

Refirm cuttings in winter when hard frost lifts them. Roots will form in spring. By fall, plants will be ready for moving to where you wish to display them.

Some roses will grow quite readily from cuttings, but others will not grow vigorously on their own roots. Commercial nurseries "bud" rose varieties on to rootstocks of wild or species roses. (Budding is a form of grafting using dormant leaf buds.)

LAYERING

Take out a 6in hole next to the plant and remove any leaves that might be buried, from the selected shoot. Make a sloping, 1½in cut through a joint in the middle of the shoot and wedge open the cut with a matchstick. Half fill the hole with a mix of equal parts sharp sand and soil and then peg the cut part of the shoot into it. Cover the shoot with more of the same mix and tie the exposed end to a cane to keep it upright. Water the layer to settle the soil around it and place a large, flat stone over it to keep the soil damp.

About a year later, when roots have formed, sever the new shrub, or layer, from its parent by cutting the stem of the parent shrub where it enters the ground. Then leave your new shrub *in situ* or transplant it to a new position in the garden.

Some shrubs may be grown from seed, but only the species will produce plants that match their parent.

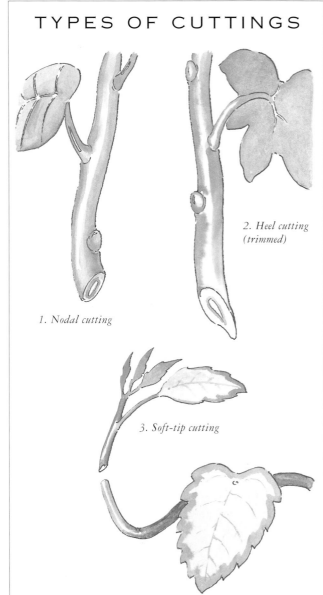

TYPES OF CUTTINGS

1. Nodal cutting

2. Heel cutting (trimmed)

3. Soft-tip cutting

CUTTINGS. *1. Nodal cuttings are made by making a clean cut ⅛in below a node (joint). 2. Heel cuttings are tugged from the main stem, to leave a tag of bark, which is trimmed back close to the base of the shoot. 3. Soft-tip cuttings are made from young, green shoot tips. Remove lower leaves (as here) before inserting in compost.*

CHOOSING A PLANT

When choosing plants at a garden center, the biggest is not always the best. Look for those that are well shaped and have a good cover of healthy leaves. Avoid plants that have woody roots protruding from drainage holes, those that are excessively tall for the pot and those that have knobbly, thickened stem bases. All these features show that the plant is pot-bound and that it should have been moved into a larger container some time ago. All plants suffer from some degree of transplanting shock, but the smaller the plant the less traumatic the move. Ideally, select plants in bloom to ensure that you are getting the color and variety you want.

SOIL PREPARATION

Because most shrubs are fairly long-lived and form a garden's permanent framework, it is worth putting in a bit of time and effort into preparing a good home for them and thus protect your investment. Shrubs planted in suitable conditions will become established more quickly, and their healthy growth will be less vulnerable to attack by pests and disease than plants that are treated more hastily.

Few shrubs tolerate heavy, waterlogged soil. If drainage is poor, you may need to consider raising the planting area or installing subsoil drains. Heavy, clay soils can be improved by adding gypsum at the rate of 7–11oz per sq yd and by working in large quantities of well-rotted, organic material. Organic matter should be dug in several weeks ahead of planting. Sandy soils, in which water and nutrients are quickly lost, benefit greatly from the addition of large amounts of organic matter before planting. All plants and soils are better for being mulched with humus-forming, well-rotted animal manure, compost, leaf mould, straw, or decayed grass clippings, as these not only retain moisture in the soil but also keep the soil and plants well nourished. Mulches should only be laid on moist soil.

STRIKING SOFT-TIP CUTTINGS

1. TO TAKE A CUTTING, gather shoots when dew-fresh and place in a plastic bag. Prepare stems by trimming to length and cutting just below a node (joint). Keep cuttings cool and shaded. Remove lower leaves, which will rot if buried.

2. FILL A SMALL POT, which has plenty of drainage holes, with gritty cutting compost. Use a pencil to make holes for inserting cuttings to half their length. Firm compost around them.

3. WATER IN CUTTINGS well, but gently, taking care not to dislodge them. They should not need watering again until new growth indicates that roots have formed. If you are unsure of how dry the compost is, and the pot feels light, add just a little water.

4. MAKE A WIRE OR BAMBOO FRAME that fits inside the pot and is tall enough to clear cuttings. Place a plastic bag over the frame and secure it to the pot. The bag will keep air and soil moist. Root cuttings in good light but not direct sunlight.

FRAMED BY STATUESQUE CONIFERS and a fiery, fall-hued tree, crimson-flowered Hebe "Great Orme" *makes a fine focal point beside this gravel path. Usefully, this evergreen shrub starts blooming in July but seldom finishes before late October.*

PLANTING

With good soil preparation and correct planting techniques your shrubs should flourish. Most container-grown shrubs are transplanted throughout the year, provided the soil is crumbly and workable and frost is not forecast. In winter, in gardens prone to hard frost, it is best to transplant only dormant, deciduous plants.

Bare-rooted shrubs, usually deciduous, are planted when leaves have fallen—from fall to early spring.

• Check that the position chosen for your shrub will allow it to develop full height and spread without your having to cut it back. You should also cater for its other needs: soil type—heavy or light, warm and free-draining—and sun or shade.

• Dig a hole at least twice as wide as the plant's root system and about the same depth. Loosen soil in the bottom of the hole and around the sides. If it is clayey, work in grit or gravel to avoid creating a sump in which roots may drown.

• Do not put fresh manure into the hole. Instead, mix a balanced fertilizer, such as fish, blood, and bone meal, Growmore, or a slow-release brand, with soil you firm around the roots. Roots must not come into direct contact with fertilizer, which may burn them.

• If you are planting a container-grown shrub bought in a stiff plastic pot, thoroughly water the compost to loosen any roots clinging to the pot sides. Invert the plant and gently tap its pot rim on a hard surface so that the rootball slides out. Carefully tease out compacted, encircling roots from the rootball.

• Trim away any roots that are damaged.

• Place the plant in its hole, at the same depth that it was previously growing. Lay a cane over the hole, next to the plant, to check this. Backfill the hole with soil that you have dug out and tread the soil firmly around the rootball. Do not tread on the rootball itself.

• Water in thoroughly to remove any air pockets and settle the soil around the feeding root hairs.

• Mulch the root area, but keep mulch well clear of the stem, because its bark could rot. Organic mulches, such as manures and composts, help to condition soil and feed plants. They break down and disappear after a year or so, so replace them annually.

MAINTENANCE

Water newly planted shrubs regularly and copiously, specially in droughty weather until they are well established.

Re-feed fall-planted shrubs in spring, and spring- planted in summer, by topdressing (sprinkling) the root area with a complete plant food. Fish, blood, and bone meal or pelleted poultry manure is ideal for most shrubs, but avoid using poultry manure on lime-hating rhododendrons and summer-flowering heathers, among others.

PRUNING

Many shrubs will never need shoots removing unless you wish to rejuvenate very old plants or take out wayward stems. If you wish to cut back a spring-flowering plant, prune it when its blooms fade. The only exception to this is plants, such as firethorn and cotoneaster, that are grown for their berries. Shrubs, such as *Buddleja davidii*, that flower from mid- to late summer are best pruned the following spring.

To train a single-stemmed standard, select a young shrub with a straight stem and shorten laterals (side shoots) to within 1in of the trunk. These leafy stumps help to conduct sap to the head of the standard. If the main stem is slender—it usually is—you may need to tie it to a cane. As the stem lengthens, shorten further side shoots to an inch or so until the stem is as high as required—normally 4–6ft. Then, when the head is developing well, trim it to a ball shape and cut off side shoots flush with the stem.

HARDINESS

All plants mentioned flourish outdoors, apart from frost-tender ardisia, echium, oleander, plumbago, pomegranate, and heliotrope, which are normally overwintered in a greenhouse or conservatory and moved to a sheltered, sunny place for summer. Of the relatively hardy kinds, some in very cold, windswept, or frost-pocket gardens may need tucking up for winter. The best way to protect them is to cover them with an open-topped wigwam of bubble plastic or several layers of fiber fleece. Make sure the material does not touch the leaves or stems, or, if moist, it might rot them.

WHAT CAN GO WRONG?

Yellow leaves
• Plants have been overwatered or are too dry.
• Plants may need feeding: fertilize the plant with a high-nitrogen tonic if this has not been done for two or three months and see if there is any improvement within the next two or three weeks.
• Older leaves may turn bright yellow before dropping. Do not worry; they have finished their useful life.
• When new leaves on azaleas are pale yellow yet the veins are green, they probably require a dose of iron chelates, which aids chlorophyll production. Apply this in spring and early summer, carefully following the manufacturer's directions on the label.

Curled or distorted leaves
• Look for aphids (greenfly)—tiny, sticky, reddish-brown, gray, or green, sap-sucking insects clustering on new growth. Control them with an insecticide containing pirimicarb, permethrin, biollethrin, horticultural soap, rotenone, or pyrethrins. Spray at dusk when bees and other beneficial insects have retired for the night. Avoid spraying when it is hot, too, because foliage may be scorched by high temperatures.
• Some viruses manifest themselves this way and there is no cure. Consult reference books or experts to see if your plant has succumbed to one of these diseases. If affected, dig it up and burn it.
• Check that there has been no drift of any herbicide from nearby spraying. Even very small amounts of spray drift, especially from selective lawn weedkillers, can distort leaves of very sensitive plants, such as tomatoes and roses.

Black spots on leaves
• These may be fungal leaf spots. On roses, they are probably caused by black spot, a common disease that badly blotches leaves. Control it by spraying with bupirimate with triforine, penconazole, or myclobutanil. Ideally, improve air circulation around plants and avoid wetting leaves when watering, which should not be done late in the day. Large, brownish-black spots on camellias probably resulted from sunburn.

Gray-white powder on leaf surfaces
• This deposit is probably powdery mildew, which affects a wide range of plants. Roses, azaleas, hydrangeas, and many other shrubs are prone to this disease. Avoid watering late in the day and spray plants with bupirimate with triforine, myclobutanil, sulfur or penconazole. It is worse on wall shrubs in dry areas where air does not freely circulate.

Mottled leaves
• This is usually associated with sap-sucking insects such as scale, thrip, lace bug, and red spider mite, which is not a true insect. Stressed, rather than healthy, plants are more liable to be attacked by these insects. Plants may be stressed by drought or overwatering, or by simply growing them away from their favored aspect.
• Limpet-like scale insects come in various sizes and colors. Control small infestations by using a damp cloth to wipe them off leaves and stems. Eradicate severe infestations by spraying plants with malathion
• Thrips and lace bugs may be reduced by hosing the underside of leaves or by spraying with pyrethrins, malathion, pirimiphos-methyl, permethrin or insecticidal soap.
• In hot, dry weather, red spider mite can be a problem on shrubs growing in rain-sheltered spots, such as under the house eaves. Hosing the foliage helps to keep them down and obviate the need for spraying. If you have to resort to insecticides, malathion, bifenthrin, and pirimiphos-methyl are effective.

Holes in leaves or on leaf margins
• This may be snail or slug damage. Snails often lurk high up on the foliage. Baiting is not effective in this instance, so pick off and kill pests. Eradicate the ground-hugging tribe by sprinkling blue-dyed molluscicide pellets containing metaldehyde or methiocarb, thinly around susceptible, soft-stemmed plants. Alternatively, ring them with grit.
• Caterpillars also chew leaves. Tackle them by hand

picking or biologically controlling them with *Bacillus thuringiensis*. Effective insecticides include permethrin, bifenthrin, and pirimiphos-methyl.

Stems and leaves webbed or matted together
• Webbing caterpillars, such as those of the lackey moth, can cover buds and new shoots and extensively defoliate trees and shrubs. Pull out the webbing with a gloved hand or cut out the damaged section. Spray with permethrin, bifenthrin or pirimiphos-methyl, or control the pest biologically with *Bacillus thuringiensis*. Inspect shrubs several times a year to control this pest in its early stages.

Sooty mould (a dry, black coating on leaf surfaces)
• A fungus, sooty mould feeds on sticky honeydew secreted by sap-sucking insects, such as aphids and scales. Once the pest is controlled, the mould will gradually disappear. Hosing helps. Wipe large-leaved plants with a damp cloth.

Sudden death of plant
• If leaves turn brown but remain attached to the plant, the plant has probably died from root rot. Root systems may have been damaged by excessive watering—from rain or irrigation—quite some time before the plant expires, especially in cool weather. When plants are stressed by extreme heat or wind, damaged root systems cannot cope and death follows quickly.
• If a plant is suffering from drought, its leaves may be brown and rapidly drop when watered.

Pomegranate fruits may appear in a warm garden.

ABELIA
Abelia

Abelia's pretty pink flowers appear at the end of summer. Striking, red calyces prolong the display.

An informal abelia hedge adds a little magic to a sunny and sheltered garden. Trim it lightly in spring.

FEATURES

Semi-evergreen and vigorous in mild districts, *Abelia × grandiflora* makes a dashing statement and a fine flowering hedge. From July to September, its arching shoots, clad with small, oval, pointed leaves, 4–5ft long, are sleeved with showy heads of tubular, pale pink flowers with reddish calyces. The decorative calyx persists into late fall.
"Francis Mason" is a stunning variety with golden-variegated leaves that complement a wealth of pink blossom. Other prized kinds are lilac-pink *A. chinensis* "Edward Goucher" and rosy-lilac *A. schumannii*.

ABELIA AT A GLANCE

Sporting clusters of pink or lilac flowers from late summer to fall, it needs a sheltered position. Hardy to 14°F (zone 8).

Month	Activity	Recommended Varieties
Jan	/	
Feb	/	*A. chinensis* "Edward Goucher"
Mar	prune	
Apr	plant, prune	*A. × grandiflora*
May	plant	*A. × grandiflora* "Francis Mason"
June	plant	*A. schumannii*
July	plant, flower	
Aug	plant, flower	
Sept	plant, flower	
Oct	/	
Nov	/	
Dec	/	

CONDITIONS

Aspect — Thriving in full sun and tolerating very light shade, abelia is best planted against a sheltered, south- or west-facing wall.

Site — Abelia prospers in a wide range of well-drained soils, from clay-loam to sand. Enrich rapid-draining, chalky, and sandy soils with well-rotted and moisture-conserving, bulky organic materials.

GROWING METHOD

Feeding — Topdress the root area with bone meal in spring and fall to encourage sturdy growth and profuse blooms.
Water freely after planting and mulch thickly with old manure, bark, cocoa shell, or rotted garden compost to keep roots cool and active.

Propagation — Take soft-tip cuttings in late spring and semi-ripe cuttings from mid- to late summer.

Problems — Shoots are brittle and easily snapped, so be careful when pruning and planting.

PRUNING

Flowers form on current-year shoots. Once mature, keep it youthful by cutting out a third of its oldest branches in spring.

ABUTILON VITIFOLIUM
Abutilon

In a sheltered, sunny spot, Abutilon vitifolium *becomes a glowing sentinel of saucer-shaped, pale to deep mauve blooms in early summer.*

Plant award-winning "Canary Bird" in a fertile, sun-soaked spot and enjoy a summer-long succession of pendent blooms.

FEATURES

There are few more exhilarating, summer sights than a mature shrub of *Abutilon vitifolium* festooned with white to purple-blue, saucer-shaped blooms. Studding stems clothed with three- to five-lobed, soft,gray, hairy leaves are flowers that have you looking closely at them. Making an upright "obelisk" to around 15ft, this shrub is worth a little cosseting—as are its eye-catching varieties, mauve-flowered "Veronica Tennant" and "Tennant's White".

Closely related *A.* × *suntense*, a fast-growing hybrid to 12ft, rewards us with pendent, white to violet-blue "saucers".

Choice forms of this hybrid are purple-blue "Geoffrey Gorer," white "Gorer's White," deep mauve "Jermyns," and dark violet-blue "Violetta". Look out, too, for "Canary Bird," whose radiant lemon-yellow blooms illuminate a border.

ABUTILON AT A GLANCE

Loosely branched, deciduous shrub sleeved with saucer-shaped, white, blue, or purple blooms in summer. Hardy to 32ºF (zone 10)

		Recommended Varieties
Jan	/	
Feb	/	*A.* × *suntense*
Mar	/	"Geoffrey Gorer"
Apr	plant, prune	"Gorer's White"
May	plant	"Jermyns"
June	flower, plant	"Ralph Gould"
July	flower, prune	"Violetta"
Aug	plant	*A. vitifolium* "Tennant's
Sept	plant	White"
Oct	/	*A. vitifolium* "Veronica
Nov	/	Tennant"
Dec	/	

CONDITIONS

Aspect Position all varieties in full sun where shoots grow stocky and are massed with bloom. Make sure abutilon is sheltered from shoot-killing, icy winds.

Site This shrub tolerates a wide range of well-drained soils, but for the best results enrich the planting area with plenty of crumbly organic matter.

GROWING METHOD

Feeding For the strongest shoots and bounteous blossom, topdress the root area with fish, blood, and bone meal or Growmore in spring and midsummer.

Water young plants regularly and mulch them with bulky organics to keep soil cool.

In long, dry spells, take out a moat around the plant and fill it repeatedly with water. When subsoil is soaked, replace excavated soil and cover with moisture-conserving mulch.

Propagation Increase favoured varieties from semi-ripe cuttings from mid- to late summer.

A. vitifolium produces masses of fertile seed.

Problems Control aphids colonizing soft stems by spraying with pirmicarb, pyrethrins, or insecticidal soap. Leaves may be damaged by caterpillars and other chewing insects. If damage is slight, ignore it. If severe, control these pests biologically with *Bacillus thuringiensis*, or apply rotenone or pirimiphos-methyl.

PRUNING

Keep bushes compact and packed with flowering shoots by cutting back dead or dying stems to healthy growth in mid-spring. In early summer, shorten flowered stems to two-thirds their length.

SILVER WATTLE
Acacia dealbata

Silver wattle's ferny, silvery-green leaves are appealing all year round, specially if shoots are fan-trained against a warm wall.

There are few more riveting sights in a sheltered garden in early spring than Acacia dealbata *in full flower.*

FEATURES

There are around 900 species of wattle but only *Acacia dealbata* is sufficiently hardy for planting outdoors in mild districts. Rapidly growing to around 12ft, its soft shoots are richly and appealingly clothed with ferny and silvery-sheened, evergreen leaves.

In April, year-old shoots are thickly clustered with small, double pompoms of fragrant, bright yellow blossom.

Ideally, because several days of temperatures hovering around freezing point may kill shoots, it is best fan-trained against a warm, south-facing wall.

Only in relatively frost-free districts can you successfully grow it as a free-standing shrub in the open garden. Elsewhere, set it in a large pot or tub and grow it in a conservatory, moving it outdoors into the open garden only for summer.

SILVER WATTLE AT A GLANCE

An evergreen, tender tree with silvery, ferny leaves and bobbles of yellow flowers in spring. Hardy to 32°F (zone 10).

Month		Recommended Varieties
Jan	/	
Feb	flower	*A. dealbata*
Mar	flower	
Apr	plant, flower	
May	prune, plant	
June	plant	
July	plant	
Aug	plant	
Sept	plant	
Oct	/	
Nov	/	
Dec	/	

CONDITIONS

Aspect Choose a warm, sunny site, ideally very sheltered and facing south or south-west, where it will not be exposed to leaf-blackening easterly or northerly winds.

Site Any well-drained, lime-free soil suits it. Fortify thin, sandy, or gravelly soils with bulky, humus-enriching manure, or well-rotted garden compost. Aerate heavy clay by working in plenty of grit or shingle. Alternatively, if puddles lie, dig a 18in drainage trench, leading to a soakaway, and fill it with gravel or rubble to within 8in of the soil surface.

GROWING METHOD

Feeding Encourage robust growth by annually sprinkling fish, blood, and bone meal, or Growmore over the rooting area in April and July. Water young plants regularly, especially in droughty spells, to help them develop a good, questing root system. Acacia appreciates occasional deep watering.

Propagation Increase acacia from semi-ripe cuttings in midsummer. Also grow from seed. Speed germination by soaking seeds overnight in hot water to soften the seed coat. Sow directly.

Problems Fortunately, it is seldom attacked by sap-sucking pests or caterpillars. If aphids cluster on shoots and cripple them, control them with pirimicarb, horticultural soap, or permethrin.

PRUNING

No regular pruning is necessary. In spring, shorten any stems killed by frost back to healthy side shoots. If acacia outgrows its situation, reduce wayward stems by up to two-thirds in late spring.

CORAL BERRY
Ardisia crenata

Fetching when enhancing a patio in summer, or conservatory in winter, ardisia is famed for its large clusters of scarlet berries.

A choice, compact evergreen, ardisia's panoply of white flowers in summer prelude a bounteous display of fruits.

FEATURES

Frost-sensitive, this evergreen shrub, clothed with attractive, rounded, toothed, and glossy, leathery leaves, has much to commend it. Coveted for its sprays of small, white, summer flowers, followed by a fetching and long-lasting display of bright red berries, it is easy to manage. Seldom more than 3ft high and across, it is normally grown in a large pot and confined to a frost-free conservatory in which temperatures are at least 20°F above freezing. In early summer when frosts finish, ardisia can be moved to highlight a lightly shaded patio.

CORAL BERRY AT A GLANCE

Sculptural evergreen with glossy leaves. White, summer flowers are followed by bright scarlet berries. Hardy to 50°F (zone 11).

Month	Activity	Recommended Varieties
Jan	/	
Feb	/	*A. crenata*
Mar	/	
Apr	plant, prune	
May	plant	
Jun	plant	
July	flower	
Aug	flower	
Sept	flower	
Oct	/	
Nov	/	
Dec	/	

CONDITIONS

Aspect
Outdoors, ardisia prefers a shaded to semi-shaded position sheltered from strong winds. Indoors, from early fall to late spring, display it in a lightly shaded conservatory.

Site
Help it excel by setting it in a large pot of John Innes potting compost No. 3. Based on moisture-retentive loam, it reduces the need for watering and encourages robust growth.

GROWING METHOD

Feeding
Encourage lustrous leaves and bounteous flowers and fruits by feeding weekly with a high-potash liquid fertilizer from spring to late summer. Alternatively, add a slow-release fertilizer to the compost in spring and replace it a year later. Water regularly from spring to fall to keep the compost nicely moist, but ease up from fall to winter when growth is slower. Cease feeding too.

Propagation Problems
Take soft-tip cuttings in spring or summer. Plants are occasionally attacked by sap-sucking scale insects, which cling like limpets to stems and leaves. Control them by spraying with malathion. Well-grown plants are seldom troubled by pests.

PRUNING

Ardisia is neat and symmetrical and cutting back is not normally necessary. If it grows too large, shorten stems to side shoots in spring.

BARBERRY
Berberis thunbergii

Berberis thunbergii *"Atropurpurea" glows with sunset hues in fall.*

Berberis stenophylla *brightens spring with a globe of yellow blossom. Keep it youthful by shearing off faded blooms in late spring.*

FEATURES

A huge, easy family of evergreen and deciduous species and varieties, berberis will grow almost anywhere. Small bushes enhance a rock garden; larger kinds light up a border or form a burglar-proof hedge. The most popular leaf-shedding kind is *Berberis thunbergii*. A dense, rounded shrub to about 5ft high and across, it is armed with long, sharp spines. Long-lived, with small, bright yellow flowers that sleeve slender, whippy stems and cheer spring, its leaves turn scarlet in fall. Bright red berries are a winter feature. Reddish-purple-leaved *B. thunbergii* "Atropurpurea"

becomes a firebrand in October. Other choice varieties of *B. thunbergii* ideal for small gardens are golden-leaved "Aurea," purple-blackish-leaved "Dart's Red Lady" and "Harlequin". Fetching, evergreen kinds are *B. × stenophylla* and *B. candidula*.

CONDITIONS

Aspect	Very hardy. Deciduous kinds especially resist icy winds. Berberis needs full sun to flower and fruit freely, but will tolerate light shade.
Site	Berberis prospers on a wide range of soils, from sand to heavy, often waterlogged clay.

GROWING METHOD

Feeding	Work bone meal into the root area in the fall. Water copiously and regularly in the first year after planting, to encourage good growth. Thereafter, little watering is necessary.
Propagation	Layer shoots from spring to fall, or take semi-ripe cuttings from early to mid-fall.
Problems	Control rust disease by spraying with a proprietary spray.

PRUNING

Bushes:	Apart from cutting back frost-damaged shoots in May, no regular pruning is needed. Renew old gaunt bushes by cutting back a third of the older stems to near ground level in April.
Hedges:	Trim when blooms fade in spring.

BARBERRY AT A GLANCE

Undemanding shrubs—many have fiery fall leaf tints—bearing yellow or orange spring flowers. Hardy to -13°F (zone 5).

Month		Recommended Varieties
Jan	/	
Feb	/	**Deciduous**
Mar	plant	*B. thunbergii*
Apr	flower, prune	*B. thunbergii* "Atropurpurea"
May	flower, plant	
June	plant	*B. thunbergii* "Dart's Red Lady"
July	plant	
Aug	plant	*B. thunbergii* "Aurea"
Sept	plant	*B. thunbergii* "Harlequin"
Oct	plant	**Evergreen**
Nov	plant	*B. candidula*
Dec	/	*B. × stenophylla*

BUTTERFLY BUSH

Buddleja davidii

Irresistible to butterflies that cluster on its nectar-rich flowers, varieties of Buddleja davidii *make summer special.*

Spectacular blooms, large handsome leaves and an ability to grow almost anywhere sunny, buddleja is a good choice for beginners.

FEATURES

There are three distinctive, hardy species: deciduous *Buddleja davidii*, whose cone-shaped flowers are dark purple, purplish red, pink, white, or blue; *B. alternifolia*, yielding a waterfall of shoots sleeved with soft purple flowers; and evergreen *B. globosa*, with its clusters of small orange balls.

CONDITIONS

Aspect These plants perform best in full sun, but tolerate slight shade; *B. davidii* resists chilly winds.

Site Thriving in most soils, they prefer a well-drained position enriched with organic matter.

GROWING METHOD

Feeding Boost growth by sprinkling bone meal around the shrub in April and October and hoeing it in. Take care not to damage roots. Water new plants regularly in spring and summer to encourage robust growth and bounteous blossom. Mulching helps to retain soil moisture in droughty spells.

Propagation All kinds are easily increased from soft-tip cuttings in early summer and hardwood cuttings in the fall.

Problems Control leaf-crippling aphids with pirimicarb, rotenone, permethrin, or pyrethrins. *B. alternifolia*, grown as a standard, needs staking throughout its life.

PRUNING

B. davidii: Cut back the previous year's flowering shoots to within 2in of the base in March.

B. alternifolia and globosa: Unlike *B. davidii*, which flowers on its current-year shoots, both *B. alternifolia* and *B. globosa* bloom on wood produced the previous year. Keep them youthful and flowering freely by shortening to the base a third of the oldest stems when the flowers fade.

BUTTERFLY BUSH AT A GLANCE

Hardy, deciduous, and evergreen or semi-evergreen shrubs. Cones or globes of blossom light up summer. Hardy to 14°F (zone 8).

Month	Activity	Recommended Varieties
Jan	/	
Feb	/	*B. alternifolia*
Mar	plant, prune	*B. davidii* "Black Knight"
Apr	plant	*B. davidii* "Dartmoor"
May	plant	*B. davidii* "Empire Blue"
June	flower, plant	*B. davidii* "Peace"
July	flower, plant	*B. davidii* "Pink Delight"
Aug	flower, plant	*B. davidii* "Santana"
Sept	plant	*B. fallowiana* "Alba"
Oct	plant	*B. globosa*
Nov	plant	*B. × weyeriana*
Dec	/	

BOX
Buxus

Drought-resisting common box makes a tight, neat plant in full sun. Tiny, yellow flowers stud shoots in spring.

Here, box clipped to create serpentine hedges focuses attention on the beauty of the brick paving, raised lily pond and garden bench.

FEATURES

Both common box (*Buxus sempervirens*), to around 15ft, and lower-growing, small-leaved (Japanese) box (*B. microphylla japonica*) are favored for planting in tubs and large pots and clipping into drumsticks, spirals, balls, pyramids, and other forms of topiary. *B. sempervirens* "Suffruticosa" makes the best low hedge. Box is long-lived and slow growing. If unclipped, it attains little more than 3ft within 4–5 years.

Common box has darker, more pointed foliage than the Japanese form, where leaves are shinier and lighter green. In spring, tiny, starry, and delicately perfumed, yellowish-green flowers appear in leaf axils.

BOX AT A GLANCE

A hardy evergreen for topiary or low hedges. Variegated forms must be positioned in full sun. Hardy to -13°F (zone 5).

JAN	/	
FEB	/	**RECOMMENDED VARIETIES**
MAR	/	
APR	flower, prune	*B. microphylla* "Winter Gem"
MAY	plant, prune	*B. microphylla* "Faulkner"
JUNE	flower, plant	*B. sempervirens*
JULY	plant, prune	*B. sempervirens* "Handsworthensis"
AUG	plant, prune	*B. sempervirens* "Suffruticosa"
SEPT	plant	*B. sempervirens* "Elegantissima"
OCT	/	
NOV	/	
DEC	/	

CONDITIONS

Aspect Plants are more compact in full sun than shade, in which the foliage has less appeal. Creamy-mottled forms must be grown in good light or the variegation will fade to green.

Soil Box thrives on chalk but also prospers on a wide range of other soils. Good drainage is vital. Enrich impoverished areas with bulky organic manure several weeks before planting.

GROWING METHOD

Feeding Encourage lusterous leaves by fortifying planting holes with fish, blood and bone meal or Growmore, and topdressing the root area with bone meal in spring and fall. These plants are not heavy feeders and normally flourish if you do forget to fertilize them. Established box tolerate fairly dry conditions.

Propagation Box species can be grown from seed but varieties must be increased from semi-ripe cuttings from early to mid-fall. Plants may also be divided in mid-spring.

Problems If not fed regularly, box is rather slow to establish on poor, sandy soil.

PRUNING

After planting, use hedging shears to shorten shoots by a third to encourage a bushy habit. Trim hedges and topiary from April to August. If a bush is old and gaunt and needs revitalizing, cut it hard back in April or May. Keep stumps moist to help them sprout. Cut out any all-green shoots on variegated plants.

CAMELLIA
Camellia

The exquisite beauty of delicately tinted camellia blooms—so effective in a vase—makes spring memorable.

Lime hating and thriving on deep, cool, leafy soil, flamboyant and long-flowering camellias associate stunningly with azaleas.

FEATURES

Glossy-leaved and showered with blossom, evergreen camellias are a great asset. Some species and varieties flower successively from late fall through to spring. Blooms are white, pink, deep rose, or crimson, and suffusions of these colors. Ranging in size from 4–15ft, most varieties flower when 2–3 years old and mature within ten years. They grow to a great age. Plant them to form a statement in a lawn or mixed shrub border, or set them in a large pot or tub and clip them to form a loose obelisk, pyramid or drumstick. They also make a dashing flowering hedge.

CAMELLIA AT A GLANCE

Evergreen, frost-tender, or hardy shrub with single, semi-double, or fully double blooms. Hardiness according to species.

Jan	flower	Recommended Varieties
Feb	flower	
Mar	flower	C. *japonica* "Adolphe Audusson"
Apr	plant	C. *japonica* "Berenice Boddy"
May	plant, prune	
June	plant, prune	C. *reticulata* "Captain Rawes"
July	plant	
Aug	plant	C. *sasanqua* "Fuji-No-Mine"
Sept	plant	C. *sasanqua* "Nodami-Ushiro"
Oct	flower	
Nov	flower	C. × *williamsii* "Donation"
Dec	flower	"Jury's Yellow"

Selection Most camellias species come from China and Japan; some from N. India and the Himalayas. They have now been extensively hybridised to yield a wide range of varieties. Specialist camellia nurseries and garden centers display flowering plants in spring. Choose a variety suited to the position you have in mind.

Types There are four main types of camellia. *Camellia japonica*: Large and glossy leaved, hardier varieties will prosper in sheltered spots. Its varieties brighten fall to spring. *C. sasanqua*: Fall-flowered, from October to December, it thrives outdoors in the south. In cooler areas, varieties are better planted in pots, displayed outdoors for summer and transferred to a cool conservatory, porch or greenhouse for flowering in fall. *C. reticulata*: Flowering from February to April, varieties can be grown outside in warm, sheltered, gardens. Elsewhere, display them under glass. *C. × williamsii*: Producing tough, weather-resistant foliage, and flowering from November to April, its varieties bloom freely despite low light intensity. Each group is discussed in more detail on pages 348–349.

CONDITIONS

Aspect Camellias grow best in sheltered, dappled shade. In cooler climates, set them in full sun or very light shade to ensure that blossom buds develop from July to October. Protect them from hot, drying, or frosty winds.

RIGHT: Dense, upright, and slow growing, "Wilamina" is a small, double, incurved variety of Camellia japonica. Blooms last well when cut and hold for a long time on the bush.

BELOW: Prized for its deep pink, outer petals that shade into a creamy-white center, "Buttons and Bows," is a medium-sized, formal, double hybrid of Camellia saluenensis. It flowers over a long period.

ABOVE: Vigorous and compact, Camellia japonica "Nuccio's Gem" is a formal, double variety with spirally arranged petals. Just a whiff of frost can result in brown-speckled petals.

BELOW: "Scentuous" is a small, informal, double hybrid of Camellia japonica "Tiffany" and the species C. lutchuensis. Its creamy-white flowers have pale pink outer petals and the perfume of C. lutchuensis. It blooms profusely.

RIGHT: "Wynne Rayner" is a saluenensis seedling. From early to mid-spring, a profusion of blooms is borne on freely branching stems clad with smallish, glossy green leaves

Camellia sasanqua

Sasanquas start the camellia season by producing flowers, depending on variety, from fall to mid-winter. They make a wonderful show in a sheltered border or cool conservatory.

The smaller, more compact varieties, such as single, rose-pink "Tanya" and double, bright rose-red "Shishigashira," make good container plants.

Others worth a little cosseting are fast-growing "Fuji-No-Mine," whose pure white, double blooms are borne on slender shoots; and bushy, upright

"Nodami-Ushiro," a sumptuous, semi-double, deep pink that pleases for weeks.

Camellia reticulata

This species presents us with the largest and most spectacular of all camellia blooms, but the shrubs themselves have a sparse, open-branching habit. Many of the more recently developed hybrids are crosses between C. japonica and C. reticulata. The result is a more leafy shrub that blooms longer with flowers that are more impressive.

To perform well, C. reticulata needs

lighter, more free-draining soil than other camellias. Choice varieties are rose-pink "Arbutus Gum" and carmine-rose "Captain Rawes".

Camellia japonica

This is the species that most people think of when camellias are mentioned. There is a wide range of varieties in white to pale or dark pink or red. There are picotee and bicolors. They are usually classified by flower type: that is, single, semi-double, and formal double. There are also peony and anemone forms.

VARIETIES

BELOW: "Betty Ridley," a rarely seen, sumptuous, and profusely blooming, formal, double variety of Camellia japonica, *is worth seeking from a specialist grower. Here it is compared with the tiny pink flower of the species,* C. rosiflora.

ABOVE: A rapturous but seldom seen white, flushed-pink, and semi-double variety of Camellia vernalis, *"Star Upon Star" is usually grouped with* C. sasanqua *because of similarities in habit and uses. Blooming late in spring, it is an upright grower and ideal for small gardens and patio pots.*

BELOW: "Desire," a large, formal, double variety of Camellia japonica, *bears arresting, mainly white petals, with rims delicately flushed with cerise pink.*

ABOVE: A collector's piece you may have to search for, "Lois Shinault" is a large-flowered variety of Camellia reticulata, *whose semi-double, orchid-pink flowers of fluted petals display a showy boss of golden stamens.*

Some varieties produce sports—flowers of a different color to the parent's. These "sports" are a source of new varieties. Varieties of C. japonica—they flower from late fall to spring—may be grown in patio tubs or planted as border specimens. They also provide a fabulous backcloth to smaller shrubs and herbaceous perennials. Varieties include: White—"Mary Costa": Unusual anemone form with incurving petals; upright growth. "Lily Pons": Single to semi-double with long, narrow petals around a barrel of stamens.

Pink—"Berenice Boddy": Semi-double; light pink with deeper pink under petals. Vigorous, spreading.
Red—"Adolphe Audusson": Semi double; good glossy leaves, open upright growth. "C. M. Hovey": Formal double rose red; freely produced blooms.
Bicolor—"Lavinia Maggi": Formal double; carmine-red and pink stripes on a white background.
Picotee—"Margaret Davis" Informal double to loose peony; white petals rimmed with red; upright.

Camellia × williamsii
This is a very fine group of camellias bred by crossing C. japonica with C. saluenensis. The original crosses were made in Cornwall by J.C. Williams, who gave them their name. Available in the same color range as other camellias, most are semi-double. Eagerly sought are: semi-double, orchid-pink "Donation;" anemone-centered, creamy-white "Jury's Yellow"; deep rose-pink "Elegant Beauty," also with an anemone center; and formal, vibrant, double, pink "Water Lily."

CAMELLIA

Some Camellia reticulata *varieties reward you with a breathtaking display of large, ruffled blooms from mid-winter to spring.*

Rare Camellia lutchuensis *treats you to a bounty of small and deliciously scented blooms from fall to spring.*

Site   Ideally, position plants where early morning sunlight does not heat up frosted blossom buds and cause frozen tissues to rupture. Sasanqua varieties tolerate more sun than most other camellias and reticulatas need full sun for part of the day. Some varieties of *Camellia japonica*, such as "The Czar" and "Emperor of Russia," happily take full sun. They need very acid, well-drained soil rich in decomposed organic matter. Heavy, badly drained soils cause root rot and plants often die. Fortify thin, sandy soils with well-rotted leaf mould or bulky manure, before planting.

GROWING METHOD

Feeding   Encourage lustrous leaves and a wealth of blossom by applying a balanced ericaceous fertilizer in April and July. It is vital that border soil or container compost is always moist, so water daily, if necessary, during prolonged hot spells. Mulch with crumbly, bulky organic manure to conserve moisture, but keep it well away from the stem, lest it causes bark to rot.

Propagation   Increase plants from semi-ripe cuttings in late summer, removing a thin strip of bark from the base to reveal wood and stimulate rooting. Leaf-bud cuttings, 1in or so long, again "wounding" the base of the shoot, are also taken then. Alternatively, layer low, flexible shoots from mid-spring to late summer. Some varieties, which are very hard to grow from cuttings, are grafted on to understocks of *C. sasanqua*.

Problems   You may encounter the following:
*Bud drop: This can be caused by overwet or overdry soils, root rot, or root disturbance. Some very late-flowering varieties may have buds literally pushed off the stem by new spring growth.
*Brown petals and balled blooms: This usually occurs when buds or flowers are lit by early morning sunshine while still wet with dew. Petals may be scorched and some buds "ball" and fail to open. Some varieties with clusters of big buds are prone to this. Gently breaking off some of the buds when they first form helps to reduce balling.
*Oedema: If plants are overwet and conditions overcast, small, brown, corky swellings may develop on leaves. Reduce watering and try to improve air circulation.
*Scale insects: These may be found on the upper or lower leaf surface. Limpet-like scales suck sap and debilitate plants. Spraying with malathion controls them, but spray only in cool or cloudy weather so that it does not scorch leaves.
*Leaf gall: This causes abnormal thickening and discoloration of new growth. It occurs in spring and is caused by a fungus. Pick off and destroy affected leaves before spores disperse.
*Viruses: May be responsible for variable, bright yellow patterns on leaves, or ring spot. Rings develop on leaves. As the leaf ages it becomes yellowish; the center of the ring becomes bright green. There is no cure for viruses, but plants rarely lose much vigor or have their blooming affected. Pick off the worst-looking leaves if they are spoiling your plant's appearance.

PRUNING

Little pruning is needed. Cutting blooms for the vase is usually enough to keep plants compact. However, any thin, spindly, unproductive growth should be removed from the center of the shrub after flowering. Ageing, overgrown camellias can be rejuvenated by quite heavy pruning, provided cuts are made directly above a leaf bud. If severe pruning is necessary, do it in stages, over two years, to avoid stressing the plant.

CALIFORNIAN LILAC
Ceanothus

Evergreen ceanothus, such as "Puget Blue," are best fan-trained against a warm wall.

There are few more riveting, spring- and early summer-flowering shrubs—ideal for light soils that dry out quickly—than evergreen members of the Californian lilac family.

FEATURES

Prized for their massed clusters of principally pale blue to deep violet-blue, powderpuff blooms, there are evergreen and deciduous varieties. They range from carpeters to imposing bushes of around 15ft high. Most evergreens, such as "Blue Mound" and *Ceanothus thyrsiflorus* "Edinensis," bloom from May to June. Two exceptions, "Fallal Blue" and "Burkwoodii," perform from July to September. The best of the deciduous group— pink "Marie Simon" and blue "Gloire de Versailles"—flower from July to October.

CALIFORNIAN LILAC AT A GLANCE

Evergreen or deciduous shrubs with blue or pink blooms from spring to early fall. Hardy to 14°F (zone 8).

Month		Recommended Varieties
Jan	/	
Feb	/	Evergreen
Mar	plant, prune	"Blue Mound"
Apr	plant, prune	"Cascade"
May	flower, plant	"Concha"
Jun	flower, plant	"Puget Blue"
July	flower, plant	*C. thyrsiflorus* "Repens"
Aug	flower, plant	"Zanzibar" (variegated)
Sept	flower, plant	Deciduous
Oct	flower, plant	"Gloire de Versailles"
Nov	/	"Marie Simon"
Dec	/	"Perle Rose"

CONDITIONS

Aspect   All kinds, especially evergreen varieties which are best grown against a south-facing wall, need a sunny, sheltered spot where air circulates freely.

Site   Ceanothus prospers on well-drained clay loam, sandy or humus-rich, gravelly soils. It will not thrive on heavy clay that waterlogs in winter, where roots are liable to rot.

GROWING METHOD

Feeding   Keep plants lustrous and flowering freely by applying bone meal in spring and fall. Breaking down slowly, it is rich in phosphates, which encourage robust root growth. In its native habitat, this plant receives rain only in winter and has adapted to very dry summers.

Propagation   Most varieties are grown from semi-ripe cuttings taken from mid- to late summer.

Problems   Ceanothus is susceptible to root rot, caused by wet soil. It is seldom troubled by pests.

PRUNING

Evergreen varieties: Trim spring-flowering kinds when blooms fade in early summer, and cut late summer performers in April.

Deciduous varieties: In early spring, shorten the previous year's flowered shoots to within 2–3in of the older wood.

JAPONICA
Chaenomeles

Eye-catching when grown as an espalier against a north- or east-facing wall, chaenomeles yields clusters of bloom from late winter to late spring.

Midwinter splendor: flowering quince is sleeved with blossom when many shrubs are resting.

FEATURES

Also known as japonica or flowering quince, this spiny, deciduous shrub makes a colorful bush to 7ft high or, if espalier-trained against a wall or fence, a striking drape to 9ft. Long-lived, it flowers early in life and reaches maturity in 3–5 years. It is valued for its thickly clustered blooms that transform bare branches from mid-winter to early spring. Flowers are followed by small, fragrant, quince-like fruits that ripen to bright yellow. Fruits are edible and make delicious jams and preserves. Showy varieties include apricot "Geisha Girl," pink "Moerloesii," white "Nivalis," and large, bright crimson "Rowallane". In borders, it makes a showy, rounded background plant for smaller shrubs, perennials, bulbs, and annuals.

JAPONICA AT A GLANCE

A hardy deciduous shrub, its clusters of white, pink, or red, saucer-shaped flowers brighten spring. Hardy to -13°F (zone 5).

Jan	/	Recommended Varieties
Feb	/	
Mar	flower, plant	For walls
Apr	flower, prune	"Geisha Girl"
May	flower, prune	"Moerloesii"
June	plant	"Nivalis"
July	prune	"Simonii"
Aug	plant	For bushes
Sept	plant	"Lemon and Lime"
Oct	plant	"Pink Lady"
Nov	plant	"Knaphill Scarlet"
Dec	/	"Rowallane"

CONDITIONS

Aspect Usefully adaptable, chaenomeles thrives in full sun or light shade, does not mind cold winds and colors cold, north- or east-facing walls.

Site Though it prefers well-drained soil, it tolerates heavy, waterlogged clay. Help sandy soils stay cool and moist by working in plenty of bulky manure or well-rotted garden compost.

GROWING METHOD

Feeding Unlike many other shrubs, chaenomeles thrives in poorish soil. For best results, build fertility by topdressing the root area with pelleted chicken manure, fish, blood, and bone meal, or Growmore in spring and midsummer. Water plants regularly in their first year.

Propagation Take semi-ripe cuttings in late summer or detach and replant rooted suckers in fall.

Problems If coral spot appears—shoots are pimpled with coral-pink or orange pustules—cut back to healthy, white wood and burn prunings. Paint stumps with fungicidal pruning compound.

PRUNING

Bushes: Apart from removing crowded shoots when flowers fade in spring, no regular cutting back is required.

Wall trained: Young plants: Tie espaliered shoots to a wire frame. In July, cut back to five leaves shoots growing away from the wall. Reduce to two buds further growth from shortened shoots. Established plants: Shorten the previous year's side shoots to two or three leaves when flowers fade in spring.

MEXICAN ORANGE BLOSSOM
Choisya ternata

Wafting citrus scent on a warm breeze, starry-flowered, evergreen Mexican orange blooms in spring and fall.

Harmonising beautifully with a pink-flowering Japanese cherry, Mexican orange blossom performs best in a sheltered, sunny spot.

FEATURES

A spring prince, evergreen *Choisya ternata*, to 6ft or more high, is regaled with orange-fragrant, starry, white flowers in April and May and again in October. Its glossy, trefoil leaves spill citrus scent when you brush against them.

"Sundance," a smaller, golden-leaved form, is particularly striking in winter when its foliage assumes orange-yellow tints. Intriguingly different—leaves are long and narrow—"Aztec Pearl" bears pink-budded, white blossoms.

CHOISYA AT A GLANCE

Hardy evergreen shrubs—"Sundance" has yellow leaves—with orange-scented, white flowers in spring. Hardy to 14°F (zone 8).

		Recommended Varieties
Jan	/	
Feb	/	*C. ternata*
Mar	/	*C. ternata* "Sundance"
Apr	flower, plant	*C. ternata* "Aztec Pearl"
May	flower, prune	
June	flower, prune	
July	plant	
Aug	plant	
Sept	flower, plant	
Oct	/	
Nov	/	
Dec	/	

CONDITIONS

Aspect   Full sun or light shade, but "Sundance" needs more light than *C. ternata* or "Aztec Pearl," otherwise its leaves will pale to green and lose their appeal. In northern gardens, position all three kinds against a warm, sunny wall.

Site   Choisya thrives in fertile, acid, neutral, or alkaline soil. Enrich nutrient-starved, quick-draining, sandy loam, or stony patches with bulky organic manure.

GROWING METHOD

Feeding   Apply a complete plant food, such as Growmore or fish, blood, and bone meal in early spring and midsummer. Water regularly and copiously in long, dry periods.

Propagation   Increase choisya from semi-ripe cuttings from mid- to late summer, or layer stems from early to late summer.

Problems   No specific pests or diseases but flowering diminishes if shrubs are not pruned regularly and left to become woody.

PRUNING

In cold areas, cut back frost-damaged shoots to healthy, white wood in spring. Keep mature bushes—over five years old—flowering freely by removing from the base a third of the older branches when blooms fade in May or June.

ROCK ROSE
Cistus

A rapid succession of crumpled, silky, often-blotched blooms in white, pink and cerise are your reward for planting cistus.

A Mediterranean drought resister, free-flowering rock roses are also coveted for their aromatic leaves, which distil "honey" on a warm day.

FEATURES

A dandyish Mediterranean native, evergreen cistus delights us from June to August with a daily succession of saucer-shaped, crumpled, silky blooms. Bushes range in size from carpeting, white and maroon-blotched *Cistus lusitanicus* "Decumbens," to 2ft high, to white and yellow-centered *C. laurifolius*, an imposing sentinel that rises to 5ft. There are pink-, crimson- and lilac-flowered varieties, too. All varieties perform early in life and taller kinds make stunning, informal flowering hedges. Small, pot or tub-grown species and varieties, such as neat and bushy "Silver Pink" with its grayish-silvery leaves, illuminate a sun-baked patio.

ROCK ROSE AT A GLANCE

Drought-resisting evergreen for light soil, it is smothered with white, pink, or red blooms in summer. Hardy to 23°F (zone 9).

Month	Activity	Recommended Varieties
Jan	/	
Feb	/	
Mar	/	Small—up to 3ft
Apr	plant, prune	*C.* × *corbariensis*
May	flower, plant	"Silver Pink"
June	flower, plant	*C.* × *skanbergii*
July	flower, plant	"Sunset"
Aug	plant, prune	Tall—over 3ft
Sept	plant	"Alan Fradd"
Oct	/	*C. laurifolius*
Nov	/	*C.* × *purpureus*
Dec	/	

CONDITIONS

Aspect Rock roses must have full sun all day to make compact, free-flowering plants. They do not mind exposed sites or salt-laden breezes, but may be damaged by frosty winds. Avoid growing them in areas of high rainfall as blooms are spoilt by prolonged, wet weather.

Site Plants make the strongest growth on humus-rich, sandy, or gravelly loam, which drains quickly; they are less spirited on heavy, badly drained soils. In nature, rock roses flourish on porous limestone. If your soil is acid, boost growth by adding lime before planting.

GROWING METHOD

Feeding These plants need little or no fertilizer. Apply a light dressing of bone meal in spring and fall.
Once plants are growing strongly, water is seldom needed, even during weeks of drought.

Propagation Take semi-ripe cuttings in summer. Species can be grown from seeds or cuttings. Varieties must be raised from cuttings.

Problems No particular pest or disease afflicts cistus, but hard pruning into older wood can inhibit stumps from re-growing.

PRUNING

Encourage newly planted shrubs to branch freely and make dense bushes by pinching out shoot tips several times throughout the first two summers. Cut back frost-damaged stems to healthy growth in spring.

SHRUBBY BINDWEED
Convolvulus cneorum

Canopied with dazzling white blossom from June to August, Convolvulus cneorum, *with red campion, flourishes in full sun.*

No garden? Plant silky-leaved, shrubby convolvulus to emblazon a patio pot or tub with a massed display of funnel-shaped flowers.

FEATURES

A coveted, silvery, silky-leaved evergreen whose pink buds open to flared, white and yellow-eyed, trumpet blooms from June to August, *Convolvulus cneorum* makes a low hummock to 18in high and 2.5ft across and has many uses.

Create a feature all will admire by associating it with *Ceanothus* "Zanzibar," prized for its powder-blue flowers and golden-variegated leaves.

Plant shrubby bindweed to highlight a rock garden or star in a patio pot or deep windowbox.

It is not fully hardy, so consign it to a very sheltered border and cover it in late fall with several layers of bubble plastic draped over an open-topped wigwam of canes. Make sure the plastic does not touch its foliage. If you plant it in a patio pot for summer, move it to a cold greenhouse for winter.

SHRUBBY BINDWEED AT A GLANCE

A borderline hardy evergreen with soft, silvery leaves; trumpet-shaped flowers appear from June to August. Hardy to 14°F (zone 8).

Month	Activity	Recommended Varieties
Jan	shield from frost	
Feb	shield from frost	(only the species
Mar	/	*C. cneorum* is grown)
Apr	plant, prune	
May	plant	
June	flower, plant	
July	flower, plant	
Aug	plant	
Sept	plant	
Oct	/	
Nov	/	
Dec	/	

CONDITIONS

Aspect   Find it a sheltered, sunny spot—it revels against a south- or west-facing wall—where it will not be damaged by chilly winds.

Site   Not fussy, it thrives in well-drained, acid to neutral soil. If your garden has badly drained clay, work in plenty of grit or sharp sand or set the plant on a raised bed. It is vital that roots are not "treading" water.

GROWING METHOD

Feeding   Boost growth by working fish, blood, and bone meal or Growmore into the root area in April and July. Add a slow-release fertilizer to patio tub compost. If planting coincides with a droughty spell, foliar feed weekly to help the plant absorb nutrients more quickly.

Water copiously after planting to settle soil around the roots. Follow by mulching with a 2 in layer of well-rotted organic material to conserve moisture.

Propagation   Increase shrubby bindweed from semi-ripe "heeled" cuttings of new side shoots from late summer to early fall.

Problems   If hard frost causes shoot tips to die back, prune them to just above a healthy bud in late spring.

PRUNING

Pruning is unnecessary unless the plant is ageing. Then, in early spring, reduce gaunt and woody stems by half their length, cutting to just above a joint or to new shoots. Keep stumps moist to help them sprout. The best way to do this, apart from sprinkling them with water, is to coat them with a plastic-based anti-transpirant, normally used for helping Christmas trees retain their needles.

FLOWERING DOGWOOD
Cornus

In mid-spring, white or pink-tinted flowers (bracts) transform the Pacific dogwood (Cornus nuttallii) *into a fascinating talking point.*

Late winter sees the bare branches of Cornelian cherry (Cornus mas) *studded with a multitude of tiny, primrose-yellow blossoms.*

FEATURES

Suddenly, in late winter—from February to March—sulfur-yellow, powderpuff blooms light up bare, slender stems. *Cornus mas* has few rivals.

In spring, when flowers fade, oval, pointed, vivid green leaves unfold. Small, edible, cherry-shaped, red fruits, good for jam, form in fall when leaves assume reddish-purple tints before falling.

A coveted, leaf-shedding native of Europe and Western Asia, it slowly forms a handsome globe to around 15ft high and across. It can also be planted to create a stocky, dense flowering hedge.

Dramatically different, the Pacific dogwood (*C. nuttallii*) bears a plethora of saucer-shaped white, pink-tinged bracts (flowers), which light up late spring. When its flowers fade, they are fetchingly replaced by orbs of multi-seeded fruits.

FLOWERING DOGWOOD AT A GLANCE

Cornus mas has sulfur-yellow flowers in February; *C. nuttallii* bears whitish-pink blooms in June. Hardy to 4°F (zone 7).

Jan	/	Recommended Varieties
Feb	flower	
Mar	flower, prune	*C. mas* "Aurea"
Apr	plant	*C. mas* "Aureoelegantissima"
May	flower, plant	*C. mas* "Hillier's Upright"
June	flower, plant	*C. mas* "Variegata"
July	plant	*C. nuttallii* "Colrigo Giant"
Aug	plant	
Sept	plant	
Oct	plant	
Nov	plant	
Dec	/	

CONDITIONS

Aspect
Though performing better in full sun, both species are good contenders for lightly shaded spots. In deep shade, they form a looser, less symmetrical branching system. They are not harmed by cold winds.

Site
C. mas thrives on virtually any soil, from light sand to heavy clay and chalk, provided it is not waterlogged. *C nuttallii* needs acid, fertile conditions. Enrich impoverished sand and chalk with bulky organic manure or well-rotted garden compost.

GROWING METHOD

Propagation
C. mas: Take semi-ripe cuttings of maturing side shoots—ready when the bark at the base of the stem turns brown and firms up—in late summer.
C. nuttallii: Best increased from soft-tip cuttings from early to midsummer.

Feeding
Boost growth by topdressing the root area with a granular form of complete plant food, or fish, blood, and bone meal in spring and midsummer. Water in if the soil is dry.
In droughty spells, keep shoots vigorous by soaking the root area or digging a moat around the shrub and repeatedly filling it with water. Follow by mulching thickly with moisture-retaining, well-rotted garden compost, bark, or cocoa shell.

Problems
C. mas and *C. nuttallii* have a rugged constitution and are seldom troubled by pests and diseases.

PRUNING

Pruning is not needed, apart from removing awkwardly placed shoots after flowering. Use pruning shears and cut to just above a shoot.

SMOKE BUSH
Cotinus coggygria

In early summer, Cotinus "Notcutt's Variety" treats us to a fabulous display of amber, pink, and purple "smoke-like" inflorescences.

Prized for its richly hued leaves, Cotinus "Royal Purple" contrasts fetchingly with green-leaved berberis.

FEATURES

Remarkably drought-resistant shrub, *Cotinus coggygria*, from central and southern Europe, is appealing twice a year: in June and July when its plumy, 6–8in flowers are reminiscent of pink smoke; and in fall when leaves are suffused with vibrant, fiery, or sunset hues. Growing slowly to form an obelisk 9ft by 6ft, purple-leaved varieties associate beautifully with lemon-yellow-leaved mock orange (*Philadelphus coronarius* "Aureus"). Purple-leaved kinds also make a fetching host for scrambling *Lathyrus grandiflorus*, an exuberant, pink-flowered perennial pea.

If you do not have sufficient border space for a smoke bush, set it in a large tub of tree and shrub compost and position it to form a statement on your patio or at the end of a path. Plant a pair of shrubs to frame the entrance to a wide driveway.

SMOKE BUSH AT A GLANCE

Green or purple leaves assume sunset fall tints. "Smoky" flowering plumes make summer special. Hardy to 4°F (zone 7).

Month	Activity	Recommended Varieties
Jan	/	
Feb	/	"Atropurpurea"
Mar	plant, prune	"Grace"
Apr	plant, prune	"Notcutt's Variety"
May	plant	"Royal Purple"
June	flower, plant	
July	flower, plant	
Aug	plant	
Sept	plant	
Oct	plant	
Nov	plant	
Dec	/	

CONDITIONS

Aspect   Stalwarts both, green- and purple-leaved varieties are very hardy and unaffected by cold winds.

Site   The green-leaved family excels in full sun or light shade, but purple-liveried varieties must have bright sunshine or their foliage will pale to insipid green. All prefer humus-rich soil enriched with bulky organic manure or well-rotted garden compost, but they will survive without stress on thin, sandy loam.

GROWING METHOD

Feeding   Fortify the root area with fish, blood, and bone meal, or Growmore, twice a year: in spring and midsummer. Water it in if the soil is dry.

Propagation   Increase plants from semi-ripe cuttings of new shoots from mid- to late summer. Root them in a lightly shaded garden frame or on a brightly lit windowsill.

Problems   If shoot tips die after a very hard winter, shorten them to live buds in early spring. Should mildew attack purple-leaved varieties, control it by spraying with fungicide containing carbendazim.

PRUNING

Choose one of three methods:

For a mass of flowers on a large shrub, prune only to remove dead wood.

To achieve a balance of foliage and flowers, take out a third of the oldest shoots each spring.

For dashing foliage, spectacular fall color and no flowers—ideal for purple-leaved varieties—cut back all shoots to 6in from the base in early spring. Keep cuts moist to encourage regrowth.

COTONEASTER
Cotoneaster

Herringbone cotoneaster (Cotoneaster horizontalis) *is splendid for covering walls. Pinkish-white flowers are followed by scarlet berries.*

Cotoneaster conspicuus *"Decorus's froth of white summer blossom preludes a feast of bright red fall fruits.*

FEATURES

This versatile, evergreen, semi-evergreen, or deciduous family ranges in height from carpeters of 12in to towering bushes more than 10ft high.

Choice kinds are dense and weed-suppressing, evergreen "Coral Beauty," whose glowing orange berries light up fall; semi-evergreen *Cotoneaster horizontalis*, ideal for clothing a bank or wall beneath a ground floor window; and semi-evergreen "Cornubia," an imposing, arching bush to 10ft.

Evergreen *C. lacteus* and semi-evergreen *C. simonsii* make splendid, low, flowering, and berrying hedges.

Sprays of small, white spring flowers are followed by a glowing fall to winter display of red or yellow fruits. Cotoneasters take 5–10 years to mature, depending on species and conditions, and are long-lived. Fruits are nutritious food for garden birds and winter migrants.

COTONEASTER AT A GLANCE

Deciduous, semi- or fully evergreen shrub; white blossom heralds an fall display of vibrant fruits. Hardy to -13°F (zone 5).

Jan	/	Recommended Varieties
Feb	/	
Mar	plant	Ground covering to 12in
Apr	plant	"Coral Beauty"
May	flower, prune	"Oakwood"
June	flower	"Skogholm"
July	plant	Small bushes (12–32in)
Aug	plant	*C. conspicuus* "Decorus"
Sept	plant	*C. horizontalis*
Oct	plant, prune	Taller kinds
Nov	plant, prune	"Cornubia"
Dec	/	

CONDITIONS

Aspect   All kinds grow best and flower and fruit more freely in full sun. They will tolerate partial shade, but shoots are looser and berries sparse.

Site   Cotoneasters prefer well-drained, medium to heavyish loam, but any reasonably fertile soil encourages stocky growth. Improve thin, sandy, or gravelly areas by digging in bulky, humus-forming, well-rotted manure, decayed garden compost, or leaf mould.

GROWING METHOD

Feeding   Not essential, but an application of Growmore or fish, blood, and bone meal, carefully pricked into the root area in spring and midsummer, encourages lustrous leaves. If you are growing a small-leafed, bushy variety such as *C. simonsii* as a close-planted hedge, apply fertilizer in spring and summer. Water newly planted cotoneasters regularly in spring and summer to help them grow away quickly. Once established, they will tolerate long periods without supplementary watering.

Propagation   Take semi-ripe cuttings from mid- to late summer; layer shoots from spring to summer.

Problems   Fireblight: Causing flowers to wilt and wither—they appear scorched—it is controlled by cutting back affected shoots to healthy, white wood. Burn prunings.

PRUNING

Keep plants flowering and fruiting well by removing one stem in three. Tackle evergreens in mid-spring and deciduous kinds in mid-fall.

HAWTHORN
Crataegus

Hawthorn's abundant, milky-scented, white flowers in early summer are followed by clusters of scarlet or orange berries in fall and winter.

A traditional English hedgerow shrub, hawthorn (Crataegus monogyna) also makes an elegant, small flowering tree.

FEATURES

Architectural, deciduous hawthorns—ideal for focal points or screening—can be shrubby or grow into small trees to 15ft. Clad with lobed or toothed leaves, suffused with fiery scarlet tints in fall, blossom mantles shoots in May and June. Bright orange or red berries—birds adore them—persist into winter. Stems are usually spiny and native may or quickthorn (*Crataegus monogyna*) makes a formidable barrier. Others, such as glossy-leaved *C. × lavallei*, whose large clusters of white blossom are followed by orange berries coupled with richly autumn-hued leaves, and deep red-flowered *C. laevigata* "Paul's Scarlet," make fetching sentinels.

HAWTHORN AT A GLANCE

Large, deciduous bushes or small trees, their summer blossom is followed by orange or scarlet fruits. Hardy to -13°F (zone 5).

		Recommended Varieties
Jan	/	
Feb	prune	"Crimson Cloud"
Mar	plant	*C. × grignonensis*
Apr	plant	*C. × lavallei*
May	flower, plant	"Paul's Scarlet"
June	flower	"Rosea Flore Pleno"
July	prune	
Aug	prune	
Sept	/	
Oct	plant	
Nov	plant, prune	
Dec	prune	

CONDITIONS

Aspect Stalwarts for exposed upland gardens raked by wind, or those fringing the sea, where leaves are powdered with salt, hawthorn flowers best in full sun. In light shade, bushes have a more open habit and fewer blooms.

Site Though hawthorn prefers deep and heavyish but well-drained soils, it will tolerate light, sandy, or gravelly ground. Improve thin soils by working in plenty of bulky organic matter.

GROWING METHOD

Feeding Work bone meal into the soil in spring and fall to ensure a continuous supply of root-promoting phosphates.
Water copiously in the first year after planting. Thereafter, when hawthorn is established, it is seldom stressed by drought.

Propagation Raise species from seed, from berries mixed with damp sand and placed in a flower pot. Break dormancy by positioning the pot in the coldest part of the garden. In spring, remove seeds and sow them in an outdoor seed bed. Seedlings quickly appear

Problems Powdery mildew can whiten leaves. Control it by spraying with carbendazim, mancozeb, or triforine with bupirimate.

PRUNING

Bushes: Encourage a profusion of blossom by shortening the previous year's shoots by two-thirds in late winter.

Hedges: Clip in mid-July and in winter.

BROOM
Cytisus

From May to June, Cytisus scoparius *illuminates a sunny border with golden-yellow blossom. Contrast it with a purple-leaved cotinus.*

Bearing cone-shaped, richly pineapple-scented blooms in early summer, Cytisus battandieri *is best fan-trained against a sunny wall.*

FEATURES

Treating us to whippy stemmed and thickly clustered cascades of fragrant, pea flowers, deciduous and butter-yellow-flowered *Cytisus scoparius* and its kaleidoscope-hued hybrids make May and June special.

Plant them singly to punctuate a border, or group several of one color or in harmonizing shades to create an unforgettable statement. Its fetching, leaf-shedding relation Moroccan (pineapple) broom (*C. battandieri*) is famed for its June display of pineapple-scented cones of bright yellow blooms amid silvery, tri-lobed leaves. It has a lax, floppy habit so train it to embrace a sunny wall or frame a patio door. Alternatively, plant it to entwine a tall, metal obelisk in a border or at the end of a path. When in flower, a warm, breezy day wafts crushed pineapple scent around the garden.

BROOM AT A GLANCE

Massed, tiny, pea blooms or chunky, golden flower cones brighten borders from late spring to early summer. Hardy to 14°F (zone 8).

Month	Activity	Recommended Varieties
Jan	/	
Feb	/	*C. battandieri*
Mar	plant	*C. scoparius* "Andreanus"
Apr	plant	*C. scoparius* "Burkwoodii"
May	flower, plant	*C. scoparius* "Goldfinch"
June	flower, prune	*C. scoparius* "Killeney Red"
July	plant	*C. scoparius* "Killeney Salmon"
Aug	plant	
Sept	plant	*C. scoparius* "Lena"
Oct	plant	*C. scoparius* "Zeelandia"
Nov	/	
Dec	/	

CONDITIONS

Aspect *C. scoparius* and its varieties are hardier than *C. battandieri*, which needs to be sheltered from cold winds. Both flower at their best in full sun.

Site Encourage robust growth by setting plants in free-draining and well-manured, neutral, or acid, sandy soil. Lime tends to cause weak, pale green leaves.

Feeding After adding balanced fertilizer to planting holes, encourage sturdy growth by topdressing the root area with fish, blood, and bone meal in spring and again in midsummer. If your soil is chalky and hybrids are suffering from iron deficiency, help them recover by applying a soil-acidifying fertilizer.

Propagation Increase *C. scoparius* and *C. battandieri* from semi-ripe cuttings taken from mid- to late summer.

Problems When *C. scoparius* and its hybrids become woody and flower less—after ten or so years—they cannot be refurbished by hard pruning, so it is best to replace them with young, potted plants.

Occasionally, in summer, leaf buds develop into cauliflower-like growths covered with silvery hairs. Gall mites cause them. There is no chemical control, so remove affected plants and replace them with healthy stock.

PRUNING

Keep *C. scoparius*s and its hybrids youthful and ablaze with flowers in spring by shearing flowered stems to just above older growth when pods form. *C. battandieri* isn't normally pruned, but cut out badly placed and weak stems after flowering If you are growing it against a wall, tie in new shoots then.

DAPHNE
Daphne

Sweetly scented Daphne odora "Aureomarginata" rewards us with clusters of pinkish-white flowers in late winter.

Lime-tolerant daphnes—this is Daphne odora—have an unfounded reputation for being difficult. Find them a cool, moist and sunny spot.

FEATURES

Grown primarily for their sweetly fragrant blooms, daphnes are best planted close to a living room where, on a warm day with a window open, scent wafts indoors. Alternatively, set bushes in pots or tubs beside a garden seat. Herald spring with deciduous *Daphne mezereum*, to 3ft, with upright stems sleeved with starry, purplish-red flowers. Slightly taller but spreading and evergreen *D. odora* "Aureomarginata," with its cream-edged, green leaves that complement clusters of pinkish-white blooms, also flowers then. From May to June, evergreen *D. burkwoodii* "Somerset," wondrous when filling a large pedestal urn and forming a focal point, exudes vanilla perfume from pale pink blooms.

DAPHNE AT A GLANCE

Deciduous or evergreen shrubs with purple-red to pink flowers from late winter to early summer. Hardy to 19°F (zone 8).

Jan	/	Recommended Varieties
Feb	flower	
Mar	flower, plant	*D. bholua*
Apr	flower, plant	*D. burkwoodii* "Somerset"
May	flower, prune	*D. cneorum*
June	flower, prune	*D. mezereum*
July	plant	*D. odora*
Aug	plant	"Aureomarginata"
Sept	plant	*D. retusa*
Oct	plant	
Nov	plant	
Dec	/	

CONDITIONS

Aspect   Daphne prospers in full sun or very light shade. Shelter it from strong, drying winds.

Site   It must have perfectly drained soil with a high organic content. Keep roots cool by mulching plants with well-decayed manure.

GROWING METHOD

Feeding   Sustain strong flowering shoots by feeding with bone meal in spring and fall. Encourage newly planted shrubs by liquid feeding with a high-potash fertilizer at weekly intervals from spring to summer.
Deep, regular watering is necessary for young plants in long, dry spells. Make sure the soil does not become soggy, for roots may rot.

Propagation   Multiply plants by layering shoots from mid-spring to late summer or by taking semi-ripe cuttings from mid- to late summer.

Problems   Sudden death is usually caused by root rot triggered by bad drainage. Daphne may also be attacked by blackening, leaf-spot fungi that speckle foliage. Control leaf spot by spraying with carbendazim or mancozeb. Viruses are also liable to attack daphne. Characterised by twisted and puckered leaves, there is no control, so dig up and burn affected plants.

PRUNING

No regular cutting back needed, apart from shortening young, straggly stems in spring to keep bushes tidy. Do not prune into older, black-barked wood, for stumps may not regenerate.

DEUTZIA
Deutzia

Flowering from spring to early summer, single, white-flowered Deutzia gracilis *makes a charming background to these late yellow primroses.*

Soaring to around 7ft, Deutzia scabra *flaunts sprays of double, white, or pink-tinged blooms from July to August.*

FEATURES

Profusely blooming, deciduous, upright or rounded deutzias are easy to grow and best displayed in a mixed border. All, apart from late-flowering *Deutzia monbeigii* with its small leaves, appealingly white beneath and complementing dense clusters of starry, white flowers from July to August, perform from May to July. An elegant, upright shrub, deutzia varies in height from deep carmine-pink-flowered *D. × rosea*, 32in by 24in, to *D. scabra* "Pride of Rochester," a handsome leviathan that soars to 7ft. From June to July, its double, white blooms smother pleasingly, peeling-barked branches.

CONDITIONS

Aspect	Deutzia prefers full sun but will tolerate light shade. Plants should be sheltered from strong, northerly or easterly winds.
Site	This shrub flourishes on most well-drained soils, especially if fortified with organic matter.

GROWING METHOD

Feeding	Undemanding, deutzia does not need regular feeding. If growth is poor, topdress the root area with Growmore or fish, blood, and bone meal in spring and summer.
Propagation	Multiply deutzia from hardwood cuttings from mid-fall to early winter.
Problems	Late spring frosts may damage blossom buds of May-flowering varieties, so position plants carefully if you garden in a frost pocket.

PRUNING

Encourage a wealth of blossom by cutting back to near ground level a third of the older branches when flowers fade. If stems bearing flower buds are killed by frost, shorten them to healthy wood.

DEUTZIA AT A GLANCE

Deciduous shrub with shoots clothed in single or double, pink or white blooms in spring and summer. Hardy to -13°F (zone 5).

Jan	/	Recommended Varieties
Feb	/	
Mar	plant	*D. × elegantissima* "Rosealind"
Apr	plant	
May	flower, plant	*D. × hybrida* "Magician" "Montrose"
June	flower	
July	flower, prune	*D. monbeigii*
Aug	plant, prune	*D. × rosea* "Campanulata"
Sept	plant	*D. scabra* "Pride of Rochester"
Oct	plant	
Nov	plant	
Dec	plant	

PRIDE OF MADEIRA
Echium candicans (fastuosum)

Tower of jewels is another evocative name for Echium candicans, *a remarkable, Canary Islands native.*

In a sheltered, frost-free garden, this amazing shrub will spread to 6ft across. Elsewhere, it should be grown in a container and overwintered under glass.

FEATURES

A somewhat sprawling shrub with gray-green leaves, Pride of Madeira is an exciting challenge. Growing to about 5ft high and spreading to 7ft or more, it produces long, fat spikes of sapphire to violet-blue flowers in late spring and early summer. Being frost tender, it is best grown in a pot and consigned to a high conservatory or large greenhouse. Move it to a sheltered, sunny patio or terrace in June and bring it indoors when nights turn chilly in September. It matures in 3–5 years and flowers early in life.

CONDITIONS

Aspect	Echium needs full sun all day. Under glass, air must freely circulate.
Site	Set this plant in a large pot of multipurpose compost augmented with a quarter part Perlite to ensure good drainage. Pot it on in early spring when roots fill the container and mat the compost as the need for watering increases.

GROWING METHOD

Feeding	Boost growth by liquid feeding with a high-potash fertilizer, weekly from spring to late summer. Alternatively, insert aggregates of slow-release fertilizer granules into the compost in spring.
Watering:	Echium tolerates very dry conditions and needs only an occasional soaking in prolonged droughty weather.
Propagation	Echium is raised from seed in spring or early summer. Alternatively, take semi-ripe heeled cuttings tugged from older stems, in midsummer. Root cuttings in a propagator heated to around 70°F.
Problems	No particular pest or disease troubles this plant. If aphids colonize shoot tips, tackle them with pirimicarb or natural pyrethrins.

PRUNING

Remove spent flower heads and shorten shoots outgrowing their allotted space.

PRIDE OF MADEIRA AT A GLANCE

Frost tender, with blue flowers in summer. In chilly areas, it must be overwintered under glass. Hardy to 30°F (zone 9).

Jan	shield from frost	Recommended Varieties
Feb	shield from frost	*E. candicans*
Mar	shield from frost	
Apr	plant	
May	plant	
June	flower, plant	
July	flower, prune	
Aug	flower, prune	
Sept	flower, plant	
Oct	/	
Nov	/	
Dec	/	

HEATH
Erica

Plant a selection of lime-hating Erica cinerea *varieties and enjoy a succession of blossom from June to November.*

Performing from November to May, Erica carnea, *here complementing a golden-flowered berberis, is prized for its white, pink, red, lavender, or mauve display.*

FEATURES

A large, vibrant-flowered group of bushy and carpeting, evergreen shrubs, 9in–5ft high, their thickly clustered, tubular or bell-shaped blooms in white and a confection of pink, purple, coral, and crimson hues illuminate the year. Color winter with varieties of *Erica* x *darleyensis* and *E. carnea;* cheer spring by grouping *E. arborea,* and *E. erigena;* glorify summer and fall with *E. cinerea*, *E. tetralix,* and *E. vagans.*

Use them to brighten borders and rock gardens and suppress weeds. Ideally, associate them with dwarf conifers.

Create a tapestry of blossom by combining ericas with closely related varieties of ling (*Calluna vulgaris*), which flower from July to November, and Irish heath (*Daboecia cantabrica*). Some callunas, such as "Beoley Gold," yield radiant golden foliage.

CONDITIONS

Aspect Most are very hardy, tolerate chilly winds and are ideal for exposed, upland gardens. Heathers must have full sun and good air circulation. Do not crowd plants.

Site While all varieties prefer acid soil, winter-flowering *Erica carnea* tolerates slightly alkaline conditions. Good drainage is vital. Mulch plants annually, in spring, with leaf mould or well-rotted garden compost.

GROWING METHOD

Feeding Established plants need little or no fertilizer. If the soil is very poor, fortify the root area with a balanced, acidifying fertilizer in spring.

Propagation Take semi-ripe heeled cuttings from early to late summer; layer shoots in mid-spring.

Problems Heathers quickly succumb to root rot in heavy or overwet soils.

PRUNING

Lightly shear flowered shoots when blooms fade. Never cut back into older wood. Tackle fall- and winter-flowering varieties when new shoots appear in spring.

HEATH AT A GLANCE

Carpeting evergreens whose succession of blossom or foliage enchants us every month of the year. Hardy to 4°F (zone 7).

Jan	flower	Recommended Varieties
Feb	flower	
Mar	flower	Spring flowering
Apr	plant, prune	"Albert's Gold"
May	flower, plant	"Viking"
June	flower, prune	Summer flowering
July	flower, prune	"C.D. Eason"
Aug	flower, plant	"Pink Ice"
Sept	flower, plant	Fall flowering
Oct	flower	"Andrew Proudley"
Nov	flower	"Stefanie"
Dec	flower	Winter flowering
		"Ann Sparkes"

ESCALLONIA
Escallonia

A prized and colorful shrub, especially for windy gardens, Escallonia "Pride of Donard" rewards us with sprays of pink blossom.

Semi-evergreen and summer-blossoming escallonia can be trained to form a fetching, flowering hedge in mild districts.

FEATURES

Escallonia is evergreen in mild districts but semi-evergreen elsewhere. Its arching shoots, festooned with sprays of clustered, tubular, white, pink, or red flowers amid small, glossy leaves, highlight the summer months. Long-lived, it makes a stunning sentinel to around 6ft and as a flowering hedge.
The hardiest species—ideal for windswept, seaside gardens—*Escallonia rubra macrantha* delights us with many rose-crimson flowers. Other choice kinds are rich pink "Donard Radiance," rose-pink "Donard Star" and golden-leaved and rosy-red-flowered "Gold Brian."

ESCALLONIA AT A GLANCE

Evergreen or semi-evergreen, its arching shoots are sleeved with white, pink or red flowers in summer. Hardy to 14°F (zone 8).

Month		Recommended Varieties
Jan	/	
Feb	/	"Donard Radiance"
Mar	/	"Donard Seedling"
Apr	plant, prune	"Glory of Donard"
May	plant, prune	"Gold Brian"
June	flower, plant	"Iveyi"
July	flower, plant	*E. rubra macrantha*
Aug	flower, plant	"Slieve Donard"
Sept	flower, plant	
Oct	/	
Nov	/	
Dec	/	

CONDITIONS

Aspect Though escallonia needs full sun to flower best, it does not object to light shade. Most hybrids tolerate buffeting wind. In chilly or northern gardens, it should be planted against a sheltered, south-facing wall.

Site This splendid shrub thrives in any well-drained soil. Aerate heavy clay by working in grit or gravel; fortify light and nutrient-starved, sandy soils by working in plenty of bulky, moisture-conserving organic materials.

GROWING METHOD

Feeding Ensure a steady release of plant foods by applying bone meal in spring and fall. After planting, water freely and regularly in dry spells to encourage strong new growth. Keep roots cool and questing freely by mulching with shredded bark, cocoa shell, crumbly manure, or rotted garden compost.

Propagation Multiply choice varieties from semi-ripe cuttings from the middle of summer to the middle of fall.

Problems Cut darkly stained shoots infected with silver leaf back to healthy, white wood 6in beyond the point of infection.

PRUNING

Shorten a third of the oldest stems to near ground level when blooms fade. In cold gardens, cut back frost-damaged growth to strong, new shoots in late spring.

SPURGE
Euphorbia species

The showiest part of a euphorbia 'flower' is a pair of lime-green bracts (modified leaves). The true flower is a small, yellow 'button'.

Perfect for tempering hot orange and yellow flowers, Euphorbia characias wulfenii *performs best in full sun.*

FEATURES

Pleasing us with a spring to early summer display of yellowish-green, bottlebrush blooms on stems clad with whorls of evergreen leaves, *Euphorbia characias wulfenii* is architecturally magnificent. Forming a dense bush to 1.2m (4ft), it is ideal for interplanting and tempering vibrant orange, yellow and red-flowered border perennials. This euphorbia lives for around ten or more years and matures within 2–3 years. Use it in a shrub border or as a background for annuals and perennials. A related sculptural gem, for sheltered gardens only, is Madeiran honey spurge (*E. mellifera*).

Seducing us with large and exotic, lance-shaped leaves, its honey-scented, brownish flower clusters form on shoot tips in spring.

CONDITIONS

Aspect	Hardy *E. characias* needs full sun; more tender *E. mellifera* requires a sheltered spot.
Site	These sub-shrubs thrive almost anywhere, even in heavy soils, provided drainage is good. Boost growth in light, sandy soil by incorporating bulky organic manure.

GROWING METHOD

Feeding	Feeding is not essential but apply fish, blood and bone meal, Growmore or pelleted chicken manure in spring.
Propagation	Take soft-tip cuttings from mid-spring to early summer.
Problems	When crowded, euphorbia may become infected with grey mould, a disease that coats leaves and stems with furry, brownish-grey mould. Control it by cutting infected shoots back to healthy tissue and spraying with carbendazim.

PRUNING

Wear gloves and safety glasses to cut back flowered stems to ground level in early summer. Strong, new shoots replace them and bloom the following year.

SPURGE AT A GLANCE

Evergreen shrub, *E. characias wulfenii* produces huge, bottlebrush blooms from spring to early summer. Hardy to -12ºC (10ºF).

		Recommended Varieties
JAN	/	
FEB	/	*E. characias:*
MAR	/	'John Tomlinson'
APR	flower, plant	'Lambrook Gold'
MAY	flower, plant	'Margery Fish Group'
JUNE	flower, prune	'Purple and Gold'
JULY	prune, plant	*E. characias wulfenii*
AUG	plant	*E. mellifera*
SEPT	plant	
OCT	/	
NOV	/	
DEC	/	

FIG-LEAVED PALM
Fatsia japonica

Exotic-fingered leaves are your reward for growing evergreen Fatsia japonica. *Plant it in a tub to light up a shady patio or terrace.*

Delighting us with its large heads of creamy, bobble-like blooms in fall, when most other shrubs are resting, fatsia tolerates dry soil.

FEATURES

Stunningly architectural, the large, glossy, palmate leaves of *Fatsia japonica* have an appealing leathery texture. In fall, it delights us with an exotic candelabrum of golf-ball-sized, white flower heads. Each comprises many tiny, five-petalled flowers. Large, handsome, black berries follow them. A native of South Korea and Japan, it has a spreading, suckering habit and makes a dome to 6ft high and 8ft across. Plant it to enhance a large patio tub. It tolerates air pollution, so is a good shrub for towns or cities. It resists salty sea breezes, too. Dramatise a sunny border by grouping it with golden-leaved yuccas.

If you plant fatsia in a border, create a striking feature by embracing it with tussock-forming and ground-covering *Liriope muscari*, whose spikes of bell-shaped, violet flowers complement the fatsia's white bobbles.

FIG-LEAVED PALM AT A GLANCE

Dashing focal point for a lightly shaded spot. Intriguing bobbles of white blossom appear in fall. Hardy to 4°F (zone 7).

Month	Activity	Recommended Varieties
Jan	/	
Feb	/	"Variegata"
Mar	/	
Apr	prune, plant	
May	plant	
June	plant	
July	plant	
Aug	plant	
Sept	plant, flower	
Oct	flower	
Nov	flower	
Dec	/	

CONDITIONS

Aspect Ideal for brightening sheltered and lightly shaded spots, it objects to hot sunshine, which may scorch its leaves. Protect from icy winds, which also brown its foliage.

Site It is not fussy about soil but prefers deep, rich loam, which encourages the largest, most sculpturally appealing leaves. Add grit or gravel to soggy clay to improve drainage. Apply an acidifying fertilizer, such as sequestered iron, to chalky soil to reduce risk of chlorosis. When iron is "locked up" by calcium, roots cannot absorb it and leaves turn yellow and die.

GROWING METHOD

Feeding Boost lustrous foliage by topdressing the root area in spring, and again in summer, with fish, blood, and bone meal, which enriches the soil's humus content and encourages beneficial micro-organisms. Alternatively, use quick-acting but short-lived Growmore to accelerate shoot development.

Water freely after planting to settle soil around roots. Follow with a 2in mulch of old manure, bark, or cocoa shell.

Propagation Take semi-ripe cuttings in summer and strike them in a closed cold frame or on a sunny windowsill.

Problems Control aphids, which colonize and cripple shoot tips, by spraying with a systemic insecticide.

PRUNING

Apart from maintaining its symmetry by shortening long branches or frost-damaged shoots in spring, cutting to a joint or lower shoot, no regular attention is necessary.

GOLDEN BELL BUSH
Forsythia

Forming a bushy shrub to around 6ft, generous flowering and sun-loving Forsythia *"Lynwood" is draped with blossom in spring.*

Create a vibrant March marriage of yellow blossom and scarlet bark by associating forsythia with a coppiced clumps of Cornus alba *"Sibirica".*

FEATURES

Heartening indeed is the spring sight of a bush thickly laden with starry, sulfur-yellow, or deep golden blooms. Flowers open naturally from March to April. Enjoy an earlier show by cutting fat-budded stems in February and forcing them into bloom in a warm room. There are two principal kinds: border forsythia (*Forsythia* × *intermedia*), which makes a rounded shrub to 8ft high and across, and *F. suspensa*, a snaking, weeping, or trailing form, enchanting when cascading over a wall or over the lower branches of pink, weeping cherry. Border forsythia can be also grown as a flowering hedge or trained to frame a window or doorway. Neat and compact "Golden Curls," just 2ft high and 3ft across, is ideal for a small yard.

GOLDEN BELL BUSH AT A GLANCE

Deciduous, bush and trailing/weeping varieties have flowers clothing year-old shoots in spring. Hardy to -13°F (zone 5).

Month	Activity	Recommended Varieties
Jan	/	
Feb	/	"Fiesta"
Mar	flower, plant	"Gold Cluster"
Apr	flower, plant	"Golden Curls"
May	plant, prune	"Gold Tide"
June	plant	"Lynwood"
July	plant	"Spring Glory"
Aug	plant	"Suspensa"
Sept	plant	"Weekend"
Oct	plant	
Nov	plant	
Dec	plant	

CONDITIONS

Aspect A sunny position is vital. In shade a multitude of shoots form but many will refuse to flower. Growth also becomes loose and weak. Forsythia braves cold wind.

Site This plant grows strongly in most well-drained soils, from heavy clay to light sand and chalk. Fortify impoverished borders, especially where roots from nearby trees invade, with humus-forming, old, crumbly, or proprietary composted manure, well-rotted garden compost, shredded bark, or leaf mould.

GROWING METHOD

Feeding If the soil was initially enriched with plant foods, forsythia seldom needs further feeding. If growth is slow, boost it by topdressing with a balanced granular fertilizer. Alternatively, liquid feed weekly with a high-nitrogen fertilizer from spring to midsummer. Water newly planted shrubs copiously and frequently to help them recover quickly.

Propagation Layer low flexible shoots from spring to late summer or take hardwood cuttings in the fall.

Problems Occasionally—the cause is not known—warty galls distort stems. Overcome them by cutting back affected shoots to healthy wood and burning them.

PRUNING

Once established, keep plants youthful and flowering freely by removing from the base a third of the oldest shoots when flowers fade. Clip hedges at the same time of year, so that flower buds form for the following year.

GENISTA
Genista

Swagged with golden flowers in midsummer, the Mount Etna broom makes a striking shrubby tree and revels in a warm, dry spot.

Here Genista lydia, *a hummock of blossom in June, looks good with silvery-leaved and yellow-flowered* Brachyglottis "Sunshine".

FEATURES

Small or rushy leaved and wiry stemmed, this accommodating deciduous family, related to broom, embraces showy, prostrate carpeters and small or large bushes to several yards high. All sport pea-like flowers in various shades of yellow.

From May to June, cushion-like Spanish gorse (*Genista hispanica*), hummocky and cascading *G. lydia* and dazzling, carpeting *G. pilosa* "Vancouver Gold" treat us to a display so radiant that it deceives you into thinking it is sunny when it is not.

Come July and August, the spring brigade is eclipsed by bushy *G. tinctoria* "Royal Gold" and the imposing and fragrant Mount Etna broom (*G. aetnensis*), with its pendulous, rush-like shoots that shower from branches 9ft high.

CONDITIONS

Aspect   Hardy and tolerating exposed positions, all genistas perform best in full sun. Drought resisting, they are ideal for hot spots that cannot easily be watered.

Site   Happiest in humus-rich and light, free-draining sand and loam, they also prosper in clay if you work in gravel and crumbly organic materials to improve drainage.
Usefully, *G. tinctoria* excels in chalky soil.

GROWING METHOD

Feeding   Encourage robust growth by topdressing the root area with a slow-release organic fertilizer, such as bone meal, in spring and fall. Water freely in droughty periods and keep roots cool and active by mulching with old manure, well-rotted garden compost, or bark.

Propagation   Increase genista from semi-ripe cuttings of side shoots from mid- to late summer. Root them in pots on a bright windowsill or in a lightly shaded cold frame.

Problems   Normally trouble free.

PRUNING

Avoid cutting back *G. aetnensis*, *G. lydia*, and *G. tinctoria*, whose stumps may not regrow. You can, however, rejuvenate ageing *G. hispanica* by shortening old woody stems by two-thirds their length in spring. Keep large stumps moist in dry, windy weather to help them regenerate.

GENISTA AT A GLANCE

Deciduous spring- or summer-flowering bushes, they need full sunshine to flower bounteously. Hardy to 14°F (zone 8).

Month	Activity	Recommended Varieties
Jan	/	
Feb	/	*G. aetnensis*
Mar	plant	*G. hispanica*
Apr	plant, prune	*G. pilosa* "Vancouver Gold"
May	flower, prune	
June	flower, plant	*G. tinctoria* "Flore Pleno"
July	flower, plant	*G. tinctoria* "Royal Gold"
Aug	flower, plant	
Sept	plant	
Oct	plant	
Nov	plant	
Dec	/	

WITCH HAZEL
Hamamelis

A heartening winter vision is spidery, sulfur-yellow-flowered Hamamelis x intermedia *"Pallida" underplanted with snowdrops.*

A bonus of orange, scarlet and red fall tints prelude Hamamelis vernalis, *Sandra's late winter display of cadmium-yellow "spiders."*

FEATURES

Shining like a beacon on a winter's day, witch hazel's twisted, spidery perfumed flowers thickly clothe bare, spreading branches. Hardy and bushy, 8–10ft high and across, this deciduous shrub is a slow but worthwhile grower that rewards patience. Ideally, set it in a lawn with snowdrops and daffodils.

Choice kinds among several undemanding species and varieties are large, golden-flowered Chinese witch hazel (*Hamamelis mollis*), which blooms from December to March. *H. x intermedia* is a hybrid that flowers from February to March and has given us upright and primrose-hued "Westerstede," sulfur-yellow "Pallida," orange and yellow "Diane," and coppery orange "Jelena."

The large, soft-hairy leaves of *H. mollis* turn butter-yellow in the fall. The foliage of "Diane" and "Jelena" is suffused with orange-red before falling. Equally fascinating is the less fragrant Japanese witch hazel (*H. japonica* "Zuccariniana"), which from January to March produces a multitude of pale lemon "spiders."

CONDITIONS

Aspect Hamamelis flowers more freely in full sun and makes a shapelier, more compact bush than in light shade, in which branches are thinner and further apart and leaves larger. Position coppery red-flowered varieties where the sun shines at an angle through their petals and renders them fetchingly translucent.

Site Preferring well-drained, fertile, neutral to acid soil, hamamelis dislikes alkaline, chalky conditions, which causes leaves to become chlorotic. Enrich sandy soils with old manure.

GROWING METHOD

Feeding Water freely after planting to encourage rapid recovery. Each spring, mulch with crumbly manure, bark or well-rotted garden compost to keep roots cool and active. In April, topdress the root area with fish, blood and bone meal or Growmore, repeating in July.

Propagation Layer shoots from mid-spring to late summer. Alternatively, take soft-tip cuttings in late spring and root them in a mist propagating unit in a temperature of 70°F.

Problems When buying plants, opt for those more than four years old, which, unlike younger ones, have a greater chance of succeeding.

PRUNING

Not necessary, but if badly placed stems need removing or shortening, to improve symmetry, use sharp secateurs or loppers when flowers fade, in early spring.

WITCH HAZEL AT A GLANCE

Deciduous and forming a chalice of spreading branches, yellow or orange blooms sleeve stems in winter. Hardy to -13°F (zone 5).

JAN	flower	
FEB	flower	
MAR	plant, prune	RECOMMENDED VARIETIES
APR	plant	*H. japonica* "Zuccariniana"
MAY	plant	*H. x intermedia* "Diane"
JUN	plant	*H. x intermedia* "Jelena"
JULY	plant	*H. x intermedia* "Pallida"
AUG	plant	*H. x intermedia* "Westerstede"
SEPT	plant	*H. mollis*
OCT	plant	
NOV	plant	
DEC	flower	

SHRUBBY VERONICA
Hebe

Salt-spray resistant, hebes are ideal for brightening coastal gardens in mild districts. They also tolerate air pollution.

Hebe *"Great Orme,"* here contrasting effectively with an upright cypress, is studded with shapely spikes of blossom from July to October.

FEATURES

An immense and handsome family of small, rounded-leaved or larger, willow-leaved, evergreen New Zealanders, hebes' clustered or cone-shaped spikes of massed, tiny flowers illuminate May to late October. Resisting air pollution, these shrubs are ideal for seaside gardens in mild districts. There are three main, easy and reliable groups:

Carpeters: Forming a dense mat of weed-suppressing foliage to around 12in high, choice kinds include silvery gray-leaved and white-flowered *Hebe pinguifolia* "Pagei".

Bushes: Making bushy globes to 4ft, stunning varieties are "Fall Glory," whose violet-blue blossoms color June to November, and "Great Orme," smothered with bright pink flowers from July to October.

Taller kinds: Imposing sentinels to 6–10ft, lilac-white *H. salicifolia* is a prince among them.

CONDITIONS

Aspect Hebes need an open position in full sun to make robust and free-flowering growth.

Site Most well-drained soils suit these plants, but they perform best in humus-rich, sandy loam.

GROWING METHOD

Feeding Boost growth by sprinkling fish, blood, and bone meal, Growmore or pelleted chicken manure over the root area in April and July. Water copiously to establish new plants. Once growing strongly, little water is needed.

Propagation Take soft-tip cuttings in early summer and semi-ripe cuttings in midsummer.

Problems Control leaf spot disease by spraying with carbendazim or mancozeb.

PRUNING

Cut back late-flowering varieties to within 6in of the base, every two years in spring, to encourage bounteous blossom. Remove any reverted, green-leaved stems from variegated varieties as soon as they appear.

SHRUBBY VERONICA AT A GLANCE

Evergreen carpeters or bushes clothed with clustered, cone-shaped flowers in white and many other colors. Hardy to 23°F (zone 9).

Month	Activity	Recommended Varieties
Jan	/	
Feb	/	"Carl Teschner"
Mar	/	*H.* ×*franciscana* "Blue Gem"
Apr	plant, prune	
May	flower, prune	"Great Orme"
June	flower, plant	*H. hulkeana*
July	flower, plant	"Midsummer Beauty"
Aug	flower, plant	*H. pinguifolia* "Pagei"
Sept	flower, plant	*H. speciosa* "Gauntlettii"
Oct	flower	"Wiri Charm"
Nov	/	
Dec	/	

SUN ROSE
Helianthemum

Deep red and yellow-eyed blooms and silvery leaves make "Supreme" a prized variety.

Enjoy a tapestry of blossom by growing sun roses to cascade from a retaining wall. Here plants are camouflaging gaunt, leggy, rose stems.

FEATURES

Varieties of evergreen *Helianthemem nummularium*, commonly called rock or sun rose, make a spreading 4–12in mound to 36in across. From May to July, a network of wiry stems clothed with small, oval leaves are almost hidden beneath a daily succession of single or double flowers in glowing shades of yellow, pink, red, orange, white, or terracotta. Flowers tend to close up on dull days. Sun roses are perfect for draping rock garden pockets, cascading from retaining walls and aproning roses and other bushes flanking a path. They are not long-lived but easily raised from cuttings of maturing, current-year shoots.

CONDITIONS

Aspect Sun rose performs best in an open, brightly lit and airy position where it has room to spread and is not crowded by other plants. Avoid even a hint of shade in which growth is looser, less comely and flowering is inhibited.

Site This shrub needs well-drained and slightly alkaline conditions. Add garden lime to raise the pH of acid soil.

GROWING METHOD

Feeding Boost lustrous foliage and a wealth of blossom by applying a high-potash rose fertilizer in spring and the middle of summer.
Water newly planted shrubs regularly and copiously to help them recover quickly and make good root growth in their first year. Thereafter, they will need watering only in droughty weather. Mulch plants generously with spent mushroom compost.

Propagation Take semi-ripe heeled cuttings in midsummer. These should make flowering-sized plants by the following spring.

Problems Poor drainage or overwatering may kill plants. Powdery mildew can be a problem in crowded borders where air circulates sluggishly. Control this disease by thinning growth and spraying with carbendazim or bupirimate with triforine.

PRUNING

From early to midsummer, when blooms fade, shear back shoots to two-thirds their length. This not only keeps bushes trim and flowering well in spring, but often results in a second, smaller, flush of blossom in fall.

SUN ROSE AT A GLANCE

A carpeting evergreen so thickly clothed with flowers from May to July that leaves are concealed by them. Hardy to 14°F (zone 8).

Month	Activity	Recommended Varieties
Jan	/	
Feb	/	
Mar	/	
Apr	plant	"Golden Queen"
May	flower, plant	"Henfield Brilliant"
Jun	flower, plant	"Raspberry Ripple"
July	flower, plant	"Red Orient"
Aug	plant, prune	"Supreme"
Sept	plant	"The Bride"
Oct	/	"Wisley Pink"
Nov	/	"Wisley Primrose"
Dec	/	

HELIOTROPE
Heliotropium

Old-fashioned heliotrope or cherry pie is festooned with spicy-perfumed blooms from early summer until the fall, when chilly nights halt the display.

"Marine" is captivating if planted to cascade its deep violet flowers from a patio or terrace tub.

FEATURES

Heliotropium arborescens, also known as cherry pie, is a half-hardy, soft-stemmed, evergreen Peruvian shrub. Growing to 4ft high and across, it is usually bedded out for summer and overwintered in a frost-free greenhouse. A succession of vanilla-fragrant, mauve to purple flowers are borne from summer to the middle of fall, or even longer under glass.

Plant it to spill from a border and on to paving, waterfall from a raised bed or beautify a patio tub. "Lord Roberts," with very dark purple-green leaves and deep violet flowers, is probably the most popular variety.

HELIOTROPIUM AT A GLANCE

Frost-sensitive evergreen with richly fragrant, pink, purple, violet, or white flowers, bedded out for summer. Hardy to 40°F (zone 10).

Jan	/	Recommended Varieties
Feb	/	
Mar	/	"Dame Alice de Hales"
Apr	plant, prune	"Chatsworth"
May	plant, prune	"Lord Roberts"
June	flower, plant	"White Lady"
July	flower	"Netherhall White"
Aug	flower	"Princess Marina"
Sept	flower	
Oct	flower	
Nov	flower	
Dec	/	

CONDITIONS

Aspect   Outdoors: Heliotrope needs a warm position sheltered from chilly winds. It flowers best in full sunshine.
Under glass: Provide full sun but reduce risk of leaf scorch by shading plants when the temperature rises above 75°F.

Site   Outdoors: The soil should be crumbly and well drained. Enrich thin, sandy patches with humus-forming, well-decayed manure.

GROWING METHOD

Feeding   Outdoors and under glass: liquid feed weekly with a high-potash fertilizer from spring to late summer.
In late summer or early fall, lift and pot up plants bedded out in borders and patio tub plants. Move them to a frost-free greenhouse or conservatory and keep the compost dry until late winter or early spring.

Propagation   Heliotrope is easily increased from soft-tip cuttings taken in spring, and semi-ripe cuttings struck in late summer.

Problems   Being half-hardy, this shrub must not be moved outdoors until frosts have finished in late May or early June.

PRUNING

Encourage new flowering stems by shortening a third of older, woody branches by half their length in early spring.

HIBISCUS

Hibiscus

A late-summer bonus of exotic, single, or double, saucer-shaped blooms are your reward for growing a hardy hibiscus.

Healthy and seldom attracting pests and diseases, hibiscus is best planted in a sunny position so shoots ripen and flower well.

FEATURES

Also known as shrubby mallow, this deciduous, late summer statement is festooned with saucer-shaped blooms from July to September. Flowers are single or double and range in color from white, pink and blue, to purple. Several are bicolored. Most popular varieties are violet-blue and white-eyed "Blue Bird," white and crimson-eyed "Hamabo" and rose-pink and dark-centerd "Woodbridge." Long-lived, it makes an upright bush to 8ft high and across and flowers early in its life. It is very hardy.

CONDITIONS

Aspect   Hibiscus grows best and flowers prolifically in full sun. Shield it from icy winds. Avoid even light shade, for shoots will not ripen well and so flowering is impaired.

Site   This shrub thrives on well-drained, fertile, sandy loam but tolerates poorer soils. Enjoy good results by enriching the planting area with plenty of well-rotted organic matter.

GROWING METHOD

Feeding   Apply all-purpose plant food, such as fish, blood, and bone meal, or Growmore, in spring and again in midsummer.
Water regularly in spring and summer to help

newly planted hibiscus recover quickly.

Propagation   Layer whippy shoots from mid-spring to late summer, and take semi-ripe heeled cuttings from late summer to early fall.

Problems   Control aphids with pirimicarb, horticultural soap, or natural pyrethrins.

PRUNING

Rejuvenate ageing shrubs by shortening them to half their height in spring. This is also the best time to cut back frost-damaged shoots.

HIBISCUS AT A GLANCE

Deciduous and slow growing, large, saucer-shaped, pink, blue, or white blooms appear in late summer. Hardy to 4°F (zone 7).

		Recommended Varieties
Jan	/	
Feb	/	"Blue Bird"
Mar	plant	"Bredon Springs"
Apr	plant, prune	"Hamabo"
May	plant	"Lady Stanley"
June	plant	"Lenny"
July	flower, plant	"Meehanii"
Aug	flower, plant	"Woodbridge"
Sept	flower, plant	"William R. Smith"
Oct	plant	
Nov	plant	
Dec	/	

HYDRANGEA
Hydrangea

Ever popular hydrangea is a native of China and Japan. Ensure pink blossom by adding lime to the soil in spring. For ultramarine-blue flowers, feed with aluminium sulphate.

Position mophead and other hydrangeas in a sheltered spot in dappled shade.

FEATURES

Brightly studded with large, globular, mushroom-headed, or broadly conical flowers, hydrangeas richly color borders from July to September. Blooms come in white and shades of pink, blue, or red. Long-lived, this deciduous shrub grows 20in–8ft high and across.

Most widely grown are aptly named mophead and lacecap varieties of *Hydrangea macrophylla*. Yielding pink, mauve, or red blooms on alkaline soils and blue heads in acid conditions, they thrive in fertile ground. Characteristically, lacecaps have an outer ring of large, sterile flowers enclosing tiny, pink, or blue, fertile ones.

Other choice kinds are white, football-headed *H. arborescens* "Annabelle" and light pink, cone-flowered *H. paniculata* "Pink Diamond." *H. quercifolia* has oak-leaved foliage which complement trusses of rich creamy flowers and *H. villosa* is a gem with porcelain-blue

mushrooms poised above stems clad with huge, velvety leaves.

A self-clinging climber, white, disc-flowered *H. petiolaris* beautifully transforms a cold, north-facing wall.

CONDITIONS

Aspect   Dappled sunlight or morning sun and afternoon shade suit hydrangeas. Make sure they are sheltered from frosty winds, which will damage embryo blossoms.
H. macrophylla varieties are reliable seaside plants for relatively frost-free areas.

Site   These shrubs need damp soil high in organic matter, so improve poor areas by digging in plenty of well-decayed manure or compost a few months ahead of planting. Also mulch plants with well-rotted organic matter.

GROWING METHOD

Feeding   Apply acidifying fertilizer like sulphate of ammonia in spring and midsummer to ensure a steady release of plant foods and encourage blue flowers.

Propagation   Multiply favoured varieties by layering flexible shoots from mid-spring to late summer. Take soft-tip cuttings from late spring to early summer and semi-ripe cuttings from mid- to late summer.

Problems   Excessive lime prevents chlorophyll from forming and causes leaves to yellow and die. Overcome it by applying iron chelates.

PRUNING

H. macrophylla: Cut off spent flowers in spring and remove crowding shoots.

H. paniculata: Prune stems to within two buds of the base in late March.

H. petiolaris: Cut out unwanted shoots when flowers fade.

H. villosa: Remove a third of older stems in spring.

HYDRANGEA AT A GLANCE

Deciduous shrubs bearing large heads of white, pink, red, or blue flowers from mid- to late summer. Hardy to 4°F (zone 7).

Month	Activity	Recommended Varieties
Jan	/	
Feb	/	**Mopheads**
Mar	plant, prune	"Hamburgh"
Apr	plant, prune	"Madame E. Moullière"
May	plant	**Lacecaps**
June	plant	"Blue Wave"
July	flower, plant	"White Wave"
Aug	flower, plant	*H. arborescens* "Annabelle"
Sept	flower, plant	*H. paniculata* "Kyushu"
Oct	plant	*H. quercifolia*
Nov	plant	*H. villosa*
Dec	/	

JASMINE
Jasminum

Illuminating a north or east-facing wall from November to March, Jasminum nudiflorum *flowers very freely on cascading shoots.*

Ideal for clothing a pergola or trellis work, twining Jasminum officinale affine *is swathed with scented flowers in summer.*

FEATURES

There are two forms of jasmine—climbing and bushy—both of which flower generously. Choice and reliable twining climbers—ideal for screening—are *Jasminum affine*, to 25ft, whose pink buds open to sweetly scented, white flowers from July to September; and *J. × stephanense*, to 15ft, which from early to midsummer pleases with a profusion of perfumed, pale pink blooms amid colorful, cream-flushed, green leaves.

Among bushy kinds, the popular, yellow-flowered winter jasmine (*J. nudiflorum*) is usually trained to transform a wall or fence from November to late February. After establishing a main framework, leave it to flower freely on cascading shoots. Aspiring to half that height, semi-evergreen *J. humile* "Revolutum" is dashingly clad with larger, fragrant, yellow blossoms from late spring to fall. Even smaller is yellow-flowered, mound

forming *J. parkeri*, which when planted on a rock garden brightens it in early summer.

CONDITIONS

Aspect   While climbing kinds need a sheltered spot and full sunshine for most of the day, the most popular bushy member—*G. nudiflorum*—thrives on a shaded, north wall lashed by frosty winds.

Site   Undemanding, all flourish on most well-drained soils. Enrich and improve the water retention of thin, sandy areas by digging in bulky organics several months before planting. Help clay drain better by forking in grit.

GROWING METHOD

Feeding   Give young plants a good start by consigning them to generous planting holes fortified with bone meal or Growmore fertilizer. Soak the soil after planting to settle it around roots and remove air pockets. Encourage robust growth by working bone meal into the root area in spring and the fall.

Propagation   Layer whippy shoots from spring to late summer or take semi-ripe cuttings from mid- to late summer.

Problems   Gray mold, a fungus covering leaves with a grayish, furry patina, may occur if shoots are crowded. Control it by removing affected parts and spraying with carbendazim.

PRUNING

Climbing kinds are not normally cut back. If they outgrow their situation, shorten shoots after flowering. Keep *J. nudiflorum* youthful and massed with bloom by removing a third of the older flowered stems when flowers fade in early spring.

JASMINE AT A GLANCE

Semi-evergreen or deciduous, twining or bush forms color walls and fences in winter and summer. Hardy to 4°F (zone 7).

Month	Activity	Recommended Varieties
Jan	flower	
Feb	flower	*J. affine*
Mar	prune	*J. humile* "Revolutum"
Apr	plant	*J. nudiflorum*
May	flower, plant	*J. parkeri*
Jun	flower, plant	*J. × stephanense*
July	flower, plant	
Aug	flower, prune	
Sept	flower, plant	
Oct	plant	
Nov	plant	
Dec	/	

KERRIA
Kerria japonica

A charmingly tangled mass of bright yellow flowers in spring makes kerria an attractive screening plant, even at dusk.

Kerria has single or double flowers and leaves that develop radiant yellow tints in fall. This is the double "Pleniflora" version.

FEATURES

Graceful and arching, deciduous *Kerria japonica* makes a fascinating focus to about 6ft high. From April to May, its radiant orange-yellow blooms clothe a profusion of suckering, cane-like, green stems.
Coveted forms are "Pleniflora," magnificent with its double, golden pompons; "Golden Guinea," with beautiful, single, buttercup-yellow flowers; and smaller "Picta"—just 3ft high—whose single, yellow blossoms complement cream-edged, green leaves. Very hardy and happy almost anywhere, taller kinds making dense and colorful hedges.

CONDITIONS

Aspect This shrub flowers best in full sun and performs passably well in shade.
Site Kerria will thrive almost anywhere.

GROWING METHOD

Feeding Keep growth vigorous and packed with blossom in spring by applying bone meal in March and October. Water new plants frequently to help them establish quickly.
Propagation Probably the easiest shrub to multiply, it can be increased from semi-ripe cuttings in midsummer; layered shoots from mid-spring to late summer; hardwood cuttings in late fall; and suckers in early spring.
Problems No particular pests or diseases.

PRUNING

Cut out from the base a third of older shoots when blooms fade in early summer. Remove green-leaved stems on variegated bushes.

KERRIA AT A GLANCE

Deciduous shrub with green stems dotted with single or double, yellow blooms in spring. Hardy to -13°F (zone 5).

Month	Activity	Recommended Varieties
Jan	/	
Feb	/	"Albescens"
Mar	plant	"Golden Guinea"
Apr	flower, plant	"Picta"
May	flower, plant	"Pleniflora"
June	plant, prune	"Simplex"
July	plant	
Aug	plant	
Sept	plant	
Oct	plant	
Nov	plant	
Dec	/	

LAVENDER
Lavendula

Blooming from July to September, evergreen lavender excels in free-draining "hot spots". Make sure you get the plant you want by buying it in flower.

Aromatic French lavender is a delightful cottage-garden plant. Brush against it and citrus scent fills the air.

FEATURES

Never out of fashion, hardy, evergreen lavender forms a rounded shrub 12–30in high. From July to September, its aromatic, gray-green foliage complements spikes of tightly clustered, pale blue, purple, pink, or white flowers. Interplant it with other shrubs or border perennials or set it to form a fetching divide between open-plan gardens.

Choice varieties are: dwarf, compact and rich purple-blue "Hidcote"; equally neat, lavender-blue "Munstead"; and taller French lavender (*Lavandula stoechas* "Papillon"), the dark purple flowers of which are borne in dense, lozenge-shaped heads. Flowers are used fresh in posies and dried for pot-pourri or cosmetics.

Lavender is an archetypal cottage-garden plant. Its common names of French, English, or Italian lavender apply to different species, but even experts find it hard to agree upon which is which.

LAVENDER AT A GLANCE

Aromatic, grayish-leaved evergreen with scented, lavender, purple, pink, or white flowers in summer. Hardy to 14°F (zone 8).

Month	Activity	Recommended Varieties
Jan	/	
Feb	/	
Mar	/	"Hidcote"
Apr	plant, prune	"Loddon Pink"
May	plant	"Munstead"
June	plant	"Nana Alba"
July	flower, plant	"Twickel Purple"
Aug	flower, plant	*L. vera*
Sept	flower, plant	*L. stoechas* "Papillon"
Oct	/	
Nov	/	
Dec	/	

CONDITIONS

Aspect
Lavender needs an open situation in full sun with good air circulation. Do not crowd it with other plantings.

Site
Thriving on most well-drained soils, it prefers coarse, sandy, or gravelly loam. Lime acid soils before planting.

GROWING METHOD

Feeding
Boost growth of young plants by topdressing the root area with fish, blood, and bone meal in spring and midsummer. When established, after two years, no regular fertilizing is necessary.

Water new plantings copiously to help them recover quickly. When well established, lavender is seldom stressed by droughty spells.

Propagation
Take semi-ripe cuttings from early to mid-fall. Alternatively, work sharp sand into the crown in spring, watering it well, so lower branches are buried. Detach rooted layers in fall and move them to their new positions.

Problems
Lavender is seldom troubled by pests or diseases but may succumb to root rot in heavy or overwet soils. If crowded, in sheltered gardens, the foliage may die back. Remove dead growth and thin out stems to improve air circulation.

PRUNING

Use shears to trim dead blooms from bushes and hedges after flowering.

Rejuvenate older, "tired" plants and help them bloom freely by shortening the previous year's flowered stems to new shoots within 2–4in of the base. Do this from early to mid-spring. Never cut back into older wood, for it seldom regenerates and plants may die.

NEW ZEALAND TEA TREE
Leptospermum scoparium

Smothered with tiny, disc-like blooms from May to June, Leptospermum "Red Damask" is best fan-trained against a warm, sunny wall in all but very mild areas.

Keep tea tree youthful and glowing with blossom by removing a third of the older shoots when flowers fade.

FEATURES

Bejewelled from May to June with stalkless, disc-like blooms amid small, narrow leaves, twiggy and slender, purplish-stemmed *Leptospermum scoparium* is an evergreen worth caring for. Forming a rounded bush, 6–8ft high, it is usually grown against a sheltered wall. Alternatively, set it among other shrubs that shield it from biting winds.

Trained as a mini-standard, it makes a fetching feature for a sun-soaked patio.

Favoured varieties are double "Red Damask," single, clear pink "Huia," and double, white "Snow Flurry". Be warned: tea trees may be short-lived unless conditions are ideal.

TEA TREE AT A GLANCE

A slightly frost-tender evergreen, it is studded with tiny, red, pink, or white blooms from May to June. Hardy to 23°F (zone 9).

Jan	/	Recommended Varieties
Feb	/	
Mar	/	"Huia"
Apr	plant	"Kiwi"
May	flower, plant	"Red Damask"
June	flower, plant	"Snow Flurry"
July	plant, prune	
Aug	plant	
Sept	plant	
Oct	/	
Nov	/	
Dec	/	

CONDITIONS

Aspect Leptospermum needs full sun and protection from cold, north or east winds. Ideally fan-train it against a south- or west-facing wall. Make sure air freely circulates to reduce risk of mildew felting and crippling leaves.

Site The planting area must be well drained. Improve light, sandy soils by digging in old manure or well-rotted garden compost.

GROWING METHOD

Feeding Encourage robust flowering growth by applying an acidifying fertilizer in spring and midsummer. Water young plants regularly in their first year after planting. Thereafter, soak the root area periodically in dry periods and mulch with shredded bark.

Propagation Multiply plants from soft-tip cuttings in June or semi-ripe cuttings in late summer.

Problems Plants are susceptible to root rot in clay soils. Avoid it by forking in grit or gravel before planting. Webbing caterpillars, such as lackey moth, can cause leaves to drop. Cut off and destroy egg bands or webbed shoots and spray with permethrin, bifenthrin, or fenitrothion.

PRUNING

If leptospermum outgrows its allotted space, remove one shoot in three from the base, when flowers fade in midsummer. Do not cut back into older wood as it seldom re-grows. Remove straggly shoots in spring.

HONEYSUCKLE
Lonicera

Small and bushy Lonicera fragrantissima *treats us to a massed display of vanilla-perfumed, creamy flowers from mid- to late winter.*

Clothed with sweetly scented blooms from June to October, Lonicera japonica *"Halliana" makes a fetching screen for a sunny patio.*

FEATURES

A trio of sweetly scented, bushy honeysuckles worth cultivating are: *Lonicera fragrantissima*, with its vanilla-perfumed, creamy-white, bell-shaped blooms, which are freely borne on twiggy shoots to 6ft from January to March; slightly smaller *L. × purpusii*, which treats us to a similar display from November to March; and *L. syringantha*, with its profusion of clustered, lilac flowers on 3ft stems from late spring to early summer.

Twining varieties, trained to frame a door or clothe a wall, fence, arbour, pergola, or arch or to scramble through a tree, enhance a garden. Color spring by planting yellow and red *L. periclymenum* "Belgica" and continue the show—from June to October—with white and red *L.p.* "Serotina."

CONDITIONS

Aspect   Plant lonicera in full or lightly dappled shade to grow strongly and flower freely.

Site   These shrubs and climbers prefer well-drained and humus-rich, sandy loam, or clay loam but also tolerate chalky soil. Improve light soils, which dry out quickly, by working in bulky organic materials well before planting.

GROWING METHOD

Feeding   Speed robust growth and a panoply of blossom by enriching the root area with bone meal in spring and fall.
Water liberally to encourage young plants to establish quickly. Once growing strongly, all varieties are unstressed by droughty periods. In spring, mulch thickly with humus-forming organics to keep roots cool and questing and encourage a fine display of blossom.

Propagation Shrubs: Take hardwood cuttings in late fall or early winter, or layer whippy stems from mid-spring to late summer.

Climbers: Take semi-ripe cuttings from early to midsummer.

Problems   Blackfly are attracted to new shoots, which they quickly smother. Control them with pirimicarb, natural pyrethrins, bifenthrin, or horticultural soap.

PRUNING

Keep winter-flowering *L. fragrantissima* and *L. × purpusii* shapely and full of young shoots, which flower freely, by removing one stem in three in mid-spring. Help spring- and early summer-blooming *L. syringantha* prosper by cutting back flowered shoots to new growth when blooms fade.
Prune *L. periclymenum* varieties and *L. japonica* "Halliana" by shortening flowered stems to new shoots when blooms fade.

HONEYSUCKLE AT A GLANCE		
Semi-evergreen bushes and deciduous and evergreen climbers light up spring, summer and winter. Hardy to -13°F (zone 5).		
Jan	flower	
Feb	flower	Recommended Varieties
Mar	plant	
Apr	flower, prune	Bushes
May	flower, prune	*L. fragrantissima*
		L. × purpusii
June	flower, prune	*L. syringantha*
July	flower, plant	*L. tartarica*
Aug	flower, prune	Climbers
Sept	flower, prune	"Belgica"
		L. heckrottii "Goldflame"
Oct	plant	"Serotina"
Nov	plant	*L. japonica* "Halliana"
Dec	/	*L. tragophylla*

MAGNOLIA
Magnolia

Unfolding in March and April, before leaves appear, starry-flowered Magnolia stellata *lights up dappled shade.*

Planted to contrast with a dark green-leaved shrub, the star magnolia *makes a statement. Underplant it with blue-flowered grape hyacinths.*

FEATURES

Heralding spring, *Magnolia stellata*, a deciduous, bushy shrub to around 7ft, illuminates borders with a multitude of fragrant, strap-petalled, starry, white flowers from March to April. Also called star magnolia, it is ideal for small gardens. Fetching varieties are pink-budded, white-flowered "Royal Star," white-flowered "Centennial," whose blooms are 5½in across, and "Waterlily," another handsome, white variety with flared, double chalices that command close attention.

Most other magnolias, such as evergreen *M. grandiflora*, which flowers best if fan-trained on a sunny, sheltered wall, and varieties of *M. soulangeana*, soar to around 15ft.

CONDITIONS

Aspect No matter how large or small the variety, magnolias should be sheltered from strong winds. To flower well, they must receive at least half a day's sunshine.

Site *M. stellata* and *M. grandiflora* prosper in well-drained, acid, neutral, or alkaline soil. *M. soulangeana* abhors chalk. Dig in plenty of organic matter well ahead of planting.

GROWING METHOD

Feeding Encourage bountiful blooms by applying an acidifying fertilizer—brands for azaleas and camellias are ideal—in April and July.

Propagation Take soft-tip cuttings from late spring to early summer. Increase *M. grandiflora* from semi-ripe cuttings in midsummer. Layering is more reliable but takes longer. Peg down shoots from spring to late summer and detach rooted stems a year later in fall.

Problems Soft, unfolding leaves can be scorched by hot, dry, or salty winds, so position plants carefully.

PRUNING

Seldom necessary. If a shrub requires shaping or crowded branches need removing, tackle it when flowers fade in mid-spring. Never prune in winter, as corky tissues are liable to rot.

MAGNOLIA AT A GLANCE

White or pink flowers are thickly borne on leafless branches in early spring. *M. stellata* is hardy to -13° (zone 5).

		Recommended Varieties
Jan	/	
Feb	/	*M. grandiflora**
Mar	flower, plant	*M. grandiflora* "Heaven Scent"*
Apr	flower, plant	
May	flower, prune	*M. grandiflora* "Little Gem"*
Jun	plant, prune	
July	plant, flower*	*M. soulangeana* "Lennei"
Aug	plant, flower*	*M. soulangeana* "Picture"
Sept	plant, flower*	*M. stellata*
Oct	/	*M. stellata* "Centennial"
Nov	/	*M. stellata* "Royal Star"
Dec	/	* summer flowering

MAHONIA
Mahonia

Tall, bushy mahonias display shuttlecocks of citrus-scented, pale lemon to golden flowers from early winter to early spring. Decorative, blue berries follow in the fall.

Mahonia × media "Charity" illuminates a dry, shady spot from mid- to late winter.

FEATURES

Ground-hugging, weed-suppressing, and good for stabilizing steep banks, tall and sculptural, evergreen mahonias have shiny, spiky, holly-like leaves that develop burnished coppery or reddish tints in winter. Flamboyant, citrus-scented heads of yellow or golden-clustered, slender, cone-like flowers appear from November to May. Blooms are followed by decorative, bluish-black berries. From 2ft to 8ft high, depending on the species, taller kinds make fetching focal points, dense screens or dashing background plants.

Varieties of suckering, ground-covering *Mahonia aquifolium*, which thrives in light shade, effectively carpet rooty areas around trees and shrubs. Position orb-shaped and free-flowering *M. × media* "Charity" and more upright "Lionel Fortescue" to light up winter.

CONDITIONS

Aspect	Thriving in sun or dappled shade, mahonias resist cold winds.
Site	These shrubs flourish in all but very chalky conditions. Improve poor soils by adding bulky organic matter several weeks before planting.

GROWING METHOD

Feeding	Boost growth by working fish, blood, and bone meal or Growmore into the root area in mid-spring and midsummer. If they are growing where there is root competition, mulch thickly to help conserve moisture.
Propagation	Raise species from seeds in early to mid-spring, in a garden frame. Take leaf-bud cuttings in mid-fall or mid-spring and root in a heated propagator. Divide *M. aquifolium* into well-rooted portions in mid-spring.
Problems	Control mahonia rust by spraying with penconazole, mancozeb, or bupirimate with triforine. *M. aquifolium* and *M. bealei* have some resistance to this disease.

PRUNING

M. aquifolium:	Prevent plants from becoming leggy by removing one stem in three after flowering.
Tall, bushy hybrids:	Remove flower heads when blooms fade; rejuvenate old, gaunt plants by shortening stems by half their height in May.

MAHONIA AT A GLANCE

Carpeting or upright evergreens, with holly-like leaves, color borders from November to March. Hardy to -13°F (zone 5).

Jan	flower	Recommended Varieties
Feb	flower	
Mar	flower	*M. aquifolium* "Apollo"
Apr	flower, plant	*M. aquifolium* "Atropurpurea"
May	prune, flower	*M. aquifolium* "Smaragd"
June	plant	*M. japonica*
July	feed	*M. lomariifolia*
Aug	plant	*M. × media* "Charity"
Sept	plant	"Lionel Fortescue"
Oct	plant	"Winter Sun"
Nov	flower	
Dec	flower	

SACRED BAMBOO
Nandina domestica

Nandina's fall bounty of bright red berries follows a summer display of white flowers. Leaves are greenish but tinted cream, pink, orange, and red.

Unlike true bamboo, the sacred version is light, airy, and not invasive and is ideal for colonising a restricted space.

FEATURES

Reminiscent of bamboo, nandina is a slender-stemmed evergreen that slowly spreads by suckers to make a fascinating focal point. Grown for its brightly hued, cream, orange, pink, and red leaves, its "airy" shoots create an impression of "lightness". Nandina, much prized for Japanese-style gardens, may also be sited elsewhere to contrast effectively with darker-toned and heavier-textured plants. Small, white flowers from June to July are followed by attractive, red berries, which linger into fall. Makes a handsome bush to 4ft high by 3ft across.

SACRED BAMBOO AT A GLANCE

Bamboo-like evergreen whose cream-, orange-, and pink-tinted leaves complement white flowers. Hardy to 14°F (zone 8).

Month		Recommended Varieties
Jan	/	
Feb	/	"Firepower"
Mar		"Nana Purpurea"
Apr	plant	"Richmond"
May	prune	
June	plant, flower	
July	plant, flower	
Aug	plant, flower	
Sept	plant	
Oct	/	
Nov	/	
Dec	/	

CONDITIONS

Aspect   Thriving in full sun or semi-shade, it needs shielding from cold winds, which can blacken leaves. Ideally, plant it at the foot of a south- or west-facing wall.

Soil   Nandina prefers well-drained and humus rich, sandy loam. Augment chalk or heavy clay soils with bulky organic materials a month or two before planting.

GROWING METHOD

Feeding   Encourage luxuriant foliage and large clusters of fruit by working bone meal into the root area in spring and the fall.
Once established, nandina is fairly drought resistant. Mulch with well-rotted garden compost, manure, shredded bark, or cocoa shell in spring to insulate roots from moisture-extracting sunshine.

Propagation   In the fall, extract seeds from ripe berries, sow in pots and raise in a garden frame. Take semi-ripe cuttings from mid- to late summer. Use a spade to split up large clumps in mid-spring.

Problems   Severe winter weather may kill shoots to ground level and new growth from roots may be slow in appearing.

PRUNING

No regular cutting back is necessary.
Rejuvenate old clumps in May by removing a third of the older stems at ground level.

OLEANDER
Nerium oleander

Delighting us with white, yellow, apricot, pink, or crimson blooms from spring to fall, evergreen but poisonous oleander is easy to grow.

Create a Mediterranean tapestry by grouping a pot-grown oleander next to a spiky-leaved yucca and scarlet pelargonium.

FEATURES

Frost-tender and principally a conservatory plant, evergreen oleander enjoys a summer airing on a sunny, sheltered patio or terrace. Depending on variety, it makes a handsome shrub, 4–6ft high. Sumptuous heads of white, yellow, pink, apricot, cerise, or scarlet, single or double blooms appear from June to November. Thrusting, upright stems are clad with slender, leathery leaves. Oleanders are long-lived and flower early in life. Choice varieties include: semi-double, light pink "Clare"; single, apricot "Madame Leon Blum"; double, white "Soeur Agnes"; and single, deep red "Hardy's Red." Double, pink-flowered "Variegatum," with cream or yellow-rimmed leaves, is very popular with flower arrangers. The plant is poisonous if eaten.

OLEANDER AT A GLANCE

Studded with showy blooms in many colors, frost-tender oleander is usually grown in a conservatory. Hardy to 45°F (zone 11).

Jan	/	Recommended Varieties
Feb	/	
Mar	plant	"Clare"
Apr	plant, prune	"Emile"
May	flower, plant	"Géant des Batailles"
June	flower, plant	"Luteum Plenum"
July	flower, plant	"Professor Granel"
Aug	flower, plant	"Soeur Agnes"
Sept	flower, plant	"Soleil Levant"
Oct	flower	"Variegatum"
Nov	flower	
Dec	/	

CONDITIONS

Aspect Oleander needs full sun and shelter from cold winds to prosper and flower freely. Only in frost-free gardens can it be grown outdoors all year round. Elsewhere, grow it in a pot indoors—in a lounge or conservatory—and move it outside when frosts finish in late May.

Site This shrub thrives in most free-draining soil types but abhors heavy, waterlogged clay. If growing it in a large pot or tub, set it in proprietary tub or hanging basket compost.

GROWING METHOD

Feeding Border plants: Encourage large clusters of blossom by sprinkling bone meal over the root area in spring and fall and hoeing it in.
Tub grown (indoors in winter): Insert slow-release fertilizer granules into the compost in spring. Repot root-bound plants in spring. Though oleander tolerates long, dry periods, soak roots occasionally in hot, dry weather.

Propagation Raise plants from seeds sown in a heated propagator in spring or take semi-ripe cuttings in midsummer.

Problems If plants are attacked by limpet-like scale insects, control them by spraying two or three times, fortnightly, with malathion or horticultural soap.

PRUNING

Keep oleander youthful and blooming freely by shortening flowered shoots by half their length when blossoms fade. Ensure plants stay neat and bushy by shortening side shoots to 4in in spring.

OSMANTHUS
Osmanthus

Forming an umbrella of small, evergreen shoots, Osmanthus delavayi's *thickly clustered, tubular flowers sleeve shoots in spring.*

A beacon of bright, cream-rimmed, evergreen leaves from Osmanthus heterophyllus *"Variegatus" illuminates dull, winter days.*

FEATURES

An easy, enchanting, and small, glossy, leathery-leaved evergreen from western China and Japan, osmanthus forms an orb of shoots and colors spring and fall.

Light up April and May with *Osmanthus × burkwoodii*. Growing to around 6ft high by 4ft across, its toothed, pointed leaves foil slender stems massed with clusters of small, white, vanilla-fragrant, tubular blooms. Create a riveting feature by grouping it with orange or yellow deciduous azaleas. It also makes a dense, wind-proof hedge.

Closely related *O. delavayi* is another spring-flowering treasure. Arching to 5ft high, it too is smothered with bunches of small, white blooms that spill jasmine perfume on to the air. Small, black fruits follow them.

Later, from September to October, comes taller *O. heterophyllus*, to 10ft high and across, the soft leaves of which deceive you into thinking it is a form of holly. It does a sterling job in coloring the closing year with a profusion of tiny, white blossoms.

Its colored-leaved varieties—purple "Purpureus" and creamy "Aureomarginatus"—are stunning throughout the year.

CONDITIONS

Aspect All, apart from *O. delavayi* which is best grown again against a sheltering, warm wall in cold districts, thrive in the open.

Site If possible, set plants in free-draining, humus-rich soil that does not dry out or become waterlogged. Fortify sandy or chalky soils with bulky organic manure.

GROWING METHOD

Feeding Boost growth by sprinkling Growmore or some other balanced fertilizer over the root area in spring, repeating in midsummer. Water it in if the soil is dry.
Foliar feed in droughty spells, when roots have difficulty absorbing plant foods, to speed uptake of nutrients. Water new plants copiously and follow with a mulch of bark, cocoa shell, or well-rotted garden compost.

Propagation Increase varieties by layering flexible shoots from late spring to late summer or take semi-ripe cuttings from mid- to late summer.

Problems Seldom attacked by pests or diseases.

PRUNING

No regular cutting back is necessary. If awkward shoots need removing, do it in spring when flowers have finished. Shorten stems to just above a joint or to new shoots. Trim a hedge of *O. × burkwoodii* when flowers fade in May.

OSMANTHUS AT A GLANCE

Spring- or fall-flowering evergreens for sun or light shade, *O. × burkwoodii* makes a stocky hedge. Hardy to 23°F (zone 9).

Month	Activity	Recommended Varieties
Jan	/	
Feb	/	*O. × burkwoodii*
Mar		*O. delavayi*
Apr	flower, plant	*O. heterophyllus*
May	flower, plant	*O. heterophyllus* "Aureomarginatus"
June	prune	
July	/	*O. heterophyllus* "Purpureus"
Aug	/	
Sept	flower, plant	*O. heterophyllus* "Variegatus"
Oct	flower	
Nov	/	
Dec	/	

MOCK ORANGE
Philadelphus

Semi-arching "Belle Etoile" is thickly clothed with richly vanilla-scented, single, large, white and flushed-yellow blooms from June to July.

Plant soaring Philadelphus lemoinei "Erectus" to brighten a sunny spot with a myriad perfumed blooms sleeving upright shoots.

FEATURES

Often but erroneously called syringa—the correct name for lilac—its sumptuous, creamy white, single, or double and richly citrus-vanilla-scented blooms fill and brighten the high-summer gap, when the spring display of shrubs is fading and fall contenders have yet to form flower buds. Ranging in height from 2ft to over 10ft, there are candidates for most situations.

Coveted tall varieties, 6–10ft, are: large, single, and pink-centerd "Beauclerk"; semi-double and yellowish-white *Philadelphus coronarius*; and double or semi-double, pure white "Virginal". Couple flowers with striking foliage by planting semi-double, creamy white *P. coronarius* "Aureus," the leaves of which open lemon-yellow and mature to greenish yellow. This plant is perfect for lighting up a sunny or dappled shady border.

Set the smallest member, "Manteau d'Hermine," just 2–3ft high, on a rock garden and enjoy its massed, double, creamy white blossoms. Taller kinds are good for hedging.

CONDITIONS

Aspect   Ideal for windswept, hillside gardens and for tolerating salty breezes, mock orange thrives almost anywhere. All flower best in full sun and lemon-leaved *P. coronarius* "Aureus" keeps its radiant leaf color in light shade.

Site   Thriving in most soils—acid sand, chalk, or heavy clay—it is best to enrich poor patches with bulky organic matter dug in several months before planting.

GROWING METHOD

Feeding   Encourage bounteous blossom on sandy soil by applying annually sulfate of potash in late winter and late summer. Regardless of soil, topdress the root area with a balanced fertilizer in April and July.

In a dry spring, water regularly to encourage strong, new shoots, which will flower the following year.

Propagation   Strike cuttings of semi-ripe shoots from mid- to late summer. Root them in a cold frame or on a sunny windowsill.

Problems   Blackfly can colonize and cripple soft shoot tips. Control them by spraying with pirimicarb, which does not harm beneficial insects.

PRUNING

When blooms fade, cut back flowered shoots to current-year stems, which will perform the following year.

MOCK ORANGE AT A GLANCE

A deciduous shrub whose single or fully double, creamy white flowers appear from June to July. Hardy to -13°F (zone 5).

Month		Recommended Varieties
Jan	/	
Feb	/	Under 1.8m (6ft)
Mar	plant	"Belle Etoile"
Apr	plant	*Coronarius* "Aureus"
May	plant	"Manteau d'Hermine"
June	flower	"Sybille"
July	flower	Over 1.8m (6ft)
Aug	prune	"Beauclerk"
Sept	/	*Coronarius*
Oct	plant	"Virginal"
Nov	plant	
Dec	/	

PHOTINIA
Photinia

The awakening year sees Photinia fraseri *draped with clusters of tiny, white flowers, occasionally followed by red berries.*

In spring and early summer, Photinia *"Red Robin" is a beacon of shining maroon-scarlet leaves. Here it is contrasting with an apple-green hebe.*

FEATURES

A valued New Zealand evergreen to around 6ft high by 5ft across, *Photinia × fraseri* "Red Robin" is a visual delight. From mid- to late spring, a foam of fluffy, white flowers, sometimes followed by scarlet berries, complements brilliant red, shiny leaves that mature to green. Riveting in a winter-color border, it is also appealing when fan-trained against a sunny, sheltered wall or fence. Alternatively, plant it in a large pot or tub and train it as a globe, pyramid, or drumstick. Clip trained forms in spring and summer. Photinia also makes a dense, low hedge.

PHOTINIA AT A GLANCE

The most popular kind, *P. × fraseri* "Red Robin," enchants us with a wealth of scarlet, new leaves. Hardy to 4°F (zone 7).

		Recommended Varieties
Jan	/	
Feb	/	"Birmingham"
Mar	/	"Red Robin"
Apr	flower, plant	"Robusta"
May	flower, prune	"Rubens"
June	flower, plant	
July	plant	
Aug	plant	
Sept	plant	
Oct	/	
Nov	/	
Dec	/	

CONDITIONS

Aspect Not the hardiest of shrubs, photinia prefers a sheltered, sunny situation in which its foliage colors magnificently. It tolerates light shade.

Site This shrub thrives on most well-drained soils but hates heavy clay and chalk. Improve sandy patches by incorporating bulky organic manures several weeks before planting.

GROWING METHOD

Feeding Encourage stocky shoots and lusterous leaves by topdressing the root area with fish, blood, and bone meal, or some other balanced fertilizer, in spring and midsummer. Water young plants copiously in dry spells in their first year to initiate strong, new shoots.

Propagation Layer young stems from spring to late summer; take semi-ripe cuttings in late summer.

Problems Photinia is susceptible to apple scab, a fungus that causes leaves to develop grayish-green spots and fall early. Control it by raking up diseased leaves, pruning out and burning scabby shoots and spraying with carbendazim, mancozeb, or bupirimate with triforine.

PRUNING

Rejuvenate old, leggy bushes by shortening stems by a third of their length in mid-spring. Remove shoot tips periodically throughout spring and summer, to encourage flushes of new, red leaves.

PIERIS
Pieris

Young pieris leaves open a vivid shade of pink or scarlet before turning yellow and ultimately green.

Some varieties, such as "Wakehurst," not only produce scarlet, flower-bright leaves but also combine them with an unstinting display of lily-of-the-valley-like blossom.

FEATURES

A captivating, evergreen shrub, 16in–9ft high and across, its bell-shaped, white, pink, or red flowers glorify spring. Its other, equally prized asset is its glowing pink or reddish shuttlecocks of new leaves.

There are many varieties. Aptly named "Flaming Silver"—2ft high, ideal for a narrow border—has fiery, new leaves which when mature are suffused with silver.

PIERIS AT A GLANCE

New, red, evergreen leaves complement sprays of white, pink, or red, bell-shaped flowers in spring. Hardy to 14°F (zone 8).

		Recommended Varieties
Jan	/	
Feb	/	"Debutante"
Mar	flower	"Firecrest"
Apr	flower, plant	"Flaming Silver"
May	flower, prune	"Forest Flame"
June	plant, prune	"Mountain Fire"
July	plant	"Pink Delight"
Aug	plant	"Valley Valentine"
Sept	plant	
Oct	/	
Nov	/	
Dec	/	

CONDITIONS

Aspect   Not a candidate for exposed gardens, pieris needs shielding from strong, cold winds and hot, leaf-scorching sunshine.

Site   Abhorring any degree of lime, this shrub needs deep, rich, well-drained soil. Create a good home for it by digging in generous amounts of organic material well ahead of planting time.

GROWING METHOD

Feeding   Boost robust growth by applying an acidifying fertilizer in spring and midsummer. Help young plants recover quickly from transplanting by watering regularly in droughty spells and mulching with moisture-conserving organics.

Propagation   Multiply plants by pegging down low shoots from mid-spring to late summer or take semi-ripe cuttings from mid- to late summer.

Problems   New leaves may be damaged by wind frost.

PRUNING

Cut off faded blooms and dead or damaged shoots in early summer. Rejuvenate old bushes by shortening gaunt shoots to half their height in mid-spring. Keep cuts moist in dry spells to encourage rapid regrowth.

SHRUBBY CINQUEFOIL
Potentilla fruticosa

Forming a spreading clump, "Red Ace"—riveting when interplanted with Artemisia *"Powis Castle"—fires a border from May to October.*

Prized for its display of butter-yellow flowers, "Dart's Golddigger" contrasts stunningly with rosy-pink bedding geraniums.

FEATURES

Potentilla fruticosa flowers continuously from late May to September, its small, saucer-shaped blossoms clustering on dense, wiry stems.

Carpeting or bushy, to 5ft—taller kinds making colorful hedges—it is hardy and a good choice for cold gardens.

Easy, eye-catching varieties are: grayish-green-leaved and white-flowered "Abbotswood"; creamy-yellow "Tilford Cream"; ground-covering "Dart's Golddigger"; chrome-yellow "Goldstar"; salmon-pink "Pretty Polly"; vermilion-flame "Red Ace"; and deep orange to brick-red "Sunset".

All are good contenders for patio and terrace tubs and pots or deep, generous windowboxes. Arrange a potted group in several harmonizing colors to flank a doorway or form a focal point at the end of a path. Shrubby cinquefoil can also be grown to embrace pergola posts.

SHRUBBY CINQUEFOIL AT A GLANCE

Deciduous, bushy plants, which also make good hedges, they flower from May to September. Hardy to -13°F (zone 5).

Month	Activity	Recommended Varieties
Jan	/	
Feb	/	Carpeting
Mar	plant	"Dart's Golddigger"
Apr	plant, prune	"Pretty Polly"
May	plant, flower	"Red Ace"
June	plant, flower	"Sunset"
July	plant, flower	Bushy
Aug	plant, flower	"Goldfinger"
Sept	plant, flower	"Goldstar"
Oct	plant, flower	"Red Robin"
Nov	plant	"Tilford Cream"
Dec	/	

CONDITIONS

Aspect A good choice for borders exposed to cold winds, shrubby cinquefoil flowers profusely in an open, sunny position or very light shade. If possible, plant it facing south or west where trees will not overshadow it.

Site A very adaptable plant, it thrives in most soils, from heavy, often waterlogged clay to light, sandy areas that become parched in summer. It does not mind a little lime but on very chalky soils it is liable to become stressed and suffer from chlorosis, when leaves turn creamy or yellowish and die.

GROWING METHOD

Feeding Encourage robust flowering shoots by working fish, blood, and bone meal or some other balanced fertilizer into the root area in spring and midsummer. Apply bone meal in the fall to release plant foods in spring. If, in sandy soil, leaf margins turn brown, indicating potash deficiency, rectify by applying sulfate of potash in February and watering it in.
Once the plant is established, watering is seldom needed, but soak newly planted shrubs to settle the soil around the roots.

Propagation Increase plants from cuttings of semi-ripe shoots in midsummer. Root them in a garden frame or on a sunny windowsill.

Problems Shoots produce their leaves very late in spring, deceiving us into thinking them dead.

PRUNING

Keep bushes youthful and flowering freely year after year by removing a third of the older shoots in spring. Rejuvenate very old, woody plants at the same time by cutting them back to within 4in of the base. Trim hedges in spring.

CAPE LEADWORT
Plumbago

Commonly called Cape leadwort, plumbago rewards us with a succession of silvery-blue flowers from mid- to late summer.

Encourage plumbago to flower bounteously every year by shortening the previous year's flowered stems in February.

FEATURES

Usually grown to color a conservatory, greenhouse, or windowsill with a mist of starry, sky-blue flowers from midsummer to fall, *Plumbago auriculata* is a rambling, evergreen climber. Ideally, grow it in a large pot or tub to allow you to move it on to a patio when frosts finish in late May or early June. Growing to 15ft or so, in cultivation it is best pruned regularly to keep it neat, compact, and floriferous. In very sheltered, frost-free gardens, create a sensation in summer by training it over an arch, arbour, obelisk or trellis.

CAPE LEADWORT AT A GLANCE

Scrambling, frost-tender climber studded with pale blue flowers from midsummer to early fall. Hardy to 46°F (zone 11).

Jan	/	Recommended Varieties
Feb	prune	
Mar	/	*P. auriculata*
Apr	plant	*P. auriculata alba*
May	plant	"Royal Cape"
June	plant	
July	flower	
Aug	flower	
Sept	flower	
Oct	flower	
Nov	/	
Dec	/	

CONDITIONS

Aspect Though plumbago flowers best in full sun, it tolerates very light shade.

Site Set this shrub in a large, well-drained pot or small tub of multi-purpose compost.

GROWING METHOD

Feeding Insert clusters of slow-release fertilizer granules into the compost in spring. From late spring to summer, apply a high-potash tomato feed.
When potting plants, add moisture-storage granules to help keep the compost damp during long, dry spells.
In late summer, when nights turn cold, return plumbago to a frost-free spot in good light. Keep the compost dryish from fall to spring.

Propagation Take semi-ripe cuttings from early to midsummer.

Problems Under glass, fluffy, waxy, white mealy bugs may colonize leaf joints and cripple growth. Control them biologically with *Aphidius colemani*, a parasitic wasp, or spray with horticultural soap.

PRUNING

Shorten the previous year's flowering shoots to within 2in of the older wood in February.

ORNAMENTAL CHERRY
Prunus

From early to mid-spring, a wealth of disc-shaped, double pink blooms transform Prunus × blireana's *bare, twiggy branches.*

Heralding spring and suitable for all sizes of garden, white-, pink-, or red-flowering cherries associate beautifully with magnolias.

FEATURES

Deciduous or evergreen shrubs or trees 4–14ft tall, the prunus family embraces a wide range of forms. Flowers are single or double, in white, pink, and red shades. Neat dwarf Russian almond (*Prunus tenella* "Firehill") has semi-double, rosy-crimson flowers, which sleeve 4ft stems in April. Also useful for small gardens is
P. × cistena "Crimson Dwarf," whose white flowers appear just before coppery-red leaves.
White-flowering and low-growing evergreen kinds—*P.* "Otto Luyken" among them—are excellent for carpeting shady spots. Taller laurel (*P. laurocerasus* "Rotundifolia") makes a dense evergreen hedge to 6ft.

CONDITIONS

Aspect	Deciduous flowering cherries, needing full sun to perform well, should be sheltered from strong winds. Evergreens thrive in light shade.
Site	All prunus prosper on any well-drained soil enriched with organic matter. Evergreen varieties also thrive on thin, sandy soils.

GROWING METHOD

Feeding	Work bone meal into the root area in spring and fall. Water freely in dry spells, especially when flower buds are forming.
Propagation	Increase evergreen, carpeting and hedging varieties from semi-ripe cuttings from mid- to late summer. Flowering cherry trees, however, are normally grafted on to *P. avium* rootstock.
Problems	Control silver leaf disease by cutting back and burning affected shoots to 6in beyond infected, purple-stained tissue, in midsummer.

PRUNING

Evergreens:	Shear laurel hedges in spring and late summer.
Deciduous varieties:	No regular pruning is necessary. Cut out crowding shoots from mid- to late summer.

ORNAMENTAL CHERRY AT A GLANCE

A huge family of deciduous, spring-flowering cherries and carpeting or hedging evergreens. Hardiness rating, according to species.

Jan	/	Recommended Varieties
Feb	/	
Mar	plant, flower	Evergreen
Apr	prune, flower	"Otto Luyken"
May	flower, plant	*P. laurocerasus*
June	plant, flower	"Rotundifolia"
July	plant, prune	"Zabeliana"
Aug	plant, prune	Deciduous
Sept	plant	"Amanogawa"
Oct	plant	*P. × blireana*
Nov	plant	"Cheal's Weeping"
Dec	/	*P. mume*
		P. tenella "Firehill"

POMEGRANATE
Punica

Showy, bell-shaped, orange-scarlet flowers are your reward for growing a pomegranate in a warm garden or conservatory.

Delicious fruits appear on outdoor or patio pot plants after a long, warm summer. Under glass, in a higher temperature, fruits swell to a greater size.

FEATURES

Deciduous and bearing carnation-like, single or double, brilliant orange-red flowers for most of the summer, *Punica granatum* makes a bushy shrub to 7ft high and across. Only single-flowered varieties bear fruits. Grow them as specimen plants in very sheltered borders in frost-free gardens. Elsewhere, treat this shrub as a pot plant and confine it to a conservatory from fall to late spring. Move it on to a sunny patio or terrace when frosts finish in late May or early June.

POMEGRANATE AT A GLANCE

Deciduous and bearing orange flowers in summer, it can be grown outside only in very sheltered areas. Hardy to 39°F (zone 10).

Jan	/	Recommended Varieties
Feb	/	"Flore Pleno Luteo"
Mar	/	"Flore Pleno Rubro"
Apr	plant, prune	*P. granatum nana*
May	plant, prune	"Striata"
June	flower, plant	
July	flower, plant	
Aug	flower, plant	
Sept	plant	
Oct	/	
Nov	/	
Dec	/	

CONDITIONS

Aspect If you are growing pomegranate outdoors, it must be in full sunshine and protected from cold winds.

Site To excel, this shrub needs well-drained loam or clay-loam soil enriched with humus-forming organics.

GROWING METHOD

Feeding Boost growth and stimulate plenty of blossom-bearing shoots by applying bone meal in spring and the fall.
Encourage young plants to establish quickly by watering liberally in the first spring and summer after planting.
In September, return potted plants that have decorated a patio for summer to a frost-free conservatory or greenhouse.

Propagation Increase this plant from semi-ripe cuttings taken from mid- to late summer.

Problems New shoots on outdoor plants can be damaged by late spring frosts, so site the shrubs carefully.

PRUNING

Remove badly placed shoots from late spring to early summer. Keep wall-trained specimens shapely by shortening flowered shoots to within four leaves of the main framework when blooms fade.

FIRETHORN
Pyracantha

A spectacular fall display of orange, red, or yellow berries, following a foam of creamy blossom, makes firethorn popular for transforming cold walls.

Planted to screen out ugly objects, firethorn's late-season bonanza of berries is a welcome winter feast for garden birds.

FEATURES

Planted mainly for screening, hedging, and training as an espalier, evergreen and hardy firethorn's spiky stems are clad with small, glossy green leaves. In early summer, showy clusters of white flowers, appearing early in the plant's life, are followed by a dramatic cloak of bright orange, yellow, or red berries from fall to winter. Garden birds feast on them. There are many long-lived varieties. Choice kinds include a trio of recently bred fireblight-resistant forms: orange-berried "Saphyr Orange"; red-berried "Saphyr Red"; and yellow-berried "Saphyr Yellow". These shrubs grow 6–10ft high, which they reach after 5–10 years.

FIRETHORN AT A GLANCE

An evergreen shrub coveted for its white flowers and display of red, orange, or yellow berries. Hardy to -13°F (zone 5).

		Recommended Varieties
Jan	/	
Feb	/	"Alexander Pendula"
Mar	/	"Dart's Red"
Apr	plant, prune	"Golden Charmer"
May	plant	*P. rogersiana*
June	flower, plant	"Saphyr Orange"
July	plant	"Saphyr Red"
Aug	plant	"Saphyr Yellow"
Sept	plant	
Oct	/	
Nov	/	
Dec	/	

CONDITIONS

Aspect Needing full sun for healthy, compact growth, firethorn flowers less and is more loosely branched in light shade. It tolerates strong gusts and is often grown as a windbreak.

Site Tolerating a wide range of soil types including chalk, it prefers well-drained loam or clay-loam enriched with organic matter. It also prospers on humus-rich, gravelly patches.

GROWING METHOD

Feeding Keep firethorn lustrous and flowering and berrying freely by working bone meal into the root area in spring and fall.
Help newly planted shrubs establish quickly by watering copiously in dry spells during their first spring and summer. Mulch thickly.

Propagation Take semi-ripe cuttings from mid- to late summer.

Problems Disfiguring leaves and berries with patches, pyracantha scab is a debilitating disease.
Control it by pruning out and burning infected shoots and spraying fortnightly with carbendazim from March to July. Grow orange-red berried "Mohave," which is resistant to it.

PRUNING

Free-standing shrubs: Cut back overgrown plants in April to keep them flowering and berrying profusely.

Wall-trained espaliers: In spring, shorten non-blossoming side shoots to 4in from the base. In midsummer, reduce current-year shoots to three leaves.

RHODODENDRON
Rhododendron

Few shrubs can equal rhododendrons for a spectacular display of blossom from late winter to summer. This skillfully planned garden features a bold planting of white and rosy-red hardy hybrids framed by dark foliage that enhances rather than competes with the flowers.

FEATURES

Enriching gardens with spectacular trusses of vibrant or delicate pastel-hued blooms from December to August, there is an enormous range of evergreen and deciduous varieties. Without doubt, they are the key to creating fetching features on acid soil.

Yielding thickly or sparsely clustered, bell- or trumpet-shaped blooms, rhododendrons are long-lived and mature within 5–10 years. Plant them to enhance woodland glades, borders, rock gardens, patio pots, and conservatories. Associate them with other lime-hating plants, such as azaleas, Japanese maples, lilies, camellias, conifers, eucryphia, pieris, and embothrium.

TYPES

Hardy hybrids: Valued for their resistance to severe weather and ability to prosper in windy gardens, hardy hybrids flower from April to June. Most grow 5–8ft high and across.

They are easy to manage and the blooms, in white and shades of red, pink, lavender, purple, and yellow, are borne in large, showy trusses amid broad, pointed leaves.

Red hues: Outstanding are: ruby red "Bagshot Ruby"; bright brick-red "Vulcan"; bright red, black-speckled "Windlesham Scarlet"; dark red "Doncaster", black-veined within; and medium-red "Cynthia".

Pink hues: A trio no garden should be without is: dark green-leaved and rose-pink "Alice"; "Pink Pearl", whose rosy buds open to flesh-pink blooms; and "Furnivall's Daughter", a gem with rose-pink and dark-spotted flowers.

Purple, blue and mauve hues: Stunning among these are: violet-blue "Blue Boy"; semi-double and bluish-mauve "Fastuosum Flore Pleno"; and rosy-purple "Variegatum", whose white-rimmed leaves illuminate shady places.

White hues: White and pale yellow-eyed "Cunningham's White" and lavender-budded and white-flowered "Loder's White" light up mid-spring.

RHODODENDRON AT A GLANCE

Evergreen shrubs mantled with blooms from late winter to midsummer. All need acid soil. Hardiness ratings vary.

Month		Recommended Varieties
Jan	/	
Feb	flower	Hardy hybrids
Mar	flower	"Doncaster"
Apr	flower, plant	"Furnivall's Daughter"
May	flower, prune	"Pink Pearl"
Jun	flower, prune	"Fastuosum Flore-Pleno"
July	plant	"Cunningham's White"
Aug	plant	"Praecox"
Sept	/	Yakushimanum hybrids
Oct	/	"Astrid"
Nov	/	"Chelsea Seventy"
Dec	/	"Grumpy"

TOP: *Sun-loving, hardy hybrid "Blue Peter."*
ABOVE: *An exquisite-flowered Vireya rhododendron.*

A 19th-century Malaysian variety used for breeding, "Pink Delight" is spectacular for a shaded conservatory or very mild, frost-free garden, but it needs cosseting.

Low-growing varieties: Equally hardy, low-growing varieties make dense bushes 18–48in high.
Heralding spring, "Praecox" opens its rosy-lilac-to-mauve blooms in February and March; "Snow Lady" bears lovely, white flowers from March to April; and "Princess Anne" is smothered with clear yellow blooms from April to May.
Stunning, too, are drought-resisting hybrids of *Rhododendron yakushimanum*. Making dense bushes to 3ft, alluring varieties are: cerise-pink "Astrid"; salmon and carmine-rose "Chelsea Seventy"; and yellowish-white and shell-pink "Grumpy".
The sumptuous and very colorful Malaysian (Vireya) rhododendrons make exciting focal points for a frost-free greenhouse or lightly shaded and very sheltered patio or terrace in summer.

CONDITIONS

Aspect Hardy hybrids and species grow and flower best in a dappled, shady spot shielded from strong wind.

Site Soil must be acid and well-drained, cool and moist throughout the year and fortified with moisture-conserving organic matter. Dig in plenty of well-rotted manure, garden compost, or leaf mould before planting. Set greenhouse varieties in large pots of orchid-bark, mixed with ericaceous compost.

GROWING METHOD

Feeding Nourish plants with an acidifying fertilizer in spring and midsummer and mulch thickly with bulky organic materials to keep roots active and leaves lustrous in long, dry spells.

Use lime-free rain water to moisten dry soil or compost.

Propagation Take softwood cuttings from mid-spring to early summer and semi-ripe cuttings in early fall; layer stems from mid-spring to late summer.

Problems *Bud blast: This fungus turns flower buds brown and is characterised by bristly black outgrowths, is spread by rhododendron leaf hopper. This is also a pest, which lays its eggs in the bud scales. Control bud blast by picking off and burning affected buds and spraying with pirimiphos-methyl to eradicate hoppers.
*Leaf spot disease: Speckling leaves with brownish-purple spots containing raised, black, fungal fruiting bodies, it is best eradicated by spraying with mancozeb when symptoms appear.
If aphids colonize soft shoot tips, control them with pirimicarb, which is selective to this pest and does not harm beneficial insects.
*Lime-induced chlorosis: Caused by a deficiency of iron and manganese in alkaline soils, which inhibits chlorophyll production, leaves develop brown rims and yellow patches between bright green veins. Rectify it by applying a chelated compound based on iron, manganese, and other trace elements.

PRUNING

Snap off spent blooms when petals fall, to channel energy away from seed production and into strong new growth. Take care not to damage new leaves.
Keep mature bushes youthful and packed with blossom in spring by removing one in three of older, black-barked stems when flowers fade. Dwarf and low-growing varieties and species are best left unpruned.

AZALEA
Rhododendron

Planted to light up a woodland glade, evergreen Kurume azalea "Kirin" treats us to a massed display of small blooms in May.

Leaf-shedding Mollis azaleas yield an unforgettable display of large clusters of vibrantly hued, trumpet blooms before leaves fully unfold.

FEATURES

Enchanting us from April to June, deciduous and evergreen azaleas come in a kaleidoscope of colors and range in height, 2–8ft. They are derived from various species of rhododendron and are among the world's most widely hybridized plants. Long-lived, azaleas mature within 3–5 years and flower from the first year of planting. Grouped in mixed shrub borders, taller varieties make a stunning backcloth for annuals or small perennials. It is best to buy plants in flower so that you can be sure of getting exactly what you want. Azaleas are often planted with acid-soil-loving camellias and purple- and green-leaved Japanese maples, where the foliage tempers the more vibrant-hued varieties.

Deciduous groups: Cherished for their May to June performance of clustered, trumpet blooms in glowing pastel and strident hues and vivid fall leaf tints, there are four deciduous types:

Mollis hybrids: Making stocky bushes to about 6ft high, their large heads of scentless, bright yellow, orange, red, cream, and salmon blooms open before leaves appear. Choice among them are orange-scarlet "Spek's Brilliant" and "Koster's Brilliant Red."

Knaphill and Exbury hybrids: Also unperfumed, their May blooms can be as large as a hardy hybrid rhododendron's. Dramatic varieties are: light yellow "April Showers"; salmon-pink "Coronation Lady"; and deep carmine "Homebush."

Ghent hybrids: Making neat, twiggy bushes clothed in long-tubed, sweet-smelling, honeysuckle-like flowers with showy stamens, blossoms peak in late May and June. Fine forms are soft yellow "Narcissiflorum" and rose-pink "Norma".

Occidentalis hybrids: Flowering from mid- to late May, they reward us with trusses of sumptuous, fragrant, pastel-hued blooms. Pure white and yellow-eyed "Bridesmaid" is a good example.

Evergreen and semi-evergreen groups: There are four widely grown divisions. Largest flowering are the prolific Vuyk and Glendale hybrids, whose blooms can be 3in in diameter. The Kaempferi hybrids, such as violet "Blue Danube," have slightly smaller flowers.
Smallest of all are the very popular and bounteous-performing Kurume hybrids. These have slightly greater tolerance to low temperatures than other evergreen varieties and blooms are single or hose-in-hose—when one flower appears inside another.

CONDITIONS

Aspect Most azaleas prefer semi-shade and shelter from strong winds and hot afternoon sunshine. A new race of "sun-loving" varieties is being

AZALEA AT A GLANCE

A form of deciduous or evergreen rhododendron bearing trumpet blooms, it colors lightly shaded spots. Hardy to 4°F (zone 7).

		Recommended Varieties
Jan	/	
Feb	/	Deciduous
Mar	plant, prune	"Bridesmaid"
Apr	flower, prune	"Coronation Lady"
May	flower, prune	"Firefly"
Jun	flower, prune	"Gibraltar"
July	plant	"Koster's Brilliant Red"
Aug	plant	Evergreen
Sept	plant	"Addy Wery"
Oct	plant	"Blue Danube"
Nov	plant	"Driven Snow"
Dec	/	"Hinode-giri"

A riot of spring blossom in yellow, orange, and other sunny shades makes it worthwhile finding a choice site for a Mollis azalea.

Site

bred for more open situations.
The soil should be acid, well-drained, and humus-rich and fortified with plenty of well-decayed organic matter several weeks before planting. In even slightly alkaline conditions, when the pH hovers just above 7.0, azaleas will suffer from iron deficiency and creamy-green, chlorophyll-deficient leaves will die. Keep plants perky in hot spells by mulching with a thick layer of organic material, such as well-rotted manure, leaf mould, compost, or decayed grass clippings.

GROWING METHOD

Feeding

Nourish plants by applying an acidifying fertilizer in spring and summer and watering it in if the soil is dry.
Water new plants regularly in droughty periods to help them establish quickly. In prolonged dry weather, gently dig a moat around a bush and fill it with water. Refill it several times when the water has soaked away. Finish by replacing the soil.

Propagation

Azaleas are easily increased from soft-tip cuttings taken from mid-spring to early summer; semi-ripe cuttings from mid- to late summer; and layers pegged down from mid-spring to late summer.

Problems

Unfortunately azaleas suffer from a number of pests and diseases.
*Powdery mildew: Causing yellow patches to blemish upper leaf surfaces it can, occasionally, trouble heavily shaded plants in areas of high rainfall. It can also be aggravated by sluggish air flow, so remove crowded plants and set them elsewhere. Pick off and burn badly affected leaves and avoid wetting the foliage. Do not grow *Rhododendron cinnabarinum* or its hybrids, which are prone to this fungus. Control the disease chemically by spraying

with bupirimate with triforine or mancozeb the moment symptoms appear.
*Azalea gall: Blame the fungus *Exobasidium vaccinii*, which causes leaves to become swollen, fleshy, and pinkish red. Later, ripe, white spores powder the surface. In the fall, galls wither and turn brown. Fortunately, the plant does not appear to suffer from its presence. Some varieties are more susceptible than others to azalea gall. Remove and destroy affected leaves. There are no chemical controls.
*Rhododendron lace bug damages azalea and rhododendron leaves in spring, summer and into the fall in mild seasons. Affected foliage is heavily mottled grayish white. Black or brown, shiny spots, the insect's excreta, are seen on the underside of leaves. When damage first appears, it may be possible to reduce the outbreak by hosing up under the foliage; otherwise, spray with horticultural soap, pyrethrins, pirimiphos-methyl, or permethrin as soon as the symptoms are seen.
*Thrips—brownish black and ⅛in long—suck sap from the leaves. The damage is similar to that of lace bug but the leaves may have a more silvery appearance. Control these pests by spraying with pirimiphos-methyl, malathion, or dimethoate. If the infestation is severe, in dry, warm weather when thrips multiply rapidly, you may need to repeat the dosage every three weeks.
*Two-spotted mite, commonly known as red spider mite, also sucks sap from the underside of leaves. Using a magnifying glass, it is possible to see the mites. Almost colorless, with two black spots on their backs, they are usually carrying clear, round eggs.
An attack is first noticed when leaves turn bronzy, tiny webs can be seen and minute creatures, with the aid of a hand lens, can be seen on the backs of leaves. Mites are more prevalent in hot, dry weather and more inclined to infest plants in sheltered spots, such as under eaves, than in open, airy situations. If the plants are not in flower when red spider mite invades, direct a hose up into the bush every couple of days to help reduce their numbers. Alternatively, spray with bifenthrin or horticultural soap.

PRUNING

Cutting flowers for a vase is usually all the pruning these plants need. But deadhead, too, to channel energy into new growth, by nipping out faded blooms when petals fall. Rejuvenate overgrown deciduous varieties by cutting back branches to within 2ft of the ground in March, before buds burst. Try and keep cuts moist to keep alive invisible buds around the stump edge. An easy way to achieve this, apart from splashing them with water, is to coat them with Christmas tree needle spray, which covers them with a plastic film that seals in moisture. If the bush is very old, prune back half the branches in the first year and the remainder the following year. Wayward stems may be cut back at any time.

ROSE
Rosa

A *sport of the famous "Peace" rose, "Chicago Peace" is a vibrant Large Flowered variety that forms a stocky bush to 4ft high.*

For sheltered, frost-free gardens, there are few more wonderful sights than the Cherokee rose (Rosa laevigata) *draping a sunny wall.*

FEATURES

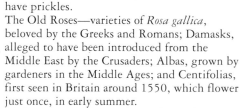

For over two millennia, roses have played an important role in garden design. However, it was not until the 19th century, from an amalgam of new developments—Hybrid Musk, Hybrid Perpetual, and Large Flowered (Hybrid Tea) roses—that modern varieties evolved. Since the late 1960s, there has been great interest in what are known as "English" roses. Bred by David Austin, they are varieties that combine the many-petalled form, lovely fragrance and full vigour of an old-fashioned rose with the wide color range and repeat-flowering qualities of a modern rose.

Roses are cherished for their form and colorful blooms, and many are very fragrant. They can be evergreen or deciduous, and most varieties have prickles.

The Old Roses—varieties of *Rosa gallica*, beloved by the Greeks and Romans; Damasks, alleged to have been introduced from the Middle East by the Crusaders; Albas, grown by gardeners in the Middle Ages; and Centifolias, first seen in Britain around 1550, which flower just once, in early summer.

Modern roses—Cluster Flowered (Floribunda), Large Flowered (Hybrid Tea) produce successive flushes of bloom. Flowers may be single, semi-double, or fully double, in a wide range of colors: white, cream, yellow, apricot, orange, every shade of pink, and red. There are bicolors, too, but a true blue rose has yet to be borne. Weed-suppressing and ideal for covering banks too steep to mow, the County Series of ground-hugging roses, such as blush-pink "Avon," gold, cerise, pink, and scarlet "Cambridgeshire" and pure white "Kent," color summer with repeat pulses of bloom. Ramblers, including coppery pink and richly scented "Albertine" flower only in midsummer. Climbers particularly modern varieties, such as "Golden Showers," salmon-pink "Compassion"

and honey-champagne "Penny Lane," have Hybrid Tea-like flowers and bloom repeatedly from June to October.

Some species, such as *R. moyesii*, produce brilliant red hips in fall and are planted specially for these, although the flowers are good too!

Uses Roses may be mass-planted in beds and borders or planted singly as sentinels. Large Flowered, Cluster Flowered and some other bush varieties are also grown as round-headed or weeping standards to flank a path or add height to a bed of roses. Thrusting through an obelisk strategically positioned in a shrub border, "Handel," a short, creamy-white and rose-pink climber, makes a riveting focal point.

Climbers and ramblers also associate strikingly with pink, red, blue, and white varieties of *Clematis viticella*, which are pruned to within 12in of the base in spring. Create a sensation by planting violet-blue C. "Etoile Violette" to entwine the climbing rose "Compassion," whose fragrant, double, light salmon-shaded, orange blooms stud strong, healthy shoots all summer.

Miniature and patio roses are ideal for planting in pots or tubs to decorate a patio or terrace. Very hardy varieties of *Rosa rugosa* are often used as hedges. Set a Large Flowered or Cluster Flowered variety *en masse* to illuminate a bed or border, or embrace a single bush with annuals, perennials, or bulbs.

CONDITIONS

Aspect The hardiness of roses is variable. Many tolerate extreme cold while others can be singed by frost.

To form stocky shoots and flower bounteously, roses need full sun all day. Good air circulation is important, too, but some shelter from strong wind is desirable to avoid flower damage.

Site These shrubs prefer heavy but well-drained,

Flowering profusely in early summer and sporadically thereafter, leggy "Felicia," a Hybrid Musk, is ideal for screening eyesores.

humus-rich loam. Improve light, sandy, gravelly, or chalky soils by adding large amounts of well-rotted manure or decomposed garden compost several few weeks before planting. Add garden lime to very acid soil.

GROWING METHOD

Feeding   Encourage lustrous leaves and fine, large blooms by feeding with a proprietary rose fertilizer, containing magnesium, in mid-April and early July.

Propagation   Vigorous Cluster Flowered varieties, most shrub roses and ramblers and climbers are easily increased from hardwood cuttings in September. The only way to multiply Large Flowered varieties is to implant a bud of the variety, in July, on to a rootstock.

Problems   *Aphids, which are sap suckers, may cover new growth quite thickly. Spray with pirimicarb, horticultural soap, permethrin, pirimiphos-methyl, or derris.
*Leaf-rolling sawfly damages roses from late spring to early summer. When females lay eggs on leaves, they inject a chemical into the leaf, which causes it to roll up and protect the eggs. Affected leaflets hang down. When caterpillars emerge, they feed on the leaves. Control with heptenophos with permethrin or pirimiphos-methyl.
*Black spot causes large black blotches to disfigure leaves. Collect and burn fallen leaves and avoid overhead watering. Some roses are less prone to this disease than others. Resistant Large Flowered varieties: "Alec's Red," "Alexander," "Blessings," "Champs Elysees," "Chicago Peace," "Honey Favorite."
Resistant Cluster Flowered varieties: "Allgold," "Arthur Bell," "City of Belfast," "City of Leeds," "Manx Queen," "The Queen Elizabeth," "Tip Top."
*Powdery mildew, worse in dry spots and where air circulates sluggishly, distorts leaves, stems, and flower buds and felts them with grayish-white patches.
Control it by opening up crowded areas, watering and liquid feeding every ten days, from spring to late summer, with a high-potash fertilizer to encourage robust growth. Also guard against infection by spraying fortnightly from spring to late summer, with triforine with bupirimate, penconazole, mancozeb, or copper with ammonium hydroxide.
*Rust is another fungus that is worse in areas of high rainfall. In early summer, bright orange spots appear on the upper leaf surface and corresponding, orange spore clusters disfigure the lower surface. In late summer, dark brown winter spore masses replace summer pustules. Badly infected leaves are shed prematurely. Control rust by pruning out and burning affected stems and spraying regularly with myclobutanil, penconazole, bupirimate with triforine or mancozeb.

PRUNING

Tackle pruning in early spring before buds burst. In fall, shorten extra long stems on bush roses to avoid them catching the wind and loosening the stem. Always cut to just above a bud.

After planting: Large Flowered and Cluster Flowered bush varieties: Shorten stems to within 6in of the base.
Shrub roses: No pruning necessary.
Ramblers: Cut back shoots to 12in from the ground.
Climbers: Shorten withered tips to healthy buds.

When established: Large Flowered and Cluster Flowered: Shorten main stems by half their length; side shoots to two buds.
Shrub roses: Cut back dead and dying shoots to healthy buds.
Ramblers: Most varieties are pruned in fall; cut out flowered stems and replace with current-year shoots.
Climbers: Shorten flowered side shoots to two or three buds.
Deadhead all roses weekly to channel energy into new shoots and more flowers.

ROSE AT A GLANCE		
Bushes, standards, weepers, carpeters, and climbers flower from spring to fall. Most roses are hardy to 3°F (zone 7).		
Jan	/	
Feb	/	Recommended Varieties
Mar	plant, prune	Large Flowered
Apr	plant, prune	"Alec's Red"
May	flower, plant	"Elizabeth Harkness"
Jun	flower, plant	English roses
July	flower, plant	"Graham Thomas"
Aug	flower, plant	Cluster Flowered
Sept	flower, plant	"English Miss"
Oct	flower, plant	Patio roses
Nov	plant	"Sweet Dream"
Dec	/	Climbers
		"Breath of life"

LEFT: A Large Flowered and upright grower to 4ft, richly scented "Double Delight" was introduced from America around 20 years ago. Its popularity has never waned.

RIGHT: Associating roses with other plants is an exciting challenge. Here this sumptuous Cluster Flowered variety is harmonising with Crambe cordifolia blossom.

BELOW: Because they absorb light, it is vital to plant scarlet and other deeply hued roses in a bright, sunny spot. In even, light shade, blooms tend to disappear on dull days.

RIGHT: Vigorous and healthy bush to 3ft, "Sunblest" is a profuse Large Flowered variety, the strong stems of which are topped with tightly formed buds that open to reveal unfading, bright yellow blooms.

Varieties

LEFT: *Though lacking the impact of semi- and fully double Large Flowered roses, single-flowered Polyantha varieties have innate charm and flower for months.*

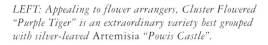

ABOVE: *"Bernina," a Cluster Flowered rose yet to come to Britain, was developed for and named after the Swiss sewing machine company. It bears a multitude of scented and perfectly formed flowers.*

LEFT: *Appealing to flower arrangers, Cluster Flowered "Purple Tiger" is an extraordinary variety best grouped with silver-leaved* Artemisia *"Powis Castle".*

RIGHT: *Bicolored roses have special appeal. When cutting these and other varieties, plunge them to their necks in a bucket of water for a day, before arranging them.*

FLOWERING CURRANT
Ribes

Blooming generously from April to May, sun-loving Ribes *"Pulborough Scarlet," a flowering currant, also performs in light shade.*

Trained against a warm wall and almost evergreen, the fuchsia-flowered currant (Ribes speciosum) *makes a fascinating feature.*

FEATURES

A deciduous family that heralds spring, the most popular kind—*Ribes sanguineum* "Pulborough Scarlet"—is very hardy. Growing to around 8ft high and 6ft across, its upright shoots are thickly sleeved with pendent clusters of deep red, tubular flowers. "White Icicle," another choice form of *R. sanguineum*, has drooping, creamy-white candelabra blooms, dramatic when embraced with purple-red *Bergenia* "Evening Glow." *Ribes sanguineum* "Brocklebankii," to 4ft, is illuminatingly different, rewarding us with a heartening display of golden leaves and pink flowers. All varieties of *R. sanguineum* can be planted to form a stocky, flowering boundary hedge.

Starry, yellow-flowered *R. odoratum*, to 6ft, has leaves that assume purple tints in fall, and less hardy *R. speciosum*, prized for its scarlet, fuchsia-like flowers on upright spiny shoots and best grown against a warm wall, are also generous performers.

CONDITIONS

Aspect Ribes is ideal for brightening a lightly shaded spot, but *R.* "Brocklebankii" must be shielded from hot sunlight otherwise its leaves will scorch. All, apart from slightly tender *R. speciosum*, prosper in exposed gardens. Make a statement by espalier training *R. speciosum* against a warm, sunny wall or set it to cascade from a pedestal pot.

Site Undemanding ribes thrives almost anywhere. Fortify sandy spots, which parch in summer, with bulky, moisture-conserving organics. If you plant this shrub on heavy clay, add gravel to improve drainage. Chalky soils can cause leaves to become chlorotic (yellowish green). Avoid this by adding acidifying fertilizer to lower the pH level.

GROWING METHOD

Feeding Provided the soil is reasonably fertile, a single application of bone meal in the fall is all that is necessary. After planting, no matter how damp the ground, water well to settle soil around the roots.

Propagation Take hardwood cuttings in late fall.

Problems This genus is prone to coral spot fungus. Causing a rash of coral-pink or orange pustules that kills shoots, it should be controlled by cutting out and burning infected plant tissue. Remove crowded shoots to improve air flow.

PRUNING

Keep ribes youthful, shapely and flowering freely by shortening a third of older shoots to new growth or near ground level when blooms fade. Remove crowding branches and cut back diseased stems to healthy wood in spring.

FLOWERING CURRANT AT A GLANCE

Deciduous bush festooned with clusters of flowers from late March to mid-May. Hardiness rating according to species.

Month	Activity	Recommended Varieties
Jan	/	*R. odoratum*
Feb	/	
Mar	flower, plant	*R. sanguineum* "Brocklebankii"
Apr	flower, plant	
May	flower, plant	*R. sanguineum* "Icicle"
Jun	plant, prune	*R. sanguineum* "Porky Pink"
July	plant	
Aug	plant	*R. sanguineum* "Pulborough Scarlet"
Sept	plant	
Oct	/	*R. speciosum*
Nov	/	
Dec	/	

ROSEMARY
Rosmarinus

An aromatic shrub and herb, rosemary embellishes a bed, border or patio tub with spires of blue, pink, or white flowers in mid-spring.

Exploit the beauty of prostrate varieties by planting them to soften a hard corner or spill over a retaining wall.

FEATURES

Grown for its aromatic, evergreen foliage, *Rosmarinus officinalis*—there is only one species—embraces varieties with hooded, blue, pale violet, pink, or white flowers in April and May. There are upright kinds to 6ft and compact, ground-covering forms to 2ft across. Rosemary also makes a fetching, informal hedge. Plant it to enhance a mixed shrub and perennial border, or in patio pots. If possible, position it where you will brush against it and detect its pleasing aroma. It is long-lived, matures within 3–5 years and flowers early in life. Rosemary, also a culinary herb, symbolises remembrance, love, and fidelity.

CONDITIONS

Aspect	Rosemary, which must have full sun to develop stocky, free-flowering shoots, prospers in exposed inland and coastal gardens.
Site	Preferring well-drained, poor, sandy, or gravelly soils, it abhors heavy clay.

GROWING METHOD

Feeding	Apart from working bone meal into the planting hole, no further fertilizer is usually necessary to ensure that rosemary flourishes.
Propagation	This shrub is easily increased from semi-ripe cuttings taken from mid- to late summer.
Problems	It is seldom attacked by pests and diseases, but its roots are liable to rot in soggy clay.

PRUNING

Upright varieties and hedges:	Keep plants compact and full of young growth by trimming them fairly hard with shears when flowers fade in late spring.
Carpeters:	Prune unwanted shoots in spring.

ROSEMARY AT A GLANCE

A hardy, small-leaved, aromatic, upright, or carpeting evergreen, with usually blue, spring flowers. Hardy to 14°F (zone 8).

Month	Activity	Recommended Varieties
Jan	/	
Feb	/	"Aureus"
Mar	/	"Benenden Blue"
Apr	flower, plant	"Corsicus Prostratus"
May	flower, plant	"Miss Jessopp's Upright"
Jun	prune, plant	Prostratus Group
July	plant	"Tuscan Blue"
Aug	plant	
Sept	plant	
Oct	/	
Nov	/	
Dec	/	

COTTON LAVENDER
Santolina

Effectively mantling and silvering this border edge, the dwarf form of cotton lavender, Santolina chamaecyparissus nana, *is a hardy evergreen.*

An arresting succession of lemon-yellow flowers clothe Santolina rosmarinifolia's *feathery, deep green stems from June to August.*

FEATURES

Mound forming, evergreen and ideal for making a low hedge to divide a lawn from a path or to segregate open-plan gardens, cotton lavender is prized for its aromatic, feathery, silvery-white, or gray foliage. There is also a green-leaved form.

If cotton lavender is left to mature, a wealth of button-like, yellow flowers appear from June to August. Flowers, however, tend to spoil its symmetry and give it a ragged look. If you prefer foliage to blooms, prune bushes hard each year.

It is a tough shrub and unaffected by salty winds, so makes a good seaside plant. It also has few enemies.

Widely planted *Santolina chamecyparissus*, grows to around 18in high and 30in across and is favoured for hedging or punctuating a border. Its dwarf form, *nana*, just 12in high, is fetching for edging a border or highlighting a rock garden.

Even whiter and more feathery is *S. pinnata neopolitana*, to 32in high.

Equally decorative but with thread-like, green leaves, *S. rosmarinifolia* (*virens*) is massed with long-stemmed, yellow flowers in summer.

CONDITIONS

Aspect
Santolina is very hardy and braves low temperatures. Provided you set plants in full sun, where silvery-white-leaved varieties develop full radiance, they will excel for you. The green-leaved species tolerates light shade.

Site
This shrub performs zestfully on sandy loam but abhors heavy clay, which becomes soggy and airless in winter. If you are stuck with heavy clay, drain it by working in grit and channelling a gravel-lined drainage trench to a soakaway.

GROWING METHOD

Feeding
There is little need to be diligent with feeding, for cotton lavender prospers on thin and nutrient-sparse soils. However, lush growth will please you if in spring and fall you work a dressing of bone meal into the root area.

Propagation
Increase your favorites from semi-ripe cuttings taken from early to mid-fall and rooted in a garden frame or multiply plants from hardwood cuttings in late fall.

Problems
Normally trouble free.

PRUNING

Shear off faded blooms in late August. Periodically—every 3 years or so when lower shoots are becoming woody—shorten stems to 6in from the base to stimulate new basal growth.

COTTON LAVENDER AT A GLANCE

Evergreen bush with ferny or thread-like leaves and yellow, "button" flowers from June to August. Hardy to 14°F (zone 8).

Month	Activity	Recommended Varieties
Jan	/	
Feb	/	*S. chamaecyparissus*
Mar	/	*S. chamaecyparissus nana*
Apr	plant, prune	*S. pinnata neopolitana*
May	plant, prune	*S. virens*
Jun	flower, plant	
July	flower, plant	
Aug	flower, plant	
Sept	flower, plant	
Oct	/	
Nov	/	
Dec	/	

CHRISTMAS BOX
Sarcococca

Vanilla scent from the tiny flowers of Sarcococca hookeriana *"Digyna," a suckering evergreen to 6ft, can waft for yards.*

Glossy leaved and smothered with scented, white blooms in winter, undemanding Sarcococca confusa *thrives in light shade.*

FEATURES

An easy, suckering, lance- or oval-leaved evergreen, sarcococca is a delight in February when tufted flowers of white or creamy male petals and smaller female blooms sleeve stems and release rich vanilla fragrance.

On a warm, breezy day, scent is detectable many yards from the bush. If you plant a group of it beneath a living-room window, the perfume will waft indoors. Cut blooms will scent a room.

Carpeting thickly and suppressing weeds, *Sarcococca hookeriana* forms a 12in high thicket, 3ft across. *Digyna*, a form of *S. hookeriana*, has purple-tinged leaves and thrusts to 4ft. Its flowers are followed by black berries. Resembling privet, *S. confusa* is a neater version, to 2.5ft. Appealingly different, *S. ruscifolia* forms a rugged bush of broader leaves, to 3ft high and across, and blooms are followed by red berries.

CONDITIONS

Aspect Ideal for clothing dappled shady areas beneath trees or borders on the north side of a wall or fence and between houses, it prospers in full sun, too. Avoid deeply shaded sites where growth is less compact and flowering inhibited.

Site Sarcococca favours deep, humus- and nutrient-rich, acid or alkaline soils that drain freely. Improve poor, sandy patches by working in bulky organic manure. Lighten and aerate heavy clay by digging in some grit or pea shingle.

Plant it in a large tub or pot to perfume a patio or terrace in mild spells during winter. Alternatively, set it to flank a path or driveway where you will brush against it and enjoy its "clean," rich scent.

GROWING METHOD

Feeding Encourage robust growth by working bone meal into the planting hole and pricking it into the root area in spring and fall. Help young plants establish quickly by watering copiously after planting and in dry spells in their first year.

Propagation Increase your stock by using a spade to slice off rooted suckers in spring or take semi-ripe cuttings of new shoots in midsummer.

Problems Small, young plants may take several months to settle down and grow enthusiastically. Encourage them to develop quickly by liquid feeding fortnightly with a high-nitrogen fertilizer in spring and summer.

PRUNING

No regular cutting back is necessary. Remove dead or damaged shoots in spring.

CHRISTMAS BOX AT A GLANCE

White-flowered and sweetly scented, bushy or carpeting evergreen for sunny or lightly shaded places. Hardy to 4°F (zone 7).

Month		Recommended Varieties
Jan	/	
Feb	flower	*S. confusa*
Mar	plant	*S. hookeriana digyna*
Apr	plant, prune	*S. hookeriana humilis*
May	plant	*S. ruscifolia*
Jun	/	
July	/	
Aug	plant	
Sept	plant	
Oct	/	
Nov	/	
Dec	/	

SPIRAEA
Spiraea

Transforming mid-spring with a fountain of snowy blossom on arching stems to 6ft, bridal wreath (Spiraea arguta) *is magnificent.*

Unusually, late summer-flowering Spiraea *"Shirobana" yields a mix of mushroom-headed, white and rose-purple flowers.*

FEATURES

An easy and floriferous family of deciduous shrubs, 18in–8ft high, spiraea rewards us with cone- or dome-shaped blooms on upright shoots or on pendulous or arching stems. There are two groups: spring flowering and summer flowering.

The finest early performers, from March to May, are epitomised by the aptly named bridal wreath (*Spiraea arguta*). Its arching stems, to 6ft, are so thickly enveloped with snowy blossom that its leaves are concealed.

Most popular summer-flowering members are forms of *S. japonica*: "Anthony Waterer," aglow with domes of carmine-pink flowers amid pink or cream-tinged leaves; and "Goldflame," prized for its dark pink flowers and radiant golden-orange leaves in spring. Another kind, *S. billiardii* "Triumphans," is ablaze with rose-purple flower cones in July and August.

Plant spiraea to punctuate a border, carpet a rock garden pocket, adorn a patio tub, or screen out an ugly view.

CONDITIONS

Aspect Very hardy, these shrubs prefer full sun in which stocky shoots flower well and colored-leaved varieties develop vivid hues.

Site They also thrive in a wide range of well-drained soils but dislike dry or very alkaline conditions. Improve sandy patches by digging in plenty of rotted organic matter.

GROWING METHOD

Feeding Encourage robust growth by gently working bone meal into the root area in spring and fall. Help new plants recover quickly from transplanting by watering liberally and mulching in dry spells in spring and summer.

Propagation Take soft-tip cuttings in early summer; semi-ripe cuttings from mid- to late summer; or hardwood cuttings in fall. Some varieties can be divided or increased from suckers in early spring.

Problems Control sap-sucking aphids, which colonize soft shoot tips, by spraying with pirimicarb, derris, or horticultural soap.

PRUNING

Spring- and summer-flowering kinds that flower on older shoots: Cut out from the base one older stem in three when blooms fade. Summer-flowering varieties that bloom on the current-year shoots: Shorten all stems to 4in from the base from early to mid-spring. Rejuvenate tall, old, woody varieties making little new growth by cutting all shoots to within 12in of the base in early spring.

SPIRAEA AT A GLANCE

Spring- or summer-flowering shrubs with white, pink, or purple-rose blooms. Some have orange foliage. Hardy to -13°F (zone 8).

Month	Activity	Recommended Varieties
Jan	/	
Feb	/	**Spring flowering**
Mar	plant, flower	*S. arguta*
Apr	plant, flower	*S. thunbergii*
May	flower, prune	"Snowmound"
Jun	flower, prune	**Summer flowering**
July	flower, prune	"Anthony Waterer"
Aug	flower, prune	*S. × billiardii*
Sept	flower, prune	"Gold Mound"
Oct	plant	"Little Princess"
Nov	plant	"Triumphans"
Dec	/	

LILAC
Syringa

Fragrant trusses of lilac blossom are a spring highlight. Syringa vulgaris *varieties bloom best in an open, sunny position.*

Cottage-garden pleasure: this white "Mme Lemoine" lilac has been skillfully pruned to form a globe of blossom in mid-May.

FEATURES

A vast and fragrant, deciduous family from S.E. Europe to E. Asia, its cone or plume-like flowers light up May and June. Most popular are varieties of *Syringa vulgaris*. Enchanting, double-flowered forms are mauve-pink "Belle de Nancy," dark purple "Charles Joly," and violet-red "Paul Hariot". Captivating singles include white "Maud Notcutt" and creamy-yellow "Primrose". All make upright focal points to 8–10ft.

The Canadian Hybrids—rose-hued "Bellicent" and pale lilac "Elinor"—tolerate shade better than *S. vulgaris* and bear plumy blossom. Accommodating dwarf varieties, to 4ft, for small gardens or rockeries, are lilac-pink *S. meyeri* "Palibin" and *S. pubescens* "Superba".

LILAC AT A GLANCE

Perfumed, cone- or plume-shaped blooms in many shades appear in spring. Hardiness rating according to species.

		Recommended Varieties
Jan	/	
Feb	/	*S. pubescens* "Miss Kim"
Mar	plant	*S. pubescens* "Superba"
Apr	plant	*S. vulgaris* "Belle de Nancy"
May	flower, plant	
Jun	flower, plant	*S. vulgaris* "Charles Joly"
July	plant	*S. vulgaris* "Mme Lemoine"
Aug	plant	
Sept	plant	*S. vulgaris* "Mrs Edward Harding"
Oct	plant	*S. vulgaris* "Primrose"
Nov	plant, prune	*S. × prestoniae* "Elinor"
Dec	prune	

CONDITIONS

Aspect Lilac flowers best in full sun but tolerates light shade. Choose an open site, protected from strong, drying winds, where air circulates freely, to reduce risk of leaves becoming mildewed.

Site These shrubs need well-drained, organically rich soil. Avoid chalky spots, which may cause lime-induced chlorosis, when leaves turn creamy yellow and die.

GROWING METHOD

Feeding Apply a complete plant food, such as Growmore or fish, blood, and bone meal in spring and midsummer.

Propagation Commercially, varieties are usually budded or grafted on to privet rootstock. Alternatively, take soft-tip cuttings in early summer or semi-ripe cuttings from mid- to late summer.

Problems Lilac blight, characterised by angular, brown spots, destroys leaves and buds. There are no chemical controls, so cut back affected shoots to healthy, white tissue and burn prunings. When mildew strikes, leaves are felted with powdery white mold. Improve air flow by thinning crowded shoots and spraying with carbendazim, mancozeb, or sulfur when symptoms appear.

PRUNING

Cut out spent flowers when petals fade. Keep bushes youthful and blooming freely by pruning out a quarter of the older shoots each year in winter. Remove basal suckers.

VIBURNUM
Viburnum

Horizontally-tiered Viburnum plicatum *"Mariesii" displays its large, lacy, sterile blossoms embracing small, fertile flowers in spring.*

A spring star is Viburnum x burkwoodii, *whose multitude of orb-shaped, pinkish-white blooms spill rich vanilla scent into the air.*

FEATURES

Coveted for their blossom, berries, foliage and architectural habit, deciduous and evergreen viburnums have year-round appeal. Flowers—clusters, globes, and sprays—in pink or white, thickly clothe shoots. Most varieties are sweetly perfumed. Growing 30in–10ft or more, most species and varieties bloom within three years of planting. All make fetching statements: such as evergreen *Viburnum tinus*, which also makes a dense, winter-flowering hedge; carpeting *V. davidii*, whose female plants are studded with turquoise-blue berries; *V carlesii*, studded with vanilla-scented, whitish-pink orbs in spring; and *V. × bodnantense* "Dawn," clustered with rose-pink flowers from October to March.

VIBURNUM AT A GLANCE

Light up winter to summer with showy flowers and fall with spectacular, scarlet berries. Hardiness according to species.

Jan	flower	Recommended Varieties
Feb	flower	
Mar	plant, flower	Winter flowering
Apr	flower, prune	"Dawn"
May	flower, plant	"Deben"
Jun	flower, plant	*V. × bodnantense*
July	plant, prune	Spring flowering
Aug	plant	*V. carlesii* "Aurora"
Sept	plant	*V. × carlcephalum*
Oct	plant	*V. × opulus* "Roseum"
Nov	plant	Fall berrying
Dec	/	*V. betulifolium*
		V. davidii

CONDITIONS

Aspect   Viburnums need at least half a day's full sunshine to prosper. Shield large-flowering varieties from cold wind.

Site   These shrubs prefer well-drained soil enriched with well-rotted organic matter several weeks before planting.
In light soils that parch quickly, mulch in spring with moisture-conserving, bulky organics to keep roots cool and active.

GROWING METHOD

Feeding   Nourish growth by applying a balanced fertilizer, such as Growmore, chicken pellets, or fish, blood, and bone meal, in spring and midsummer. In a cold spring, boost growth of young plants by foliar feeding fortnightly with a high-potash fertilizer.
Water frequently newly planted viburnums in warm, dry weather.

Propagation   Take soft-tip cuttings in spring; semi-ripe cuttings from mid- to late summer; and hardwood cuttings in late fall. Layer shoots from mid-spring to late summer.

Problems   Tackle viburnum beetle, which shreds leaves in summer, by spraying in late spring with permethrin, bifenthrin, or pyrethrum.

PRUNING

V. tinus: Trim shoots lightly in early spring. Deciduous, winter-flowering species: Remove one stem in three every 2–3 years in spring. Evergreens: Cut out one stem in three, in midsummer, every four years.

WEIGELA
Weigela

Weigela florida *"Variegata" brightens late spring with a generous confection of pinkish blossom on year-old shoots.*

Compact and low growing, so ideal for small gardens, Weigela *'Rumba's shoots are thickly sleeved with radiant blooms.*

FEATURES

Flowering unstintingly from May to June, weigela is a reliable, hardy, deciduous shrub. Growing 4–6ft high and across, there are two main divisions: varieties of *Weigela florida* and a range of hybrids.

Two of the showiest forms of *W. florida* are dark purple-leaved and rose-pink-flowered "Foliis Purpureis" and widely grown "Variegata," whose green-and-yellow foliage complements pale pink blooms.

Appealing hybrids include "Briant Rubidor," where golden-yellow to green leaves combine pleasingly with a wealth of vibrant, ruby-red flowers. Very different is *W.* "Looymansii Aurea," which must be grown in light shade or its leaves, bright gold in spring, will scorch.

CONDITIONS

Aspect	Most varieties flower best if planted in full sun. Shield them from strong wind, too, which can damage flowers and "burn" soft, new leaves.
Site	Encourage vigorous growth by setting plants in well-drained soil, including chalk, enriched with plenty of well-decayed manure.

GROWING METHOD

Feeding	Boost sturdy shoots sleeved with blossom by topdressing the root area with bone meal in spring and fall and mulching in spring.
Propagation	Take soft-tip cuttings in early summer; semi-ripe cuttings from mid- to late summer; and hardwood cuttings in the fall.
Problems	Pale green capsid bugs, about ¼in long, suck sap from shoot tips and secrete a toxin that kills cells. When leaves unfold, damaged areas become ragged holes. Control by spraying with pirimiphos-methyl or fenitrothion when symptoms seen.

PRUNING

Keep bushes young and packed with blossom by removing from the base one in three of the oldest flowering stems when blooms turn fade.

WEIGELA AT A GLANCE

Bushy shrubs bearing trumpet-shaped, white, pink, red, or purple-red blooms from May to June. Hardy to -13°F (zone 5).

Jan	/	Recommended Varieties
Feb	/	"Abel Carriere"
Mar	plant	"Briant Rubidor"
Apr	plant	"Carnival"
May	flower, plant	"Foliis Purpureis"
Jun	flower, plant	*W. middendorffiana*
July	prune, plant	"Newport Red"
Aug	plant	"Rumba"
Sept	plant	"Variegata"
Oct	plant	
Nov	plant	
Dec	/	

Growing Cacti

GROWING CACTI

*Although they are part of the large family of succulents,
cacti are unlike any other group of plants. With
distinguishing features such as ribbed surfaces, waxy
coating and, of course, their spines, cacti deserve a
special place in any creative display, invariably being
grown in pots and used as focal points that
are easily admired.*

Cacti are magnificent plants giving architectural shapes of all kinds
from tiny round balls to enormous tree-like growths, the kind of thing
you see in cowboy films, and often superb flowers. In many cases the
flowers only open at night, and can be wonderfully scented. Cacti need
to be grown in pots, at least in winter, when the amount of drinking
water they are given is strictly controlled. Too much is inevitably
fatal. If they are not too heavy, pot-grown plants can be moved outside
in summer, making the focal point in a bed of architectural plants.
They can even be taken out of their pots, and placed in, for example, a
special gravel bed, where there is excellent drainage. Alternatively,
they can be grown in a special display bed in a large conservatory or
greenhouse. Take care though not to confuse epiphytic cacti with the
desert kind. The former tend to grow high up in trees, under the leafy
canopy, in shady conditions. The latter demand day-long bright light.

KEY TO AT A GLANCE TABLES

PLANTING

FLOWERING

At a glance charts are your quick guide.
For full information, consult the accompanying text.

---

*LEFT: A fine collection of well-grown cacti shows some of the extensive range of these
fascinating plants. Variations in shapes and heights of the rounded barrel types with
the vertical column cactus adds interest to the display.*

GROWING CACTI

What is a cactus? What is a succulent?

A cactus is a succulent plant—but not all succulent plants are cacti. Succulent plants are xerophytes, plants able to escape or endure prolonged drought conditions. Succulents have the capacity to store water in swollen stems and roots, while some withdraw into the soil or shed their foliage in times of stress. Although succulent plants and cacti do share some characteristics, cacti have certain features that distinguish them from other plant families, including other forms of succulent plants.

FEATURES OF CACTI

Plant structure

Cacti are mainly round or cylindrical in shape, with a ribbed surface that allows for shrinkage as water is lost from the plant. The ribbed edges of cactus plants expose less surface area to the sun, which helps to reduce moisture loss. Waxy coatings on their outer surfaces also cut down moisture loss in extreme heat. Cacti have sharp, sometimes horny spines that deter animals from grazing and also provide some shade for the body of the plant. Cactus spines are in fact modified

GOLDEN BARREL CACTI dominate this carefully planned landscape of cactuses and succulents. These plants are growing in raised beds to ensure that they have perfect drainage.

leaves that have evolved to cut down moisture loss in the usually dry conditions of their native environment. There is a considerable range of spine types and sizes.

In cacti the breathing pores (stomates) enabling gas exchange between the plant and the atmosphere are located deep inside the plant walls and tend to be less numerous than those of many other plants. These stomates generally open only at night, avoiding water evaporation in the heat of the day. All cacti possess areoles, which are small woolly cushions from which emerge the spines and flower buds. These are found on top of warty protrusions known as tubercles. Many cacti have jointed parts that can be shed from the plant; these strike roots as they touch the ground and so aid in the distribution and continuity of the species.

Flowers

Cactus flowers are like jewels, glorious and showy, but they are also very short lived. Many last only one or two days while others are nocturnal, opening in the middle of the night and fading before dawn. The flowers have a silky or satiny texture and come in all colors except a true blue, although violet and purple are well represented. Many cacti have flowers in shades of pink, red, or yellow. After the flowers have been pollinated, brightly colored fruits form—these are usually red and very long lasting. In their native habitats, many cacti are pollinated by birds, especially humming-birds, while the night-flowering types are pollinated by moths, bats, or other nocturnal creatures.

Types of cacti

Cacti are roughly grouped into three types: round or barrel cacti such as the golden barrel (*Echinocactus* species) and *Mammillaria* species; elongated cacti such as column cactus (*Cereus* species) and silver torch (*Cleistocactus* species); and jointed cacti such as *Opuntia* species and crab cactus (*Schlumbergera* species).

The cristate or crested cacti are the result of mutations that cause the growing tip of a shoot to broaden out into a band, forming strange, tortuous shapes. These mutations may be due to genetic changes or they may be due to the plant suffering unusual stress.

Native habitat

True cacti, almost without exception, are native to the Americas. Although not all cacti have their origins in real deserts, the greatest number of species occur in the low rainfall areas of the south-western United States and Mexico.

Cacti in these regions of desert plains endure scorching heat by day and often freezing nights. Sporadic rainfall of generally less than 10in per annum allows the plants to store just enough water to survive. Heavy dews and the occasional snowfall augment the water supply. Snow insulates plants against cold and, when it melts, the water is directed to the plant roots.

The next largest group of species originates in the dry areas of central and eastern Brazil. Some cacti come from quite high elevations where conditions are still very harsh, but where the daytime temperatures do not reach the extremes of the true deserts.

On rocky slopes of mountains and high plateaus, the soil is often poor and the water drains away rapidly. Plants are exposed to intense sunlight and freezing night temperatures, high wind and often snow. Small cacti find a foothold among rocks and crevices that hold just enough water for survival while affording some shelter from wind. Many cacti from these habitats have dense woolly spines that provide protection from both searing sun and intense cold. Lower down the slope, large column cacti branching from heavy bases start to be seen. These and the large barrel types are able to withstand exposure to very strong winds.

A few species of cactus such as *Epiphyllum* and *Schlumbergera* are native to humid jungle environments where they grow as epiphytes on trees and sometimes on rocks. Although adapted to low light, they can also tolerate dry seasons. Some remain high in the tree canopy where there is more light while others start lower down, scrambling up as they grow towards the light.

Human use

A number of cacti have long been used by humans as food and in medicines. The fruit of some species is eaten fresh, cooked, or dried. Indian fig (*Opuntia ficus-indica*) is probably the best known of these edible cacti, but the fruits of some of the hedgehog cacti (*Echinocereus* species) and the tiny fruits of some *Mammillaria* species are also considered delicacies. In Mexico, the aromatic fruits of *Ferocactus wislizenii* are stewed, candied, and made into sweets, giving this species the common name of candy cactus. However, it is not recommended that you taste any part of a cactus unless you are certain that it is an Indian fig or another known edible variety. Many cacti contain alkaloids, which can be extremely damaging to health. On the other hand, heart-stimulant drugs are made from species of the cactus *Selenicereus*, which is widely cultivated both in the United States and Europe for this purpose.

Growing cacti under glass

It is very hard trying to group cacti with other plants; somehow they never look right. They are generally best arranged together, possibly with some excellent succulents. Fortunately, cacti come in such a wide range of shapes, from tiny quirky balls to grand theatrical vertical pillars, that you can always create a lively, contrasting mix.

The best displays of cacti are invariably in a large glasshouse where you can create a small scene from say South America. This gives you the space to plant the cacti reasonably well apart so that they can be seen from all angles, and with space to the front so that you are not endangered when they have got sharp, vicious spines. The cactus' shape is often so striking that its poor flowers seem unimportant.

Generally speaking, a dry environment must be provided, especially in winter, with bright light and excellent drainage. But when buying a cactus do try and find out where it comes from, so that you can provide the correct growing conditions. Unless you are very lucky, that almost certainly means growing them under glass, indoors or in a conservatory, where you can manufacture their special needs. And these needs mean either replicating desert or jungle conditions.

Established desert cacti grown in pots need three parts John Innes No. 2 with one part grit, well mixed together giving an open, free-draining soil. In summer they need watering (letting them dry out between each drink) and feeding as much as any thriving plant. Use special cactus feed or tomato fertilizer to encourage flowering. Over winter keep the plants dormant at about 45°F, only occasionally watering to prevent them from completely drying out and shrivelling. In fact over-watering is the commonest cause of death. When in doubt, do not water. Good light does though remain essential.

Strangely enough, some cacti prefer steamy, jungle-like conditions, which are harder to provide. Such cacti tend to be epiphytes which grow high in the branches of trees, not exposed in the open ground. You can still grow them in pots but you must provide a winter temperature nearly 50°F higher than that for the desert kind, with year-round

A PROFUSION of clear yellow flowers conceals the whole top of this Trichocereus huascha *(previously called* Echinopsis*).*

TERRACOTTA POTS make ideal containers for growing cacti and succulents. Displayed at different levels, all plants can be easily seen.

humidity. The key to success remains open, free-draining compost, and in summer constant shade from strong sunlight (in the wild they would grow well protected by the tree canopy). A summer feed will boost the show of flowers.

Growing high up, these cacti tend to send out tumbling, trailing stems and they make good ingredients for a hanging basket. The Christmas cactus (see page 484) is an astonishing sight in full flower, especially when it is a flashy scarlet. Most people grow it as a pot plant on a table, and though fine, it is never as good a spectacle as when seen from below.

GROWING CACTI IN CONTAINERS

Cacti are easy-care potted plants and can be grown as single specimens or combined in shallow bowls to make a miniature cactus garden. Miniature cactus gardens can be of great interest. You could feature a mixture of several small-growing species or you may want to display a single fine, clustering plant that has been increasing over the years. Cacti are ideal for growing on balconies or patios as they do not mind drying out and appreciate shelter from the rain.

Cactus plants definitely look most attractive when grown in terracotta pots or glazed ceramic pots; in the glazed pot range, the ones decorated in blues and greens seem to suit the cactus best. When you are choosing a pot for an individual specimen, try to find one that is not much larger than the plant's rootball.

HANDLING A CACTUS USING FOLDED PAPER

WHEN HANDLING CACTI, use a band of cardboard or folded paper held firmly around the cactus to avoid the spines.

Cacti grown in containers must be potted into a very sharp-draining mix. For a small number of pots, it may be best to purchase a cactus mix from your local nursery. If you are potting a large number of plants or filling large pots, it will probably be more economical to buy the mix in bulk (if possible), or to buy the ingredients for making your own mix: this should include bags of special horticultural sand or grit (avoid builder's sand) and John Innes No. 2. Though you may think that desert cacti in particular grow in sand alone, that is not true. They need rather more soil than added drainage material. A ratio of three parts of soil to one of grit is fine.

Pots can be displayed on purpose-built stands, on pedestals, or on the ground. Pots to be put on the ground should not be in direct contact with the soil and must be elevated very slightly to allow air to circulate under the pot base. You can purchase "pot feet" or simply use pieces of broken terracotta or stone to elevate your pot.

Potted cacti team well with Mexican and Mediterranean style decor, for example, black wrought-iron furniture or rustic unpainted timber pieces. You could extend this decorating idea by adding some feature wall tiles.

Growing cacti outdoors in summer

Like most pot plants, cacti like to stand outside during the summer. Alternatively, they can be tapped out of the pot and planted in a special bed which is very free draining. This guarantees them excellent light levels while they are in full growth and ensures that they have plenty of fresh air. It also avoids the danger of baking in an inadequately ventilated or poorly shaded glasshouse. The chances of being attacked by greenhouse pests is also reduced. Overall, a spell outside gives healthier, sturdier plants.

What is more, creating a special group of cacti in a gravel garden which sets off their shapes, or on a rockery, adds style and interest to your garden. If you are growing the taller, column cacti try moving them outside before they become too big and then experiment with uplighting them at night. In a bare, minimalist garden they make quite an impact. It is absolutely essential to keep all spiny cacti well away from sites where children play.

HANDLING CACTI

To avoid injury from the spines when handling a cactus, use a band made of cardboard or folded newspaper. Place the band around the plant to steady it and hold firmly where the two pieces come together. This should prevent your hands from coming into contact with the spines and should not damage the cactus. You should, of course, also wear sturdy gloves. When handling larger specimens of cactus plants, you may need another person to help you. In this case, you should each use a paper band, or wooden or plastic tongs such as kitchen tongs, to lift and move the cactus. It is a difficult, heavy job to move large cactus plants but careful planning before planting—deciding on the new, permanent location of your cactus and preparing the planting hole—should help you to avoid problems in the future.

WATERING

It is important to remember that at any time of the year, cacti should only be watered when the soil or potting mix has dried out completely. Withholding water from plants may result in slower growth, but this is better than killing the plants through

RICHLY COLORED SILKY FLOWERS on a cactus can look greatly at odds with the spines. In fact the flowers are often short-lived, though flowering reliably occurs each year. Two of the most reliable flowering kind are Rebutia and Mammillaria species.

watering too much or too often. Plants watered too often while they are dormant and unable to use or store water will rot and die. Large plants, because of their greater ability to store water, will need watering much less often than smaller plants. Potted plants will need watering more often than plants in the ground, especially during warmer weather, and the larger the container the less often it will need watering.

Until you feel confident about the frequency of watering needed, it is a good idea to dig into the soil or growing mix with a stick, a pencil or a thin bamboo stake to check the degree of dryness. In small pots, up to 4in diameter, the top 1–2in must be dry before more water is applied. In a 8in pot, the soil should be dry at a depth of 3in or more. Plants that have just been repotted should not be watered for at least a week afterwards. With any cactus, enough water should be applied at any one watering to thoroughly saturate the soil or mix. The frequency of watering will, of course, depend on the weather. If it is very hot and windy, plants will dry out much faster than they would in either warm, calm weather or cold conditions. In cold weather, plants may need watering only every 4–6 weeks or even less often, while in very hot weather they may need watering every few days.

Overhead watering will not hurt the cacti as it also washes dust off their surfaces, but do not do this late in the day, especially in humid districts, as water remaining on the plant overnight may predispose it to rotting. (You should note that some succulents should not be watered this way because of the waxy bloom on their foliage.) Alternatively, you should simply water the soil surface using a watering can or sit the whole pot in a container of water and allow the moisture to be drawn up from below. If available, rainwater is ideal for cacti. Cacti do not like alkaline water, so if your water supply is known to be alkaline, it may be worth collecting rainwater.

FERTILIZING

The most convenient method of fertilizing cacti is to use granular, slow-release fertilizers. A formulation containing trace elements, but low in nitrogen, is ideal. These fertilizers should be applied in spring to feed the plants slowly throughout their growing season. Follow the label directions and do not exceed the recommended amount. Feeding when plants are dormant may damage them and is a waste of fertilizer, which only starts to be released once soil temperatures rise. In the garden, you can use pelleted poultry manure as an alternative, but do not be too heavy handed.

PROPAGATION

Growing from seed

Seed is best sown in spring. Cactus seed should be sprinkled or placed on the surface of a seed-raising mix and lightly covered with the mix. You can mix very small seeds with fine sand for a more even sowing or put the seeds in a cone of paper from which you can gently shake them. Seed may germinate in a few days or a few weeks depending on the species. Keep the growing mix damp, but not soggy, by standing the pot in a container of water to draw up moisture, and then drain off any excess water from the seed-raising pot. Overhead watering will dislodge the seed. Once the seed has germinated, it may be several months before the seedlings are large enough to handle and pot up individually.

Although many home-grown cactus will not set viable seed because of the lack of suitable pollinators, it is possible to hand pollinate sometimes with good results. Use a small paintbrush to collect the pollen from one flower then gently

PROPAGATING BY CUTTINGS

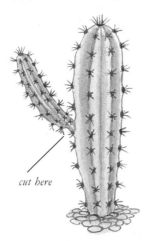

1. TAKE CACTUS cuttings by cleanly removing an offshoot from the parent plant.

cut here

2. THE BASE of the cutting should be slanted towards the central core of the stem. Dry the cutting for a few days before planting.

3. ROOTS are formed at the center stem core. The amount of time taken to form roots varies with the species of cactus and the season of the year.

dust this into the center of another flower. Pollen should go on to the stigma which is the organ in the center of the flower surrounded by numerous pollen-bearing stamens.

It is fairly easy to collect seed from cacti with fleshy fruits. Once the fruit is fully colored and ripe, pick off the fruit, slit open and squeeze out the seeds which should be cleaned and dried before sowing. It is more difficult to obtain the seed of cacti which normally shed their seed as the fruits dry and split. As the fruit is nearing maturity, a paper or mesh bag can be tied around the fruit to catch the seeds as they are dispersed from the maturing fruit.

Growing from cuttings

Some cacti form numerous offsets, which you can remove and pot up separately to start a new plant. Cut away any offsets from the parent plant by pushing a sharp knife down into the soil to sever any underground joints.

Some cacti can be propagated from cuttings of the plant, which must be taken with a very sharp, clean knife or pruning shears. You should take cactus cuttings in spring, as the new growth begins. The cuttings or offsets with wounds must be allowed to dry for a few days, or a few weeks if necessary, until the cut area is completely dry and callused over. Cuttings can be taken from side shoots or even the head of the main stem. Slant the cut towards the core of the stem and allow the cutting to dry; this should encourage roots to develop from the stem core. When the cuttings have dried, insert them into very coarse sand. Plants should not be watered until roots start to form. The time that it takes for this to happen varies from one to six months.

Propagating by grafting

Grafting of cacti is usually done simply to produce unusual effects. Different colored cacti may be joined together, or a barrel-shaped cactus may be grafted on the top of a column type. A flat graft is the easiest technique to use. Simply cut both the understock and the scion (the piece to be grafted on to the top of the understock) straight across, join the two sections neatly, and hold them in place with rubber bands or fine, strong cactus spines. At the optimum time of year—mid-spring to early fall—the graft may "take" within two weeks. Cleft and side grafts are also used, but these are not so easy for beginners.

BUYING A CACTUS

Many of the larger garden centers and nurseries will sell good-quality cactus plants that have been obtained from specialist growers. These are often small, reasonably priced plants, which will introduce you to the amazing range of cactus forms and become the beginning of a collection. Some specialist cactus nurseries sell direct to the public or by mail order. Garden centers and specialist growers are generally able to give you the right advice about the care and culture of your new plants. Novelty cactus are also on sale from florists or department stores, but the sales staff in these places are not, as a rule, qualified to give correct advice on cultivation.

Any cactus you buy must look clean and firm, and there must be no soft or decaying areas anywhere on the plant. It should not look pale or elongated, which would indicate that the cactus may have been kept for too long in poor light. The cactus must also be free of insect pests such as mealybugs, which resemble small, white, sticky patches of cotton wool and are often found between the spines.

WHAT CAN GO WRONG?

Cacti can be attacked by a range of sap-sucking insects such as aphids, mealybugs, scale insects, thrips, and two-spotted mites. Healthy, vigorous plants grown in good conditions are much less likely to succumb to an attack of these pests.

If your plants are attacked—and if you cannot manually remove the pests—you may need to spray with a registered insecticide. You will sometimes be able to dislodge mealybugs and scale insects with a cotton bud dipped in methylated spirit. Overhead watering will often discourage mites and aphids.

Soft rots and root decay are almost impossible to treat if they have become well established. If this is the case, cut away the rotted section with a sharp, clean knife to expose any healthy tissue, remove a healthy section of the plant, and then dry it and treat it as a cutting. Dusting the exposed clean tissue of the cactus with sulfur is sometimes also helpful. Most rots are caused by overwatering, especially when plants are not in active growth. If you are unsure whether or not to water, do not! When you do water, soak the cactus thoroughly and then allow the soil to dry out before you water again.

GLASSHOUSE COLLECTIONS offer a variety of shapes, like this magnificent vertical Euphorbia and Pandanus with pendulous leaves.

PROPAGATING BY GRAFTING

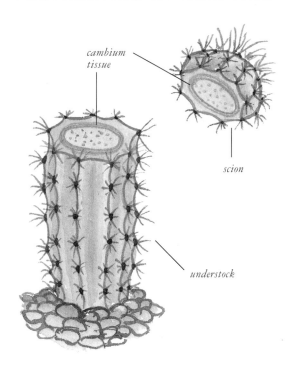

cambium tissue

scion

understock

1. WHEN GRAFTING, is most important to line up the cambium tissue of both the understock and scion to ensure a good graft union.

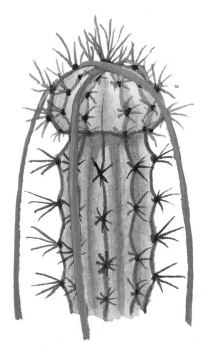

2. ONCE ALIGNED, firm pressure must be maintained. Rubber bands can be used to go right around the graft and the pot, or use fine pins, cactus spines, or toothpicks to hold the graft in place.

APOROCACTUS
Rat's Tail Cactus

APOROCACTUS FLAGELLI *IS ONE of the most common types to be found and is quite easy to grow, it's colorful purple-red blooms adding a touch of vibrant color to the garden in summer.*

FEATURES

Partial
Shade

A good group of cacti with its botanical name in dispute; this is now classified as *Aporocactus*. These lovely, epiphytic plants are native to rainforests or damp mountainous areas of tropical and subtropical regions of the Americas where they grow from the branches of trees. Their stems are mainly jointed and flattened, tending to be long and narrow with few if any spines. They are pendulous and branching, bearing scarlet or pink flowers on the tips of the branches in late spring or early summer. These plants are delightful when grown in pots or hanging baskets which can be used for indoor decoration while the cactus is in flower. Where temperatures fall below 50°F they should be grown in a glasshouse.

APOROCACTUS AT A GLANCE		
Dramatic cactuses for a hanging basket, with long trailing stems and bright showy flowers. 43°F min (zone 11).		
Jan	/	Recommended Varieties
Feb	/	*Aporocactus flagelliformis*
Mar	transplant	*A. martianus*
Apr	repotting	
May	flowering	COMPANION PLANTS
Jun	flowering	Epiphyllum
July	/	Hatiora
Aug	/	Schlumbergera
Sept	/	Selenicereus
Oct	/	
Nov	sow	
Dec	/	

Varieties The two most commonly found plants are *Aporocactus flagelliformis* and *A. martianus*. The latter has larger flowers than the former. Appearing in early summer, they are vivid red on gray-green stems. The plant only grows to 5in high, but can spread up to 3ft. *A. flagelliformis* is easier to grow. Its hanging growth may reach 5ft. Its purple-red blooms appear in spring when it makes a terrific sight with its snake-like stems topped by the colorful flowers.

CONDITIONS

Aspect Being epiphytic, the plants need to be grown with some degree of shade during the day. It is particularly important during the hottest, brightest part of the day. A morning of sun, and afternoon of shade is fine.

Site Grow in special epiphytic compost. Make sure that it is extremely free-draining.

GROWING METHOD

Propagation Plants can be grown from seed sown in spring, but are easier to grow from stem cuttings taken in spring or summer.

Feeding From late spring until late summer, provide a high potash or tomato feed once a month. Exceeding this dose is counter productive.

Problems Will not thrive in full sun or if overwatered.

FLOWERING

Season Rat's tail cactuses will flower either in late spring or early summer.

Fruits Flowers are followed by papery fruits.

ASTROPHYTUM
Bishop's Cap

FASTEST GROWING of all species of bishop's cap, Astrophytum
ornatum *bears many yellow flowers annually after about five years.*

*DEEPLY DEFINED RIBS and white scales around the upper body
characterise* Astrophytum ornatum, *also known as star cactus.*

FEATURES

Sun

This very small genus originates in Texas and
Mexico. The two most sought-after species are
virtually spineless and covered in white scales
instead. The bishop's cap or bishop's mitre,
Astrophytum myriostigma, has an unusual dull
purple, bluish, or green body that is speckled
all over with white scales. In the wild it may
be 2ft high and 8in across, but in cultivation it
is unlikely to reach melon size—and then only
after many years. Its flowers are bright yellow,
with the outer petals black tipped. *A. asterias*,
known as the sea urchin or sand dollar cactus,
is gray-green, slow growing and rarely more
than 2–3in high, eventually growing to a
width of about 4in. It has spectacular bright
yellow flowers with deep red centers.

ASTROPHYTUM AT A GLANCE

There are four species of these slow growing, attractive
roundish cactuses that like arid conditions. 50°F min (zone 11).

Jan	/	Recommended Varieties
Feb	/	*Astrophytum asterias*
Mar	/	*A. capricorne*
Apr	sow 🖐	*A. myriostigma*
May	transplant 🖐	*A. ornatum*
Jun	flowering ❀	
July	flowering ❀	
Aug	flowering ❀	COMPANION PLANTS
Sept	/	Echinocactus
Oct	/	Epostoa
Nov	/	Gymnocalycium
Dec	/	Mammillaria
		Rebutia

Varieties

A. ornatum has pronounced spines on its very
well-defined ribs. It is a cylindrical shape and it
grows to about 1ft. During the summer it
produces yellow flower. There are many different
varieties and hybrids of these popular and
attractive species. If you are just starting a
collection of astrophytum, it is well worth
growing *A. capricorne*, known as the goat's horn
cactus. It is quite a small cactus, reaching a
height of only about 8in. Its common name was
inspired by the bizarre form of its twisted spines
which wrap themselves around the cactus
instead of sticking up vertically in the usual way.
This makes handling the plant quite a problem
as its spines tend to get snapped off very easily.

CONDITIONS

Aspect Plants grow best in full sun, but may need a
little shading if grown under glass.
Site Soil must be very free draining and should
contain very little organic matter.

GROWING METHOD

Propagation Easy to raise from seed sown in spring.
Feeding Give low-nitrogen liquid plant food in spring
and mid-summer or use slow-release granules.
Problems Overwatering causes them to rot and die.

FLOWERING

Season Warm spring or summer flowering.
Fruits Flowers followed by fleshy, ovoid green or red
berries with long seeds within.

CEREUS
Column Cactus

THE LARGE AND VERY BEAUTIFUL flowers of Cereus uruguayanus *appear after dark and are worth waiting up for.*

THE BLUE-GREEN STEMS of Cereus *species are distinctly notched where the areoles and spines emerge.*

FEATURES

Sun

With a diverse range of origins from the West Indies to eastern South America, many of these cactuses are almost tree-like, while most form upright sturdy columns. The best-known species, *Cereus uruguayanus* (syn. *C. peruvianus*), is tree-like and can grow to 10ft or more with a stout, blue-green body notched where spines emerge. The "Monstrose" form makes a jumble of oddly shaped, blue-gray stems. Another tree-like species, *C. validus*, can also reach about 10ft high. Once established, it has pink-tinged white flowers in summer.
C. chalybaeus is a column cactus, often tinged blue or purple, with well-defined ribs bearing spines that mature to black. Its flowers are also white with the outer petals magenta or red.

CEREUS AT A GLANCE

A good choice if you like tall, quick growing vertical cacti, many with night-opening flowers. 45°F min (zone 11).

		Recommended Varieties
Jan	/	*Cereus aethiops*
Feb	/	*C. chalybaeus*
Mar	sow	*C. hildmannianus*
Apr	transplant	*C. uruguayanus*
May	repotting	*C. validus*
Jun	flowering	
July	flowering	
Aug	/	Companion Plants
Sept	flowering	Astrophytum
Oct	/	Echinocactus
Nov	/	Gymnocalycium
Dec	/	Mammillaria

CONDITIONS

Aspect These cactuses prefer to be grown in an open situation in full sun. Keep them well away from even the lightest shade.

Site The soil must be free draining, but need not be rich. Column cactuses come from areas with poor rocky soil. Although the size and proportion of these plants make them easiest to accommodate in a desert garden, column cactuses can also be grown in containers, which may need some extra weight such as stones or gravel in the base to stop them tipping over. Note however that some, such as the columnar *C. validus* and *C. hildmannianus monstrose*, have the potential to reach 20ft and 15ft. Of the two, the latter makes the most interesting shape with a contorted vertical stem.

GROWING METHOD

Propagation Grow plants from seed sown in spring or from cuttings of side branches.

Feeding Feed container-grown plants low-nitrogen liquid fertilizer monthly in summer. Ground-grown plants do not need feeding.

Problems No pest or disease problems are known.

FLOWERING

Season The large and lovely nocturnal flowers appear during spring and summer. The flowers usually appear after dark and fade before dawn.

Fruits Flowers are followed by round or oval fleshy fruits that ripen to yellow or red or purple.

CLEISTOCACTUS
Cleistocactus

TUBULAR FLOWERS grow directly from the stem of the silver torch cactus. A single flower near the crown creates a bird-like appearance.

BACK-LIT BY LOW SUN, the fine silvery spines of this cactus become a real feature as the silhouette of the narrow column is defined.

FEATURES

Sun

Although there are 45 species of *Cleistocactus*, all native to South America, very few are in general cultivation. Mostly branching from the base, these are upright column cactuses densely covered with fine spines that give them a silvery, woolly look. Although they look interesting as single stems, these cactuses are most spectacular when they are mass-planted. Their heights vary from 3–10ft but they are all fairly slender. The flowers, which emerge almost at right angles from the sides of the column, are mostly in shades of red and are pollinated by humming-birds in their natural habitats. The flowers never open very wide. These cactuses are fairly slow growing, making them ideal for pot culture, but they also can be grown in the open ground in conservatories. For plants in containers, regular potting on seems to produce the best growth.

CLEISTOCACTUS AT A GLANCE		
These are generally quick-growing, spreading plants requiring plenty of space. Dramatic at full size. 45°F min (zone 11).		
Jan	/	Recommended Varieties
Feb	/	*Cleistocactus brookei*
Mar	sow	*C. hyalacanthus*
Apr	/	*C. jujuyensis*
May	transplant	*C. strausii*
Jun	flowering	*C. winteri*
July	flowering	
Aug	flowering	Companion Plants
Sept	/	Aeonium
Oct	/	Espostoa
Nov	/	*Kalanchoe tomentosa*
Dec	/	Ferocactus
		Sansevieria trifasciata
		Yucca

Varieties The most commonly cultivated species is *C. strausii*. It grows about 6½ft high and forms clumps almost as wide. It is the species most often known by the name silver torch, and has cerise-red flowers in summer. *C. hyalacanthus* (syn. *C. jujuyensis*) is usually less than 3ft high, with columns covered in hairy, brownish to cream spines and flowers that may be bright scarlet to orange-red. *C. brookei* has one of the biggest growth potentials. Its height and spread are indefinite. In the wild it forms a superb show of red or orange flowers.

CONDITIONS

Aspect The plants need a position with continuous bright light and frequent watering during the growing season when the summer is hot. Over winter they must be kept bone dry, with a severe reduction in water from late fall.

Site Must have free-draining soil or cactus mix.

GROWING METHOD

Propagation Can be grown from seed or from stem cuttings or offsets during the warmer months.

Feeding Apply granular slow-release fertilizer in spring or feed the plants with weak solutions of liquid plant food through the growing season.

Problems Very susceptible to overwatering. If plants are indoors, mealybugs may be a problem.

FLOWERING

Season Flowers are red or pink, but also yellow, orange, or green. Most flower in summer.

Fruits Small, rounded, yellow, green, or red.

ECHINOCEREUS
Hedgehog Cactus

CYCLAMEN-PINK flowers stand like coronets to envelop the entire crown of this hedgehog cactus.

PRETTY LAVENDER-PINK flowers on Echinocereus pectinatus *may be followed by edible fruits in ideal growing conditions.*

FEATURES

Sun

Hailing from the south-west of North America, all 47 species in this group are in cultivation. It is a very variable genus: some types are globular, while others form short columns, some of which are pencil thin.

The group is also split when it comes to their spines. Some species are heavily spined, while others are relatively smooth. Most are clump-forming or clustering, and in ideal conditions clumps of up to 3ft wide are found. Some species have edible fruits reputed to taste like strawberries. The best known of these are *Echinocereus pectinatus*, *E. engelmannii*, *E.reichenbachii,* and *E. subinermis*. The range of flower color in this group extends from white to yellow, orange, bright red, pale pink, magenta, and violet.

ECHINOCEREUS AT A GLANCE

Dramatic small cactuses, with flowers bursting through the skin. Many attractive species. 50°F min (zone 11).

		Recommended Varieties
Jan	/	*Echinocereus chloranthus*
Feb	/	*E. cinerascens*
Mar	sow 🖐	*E. engelmannii*
Apr	transplant 🖐	*E. knippelianus*
May	flowering ❀	*E. pectinatus*
Jun	flowering ❀	*E. reichenbachii*
July	/	*E. scheeri*
Aug	/	*E. subinermis*
Sept	/	*E. triglochidiatus*
Oct	/	
Nov	/	
Dec	/	

Varieties

E. knippelianus is a striking cactus, with a dark green, almost smooth body, few spines, and pink to purple spring flowers. *E. subinermis* is one of the few yellow-flowered species, while *E. triglochidiatus* has brilliant scarlet flowers and a great range of forms. The "must have" hedgehog cactus for any collector is *E. reichenbachii* with purple-pink flowers; it makes a tidy smallish shape being 1ft high and 8in wide.

CONDITIONS

Aspect Prefers full sun with good air circulation.
Site Use a well-drained standard cactus mix. If being planted outside over summer, dig plenty of grit into the soil.

GROWING METHOD

Propagation Can be grown from seed sown in spring or from offsets taken in spring or summer.
Feeding Apply slow-release granules in spring or use weak liquid plant food in the growing season.
Problems Outdoors, few problems are encountered. If plants are grown under glasss, mealybugs or scales may be troublesome.

FLOWERING

Season Flowers appear some time during spring or summer. The flower buds form inside the plant body and then burst through the skin near the stem tips, often leaving scars.
Fruits Flowers are followed by fleshy fruits, most of which ripen to red although some fruits are green or purple.

EPIPHYLLUM
Orchid Cactus

THE CENTER *of a lovely orchid cactus is dominated by a branched, star-like stigma surrounded by pollen-bearing stems.*

EMERGING FROM *the edge of the flattened stems, the rich red flowers of a hybrid orchid cactus cascade down from a basket.*

FEATURES

Shade

Partial Shade

This group of epiphytic tropical American cactuses is known as orchid cactus because of the gorgeous, large flowers. Few of the true species are available, but the many spectacular named varieties have huge flowers 4–8in across, in shades of cream, yellow, salmon, various pinks, and reds. Some of these cultivars have a tendency to change color according to light levels and temperatures. Stems of the orchid cactus are almost spineless, broad, flattened, and leaf-like with flowers emerging from buds that are formed on the edges of these stems. These cactuses are natural epiphytes growing in tree canopies in tropical forests. As a result, they do well growing in hanging baskets or against a wall or tree that they can use for support as they scramble up.

EPIPHYLLUM AT A GLANCE

Stunning, beautiful, often scented flowers on cactuses that look highly impressive in hanging baskets. 50°F min (zone 11).

		Recommended Varieties
Jan	/	*Epiphyllum crenatum*
Feb	/	"Fantasy"
Mar	sow	"Hollywood"
Apr	transplant	"Jennifer Anne"
May	flowering	*E. oxypetalum*
Jun	flowering	*E. pumilum*
July	flowering	"Reward"
Aug	/	
Sept	/	
Oct	/	
Nov	/	
Dec	/	

Varieties

Varieties Some of the large-flowered types are slow to produce their first blooms and must be very mature before they flower regularly. However, the lovely species *Epiphyllum oxypetalum*, known as "Belle de Nuit," is nocturnal with huge white, scented flowers unfolding on warm nights to close again by daybreak. If you only have room for one small orchid, *E. laui* is an excellent choice. It grows 1ft high by 1½ft wide, and produces scented white flowers about 6in long.

CONDITIONS

Aspect Unlike many cactuses, they prefer dappled, filtered shade out of direct sunlight.

Site The soil mix must be relatively fertile, but above all open and free draining.

GROWING METHOD

Propagation Can be grown from seed sown in spring, but hybrids must be increased from stem cuttings taken during summer to early fall.

Feeding Apply granular slow-release fertilizer in spring or regular liquid feeds in the growing season.

Problems Usually trouble free in the right conditions.

FLOWERING

Season Flowers are produced on mature plants from late spring through summer. Some flowers are quite long lasting. The original species are mostly night blooming, but the majority of those available today are day flowering.

Fruits Red fruits may form on some plants.

HATIORA SALICORNIOIDES
Drunkard's dream

UNOPENED BUDS FORMING on the tips of each slender segment of this plant are like small, glowing torches.

A LOVELY MATURE specimen of drunkard's dream in a hanging basket allows its fine shape to be appreciated in or out of flower.

FEATURES

Partial Shade

These plants bear no apparent likeness to the spiny plants so readily recognised as cactuses. They tend to be upright in early stages, but become pendulous under their own weight and so are ideal for hanging baskets. A large potted plant may need heavy stones in the container base to counterbalance the cactus's weight. The stem segments are mid-green to bronze and are topped by small, yellow to orange tubular, or funnel-shaped flowers in spring. This Brazilian group of plants includes ground growers and epiphytes and it is easy to imagine them growing from the fork or branch of a tree. *Hatiora salicornioides* is called drunkard's dream because the dense growth of tiny jointed stems resembles hundreds of tiny bottles. In Australia it is also called dancing bones.

HATIORA AT A GLANCE

Genus with many excellent species, well worth including in any collection of first-rate cactuses. 50°F min (zone 11).

		Recommended Varieties
Jan	/	*Hatiora ephiphylloides*
Feb	/	*H. gaertneri*
Mar	sow	*H. rosea*
Apr	transplant	*H. salicornioides*
May	flowering	
Jun	flowering	
July	/	Companion Plants
Aug	/	Astrophyllum
Sept	/	Epiphyllum
Oct	/	Rebutia
Nov	/	Schlumbergera
Dec	/	Selenicereus

CONDITIONS

Aspect Drunkard's dream grows best in filtered sunlight or in a position that has morning sun and afternoon shade.

Site The epiphytic kind need some shade to replicate their natural growing conditions, just under the tree canopy. Either provide filtered sunlight, or a position with morning sun and reasonable afternoon shade. Spray regularly to provide high levels of humidity, especially on hot days, when in full growth from spring to fall.

GROWING METHOD

Propagation These plants can be grown from seed sown in spring, but it is much easier to strike cuttings from the jointed stems in spring through to early fall.

Feeding Apply a low-level nitrogen liquid feed once a month during the growing season.

Problems This is generally a very easy plant to grow and it has no specific pest or disease problems.

FLOWERING

Season Small, orange to yellow tubular flowers appear from the lower half of the plant in spring. Although the flowers are not spectacular, they give the impression of tiny lights on the ends of the stems. The most impressive thing about most of these plants, is their distinctive, unusual, non-cactus like dangling growth. From a distance *H. salicornioides* looks a bit like the jangled stems of a mistletoe.

Fruits The flowers of drunkard's dream are followed by tiny white fruits.

MAMMILLARIA
Mammillaria

THE MATURING RED FRUITS of Mammillaria prolifera *surround each rounded stem. This species readily forms large colonies which makes it a satisfying plant to cultivate, both for the novice and more experienced growers.*

FEATURES

Sun

This is probably the most popular group of cactus among growers and collectors and there are about 150 species in the genus. The largest number of these cactuses are native to Mexico, but their habitat also extends through the south-western United States south to Colombia and Venezuela. Instead of ribs, these cactuses all have tubercles which vary greatly in shape. These plants are sometimes also known as pincushion cactuses.

MAMMILLARIA AT A GLANCE

Some Mammillaria should be in every collection, for their flowers and shape, especially the terrific white snowballs. 45°F min (zone 11).

		Recommended Varieties
Jan	/	*Mammillaria baumii*
Feb	/	M. *bocasana*
Mar	sow	M. *bombycina*
Apr	transplant	M. *candida*
May	flowering	M. *carmenae*
Jun	flowering	M. *elongata*
July	flowering	M. *geminispina*
Aug	flowering	M. *hahniana*
Sept	flowering	M. *plumosa*
Oct	/	M. *zeilmanniana*
Nov	/	
Dec	/	

Varieties
While it is impossible to cater for all tastes, the following few species indicate the variety within the group. *Mammillaria carmenae* has feathery, white or cream spines fanning out from the woolly body, and rich creamy flowers. It rarely grows more than 4in high, forming pretty clusters. M. *bombycina* has red, brown, or yellow spines pushing through the woolly surface of the plant. This species is quick to make offsets to form a good-looking specimen, especially when topped with a ring of pretty cerise-pink flowers. M. *longimamma*, called the finger mound cactus, has fat, stubby tubercles like smooth, dark green fingers with tufts of yellow spines on each tip. Flowers borne in late spring are quite large and rich yellow, while fruits that follow are fleshy and green, not unlike the cactus itself. M. *geminispina* is another excellent cactus with small rounded shapes, and is distinguished by a covering of white spines, white areoles, and white flowers. Even better, after a few years it will start to produce plenty of young plants, eventually creating an eye-catching mound. Old lady or birthday cake cactus, M. *hahniana*, is named for the almost perfect ring of cerise flowers on the crown of the plant, which is followed by another ring of red candle-like fruits.

Snowballs
M. *plumosa*, M. *bocasana,* and M. *sempervivi* are so densely covered in white wool below the spines that they resemble snowballs or powder puffs—they are sometimes referred to by these common names.

THE SMALL CERISE FLOWERS of Mammillaria hahniana *encircle the crown of the plant when fully developed.*

THIS COLUMNAR SPECIES of Mammillaria *has its crown covered with buds and flowers in spring. It is very rewarding to grow.*

Growth habit Most of these cactuses are small and rounded and thickly covered with spines, but some have finger-like stems. Most produce offsets freely, making a good show in pots or in a bed, but a few, however, are solitary growers. These cactuses are popular and satisfying to grow not only because of their easy cultivation, but because they produce rings of beautiful flowers around the crown of the plant in spring to early summer even when quite young. Spines vary from straight to curved, soft and feathery to almost rigid, and come in variable colors.

Size There is a great variation in height and size, and although a few of these cactuses may reach 12–16in in height, by far the greatest number will never exceed 6in. The ultimate spread of these species is harder to determine, but where there is space and where growing conditions are suitable, some may keep on spreading indefinitely. However, as it is easy to remove the offsets, their vigour need never be a problem.

CONDITIONS

Aspect Grow plants outdoors in full sun, but if they are under glass provide shading at the hottest time of day.

Site These cactuses are easy to grow. In pots, provide the standard cactus compost which will be free draining. When growing them in outdoor beds over summer, or in conservatory beds, make sure that the soil is on the poor side.

GROWING METHOD

Propagation These plants can be grown from seed sown in spring or by division of offsets in spring and summer. When the cactuses become quite prolific, as in the case of *M. geminispina*, it is worth removing smaller plantlets as they appear, not so much to create new plants as to maintain an aesthetically pleasing shape. It is also worth ensuring that one particularly good plant is always kept alone, without offspring, so its shape can be fully appreciated.

Feeding Apply small quantities of granular slow-release fertilizer in spring. You can also use low-nitrogen soluble liquid fertilizer at weak concentrations every month through the growing season.

Problems Some species form a thick tuberous root and these will rot if overwatered. *M. longimamma* is one of these, but all species must be considered vulnerable to overwatering.

FLOWERING

Season This cactus group produces its flowers during spring or summer, sometimes giving a second flush later in the season. They also tend to flower reliably year after year. The range of flower colors includes white, yellow, and orange with a wide range of shades of pink, red, and purple.

Fruits The berry-like fruits that follow the flowers are often bright red, but may also be green.

OPUNTIA
Opuntia

AN IMPENETRABLE BARRIER *has been formed where two species of* Opuntia *have become intermingled.*

FLAT, PADDLE-SHAPED *segments and the sizeable growth of the edible* Opuntia ficus-indica *make an impact in the landscape.*

FEATURES

Sun

Variously known as prickly pear, Indian fig, and cholla, with many more local common names, this is a very large genus of cactus with a vast geographical range. Opuntia are jointed or segmented cactuses with mainly padded and flattened joints, although sometimes these are cylindrical or rounded. Species occur naturally from southern Canada and throughout the Americas, continuing to Patagonia on the tip of South America. Long grown as living fences in their native areas, many prickly pears were introduced to other countries for this purpose, with disastrous results.

OPUNTIA AT A GLANCE

The largest group of cactus with some outstanding plants; excellent shapes and dangerous spines. 41°F min (zone 11).

		Recommended Varieties
Jan	/	*Opuntia basiliaris*
Feb	/	*O. clavarioides*
Mar	sow	*O. ficus-indica*
Apr	transplant	*O. microdasys*
May	flowering	*O. imbricata*
Jun	flowering	*O. tunicata*
July	flowering	*O. verschaffeltii*
Aug	flowering	*O. vestica*
Sept	flowering	
Oct	/	
Nov	/	
Dec	/	

Prickly pear — *O. aurantiaca*, *O. stricta,* and *O. vulgaris* and a number of other species have become quite appalling weeds in Australia, Africa, and India. By 1925, there was estimated to be above 10 million acres (25 million hectares) of land infested by prickly pear in Australia. A huge program of biological control was initiated, involving the introduction of the *Cactoblastis* moth and cochineal insects.

Indian fig — The Indian fig, *O. ficus-indica*, is widely grown in many parts of the world for its fruit. It is a tree-like cactus up to 17ft high and wide.

Other types — Although many species of opuntia are too large to place anywhere except in a large desert garden, there are numerous other shapes and sizes, with some that are suitable for pot culture. Bunny ears, *O. microdasys*, has dark green pads dotted with white areoles, and white, yellow, or brown bristles. The brown-bristled form is known as teddy bear ears. These plants rarely grow more than 16–24in high and wide, and suit both containers or the yard. *O. tunicata* is a small, spreading bush about 24in high and up to 3ft wide. Its thick, creamy spines take on a satin sheen in sunlight. Beaver tail, *O. basilaris*, has purple-gray flat pads with few spines and spreads by branching from the base, so is rarely more than 16in high. *O. erinacea* is clump-forming with flattened blue-green pads, but it is the variety *ursina* with masses of fine hair-like spines—known as grizzly bear cactus—that attracts many growers. In the wild it grows in California and Arizona, has 4in long pinky orange flowers, and grows about 18in high.

THE VIVID RED FLOWERS are tightly ridged across the top of the young leaves of this Opuntia. *The flowers of most species are usually produced in spring or summer, and are followed by succulent fruits later in the season.*

Chollas   It is well worth knowing something about this rare group, which are rarely seen outside specialist botanical collections. The chollas (pronounced "choyas") are enormously variable in their habit of growth. They include the very spiny, almost furry-looking *O. bigelovii*, which grows to about 3–6½ft high, and the more open, tree-like *O. versicolor*, which may reach almost 13ft in height. Most of this group have easily detached segments, in particular the jumping cholla, *O. fulgida*, which hooks on to anything that passes, usually taking root and growing where it falls.

CONDITIONS

Aspect   Best grown in an open, sunny situation.
Site   Provide container-grown plants with sharply drained, standard cactus mix. In the garden, they tolerate a wide range of soils as long as they drain well. All opuntias dislike having their roots cramped in a small space. The larger plants should eventually be moved to a border in the glasshouse. If you opt for a regime of constant potting up, note that the spines are vicious.

GROWING METHOD

Propagation   Easily grown from stem segments which should be separated from the parent plant from spring to fall. They can also be grown successfully from seed sown in spring.
Feeding   In spring and mid-summer, plants in the ground can be given pelletted poultry manure or granular slow-release fertilizer. Potted plants should have a dose of slow-release fertilizer in the spring or an occasional liquid feed during the growing season.

Problems   Few problems are encountered if growing conditions are suitable. The two worst offenders to look out for are scale insects and mealybugs. You will invariably need to spray to remove them, since the dangerous spines prevent you from getting in close to carry out treatment with a swab.

FLOWERING

Season   The flowers of opuntia are produced sometime during spring or summer, depending on species. The majority of species has yellow flowers, but these may also be orange, purple, or white. For example, the bright yellow flowers of *O. tunicata* appear from spring to summer, while *O. basilaris* bears its bright rose-pink flowers in summer.
Fruits   Berry-like fruits form after the flowers fade, and in some species these are edible. The Indian fig has bright yellow flowers that are followed by deep red to purple fruit. It is widely cultivated around the world for its fruit. Prepare the fruit for eating by washing and using a brush to remove the spines. Slice off the top and bottom, slit the skin, and peel. Serve in slices with a squeeze of lemon or lime juice. You can also use the pulp to make jam. *O. cochenillifera* is a source of cochineal—although today this dye is mainly synthesized.

PARODIA
Ball Cactus

DENSELY COVERED with fine yellow spines, the species Parodia claviceps *can be slow to form colonies.*

BRIGHT YELLOW FLOWERS are a feature of Parodia magnifica, *a deeply furrowed species which is not heavily spined.*

FEATURES

Sun

Partial Shade

While the species is now known as parodia, you will find that many ball cactuses are still under the old name of notocactus. These superb cactuses are native to Brazil, Paraguay, Uruguay, and Argentina. Mostly rounded in form, although a few are column shaped, they are easy to grow and flower profusely. Many ball cactuses have deeply furrowed surfaces, but the coverage of spines varies greatly; some forms are thickly covered and others have quite sparse spines. *P. concinnus* is a small tubby shape with primrose-yellow flowers, while *P. leninghausii* can form a thick column up to 3ft high and has large yellow flowers. *P. herteri*, prized for its hot pink-purple flowers, is squat-shaped and blooms when it reaches tennis-ball size. *N. uebelmannianus* is another squat grower, with large purple or yellow flowers.

PARODIA AT A GLANCE

Generally globular or spherical, ribbed spiny cactuses from South America. Funnel-shaped blooms. 45°F min (zone 11).

		Recommended Varieties
Jan	/	*Parodia chrysacanthion*
Feb	/	*P. concinna*
Mar	transplant	*P. herteri*
Apr	flowering	*P. horstii*
May	flowering	*P. leninghausii*
Jun	flowering	*P. magnifica*
July	flowering	*P. mammulosa*
Aug	sow	*P. nivosa*
Sept	/	*P. rutilans*
Oct	/	*P. schwebsiana*
Nov	/	
Dec	/	

CONDITIONS

Aspect   Ball cactuses will grow in full sun or in very light shade. When standing pots outdoors in summer, make sure that the plants receive some shade around midday.

Site   When growing in pots, use a standard well-drained compost. In the ground, ball cactuses like equally well-drained soil with some well-rotted compost that slightly increases fertility.

GROWING METHOD

Propagation   Grow from seed in spring or from offsets taken in summer. None of the species will produce offsets until quite mature. Increase watering in the spring and allow the soil to dry out between waterings during the summer.

Feeding   Apply slow-release fertilizer in spring, or feed the plants with some low-nitrogen liquid fertilizer every 6–8 weeks throughout the growing season.

Problems   This is generally a trouble-free type of cactus that is easy to grow.

FLOWERING

Season   The flowers appear on the crown of ball cactuses during the spring or summer months. The central stigma of the flower is nearly always a deep reddish-purple to pink color. While the majority of the ball cactuses have yellow flowers, it is possible to obtain other species that have attractive flowers in red, pink, purple, or even orange colors. Contact a cactus nursery which specialises in parodia.

Fruits   In ideal growing conditions, as in the wild, you may find that after the flowers fade fleshy fruits ripen to red.

SCHLUMBERGERA
Christmas Cactus

A VIVID SCARLET HYBRID of Schlumbergera truncata *makes a desirable potted plant to brighten winter days.*

FLOURISHING IN LIGHT SHADE, this Christmas cactus is the cerise-pink color that most people associate with the species.

FEATURES

Partial Shade

This group of easily grown cacti originated from only about six species, and now features almost 200 cultivars of popular flowering pot plants which are more familiar to some as *Zygocactus*. *Schlumbergera* species, or Christmas cacti, are epiphytic and grow on trees or sometimes rocks in their native Brazilian habitat where their flowers are pollinated by humming-birds. Their popularity as pot plants is assured because most of them flower in fall or winter, hence their common name. They have flat, jointed stems arching into small bushes, making them ideal for hanging baskets as well as pots. They come into vigorous growth in summer, and start flowering once the day length is less than 12 hours. Christmas cacti make excellent gifts.

SCHLUMBERGERA AT A GLANCE

High performance pot plants which give a big show of bright color around Christmas. Easily grown. 45°F min (zone 11).

Jan	flowering ❀	Recommended Varieties
Feb	flowering ❀	*Schlumbergera "Bristol Beauty"*
Mar	/	*S.* x *buckleyi*
Apr	sow 🖐	"Gold Charm"
May	flowering ❀	"Joanne"
Jun	transplant 🖐	"Lilac Beauty"
July	/	*S. opuntioides*
Aug	/	*S. truncata*
Sept	/	
Oct	/	
Nov	flowering ❀	
Dec	flowering ❀	

Varieties

The silky, irregularly-shaped flowers are mainly in shades of pink or red, but hybrids can be almost pure white to cream, salmon, apricot, cerise, violet, and scarlet. Some display yellow tones that revert to pink as temperatures fall. *S. truncata*, the crab cactus, and *S.* x *buckleyi*, the Christmas cactus, provide the origins of many of the modern hybrids.

CONDITIONS

Aspect Best in partial shade or with morning sun and afternoon shade in a sheltered situation.

Site For an established pot plant, John Innes No. 2 with added grit for good drainage is ideal. Repot every three years in the spring. It is too tender to be grown outdoors.

GROWING METHOD

Propagation These plants are easy to grow from cuttings of stem sections taken in spring or summer.

Feeding A light, regular summer feed will promote plenty of new growth and guarantee an excellent display of flowers.

Problems Generally easy to grow, these plants will suffer if grown in full sun and may not flower. Overwatering causes root rot and subsequent collapse of stems.

FLOWERING

Season Masses of flowers appear in fall or winter. Once flower buds have formed, do not move the plants until buds begin to open. Flowers in spring if kept at 36–39°F over winter. Gradually increase the temperature in spring.

SELENICEREUS
Selenicereus

THESE PLANTS ARE CULTIVATED for their beautiful white, cream, or pale pink fragrant flowers, which open at night. It is amazing to see such a glorious flower emerge at dusk from a fairly ugly-looking stem but, of course, it will have faded by the following morning.

FEATURES

Partial Shade

There are about 20 species in this group of very long-stemmed climbing epiphytic cactuses. They are native to the forests of the south-western United States, central America, the West Indies, and Colombia, where they live on trees or rocks. *Selenicereus* species have long been cultivated in Mexico for a drug used in the treatment of rheumatism and in Costa Rica for a heart-stimulant drug. They are now being cultivated in Germany and elsewhere for use in medicine, especially in the treatment of heart disorders. These plants have long, angled, or tubular stems bearing small spines on the ribs, but it is their aerial roots that enable them to climb and cling on to their host plants. They will continue to grow up-wards and spread as long as they find support.

SELENICEREUS AT A GLANCE

Strange, thin climbing stems with outstanding scented flowers, from South American forests. 59°F min (zone 11).

Jan	/	Recommended Varieties
Feb	/	*Selenicereus grandiflorus*
Mar	sow	*S. hamatus*
Apr	/	*S. innesii*
May	transplant	*S. pteranthus*
Jun	flowering	*S. spinulosus*
July	flowering	
Aug	flowering	Companion Plants
Sept	/	Epiphyllum
Oct	sow	Hatiora
Nov	/	Schlumbergera
Dec	/	Selenicereus

Varieties   *S. grandiflorus* is the species most often grown. Its flowers have outer petals that are yellow to brown, but the inner flower is pure white. Two other species found in cultivation are *S. pteranthus* and *S. spinulosus*. Both have cream, white, or pale pink flowers. These plants can be grown in the ground, or rooted in large pots set against some strong support.

CONDITIONS

Aspect   Being epiphytic, these extraordinary cactuses need to be kept out of direct sunlight. They like filtered, dappled light, or as second best, light for half the day, shade for the rest.

Site   Plants need well-drained compost with added decayed organic matter. An orchid mix would suit them.

GROWING METHOD

Propagation   Plants are easily grown from stem segments taken from spring to early fall. They can also be grown from seed sown in spring.

Feeding   Apply slow-release fertilizer in spring, or liquid feed occasionally in the growing season.

Problems   No specific pests or diseases are known, but keep an eye out in the summer for scale insects and mealybugs.

FLOWERING

Season   The spectacular, scented flowers do not appear until the plants have become quite mature. They open on summer evenings.

Fruits   The fleshy fruits are hairy or spiny.

Growing Climbers

GROWING CLIMBERS

Climbers are among the most useful of garden plants. They provide color and interest on a higher level without taking up much space near the ground. They are very versatile and can be used in many ways, primarily for covering fences, walls, and outbuildings. They can be grown up trellis screens in the garden, and when trained over pergolas will provide shade for a patio or terrace. Suitable climbers can be trained up trees and over large shrubs, and some can be used as groundcover. They can also be grown on free-standing supports in borders.

Climbers can also be used as focal points in a garden by training them over an ornamental arch, say at the end of a pathway. Although few people think of them when planning balcony gardens, they are ideal for this purpose as they take up little horizontal space while decorating an otherwise blank wall.

LEFT: This glorious display of wisteria is at its peak, and it perfectly complements the iron lacework on this long verandah.

WISTERIA SINENSIS *and a white climbing rose have been trained to grow up opposing ends of this metallic arch. With a few more years' growth these plants should tangle together delightfully. The shape of the structure will create a pleasant flowering window between two areas of the garden.*

HABITS OF GROWTH

Unlike the other groups of woody plants, the trees and shrubs, climbing plants do not have self-supporting trunks or stems and therefore use various modifications to lift themselves up toward the light. In their natural habitats there may not always be a convenient support for the plant and so it may trail over the ground or over a rock. We can make use of this method of growth in gardens by using some climbers are groundcover, just allowing them to sprawl over the soil surface. It is a good way of quickly covering large areas, especially banks.

Climbers are grouped into four broad groups according to the mechanism they use to climb: tendril climbers, twiners, scramblers, and self-clinging climbers.

Tendril climbers
Tendril climbers have thin, curling tendrils that coil around their supports, whether it's wire, netting, or trellis. Tendrils are modified organs; in the case of climbers they are generally modified leaves. The grape vine, *Vitis vinifera*, is a good example of a tendril climber. Some tendril climbers, such as *Parthenocissus tricuspidata* (Boston ivy) have adhesive suckers or disks on the tips of their tendrils that stick to smooth surfaces such as walls.

Twiners
Twiners are climbing plants that twine their new shoots entirely around a support. *Wisteria*, which is among our best-loved climbers, is a twiner, and a vigorous one at that. This group of climbers will twine either clockwise or anticlockwise according to species.

Scramblers
Scramblers often climb and support themselves by means of thorns that usually curve downwards, acting as hooks. Climber and Rambler roses come in this group, as do the brambles or *Rubus* species, such as *Rubus henryi* var. *bambusarum*. Scramblers attach themselves to other plants or supports to pull themselves up. Some scrambling plants

TYPES OF CLIMBERS

Tendril climber

Twining climber

Scrambler

Self-clinging climber

are described as lax, having very long thin thornless stems, an example being *Jasminum nudiflorum* (Winter jasmine). In the wild these just sprawl over other plants or rocks but when grown in gardens they need to have their stems tied in to supports to help them climb.

Self-clinging climbers

Self-clinging climbers are not as common as the other kinds. They produce short roots from their stems, known as aerial roots, that attach themselves firmly to supports. Self-clinging climbers are capable of attaching to completely flat, relatively smooth surfaces such as walls. In the wild they would attach themselves to tree trunks or rock faces. These adventurous roots make their way into any tiny crack or rough patch in the surface of the support. The best-known examples of self-clinging climbers are *Hedera* species (Ivy), *Hydrangea anomala* subsp. *petiolaris* (Climbing hydrangea) and *Schizophragma hydrangeoides*, a relation of the hydrangea.

Matching climbers to supports

Now that we know the methods that climbers use to climb and to support themselves, we can choose suitable plants for the existing supports. On the other hand, if you want to grow a particular climber, you could provide a custom-made support if necessary. Climbers vary tremendously in height and this is an important consideration when choosing plants for the garden.

Some are capable of reaching to the tops of the tallest walls or trees, while others are much less vigorous and will not grow any taller than an ordinary garden fence.

Flamboyant flowers

Apart from their methods of supporting themselves, climbers are diverse in other respects, too. Many are noted for their colorful flower displays. Many hardy climbers have quite flamboyant flowers and are capable of providing an exotic effect in gardens. *Wisteria* is a good example, with its long trusses of pea-flowers, but there are many others such as *Abutilon megapotamicum* (Flowering maple) with red and yellow bells, *Campsis radicans* (Common trumpet creeper) with large orange trumpet-shaped flowers, *Clianthus puniceus* (Glory pea, Lobster claw) with bright red claw-like flowers, *Fremontodendron californicum* with large saucer-shaped yellow flowers, and *Passiflora caerulea* (Blue passion flower), which looks as though it should be grown under glass but which is in fact hardy enough to survive outdoors in many areas.

For sheer quantity of flowers over a long period in summer there is nothing to beat the Climbing and Rambler roses. Some have only one flush of flowers in summer, but if you choose the right cultivars you will get several flushes throughout summer.

Many roses have fragrant flowers, and this is a characteristic of numerous other climbers. For many people the first choice for fragrance, apart from roses,

THIS FINE Clematis *"Etoile Violette" has large, violet flowers with contrasting yellow stamens. The Viticella Group of clematis of which this is one, contains a host of vigorous, free-flowering varieties. These clematis bloom from the midsummer to late fall.*

is honeysuckle such as *Lonicera caprifolium* (Italian honeysuckle), *L. japonica* "Halliana" (Japanese honeysuckle), and *L. periclymenum* cultivars (Common honeysuckle, Woodbine). Some jasmines also have highly fragrant blooms, especially *Jasminum beesianum*, *J. humile* "Revolutum" and, the most fragrant of all, *J. officinale* (Common jasmine). Not related to jasmine, but still with very fragrant flowers, is *Trachelospermum jasminoides* (Star jasmine). And don't forget the reliable *Wisteria* when it comes to fragrance, particularly *W. floribunda* and *W. sinensis* and their various cultivars.

Attractive foliage

Climbers may be deciduous, in other words they lose their leaves in the fall, or evergreen—retaining their leaves all the year round. The latter are particularly valuable where an object such as a wall needs to be covered all the time. Many climbers are, in fact, grown for their attractive foliage, some of which can be quite exotic-looking, especially the large leaves of the deciduous *Actinidia kolomikta*, which are dark green, pink, and white. The evergreen *Euonymus fortunei* cultivars are often brightly variegated and make a splash of color in a shady situation. The same is true of ivies, both the small-leaved *Hedera helix* (Common ivy) and cultivars of the large-leaved kinds such as *H. canariensis* (Canary Island ivy) and *H. colchica* (Persian ivy). All have green-leaved cultivars, too. The related X *Fatshedera lizei* (Tree ivy), has large

dark green ivy-like leaves, or variegated in some of the cultivars. *Humulus lupulus* "Aureus" (Golden hop) is one of the most colorful foliage climbers with its golden-yellow, deciduous leaves.

Several deciduous climbers are grown for their fall leaf color. Supreme in this respect are species of *Parthenocissus*. Probably the best known and most widely planted is *P. quinquefolia* (Virginia creeper) whose leaves become brilliant red in fall. Also good are *P. tricuspidata* (Boston ivy) and *P. henryana* (Chinese Virginia creeper). Another superb climber for fall leaf color is *Vitis coignetiae*, an ornamental vine, one of the largest-leaved hardy climbers available, whose foliage becomes bright red before it falls.

USES IN GARDENS

Climbers are a highly versatile group of plants and can be used in many ways in the garden. Do not think only in terms of using them to cover a wall. Be more imaginative and adventurous and try using them as free-standing features in beds and borders, growing them over large shrubs, or even using them as groundcover.

It is important that climbers are matched to their supports, so bear this in mind when choosing plants for your garden. Some climbers are very vigorous and only suitable for covering the largest walls, and would therefore need a lot of pruning to keep them within

DESPITE ITS YOUTH, a young honeysuckle plant nevertheless provides a bright show of vibrant red flowers. This species, Lonicera x brownii *"Fuchsioides," is quite hardy and will make a good wall-covering climber. It flowers throughout the summer.*

A TRELLIS makes the perfect support for this Clematis macropetala *"Markham's Pink." The plant will grow leaving decorative windows.*

THE LINES of this trellis are consumed by a mass of Parthenocissus *leaves. Climbers will help any object to blend into the garden.*

bounds. On the other hand there are many of more modest stature, suitable for even small gardens.

Walls and fences

It is safe to say that all climbers can be grown on walls. On the walls of the house it is probably best to avoid those that produce aerial roots such as ivies, and tendril climbers with adhesive suckers like *Parthenocissus*, for not only are they vigorous but once attached are very difficult to remove. These would be better for tall boundary walls. Instead, for the average house, go for more manageable climbers such as roses, *Clematis* and jasmines; or wall shrubs such as *Abutilon megapotamicum* (Flowering maple), *Chaenomeles speciosa* (Flowering quince), *Cotoneaster horizontalis* (Fishbone cotoneaster), and *Fremontodendron californicum* (Flannel bush). Wisterias are often grown on house walls but bear in mind that they are tall, vigorous climbers and need a lot of pruning. They are probably better for large houses.

For boundary fences, which are generally about 6ft high maximum, such as close-boarded or panel fences, again use the smaller, more manageable climbers as suggested above. If you have a chain-link fence you could choose from the group known as twiners. These will support themselves by twining their shoots through the mesh. Wisterias are twiners, and although very tall, they can be grown on low fences by training the stems horizontally. *Muehlenbeckia complexa* is another twiner suitable for covering chain-link fencing.

Pergolas, arches and arbours

These are excellent supports for many climbers but not for those that produce aerial roots like ivies, or adhesive suckers such as *Parthenocissus*. Favorites for pergolas are grape vines, *Vitis vinifera*, either fruiting or ornamental kinds, which quickly provide welcome shade over a patio. Climbing roses are also popular, and look especially attractive trained over an arch or arbour. Roses can be grown with *Clematis*, allowing the two to intertwine for some really stunning effects. *Wisteria*, again, is a favorite for larger pergolas, especially as the dense flower trusses hang down inside the structure.

Obelisks for borders

Few people think of growing climbers in beds and borders as free-standing specimens. Yet this is an excellent way to grow the smaller kinds such as Large-flowered climbing roses, *Clematis* (try combining the two), and *Humulus lupulus* "Aureus" (Golden hop). Obelisks make ideal supports, and are obtainable in steel or wood. Woven hazel or willow obelisks are also available and their rustic appearance makes them ideal for cottage or country gardens. DIY enthusiasts could probably save some money by making their own obelisks out of timber.

Trees and shrubs

Large mature trees make suitable supports for tall vigorous climbers such as *Rosa filipes*, particularly the cultivar "Kiftsgate." With its white flowers, this is very effective when grown through a large mature dark green conifer. Ivies, *Parthenocissus*, *Hydrangea anomala* subsp. *petiolaris* (Climbing hydrangea), and other self-clinging climbers are suitable for big deciduous trees. Thin-stemmed, light and airy climbers such as *Clematis viticella* cultivars can be grown through large mature shrubs.

THIS SOLANUM CRISPUM *hangs lush and colorful over a bed of assorted plants. The addition of a climber can lift an entire bed and completes the decorative effect. Plantings should be thought out with the use of climbers in mind—they can revolutionize your entire garden look.*

Ugly outbuildings

To quickly cover and hide ugly outbuildings such as sheds and garages choose a vigorous climber. These include plants such as *Ampelopsis glandulosa* var. *brevipedunculata* "Elegans," *Campsis radicans* (Common trumpet creeper), *Celastrus orbiculatus* (Staff vine), the extremely vigorous *Fallopia baldschuanica* (Russian vine), *Hedera colchica* (Persian ivy), or *Parthenocissus* species.

Pots and tubs

While most climbers are planted directly in the open ground, some can also be grown in tubs and pots. For example, if you have a pergola built over a paved area such as a patio, or you want to grow a climber on a patio wall, there may be no soil available in which to plant. Large containers filled with soil-based potting compost will make suitable homes for the less-vigorous climbers. The container needs to be a minimum of 12in in diameter and depth; 18in or larger would be better. A good depth is particularly important as then the compost will not dry out quickly and the climber will be able to root deeply, resulting in better growth.

Less-vigorous climbers are best suited to containers as then they will not quickly outgrow them. Many *Clematis* are ideal, particularly the summer-flowering Large-flowered hybrids and the *C. viticella* cultivars. Other suitable plants you might like to try include *Abutilon megapotamicum* (Flowering maple), *Clianthus puniceus* (Glory pea, lobster claw), X *Fatshedera lizei* (Tree ivy), hederas (Ivies), *Humulus lupulus* "Aureus" (Golden hop), and Large-flowered climbing roses (these need a large tub). Very vigorous climbers should not be attempted, although wisterias are sometimes trained as standards (like small trees, with a single stem) in large tubs, and they make unusual features on a patio. *Vitis vinifera* (Grape vines) can be grown in the same way.

Container-grown plants will need extra maintenance in the way of regular watering and feeding through the year, but the results are certainly worthwhile.

Groundcover

Some climbers make excellent groundcover, say among shrubs, under trees, or even for covering a steep bank. *Cotoneaster horizontalis* (Fishbone cotoneaster), although a wall shrub rather than a climber, is often used for this purpose. It has a prostrate, spreading habit of growth when used for ground cover.

Euonymus fortunei cultivars make excellent evergreen groundcover and are particularly good for growing in shady areas of the garden, although the variegated cultivars develop a better color when exposed to at least some sun. The same applies to ivies. The small-leaved *Hedera helix* cultivars (Common ivy) create a marvelous flowing texture when grown as groundcover, and the large-leaved ones such as *H. colchica* (Persian ivy) create a different but still pleasing effect.

THIS CLIMBING ROSE has managed to extend itself across the entire width of this house, and is enlivening the whole of the front of the house with an amazing abundance of light pink flowers. At this height, dead-heading becomes a major effort—but as this picture shows it is well worth the trouble.

Parthenocissus can be used for covering large areas and is effective when cascading down a bank, especially in fall when the leaves turn brilliant red, giving the effect of a stream of molten lava.

PROVIDING SUPPORTS

Many climbers, apart from the self-clinging kinds, need a bit of extra help to climb their supports. For example, they will not be able to hold on to a wall or fence, or the pillars of a pergola, without some additional support. And free-standing climbers in beds and borders, for instance, will need some kind of structure to climb.

Walls and fences
The traditional method of supporting climbers on walls and fences is with a system of horizontal wires, to which the stems of the climbers can be tied as they grow. Heavy gauge galvanized or plastic-coated wire is recommended for this purpose. The wires, which can be spaced about 12–18in apart up the wall or fence, can be stretched tightly between vine eyes, which are like screws but with a ring at the top. Provide one of these at each end of the wire, and if it is a long stretch insert one or two in between to prevent the wire from sagging too much. To achieve really tight wires you may have to use stronger devices such as straining bolts instead of vine eyes.

CLIMBERS FOR GROWING AS GROUNDCOVER

- *Akebia quinata* (Chocolate vine)
- *Ampelopsis glandulosa* var. *bevipedunculata* "Elegans"
- *Clematis*, Viticella Group
- *Cotoneaster horizontalis* (Fishbone cotoneaster)
- *Decumaria barbara*
- *Euonymus fortunei*
- *Hedera canariensis* (Canary Island ivy)
- *Hedera colchica* (Persian ivy)
- *Hedera helix* (Common or English ivy)
- *Hydrangea anomala* subsp. *petiolaris* (Climbing hydrangea)
- *Lonicera periclymenum* (Common honeysuckle)
- *Parthenocissus henryana* (Chinese Virginia creeper)
- *Parthenocissus quinquefolia* (Virginia creeper)
- *Parthenocissus tricuspidata* (Boston ivy)
- *Rubus henryi* var. *bambusarum* (Bramble)
- *Schisandra chinensis*
- *Schizophragma hydrangeoides*
- *Trachelospermum jasminoides* (Star jasmine)
- *Vitis coignetiae* (Vine)
- *Vitis vinifera* "Purpurea" (Grape vine)

Vine eyes hold the wires a short distance away from the wall, and this allows free circulation of air between the wall and the plants. Good air circulation is particularly recommended for house walls to prevent the possible development of dampness. It also lessens the risk of diseases attacking the plants.

The alternative to horizontal wires is to fix trellis panels to walls and fences, to which climbers can be tied. Available in wood, metal, or plastic, they can generally be fixed to the wall with rust-proof screws, placing a wooden block between the wall and the panel wherever screws are used, to ensure a space of at least 2in for air circulation. Old cotton reels make good "buffers."

Wires or trellis panels can also be used on outbuildings to support climbers. A particularly unsightly building can be made more attractive by completely covering the walls with attractive wooden trellis.

Substantial and long-lasting materials are needed to tie in climbers to their supports. The traditional material is tarred string which has a long life. Otherwise use ordinary thick garden string or twine. Small proprietary plastic ties of various kinds are also suitable. Do not use wire, as this will cut into the stems.

Pergolas, arbours, and arches

A pergola is one of the most popular supports for climbers. It is a tall garden structure that can take various forms. Basically it consists of a series of pillars. These are generally made of timber, but pillars can be constructed with brick or natural stone, these being more suitable for large gardens as they are bulky structures. The pillars support horizontal beams.

Pergolas can be various shapes but the most popular is to have pillars along each side of a path linked by cross beams, thus creating a covered walk. Also popular is a square or rectangular pergola covering or partially covering a patio or other paved area that is used for outdoor living, the idea here being to create a pleasant shady area in which to sit, relax, and enjoy alfresco meals.

It is possible to buy pergola kits. Timber is the most popular material for construction and is available from many DIY superstores and garden centers. Metal pergolas, available from specialist suppliers, are more expensive. DIY enthusiasts may be able to construct their own timber pergola, using smooth, pressure-treated timber or, for a country or cottage garden, rustic poles.

Arches also make good supports for climbers, again available in kit form, timber, or metal. They consist of upright pillars with cross pieces at the top and are generally used to form an entrance—again, perhaps, placed over a path. These can be highly effective with a flowering climber draping itself overhead.

An arbour or bower is a traditional support for climbing plants. These are essentially intimate alcoves where one can sit and enjoy a pleasant view of the garden. An arbour is often combined with a pergola, being placed

A FETCHING ARCH over a path, seating area and lavender bed benefits from a climber. Used with architectural elements, climbers act to soften harsh lines and help to make objects such as this arch to merge into the general flow of the garden.

BIRDS LOVE the twisting branches of climbers as sites for their nests. Here a clematis provides decoration and a home.

THIS LARGE-FLOWERED Clematis cultivar has a good hold on a timber post, and provides a column of vibrant colors.

at the end of a path. There are timber or metal versions available, but the DIY enthusiast may be able to construct one from wooden trellis panels.

Most climbing plants will need some help to grow up the timber pillars used for garden structures, as well as brick or stone pergola pillars. Vertical wires can be fixed to pillars, to which the climbers can be tied, again using vine eyes or even ordinary screws which end up looking less conspicuous. Generally there is no problem tying in climbers to metal structures, and no additional support is needed to keep the plants in place.

Free-standing supports

To grow climbers, such as clematis and roses, in a bed or border you will need to provide some kind of support. Very popular are obelisks, specially designed for the purpose. Proprietary ones are available in metal or wood. If you want a more rustic kind, opt for woven willow or hazel designs. Obelisks come in various heights—make sure you choose a suitable height for your subject. For most climbers 6ft would be the minimum. Pot obelisks are also available for patio tubs. Simply tie in climbers to these supports with garden twine.

Alternative supports for climbers in beds and borders are wooden pillars. Stout fencing posts about 8ft long are ideal for the purpose, and should be sunk about 24in into the ground. Provide a vertical wire on each side of the post for tying in the climber.

Growing up trees

Climbers other than self-clinging kinds will need additional means of support on large trees until they reach the branches, which will then take over as supports. So to start with insert long bamboo canes into the ground against the trunk of the tree, one for each stem. The young stems can then be tied into these with garden twine. Self-clinging climbers generally need to be provided with just one shorter cane after planting to initially guide the young stem to the trunk.

GROWING CONDITIONS

To ensure optimum growth and flowering from your climbers you must grow them in the right conditions. It is a case of choosing exactly the right spot in your garden for the particular plant, taking into account aspect and soil conditions. Specific conditions are given for each climber in the plant section (see pages 692–723).

Aspect

The majority of climbers grow best in sites with full sun but there are some that tolerate partial shade, in other words, where the sun reaches for part of the day only. Others will take full shade, with no sun at all. Some climbers like the best of both worlds—an example being clematis, which like a cool shaded root run but their heads in the sun. To achieve this, grow them in a sunny spot but ensure their roots are shaded by shallow rooting, low growing or groundcover plants. Heavy mulching over the root area will achieve the same result.

South- and west-facing walls and fences are usually the sunniest and warmest areas of the garden, while north- and east-facing ones are the coolest and shadiest. Those facing east receive some sun in the morning while northerly aspects receive no sun at all.

Many climbers need shelter from strong winds, not only to prevent their stems being whipped around and damaged (although if tied in properly this should not happen), but also to prevent the foliage being scorched by cold drying winds. Some of the less hardy climbers in particular need a warm, sheltered spot to ensure good growth and flowering. If the garden is not naturally sheltered, wind protection can be provided in various ways, for example by planting large wind-resistant shrubs on the windward side of the garden to filter and slow down the wind. Also large shrubs planted further in the garden to form a screen can have the effect of creating a favourable microclimate for less-hardy plants. Sheltered courtyards are also ideal for the less-hardy climbers.

Soil

There are climbers to suit all types of soil, from heavy clay, through loams, to chalky types and light sandy soils, and from moisture-retentive to dry. The majority of climbers will grow well in any type of soil if it has been well prepared, and in both acid (lime-free) and alkaline (limy) soils. Some, however, prefer limy or chalky soils, such as clematis, while others must have acid conditions,

an example being *Berberidopsis corallina*, although it would survive in neutral soil. Check your soil for acidity or alkalinity (also called its pH) with a simple soil-testing kit, obtainable from many good garden centers.

Many climbers are long-lived plants and respond well to thorough soil preparation and improvement before planting. In particular it is important to ensure that the soil is adequately drained and does not become waterlogged in the winter. Soil is prepared by digging to the depth of the spade blade and at the same time any improvements can be carried out.

Loamy soils are the best, being fertile and well-drained, and need little in the way of improvement. However, even these benefit from the addition of bulky organic matter during digging, adding it to the bottom of each trench and then forking it in. You can use garden compost, well-rotted manure, or composted bark. These all break down in the soil and become humus that helps to improve the structure of all soils and also aids in the retention of moisture and nutrients.

Clay soils may be poorly drained. To improve drainage, again incorporate bulky organic matter, but also add copious amounts of horticultural grit or coarse sand if

A POPULAR CLIMBER, Wisteria floribunda "Multijuga" arranges itself in a pleasantly regular fashion over the rear of this house. Its pendulous blooms of lilac-blue make a striking textural as well as colorful display. These flowers appear in late spring and early summer.

drainage is poor. These materials open up the soil and improve both drainage and air circulation. Add sand or grit to the bottom of the trenches during digging and also mix it into the top 12in of soil.

Adding bulky organic matter to the freely drained chalky and sandy soils, which are inclined to dry out rapidly, will help them to retain moisture during dry periods. Unfortunately the humus thus created does not last long in these soils, but can be replaced by the application of a heavy mulch.

Following the initial preparation of a planting site, leave the ground to settle for a few months before planting. Then just before the plants go in fork a general-purpose fertilizer into the surface.

Planting

As with most plants these days, climbers are bought in pots, whether from a garden center or from a mail-order nursery. So they can be planted at any time of year because their roots are not disturbed when planting. However, never plant when the soil is cold and wet, or frozen, in the winter as the roots may rot before the plant has a chance to become established. It is not a good idea to plant during drought conditions as then much more water will be needed to get plants established. The ideal time to plant is in the spring, as the soil is warming up and drying out. Then the plants will quickly root into the soil and become established. Some gardeners also favor fall planting, while the soil is still warm.

To plant a pot-grown climber, make a planting hole slightly wider than the rootball, and of such a depth that after planting the top of the rootball is only just below the soil surface. Return fine soil around the rootball, firming it well with your heels or fist as you proceed.

If initial supports are needed, such as a bamboo cane to guide the stems to the main support, insert this before returning soil around the plant, to avoid pushing it through the roots, which may damage them.

It is the usual practice to set climbers at least 12in away from a wall or fence and to guide the stems to the support with bamboo canes angled in towards it. This is because the soil can be very dry immediately in front of a wall or fence, because rain is deflected, so climbers may not establish well in this "rain shadow." The same applies when planting against a large tree. After planting, mulch the plants with bulky organic matter.

When planting in pots and tubs, first put a 2in deep layer of drainage material in the bottom (broken clay flower pots or pebbles), cover this with a layer of chipped bark, then use a good soil-based potting compost to fill the container. Half fill the container, set the plant in the center, then fill up with more compost.

GENERAL CARE

Having taken care to get your new climbers off to a good start by preparing the soil well and planting them correctly and in the best positions, it is sensible to look after them well for the rest of their lives. They will repay you with healthy growth and prolific flower displays.

Mulching

A modern gardening trend is to permanently mulch the ground between plants in beds, including shrubs, climbers, and hardy perennials. This will help to prevent

STAR JASMINE is widely grown for its dark, glossy foliage and heavily scented white flowers. It will soon twine around this post.

the soil from losing moisture rapidly during dry periods and also acts to prevent weeds establishing themselves. It can also give the bed a neater appearance than bare soil.

However, the ground must first be completely free from weeds, particularly perennial kinds, before laying a mulch. Perennial weeds will force their way up through organic mulching materials, so if necessary kill them off first with glyphosate weedkiller. A modern idea is to lay a geotextile sheet mulch, such as bonded fibre fleece or woven polypropylene, around plants to suppress weeds and then cover it with a more decorative, such as an organic, mulching material. Sheet mulches allow air and water to pass through, but do make it quite difficult to apply fertilizer around plants.

Organic mulches are widely used. A particular favorite is chipped bark or wood, used both fresh and composted, and available in various grades and wood to bark ratios. Garden compost and well-rotted manure are also good but not as attractive as bark. These materials are laid about 2in deep over the entire bed or border, but not hard up against the stems of plants.

An organic mulch can initially be laid in the spring and then topped up as necessary. The soil must be moist rather than dry before laying a mulch.

Watering

All newly planted climbers, like any other plants, will need regular watering if the soil starts to dry out, until they become established. Until new roots have made their way into the soil plants are very susceptible to water stress. Check new plantings every few days during dry weather in spring, summer and fall and if the soil feels dry water heavily. When plants are established they usually need watering only during long periods of dry weather, if the soil is drying out.

Apply sufficient water for it to penetrate the soil to at least 6in. This means about (4 gal per sq/yd. This equals about 1in of rain. Use a garden sprinkler or, even better, a permanent seep hose laid among the plants, ideally under a mulch.

Pots and tubs will need checking daily in spring, summer and into fall for water requirements. Remember they can dry out rapidly in warm weather, especially when plants are well rooted in them. Fill up the space, usually about 1in, between the compost surface and the rim of the pot with water to ensure the entire depth of compost is moistened.

Feeding

Established climbers benefit from an annual application of fertilizer in the spring. Use a general purpose slow-release fertilizer. A good organic one is blood, fish, and bone. The soil should be moist, but not sodden, when the fertilizer is applied. If the soil has a mulch over it you will need to scrape this away from the plants before applying fertilizer. Ideally fertilizer should be lightly forked into the soil surface to speed up its absorption.

Climbers in pots and tubs can also be fed once a year in the spring, again using a slow-release fertilizer that will keep them going throughout the growing season.

Tying in

If necessary, the young stems of climbers should be tied in to their supports as they grow. This will prevent them being whipped around by the wind or snagged by passers-by and damaged. It is always easier to train stems when they are young and supple, because as they age they become more woody and therefore difficult to position exactly where you want them. Mature stems are also more prone to snapping. Stems should always be spaced out evenly on the support and tied in with tarred or ordinary garden twine or small plastic ties.

Winter protection

Some climbers and wall shrubs are less hardy than others and could be damaged by hard frosts. If you are tempted to grow any of these and live in a cold part of the country it would be advisable to provide some form of protection during the winter, particularly for the lower parts of the stems to prevent these being killed off. A protective screen about 6ft high can be formed from two sheets of wire netting with a layer of bracken or straw sandwiched in between them. Wire them together then form the

THIS PRETTY PINK jasmine, Jasminum beesianum, *has found itself a pleasant spot nestled in the corner of a large pergola. It makes a wonderfully bright highlight in what would otherwise have been a rather dull and uninteresting corner. It also provides scent to fragrance the area.*

MAKING FULL USE of each plant's habit of growth, this meeting of white foxgloves from below and white climbing roses from above makes for an upward sweeping movement.

ENJOYING PERFECT health, this clematis shines forth with an abundance of scarlet flowers, enhanced with bright yellow stamens.

"sandwich" into a half cylinder and place it in front of the climber, hard up against the wall or fence. This should provide sufficient protection from hard frosts. If the tops of the stems are killed by frost, cut them back to live tissue in the spring, and they should re-grow.

Pests and diseases

Fortunately most climbers are not troubled much by pests and diseases. Occasionally they may be attacked by aphids or greenfly but these are easily controlled by spraying with an insecticidal soap or pyrethrum. These products will also control any infestations of caterpillars. Powdery mildew may crop up occasionally, particularly on grape vines, creating a white deposit on the leaves and shoot tips. If you notice this on the plant, spray it with a fungicide such as carbendazim.

One or two climbers, however, have more than their fair share of troubles, particularly roses. These may be attacked by the diseases rose black spot (black spots on leaves), rose rust (rust-colored spots on leaves), and rose powdery mildew. Aphids (greenfly) are also very fond of roses. Wherever possible buy cultivars that are resistant to diseases, particularly black spot. If you have to resort to spraying, opt for a combined rose spray that controls pests and diseases. Very often rose diseases can be prevented by spraying regularly before they appear.

Clematis are prone to a very serious fungal disease known as clematis wilt, which causes shoots and foliage to wilt and die back. If this occurs, cut back affected stems to healthy wood. It may even be necessary to remove stems at ground level or below. If the attack is not too severe, the plant should produce new growth.

PRUNING AND TRAINING

Many climbers do not need regular pruning, only the occasional removal of old and congested growth. This is just as well as pruning these plants is a time-consuming process, much of which may have to be done from ladders or stepladders. However, some climbers do need annual pruning to keep them under control and to ensure good growth and flowering. These need to be grown where they are easily reached and not, for example, up a tall tree or very high wall. Specific pruning requirements and when to prune are given for each climber in the plant section (see pages 692–723). The various techniques for pruning climbers are discussed here.

Basic techniques

You will need a good pair of parrot-bill pruning shears for pruning thin stems, for example when you are spur pruning a wisteria. You will also need a pruning saw or heavy-duty loppers (like long handled pruning shears) to tackle thick growth, such as when you are renovating an old climber. Shears are useful for pruning or trimming some climbers, particularly those which produce a mass of thin stems such as hederas (ivies) and loniceras (honeysuckles). It would be too time consuming to prune these stems individually with pruning shears so shears are used to considerably speed up the job.

Always use really sharp tools to ensure clean cuts that heal more rapidly than ragged cuts made with blunt implements. The latter may encourage the entry of diseases, resulting in stems dying back.

IVIES ARE among the most frequently seen climbers. Many varieties are vigorous growers and some can be invasive, smothering formal beds. Under close supervision, however, they make superb groundcover (above) as well as excellent climbers, with some species displaying variegated foliage.

Individual pruning cuts, for example when spur pruning, are made directly above a bud on the stem. Always cut to a bud that points in the direction that you want growth to occur. Never cut back to buds that face in towards the wall or other support. Do not leave a length of stem or "stub" above a bud, as it will only die back and look unsightly and may create an entry point for diseases. If stems have buds arranged alternately, make the cut slightly slanting, in the direction that the bud is pointing, to allow rainwater to run off. If there are pairs of opposite buds, as in clematis for example, make a straight cut just above them.

There is no need to seal pruning cuts, although very large wounds, such as occur when cutting out old, thick wood, could be sealed with proprietary pruning "paint" to prevent moisture and diseases from entering. If you are pruning plants that are diseased, you should regularly disinfect your tools by wiping the blades with methylated spirit or dipping them in horticultural disinfectant.

It is important to prune climbers at the right time of year. Generally deciduous climbers are pruned in the winter while they are dormant, ideally in late winter, and evergreens in the spring, when they will rapidly produce new shoots to hide the pruning cuts. Some flowering climbers are pruned in spring or summer immediately after the flower display is over.

Initial training

Before planting a new climber, remove any weak, dead or damaged stems. If it has only one or two stems and you want more, cut out the tips to encourage new shoots to be produced from lower down. Some young climbers have only a single stem when purchased, including many clematis. It is best to allow such plants to become established over a complete growing season before cutting back the stem in early spring to encourage more stems to grow. With clematis the stem can be cut back really hard, near to the soil. Other climbers can have their stem reduced by one-third to half its length.

Tie in the stems of all climbers after planting, whatever their habit of growth may be, and keep them tied in as they grow. Self-clinging climbers do not adopt this habit to start with so keep them tied in until they can support themselves.

In the first few years young climbers do not need much pruning but you should concentrate on training the stems to their supports. If the plant is neither branching enough nor making sufficient stems to cover a given area, then cut back the leading shoots to encourage the production of side shoots.

Aim to develop a basic framework of stems that covers the support well. Train the stems as evenly as possible, making sure they are well spaced out, especially on a wall or fence where they can be trained to a fan shape. Bear in mind that stems trained horizontally often flower much better than those trained vertically. The same applies to stems spiralled around the support, such as a post or pillar. Some flowering climbers, such as wisterias, can have all their stems trained horizontally, on a low fence or wall for example, which will encourage prolific flowering. Climbing and Rambler roses also respond especially well to horizontal training.

Stems are trained vertically on pillars and posts, or they can be spiralled around the support to encourage better flowering. When the stems reach the top of structures such as pergolas, arches, and arbours they are trained horizontally over the structure.

Regularly cut out any shoots that are growing in toward the wall or growing outward, or train them in a different direction. Do not allow stems to grow across each other. Any shoots that are not needed for the main framework can be cut back to at least three buds. They may then produce flowers.

Annual spur pruning

Much annual pruning of established climbers to encourage the production of flowers or fruits, and prevent congested growth, takes the form of spur pruning. It is generally deciduous climbers that produce their flowers on shoots produced in the current season, such as climbing roses, that are spur pruned. In late winter side shoots produced from the main framework are cut back to within three to six buds of their base. These spurs develop to produce flowers later in the year.

However, if the climber flowers on shoots produced in the previous year, it should be spur pruned as soon as flowering season is over, an example of this being *Jasminum nudiflorum* (Winter jasmine).

Very vigorous climbers such as wisteria are pruned twice a year, once in summer to reduce the length of the vigorous side shoots, and then in winter when they are reduced further, to within two or three buds of their base.

Trimming

Established climbers that do not need regular pruning, such as hederas (ivies), *Clematis montana* and its cultivars and *Lonicera* (honeysuckle) species and cultivars, produce a heavy mass of growth over a period of time and need cutting back with shears to reduce their bulk. They can be pruned hard back to their support in late winter or early spring, just leaving the main framework of stems which will then produce a fresh crop of new growth. To prevent ivies from becoming bulky they can, alternatively, be trimmed annually in spring.

Thinning and renovating

Established climbers that are not pruned regularly may eventually need to have their main body of growth thinned out. It is not advisable to allow plants to become too congested before pruning, as it will then involve a large amount of work and may end up spoiling the overall appearance of the plant. Thinning will help to prevent the plant from becoming too heavy and congested and allows light and air to reach the center, which is necessary for continued healthy growth.

The technique involves cutting back some of the older stems to younger shoots lower down which will then replace them. Alternatively old stems may be cut down fairly close to the ground to encourage them to produce

AN OLD WISTERIA in full bloom grows over an arch where the lovely pendulous flowers can be best appreciated.

THE FROTHY flowers of this rose are trained to poke through the trellis. Intertwined ivy is set off beautifully by the stained blue wood.

new shoots from very low down. Always cut out stems in short sections as it makes the job easier. Trying to pull out a long stem from a congested mass of growth is not only difficult but can also damage the plant. In a dense mass of growth it is not always easy trace the entire length of a stem, and you may cut out a young vigorous stem by mistake. To overcome this problem, cut back an old stem, even close to the ground, and then wait a few days for it to wilt so that it can be easily seen.

If a climber has been badly neglected and not pruned for years (perhaps in a garden that you have recently inherited from a previous owner) some drastic action may be called for to rejuvenate it. If the plant is a species that is known to respond well to severe pruning, be brave and cut it down almost to ground level—within 12–24in. This hard pruning should be carried out in the winter. In the spring the plant will produce new shoots. For plants that will not tolerate such drastic action, such as many evergreens, do the job over several years, cutting back only one or two of the oldest stems each time. During this renovation remove any dead wood and tie in young replacement stems.

Dead growth

Always cut out dead, dying, diseased and damaged stems as soon as they are noticed, regardless of time of year. Prune the shoots right back to healthy tissue. If you have the time it is always a good idea to remove dead flowers

regularly, as not only does this make the plant look tidier, but also often results in more flowers following in the same season. This is certainly true of many climbing roses, for instance. It also reduces the risk of disease moving in to dead areas. However, some climbers are grown for their fruits or attractive seed heads, including various clematis species, so do not dead-head these.

Standard climbers

Some climbers can be grown as standards in large tubs to make unusual patio features. Standards are like small trees, with a single stem and a head of branches at the top. Climbers that are spur pruned, such as grape vines, *Wisteria*, *Solanum crispum,* and *S. jasminoides*, are ideal for training as standards, as are *Lonicera* species (honeysuckles) that do not mind regular pruning.

To create a standard, first pot and stake a single-stemmed young plant, then cut back the stem by about one-third. Lateral or side shoots are allowed to grow on this to encourage it to thicken, and are removed gradually over three years, those remaining being shortened by two-thirds in the summer. In the first winter remove the lower third of laterals, in the second winter the middle third and in the third winter the top laterals. Lightly cut back the leading shoot each year, again to help strengthen and thicken the stem. When the desired height is reached, normally about 5ft, allow laterals to develop at the top of the stem to form a head of branches.

A WONDERFUL MIXTURE of colors brings life to this classic garden scene. Note how the blooms of the climbing rose combine well with the bed in the foreground and the light brown stone of the house wall. Such roses can be dead-headed through the flowering season to prolong the display.

GLORIOUS YELLOW Clematis tangutica *flowers and frothy foliage merge with flowering plants in a decorative border.*

The procedure for pruning the head of established standards is the same as for climbing plants, and a permanent wooden stake will be needed for support.

PROPAGATION

Propagating your own climbers is an economical way of obtaining new plants. Rooting cuttings is a widely used method, especially where many new plants are required. The same is true of raising plants from seeds, but this method is suitable only for species, not cultivars and hybrids that do not come true to type. Many climbers can be propagated by layering, which involves rooting a stem while it is still attached to the parent plant. This technique is ideal where only a few new plants are needed.

Taking cuttings

Stem cuttings are the most widely used, consisting of a portion of stem in various degrees of ripeness or maturity: one can take softwood, semi-ripe, and hardwood cuttings. You need to choose the best type of cutting for the particular plant being propagated.

Softwood cuttings taken in spring and early summer are the most challenging to root because very soft shoots are used, which wilt all too easily. They are suitable for many deciduous climbers. Select new soft shoots 1½–2in long and cut just below a node or leaf joint at the base. Remove the lower leaves (leave two or three pairs of leaves at the top) and the soft tip, and dip the base of the cutting in hormone rooting powder. Insert in pots of cuttings compost (equal parts peat and coarse sand), water in and place in a heated, humid propagating case with a temperature of 59°F. The cuttings should develop roots in a few weeks.

Semi-ripe cuttings, taken in mid- to late summer, are also prepared from current season's shoots, but are soft at the tip and hard or ripening at the base. They are suitable for a very wide range of deciduous and evergreen climbers. Cuttings vary in length from 2½–4in depending on growth. Cut the shoot immediately below a node or leaf joint at the base, remove the lower third of leaves and then

A LUSH CORNER, brimming with foliage and flowers. The climbing rose and Vitis *vine sweep in from above and complete the picture.*

CLIMBERS FOR TRAINING AS STANDARDS

- *Actinidia kolomikta*
- *Campsis radicans* (Common trumpet creeper)
- X *Fatshedera lizei* (Tree ivy)
- *Hedera helix* (Common or English ivy)
- *Hydrangea anomala* subsp. *petiolaris* (Climbing hydrangea)
- *Lonicera japonica* (Japanese honeysuckle)
- *Lonicera periclymenum* (Common honeysuckle)
- *Schizophragma hydrangeoides*
- *Solanum crispum* (Chilean potato tree)
- *Solanum jasminoides* (Potato vine)
- *Vitis vinifera* (Grape vine)
- *Wisteria floribunda* (Japanese wisteria)
- *Wisteria sinensis* (Chinese wisteria)

dip the base of the cutting in hormone rooting powder. Insert the cuttings in pots of cuttings compost, water in and place in a cold frame to root, or in a propagating case if the subject needs heat to root. A humid atmosphere is required for rooting. Cuttings should be rooted by the following growing season.

Hardwood cuttings are prepared from late fall to mid-winter from current-season's shoots that are fully ripe or hard. They are suitable for various deciduous climbers such as *Vitis* (Grape vines) and *Fallopia baldschuanica*. Select leafless stems and cut them into lengths of 8in with pruning shears, below a bud at the base and above a bud at the top. Dip in hormone rooting powder, insert in deep pots of cuttings compost and place in a cold frame. Hardwood cuttings are slow rooting, often producing leaves in spring before they have rooted. Allow a year before lifting and planting out. Rooting can be speeded up by placing cuttings in a heated propagating case, as is usually practiced with vines.

Leaf-bud cuttings are modified versions of stem cuttings and are useful for several deciduous and evergreen climbers. They can be softwood or semi-ripe. Climbers commonly propagated from leaf-bud cuttings include clematis (softwood or semi-ripe) and ivies (semi-ripe). You get more cuttings from a length stem than with conventional stem cuttings. Each cutting consists of a 1in length of stem, cut between nodes at the base but just above a node at the top, with a leaf or pair of leaves at the top containing a growth bud in the leaf axil. Otherwise treat leaf-bud cuttings as for softwood or semi-ripe stem cuttings.

Layering

Layering involves encouraging a stem to root while still attached to the plant. It is a suitable and easy method of propagating many deciduous and evergreen climbers such as clematis, wisterias, and akebias. Some climbers may self-layer if the stem comes into contact with the soil, such as ivies used as ground cover. Layering is carried out in the spring and stems can take up to a year to root.

Serpentine layering is used for climbers, rooting the stem in a number of places along its length. Use one of the previous year's stems. You need to wound the underside of the stem where you want it to root, by making a slanting cut about 1in long between nodes to form a tongue. Keep this cut open with a matchstick and dust it with hormone rooting powder. Using a V-shaped wire pin, peg down the stem where wounded into an 3in deep depression in the ground and cover with soil. The stem is "snaked" in and out of the soil, ensuring that at least one bud stays above soil between the wounded areas. An alternative technique is to wound through nodes or

BOSTON IVY is being trained against this brick wall, which it will eventually cover. In the meantime it still looks decorative.

A HEAVY SWATHE of star jasmine hangs across the top of this gate and down beside the steps. In full bloom the perfume is all-pervading.

A TRADITIONAL "English garden" combination of roses, delphiniums, and wisteria creates a delightful effect in early summer. Wisteria, a twining climber, is easily trained to any shape desired, on both high and low supports.

leaf joints, or just behind them, and pin the stem where wounded to the soil surface. Keep layers moist at all times. Lift the new plant when it has rooted and sever from parent plant.

Growing from seeds

Seeds of some climbers need a cold period in winter before they will germinate in the spring, examples being members of the rose family such as climbing roses and cotoneaster. Fleshy fruits and berries of other climbers generally need the same treatment. Sow these as soon as collected in late summer or fall and stand the pots in a cold place to alternately freeze and thaw throughout winter, a technique known as stratification.

Seeds of other climbers can be sown in spring. Seeds with very hard coats, such as those of the pea family, need to have their coats scarified to allow moisture to penetrate before they will germinate. Rub the seeds between two sheets of sandpaper to scratch the surface, or pour boiling water over them and let them soak for 24 hours.

Sow seeds in pots of soil-based seed compost and for spring sowings cover very lightly with compost, followed by a ½in layer of fine-grade vermiculite (a natural mineral). Seeds to be stratified over winter are also lightly covered with compost followed by a ¼in layer of grit. Spring sowings are best germinated in a heated propagating case, a temperature of 59–68°F being suitable for most subjects.

CONTRASTING COLORS are used here to great effect. Using Clematis *species and a cultivar with different foliage textures and flower colors makes a lively display—rather like a vertical border.*

AKEBIA QUINATA
Chocolate vine

THE CHOCOLATE VINE is not over-vigorous but this particular vine is producing a great show of flowers. It is hard to describe their color but it is a dark pinkish or purplish brown, and they have an unusual chocolate smell. Leaves consist of five deep green leaflets.

FEATURES

Twiner

The fascinating and unusual purple-brown flowers of the Chocolate vine, a native of China, Japan and Korea, have a light but distinctive smell of chocolate. The foliage is also decorative, and therefore this climber looks good even when not in flower. It is a long-lived twining semi-evergreen climber capable of growing up to 30ft, although it may be less in some gardens. Growth is fairly vigorous once the plant is established but it is rather open in habit and never ends up looking heavy. This climber is seen to best advantage when grown over a trellis screen, pergola or arch, and is also a suitable subject for growing into a large tree.

AKEBIA QUINATA AT A GLANCE

One of the earliest climbers to flower, with unusual chocolate-scented blooms. Hardy to 5°F (zone 7).

Jan	/	Companion Plants
Feb	planting 🖐	Strong-growing summer-flowering clematis or climbing roses will take over from the spring display.
Mar	flowering ✾	
Apr	flowering ✾	
May	flowering ✾	
Jun	/	
July	/	
Aug	/	
Sep	/	
Oct	/	
Nov	/	
Dec	/	

CONDITIONS

Aspect   Akebia will grow equally well in full sun or partial shade.
Site   The soil must be well-drained, moisture-retentive, and reasonably fertile.

GROWING METHOD

Propagation   Sow seeds in fall and place in a cold frame. Take semi-ripe cuttings in summer. Carry out serpentine layering in the spring.
Watering   Make sure the soil does not dry in the summer.
Feeding   This is necessary only once a year in spring. Apply a slow-release organic fertilizer such as blood, fish, and bone.
Problems   Not troubled by pests or diseases.

FLOWERING/FOLIAGE

Flowers   The scented flowers are produced throughout spring and followed by long fleshy fruits. Warm conditions throughout spring and summer are necessary for fruit to be produced.
Foliage   The foliage consists of five deep green leaflets. Leaves may become flushed with an attractive purple color in the winter.

PRUNING

Requirements If necessary trim the plant after flowering to keep it within bounds. It may eventually need some of the oldest stems thinned out, or renovation pruning.

BERBERIDOPSIS CORALLINA
Coral vine

THE INTENSE SCARLET of these Berberidopsis corallina *flowers makes up for their small size, and they blaze amid the rich foliage.*

THE DEEP GREEN foliage of B. corallina *makes a marvelous background for the vibrant flowers.*

FEATURES

Twiner

A spectacular evergreen climber from Chile, valued for its exotic-looking pendulous red flowers, and ideal for a shady wall or fence. It can be especially recommended for a shady courtyard that is well protected from cold winds, but it also looks at home in a woodland garden, with suitable perennials and shrubs, as it grows in woodland in the wild. The Coral vine can also be grown through large shrubs or up mature trees. It can reach a height of up to 15ft. A severe winter may kill back the stems but it may still go on to produce new shoots from the base in the spring.

CONDITIONS

Aspect   The Coral vine needs a position in shade or

BERBERIDOPSIS AT A GLANCE

Pendulous red flowers and deep green spiny foliage. Hardy to temperatures of 23°F (zone 9).

		Companion Plants
Jan	/	Looks good with x *Fatshedera lizei*, which will also take shade. Also woodland-garden shrubs and perennials, including ferns.
Feb	/	
Mar	/	
Apr	planting 🖐	
May	planting 🖐	
Jun	flowering ✽	
July	flowering ✽	
Aug	flowering ✽	
Sep	flowering ✽	
Oct	/	
Nov	/	
Dec	/	

Site   partial shade, with shelter from cold winds. The soil must be acid or neutral, contain plenty of humus, and be able to retain moisture yet well drained. A deep organic mulch applied in fall will protect the roots from severe frosts. Coral vine grows best on wire or trellis but will also scramble over fences, tree stumps, and other objects.

GROWING METHOD

Propagation   Sow seeds in spring and germinate in a cold frame. Carry out serpentine layering in spring. Take semi-ripe cuttings toward the end of summer.

Watering   Do not allow the plant to dry out at any time. Keep the soil steadily moist.

Feeding   Once a year in spring, using a slow-release fertilizer, but avoid alkaline types.

Problems   Neither pests nor diseases are a problem.

FLOWERING/FOLIAGE

Flowers   Long-stalked pendulous flowers are carried in rows on the shoots.

Foliage   Elliptical deep green leaves have spiny edges and gray-green undersides.

PRUNING

Requirements Minimal pruning is needed for this climber. It is best not to prune unless it is considered essential. The Coral vine certainly does not like hard cutting back. Spring is the best time for pruning, removing dead growth and any very weak stems. Eventually, as the plant matures, some judicious thinning may be necessary.

CHAENOMELES SPECIOSA
Flowering quince

THERE IS A DEEP GLOSSY SHEEN to the oval leaves, which usually emerge after the flowers have bloomed on the bare branches.

THIS ADAPTABLE PLANT makes a good hedge, does well in a flower border and can be trained to grow up a sunny wall.

FEATURES

Wall shrub

This deciduous spiny shrub, a native of China, is very amenable to training flat against a wall or fence. The spines and thick growth of this plant make it a practical barrier shrub—and it can also be trained as a hedge. It flowers only from young shoots, so build up a system of permanent stems, tying them in to their support, and the flowers will be produced on the previous year's side shoots. The rich red blooms appear in spring, often very early in the season. Although of vigorous habit, growing up to 8ft high with a spread of 15ft, it is ideally suited to growing on a wall of the house, or on a fence of normal height, as it can be kept smaller if desired by pruning.

CHAENOMELES AT A GLANCE

A spiny shrub with cup-shaped flowers, often on bare stems, in the spring. Hardy to 5°F (zone 7).

Jan	/	Recommended Varieties
Feb	planting	"Geisha Girl," double, deep
Mar	planting	apricot
Apr	flowering	"Moerloosei," white and pink
May	flowering	"Nivalis," white
Jun	/	"Simonii," double, deep red
July	/	
Aug	/	
Sep	/	
Oct	/	
Nov	/	
Dec	/	

CONDITIONS

Aspect The Flowering quince should be grown in full sun or partial shade. However, flowering is most prolific in sun.

Site This shrub will thrive in any well-drained soil that is reasonably fertile.

GROWING METHOD

Propagation Sow seeds in fall and stratify them over winter. Take semi-ripe cuttings in summer.

Watering Watering is only needed if the soil starts to dry out excessively in the summer.

Feeding In the spring apply a slow-release organic fertilizer such as blood, fish and bone.

Problems The plant may be attacked by pests including aphids and scale insects.

FLOWERING/FOLIAGE

Flowers Bowl-shaped flowers, which are usually red with yellow anthers, are produced in the spring. They are followed by fragrant, apple-shaped, greenish yellow edible fruits, which can be used to make jelly.

Foliage The oval leaves are shiny and deep green.

PRUNING

Requirements Build up a permanent framework of stems and then spur prune annually after flowering—cut back the old flowered shoots to within two to four buds of the framework.

CLEMATIS
Clematis species and cultivars

THE FIRST FLOWER of this C. montana *cultivar is fully open and the plump buds promise more in the near future.*

C. armandii *"Apple Blossom" is a vigorous spring-flowering evergreen that needs to be grown in a warm, sheltered position.*

FLOWERS of the Jackmanii hybrids are by far the largest of all cultivated clematis. These large lavender-blue ones are quite lovely.

FEATURES

Twiner

There are at least 200 species, deciduous and evergreen, and countless cultivars and hybrids of clematis, the most popular of all climbers. They are native mostly to the northern hemisphere. *Clematis vitalba* (Traveller's joy, Old man's beard), sprawls over hedgerows and produces greeny white flowers in summer followed by silky seed heads. This is not generally grown in gardens as it is not sufficiently decorative. The many other species, cultivars and hybrids are more preferable.

The deciduous spring-flowering *C. montana* and its cultivars are especially popular, with flowers in white or in shades of pink. *C. armandii* and its cultivar "Apple Blossom" are vigorous spring-flowering evergreens, with white and pink-tinged flowers respectively.

The large-flowered hybrids are the most popular of all, flowering in the summer. They have some of the most spectacular flowers imaginable. All are deciduous and of modest growth. They come in a range of colors, including white, blue, purple, mauve, and red shades, and some are bicolored. Perhaps the best known is "Jackmanii" with deep purple flowers.

Tall clematis such as *C. montana* are often allowed to climb into mature trees where their flowers tumble out over the canopy. Less-vigorous clematis, such as the large-flowered hybrids, are excellent for walls, fences, pergolas, arches, arbors, obelisks, and tubs. Thin stemmed, light and airy clematis, such as the Viticella Group, are ideal for growing over large shrubs or for use as ground cover. They are also good for containers.

CONDITIONS

Aspect Clematis like to have their top growth in full sun but their roots in the shade. Roots can be shaded with plantings of groundcover plants or with other low-growing subjects, with paving slabs or with even a deep mulch of organic matter.

Site Clematis grow well in any well-drained, reasonably rich soil containing plenty of humus. They are particularly suitable for chalky soils. Keep the plants permanently mulched with organic matter.

GROWING METHOD

Propagation Sow seeds as soon as collected in the fall and stratify them over winter. They should then go on to germinate in the spring. Take softwood or semi-ripe leaf-bud cuttings in spring or summer. Carry out serpentine layering in the spring.

THIS TRANQUIL RURAL VIEW is beautifully framed by a fence covered with a rambling Clematis montana. *The delicate tracery of the stems and the scattering of white flowers would be just as attractive in a city garden.*

Watering — Clematis should not be allowed to suffer from lack of moisture, so water plants well during rainless periods if the soil starts to dry out.

Feeding — An annual application of slow-release organic fertilizer, such as blood, fish, and bone, should be applied in the spring.

Problems — Clematis wilt is the biggest problem. To help overcome this disease, plant clematis deeply, covering the top of the rootball with 3in of soil. This also ensures that new stems grow from below ground. Aphids may infest plants in the summer.

FLOWERING/FOLIAGE

Flowers — Clematis flower mainly in the spring, summer and fall, according to type. A few species bloom in the winter. Flowers come in all colors and they may be flat, bell-shaped, or cup-shaped.

Foliage — This may be deciduous or evergreen, according to the individual species. Generally the leaves have twining stalks.

PRUNING

Requirements — Pruning varies according to the group that clematis are in. Group 1 contains clematis that flower early in the year on previous year's shoots, including *C. montana* and cultivars, *C. alpina, C. cirrhosa* var. *balearica, C. macropetala,* and *C. armandii.* The only pruning these plants need is thinning when they become congested. This is done after flowering. If renovation pruning is needed, cut down the complete plant to within 12in of the ground after flowering.

Group 2 contains large-flowered hybrids that produce a flush of flowers in early summer on last-year's shoots, and then another flush of blooms in late summer and fall on current year's shoots. These are pruned in late winter or early spring. Established plants can get by with very little pruning. The simplest technique is to cut them to within about 12in of the ground, every three to four years. After pruning you will lose the early summer flowers but they will bloom in late summer.

Group 3 contains clematis that flower in late summer and early fall on current season's shoots. This growth comes from the base of the plant. Included in this group are *C. viticella* and its cultivars and hybrids, *C. orientalis,* and "Jackmanii." Plants are pruned annually in late winter or early spring down to within 12in of the ground.

CLEMATIS AT A GLANCE

Very variable climbers, suitable for many situations. Flat, bell-shaped or cup-shaped flowers. Most are hardy to 5°F (zone 7).

Jan	/	**Recommended Varieties**
Feb	planting	Other clematis worth growing:
Mar	planting	
Apr	flowering	*C. alpina,* blue flowers, spring
May	flowering	
Jun	flowering	*C. cirrhosa* var. *balearica,* cream, winter/spring
July	flowering	
Aug	flowering	*C. macropetala,* blue, spring
Sep	flowering	*C. orientalis,* yellow, summer
Oct	flowering	*C. tangutica,* yellow, summer/fall
Nov	/	
Dec	/	

CLIANTHUS PUNICEUS
Glory pea

IN AREAS SUBJECT to hard frosts in winter, grow Clianthus puniceus *in a cool conservatory or greenhouse.*

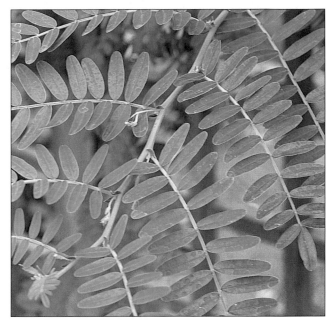

AS WELL AS its eyecatching red blooms in spring, C. puniceus *is grown for the all-year interest of its attractive pinnate leaves.*

FEATURES

Scrambler

This flamboyant semi-evergreen or evergreen climber will provide a touch of the southern hemisphere, as it is a native of the north island of New Zealand. Flowering in spring and early summer, it produces clusters of unusual, scarlet, claw-like flowers, another of its popular names being Lobster claw. These flowers are the plant's principal attraction. It will grow up to 12ft tall and needs to be grown against a warm sheltered wall. When grown unsupported it tends to spread horizontally. The Glory pea is an ideal subject for a small courtyard or other enclosed area. In parts of the country that are subject to hard frosts, it would be better to grow this climber in a frost-free conservatory or glasshouse.

CLIANTHUS AT A GLANCE

Scarlet claw-like flowers and handsome pinnate foliage. Hardy to temperatures of 23°F (zone 9).

Jan	/	Recommended Varieties
Feb	/	"Albus," white flowers
Mar	/	"Roseus," deep rose-pink
Apr	planting 🖐	flowers
May	flowering ✿	
Jun	flowering ✿	
July	/	
Aug	/	
Sep	/	
Oct	/	
Nov	/	
Dec	/	

CONDITIONS

Aspect   It must have a position in full sun and be well sheltered from cold winds.

Site   The soil should be very well drained. This climber will thrive in quite poor soils. A deep permanent mulch of organic matter is recommended to protect roots from frost.

GROWING METHOD

Propagation   Take softwood or semi-ripe cuttings in spring or summer. Sow seeds in spring, first soaking them in water or abrading them (see pages 690–691). Germinate at 64°F.

Watering   Fairly drought tolerant but apply water if the soil dries out excessively in the summer.

Feeding   Give an annual spring application of a general purpose slow-release organic fertilizer, such as blood, fish, and bone.

Problems   There are no problems from pests or diseases.

FLOWERING/FOLIAGE

Flowers   Valued for its early, exotic-looking flowers.
Foliage   The shiny pinnate leaves are attractive.

PRUNING

Requirements   Very little needed. This climber will not survive severe pruning. Cut out any weak or dead shoots as necessary. Stems may be killed back by hard frosts, but the plant may produce new shoots from the base in spring. Cut back dead growth to live tissue.

DECUMARIA BARBARA
Decumaria

APPEARING IN EARLY summer, the delightful puffs of cream-colored sweetly-scented flowers are the main attraction of Decumaria barbara. *This plants is a sturdy climber and can easily scale and cover large walls and substantial trees.*

FEATURES

Self-clinging climber

This deciduous climber from the south-east USA has stems that produce aerial roots, so eventually it is self-supporting. Decumaria is grown for its flat heads of fragrant, cream flowers that are produced in early summer. Attaining a height of 30ft, it is ideal for growing up a tall mature tree or high wall. Be wary about growing this climber on a house wall, as it will be impossible to remove it for house maintenance without damaging the stems. There is also the risk of damaging the wall itself. This plant makes good and unusual groundcover in a woodland garden or shrub border. It will also enjoy the partial or dappled shade of these situations.

DECUMARIA AT A GLANCE

A self-clinging climber with flat heads of cream flowers and handsome glossy foliage. Hardy to 23°F (zone 9).

Jan	/	Companion Plants
Feb	/	Looks good with climbing
Mar	planting ✎	roses, which should flower at
Apr	planting ✎	the same time.
May	/	
Jun	flowering ✳	
July	/	
Aug	/	
Sep	/	
Oct	/	
Nov	/	
Dec	/	

CONDITIONS

Aspect   Grows well in full sun or partial shade. Provide shelter from cold drying winds as this climber is not fully hardy and may therefore be damaged in an exposed situation.

Site   Any well-drained fertile soil will be suitable for this climber.

GROWING METHOD

Propagation   Take semi-ripe cuttings in late summer. When grown as ground cover it will self-layer, so simply remove rooted portions of stem, complete with buds or young shoots, if new plants are required.

Watering   If the soil starts to dry out in summer water the plant well. It dislikes drying out.

Feeding   An annual spring application of slow-release fertilizer, such as the organic blood, fish, and bone, will be sufficient.

Problems   Not troubled by pests or diseases.

FLOWERING/FOLIAGE

Flowers   The cream flowers, which are produced in early summer, smell of honey.

Foliage   The large deep green leaves are attractive and make a good background for the flowers.

PRUNING

Requirements No regular pruning needed. If necessary trim after flowering to keep within allotted space.

X FATSHEDERA LIZEI
Tree ivy

THE STUNNING LEAVES of X Fatshedera lizei *are evergreen, and very deply lobed. Being deep green and very shiny they create a luxuriant effect in any garden. The Tree ivy can be grown as a climber, as groundcover, or even as a standard in a tub.*

FEATURES

Scrambler

An evergreen shrub of spreading habit. It is not a true climber but can be trained against a wall, on an obelisk, or as a standard in a tub. The Tree ivy also makes good ground cover. It is a hybrid of *Fatsia* and *Hedera* (ivy) that originated under cultivation, and has the characteristics of both parents. The Tree ivy is valued for its lush foliage that looks good all the year round. Highly adaptable, it is a very good choice for shady town and city gardens, and takes atmospheric pollution in its stride. The plant is of modest stature, growing to a height of 4–6ft, or more when trained to a support.

X FATSHEDERA LIZEI AT A GLANCE

An ivy-like shrub with lustrous dark green foliage. Hardy to 23°F (zone 9).

Jan	foliage	
Feb	foliage	**Recommended Varieties**
Mar	foliage	"Annemieke," yellow
Apr	planting	variegated leaves
May	planting	"Variegata," white-edged
Jun	foliage	leaves
July	foliage	These two are half-hardy and
Aug	foliage	should be grown in pots
Sep	flowering	under glass.
Oct	flowering	
Nov	foliage	
Dec	foliage	

CONDITIONS

Aspect Good for partial shade but also grows well in a sunny spot.

Site Thrives in any soil. The ideal soil is reasonably rich, moisture-retentive yet well-drained.

GROWING METHOD

Propagation Take semi-ripe leaf-bud cuttings in summer. Stems can also be layered.

Watering Keep the soil moist in summer during dry spells as the plant dislikes drying out.

Feeding Give an annual spring application of slow-release organic fertilizer such as blood, fish, and bone.

Problems Generally free from pests and diseases.

FLOWERING/FOLIAGE

Flowers Heads of tiny green-white flowers are produced in fall. These are not the most showy of flowers and the plant is grown primarily for its decorative foliage.

Foliage The evergreen deeply lobed leaves are deep green and shiny, creating a luxuriant effect.

PRUNING

Requirements Does not need pruning, only the removal or cutting back of any shoots that spoil the overall shape. Pruning should be carried out in late winter or early spring.

FREMONTODENDRON
Flannel bush

A GENEROUS DISPLAY OF yellow blooms cover this plant for months at a time, but flowering may be affected if the soil is too rich.

THE DARK GREEN leaves of Fremontodendron "California Glory" provide the perfect canvas for its vibrant yellow blooms.

FEATURES

Wall shrub

This large evergreen shrub, the full name of which is *Fremontodendron californicum*, is spectacular when laden with its large bowl-shaped bright yellow flowers in summer and fall. It grows up to 20ft tall and so needs a reasonable amount of headroom. It is a native of the USA, especially California.
Unfortunately the Flannel bush can be quite a short-lived plant so it is best to propagate it to ensure you have some young replacement plants should it suddenly expire. It is a great choice for a house or other high wall and relishes a sheltered courtyard garden or other secluded area. It looks good growing with a blue-flowered ceanothus.

FREMONTODENDRON AT A GLANCE

A large vigorous shrub with shallow bowl-shaped yellow flowers over a very long period. Hardy to 23°F (zone 9).

Jan	/	Recommended Varieties
Feb	/	*Fremontodendron* "California
Mar	/	Glory," deep yellow flowers.
Apr	planting ✿	
May	planting ✿	
Jun	flowering ✾	
July	flowering ✾	
Aug	flowering ✾	
Sep	flowering ✾	
Oct	flowering ✾	
Nov	/	
Dec	/	

CONDITIONS

Aspect Grow against a warm sunny wall. Needs to be well sheltered from wind.

Site Can be grown in a wide range of well-drained soils, from dry to moist, but prefers alkaline or neutral conditions. Ideally suited to poor soils.

GROWING METHOD

Propagation Sow seeds in spring and germinate at 59–68°F. Take semi-ripe cuttings in late summer and root in a heated propagating case. Hardwood cuttings in late fall or winter are easier. Root them in a cool glasshouse.

Watering This plant takes quite dry conditions, so it is not necessary to water unless the soil becomes excessively dry.

Feeding Give an annual application of slow-release organic fertilizer in the spring.

Problems Not generally troubled by pests or diseases.

FLOWERING/FOLIAGE

Flowers It is grown for its flamboyant yellow flowers produced over a very long period.

Foliage Dark green lobed leaves. Shoots hairy and covered in scales.

PRUNING

Requirements Minimal pruning in midsummer after the first flowers. Wear goggles: the mealy coating on the shoots and leaves can irritate the eyes.

HEBE HULKEANA
New Zealand lilac

THIS YOUNG Hebe hulkeana *needs careful training to contain its loose growth habit. It tolerates some shade, but does best in full sun.*

SHAPELY LEAVES ARE a key attraction of the hebes, and many have subtle distinguishing features, such as the thin red edging here.

FEATURES

Wall shrub

This is an evergreen shrub from New Zealand, with a slender, loose, sprawling habit of growth. It is best grown by training it to a warm sunny wall, where it will benefit from the protection afforded, as it is not one of the hardiest subjects. The New Zealand lilac is a beautiful shrub, though, and well worth growing for its spring and summer display of lavender-blue flowers. As a free-standing shrub it grows to about 3ft high, but will grow taller against a wall, up to 6ft. For those who live in areas subject to very hard winters, this hebe can be grown in a cool conservatory. It will particularly enjoy and thrive in mild seaside gardens. The *Hebe* genus as a whole is valued by gardeners for its versatility, fine flowers and neat foliage.

HEBE HULKEANA AT A GLANCE

A loose, slender evergreen shrub with heads of lavender-blue flowers. Hardy to 23°F (zone 9).

Jan	/	**Companion Plants**
Feb	/	Associates well with early-
Mar	/	flowering climbing roses
Apr	planting 🍃	with pink or red flowers.
May	flowering ❀	
Jun	flowering ❀	
July	/	
Aug	/	
Sep	/	
Oct	/	
Nov	/	
Dec	/	

CONDITIONS

Aspect Will grow in sun or partial shade, but needs to be well protected from cold drying winds.

Site This plant requires well-drained yet moisture-retentive soil, ranging from alkaline to neutral and low to moderate fertility.

GROWING METHOD

Propagation Take softwood cuttings in spring or early summer, or semi-ripe cuttings in summer. It is best to have some young plants in reserve to replace the main plant if it is killed off by hard frosts.

Watering Do not let the plant dry out. Water if the soil starts to become dry in summer.

Feeding Once a year, in spring, apply a slow-release organic fertilizer, such as blood, fish, and bone.

Problems These plants may be attacked by aphids in spring or summer.

FLOWERING/FOLIAGE

Flowers This shrub is grown primarily for its flowers, which are produced in decorative trusses on the ends of the shoots.

Foliage The shiny evergreen elliptic leaves with red edges are attractive.

PRUNING

Requirements No regular pruning needed. Spread out and train young stems to their supports. Cut back any frost-damaged or dead growth in spring. Remove dead flower heads.

HOLBOELLIA LATIFOLIA
Holboellia

THE GLOSSY eye-shaped leaves of Holboellia latifolia are a principal attraction of this appealing climber.

HANGING IN GENTLE cascades from a house wall, H. latifolia *creates a verdure of pleasant sun-catching foliage.*

FEATURES

Twiner

This unusual spring-flowering evergreen climber is originally a native of Asia, and is particularly at home in the foothills of the Himalaya mountain range. It is not one of the hardiest climbers but it will thrive in gardens in the milder parts of the country if it is provided with a warm and sheltered situation. Holboellia is grown just as much for its attractive foliage as for its decorative purple female flowers. When situated in suitable conditions it is a vigorous climber, growing up to 15ft tall. It is suitable for growing on a pergola, arbor or arch, or for growing up a mature tree. A high wall makes another suitable support, as does a trellis screen.

HOLBOELLIA AT A GLANCE

Spring-flowering evergreen climber with purple flowers and handsome deep green foliage. Hardy to 23°F (zone 9).

Jan	foliage
Feb	foliage
Mar	planting
Apr	flowering
May	flowering
Jun	foliage
July	foliage
Sep	foliage
Oct	foliage
Nov	foliage
Dec	foliage

Companion Plants

Makes a good partner for spring-flowering clematis.

CONDITIONS

Aspect Grows in full sun or partial shade. Must provide shelter from wind, which could result in damage to the plant.

Site Any well-drained yet moisture-retentive soil that contains plenty of humus.

GROWING METHOD

Propagation Sow seeds in the spring and germinate in a temperature of 61°F. Take semi-ripe cuttings in late summer. Layer stems in spring.

Watering If the soil starts to become excessively dry in summer, water the plant well.

Feeding In the spring each year apply a slow-release organic fertilizer, such as blood, fish, and bone.

Problems Not troubled by pests or diseases.

FLOWERING/FOLIAGE

Flowers Male flowers are green-white, female flowers are purple. Both are borne on the same plant. Long red or purple fruits may follow, but cannot be guaranteed.

Foliage Deep green, consisting of elliptical leaflets.

PRUNING

Requirements Needs no regular pruning but you can, if desired, shorten side shoots to six buds in summer, as these tend to be vigorous and spread outward. Or just trim the plant in summer to fit allotted space.

JASMINUM
Jasmine

THE GLOSSY lance-shaped leaves of jasmine are decorative enough to earn it a place in the garden even if it didn't produce its flowers.

TREASURED for their subtle fragrance, the flowers of Jasminum officinale *also make a delightful display in summer and fall.*

FEATURES

Scramblers
twiners

These deciduous and evergreen climbers are among the most popular of all, many being valued for their sweetly fragrant flowers. Due to their informal habit they are great favorites for cottage and country gardens, where they combine well with old-fashioned flowers. Try grouping them with old-fashioned roses, for instance, and shrubs such as philadelphus (Mock orange), which is also highly scented. But the versatile jasmines can be used in any type of garden. They can be grown up and over various kinds of support. Use them to cover walls, fences, trellis screens, pergolas, arches and arbors. They can even be trained up large mature trees. Large mature shrubs might also make good hosts, but then pruning of the jasmines becomes more difficult.

There are many species of jasmine but some are too tender to be grown out of doors in cold climates. These are best grown in a cool conservatory. However, there are still many good species suitable for growing in gardens, including *Jasminum beesianum*, a Chinese twiner that is evergreen in milder gardens but deciduous in colder areas. The flowers, produced in the first half of the summer, are fragrant and red-pink in color. It grows to a height of 15ft so would be suitable for training on a wall of the house.

Jasminum humile "Revolutum" (Yellow jasmine), is of garden origin, but the species is a native of China, Afghanistan and the Himalayas. This semi-evergreen scrambler has bright yellow scented flowers in late spring and early summer and reaches a height of at least 8ft. Again this is another suitable species for the walls of the house.

The ever-popular Winter jasmine, *J. nudiflorum*, is a scrambling, deciduous, Chinese shrub that is ideally suited to training to a wall. The green stems and shoots carry bright yellow flowers in winter and into spring. Height 10ft. It can also be used as groundcover to clothe a bank.

Jasminum officinale (Common jasmine), a twining, deciduous climber from China and the Himalayas, can grow up to 40ft in height, but may be kept shorter by pruning. It is an extremely popular species and an essential choice for cottage gardens. Sweetly scented white flowers appear in summer and fall. There are several good cultivars and forms including *J. o.* f. *affine* whose white flowers are tinted with pink; "Aureum" with yellow-variegated leaves; and "Argenteovariegatum" with white-edged leaves.

JASMINUM AT A GLANCE

Scrambling climbers. The species in the main text are hardy to 23°F (zone 9), *J. nudiflorum* is hardy to 5°F (zone 7).

Jan	flowering ❀	**Companion Plants**
Feb	flowering ❀	Jasmines look lovely
Mar	planting ✎	intertwining with climbing
Apr	planting ✎	or rambler roses. Ivy is a
May	flowering ❀	good companion for the
Jun	flowering ❀	winter jasmine.
July	flowering ❀	
Aug	flowering ❀	
Sep	flowering ❀	
Oct	/	
Nov	/	
Dec	flowering ❀	

JASMINE MAKES a perfect plant to drape over various garden structures, and here forms a scented canopy over an arbor.

MASSES OF FLOWERS adorn Jasminum nudiflorum *from late fall to early spring, providing a wall of color.*

CONDITIONS

Aspect   Ideally jasmines should be grown in full sun, where they flower most freely, but partial shade is acceptable. The Winter jasmine, especially, is suitable for partial shade.

Site   Jasmines are highly adaptable plants and will grow in any well-drained and reasonably fertile soil. The soil should be capable of retaining moisture during dry weather—so add bulky organic matter before planting.

GROWING METHOD

Propagation   The easiest way to propagate jasmines is to carry out serpentine layering in the spring. Alternatively take semi-ripe cuttings in summer. However, hardwood cuttings in winter are better for *J. nudiflorum* and *J. officinale*, rooting them in a cold frame or in a cool glasshouse.

Watering   It is important not to allow jasmines to suffer from extended lack of moisture, try to keep the plants well watered during any prolonged dry spells if necessary.

Feeding   Apply a slow-release fertilizer annually in the spring just as growth is starting. Blood, fish, and bone is a good organic choice.

Problems   Jasmines may be attacked by aphids, but these pests are easily controlled by spraying with a suitable insecticide.

FLOWERING/FOLIAGE

Flowers   Jasmines are grown primarily for their flowers, which are often highly fragrant.

Foliage   Many jasmines have pinnate foliage. It may be evergreen or deciduous, depending on species and/or climate.

PRUNING

Requirements   Jasmines vary in their pruning requirements according to species. *Jasminum humile* "Revolutum" needs thinning out regularly to prevent congested growth. When flowering is over, cut out completely no more than two of the oldest stems. Neglected and overgrown plants can be renovated by cutting them back hard in early spring.

Jasminum nudiflorum requires annual pruning. This should take place as soon as flowering is over. Carry out spur pruning by cutting back the old flowered shoots to within two or three pairs of buds of the main framework of the plant.

For established plants of *J. officinale* and *J. beesianum* thin out congested growth as soon as flowering is over by cutting back the flowered shoots. If necessary neglected plants can be hard pruned by cutting back old stems to within 3ft of the ground in late winter or early spring.

LONICERA
Honeysuckle

*TOLERANT OF PARTIAL shade, Lonicera japonica "Halliana"
is also fast-growing and makes an ideal cover for pergolas.*

*THE FLUTED BLOOMS of Lonicera sempervirens hang in
attractive bunches that add to their visual impact.*

FEATURES

Twiners

Honeysuckles are widely grown climbers,
ranking in popularity with clematis and
jasmines. Like the latter, many have highly
fragrant flowers and are valued for this alone,
but the blooms also make a colorful display in
the summer.

They have a very informal habit of growth,
making them ideally suited to cottage and
country gardens, where they could be grown
with old-fashioned flowers and other plants,
such as old roses. Try growing them with
climbing roses and let them intertwine for
some really stunning effects, although bear in
mind that pruning of both may then be more
difficult. Owners of more modern gardens
should also consider growing honeysuckles as
they will not look out of place.

Honeysuckles can be grown up a variety of
supports, including walls, fences, pergolas,
arbors, arches, obelisks in a shrub border, and
large mature trees. They look particularly at
home in a woodland garden, as they often grow
in woodland conditions in the wild. The
Common honeysuckle or Woodbine, *Lonicera
periclymenum* and its cultivars, makes good
groundcover in shrub borders and woodland
gardens. Some species can be grown in tubs
and trained as standards, including *L. japonica*
"Halliana" (Japanese honeysuckle) and
L. periclymenum cultivars.

There are many species and cultivars to
choose from but the following are probably
among the best loved. *Lonicera* x *brownii*
"Fuchsioides" (Scarlet trumpet honeysuckle),
has clusters of slightly fragrant, tubular,
orange-scarlet flowers in summer. A twiner
of garden origin, it is deciduous or, in some
climates, evergreen, and can attain a height
of 12ft.

Lonicera caprifolium, (Italian honeysuckle),
a native of Europe and western Asia, is a
deciduous twiner producing, in summer,
clusters of highly fragrant, tubular, cream or
yellow flowers flushed with pink. It can grow
to a height of 20ft.

The extremely vigorous *L. japonica*
"Halliana" (Japanese honeysuckle), is a semi-
evergreen or evergreen twiner with white
tubular flowers which turn yellow as they age.
The blooms are highly fragrant and the
flowering period is from spring to the end of
summer. It grows to a height of 30ft. The
species is a native of eastern Asia.

The Common honeysuckle, also known as
Woodbine, *L. periclymenum*, is a native of
Britain where it scrambles over hedgerows.

LONICERA AT A GLANCE		
Vigorous twiners with tubular flowers in summer. Hardy to temperatures of up to 5°F (zone 7).		
Jan	/	Companion Plants
Feb	planting	Honeysuckles look good
Mar	planting	accompanied by climbing
Apr	planting	or rambler roses.
May	flowering	
Jun	flowering	
July	flowering	
Aug	flowering	
Sep	flowering	
Oct	/	
Nov	/	
Dec	/	

A PROFUSION of flowers smothers this Lonicera pericylmenum *"Belgica". The flowers fill the air with their powerful fragrance.*

THE DELICATE TUBULAR flowers of Lonicera pericylmenum *"Belgica" are prized for their perfume and distinctive appearance.*

It is a very vigorous twiner that produces fragrant flowers from mid- to late summer. The species is not generally grown in gardens, most gardeners preferring to use its cultivars. *L. p.* "Belgica" is popularly known as the Early Dutch honeysuckle and has white blooms that age to yellow. These are flushed with red on the outside. *L. p.* "Serotina" is the Late Dutch honeysuckle with cream flowers that are flushed with reddish-purple on the outside. Both of these decorative cultivars can grow up to 20ft tall.

Hailing from the USA, *Lonicera sempervirens,* known as Trumpet honeysuckle, is an evergreen or deciduous twiner with tubular flowers that are reddish orange on the outside but yellow-orange within. The flowers are produced throughout summer and into fall. It reaches up to 12ft in height.

CONDITIONS

Aspect	All species and their cultivars will grow in full sun or partial shade.
Site	Honeysuckles are very adaptable and will grow in any well-drained but moisture-retentive, humus-rich soil of reasonable fertility.

GROWING METHOD

Propagation	The easiest method of propagation is to carry out serpentine layering in the spring. Alternatively take softwood or semi-ripe cuttings in spring and summer. Sow seeds in fall and stratify over winter.
Watering	Do not let honeysuckles suffer from prolonged lack of moisture. Water the plants thoroughly if the soil starts to dry out during long dry periods in the summer.
Feeding	Apply a slow-release fertilizer, such as the organic blood, fish and bone, in the spring.
Problems	Plants may become infested with aphids during the summer.

FLOWERING/FOLIAGE

Flowers	Honeysuckles are grown primarily for their flowers, and the scented kinds are most popular.
Foliage	Evergreen or deciduous, the leaves being arranged in opposite pairs.

PRUNING

Requirements	The congested growth of *Lonicera japonica* can be thinned out in early spring. Prune back any very long shoots. If renovation is needed, cut back the entire plant to within 3ft of the ground in late winter or early spring. With the species *L. periclymenum, L. x brownii, L. caprifolium,* and *L. sempervirens,* you can either allow them to grow at will or reduce the flowered shoots by one-third in early spring to restrict the size of the plant. Shears may be used to trim the entire plant. Renovation pruning is the same as for *L. japonica.*

PASSIFLORA CAERULEA
Blue passion flower

THE FLOWERS of Passiflora *are famous for their intricate petals and stamens. Only P.* caerulea *is hardy enough to be grown outside.*

MILDLY FRAGRANCED and producing yellow or orange fruit in late summer and early fall, P. caerulea *provides plenty of interest.*

FEATURES

Tendril climber

The Blue passion flower is a fast-growing climber from Brazil and Argentina with evergreen or semi-evergreen foliage. The very complex flowers, basically bowl shaped, come in a striking color combination of white and green, zoned with blue, purple, and white. This species grows to at least 30ft tall. As it is not one of the hardiest climbers available the Blue passion flower is best grown against a warm, sunny, sheltered wall. This makes it an ideal subject for a courtyard garden or any similar enclosed area. Alternatively, it could be grown on the wall of the house. It really flourishes in mild parts of the country, and in colder areas this plant will need adequate protection from cold drying winds.

PASSIFLORA AT A GLANCE

A vigorous tendril climber producing exotic-looking flowers followed by orange fruits. Hardy to 23°F (zone 9).

Jan	/	**Recommended Varieties**
Feb	/	*P. c.* "Constance Elliot" has
Mar	/	white flowers.
Apr	planting 🖐	
May	planting 🖐	
Jun	flowering ✽	
July	flowering ✽	
Aug	flowering ✽	
Sep	flowering ✽	
Oct	flowering ✽	
Nov	/	
Dec	/	

CONDITIONS

Aspect Best in full sun but can also be grown in partial shade. This plant needs to be well sheltered from cold winds.

Site Grows in any reasonably fertile, well-drained yet moisture-retentive soil.

GROWING METHOD

Propagation Take softwood or semi-ripe leaf-bud cuttings in spring and summer. Carry out serpentine layering in the spring. Sow seeds in spring, after soaking in hot water for 24 hours. Germinate at 64°F.

Watering If the soil starts to dry out in the summer water the plant well.

Feeding Apply a slow-release fertilizer in the spring, such as the organic blood, fish, and bone.

Problems Passifloras are not usually troubled by pests and diseases out of doors.

FLOWERING/FOLIAGE

Flowers Bowl shaped flowers over a very long period, followed by egg-shaped light orange fruits.

Foliage Dark green and deeply lobed.

PRUNING

Requirements Train a framework of permanent stems on the support and in spring just before growth starts, carry out spur pruning by cutting back flowered shoots to within two or three buds of this framework.

PERIPLOCA GRAECA
Silk vine

THE STAR-SHAPED flowers of Periploca graeca, *the Silk vine, are followed by silky seeds, hence the common name.*

THIS EXOTIC VARIETY, Periploca laevigata, *a native of north Africa and the Canary Islands, produces amazing star-shaped flowers.*

FEATURES

Twiner

This is a vigorous deciduous climber, a native of south-west Europe and south-west Asia. The Silk vine is grown primarily for its attractive-looking star-shaped flowers in the summer. Unfortunately these flowers also have a rather unpleasant fragrance. It is the most commonly grown species, of which there are about 11 altogether in the genus. Growing to a height of 28ft, the Silk vine is suitable for a warm sheltered wall or close-boarded fence where it will be well protected. This plant is also suitable for a pergola or trellis screen, as long as the chosen site is well sheltered from cold and drying winds. It will make an ideal climber for a courtyard garden with its own favorable microclimate.

PERIPLOCA GRAECA AT A GLANCE

A vigorous deciduous climber with star-shaped yellow-green and purple flowers in summer. Hardy to 23°F (zone 9).

Jan	/	Companion Plants
Feb	/	Grow with other climbers
Mar	planting 🖐	and wall shrubs that need
Apr	planting 🖐	similar conditions, such as
May	/	*Abutilon megapotamicum.*
Jun	/	
July	flowering ❋	
Aug	flowering ❋	
Sep	/	
Oct	/	
Nov	/	
Dec	/	

CONDITIONS

Aspect The Silk vine requires a position in full sun that is also warm and sheltered.

Site Any soil is suitable provided it is well drained.

GROWING METHOD

Propagation Sow seeds in the spring and germinate them in a temperature of 61°F. Root semi-ripe cuttings during the summer.

Watering Do not let this climber suffer from drought. Water the plant well if the soil starts to dry out excessively.

Feeding An annual application, during the spring, of a slow-release fertilizer will keep the plant going. The organic blood, fish and bone is a suitable choice.

Problems The Silk vine is not usually troubled by any pests or diseases.

FLOWERING/FOLIAGE

Flowers Star shaped, yellow-green, and purple, followed by long thin seed pods that split open to reveal silky seeds, hence the common name.

Foliage Deep green shiny leaves make a good background for the flowers.

PRUNING

Requirements In early spring simply trim if necessary to keep the plant within its allotted space. Eventually renovation pruning may be needed by thinning out the oldest stems.

PILEOSTEGIA VIBURNOIDES
Pileostegia

PILEOSTEGIA VIBURNOIDES *shows a fetching contrast between its bold leaves and its lacy puffs of cream-white flowers.*

DRAMATIC FIREWORK *bursts of white, the flowers of* P. viburnoides *reveal their intricate beauty on close inspection.*

FEATURES

Self-clinging climber

This is a very vigorous, tall-growing evergreen climber that supports itself by means of aerial roots produced from the stems. It is related to schizophragma (see page 717). Pileostegia is a native of China, Taiwan and India. This climber is grown for its flowers, which are produced in summer and fall, and for its dense, good-looking foliage that effectively hides the support. Growing up to 20ft in height, pileostegia is suitable for growing on high walls or up large mature trees but is not a suitable subject for small gardens or where space is restricted. It is also a good shade survivor, which might make it a suitable choice for shaded areas that other climbers cannot endure.

PILEOSTEGIA AT A GLANCE

Vigorous evergreen climber with deep green foliage and cream-white flowers in late summer and fall. Hardy to 23°F (zone 9).

Jan	/	Companion Plants
Feb	/	Due to its vigour, best grown
Mar	planting 🌱	alone, but could combine
Apr	planting 🌱	with a vigorous rambler rose.
May	/	
Jun	/	
July	/	
Aug	flowering ❀	
Sep	flowering ❀	
Oct	flowering ❀	
Nov	/	
Dec	/	

CONDITIONS

Aspect	Pileostegia will endure most light conditions, from full sun to full shade.
Site	This climber will grow in any reasonably rich soil provided the drainage is good.

GROWING METHOD

Propagation	Take semi-ripe cuttings in summer and ideally root them in a cold frame.
Watering	Do not let this climber dry out excessively, so water well in prolonged dry spells in summer.
Feeding	An annual feed, in spring, of slow-release fertilizer, such as the organic blood, fish, and bone, is all that is required.
Problems	Pileostegia is not troubled by pests or diseases.

FLOWERING/FOLIAGE

Flowers	The heads of cream-white flowers are produced late in the summer.
Foliage	The deep green elliptical leaves have a leathery texture.

PRUNING

Requirements	Prune in early spring. Minimal pruning needed. Shorten any over-long or badly placed shoots as necessary. This climber produces most flowers at the top so do not prune to reduce height. Hard renovation pruning is acceptable if necessary—simply leave a main framework of stems. Ideally spread this type of pruning over several years to prevent too much loss of flower following pruning.

ROSA
Rose species and hybrids

ROSA "ALBERTINE" is a beautiful, heavily scented rambler rose, shown in this garden in its full glory. Although it produces only one long blooming each year, its lovely salmon-pink color and scent are well worth the wait. It is one of the most popular rambler roses.

FEATURES

Scramblers

The climbing roses rank among the most popular of all climbing plants. There are climbing roses suitable for walls and fences of all sizes, and vigorous ramblers and climbers that can be allowed to grow up through large mature trees and evergreen conifers. Many climbers and ramblers are ideal for pergolas, arches, arbors, and obelisks.

Modern hybrid climbers such as "Alchemist" are the most popular. They are recurrent flowering, producing several flushes of flowers in summer, and there is a large range to choose from in a wide selection of colors. Older cultivars may have only one flush of blooms.

Ramblers, both species and cultivars, are generally more vigorous than modern hybrid climbers and need plenty of space. Many have only one main flush of flowers in the summer, such as the popular old "Albertine" and "Wedding Day."

Species roses are also well worth considering, including *Rosa banksiae*, the double white Banksian rose. This climber has double, sweetly scented, white flowers in late spring and is one of the earliest roses to flower. Also recommended is the yellow Banksian

rose, *R. b.* "Lutea," with double yellow flowers. The species itself is very tall, up to 40ft, but the yellow cultivar is much shorter, about 20ft. The Banksian roses are hardy to 23°F and are best grown on a warm sunny sheltered wall or fence.

CONDITIONS

Aspect	Full sun is required for best flowering.
Site	Roses like a fertile, deep, moisture-retentive, yet well-drained soil. Dig in plenty of bulky organic matter before planting to provide humus, which helps to retain moisture during dry periods. Keep roses well mulched with bulky organic matter.

GROWING METHOD

Propagation	It is not really feasible for home gardeners to propagate many of the climbing roses. Commercially they are propagated by budding onto suitable rootstocks. You could try ramblers and species roses from hardwood cuttings in winter. Root them in a cold frame.
Watering	Keep roses well watered if the soil dries. They dislike very dry or drought conditions.

Feeding	You could use a proprietary rose fertilizer. Alternatively apply blood, fish, and bone fertilizer. Apply in the spring as growth is starting, and after the first flush of flowers.
Problems	Roses have more than their fair share of problems: aphids, rose black spot, rose powdery mildew and rose rust, to name some of the most troublesome. Wherever possible buy disease-resistant roses. Carry out preventative spraying to control diseases, starting as soon as new foliage appears. Use a combined rose spray.

FLOWERING/FOLIAGE

Flowers	May be single, semi-double, or fully double, fragrant or without scent. Flowering may be a single flush in the summer, or repeat-flowering throughout summer.
Foliage	The leaves are made up of leaflets in varying shades of green, often shiny, but generally not particularly attractive.

PRUNING

Requirements Roses flower on current or previous year's shoots, so prune annually. Wherever possible train stems horizontally as they then produce better distributed flowers, instead of blooming only at the top. Of course, this method of training is not possible when growing on pergola pillars and obelisks. There are hybrid climbing roses that are suitable for these types of supports, or spiral training could be used to give you blooms all the way up the support.

Ramblers flower best on stems produced in the previous year, but will also flower on older ones. Prune after flowering by cutting out some of the oldest flowered stems to ground level. Then space out and tie in the remaining stems.

For modern hybrid climbers train a main framework of stems to the support. This produces side shoots that in turn produce flowers. Prune in late winter or early spring by cutting back side shoots to two or three buds from the main stems. Cut back the oldest stems once they start producing fewer flowers.

R. "WEDDING DAY," a lovely single white rambler rose, bears a great profusion of blooms. Here it has a sturdy metal frame for support.

WELL-SPACED STEMS encourage the best flowering and allow all flowers to be seen. This peachy-apricot climbing rose is R. "Alchemist."

THE WEIGHT of growth from this prolific pink-flowering climbing rose may require an extra cross-bar support for the pergola.

ROSA AT A GLANCE		
Summer-flowering scramblers, with flowers in a wide range of colors, many being fragrant. Most roses are hardy to 5°F (zone		
Jan	planting 🌱	Companion Plants
Feb	planting 🌱	Summer-flowering clematis
Mar	planting 🌱	are particularly good
Apr	planting 🌱	companions. You can allow
May	flowering ❁	the two to intertwine.
Jun	flowering ❁	
July	flowering ❁	
Aug	flowering ❁	
Sep	flowering ❁	
Oct	planting 🌱	
Nov	planting 🌱	
Dec	planting 🌱	

RUBUS HENRYI
Rubus

THE DISTINCTIVE three-fingered leaves of Rubus henryi *var.* bambusarum *are joined by pink flowers in early summer.*

MANY OF the decorative members of the Rubus *genus are grown for their glossy and pleasantly-shaped leaves.*

FEATURES

Scrambler

The genus *Rubus* is huge, containing over 250 species, some of which are well-known edible fruits such as blackberries and raspberries. There are also numerous ornamental species and one of the most decorative is *R. henryi* var. *bambusarum*. This handsome evergreen climber from China has long spiny stems with white hairs. It is grown for these attractive stems, as well as for the foliage and summer flowers. It is a vigorous plant, growing 20ft tall, and is a good subject for a shrub border or woodland garden. In these situations it can be grown either as a climber, perhaps over a large shrub, up a mature tree, or on an obelisk or as a groundcover plant.

RUBUS HENRYI AT A GLANCE

R.h. var. *bambusarum* is a handsome blackberry relation with spiny stems and pink summer flowers. Hardy to 5°F (zone 7).

Jan	/	**Companion Plants**
Feb	planting 🌿	This climber looks good
Mar	planting 🌿	with shrubs, particularly
Apr	planting 🌿	woodland-garden kinds.
May	/	
Jun	flowering ✿	
July	flowering ✿	
Aug	flowering ✿	
Sep	/	
Oct	/	
Nov	/	
Dec	/	

CONDITIONS

Aspect   Suitable for sun or partial shade.
Site   *R. h.* var. *bambusarum* will grow in any soil that is well drained and reasonably fertile.

GROWING METHOD

Propagation   Take semi-ripe cuttings in summer. You can also use semi-ripe leaf-bud cuttings. Layer stems in the spring. Groundcover plants may self-layer.
Watering   It likes moist conditions so do not allow the plant to dry out during prolonged dry spells in summer.
Feeding   Apply a slow-release fertilizer in the spring, such as the organic blood, fish, and bone.
Problems   Not generally troubled by pests or diseases.

FLOWERING/FOLIAGE

Flowers   Clusters of small bowl-shaped pink flowers are followed by shiny black berries.
Foliage   The shiny deep green three-lobed leaves with white undersides are very attractive.

PRUNING

Requirements   Pruning aims to ensure plenty of new stems, so in late winter or early spring each year cut some of the stems that produced flowers the previous year down to ground level. New shoots will then appear from the base of the plant in the spring.

SCHIZOPHRAGMA
Schizophragma

SCHIZOPHRAGMA HYDRANGEOIDES *has plenty to shout about, with rich green leaves in season and ebullient white blooms.*

IN THE SUMMER, S. hydrangeoides *is a seething mass of pleasant white flowers, so densely packed that the foliage is hardly visible.*

FEATURES

Self-clinging climber

Schizophragma hydrangeoides is a deciduous climber from Japan and Korea. It supports itself by means of aerial roots. It is a lofty climber, growing up to 40ft tall, so it preferably needs a high wall or fence. Alternatively, grow it through a large tree, or use it as groundcover, for example in a woodland garden or shrub border. This climber is grown mainly for its unusual and conspicuous heads of flowers produced in summer, but the foliage is also attractive and covers its support well. There is one other species in the genus, *S. integrifolium*, which is not quite so hardy.

SCHIZOPHRAGMA AT A GLANCE

A self-clinging climber with large flat heads of cream flowers surrounded by conspicuous bracts. Hardy to 5°F (zone 7).

Jan	/	Recommended Varieties
Feb	/	*S. h.* "Moonlight" has variegated foliage.
Mar	planting 🖐	*S. h.* "Roseum" has rose-tinted bracts.
Apr	planting 🖐	
May	/	
Jun	/	
July	flowering ❋	
Aug	flowering ❋	
Sep	/	
Oct	/	
Nov	/	
Dec	/	

CONDITIONS

Aspect A good choice of plant for partial shade but it also grows well in full sun. Must be well sheltered from cold drying winds.

Site Well-drained yet moisture-retentive soil that contains plenty of humus.

GROWING METHOD

Propagation Take semi-ripe cuttings in summer. Sow seeds in fall and stratify over winter.

Watering Do not let the plant suffer from lack of moisture, so water well if the soil starts to dry out in summer.

Feeding An annual spring application of slow-release fertilizer such as the organic blood, fish, and bone will keep the plant going all season.

Problems This climber is not usually troubled by pests or diseases.

FLOWERING/FOLIAGE

Flowers Flat heads of cream flowers with large oval bracts of the same color around the edge.

Foliage The large, oval, deep green leaves are attractive in season.

PRUNING

Requirements No regular pruning needed. If necessary, after flowering, cut back by about two-thirds any overlong shoots and trim the plant to fit the available space.

Solanum
Potato tree, Potato vine

THESE DAINTY FLOWERS *belie the vigor of* Solanum crispum.
It may put forth flowers over many months of the summer.

THE POTATO VINE, S. jasminoides, *here in its cultivar "Album,"*
is a half-hardy climber, needing conservatory protection in most areas.

FEATURES

Scramblers

Two evergreen or partially evergreen species of this genus are generally grown. Both of these are very vigorous, growing to 20ft tall. *Solanum crispum* (Chilean potato tree) from Chile and Peru has fragrant blue flowers in the summer. The cultivar "Glasnevin," with purple-blue flowers, is more widely grown than the species. The Chilean potato tree can be grown on a wall or fence, or used to cover an unsightly outbuilding. *S. jasminoides* (Potato vine) is a half-hardy climber originating from the jungles of Brazil and will need the protection of a cool conservatory in most areas. In the garden it must have a very well sheltered sunny wall. It bears scented, pale blue flower in summer and fall. Both species can be grown as standards.

SOLANUM AT A GLANCE

Vigorous climbers with clusters of potato-like flowers. *S. crispum* is hardy to 23°F (zone 9), *S. jasminoides* to 32°F (zone 10).

Jan	/	
Feb	/	Companion Plants
Mar	/	Solanums look lovely with
Apr	planting 🌱	red or pink climbing or
May	planting 🌱	rambler roses
Jun	flowering ✿	
July	flowering ✿	
Aug	flowering ✿	
Sep	flowering ✿	
Oct	/	
Nov	/	
Dec	/	

CONDITIONS

Aspect   These plants need a warm, very sheltered position in full sun.
Site   Well-drained yet moisture-retentive, reasonably fertile soil, ideally slightly alkaline.

GROWING METHOD

Propagation   Take semi-ripe cuttings in summer.
Watering   Water only if the soil starts to dry out excessively in the summer.
Feeding   An annual application of slow-release fertilizer such as blood, fish, and bone, preferably in the spring, will be sufficient.
Problems   Plants are prone to attacks from aphids.

FLOWERING/FOLIAGE

Flowers   Produces large clusters of potato-like (star-shaped) flowers.
Foliage   The deep green oval leaves of these plants are not particularly attractive.

PRUNING

Requirements   Solanums flower on the current year's shoots. Train a permanent framework of stems and spur prune back to this in early spring each year by cutting back lateral shoots to within two or three buds of the main stems. Also prune the plant back to fit the available space. Renovation pruning is not recommended—better to replace overgrown plants. Wear gloves when pruning as the sap can cause an allergic reaction in some people.

STAUNTONIA HEXAPHYLLA
Stauntonia

JUST AS IN its natural habitat in Japan and south Korea, this Stauntonia hexaphylla *has found a tree to twine its way around.*

ALTHOUGH IT DOES produce attractive flowers, S. hexaphylla *is also grown for its pleasant, lush, evergreen foliage.*

FEATURES

Twiner

This is a vigorous, evergreen climber from Japan and south Korea, where it is largely found growing in woodland conditions. It is related and similar to *Holboellia latifolia* (see page 705). Stauntonias are grown for their attractive bell-shaped flowers, which are produced in spring, and for their lush foliage that serves to cover their support well. Grow this climber on a sheltered wall or fence, or allow it to scramble through a large mature shrub or up a tree. Although this plant is frost hardy it will not survive severe cold spells. In areas that suffer from hard frosts it is best to grow it in a cool conservatory. The eventual height of this plant is 30ft.

STAUNTONIA AT A GLANCE

A vigorous twiner with white, violet-flushed, bell-shaped flowers in spring. Hardy to 23°F (zone 9).

Jan	/	Companion Plants
Feb	/	Try growing this climber
Mar	/	with spring-flowering
Apr	planting 🖐	clematis.
May	flowering ❀	
Jun	/	
July	/	
Oct	/	
Nov	/	
Dec	/	

CONDITIONS

Aspect	Full sun or partial shade, warm and well sheltered from cold winds.
Site	Stauntonia will get by in any well-drained soil that is reasonably fertile.

GROWING METHOD

Propagation	Semi-ripe cuttings taken in summer. Sow seeds in spring and germinate in a temperature of 61°F.
Watering	Water the plant well if the soil starts to dry out excessively in the summer.
Feeding	Feed annually in the spring. The slow-release organic fertilizer, blood, fish, and bone can be recommended.
Problems	There are no problems from pests or diseases.

FLOWERING/FOLIAGE

Flowers	Pendulous clusters of scented, white, bell-shaped flowers, tinted with violet may be followed by edible, purple fruits (a male and female plant are necessary to obtain fruits).
Foliage	Deep green, shiny, leathery, hand-shaped leaves make a good background for the flowers.

PRUNING

Requirements	Spur pruning. To keep growth under control, shorten lateral shoots to six buds in summer, and then in early spring cut them back again, to within two or three buds of the main stems.

TRACHELOSPERMUM
Star jasmine

THE WHITE FLOWERS of Trachelospermum jasminoides are enjoyed for their appearance as well as their strong perfume.

THIS LUSH PLANT of T. jasminoides has been trained and pruned most effectively to echo the angle of the steps and then curve up again.

FEATURES

Twiner

Trachelospermum jasminoides is a handsome, evergreen, twining climber from China, Japan and Korea. It is valued for its pleasing foliage and for its clusters of strongly perfumed white flowers, which appear in mid- to late summer and age to cream through the flowering season. The blooms are reminiscent of the true jasmine (see pages 706–707). It is an ideal subject for growing on walls, fences, trellis screens, pergolas, arches and arbours. Star jasmine can also be grown as ground cover, for example in a shrub border, or used for covering a bank. Once established it grows quite quickly, and in maturity it reaches a height of 28ft. In areas subject to very hard winters this climber should be grown in a cool conservatory or glasshouse.

TRACHELOSPERMUM AT A GLANCE

A jasmine-like climber with very dense growth and sweetly fragrant white flowers. Hardy to 23°F (zone 9).

Jan	/	**Companion Plants**
Feb	/	A good companion for red or
Mar	planting 🍃	pink climbing roses.
Apr	planting 🍃	
May	planting 🍃	
Jun	/	
July	flowering ✻	
Aug	flowering ✻	
Sep	/	
Oct	/	
Nov	/	
Dec	/	

CONDITIONS

Aspect   Must be very well sheltered and warm. Full sun or partial shade are acceptable.

Site   This climber likes a good, reasonably rich soil that is well drained.

GROWING METHOD

Propagation   Take semi-ripe cuttings in the summer and then provide them with bottom heat—about 68°F. Carry out serpentine layering in the spring.

Watering   Do not let the star jasmine suffer from lack of moisture. Water well in summer if the soil starts to become excessively dry.

Feeding   Give an annual spring application of slow-release fertilizer, such as blood, fish, and bone.

Problems   There are no problems from pests or diseases.

FLOWERING/FOLIAGE

Flowers   Clusters of white, star-shaped, highly fragrant flowers reminiscent of jasmine.

Foliage   Deep green, shiny, oval leaves.

PRUNING

Requirements   Needs little pruning. In early spring thin out some of the oldest stems if necessary. Bear in mind that this climber is naturally very dense in habit so do not attempt to thin it out too much. Prune back the plant as necessary to keep it within its allotted space, but avoid hard pruning. It is best to replace very old neglected plants rather than renovate them.

VITIS
Vine, grape vine

THE LEAVES OF Vitis vinifera "Pupurea" are purple in summer and become darker in fall before they fall.

GROWING UP OUT of a bed, this V. vinifera "Pupurea" adds a vertical element to the planting, and fills the blank space of the fence.

FEATURES

Tendril
climbers

Apart from the well-known edible grape vine, cultivars of *Vitis vinifera*, there are several ornamental vines that are valued for their fall leaf color. *Vitis coignetiae* is a very vigorous species from Japan and Korea and is also one of the largest leaved. In fall the leaves turn brilliant red. It reaches 50ft in height. *V. vinifera* "Purpurea" has purple leaves in summer that become darker in fall, and reaches 22ft. These vines, whose summer foliage is also attractive, are ideal for pergolas, arches and arbours; also trellis screens, walls and fences. They can be used for groundcover, and *V. vinifera* "Purpurea" makes a good standard for the patio.

VITIS AT A GLANCE

Tendril climbers valued for their large lobed leaves. Hardy to temperatures of 5°F (zone 7).

Jan	/	
Feb	/	
Mar	planting 🖐	**Companion Plants**
Apr	planting 🖐	These vines look good with
May	foliage 🍃	large-leaved ivies such as
Jun	foliage 🍃	*Hedera colchica* and
July	foliage 🍃	*H. canariensis.*
Aug	foliage 🍃	
Sep	foliage 🍃	
Oct	foliage 🍃	
Nov	/	
Dec	/	

CONDITIONS

Aspect Full sun or partial shade.
Site Any well-drained soil, but alkaline or neutral conditions preferred. Soil should also contain plenty of humus.

GROWING METHOD

Propagation Take hardwood cuttings in late fall or winter, rooting them in a bottom-heat temperature of 70°F. Carry out serpentine layering in spring.
Watering Vines will tolerate fairly dry conditions but it is best to water them well if the soil starts to dry out excessively.
Feeding Apply a slow-release organic fertilizer in the spring, such as blood, fish and bone.
Problems Leaves may be affected by powdery mildew.

FLOWERING/FOLIAGE

Flowers Trusses of tiny green flowers followed by purple or black grapes which, in the ornamental vines, are not palatable.
Foliage Handsome, large lobed leaves.

PRUNING

Requirements Build up a permanent framework of stems and spur prune annually in mid-winter. Cut back side shoots to within two or three buds of their base. During the summer any very long shoots can be shortened if desired.

WISTERIA
Wisteria

EVEN THE STEMS of this wisteria have disappeared beneath an abundance of bloom—and there is no foliage yet to distract the eye.

THIS WHITE WISTERIA has been trained along a wire frame. The cascades of flower make it a high point of the garden in spring.

FEATURES

Twiner

These very vigorous, fast-growing, long-lived deciduous climbers are desired by most garden owners for their spectacular spring display of pendulous, often fragrant flowers that generally appear just before or with the new leaves. The plants eventually develop thick stems and therefore are very weighty, needing strong supports. They are very amenable to training and can be formed into virtually any shape desired. Wisterias are often used to cover large pergolas, when the flowers "drip" down inside in a very dramatic fashion. They can also be trained vertically along veranda railings or low walls. These climbers are often seen on house walls. Wisterias are ideal, too, for growing up large mature trees.

If you do not have the wall space or other suitable support for one of these magnificent climbers, then consider growing one in a tub and training it into a standard to decorate the patio. Bear in mind that young wisteria plants can take up to seven years, or even longer, to start flowering, so patience is needed after planting. In the meantime, simply enjoy the foliage, which looks particularly lush when newly opened in the spring.

Probably the most popular wisteria is *W. floribunda* "Multijuga," a cultivar of the Japanese wisteria. The fragrant lilac-blue flowers are carried in pendulous trusses up to 4ft in length. If this cultivar is grown on a pergola it is a truly magnificent sight when in full flower and the trusses are dangling down inside. It grows to a height of at least 28ft. There are many other cultivars of *W. floribunda*. These include *W. f.* "Kuchi-beni" ("Peaches and Cream") with its pink and white flowers, and *W. f.* 'Alba' with white flowers.

Also widely grown is *W. sinensis* (Chinese wisteria), with scented, lilac-blue flowers in trusses up to 12in in length. It is a fast-growing and vigorous climber with dense trusses of flowers, growing to the same height as *W. floribunda* 'Multijuga'. Again there are numerous cultivars.

CONDITIONS

Aspect
Wisterias ideally need a warm sheltered site in full sun. Good growth and flowering are also possible in partial shade.

Site
There is every chance that young wisterias start flowering sooner in poorish or moderately fertile soil. If the soil is too rich they will tend to produce a huge amount of leaf and stem growth instead of focusing their energy on flowers. The site should also be well-drained yet at the same time moisture-retentive.

WISTERIA AT A GLANCE

Vigorous, deciduous twiner with long trusses of pea-like flowers in spring and early summer. Hardy to 5°F (zone 7).

		Recommended Varieties
Jan	/	*W. floribunda* cultivars:
Feb	/	"Alba," white
Mar	planting 🖐	"Kuchi-beni," pink and white
Apr	planting 🖐	"Rosea," pink
May	flowering ✿	"Royal Purple," purple-violet
Jun	flowering ✿	"Violacea Plena," double,
July	/	violet-blue
Aug	/	*W. sinensis* cultivars:
Sep	/	"Alba," white
Oct	/	'Amethyst', light rose-purple
Nov	/	'Prolific', lilac-blue
Dec	/	

THE DELICATE SHADE *of this* Wisteria sinensis *and the abundance of its blooms, make it a favorite in British gardens.*

GROWING METHOD

Propagation The easiest and most reliable method of propagation for the home gardener is to carry out serpentine layering in the spring. The stems, which are pegged down in a number of places along their length, should be well rooted after a year. Hardwood cuttings of dormant wood may be taken in winter, but these may prove a little slow to root. Once established, wisterias can go on to live for hundreds of years.

Watering Keep young plants well watered. Water established plants only if the soil starts to become excessively dry in summer.

Feeding Avoid fertilizers that are very high in nitrogen as they result in vegetative growth at the expense of flowers. Instead opt for a balanced slow-release organic fertilizer such as blood, fish, and bone. One application per year, made in the spring just as growth is about to start, will be sufficient. Plants in tubs may need a further feed in the summer as plant foods are quickly leached out of containers.

Problems There are a few pests that may trouble wisterias, particularly aphids and scale insects. Also, a fungal leaf spot may appear but it is not considered to be serious. It shows itself as dark brown spots on the foliage.

FLOWERING/FOLIAGE

Flowers The flowers are similar in shape to those of garden peas, and in fact the two plants are related. Unlike peas, though, the flowers are carried in long, pendulous trusses. Blooms are generally fragrant. They appear in late spring and early summer.

Foliage Large, pinnate, mid- to deep green leaves are attractive in spring and summer.

PRUNING

Requirements Train a permanent framework of stems to the shape desired, then spur prune to this. Wisterias can be trained to virtually any shape, but on walls the espalier is a good shape as it has many horizontal branches. These flower much more freely than branches that are trained vertically. This shape also provides a stable base for heavy wisterias. The espalier is completely flat and consists of a single, upright stem with horizontal branches evenly spaced out on each side.

Routine pruning of established wisterias is carried out twice a year to keep new growth under control. In mid-summer cut back the new lateral shoots to within five or six buds of the main framework. Then in mid-winter prune them back further, to within two or three buds of the framework.

If renovation pruning ever becomes necessary, spread the task over several years, thinning out one of the oldest stems each year. Otherwise the flower display will be reduced considerably. The heads of standard wisterias are also spur pruned, in the same way as those grown as climbers.

WISTERIA IS *particularly effective for framing windows, doors and other architectural elements. Blooms can be trained to droop into view.*

INDEX

Published in 2007 by Bay Books, an imprint of Murdoch Books Pty Limited.

Murdoch Books Australia
Pier 8/9, 23 Hickson Rd, Millers Point NSW 2000
Phone: +61 2 8220 2000 Fax: +61 2 8220 2558

978 0 681630 45 1

Printed by Hang Tai Printing Company Limited, China.
PRINTED IN CHINA. Reprinted 2010.

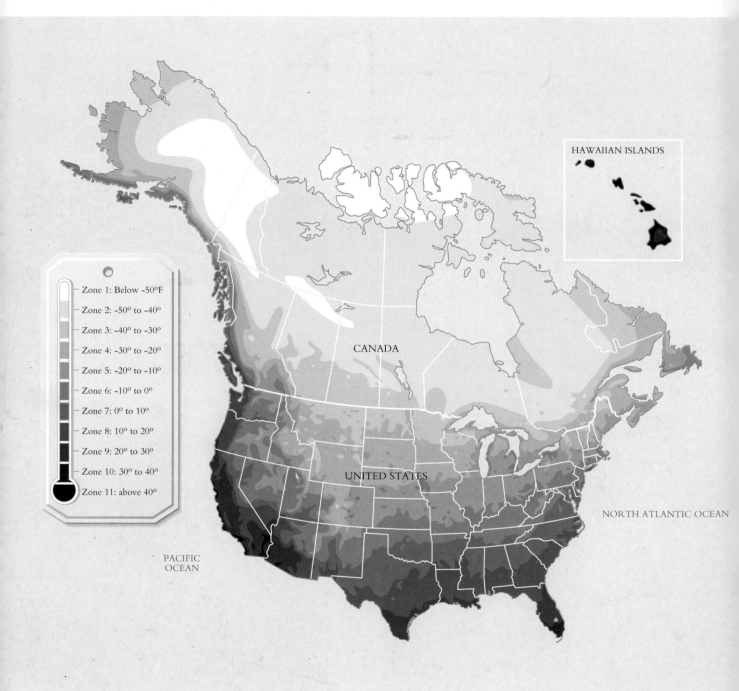

Zone 1: Below -50°F
Zone 2: -50° to -40°
Zone 3: -40° to -30°
Zone 4: -30° to -20°
Zone 5: -20° to -10°
Zone 6: -10° to 0°
Zone 7: 0° to 10°
Zone 8: 10° to 20°
Zone 9: 20° to 30°
Zone 10: 30° to 40°
Zone 11: above 40°

HAWAIIAN ISLANDS

CANADA

UNITED STATES

PACIFIC
OCEAN

NORTH ATLANTIC OCEAN